MULTINATIONAL
MARKETING
MANAGEMENT

PRENTICE-HALL INTERNATIONAL SERIES IN MANAGEMENT

second edition

MULTINATIONAL MARKETING MANAGEMENT

WARREN J. KEEGAN

Professor of Business Administration
School of Government and Business Administration
The George Washington University

PRENTICE-HALL, INC., *Englewood Cliffs, New Jersey 07632*

Library of Congress Cataloging in Publication Data
Keegan, Warren J
    Multinational marketing management.

    Bibliography: p.
    Includes index.
    1. Export marketing. 2. Marketing management.
I. Title.
HF1009.5.K39   1980   658.8'09'382   79-22948
ISBN 0-13-605055-7

Editorial production/supervision and
  interior design by Sonia Meyer
Cover design by Maureen Olsen
Manufacturing buyer: John Hall

Printed in the United States of America

10 9 8 7 6 5 4 3

Prentice-Hall International, Inc., *London*
Prentice-Hall of Australia Pty. Limited, *Sydney*
Prentice-Hall of Canada, Ltd., *Toronto*
Prentice-Hall of India Private Limited, *New Delhi*
Prentice-Hall of Japan, Inc., *Tokyo*
Prentice-Hall of Southeast Asia Pte. Ltd., *Singapore*
Whitehall Books Limited, *Wellington, New Zealand*

TO DONALD, MARK, AND TRACY ANN

contents

part five

PLANNING, ORGANIZING, AND CONTROLLING THE MULTINATIONAL PROGRAM

Decline of the United States

Marketing: A Global Profession

Type of person needed for multinational marketing;
Impact of marketing approach on job specifications

Bibliography

preface

This book introduces the student and the practitioner of international marketing to a systematic treatment of marketing on a global scale. In both teaching and practice, marketing has increasingly evolved from application in single domestic market environments to application on a global scale. In practice, this development has resulted in the exploitation of major opportunities which has yielded increasingly significant rewards for venturesome firms, and at the same time it has exposed companies to risks and problems that have resulted in an appalling number of failures and blunders. A recent study of international business blunders reveals that 53 percent were associated with marketing, 35 percent with management, and only 12 percent with legal, production, and finance functions.[1] It is hoped that this book will provide multinational marketing managers with the conceptual and analytic tools as well as a solid data base of understanding that will enable them to better exploit opportunities and better avoid the pitfalls of multinational marketing.

This second edition has been written with four objectives:

1. To update each section of the book. Since the first edition was published, there have been major changes in the world market environment, including the collapse of the old fixed exchange rate system, the devaluation of the U.S. dollar, persistent and high worldwide inflation, and an increase in the price of commodities, particularly oil, with the resulting shift in global income to producing countries. In addition, the field of international marketing has developed considerably, allowing a much deeper discussion of

[1]J.S. Arpan, D.A. Ricks, and D.J. Patton, "The Meaning of Miscues Made by Multinationals," *Management International Review,* Volume 14, 1974, p. 6.

the process of identification of global opportunities and threats, the formulation of multinational marketing programs, and of multinational planning, organization, and control.

2. To add material not developed in the first edition on economic theory as it applies to international marketing, the international financial framework, and the financing of multinational marketing programs, political risk, and legal aspects of multinational marketing.

3. To shorten the text so that it can be used with maximum effectiveness in a one-semester course.

4. To completely revise and update the case selection with cases of proven classroom effectiveness that provide an opportunity to apply concepts, tools, and knowledge of the world market environment to a cross section of actual multinational marketing situations.

Part I of the book introduces the reader to the world market environment. Part II describes the major characteristics of this environment—its complexity and diversity, and at the same time the many unifying factors and characteristics that reward integration of multinational marketing programs.

To operate effectively in the global market, methods of identifying opportunity are required. A systematic way of accomplishing this is developed in Part III of this book. Tapping opportunity with effective multinational marketing programs requires the development of specific elements of a total program involving product decisions, pricing decisions, channel decisions, and communications decisions. Each of these decision areas and the special case of export marketing are developed in Part IV. The overall process of planning, organizing, and controlling a multinational marketing program is examined in Part V. Part VI discusses the future of multinational marketing.

The book develops three basic dimensions, each of which is fundamental to the successful practice of multinational marketing. The first is the traditional consideration of the dimensions of foreign market environments. I have taken a market development approach as well as a regional approach to develop a perspective on the types of market environments that exist and are evolving in the world. A second dimension of multinational marketing is the crossing of national boundaries with elements of marketing programs, in particular with goods in export marketing, but also with other aspects of a marketing program, such as communications appeals and pricing stategies. A third dimension of the text, a new direction in the field of international marketing and a particular thrust of this book, is a consideration of multinational marketing management or the management of marketing programs being conducted simultaneously in two or more national marketing environments. The simultaneous management of marketing programs presents major opportunities for leverage or advantage and is the basis for much of the success and advantage of the multinational company. This book identifies the basic requirements and the kinds of opportunities that exist to develop leverage in marketing programs that are managed simultaneously in different national marketing environments.

ACKNOWLEDGMENTS

A textbook author can only touch the tip of the iceberg in adequately acknowledging his debt to others. My present and former colleagues at The George Washington University, School of Government and Business Administration, Bernard M. Baruch College of the City University of New York, and Columbia Business School have constantly stimulated my own interest and understanding of the field of multinational marketing. Although many colleagues have contributed, I especially want to thank Adel El-Ansary, Jean Boddewyn, William Brandt, Sal Divita, Phil Grub, Peter Lauter, Nathaniel Leff, Norma Maine Loeser, William Newman, Stefan Robock, Charles Stewart, James A. F. Stoner, David Zenoff, and Jack Zwick.

I am indebted to colleagues at other universities who have reviewed or commented on this or the first edition of this book and who have provided valuable and insightful suggestions: J. Scott Armstrong (University of Pennsylvania), James C. Baker (Kent State University), David W. Blakeslee (Rutgers University), Richard M. Clewett (Northwestern University), John S. Ewing (University of Santa Clara), John Fayerweather (New York University), Donald W. Hackett (Wichita State University), Donald Henley (Michigan State University), Richard H. Holton (University of California, Berkeley), Christopher Korth (University of Michigan), Ken Simmonds (London Business School), Ralph Sorenson (President, Babson College) and Ulrich Weichmann (Harvard Business School).

My faculty assistants, Carol Mozak, Steven C. Lowe, and Ernest M. Troth at the School of Government and Business Administration, The George Washington University, and Martin Topel at Baruch College, provided research assistance above and beyond the call of duty in the preparation of this edition. Alison Ruml, in addition to invaluable editorial and research assistance, prepared the first draft of Chapter 6 and completed a major revision of the Appendixes. I am especially grateful for her energy, enthusiasm, and talent, which spurred me to finally meet revision deadlines. Elizabeth McAleer and Pam Britnell provided indefatigable secretarial assistance.

My sincere appreciation goes to the supervisors and authors of cases included in this edition. Robert D. Buzzell for Polaroid France; Ram Charan and Lawrence D. Chrzanowski for Bancil Corporation; Donald S. Henley for Global Fasteners; Jean-Louis Lecocq for Polaroid France, S.A.; Gordon E. Miracle for Quaker Oats (A) and (B); Howard V. Perlmutter for permission to adapt his article "The Tortuous Evolution of the Multinational Corporation" into the case "Which Company Is Truly Multinational?"; Ralph Z. Sorenson for Choufont-Salva, Inc., and Mallory Batteries Limited; Hugo Uyterhoeven for Mallory Batteries Limited; and Harold Burson for Marsteller International.

Global Fasteners, Inc. case was written by Donald S. Henley, Professor of Marketing, Michigan State University; President, Donald S. Henley Associates, Inc. Reprinted with permission.

Mallory Batteries Limited case was written by W. Edward Massey, Jr., and Audrey T. Sproat, under the supervision of Ralph Z. Sorenson and Hugo Uyterhoeven. © 1968 by l'Institut pour l'Etude des Méthodes de Direction de l'Enterprise. Reprinted by permission.

Polaroid France S.A. case was written with the cooperation of Polaroid Corporation and Polaroid France S.A. by Professor Robert D. Buzzell of Harvard Business School with the assistance of M. Jean-Louis Lecocq of the Institut Europeen d'Administration des Affaires (INSEAD). © 1968 jointly by the President and Fellows of Harvard College and the Institut Europeen d'Administration des Affaires (INSEAD). Reprinted by permission.

MULTINATIONAL
MARKETING
MANAGEMENT

part one

A CONCEPTUAL OVERVIEW OF INTERNATIONAL MARKETING

an introduction to multinational marketing management

> I am not an Athenian or a Greek, but a citizen
> of the world.
>
> *Socrates, 469–399 B.C.*
>
> *(from Plutarch, Of Banishment)*

INTRODUCTION

Multinational marketing is the process of focusing the resources and objectives of an organization on global market opportunities. The post-World War II decades have been a period of unparalleled expansion of national enterprise into international markets. This book focuses on the major dimensions of multinational marketing: the environment of multinational marketing; the identification of global opportunities and threats; the formulation of multinational marketing plans; and the organization and control of multinational marketing. The major environmental dimensions of world markets are described in the book, and a set of concepts and tools specifically tailored for multinational marketing is presented. It is assumed that the reader is familiar with marketing as a discipline and with marketing practice in at least one national market environment.

Multinational marketing is both a major corporate opportunity and an important means of ensuring corporate survival. On the opportunity side, almost every company that is nationally based has larger markets abroad than at home. U.S. companies, with the largest home market in the world, today find that increasingly their biggest growth opportunities are abroad. General Electric is typical of U.S. companies:

> Sixty percent of the total world market for GE-type products is outside the United States, and it's a market that's not only larger, but growing faster than the U.S. market.[1]

[1] J. Stanford Smith, *General Electric Investor* (General Electric, Fall 1971), p. 3.

For non-U.S. companies the opportunities are even more dramatic, for they include the supergiant U.S. market.

The threat to the company that remains national is more important in many cases than opportunity abroad. This is particularly true in industries where large competitors are well entrenched. Industries that were once entirely national in character are becoming international and are dominated by international companies. There is a close parallel between the rise of the national corporation, emerging from the regional and local corporation, in the 1880s and the 1890s in the United States and the current rise of the international corporation. The plow company that remained in Illinois in the nineteenth century has disappeared, and only national companies such as Deere and International Harvester have survived. In the same way today, in an increasing number of industries, firms that remain national will disappear and only the international firms will survive to see the year 2000.

MARKETING

The building block or base for global marketing is a sound understanding of the marketing discipline. Marketing is the process of focusing the resources and objectives of an organization on environmental opportunities and needs. In a business enterprise a major objective of this process is *profit*. During the past three decades the concept of marketing has changed dramatically. The old concept of marketing focused on the product. Companies concentrated their efforts on making a "better" product. The definition of "better" was derived by referring to internal standards and values. The means of achieving the profit objective was by selling, or persuading a potential customer to buy the company's product. The new concept of marketing has shifted the focus from the product to the customers. Their needs, wants, and preferences in modern marketing are the determinants not only of product characteristics but also of pricing, distribution, advertising, promotion and selling, and service. This total set of marketing activities, sometimes called the marketing mix, is integrated into a unified program, which today, in addition to profitability, typically includes a host of broader objectives relating to current societal concerns. These concerns now focus on such areas as protection of the physical environment, product safety, and equal employment opportunity. The key difference is that under modern marketing, profits are viewed as a function of providing customer benefits; whereas under the old concept, profits were viewed as a function of sales. In sum, marketing is at the same time a concept, a business process, and a set of activities. These definitions of marketing are summarized in Table 1-1.

GLOBAL MARKETING ACTIVITIES

As companies become more involved in marketing in two or more countries, the question arises, Are there differences between domestic and global marketing?[2]

[2] See Robert Bartels, "Are Domestic and International Marketing Dissimilar?" *Journal of Marketing* (Chicago: American Marketing Association, July 1968), pp. 56–61.

TABLE 1-1. Marketing Defined

I. Marketing Concept

Concept	*Focus*	*Means*	*End*
Old :	Product/Service	Selling	Profits via sales
New :	Customers/ Competition	Integrated marketing activities	Profits via customer satisfaction

II. Marketing Activities (The Marketing Decision "Mix")

Product Decisions (Design, durability, size, etc.)
Pricing Decisions
Distribution Decisions (Physical distribution and channel structure)
Communications Decisions (Advertising, promotion, personal selling)
Service
Research

III. The Marketing Management Process

Marketing is the process of focusing the resources and objectives of an organization upon opportunities in the environment.

There are important differences, and at the same time there are basic similarities. First of all, the basic concepts, activities, and processes of marketing, summarized in Table 1-1, apply as fully to global marketing as they do to domestic marketing. When a company expands its operation to a foreign market, the basic requirements for market success are not relaxed. This seemingly obvious point is overlooked with surprising frequency. Companies enter foreign markets without analyzing both customers and competition, although they would not think of doing this at home. They fail to integrate their total marketing program, although careful attention to integration and fit is standard operating procedure in their home market. They embark upon marketing programs without a clear idea of their ultimate objective or any appraisal of the obstacles that lie in the path of sales and profits.

The differences between domestic and global marketing derive entirely from the differences in national environments within which global marketing is conducted, and the differences in the organization and programs of a company operating simultaneously in different national markets. Global marketing can be divided into two basic activities, which are described in the following section.

Foreign Marketing

Foreign marketing is marketing in an environment different from that of the home or base environment. The very concept of foreignness presumes that there is a familiar or home base. Foreign marketing requires the managing of the same activities that are involved in domestic marketing but in an unfamiliar national environment.

There is a sizable literature on foreign marketing that describes the characteristics of different national markets, often within a comparative framework. Since 1946 the *Journal of Marketing,* a major U.S. academic publication, has published over eighty articles on international and foreign marketing, the bulk of which has been foreign marketing articles with titles such as "Marketing in Spain" and "Retailing in Poland.

The interesting aspect of "foreign" marketing is that one man's or company's foreign market is also another man's or company's home or base environment. France is a foreign market to a U.S. manufacturer who has never operated there, but it is the home market to all French-based manufacturers. To the U.S. company with operations in France, the country may be simultaneously a "foreign" market to the U.S. headquarters and a "domestic" market to the company's French subsidiary.

As time passes, however, the U.S. company with operations in France may cease to think of France as a foreign market and may consider it no more "foreign" than any other area, including the United States. This occurs when French operations become truly integrated into the corporate operating structure. Thus the company has shifted its orientation from the binary foreign-domestic market concept set for operating markets to a unitary definition of operating markets by which they are all considered basic "operating" markets. In such a company nonoperating markets might still be considered as "foreign" markets, but more likely they would simply be considered markets in which the company has not yet established operations.

Foreign marketing as a dimension of global marketing still exists in most organizations, but in an increasing number of companies the concept of "foreign" is breaking down because of the growing involvement of the corporate headquarters in the company's marketing programs regardless of location. For example, IBM operates worldwide, with product and functional specialists at headquarters taking responsibility for its products and functions on a global basis. To these specialists and to the president of IBM there is no such thing as a "foreign" market in the psychological sense—there are markets in different parts of the world, at different stages of development, with different characteristics. Company operating units are expected to understand their own markets in depth. IBM knows as much about the French market for data-processing equipment as it knows about the U.S. market.

International-Multinational Marketing

A second type of global marketing, which develops as organizations gain more experience in global operations, is international or multinational marketing. The difference between an "international" company and a "multinational" company is rather subtle. An international company usually means a "national" firm operating in foreign markets. The basic orientation of an international firm is toward the home country. A multinational company is world oriented. It pursues global opportunities. There is so much interchangeability in the usage of these terms, however, that they will be used synonymously in this book to denote a company that is operating in two or more nations.

Multinational marketing has two major dimensions: the problems created by conforming to the new national markets and the opportunities that are similarly created. The first dimension arises because the firm that operates in two or more national markets is crossing national boundaries with products, prices, and advertising messages and appeals. Crossing boundaries of sovereign nations requires passing through the national "conditions of entry." For example, when a firm crosses boundaries with products, certain safety, health, and labeling regulations must be met. Duties, tariffs, and taxes must be paid on products and earnings. Product and service valuation in intracompany transactions influences prices, the location of profits, and national tax liabilities in the company's multinational system. The effect of pricing policy on the location of earnings and thus on tax liabilities in various countries has resulted in tax authority review of "transfer" or controlled prices of international companies in their intracompany sales.

The second dimension of multinational marketing arises because a company is simultaneously marketing its products in more than one national environment. The simultaneous conduct of marketing programs in two or more national environments raises issues and opportunities within an organization that are distinct from those associated with the crossing of national boundaries. The basic questions, given objectives of global or international market performance, are *what, who, how, when,* and *where.* What are the major opportunities and threats in world markets, and what are the company's capabilities and weaknesses? What are the objectives of the company, and what must be done to achieve these objectives? Who will perform what tasks, and when and where will they carry out these tasks? The basic marketing questions are: Which markets? Which products? and What price? Through what channels? With what communications? To what extent should responsibility for markets be decentralized? How much integration is required or how much is optimal?

Multinational marketing makes it possible to compare country marketing programs, either formally or informally, to identify similarities in markets and cause-and-effect relationships. If country market analogies can be established, experience from the analogous market can be transferred or translated to aid in understanding. This comparative analysis can lead to the replacing of unexplainable differences with explainable relationships. Apparent obstacles to success can be identified as being unimportant. Key measures of potential and the basic requirements for success can be identified. The technique of clustering country markets into groups, so that the distance between clusters is greater than the distance within clusters on the scaled dimensions, expands the potential usefulness of comparative analysis. In other words, the multinational marketing activity extends the possibilities for generating useful data within the organization that can be applied to planning or programs design and the analysis of results and the appraisal of programs. Of course, because no two markets are exactly alike, comparative analysis must be applied with full recognition of the differences between the markets being compared.

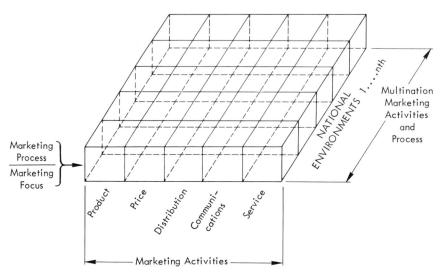

FIGURE 1-1. Relationship of Domestic and Multinational Marketing

Relationship between Domestic and Multinational Marketing

Marketing is the process of focusing the resources and objectives of an organization on opportunities within an environment. In this process, the main focus is on customers and competition. The means through which this is achieved is through the integration of decisions concerning product, price, distribution, communications, and service. Multinational marketing adds to this process the additional dimension of multiple national environments. And each environment has unique aspects that require adaptation and major elements of similarity that allow extension. Figure 1-1 illustrates these relationships.

OUTLINE OF THIS BOOK

This book is designed for the student and practitioner of multinational marketing management and is divided into six parts.

Part I presents a conceptual overview of the multinational marketing process.

Part II outlines the major dimensions of the environment of multinational marketing: the location of income and markets, trade patterns, and trade theory and the location of resources; the social and cultural dimensions of the world markets; regional market characteristics; legal aspects and political risk; and the international financial framework.

Part III focuses on systematic approaches to the identification of global opportunities and threats, and the broad strategy alternatives for tapping world opportunity.

Part IV is the core of the book. It focuses on the key decision elements of a marketing program: product, price, channel, and communications decisions. Export marketing is considered in a separate chapter.

Part V examines the integrating and managerial dimensions of multinational marketing: planning, organization, and control.

Part VI examines the future of multinational marketing.

BIBLIOGRAPHY

BOOKS

Bartels, Robert, *Comparative Marketing Wholesaling in Fifteen Countries.* Homewood, Ill.: Richard D. Irwin, 1963.

Beeth, Gunnar, *International Management Practice.* New York: AMACOM, 1973.

Carson, David, *International Marketing: A Comparative System Approach.* New York: John Wiley, 1967.

Cateora, Philip R., and John M. Hess, *International Marketing* (3rd ed.). Homewood, Ill.: Richard D. Irwin, 1975.

Daniels, John D., Ernest W. Ogram, Jr., and Lee H. Rodebaugh, *International Business Environments and Operations.* Reading, Mass.: Addison-Wesley, 1976.

Dymsza, William A., *Multinational Business Strategy.* New York: McGraw-Hill, 1972.

Fayerweather, John, *International Business Management: A Conceptual Framework.* New York: McGraw-Hill, 1969.

———, *International Marketing* (2nd ed.). Englewood Cliffs, N.J.: Prentice-Hall, 1970.

Grub, Philip D., and Mika Kaskimies, *International Marketing in Perspective.* Helsinki, Finland: Sininen Kirja Oy, 1971.

Hays, Richard D., Christopher M. Korth, and Manucher Roudiani, *International Business: An Introduction to the World of the Multinational Firm.* Englewood Cliffs, N.J.: Prentice-Hall, 1972.

ICAME, *Marketing Management: Cases from the Emerging Countries.* Reading, Mass.: Addison-Wesley, 1966.

Kramer, Roland L., *International Marketing* (3rd ed.). Cincinnati: South-Western Publishing, 1970.

Leighton, D.S.R., *International Marketing: Text and Cases.* New York: McGraw-Hill, 1966.

Miracle, Gordon E., and Gerald S. Albaum, *International Marketing Management.* Homewood, Ill.: Richard D. Irwin, 1970.

Robinson, Richard D., *International Management.* New York: Rinehart & Winston, 1967.

Sethi, S. Prakash, *Advanced Cases in Multinational Business Operations.* Pacific Palisades, Calif.: Goodyear Publishing, 1972.

Simmonds, Kenneth, and David Leighton, *Case Problems in Marketing.* Old Woking, Surrey, England: Thomas Nelson, 1973.

Terpstra, Vern, *American Marketing in the Common Market.* New York: Praeger, 1967.

——, *International Marketing.* New York: Holt, Rinehart & Winston, 1972.

Vernon, Raymond, and Louis T. Wells, Jr., *Manager in the International Economy* (3rd ed.). Englewood Cliffs, N.J.: Prentice-Hall, 1976.

Yoshino, M. Y., *The Japanese Marketing System, Adaptations and Innovations.* Cambridge, Mass.: M.I.T. Press, 1971.

ARTICLES

The following list includes all the articles on international and foreign marketing that appeared in the *Journal of Marketing* between 1968 and 1977.

1968

Bartels, Robert, "Are Domestic and International Marketing Dissimilar?" 32, No. 3 (July 1968), 56–61.

Carson, David, "Marketing Organization in British Manufacturing Firms," 32, No. 2 (1968), 34–39.

Kriesberg, Martin, "Marketing Food in Developing Nations—Second Phase of the War on Hunger," 32, No. 4 (October 1968), 55-60.

Slater, Charles C., "Marketing Processes in Developing Latin American Societies," 32, No. 3 (1968), 50–55.

Thorelli, Hans B., "South Africa: Its Multicultural Marketing System," 32, No. 2 (April 1968), 40–47.

Wells, Louis T., Jr., "A Product Life Cycle for International Trade," 32, No. 3 (July 1968), 1–6.

1969

Donnelly, James H., Jr., and John K. Ryans, Jr., "Standardized Global Advertising: A Call As Yet Unanswered," 33, No. 2 (April 1967), 57–60.

Keegan, Warren J., "Multinational Product Planning: Strategic Alternatives," 33, No. 1 (January 1969), 58–62.

Lipson, Harry A., and Douglas F. Lamont, "Marketing Policy Decisions Facing International Marketers in the Less-Developed Countries," 33, No. 4 (October 1969), 24–31.

1970

Aylmer, R. J., "Who Makes Marketing Decisions in the Multinational Firm?" 34, No. 4 (October 1970), 25–30.

Leighton, David S. R., "The Internationalization of American Business—The Third Industrial Revolution," 34, No. 3 (July 1970), 3–6.

Nagashima, Akira, "A Comparison of Japanese and U.S. Attitudes towards Foreign Products," 34, No. 1 (January 1970), 68–74.

1971

Lauter, G. Peter, "The Changing Role of Marketing in the Eastern European Socialist Economies," 35, No. 4 (October 1971), 16–20.

Thorelli, Hans B., "Consumer Information Policy in Sweden—What Can Be Learned?" 35, No. 1 (January 1971), 50–55.

1972

Arndt, Johan, "Temporal Lags in Comparative Retailing," 36, No. 4 (October 1972), 40–45.

Ostlund, Lyman E., and Kjell M. Halvorsen, "The Russian Decision Process Governing Trade," 36, April 1972, 3–11.

1973

Walker, Bruce J., and Michael J. Etzel, "The Internationalization of U.S. Franchise Systems: Progress and Procedures," 37, No. 2 (April 1973), 38–46.

Wind, Yoram, Susan P. Douglas, and Howard V. Perlmutter, "Guidelines for Developing International Marketing Strategies," 37, No. 2 (April 1973), 38–46.

1974

Cunningham, William H., Russel M. Moore, and Isabella C. M. Cunningham, "Urban Markets in Industrializing Countries: The Sao Paulo Experience," 38, No. 2 (April 1974), 2–12.

Goldman, Arieh, "Outreach of Consumers and the Modernization of Urban Food Retailing in Developing Countries," 38, No. 4 (October 1974), 8-16.

1975

Green, Robert T., and Eric Langeard, "A Cross-National Comparison of Consumer Habits and Innovator Characteristics," 39, No. 3 (July 1975), 34–41.

Lauter, G. Peter, and Paul M. Dickie, "Multinational Corporations in Eastern European Socialist Economies," 39, No. 4 (October 1975), 40–46.

Walters, J. Hart, Jr., "Marketing in Poland in the 1970's: Significant Progress," 39, No. 4 (October 1975), 47–51.

1976

Dunn, S. Watson, "Effect of National Identity on Multinational Promotional Strategy in Europe," 40, No. 4 (October 1976), 50–57.

Kaikati, Jack G., "The Reincarnation of Barter Trade as a Marketing Tool," 40, No. 2 (April 1976), 17–24.

1977

McIntyre, David R., "Your Overseas Distributor Action Plan," 41, No. 2 (April 1977), 88–90.

van Dam, André, "Marketing in the New International Economic Order," 41, No. 1 (January 1977), 19–23.

ARTICLES

The following list includes all the articles on international and foreign marketing that appeared in the *Journal of Marketing Research* between 1968 and 1976.

1968

Ehrenberg, A.S.C., and G. J Goodhardt, "Comparison and British Repeat Buying Habits," February 1968, p. 29.

Farley, A.J.U., and H. J. Leavitt, "Model of the Distribution of Branded Personal Products in Jamaica," November 1968, p. 362.

Laurent, C. K., and Aquileo A. Parra, "Use of Mail Questionnaires in Colombia," February 1968, p. 101.

Moyer, Reed, "International Market Analysis," November 1968, p. 353.

1969

Crosby, R. W., "Attitude Measurement in a Bilingual Culture," November 1969, p. 421.

Murray, J. A., "Canadian Consumer Expectational Data," February 1969, p. 54.

Wilson, Aubrey, "Industrial Marketing Research in Britain," February 1969, p. 15.

1970

Armstrong, J. Scott, "Application of Econometric Models to International Marketing," May 1970, p. 190.

1971

Boyd, Harper W., Jr., and Michael L. Ray, "What Big Agency Men in Europe Think of Copy Testing Methods," May 1971, p. 219.

Sethi, S. Prakash, "Comparative Cluster Analysis for World Markets," August 1971, p. 348.

1972

Bennett, Peter D., and Robert T. Green, "Political Instability as a Determinant of Direct Foreign Investment in Marketing," May 1972, p. 182.

1974

Hempel, Donald J., "Family Buying Decisions: A Cross-Cultural Perspective," August 1974, p. 295.

1975

Arndt, Johan, and Edgar Crane, "Response Bias, Yea-Saying and the Double Negative," May 1975, p. 218. (A Norwegian study.)

Hueges, Michel, "An Empirical Study of Media Comparison," May 1975, p. 221. (A French study.)

1976

Grønhaug, Kjell, "Exploring Environmental Influences in Organizational Buying," 13, No. 3 (August 1976), 226–29. (A Norwegian study.)

OTHER PERIODICAL SOURCES

Franko, Lawrence G., "The Move toward A Multidivisional Structure in European Organizations," *Administrative Science Quarterly,* Vol. 19, December 1974.

Gregory, Peter, "Wage Structures in Latin America," *Journal of Developing Areas,* Vol. 8, July 1974.

Macrae, Norman, "Pacific Century, 1975–2075," *Economist,* Vol. 254, January 4, 1975.

WHICH COMPANY IS TRULY MULTINATIONAL?

Four senior executives of the world's largest firms with extensive holdings outside the home country speak:

Company A: "We are a multinational firm. We distribute our products in about 100 countries. We manufacture in over 17 countries and do research and development in three countries. We look at all new investment projects—both domestic and overseas— using exactly the same criteria."

The executive from Company A continues, "Of course most of the key posts in our subsidiaries are held by home-country nationals. Whenever replacements for these men are sought, it is the practice, if not the policy, to 'look next to you at the head office' and 'pick someone (usually a home-country national) you know and trust.'"

Company B: "We are a multinational firm. Only 1 percent of the personnel in our affiliate companies are non-nationals. Most of these are U.S. executives on temporary assignments. In all major markets, the affiliate's managing director is of the local nationality."

He continues, "Of course there are very few non-Americans in the key posts at headquarters. The few we have are so Americanized that we usually don't notice their nationality. Unfortunately, you can't find good foreigners who are willing to live in the United States, where our headquarters is located. American executives are more mobile. In addition, Americans have the drive and initiative we like. In fact, the European nationals would prefer to report to an American rather than to some other European."

Company C: "We are a multinational firm. Our product division executives have worldwide profit responsibility. As our organizational chart shows, the United States is just one region on a par with Europe, Latin America, Africa, etc., in each division."

The executive from Company C goes on to explain, "the worldwide product division concept is rather difficult to implement. The senior executives in charge of these divisions have little overseas experience. They have been promoted from domestic posts and tend to view foreign consumer needs as really basically the same as ours. Also, product division executives tend to focus on the domestic market because the domestic market is larger and generates more revenue than the fragmented foreign markets. The rewards are for global performance, but strategy is to focus on domestic. Most of our senior executives simply do not understand what happens overseas and really do not trust foreign executives, even those in key positions."

Company D (non-American): "We are a multinational firm. We have at least 18 nationalities represented at our headquarters. Most senior executives speak at least two languages. About 30 percent of our staff at headquarters are foreigners."

He continues by explaining that "since the voting shareholders must by law come from the home country, the home country's interest must be given careful consideration. But we are proud of our nationality; we shouldn't be ashamed of it. In fact, many times we have been reluctant to use home-country ideas overseas, to our detriment, especially in our U.S. subsidiary. Our country produces good executives, who tend to stay with us a long time. It is harder to keep executives from the United States."

QUESTIONS

1. Which company is truly multinational?
2. What are the attributes of a truly multinational company?
3. Why quibble about how multinational a company is?

underlying forces and concepts

Something which is vitally important but which, I think is often lost sight of in the United States . . . is the fact that international life normally has in it strong competitive elements.

George F. Kennan
(Russia and the West under Lenin and Stalin, 1961)

INTRODUCTION

During the thirty-five years between 1913 and 1948, the volume of world production increased at an average annual rate of around 2 percent, according to a recent study made by the General Agreement on Tariffs and Trade in Geneva.[1] Population growth and gains in productivity each accounted for about half the increase. Over the same period the volume of world trade grew by only about 0.5 percent per year. The result was a decline in the volume of world trade per person and a commensurate decline in the degree of specialization in the world economy.

Between 1948 and 1973, total world production grew at an average annual rate of about 5 percent. Population growth accounted for about two-fifths of the rise, and productivity for about three-fifths. Trade grew at an average annual rate of 7 percent; thus, specialization was on the rise. This chapter focuses on the underlying forces and concepts that both explain and determine the degree of international specialization and trade in the world economy.

TRADE THEORY

As all students of basic economics and introductory international business courses know, it can be demonstrated that a country can profit from trade with the world

[1] General Agreement on Tariffs and Trade, "Trade Liberalization, Protectionism and Interdependence" (Geneva, 1978).

even it it has an absolute cost disadvantage in every product that it produces. I refer, of course, to the well-known demonstration of comparative advantage and how this exists for a country that has an absolute disadvantage in the production cost of every single item on a potential trade list.

Any literate international marketer should be familiar with both the existence and the demonstration of the theory of comparative advantage. However, the theory itself does not relate to the situation faced in the firm. The problem with the theory of international trade, as is so often the case with economic theories, is that reality is far more complex than the limiting assumptions upon which the theory is based. A firm's costs are based not only on factor costs such as wages and materials but also on the volume of production. It has been conclusively demonstrated in hundreds of observations of actual cost behavior that there is a relationship between cost and volume which results in a typical decline in costs of 20–30 percent with each doubling of accumulated volume in the production of manufactured items. This empirical observation, which was first suggested by the Boston Consulting Group, is now widely known as experience theory.

Thus, even though a firm may be paying higher wages and experiencing other higher-factor costs than it would encounter in other parts of the world, if it has a volume advantage over competitors in lower-cost areas its net cost position may still be lower.

Another limitation of classical trade theory is that it ignores product and program differentiation. A company's ability to compete in national or international markets is only partly determined by its cost position. Of great importance is the actual product and program differentiation and the effectiveness of the company's customer offering in relation to competitive offerings. For example, the extraordinarily robust and appreciating deutsche mark which has contributed to the rising prices of Mercedes automobiles has not resulted in a displacement of Mercedes from the high-priced segment of the U.S. automobile market. Clearly, demand for the Mercedes and other "quality" products is so great that customers are prepared to pay a significant price differential in order to obtain what they perceive to be a superior product.

Conceptually, the international marketer needs to clearly distinguish between marketing programs that both identify and incorporate customer need into the marketing mix and manufacturing or production programs that create the products called for in the marketing plan. Production and marketing may be combined in the same country, but conceptually they should be quite distinct and separate. If manufacturing is located in the market country, it should be located there because the considerations that affect manufacturing location favor the market country and not because of an automatic linking of marketing and manufacturing.

Companies may decide to locate production in a single country to take advantage of manufacturing scale economies. The scale economies may more than offset transportation, duty, and other entry costs to foreign target markets. Another strategy is to locate production in a stable country that offers a large pool of trainable, low-cost labor. U.S. and Japanese electronics companies have pursued this strategy in locating labor-intensive production operations in places like Singapore, Hong Kong, and Taiwan to take advantage of the stable political environment and the low wages. In many of these manufacturing locations 100 percent of production is sold outside the country of manufacture. Some uninformed people believe that all multinational manufacturing is of this latter variety when in fact, for the multinational companies as a group, roughly 90 percent of all overseas production is for the market in the country of manufacture and only about 10 percent of multinational production is for so-called third-country markets.

UNDERLYING FORCES OF INTERNATIONAL BUSINESS

Behind the remarkable growth of the international economy in the post–World War II decades are five basic factors that were not present before the war. It is useful to identify these underlying forces to gain an insight into the foundations of the international economy as it exists today:

1. *The international monetary framework.* In 1944 at Bretton Woods, New Hampshire, economists and diplomats from the Allied Nations gathered to plan an international monetary framework for the post–World War II era. The result of their efforts led to the creation of the International Monetary Fund, and to a framework for the establishment of international liquidity to facilitate the transfer of goods and services between nations. The system developed at Bretton Woods as it evolved over the years is far from perfect. However, despite its many flaws, the international monetary framework has proved that it is capable of responding to pressures requiring adjustment. The dollar glut that resulted from the massive balance-of-payments deficits of the United States in the 1960s was addressed by the abandonment of the fixed, or pegged, exchange rate system and the adoption of "floating," or flexible, market-determined rates. The petrodollar crisis of 1974–75 created a great deal of concern, but the system proved capable of absorbing this pressure. In the meantime the petrodollar crisis quietly disappeared as the OPEC countries increased their expenditures for foreign goods and services.

    The rapid growth of trade and investment in the post–World War II era has created an increasing need for international liquidity (i.e., money or a means of payment) to facilitate the exchange of goods and services between nations. Until 1969 the world economy limped along, with gold and foreign exchange as the entire source of international liquidity. Since 1969 the liquidity available to nations has been supplemented by the agreement of International Monetary Fund members to accept the SDRs (special drawing rights) in settling reserve transactions. For the first time an international reserve asset is available. The inherent limitations on liquidity expansion through the use of gold and foreign exchange have been overcome. The essential fact concerning the international monetary framework is that for over two decades it has functioned adequately. This evolving structure has every prospect of continuing to function adequately, thus making it possible for companies to finance trade and investment between nations, and to continue their multinational marketing efforts.

2. *Global peace.* In spite of the almost continuous local warfare that has persisted since 1945, the global condition has been characterized by the absence of a world war or warfare involving a substantial proportion of the

nations of the world. Perhaps *global peace* is an exaggerated expression to characterize this condition, but nevertheless the absence of global warfare has been an essential basis for the healthy and rapid growth of the international economy.

3. *Domestic economic growth.* Behind this growth are the more basic factors of technology and managerial skill, which have created growing markets in those domestic economies that have been receptive to the entry of international firms. When a country is growing rapidly, receptiveness is encouraged because a growing country means growing markets and therefore expanding opportunities. Under this condition it is possible for an outside or international company to enter a domestic economy and to establish itself without taking business away from local firms. The growing economy is a classic illustration of the so-called nonzero sums game whereby players can participate and "win" without doing so at the expense of others because their "play" enlarges the size of the total gains to be distributed. Without economic growth, the only way that international participation in countries could occur would be if they were able to take business away from local enterprise (assuming of course that local enterprise was not deliberately liquidating its position). If this kind of competition between international and domestic enterprise existed, it is more likely that domestic enterprise would seek governmental intervention to protect its local position.

Thus there are two reasons why economic growth has been an underlying force in the expansion of the international economy. First, growth has created market opportunities. The existence of market opportunities has been the major reason for the international expansion of enterprise. Of course, international enterprise has itself contributed to the process of development in host countries.[2] Second, economic growth has reduced the resistance that might otherwise have developed in response to the entry of foreign firms into domestic economies.

4. *Communications.* Developments that have increased the speed and capacity and lowered the cost of transportation and electronics have been a major force underlying international business expansion. The jet airplane has revolutionized the communications field by making it possible for people to travel around the world in less than forty-eight hours. One of the essential characteristics of the effective business enterprise is the face-to-face meeting of those responsible for directing the enterprise. Without the jet airplane, the face-to-face contact so essential to business management would not have been possible because the amount of time required to travel the distance involved in international operations would be too great. The jet aircraft has made it possible for executives to be in face-to-face contact at regular intervals throughout the year.

A second major communications development has been the enormous improvement in the ability to transmit data electronically. The cost of voice and data communications globally has declined continuously since World War II, and this declining cost and the increasing availability of electronic data have made it possible to knit the geographically dispersed operations more tightly together.

5. *The multinational corporation.* The multinational corporation, or any business enterprise that pursues global business objectives by relating

---

[2] See, for example, J. J. Servan-Schreiber, *The American Challenge* (New York: Atheneum, 1969), for a European view of the role of multinational enterprise in national development.

world resources to world market opportunity simultaneously in two or more countries,[3] has been the institutional device that has pulled together and taken advantage of the four basic changes outlined above. Within the international monetary framework and under the umbrella of global peace, the corporation has utilized the expanding communications technologies both to take advantage of and to contribute to economic growth throughout the world. It has identified markets, mobilized manpower and financial resources, and developed and implemented research, manufacturing, and marketing programs on a global scale.

A CONCEPTUAL FRAMEWORK

Figure 2-1 presents a strategy formulation conceptual framework. Phase 1 of this framework identifies three basic strategic dimensions: the environment, the organization, and values and aspirations. The strategic process requires an assessment of opportunities, threats, and trends in the environment. For the international company, this assessment must be conducted on a regional, national, and global basis. Since the number of countries in the world far exceeds the resource capacity of most companies, screening criteria are needed to narrow the field of potential opportunity to those that are most attractive and most related to the organization's own strengths and weaknesses.

The second phase of the strategic process consists of the assessment of the organization's strengths and weaknesses and the comparison of strengths and weaknesses with opportunities, threats, and trends. The objective of this exercise is to identify alternatives. What is possible? The strategic process of assessment continues with the assessment of values and aspirations to determine their relative importance in the firm's aspiration level.

Phase 2 should create a list of alternatives or of possibilities. In phase 3 it is necessary to confront the alternatives with the firm's own values and aspirations to make specific choices. The determination of objectives requires a specification of both product/market objectives and broader organizational objectives.

Phase 4 of the framework requires the development of integrated plans and programs to achieve the objectives specified in phase 3. Our particular concern in this book is the development of integrated marketing programs, but any marketing

[3] This is the definition we shall use in this text. Other definitions abound. A major study of the multinational corporation directed by Professor Raymond Vernon of the Harvard Business School defines *multinational corporation* as any one of the 187 business enterprises in *Fortune*'s 500 in 1967 that in 1967 or in previous years had controlled manufacturing subsidiaries in six or more foreign countries. This definition, by limiting the definition to companies on *Fortune*'s list of the five hundred largest U.S. companies, focuses on the international activities of major enterprises. The striking aspect of the remarkable growth of the international economy is the domination of the expansion of direct business operations by larger companies. It is estimated, for example, that over 80 percent of U.S. international direct investments is accounted for by the five hundred largest U.S. manufacturing enterprises. By and large, small business has not participated extensively or proportionally in expansion into international markets. Nevertheless, by our definition, any company that operates in two or more countries is multinational. This definition reflects our conviction that smaller enterprises can participate effectively in multinational marketing.

FIGURE 2-1. Strategy Formulation—A Conceptual Framework

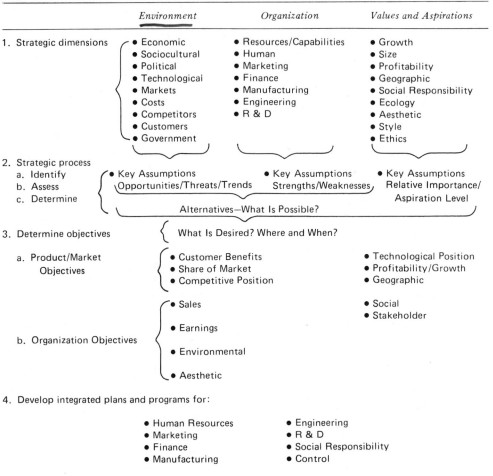

	Environment	*Organization*	*Values and Aspirations*
1. Strategic dimensions	• Economic • Sociocultural • Political • Technological • Markets • Costs • Competitors • Customers • Government	• Resources/Capabilities • Human • Marketing • Finance • Manufacturing • Engineering • R & D	• Growth • Size • Profitability • Geographic • Social Responsibility • Ecology • Aesthetic • Style • Ethics

2. Strategic process
   a. Identify
   b. Assess
   c. Determine

• Key Assumptions
Opportunities/Threats/Trends

• Key Assumptions
Strengths/Weaknesses

• Key Assumptions
Relative Importance/
Aspiration Level

Alternatives—What Is Possible?

3. Determine objectives

What Is Desired? Where and When?

a. Product/Market
   Objectives

• Customer Benefits
• Share of Market
• Competitive Position

• Technological Position
• Profitability/Growth
• Geographic

• Sales

• Social
• Stakeholder

b. Organization Objectives

• Earnings

• Environmental

• Aesthetic

4. Develop integrated plans and programs for:

• Human Resources
• Marketing
• Finance
• Manufacturing

• Engineering
• R & D
• Social Responsibility
• Control

5. Obtain and commit resource to plans and programs.
6. Control. Compare implementation results with plans. Compare environmental, organizational, and value assessment with key assumptions.
7. Timing

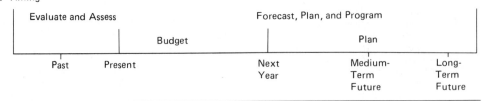

Evaluate and Assess		Forecast, Plan, and Program	
	Budget	Plan	
Past Present		Next Year	Medium- Term Future Long- Term Future

program must be integrated and related to programs for human resources, finance, manufacturing, engineering, research and development, control, and social responsibility.

Phase 5 calls for obtaining and committing resources to the plans and programs.

Phase 6 of the framework, control, overlaps with strategy implementation. In this phase implementation results are compared with plans, and any deviation from plans is reviewed to determine whether this requires an adjustment in the strategy or improvement in the implementation effort. Another aspect of control, and critically important as a part of strategy formulation, is the scanning of the external and internal environment as well as stakeholder values to compare environmental, organizational, and value assessment with key assumptions that were established at the beginning of the strategy formulation process.

Phase 7, timing, indicates the relationship of the past, present, and future to the strategy formulation process. As indicated in Figure 2-1, strategy formulation cuts across the time line. It requires an evaluation and assessment of past events, an assessment and identification of present realities, and an anticipation or forecast of future conditions. Since the past is history, and the future has not yet occurred, the only time period in which we can actually have an impact on the external world is the present. Thus strategy, even though it has a profound impact on a company's future, is implemented in the present. What a manager does on Monday morning is as much a part of the overall strategy of the organization as any thinking about what the organization might be five, ten, or fifteen years from now. Many managers fall into the trap of assuming that there is some magical distinction between future thoughts and present actions. Nothing could be further from the truth. The future is nothing more or less than an accumulation of actions in the present. Indeed, in a changing world the future is a creation of man's ego, and ego operates not only in thought but of course in the action of the moment.

Figure 2-2 suggests the major characteristics of the environment of global marketing. At the center of the diagram is the company, which is defined in terms of four major dimensions: its products, its skills (particularly the marketing skills of product, communications, distribution, pricing, and marketing research management, and also its production, R & D, financial, and managerial skills), its financial resources, and its people. The company exists in a world that contains 188 different countries and territories, each of which is characterized by seven major dimensions: economic, sociocultural, technological, physical, market, competitive, and governmental. A fundamental aspect of the global market environment is that it is characterized by nations that are both similar to and different from each other. Although each of these national environments is different, both statistical analysis of the major environmental dimensions and managerial judgment agree that it is possible to cluster these 188 different market environments in order to establish groups of countries that result in clear within-group similarities and between-group differences.[4]

---

[4] See, for example, S. Prakash Sethi, "Comparative Cluster Analysis for World Markets," *Journal of Marketing Research* (Chicago: American Marketing Association, August 1971).

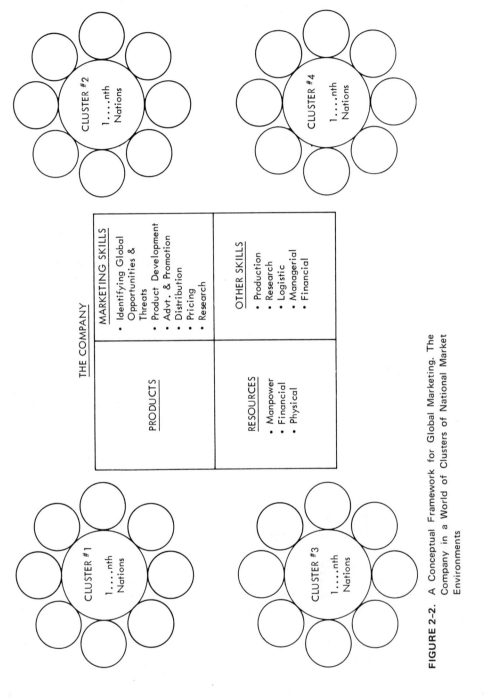

FIGURE 2-2. A Conceptual Framework for Global Marketing. The Company in a World of Clusters of National Market Environments

The economic environment in global markets is highly diverse. Per capita 1975 GNP ranged from a low of $90 per annum in Mali and Bangladesh to a high of over $15,190 in Kuwait.[5] At the extremes there is no question that income is a differentiating influence in world markets today. The similarities between the United States market and, say, the market in Malawi are so small as to be unimportant. Nevertheless, within this wide range of global per capita income, there are clusters of countries at the bottom, in the middle, and at the top that are so similar in terms of income that the income in these clusters becomes a unifying influence rather than a differentiating one.

Another important market characteristic is size. The U.S. market, with almost $2 trillion in annual income, is enormous. Other industrialized countries with incomes on a per capita basis quite similar to that of the United States are still quite small in the aggregate. A good example would be Sweden, whose per capita GNP in 1975 was $8,150 but whose GNP was only $67 billion. At these extremes, the size of markets is a highly differentiating influence. The structure, staffing, information, and control system that is appropriate for the Swedish marketing organization would be grossly inadequate for an organization that obtains a similar share of the U.S. market. A company that is simultaneously marketing in large and small markets must be flexible in its approach to organization, staffing information, and control lest it find itself in the position of enforcing some unified approach to each of these system areas—and as a consequence having organizations, information systems, and control systems that are either inadequate to the size of the market or too elaborate for a smaller market.

Governmental influences in the company's global environment, including tariffs, taxes, laws, regulations, and codes, are highly differentiated. For example, companies marketing equipment used in the construction and building trades must face the complete welter of codes and regulations that exist not only internationally but also within a particular national environment in various local political jurisdictions. Consider, for example, the situation faced by a crane manufacturer. In many countries in the world, cranes must have a free-fall capability for instantly releasing their load. This requirement has been established in order to make the cranes safer. A crane with the capability of a free-fall displacement of its load is difficult to tip over. In other countries, however, there is a requirement that a crane not have a free-fall capacity. The prohibition against free fall is also motivated by a desire to increase the safety of crane operation. The rationale behind the prohibition of free-fall capability is that any crane with this capability is liable to lose its entire load accidentally. In other words, considerations of safety for this particular product have motivated opposite conditions in the area of free fall, and any company that wishes to market this product internationally must be able to respond to these conditions and to offer products that do not have such a capability.

The company's strengths, weaknesses, and characteristics are important elements of the multinational marketing conceptual framework. One of the most important company conditions is the product or products that it offers in international markets. One useful way of looking at products internationally is to place

[5] Data source: *World Bank Atlas,* published by the World Bank, 1977.

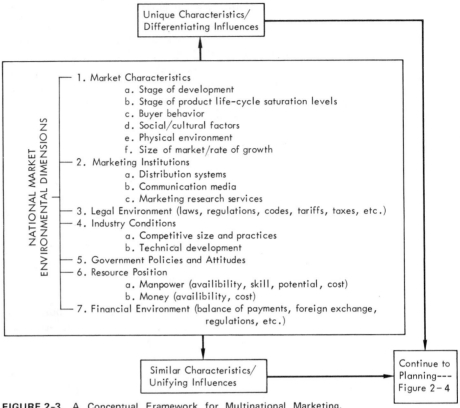

FIGURE 2-3. A Conceptual Framework for Multinational Marketing. Major Dimensions of a National Market Environment: Absolute and Compared to Other Nations

them on a continuum of environmental sensitivity. At one end of the continuum are the environmentally insensitive products, which do not require significant adaptation to the economic and social environments of markets around the world. At the other end of the continuum are those products that are highly sensitive to differences in economic, sociocultural, physical, and governmental factors in world markets. A company with environmentally insensitive products is going to have to spend relatively less time determining the specific and unique conditions of local markets because the product the company offers is basically universal. A computer line is an example of an environmentally insensitive product. At the other end of the continuum, the company in the business of marketing environmentally sensitive products is going to have to spend a great deal of time and effort learning about the way its products interact with the specific economic, social and cultural, physical and prescriptive environmental conditions that exist throughout the world. Convenience foods are an example of environmentally sensitive products.

As outlined in Figure 2-3, markets consist of seven major dimensions. These dimensions must be scanned to assess the basic characteristics of each national market environment. This will help one determine which of these characteristics are

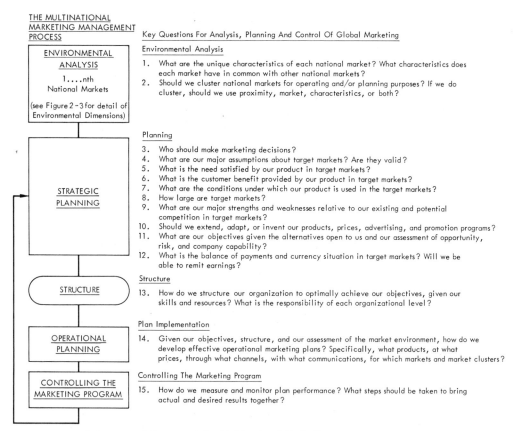

THE MULTINATIONAL
MARKETING MANAGEMENT
PROCESS

ENVIRONMENTAL
ANALYSIS

1....nth
National Markets

(see Figure 2-3 for detail of
Environmental Dimensions)

STRATEGIC
PLANNING

STRUCTURE

OPERATIONAL
PLANNING

CONTROLLING THE
MARKETING PROGRAM

Key Questions For Analysis, Planning And Control Of Global Marketing

Environmental Analysis

1. What are the unique characteristics of each national market? What characteristics does each market have in common with other national markets?
2. Should we cluster national markets for operating and/or planning purposes? If we do cluster, should we use proximity, market, characteristics, or both?

Planning

3. Who should make marketing decisions?
4. What are our major assumptions about target markets? Are they valid?
5. What is the need satisfied by our product in target markets?
6. What is the customer benefit provided by our product in target markets?
7. What are the conditions under which our product is used in the target markets?
8. How large are target markets?
9. What are our major strengths and weaknesses relative to our existing and potential competition in target markets?
10. Should we extend, adapt, or invent our products, prices, advertising, and promotion programs?
11. What are our objectives given the alternatives open to us and our assessment of opportunity, risk, and company capability?
12. What is the balance of payments and currency situation in target markets? Will we be able to remit earnings?

Structure

13. How do we structure our organization to optimally achieve our objectives, given our skills and resources? What is the responsibility of each organizational level?

Plan Implementation

14. Given our objectives, structure, and our assessment of the market environment, how do we develop effective operational marketing plans? Specifically, what products, at what prices, through what channels, with what communications, for which markets and market clusters?

Controlling The Marketing Program

15. How do we measure and monitor plan performance? What steps should be taken to bring actual and desired results together?

FIGURE 2-4. A Conceptual Framework for Multinational Marketing

similar and therefore unifying, and which are unique and therefore differentiating.[6] Information and conclusions resulting from this scanning feed into the analysis, planning, and control process shown in Figure 2-4, which is concerned with relating opportunities and threats in the world market environment to the basic strengths and weaknesses of the company. The planning process results in the selection of objectives among the alternatives open to the company. Given objectives, companies decide upon an organization appropriate to the company's basic skills and resources. Within the framework of a specified organizational structure, the implementation of decisions about objectives must be accomplished. In marketing this requires the design and specification of products, prices, channels, and communications. Given specified marketing plans, the next step is implementation. The final phase of the global marketing process is control, that is, the measurement and evaluation of performance. The results of this control activity feed back to the planning process and become an important input to the planning cycle.

[6]The concept of unifying and differentiating influences was first suggested by John Fayerweather in *International Business Management: A Conceptual Framework* (New York: McGraw-Hill, 1969).

The process of global marketing requires the marketing manager to answer a number of basic questions in order to plan and implement a global marketing strategy. He must identify opportunities and threats. He must know where global markets are located today, and where they will be in the future. The remarkable success in recent years of countries such as Japan, Brazil, and Spain is a reminder that opportunity is constantly shifting in the world. The global marketer needs to identify similarities and differences in order to know what to change and what not to change. To do this, an organization must be structured to respond to the unique aspects of country markets and at the same time be capable of identifying relevant experience and applying it across national boundaries.

LEVERAGE

One of the unique advantages of a multinational company is the opportunity to develop "leverage," or advantages that it has because it operates simultaneously in more than one national market. A multinational company can develop seven types of "leverage":

1. *Program transfers.* It can draw upon strategies, products, advertising appeals, sales management practices, promotional ideas, and so on, that have been tested in actual markets and can apply them in other comparable markets.
2. *Systems transfers.* It can introduce planning, budgeting, new-product strategies, and other successful systems developed and tested in the company into new markets.
3. *People transfers.* It can assign skilled people across national boundaries, thus drawing upon a manpower pool of international rather than merely national dimensions.
4. *Scale economies in manufacturing.* The multinational firm, in addition to obtaining traditional single-plant scale economies, can combine into finished products those components manufactured in scale-efficient plants in different countries.
5. *Economies of centralization of functional activities.* Instead of duplicating its functional staff, it can concentrate activities at single locations and thereby develop greater competence while reducing costs. This has been strikingly accomplished in financial management and engineering and is increasingly being accomplished in marketing.
6. *Resource utilization.* A major strength of the multinational company is its ability to scan the entire world to identify sources of manpower, money, and materials that will enable it to compete most effectively in world markets.
7. *Global strategy.* The multinational company scans the world for markets that will provide an opportunity for it to apply its skills, matches these markets with its resources, and—where necessary to exploit opportunity—creates and shifts resources to tap identified opportunities. The application of top management's strategic planning expertise on a global scale is an important source of leverage or advantage over the local firm.

CONCLUSION

From the turn of the century until World War II, world production increased at the rate of approximately 2 percent per annum and world trade increased at the rate of approximately 1 percent per annum. This was a period of decline in specialization in the world economy, with the trend toward greater autarchy on the part of nations. Since World War II the average increase in world production has been about 5 percent per annum and international trade about 7 percent. Thus, international specialization has gradually been increasing. The basic forces that led to the rise of the national firm have been operating in the world economy to create the international firm.

Conceptually, companies must make a clear distinction between the requirements for an effective marketing plan and the requirements for an effective production plan. The two activities may take place in the same country, but there is no reason why they *must* do so.

The chapter suggests a conceptual framework for developing both national and international strategic plans and concludes with a list of ways in which a multinational company can develop leverage or advantage vis-à-vis national competitors.

BIBLIOGRAPHY

Aharoni, Yair, *The Foreign Investment Decision Process.* Boston: Division of Research, Graduate School of Business Administration, Harvard University, 1966.

Barnet, Richard J., and Ronald E. Muller, *Global Reach.* New York: Simon & Schuster, 1974.

de Jouvenel, Bertrand, *The Art of Conjecture.* New York: Basic Books, 1967.

Galbraith, John K., *New Industrial State* (2nd and rev. eds.). Boston: Houghton Mifflin, 1972.

Gilpin, Robert, *U.S. Power and the Multinational Corporation.* New York: Basic Books, 1975.

Heilbroner, Robert L., *Business Civilization in Decline.* New York: Norton, 1976.

——, *Worldly Philosophers.* Los Angeles: S&S Enterprises, 1972.

Kindelberger, Charles P., *Foreign Trade and the National Economy.* New Haven: Yale University Press, 1962.

——, *International Economics* (5th ed.). Homewood, Ill.: Richard D. Irwin, 1973.

Korbin, S., "The Environmental Determinants of Foreign Direct Investment: An Ex Post Empirical Analysis," *Journal of International Business Studies,* Fall/Winter 1976, pp. 29–42.

Mason, R. Hal, Robert R. Miller, and Dale R. Weigel, *The Economics of International Business.* New York: John Wiley, 1975.

Ohlin, Bertil, *Interregional and International Trade.* Cambridge, Mass.: Harvard University Press, 1933.

Robock, Stefan H., and Kenneth Simmonds, *International Business and Multinational Enterprises.* Homewood, Ill.: Richard D. Irwin, 1973.

Turner, Louis, *Multinational Companies and the Third World.* New York: Hill & Wang, 1973.

Wilkins, Mira, *The Emergence of Multinational Enterprise: American Business Abroad from the Colonial Era to 1914.* Cambridge, Mass.: Harvard University Press, 1970.

——, *The Maturing of Multinational Enterprise: American Business Abroad from 1914 to 1970.* Cambridge, Mass.: Harvard University Press, 1974.

LAUNDROWASH S.p.A. (A)

In February 1961 Mr. Mario Paino, owner of Laundrowash S.p.A., was wondering what price schedules he should set for his new Turin automatic laundry. Laundrowash S.p.A., which was scheduled to open May 9, 1961, was to be the first American style automatic coin-operated laundry in Italy.

Mr. Paino, a successful Italian investor living in Rome, had recently acquired the Speed Wash coin-operated laundry equipment franchise for Italy. After acquiring the franchise, he had made many attempts to interest Italian investors in coin-operated laundries, but each time these attempts were greeted with skepticism. Many investors were interested, but felt the market risks of this radical new service were too great to justify their making the first move. After a number of unsuccessful attempts to interest investors, Mr. Paino decided to form a corporation called Laundrowash S.p.A. and open his own Speed Wash coin-operated laundry. Although his main objective remained to distribute coin-operated equipment, he felt that a successfully operating laundry would provide the evidence he needed to convince investors that coin-ops could be profitable in Italy.

DEFINITION AND DEVELOPMENT OF COIN-OPS IN THE UNITED STATES

The term "coin-op" developed in the United States. It was used there to describe unattended (or attended by one clerk) laundries where customers operated automatic washers, dryers, and soap and bleach dispensers themselves by dropping coins in the appropriate slots. In a coin-operated laundry, each machine was equipped with a coin meter that automatically operated the machine when the correct amount of change was inserted.

In the United States the forerunners of coin-ops were "laundrettes." The laundrette was a laundry where the customers' clothes were washed by laundry attendants. This type of laundry offered a same-day, rough-dry service in which the clothes were simply washed by machine, and dried in an automatic dryer. They also usually offered a more expensive "semi-finished" service in which clothes were hand folded after drying. Although most laundrettes used automatic equipment, their labor cost for attendants limited their ability to compete on a price basis with coin-ops. It also limited the hours per day that they could remain open, so that their costs were not spread over a twenty-four-hour day. Because of their higher cost structure, the cost per pound to the housewife was greater than that of the coin-ops.

Coin-ops were first introduced in the United States at the close of World War II. Their installation was on a small scale, however, and made little market impression. Initial attempts to establish them on a large scale failed, partly because then-existing machines and metering devices were unreliable.

With rising labor costs, and the development of effective coin-metering equipment and more reliable machines, the way was open for the installation of self-service laundries in America. The business got its start in California, where people were more accustomed to self-service facilities. By 1958, coin-ops were spread over the entire country, and new ones were being established at the rate of one per day.

In early 1960 *Coin-Op Magazine* estimated that there were 25,000 automatic laundries in the U.S., and that during the year another 3,000 would open their doors. Using an average figure of 20 machines per laundry, this meant that there were 500,000 coin-operated machines in the U.S. in January of 1960, and expectations were that an additional 60,000 would be installed during the year. Throughout the rise of the coin-ops, annual sales of four million automatic machines for home use remained steady.

One of the reasons for this rapid growth, according to *Barron's*[1] was the lower cost to the housewife.

> A housewife can wash a load of clothes in one (coin-operated machine) for 10 or 20 cents, and she can use a dryer which will take up to four loads of washing for one cent per minute. Indeed, all her laundering for a week can be done in an hour for no more than $1.25, or far less than the payments on a washing machine of her own.

In 1960, the average prices in the U.S. were less than 25 cents per wash, and 10 cents per five-minute drying cycle.

In America, small investors were attracted to coin-ops by the low initial cash outlay, the small claim on their time, and the prospect of a high return on investment. ALD, Inc., the largest equipment supplier to the trade, estimated that a laundry containing 20 regular 9 lb. (4 kilos) automatic machines and one large 25 lb. (11 kilos) machine for rugs, eight dryers, and all necessary auxiliary equipment such as changemakers, water softeners, boilers, heaters, and sinks would cost, completely installed, $23,000. Another estimate of laundry costs was made by an appraisal bulletin published in January 1959, which suggested that on the average the total cost of all equipment and installation charges averaged about $700 per washer.

[1] November 10, 1958. *Barron's* is a well-known U.S. financial publication.

Using this guide, the total investment for the average 20-machine laundry in the U.S. was around $14,000. It further reported:

> Income and operating information is rather sketchy but we have obtained figures in St. Louis from what we consider reliable sources. A good average sized coin-op in the St. Louis area will gross about $15,000 during this year. In order to do this volume of business, the laundry would have to be in a good location and should operate 24 hours a day, 365 days a year. We found a few coin-ops gross as high as $30,000 per year.
>
> Insofar as the expenses are concerned, on a coin-op doing an annual gross of $15,000, the breakdown will be about like this:

	Monthly	Yearly
Rent	$100	$1,200
Utilities	200	2,400
Maintenance	50	600
Insurance (including vandalism coverage)	30	360
Taxes	10	120
Miscellaneous	150	1,800
	$540	$6,480

THE ITALIAN MARKET

After forming Laundrowash S.p.A. in 1960 to operate the first coin-op laundry in Italy, Mr. Paino's first step was to investigate potential cities as sites for his automatic laundry. In checking market statistics, he quickly found that considerable variations existed in different regions. For example, average per capita Gross National Product for 1959 in Italy was listed as $545. In the same year a survey in the industrial north[2] revealed a much different figure: a sample of 97,000 workers in metallurgical and mechanical firms showed that payments to them averaged $2,200 per year including direct payments, indirect payments, and charges for social welfare. Statistics for the province of Turin, in the north, showed one car owner for every 22 persons while this figure for Nuovo, in comparatively backward Sardinia, was 272. The average figure for Italy of 77 (1956) was anything but indicative of the real picture. A close look at the figures confirmed Mr. Paino's conclusion that Italy was economically two countries: the highly-developed north and the relatively under-developed south.

Because of the much higher living standards there, Mr. Paino decided to concentrate his search in northern Italy. In the north, Turin seemed the best choice for a number of reasons. Since 1946, the city had grown from 700,000 to over one million in population. With less than 4 percent of the country's population, it paid almost 20 percent of the national tax bill. It was the fourth largest city in Italy,

[2]Turin Industrial Association, May 1959. Results published in *Setting Up a Business in Italy*. Investment Information Office, Rome, 1960.

EXHIBIT 1. Street Plan Showing the Site of the Automatic Laundry

Wine Shop	China Shop	Dress Shop	Baby Clothing Shop	Watch Shop	Furniture Shop	Automatic Laundry Shop	Health Center	Women's Purse Shop	Hard-ware Shop	Cloth Shop	Sports Shop	Cloth. Shop

VIA ROSSELLI

Coffee Bar & Billiard Hall	Butcher Shop	Shoe Shop	Fruit Shop	Milk Shop	Grocery Store	Vegetable Shop	Household Goods and Furniture Shop	

◀———————————— One city block ————————————▶

located in the heart of the industrial Po Valley, where workers enjoyed a standard of living rivalling that of the most advanced European countries. After several visits to Turin, Mr. Paino concluded that it was a dynamic modern city, whose population was receptive to new ideas. Therefore, when he was offered a chance to sign a two-year lease for a 5 × 13 metre shop on Via Rosselli, he accepted with the thought of setting up his first coin-op laundry there.

THE SITE

Via Rosselli was a wide, tree-lined street at the southwest edge of Turin. A street plan of Turin showing the location of the automatic laundry and the other shops in the block is given in Exhibit 1. The area was predominantly residential, with most families living in apartment buildings ranging from four to seven stories in height. All buildings within approximately 2,000 metres of the laundry appeared to be of post-war construction. The apartments in the immediate area were of excellent quality and had been constructed within the last five years. The average four-room apartment was renting for around $65 per month. There were no single unit dwellings in the area.

The inhabitants were mainly middle-class families, with a few professionals and managers. Occupationally they were about evenly divided between office workers and skilled factory workers, with most families having more than one wage earner. Mr. Paino estimated that average family income was around $200 per month, and that there was about one car for every 20 people in the area.

Turin was divided into 20 zones for statistical reporting. The automatic laundry site was located at the southern end of zone 17. Exhibit 2 shows population statistics for zone 17, and total figures for all 20 zones.

AVAILABLE LAUNDRY FACILITIES

For the Turin housewife, there were three ways of getting her wash done. She could have it done by a "charwoman," do it herself at home, or send it to a com-

EXHIBIT 2 . Population Statistics for the Proposed Laundrowash Zone*
(30th January, 1959)

	Blue Collar Workers		Office Workers		Managers		Self-Employed		Self Employed Professionals		Part-Time Workers		Non-Working Population		%
	Number	%	Number	%	Number	%	Number	%	Number	%	Number	%	Number	%	
LAUNDROWASH Zone (17)	26,232	24.0	17,682	16.0	790	0.7	6,033	5.0	391	0.3	2,162	2.0	57,395	52.0	110,685	100
City Total (percentages only)		21.0		14.0		1.0		7.0		1.0		2.0		54.0		100

*Note: For statistical reporting purposes, Turin was divided into 20 zones.

Source: Citta di Torino

EXHIBIT 3. Washing Machine Sales and Saturation in Italy

	Sales			Household Saturation Index		
Year	Number (000)	Average Price in Lire	Total Value in Lire (000)	Household Units (000)	Number with Machines (000)	Percentage with Machines
1950	10	80,000	800,000	5,910	11	.18
1951	20	80,000	1,600,000	6,260	30	.49
1952	23	85,000	1,955,000	6,560	50	.76
1953	30	85,000	2,550,000	6,810	80	1.17
1954	40	90,000	3,600,000	7,300	115	1.57
1955	52	90,000	4,680,000	7,600	160	2.10
1956	74	100,000	7,400,000	8,000	225	2.80
1957	90	100,000	9,020,000	8,350	300	3.60
1958	120	110,000	13,200,000	8,700	400	4.60
1959	190	110,000	20,900,000	9,100	570	6.25

Source: Apparecchi Elettrodomestici, anno 111, No. 8, Agosto 1960, page 64.

mercial laundry. A great deal of washing was done by "charwomen" who charged from 200 ($0.32) to 250 lire ($0.40) per hour plus soap. These women would come into homes and wash or would do the laundry in their own homes.

The housewife did her laundry at home by machine if she owned one, but since this was rare, the more usual method was by hand. Exhibit 3 shows washing machine sales and market saturation figures for Italy. Mr. Paino estimated that the saturation index for Turin was double the national average.

There were approximately 200 commercial laundries in Turin. Their per kilo rates for unfinished dry laundry ranged from 110 to 160 lire while finished rates per kilo were from 170 to 235 lire. Average finished piece rates ranged from 160–200 lire per shirt and from 130–150 lire per sheet.

Although confident that his laundry would succeed, Mr. Paino recognized that the success in the United States of coin-op laundries did not necessarily mean that they would be successful in Italy. The standard of living, for example, was different and there were definite customs and cultural patterns in Italy that might retard the early acceptance of the automatic laundry idea. Several people had pointed to the disappointing sales of supermarkets which had recently opened in Turin as an example of what was in store for other American ideas that were transplanted to Italy. Mr. Paino, however, felt that lessons learned from the super-market experience supported his belief in the future of automatic laundries. He noted that especially among middle- and upper-middle-class housewives it was a "status symbol" to be seen in a supermarket. By going to a supermarket, the housewife proved that she was "modern" and "up to date."

Housewives did not continue to trade in supermarkets, according to Mr. Paino, because the great majority were without cars and found supermarkets too inconvenient. He reasoned that the need to feel "modern" which motivated many women to try supermarkets would also motivate them to try an automatic laundry.

Once they had tried them, he was convinced women would continue to use the laundries.

INVESTMENT COSTS

Exhibit 4 was Mr. Paino's estimation of the cost of equipping and installing a laundry with sixteen 9 lb. (4 kilos) machines, one 25 lb. (11 kilos) rug washer, six dryers, and all necessary auxiliary equipment, leasehold improvements, and furniture. The estimated total investment cost of $31,440 shown in Exhibit 4 was almost double that of the average cost of an equivalent sized U.S. laundry.

Mr. Paino observed that "clearly the reason for the high investment cost is the expensive imported auxiliary equipment." A typical example of the cost of importing was the hot water storage tank shown below:

Cost of Imported Hot Water Storage Tank

U.S. Factory Cost	$592
Freight: Factory to New York	62
Freight: New York to Genoa	300
Duty and Misc. Import Taxes	406
Total Landed Cost in Italy	$1,360

All equipment in Exhibit 4 was imported. For the type of equipment necessary, no Italian source existed. Although Mr. Paino was concerned about the high costs, he was not completely discouraged. He did observe that "it is quite evident that if I am ever going to make a success of my Speed Wash franchise, I must find a cheaper Italian source of auxiliary equipment." He reasoned that investors

EXHIBIT 4. Investment Required for Turin Automatic-Laundry

Equipment	No. of Units	Cost per Unit	Total Cost
Four-kilo Speed Wash washers with meter	16	$ 524	$ 8,384
11-kilo washer with meter	1	1,179	1,179
Speed Wash dryers with meter	6	758	4,548
Water Extractor, with meter	1	758	758
Hot water storage tank	1	1,400	1,400
Water softener	1	2,213	2,213
Water heater	1	2,710	2,710
Soap and bleach dispenser	1	758	758
Outdoor electric sign	1	454	454
Indoor instructions signs		252	252
Furniture		179	179
Equipment Total:			22,835
Installation Costs and Leasehold Improvements			8,605
Total Investment Required			$31,440

would be concerned with the total cost of opening a laundry, and that lowering this figure by bringing down auxiliary equipment costs would lower the cost of entering the business, and therefore make it more attractive as an investment.

The cost of importing washers was not so high as the cost of the auxiliary equipment. The landed cost in Genoa of a $215 (factory price) Speed Wash automatic washer was $325. Mr. Paino planned to sell these machines to coin-op investors at the landed price plus a 38 percent markup.

Mr. Paino's estimate of monthly operating expenses is shown below:

Estimated Monthly Operating Expenses

Fixed Expenses

Rent	$175
Maintenance	80
Salaries (attendant & janitor)	140*
Insurance	30
Depreciation	500
	$925

Variable Expenses

Utilities (gas, fuel, oil and electricity).
$ 0.04 per twenty-minute washer cycle
$0.015 per five-minute dryer cycle

*Assumes there will be one attendant and that the laundry will be open 8 hours per day, 5 1/2 days per week. Attendant's salary was estimated at $110 per month. The janitor would work part time and would receive $30 per month.

The depreciation figure was based on five-year straight-line (20%) rates applied against the estimated total investment of $31,440. The variable expense for utilities was taken from an estimated income statement which ALD, Inc. (the largest U.S. coin-op distributor) mailed to prospective investors. Italian electricity costs were about the same as those in America, but gas costs were slightly higher. However, for estimating purposes, the figures given were considered satisfactory, although Mr. Paino felt they might be a bit on the low side.

EQUIPMENT CAPACITY

The four-kilo washers had a 20-minute cycle while the 11-kilo washer had a 30-minute cycle. The dryers had 5-minute cycles and were capable of drying the average four-kilo load in two cycles. With a 24-hour operation, therefore, the theoretical capacity of each washer was 72 loads per day, while each dryer had a theoretical capacity of 144 four-kilo loads per day. Loading time was the limiting factor on theoretical capacity. One estimate of actual washer capacity was published by ECON-O-WASH, a U.S. installer of coin-ops, who advised investors that a 20-minute cycle could produce about 60 loads per day.

TABLE 1

Italian Coins	U.S. $ Value (620 lire = $1)
5 lire	$0.008
10 ″	0.016
20 ″	0.032
50 ″	0.08
100 ″	0.16
500 ″	0.80

The supply vending machine was designed to sell packets of soap and bleach. An American laundry detergent would be imported and put up in individual wash packets at a total cost of 20 lire ($0.032) per packet. There was a possibility that an Italian manufacturer might be able to deliver an equivalent soap for 15 lire ($0.024) per package. Bleach was available at a price of 20 lire per packet.

Coin meters were available and capable of accepting any combination of Italian coins, except five 100-lire coins or a single 500-lire coin.

PRICING

A critical problem for Mr. Paino was to decide what prices to charge for washing, drying, and supplies. Table 1 shows Italian coins and their exchange value in U.S. dollars.

In his attempt to select prices that would maximize long-run profitability, Mr. Paino was having considerable difficulty appraising elasticity of demand for his new service. He was aware of U.S. prices, but felt they were only a very rough guide in Italy, especially because of much higher Italian investment costs.

QUESTIONS

1. Would you start a coin-operated laundry if you were Mr. Paino? Why or why not?
2. What factors will determine the success or failure of a coin-op in Italy?
3. What is Paino's objective?

part two

THE ENVIRONMENT
OF MULTINATIONAL
MARKETING

economic environment

Free trade, one of the greatest blessings which a government
can confer on a people, is in almost every country unpopular.

Lord Macaulay, 1800–1859

INTRODUCTION

A major characteristic of the multinational marketers' world is the diversity of marketing environments in which they conduct their operations. The economic dimensions of this world market environment are of vital importance. This chapter examines the characteristics of the world economic environment.

The multinational marketer is fortunate in having a substantial body of data available that charts the nature of the environment on a country-by-country basis. Every country has national accounts data indicating, at a minimum, estimates of gross national product. Also available on a global basis are demographic data indicating the number of people, their distribution by age category, and the rates of population growth. National accounts and demographic data do not exhaust the types of economic data available. A single source, *The Statistical Yearbook of the United Nations,* contains global data on manpower, agriculture, mining, manufacturing, construction, energy production and consumption, internal and external trade, railroad and air transport, wages and prices, health, housing, education, communications (mail, telegraph, and telephone), and mass communications by book, film, radio, and television. In general, all of these data are available for the richer industrialized countries. The less developed a country is, the scarcer the availability of economic data. In the least-developed countries of the world one cannot be certain of obtaining anything more than basic national accounts, and demographic and external trade data. Nevertheless, in considering the world economic environment, the initial problem is not one of an absence of data but rather of an abundance. This chapter will identify the most salient characteristics

An American often gets predictable advice on what not to *do* in a developing country, such as drink the water or denigrate local customs. Less predictably, a European expatriate urges, "You should never *think* in statistics here. When you are in a poor country, they are always misleading."

That advice may be the most widely significant, as the poor countries' demand for a "new international economic order" inevitably focuses attention on statistics about North-South inequities.

Figures on the gross national product per capita are the most common shorthand for expressing the gap between the rich and the poor countries, and the aspirations of the latter. Can they reliably reflect either? Despite all the gripes about U.S. statistics, the Commerce Department can be fairly confident in putting the U.S. average at $7,337.

But for a country like Senegal, in the middling-poor group, various exchange rate concepts and slow, shaky underlying data automatically inject uncertainty. The World Bank puts Senegal's average at $280, the U.S. embassy at $130, and local analysts generally settle on something "under $200" a year.

Money does mean something in the rural Third World. Visiting a peasant's grass hut discloses a surprising number of things that only it can buy: iron bed frames, a battery-run radio, a kerosene lantern, a roof of corrugated metal, aluminum pots, snapshots, some jars of lotion. In larger Senegalese towns, there are television sets, and there's talk of adding commercials.

To thoughtful Third World leaders, however, it isn't clear that having far more money would add proportionately to the happiness of the masses. What with pollution, crime and psychiatrists, "it is not sure that the way of life in America or Europe is the best one," softly says Fara Ndiaye, an opposition politician, businessman and economist. Even Senegal's official goal of a mere $600 per capita income by the century's end is "a wrong way" to measure development, he contends.

Whatever the right figure is for Senegal, it would be inconceivable to live on it for a year in America, what with those shocking bills for utilities, auto repairs and nursing homes. But in the West African countryside where most Senegalese live, there are no such "necessities" to joylessly soak up their money. Sunshine and wells suffice for utilities, sandals substitute for autos, and tradition assures that kinfolk care for their ailing and elderly.

Even modest development goals require the import of much technology, though, and paying requires exports, for which Third World leaders seek stable or even "indexed" rising prices. Those demands usually strike Americans as rigid and unrealistic. To see them from the Third World perspective, statistics aren't as instructive as stepping out from a modern Dakar hotel to be beset by street peddlers.

Reject the seed necklace offered by the first, and a second shouts a lower price. And a third, and a sixth. The number of necklaces thrust out multiplies, and the price per unit plummets to a fraction, sometimes to a request for whatever small change the visitor might have, lest "tonight I no chop."

The problem becomes clearer. All the necklaces—like all the Third World's raw materials—are essentially indistinguishable from one another. The surging population means more people trying to support themselves by auctioning off the same things to the relatively few who can afford them, the affluent Westerners. The peddlers rarely even attempt to sell them to other Africans, and they lack the skills or capital to make or sell anything else.

Developing countries might advance faster by trading more within their own regions. But trade tends to be locked into a North-South pattern by politics, transportation, telephone systems and habit. "If you are in the Ivory Coast and you want to buy peanut oil from Senegal, very often you have to buy it in Paris," frets Mr. Ndiaye.

To buy anything from the North, however, means paying prices set by the sellers, who do have the leeway to diversify or sell elsewhere. That's clear to a driver named Mamadou, who is proud of his new Renault taxi. It cost $7,700. "Four years ago, the same kind of car cost $4,200," he says. However well that might be explained by local taxes or wage rate statistics in far-off France, to Mamadou it means only that he needs to work longer hours to support the already-rich North.

Much the same is true on a national scale, meaning Senegal must somehow raise and sell more peanuts, or make do with fewer autos. Statistics show the lowly peanut accounts for 75% of export revenues. Elsewhere, too, one simple crop dominates the economy, and the psychology, of an entire country, making it hard for leaders to see why the West doesn't just rely on their commodities for all its needs, preferably at prices geared to the meager needs of their own people.

It is harder for them to see why the West often seeks to restrain commodity imports from them in favor of domestic farmers, especially if foreign policy is to be friendly. "How can you have a problem with vegetable oil when you are an industrial country?," puzzles a Nigerian diplomat. "Some countries depend entirely on that product, and it is a very small percent of GNP for you," he chides.

No doubt U.S. statistics tell him that. But they tell him nothing of American farm lobbies, Capitol Hill committees, or how the price of soybeans compares with the cost of tractors and tuition in the eyes of an Illinois farmer. Nor can Africa's average income statistics help an American understand how African pride and rivalries so often lead to buying military jets instead of medicines or milk.

In thinking about North-South problems, few Americans could get started without thinking in statistics. But the solutions may not be as difficult economically, or as easy politically, as numbers alone suggest.

—RICHARD F. JANSSEN

FIGURE 3–1. Three Kinds of Lies . . .*

Source: The Wall Street Journal, "The Outlook," April 26, 1976, p. 1. Reprinted with permission. © Dow Jones & Company, Inc. (1976). All rights reserved.

of the economic environment to provide the framework for further consideration of the elements of a multinational marketing program.

MARKET CHARACTERISTICS

The Location of Income

In charting a plan for multinational market expansion, the single most valuable economic variable for most products is income. For some products, particularly those that have a very low unit cost, population is a more valuable

*Lies, damned lies, and statistics.

predictor of market potential than income. Cigarettes are an excellent example of this type of product. Nevertheless, for the vast range of industrial and consumer products in international markets today, the single most valuable and important indicator of potential is income.

Income is not an accurate or a precise measure of potential; it is only a gross indicator. For example, the United States per capita GNP is approximately seven times that of Brazil ($6,670 vs. $920 in 1974). This figure is of initial interest to a manufacturer of light sockets and light bulbs and suggests a U.S. market eight times larger on a per capita basis. However, the average number of light sockets per home in Brazil is five versus twenty-seven in the United States, a difference of five and one-half times. When market potential is estimated on the basis of the number of Brazilian homes, the size of the Brazilian market can be estimated more precisely. With additional data on the average utilization of light bulbs in Brazilian households, the light-bulb marketer with data on the number of homes could identify the exact potential in Brazil. Without the household data, the marketer could estimate roughly on the basis of total GNP.

Gross national product (GNP) and other measures of national income converted to U.S. dollars or any other numéraire should ideally be calculated on the basis of purchasing power parities (i.e., what the currency will buy in the country of issue) or through direct real product comparisons. This would provide an actual comparison of the standards of living in the countries of the world. Since these data are not available in regular ststistical reports, throughout this book we use, instead, conversion of local currency measured at the year-end U.S. dollar foreign exchange rate. The reader must remember that exchange rates equate, at best, the prices of internationally traded goods and services. They often bear little relationship to the prices of those goods and services not entering the international trade, which form the bulk of the national product in most countries. Agriculture output and services, in particular, are generally priced lower in relation to industrial output in developing countries than in industrialized countries. Furthermore, agriculture typically accounts for the largest share of output in developing countries. Thus the use of exchange rates tends to exaggerate differences in real income between less-developed and more-developed countries.

The UN International Comparison Project (ICP) has developed a sophisticated method for measuring total expenditure, which has been used to derive more reliable and directly comparable estimates of per capita income. The World Bank has published a comparison of ICP findings with its own *Atlas* figures based on exchange rate conversion. Table 3-1 compares World Bank GNP data based on exchange rate conversion of local currency GNP with the ICP's more sophisticated measure. India's real income, for example, is three times greater than that indicated by the exchange comparison. The ICP income figure is one and one-half times greater than that indicated by the exchange comparison. In short, the use of exchange rates tends to distort real income or standard-of-living measures. Nevertheless, the use of exchange rates does provide a rough measure of income levels and has the merit of being an easily obtainable figure.

With these qualifications in mind the reader is referred to Table 3-2, which

TABLE 3-1. Per Capita Currency Conversion Method (Atlas GNP) Compared with International Comparison Project Method (ICP–GDP) (Indices U.S. = 100)

Country	1970		1974	
	GDP ICP (1)	GNP Atlas (2)	GDP ICP (3)	GNP Atlas (4)
Kenya	5.72	2.94	6.84	3.03
India	7.12	2.31	6.28	2.02
Colombia	15.90	7.12	17.57	7.55
Hungary*	40.30	30.60	58.20	32.70
Italy	45.80	42.00	47.40	42.30
United Kingdom	60.30	53.40	62.00	53.80
Japan	61.50	55.40	64.00	61.00
Germany, Federal Republic of	74.70	94.00	75.40	93.90
France	75.00	76.00	77.30	81.60
United States	100.00	100.00	100.00	100.00

*Hungary: All data except 1970 ICP are special World Bank estimates not based on *Atlas* method.
Col. (1): GDP ICP
Col. (2): *Atlas* 1970 current price estimates based on 1973–75 prices and exchange rates.
Col. (3): ICP 1970 estimates updated using gross domestic product (GDP) deflators and 1974 exchange rates.
Col. (4): *Atlas* 1974 current price estimates based on 1973–75 prices and exchange rates.

Source: World Bank Atlas, 1976, p. 21.

indicates the location of world income by region in 1975. The striking fact revealed by this table is the concentration of income in the three large regions of the world—North America, Europe, and Japan—which together with Oceania accounted for 81 percent of global income but only 28 percent of the world's population in 1975.

The concentration of wealth in a handful of large industrialized countries is the most striking characteristic of the global economic environment. This characteristic appears again if one examines the world regions and again if one examines the distribution of wealth and income within countries. The United States is, of course, a colossus in North America, as is the Soviet Union in Eastern Europe. These countries accounted for 91 percent and 66 percent, respectively, of their region's GDP (gross domestic products) in 1975. In Western Europe, France, West Germany, and the United Kingdom accounted for 73 percent of that region's GDP in 1975. In Asia, Japan accounted for 48 percent of the 1975 GDP. In Latin America, Argentina, Brazil, and Mexico accounted for 77 percent of LAFTA (Latin America Free Trade Area) GDP in 1975, and so on.

An examination of the distribution of wealth within countries again reveals patterns of income concentration, particularly in the less-developed countries outside the Communist bloc. Adelman and Morris found that the average share of GNP accruing to the poorest 20 percent of the population in forty-four less-developed countries included in their study was 5.6 percent as compared with 56.0 percent going to the top 20 percent. The income of the bottom 20 percent was about one-fourth of what it would have been had income been distributed uniformly throughout the population. Their study suggests that the relationship

TABLE 3-2. Global Income and Population, 1975

	GDP ($ billions)	Population (millions)	GDP per Capita ($)	% World GDP	% World Population
United States	1,514.0	213.9	7,078	26	5
Western Europe	1,763.1	404.2	4,362	30	10
Germany	423.6	61.7	6,865	7	2
France	336.9	52.9	6,369	6	1
United Kingdom	226.6	56.4	4,018	4	1
Eastern Europe	737.8*	360.4	2,047	13	9
Japan	485.5	111.1	4,370	8	3
Oceania and Canada	246.3	39.6	6,220	4	1
Latin America (LAFTA, CACM, and Caribbean)	359.3	322.4	1,110	6	8
Asia (excluding Japan)	522.6	2,129.5	245	9	53
Middle East	158.0	114.5	1,380	3	3
Africa	128.0	357.6	357	2	9
Global total	5,914.6	4,053.2		100‡	100‡
Global average			1,459		

*Net material product.

‡Column totals figures are rounded off.

Data source: Business International, "Indicators of Market Size for 132 Countries," December 3, 1976, pp. 390–91; and December 10, 1976, pp. 396–97. Table prepared by author.

between the share of income at the lowest 20 percent and economic development varies with the level of development. Economic development is associated with increases in the share of the bottom 20 percent only after relatively high levels of socioeconomic development have been attained. At the early stages of the development process, economic development works to the *relative* disadvantage of the lowest income groups. In Brazil, for example, the poorest 20 percent of the population received 3.5 percent of total national income while the top 20 percent received 61.5 percent.[1] This compares with the United States in 1976 where the lowest 20 percent received 4.0 percent and the top 20 percent received 48.3 percent.[2]

Adelman and Morris found that countries with a higher share of national income accruing to the poorest 20 percent were characterized by low or moderate degrees of dualism in their economies and by the pursuit of agriculturally oriented foreign trade policies. Countries in which the smallest portion of national income (2 percent) accrued to the lowest 20 percent were characterized by sharp dualism

[1] Irma Adelman and Cynthia Taft Morris, "An Anatomy of Income Distribution Patterns in Developing Nations—A Summary of Findings," International Bank for Reconstruction and Development, International Development Association (Economic Staff Working Paper No. 116, September 23, 1971).

[2] U.S. Department of Commerce, Bureau of the Census, *Statistical Abstract of the United States, 1977,* Table No. 724, p. 449.

in their economies, which were centered on foreign finance and foreign-managed exploitation of natural resources.

Throughout the ages, mankind has spent most of its energy making a living—finding food, clothing, and shelter. An old Armenian folk saying, "Making a living is like taking food out of a lion's mouth," captures this reality. Although the problem of poverty has not been eliminated in all of the industrialized countries, for those in the top income categories poverty results from legacies of discrimination and uneven participation in economic life rather than from a lack of sufficient aggregate resources. Those industrialized countries with homogeneous populations and an advanced collective social conscience have indeed eliminated poverty within their borders.

Today a different type of inequality has impressed itself on the conscience of the world—the vast and growing gap between the rich and the poor nations. Surendra Patel of the Economic Commission for Africa has addressed several crucial questions concerning the present economic distance between these nations. When did it evolve? How large is it? What were the dimensions of time and space that brought it about? Can it be bridged in the foreseeable future?[3]

At the beginning of the industrial revolution two hundred years ago, the economic landscape of the world was relatively flat in contrast to the present uneven world where there are very high mountains and very low plains. Even as late as 1860 more than half the population of northwestern Europe and the United States was engaged in agriculture—not much different from the share of the population engaged in agriculture in the pre-industrial countries at present. Yields per hectare of land, share of industries in total output, and illiteracy ratios were only marginally different. The peoples of Western Europe, for example, did not have the means to be economically much better off than the rest of mankind. World output of pig iron in 1850 was only 4.6 million tons, and half of it was produced in Great Britain. The most advanced countries were still in the last days of the Iron Age. Even by 1870, world output of steel was no more than seven hundred thousand tons—less than one-fifth of India's output in 1961.

Empirical evidence about the income levels in industrialized countries supports this picture. Professor S. S. Kuznets has, by applying known rates of growth, extrapolated backward the per capita income of the industrial countries in the early 1950s. The data in the following list show the years when such regression (extrapolation backward) yields a per capita income of $200 in comparable 1952-54 prices:

United States	— 1832	Germany	— 1886
United Kingdom	— 1837	Sweden	— 1889
France	— 1852	Italy	— 1909
		Japan	— 1955

A weighted average and straight-line extrapolation suggest that the average per

---

[3]The following paragraphs draw largely on Surendra J. Patel, "The Economic Distance between Nations: Its Origin, Measurement and Outlook," *The Economic Journal* 74, No. 293 (March 1964): 119–131.

capita income in industrial countries as a group was about $170 in 1850, or only 70 percent higher than that of the pre-industrial countries in the early 1960s. If the United Kingdom and the United States are excluded, the average income in the rest of this group would have been $150 in 1850.

Although these estimates make no allowance for free sunshine and the lower requirements for survival in the warmer climates, it seems clear that the economic landscape of the 1850s was relatively flat. The actual conditions of life for the masses of the two worlds could not have been significantly different. This is in sharp contrast to the condition of today's world economic landscape with the sunny mountaintops of the industrial countries and the dark valleys of the pre-industrial world.

Since 1850 the distribution of population between the industrial and the pre-industrial countries has not altered significantly. But between 1850 and 1960 the industrial countries' share of world income increased from 39 to 78 percent. The annual compound rates of growth during this period, which have so profoundly altered the world's distribution of income, were 2.7 percent in total output, and 1.8 percent in per capita output. The magnitude of change as compared with the previous six thousand years of man's civilized existence is enormous; over one-third of the real income and about two-thirds of the industrial output produced by mankind throughout its civilized history were generated in the industrialized countries in the last century. The significance of these growth figures is that relatively small average annual rates of growth have transformed the economic geography of the world. What the industrial countries have done is to systematize economic growth or, put another way, they have established a process of continuous, gradual, change. Patel has calculated that India, one of the poorest countries in the world, could reach U.S. income levels by growing at an average rate of 5 to 6 percent in real terms for forty to fifty years. This is no more than the lifetime of an average Indian, and much less than half the lifetime of an average American. To point out the possible does not of course make it a probable event, but it does underline the fact that economic distance created by sustained growth can also be removed by sustained growth, as Japan has so dramatically demonstrated in recent years.

The world has changed enormously from biblical times when Saint Matthew observed, "For ye have the poor always with you." Today, much more than was true two thousand years ago, wealth and income are concentrated regionally, nationally, and within nations. The implications of this reality are crucial for the multinational marketer. A company that decides to diversify geographically can accomplish this objective by establishing operations in a handful of national markets. As can be seen in Table 3-3, as measured by 1974 GNP the ten largest countries in the world accounted for 72 percent of world income, and the five largest accounted for 57 percent. These data underline the fact that a company can be intensely multinational in the sense that its income is derived from a number of countries instead of being concentrated in a single national market, and at the same time be operating in ten or fewer countries. Another inescapable implication of

TABLE 3-3. Ten Largest Countries in the World

	1974 GNP at Market Prices ($U.S. tens of millions)
United States	$1,414
USSR	599
Japan	446
Germany, Federal Republic	389
France	286
China, People's Republic	245
United Kingdom	201
Italy	157
Canada	139
Brazil	96
Total	$3,972
World total	$5,534

Top ten as a percentage of world total: 72%.
Top five as a percentage of world total: 57%.

Data source: World Bank Atlas, 1976. Table prepared by author.

these data is that any company that decides to enter a large number of national markets is going to find itself managing small-scale operations.[4]

The Location of Population

For products whose price is low enough, population is a more important variable than income in determining market potential. Although population is not as concentrated as income, there is, in terms of size of nations, a pattern of considerable concentration. The ten most populous countries in the world accounted for 62 percent of the world population in 1973.

Man has inhabited the earth for over 2.5 million years. The number of human beings has been small during most of this period. In Christ's lifetime there were approximately 300 million people on earth, or roughly one-third of the number of people on Mainland China today. World population increased tremendously during the eighteenth and nineteenth centuries. By 1850 world population had reached 1 billion. Between 1850 and 1925 it had increased to 2 billion, and from 1925 to 1960 it had increased to 3 billion. World population is now approximately 4 billion and at the present rate of growth will reach 7 billion by the end of the century. There is no necessary correlation between population and income level. India and China, the two most populous countries in the world, have low incomes. The United States and the Union of Soviet Socialist Republics, the third and fourth most populous countries, have high incomes.

[4] Readers interested in country detail can refer to the excerpts from the *World Bank Atlas* reprinted in Appendix IV of this book, which lists population, GNP, and average annual growth rates for 188 countries and territories for 1973.

TRADE PATTERNS

From the end of World War II until 1973, growth in world trade was stimulated primarily by increased output, incomes, and expenditures in the industrialized countries of Europe and North America and in Japan. As Table 3-4 indicates, in the late 1960s the industrial countries' share of world exports had grown to over two-thirds of the world total. Moreover, examination of the destination of industrial countries' exports reveals that almost three-quarters of their exports in 1973 were to other industrial countries. Thus the biggest competitors of the industrial countries in world trade are also their best customers. Since World War II the classical trade pattern of commodity exports from underdeveloped countries to industrialized countries, and manufactured exports from industrial countries to developing countries, has been replaced by intraindustrial country trade. In 1973 this trend was reversed by the price increases in commodity exports, petroleum in particular, which went from under $3 to over $10 per barrel. This massive shift in commodity prices overnight adjusted the terms of trade between industrial and producing regions and in 1974 resulted in a drop in the industrial country share of world exports to 62 percent, which was less than the industrial country share in 1960. The developing areas of world exports have increased recently from a low of 18 percent in 1970 to 27 percent in 1974, reflecting the reversal in the declining terms of trade in these areas during the 1960s and early 1970s. Another interesting development is the decline in the share of world exports accounted for by the Eastern trading area, from 12 percent in 1960 to 8 percent in 1974. This proportion is reduced to only 4 percent of world exports if the intra-Eastern trading area's world trade is eliminated from the total exports of this region. The proportion of the Eastern trading area's world trade is small when compared with the total annual production of the area. However, the different methods of defining income in the Eastern trading area make comparisons difficult, but based on production this area may account for perhaps 25 percent of world production. The high expectations for an increase in East-West trade that developed as a result of the Nixon-Kissinger detente initiative in the early 1970s are based largely upon the considerable gap between the proportion of income accounted for by the Eastern area and its share of world trade.

The dollar value of world exports increased by 47 percent in 1974 as compared with 38 percent in 1973, 19 percent in 1972, and 10 percent per year, on the average, in the preceding decade.

In 1971, manufactured products accounted for 63 percent of the value of world exports. By 1974 this percentage had declined to 56 percent as a result of the increase in commodity prices. The share of manufactured goods exports of the industrial countries hardly changed during this period, declining only 1 percent—from 84 to 83 percent. The biggest change was in the developing area's share of primary product exports to the world, which increased from 43 to 57 percent between 1971 and 1974. Although it would appear that in the aggregate the developing countries have dramatically improved their position and terms of trade (i.e., the price of the goods they buy), this improvement is, in fact, concentrated in a

TABLE 3-4. Network of Total Exports by Major Areas, 1963, 1968, 1970 to 1975
(Billion Dollars F.O.B. and Percentages of World Exports)

Origin	Year	Industrial Areas Value	%	Developing Areas Total Value	%	of which: Oil Importing Developing Countries Value	%	Eastern Trading Area Value	%	Total World* Value	%
Industrial areas	1963	69.80	44.9	21.95	14.2	18.10	11.7	3.75	2.4	99.25	63.9
	1968	117.75	49.4	31.10	13.0	24.95	10.4	6.70	2.8	161.10	67.5
	1970	160.90	51.4	39.70	12.6	32.00	10.2	8.75	2.8	216.45	69.1
	1971	180.75	51.6	44.20	12.6	35.05	10.0	9.60	2.7	242.25	69.2
	1972	217.95	52.2	50.00	12.0	38.45	9.2	12.65	3.0	287.85	69.0
	1973	293.60	50.8	69.10	12.0	53.05	9.2	19.30	3.3	392.40	67.9
	1974	375.70	44.8	106.40	12.7	77.75	9.3	27.50	3.3	526.10	62.7
	1975	380.65	43.3	129.30	14.7	83.95	9.6	34.40	3.9	560.90	63.8
Developing areas	1963	22.50	14.5	6.80	4.4	6.35	4.1	1.70	1.1	31.85	20.5
	1968	31.50	13.2	8.95	3.7	8.10	3.4	2.25	0.9	43.65	18.3
	1970	40.10	12.8	11.00	3.5	9.90	3.2	3.10	1.0	55.45	17.7
	1971	45.60	13.0	13.10	3.7	11.80	3.3	3.05	0.9	63.00	18.0
	1972	55.25	13.2	15.70	3.8	14.05	3.4	3.40	0.8	75.75	18.2
	1973	81.10	14.0	23.35	4.0	20.70	3.6	5.10	0.9	111.80	19.4
	1974	163.90	19.5	46.45	5.5	41.70	5.0	7.65	0.9	222.65	26.5
	1975	152.55	17.4	47.40	5.4	41.35	4.7	8.25	0.9	212.40	24.2
	1963	15.75	10.2	4.75	3.1	4.35	2.8	1.60	1.0	22.65	14.6
	1968	20.55	8.6	6.55	2.8	5.85	2.5	2.05	0.8	29.75	12.4
	1970	26.50	8.5	8.05	2.6	7.10	2.3	2.85	0.9	38.20	12.2

of which: Oil importing developing countries	1971	27.25	7.8	8.95	2.5	7.80	2.2	2.65	0.8	39.80	11.3
	1972	33.05	7.9	10.45	2.5	9.00	2.2	2.90	0.7	47.35	11.3
	1973	47.65	8.3	14.90	2.6	12.55	2.2	4.35	0.7	68.35	11.8
	1974	67.85	8.1	22.20	2.6	17.90	2.1	6.30	0.7	98.75	11.8
	1975	65.60	7.5	24.05	2.7	18.45	2.1	6.70	0.8	98.45	11.2
Eastern trading area	1963	3.75	2.4	2.80	1.8	2.60	1.7	12.40	8.0	18.95	12.2
	1968	6.45	2.7	4.10	1.7	3.60	1.5	16.70	7.0	27.30	11.4
	1970	8.10	2.6	5.15	1.6	4.20	1.3	20.05	6.4	33.35	10.6
	1971	9.10	2.6	5.25	1.4	4.35	1.2	22.00	6.3	36.40	10.4
	1972	10.80	2.6	6.00	1.4	4.90	1.1	26.30	6.3	43.15	10.3
	1973	16.20	2.8	8.80	1.5	7.10	1.2	32.70	5.7	57.90	10.0
	1974	23.55	2.8	11.50	1.4	8.85	1.1	36.80	4.4	72.00	8.6
	1975	24.60	2.8	13.30	1.5	9.85	1.1	48.75	5.5	86.80	9.9
Total world*	1963	99.75	64.3	32.25	20.8	27.70	17.9	18.20	11.7	155.10	100.0
	1968	160.40	67.3	45.25	19.0	37.75	15.8	25.90	10.8	238.40	100.0
	1970	214.70	68.7	57.30	18.3	47.50	15.2	32.20	10.3	313.10	100.0
	1971	241.30	68.9	64.45	18.4	52.90	15.1	34.85	10.0	350.10	100.0
	1972	291.60	69.9	73.70	17.7	59.30	14.2	42.65	10.2	417.20	100.0
	1973	402.10	69.6	103.95	18.0	83.25	14.4	57.65	10.0	577.50	100.0
	1974	575.10	68.6	168.65	20.1	132.00	15.7	72.60	8.6	838.90	100.0
	1975	570.65	64.9	194.40	22.1	138.70	15.8	92.25	10.5	879.10	100.0

*Including Australia, New Zealand, and South Africa.

Source: GATT, *International Trade, 1975–76*, Geneva, 1976, p. 6.

TABLE 3-5. Global Exports and Imports, 1975

	GDP ($ billions)	% World GDP	Total Exports ($ billions)	% World Exports	Total Imports ($ billions)	$ World Imports
United States	1,514	26	107,652	14.0	139,716	18.0
Western Europe	1,763	30	336,475	43.5	301,370	38.8
Germany	424	7	90,171	11.6	74,978	9.7
France	337	6	53,118	6.9	53,964	7.0
United Kingdom	227	4	44,120	5.7	53,568	6.9
Eastern Europe	738*	13	26,201	3.4	37,642	4.9
Japan	486	8	55,817	7.2	57,853	7.5
Oceania and Canada	246	4	47,635	6.2	50,569	6.5
Latin America (LAFTA, CACM, and Caribbean)	359	6	42,217	5.5	53,707	6.9
Asia (excluding Japan)	523	9	48,740	6.3	60,192	7.8
Middle East	158	3	70,489	9.1	37,165	4.8
Africa	128	2	38,780	5.0	37,858	4.9
Global total	5,915	100‡	774,006	100.0‡	776,072	100.0‡

*Net material product.
‡Totals figures are rounded off.

Data source: Business International, "Indicators of Market Size for 132 Countries," December 3, 10, 17, and 24, 1976. Table prepared by author.

handful of oil-exporting countries. Between 1970 and 1974 the index of export prices of less-developed countries increased from 100 to 291, and import prices increased from 100 to 190. However, this increase was divided between the oil-exporting countries, whose prices increased from 100 to 489, and the rest of the developing areas, whose prices increased from approximately 100 to 190. Industrial country export prices increased from 100 to 170, so there has been an improvement in the non-oil-country terms of trade, but the great fear of the non-oil-exporting developing countries is that the recent improvement in their terms of trade will be lost as industrial country prices outstrip the price increases in their commodity exports.[5]

Table 3-5 shows the dominant position of the United States, Germany, Japan, and the Middle East as world exporters. Between 1950 and 1975 Japan's exports increased seventyfold—from $800 million to $56 billion. This remarkable growth does not mean that Japan exports most of its production. As indicated in Table 3-5, the Japanese share of world GDP is actually greater than the Japanese share of world exports. For its size, the most successful exporting country in the world is Germany, whose exports of $90 billion in 1975 were only $17 billion less than U.S. exports, although German GDP is only one-fourth that of the United States. Another measure of the export intensity of the German economy is the fact that Germany accounted for 11.6 percent of world exports in 1975-76 but only 7

[5]Export and import price data are taken from International Monetary Fund, *International Financial Statistics*, April 1976, pp. 32–33.

TABLE 3–6. United States Exports ($ billions)

	1974	1976
Total Exports, including re-exports	98,506.2	114,997.2
By Geographic Regions:		
Africa	3,662.0	5,205.9
Asia	25,806.6	29,731.2
Australia and Oceania	2,696.3	2,689.9
Europe	30,089.6	35,902.9
Northern North America	19,850.1	24,113.5
Southern North America	7,949.3	8,867.7
South America	7,858.4	8,600.5
Total U.S. merchandise exports	97,143.4	114,611.6
By Commodity Groups:		
Food and live animals	13,993.8	15,434.3
Beverages and tobacco	1,247.4	1,523.3
Crude materials, inedible, ex. fuels	10,956.5	10,891.4
Mineral fuels, lubricants, etc.	3,442.5	4,226.1
Animal and vegetable oils, fats, waxes	1,423.3	978.1
Chemicals	8,821.8	9,958.2
Manufactured goods	11,165.8	11,204.8
Machinery and transport equipment	38,197.2	49,509.9
Machinery total	23,688.9	31,289.0
Transport equipment total	14,508.3	18,220.9
Miscellaneous manufactured articles	5,344.4	6,572.3
Commodities not classified	2,592.1	2,749.4

Source: Survey of Current Business, "Foreign Trade of the United States," February 1975, pp. 5–22; "Foreign Trade of the United States," May 1977, pp. 5–22.

percent of world GDP. Much of the German success in exports has been concentrated in automobiles and machinery. The success of the German export drive has resulted in a substantial revaluation or increase in the value of the German deutsche mark, which has threatened the position of German exporters in foreign markets, particularly in the United States. Volkswagen, for example, has suffered a severe share of market decline in the U.S. market because of the increasing price of its automobiles compared with the price of competing U.S. and Japanese automobiles.

United States exports for 1976 are shown in Table 3-6. Europe is the largest U.S. export market, followed closely by Asia and Canada. The three largest commodity groups are machinery, transport equipment, and food and live animals. The most important commodity group is machinery, which is almost twice as large as transport equipment and food and live animals combined.

Many observers were concerned about the declining trade surpluses of the United States in the 1960s. During the 1960s, U.S. trade surpluses declined from approximately $7 billion at the beginning of the decade to zero in the last quarter of 1969. In 1971 the United States experienced a $2 billion deficit in its trade with the world in goods and services, the first annual trade deficit since 1893. Government officials reacted with horror, and many observers predicted that the United States was going to end up as a nation of fast-food franchisers purchasing all manufactured goods from abroad. These dire predictions were not fulfilled, because the devaluation of the U.S. dollar in 1971 and the relatively lower rate of inflation in the United States as compared with other industrial countries corrected the over-evaluation of the U.S. dollar and restored the competitive position of the U.S. economy in world trade. After merchandise trade deficits in 1971, 1972, and 1974, and a virtual break-even point in 1973, the United States in 1975 reported one of its largest trade surpluses in history, over $10 billion. In 1976, as a result of the strengthening of the dollar in response to the strong U.S. balance-of-payments surplus, the U.S. surplus was expected to be much smaller. The U.S. experience in recent years is a good example of the effect of currency values on balance-of-payments results. An overvalued U.S. dollar resulted in U.S. balance-of-payments deficits; this required a devaluation of the U.S. dollar, which was then, in fact, undervalued. The undervaluation resulted in a U.S. balance-of-payments surplus, which pushed up the value of the dollar and reduced the size of the U.S. trade surpluses. This experience reflects how an essentially healthy economy relates economically to the rest of the world through currency value fluctuations.

The entire cycle was repeated in 1977 when the U.S. dollar was overvalued and the U.S. reported the largest trade deficits in its history. During this period, a decision by surplus countries such as Germany and Japan to artificially maintain the value of the dollar and resist market pressure to increase the value of their currencies contributed to their surpluses and the U.S. deficit. This experience illustrates the trade effects of major interference with market forces.

CONSUMPTION PATTERNS

Engel's Law

Income is the single most important variable affecting market potential for most products. How does income affect consumption? Every marketer is aware of the relationship between income level and consumption patterns and, therefore, frequently uses income segmentation in defining a market. The nature of income elasticity (the relationship between demand changes and changes in income) for food was first observed and formulated by the nineteenth-century Prussian statistician Ernst Engel. Engel discovered a uniform condition in European countries that he surveyed: When income grew above a certain minimum, expenditures on food as a percentage of total income decreased, although the absolute amount of food expenditures was maintained or increased. This pattern of expenditures on necessities is referred to as Engel's Law and has been confirmed by empirical budget studies. One survey, published by the United Nations Food and Agricultural Organization in Rome, recorded the elasticities of demand for food along with per capita incomes in dollars of 1955 purchasing power for various areas of the world. This survey revealed that Asia, the poorest area, had an income elasticity of demand for food of 0.9, whereas North America, the richest area, had an income elasticity of demand for food of 0.16. This means that for the 1957–59 period for which the data were accumulated, ninety cents out of every additional dollar in income in Asia was expended on food, as compared with sixteen cents for North America. By and large there is an inverse correlation between GNP per capita and income elasticity of demand for food. As incomes rise, the elasticity of demand for food declines.

Product Saturation Levels

In general, product saturation levels, or the percentage of potential buyers or households who own a particular product, increase as national income per capita increases. However, in markets where income is sufficient to enable consumers to buy a particular product, other factors may be determinant. For example, the sale of air conditioners is explained by income and climate. Average-income-level people in an underdeveloped country cannot afford an air conditioner no matter how hot it is. High-income people in a northern climate can easily afford an air conditioner but have no need for one.

In a survey made during the 1960s, the ownership of electric vacuum cleaners in the European Common Market ranged from a high of 95 percent of households in the Netherlands to a low of 7 percent of households in Italy. The differences in ownership of this appliance in Europe are only partially explained by income. A much more important factor in explaining ownership levels is the type of floor covering used in the homes of the country. Almost every home in the Netherlands contains rugs, whereas in Italy the use of rugs is uncommon. This illustrates the importance of a companion product in determining the sale potential for a product.

Within any particular economy, income is a major determinant of ownership of consumer durable goods. This is demonstrated in Table 3-7 in data from Japan for 1968. For every product except television sets, which seem to be an almost universal item of ownership in Japan, the effect of rising incomes in households is dramatic. For products that are major labor-saving tools, such as washing machines and sewing machines, rising incomes have increased ownership from less than 50 percent to more than 90 percent. Products requiring a major consumer outlay, such as the passenger car, increased from ownership levels of less than 1 percent to over 40 percent. Products that are new or highly innovative in a particular market, such as air conditioners and living room sets, are highly sensitive to rising incomes.

COMPETITION

An inevitable consequence of the expansion of international marketing activity is the growth of competition on an international basis. In industry after industry, international competition is a critical factor affecting success. In some industries, international companies have virtually excluded all other companies from their markets. An example of this phenomenon is the detergent industry where three companies—Colgate, Unilever, and Procter & Gamble—dominate an increasing number of detergent markets. Many companies can make a quality detergent, but the skills of packaging, pricing, distributing, merchandising, and advertising detergent products are so highly developed in a handful of large international companies

TABLE 3-7. Japanese Ownership of Consumer Durable Goods by Income Category of Household (Percentage of All Households Owning Item)

Annual Income	Sewing Machines	Television Sets	Passenger Cars	Refrigerators	Vacuum Cleaners	Air Conditioners	Living Room Sets	Dining Room Sets	Washing Machines	Color T.V.
Less than ¥300,000	44.6	82.1	0.7	33.8	16.4	1.1	3.9	3.3	44.4	2.2
¥300,000–599,999	74.9	97.2	4.5	65.3	33.7	1.2	6.8	9.6	75.0	1.3
¥600,000–899,999	86.4	983.	10.0	80.6	54.1	2.5	13.1	19.1	88.8	3.7
¥900,000–1,299,999	87.4	95.0	18.5	87.3	67.8	3.8	21.4	27.0	94.0	6.2
¥1,300,000–1,499,999	92.8	98.5	22.9	93.2	75.3	5.9	33.2	32.7	94.1	7.1
¥1,500,000–1,799,999	94.0	98.4	28.4	93.6	79.4	7.9	41.7	41.3	94.6	15.5
Over ¥1,800,000	95.7	96.6	40.9	95.1	88.4	23.6	60.7	53.3	97.5	26.6

Source: Shohi to Chochiku no Dōkō: Showa 43 nen ban [*A Survey of Consumption and Savings, 1968*] (Tokyo: Economic Planning Agency, 1968), pp. 108–109, as reproduced in M. Y. Yoshino, "Marketing Developments in a Rapidly Emerging Mass Consumption Society: The Case of Japan" (Unpublished manuscript, January 1970).

that they have overwhelmed local competition in market after market. A good illustration of how they have done this is provided by the excellent series of cases on the competition in the detergent industry in the Central American Common Market.[6]

The automobile industry has become increasingly competitive on an international basis. Part of the reason for the initial success of foreign cars in the United States was the reluctance of U.S. manufacturers to make a small and inexpensive product. The resistence of U.S. manufacturers was based on the economics of car production. The additional cost of a larger car is mainly in materials and not in fabrication. U.S. manufacturers had over the years established a pricing policy that linked price to size. The bigger the car, the higher the price. Under this formula, small cars meant smaller unit profits. Therefore U.S. manufacturers resisted the increasing preference in the U.S. market for smaller cars. Meanwhile, European manufacturers' product line has always been smaller than the U.S. line because of the different market conditions in Europe: less space, high taxes on engine displacement and on fuel, and a much greater market interest in functional design and engineering innovations (disc brakes, rack and pinion steering, five-speed gear boxes, small-displacement high-performance engines, and so on). These manufacturers discovered that there was a growing demand for their product in the U.S. market. Sales of imports, predominantly of small cars, multiplied twentyfold between 1954 and 1959. The introduction of the American compacts in the early 1960s blunted the import penetration of the U.S. market, but as the U.S. compacts each year included an increase in size, power, and price, import sales more than doubled between 1962 and 1967, and then doubled again between 1967 and 1972. The share of market for foreign cars in the United States increased from less than 5 percent in the early 1960s to 17 percent in 1975.

The oil embargo simply amplified the long-term trend toward a shift to smaller cars in the U.S. market. According to Lee Iacocca, former president of the Ford Motor Company, "the embargo didn't change the direction of the market; it merely accelerated the speed of the change in preferences. In the two years after the embargo, the small-car segment grew from 41 percent of the U.S. industry to 54 percent, a shift we had expected to see take place over 10 years."

The rise in gasoline prices resulting from the OPEC price increases has made consumers more cost-conscious. Even for consumers who were willing to pay higher gasoline prices, the long gas-station lines in 1973–74 demonstrated that a car with poor gas mileage could be an inconvenience as well as an expense.

In many respects the U.S. market has gradually become quite similar to European and Japanese markets. In Europe, for example, taxes on engine displacement and gasoline have made economy a necessary feature in automotive products. Although the United States has not adopted this form of control, the U.S. industry committed itself to voluntarily achieving a 40 percent improvement in gasoline mileage by 1980 if emission standards were frozen at the 1975 level. The U.S. government is aiming for a sales weighted average of twenty-eight miles per gallon by 1985.

[6] Available from Intercollegiate Case Clearing House, Boston, Mass. 02163.

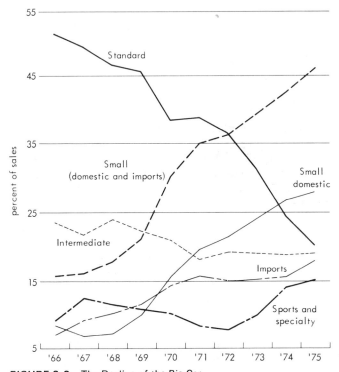

FIGURE 3-2. The Decline of the Big Car

Source: First National City Bank, "Monthly Economic Letter," February 1976, p. 14.

Figure 3-2 shows the effect of these changes on U.S. auto sales. Standard cars (consisting of high-priced, regular-sized, and medium-priced models) have shrunk from half of U.S. sales in 1966 to roughly one-fifth of the total. Small-car sales have tripled from 15.7 percent in 1966 to about 45.0 percent in 1975.

The old relationship between price and size has eroded as Detroit has learned to promote the luxury compact with automatic transmissions, luxury trim packages, air conditioning, and so forth. Meanwhile European and Japanese cars have, as a result of rising wages, become increasingly expensive. In order to hold share of market, European and Japanese manufacturers are being forced to establish manufacturing facilities in the United States. Volvo and Volkswagen have been the first foreign companies to make this move, and if wage rates in Japan continue to rise as they have in the past, the Japanese will not be far behind in making a similar move.

The effect of international competition has been highly beneficial to consumers around the world. In the two examples cited—detergents in Central America and automobiles in the United States—consumers have benefited. In Central America detergent prices have fallen as a result of international competition. In the United States consumers have obtained from foreign companies the automobile products, performance, and price characteristics that they wanted. If the imported cars of the smaller size and price had not been available, it is unlikely that Detroit manufacturers would have provided a comparable product as quickly. International competition expands the choice available to consumers and increases the likelihood that consumers will get what they want.

STAGES OF MARKET DEVELOPMENT

International markets are at different stages of development with correspondingly different characteristics. These stages fall easily into five levels of development with accompanying income ranges, which, although necessarily somewhat arbitrary, do roughly distinguish various stages of market development. The 188 countries and territories of the world are assigned to five different categories in Table 3-8.

Pre-Industrial Countries

Pre-industrial countries are those with 1973 incomes under $200 per capita. Forty-three countries and territories were in this category in 1973. The characteristics shared by the diminishing number of countries at this level are as follows:

1. Low literacy rates and a high percentage of employment in agriculture
2. Low population density and low degree of urbanization
3. Linguistic heterogeneity and a small percentage of working age population
4. Industrial sectors virtually nonexistent and undeveloped
5. Heavy reliance upon foreign sources for all manufactures and principal engagement in agricultural endeavors

Because of their low income, these countries must be examined on a case-by-case basis. Although the market for the vast majority of capital goods is even more limited in these countries than their low income suggests due to the total absence of a significant industrialized sector, they may present interesting export opportunities in particular capital goods areas to fill needs created by development projects.

Note that consumer goods markets in the pre-industrial societies are developed in certain special areas. For example, even though income levels are extremely low, there is not a pre-industrial society anywhere in the world where a mass market for soft drinks cannot be developed by a bottler. Although incomes are low, the price of a soft drink in these countries is only a few pennies because of lower costs. This is a large sum of money relative to the income. But the money is not an impossible sum to accumulate, and consumers in these countries do from time to time make a soft-drink purchase. The same is true in these markets for such products as bicycles, radios, inexpensive clothing and footwear, and cooking utensils. A limited range of basic necessities and even of items that are discretionary can be sold in the pre-industrial societies.

TABLE 3-8. Stages of Market Development, 1975

Income group [1]	Number of countries	Population (millions)	GNP (US$000 millions)	Average GNP per capita (US$)
Less than $200	28	959	131	140
$200 to $499	40	1,295	457	350
$500 to $1,999	59	576	590	1,020
$2,000 to $4,999	30	654	2,034	3,110
$5,000 and over	25	422	2,876	6,820

[1] Excludes Cambodia, Lebanon, and Viet Nam in the aggregation.

Countries with per capita income of—

Less than $200: Afghanistan, Bangladesh, Benin, Bhutan, Burma, Burundi, Chad, Ethiopia, Gambia (The), Guinea, Guinea-Bissau, Haiti, India, Lao People's Democratic Republic, Lesotho, Malawi, Maldives, Mali, Mozambique, Nepal, Niger, Pakistan, Rwanda, Somalia, Sri Lanka, Tanzania, Upper Volta, Zaire.

$200-$499: Angola, Bolivia, Botswana, Cameroon, Cape Verde, Central African Empire, China (People's Republic of), Comoros, Egypt (Arab Republic of), El Salvador, Equatorial Guinea, Grenada, Honduras, Indonesia, Jordan, Kenya, Korea (Democratic People's Republic of), Liberia, Madagascar, Mauritania, Morocco, New Hebrides, Nigeria, Papua New Guinea, Philippines, São Tome and Principe, Senegal, Sierra Leone, Solomon Islands, St. Vincent, Sudan, Swaziland, Thailand, Togo, Tonga, Uganda, Western Samoa, Yemen Arab Republic, Yemen (People's Democratic Republic of), Zambia.

$500-$1,999: Albania, Algeria, Antigua, Argentina, Barbados, Belize, Brazil, Chile, China (Republic of), Colombia, Congo (People's Republic of the), Costa Rica, Cuba, Cyprus, Djibouti, Dominica, Dominican Republic, Ecuador, Fiji, French Guiana, Ghana, Gilbert Islands, Guadeloupe, Guatemala, Guyana, Hong Kong, Iran, Iraq, Isle of Man, Ivory Coast, Jamaica, Korea (Republic of), Macao, Malaysia, Malta, Mauritius, Mexico, Mongolia, Namibia, Netherlands Antilles, Nicaragua, Panama, Paraguay, Peru, Portugal, Reunion, Rhodesia, Romania, Seychelles, South Africa, St. Kitts-Nevis, St. Lucia, Surinam, Syrian Arab Republic, Trust Territory of the Pacific Islands, Tunisia, Turkey, Uruguay, Yugoslavia.

$2,000 to $4,999: Austria, Bahamas, Bahrain, Bulgaria, Channel Islands, Czechoslovakia, French Polynesia, Gabon, German Democratic Republic, Gibraltar, Greece, Greenland, Hungary, Ireland, Israel, Italy, Japan, Martinique, New Caledonia, New Zealand, Oman, Poland, Puerto Rico, Saudi Arabia, Singapore, Spain, Trinidad and Tobago, United Kingdom, USSR, Venezuela.

$5,000 and over: American Samoa, Australia, Belgium, Bermuda, Brunei, Canada, Canal Zone, Denmark, Faeroe Islands, Finland, France, Guam, Germany (Federal Republic of), Iceland, Kuwait, Libya, Luxembourg, Netherlands, Norway, Qatar, Sweden, Switzerland, United Arab Emirates, United States, Virgin Islands (US).

Source: World Bank Atlas, 1977.

Underdeveloped Countries

Underdeveloped countries and territories are the fifty-two societies whose 1973 GNP per capita ranged from $200 to $499. The first stages of industrialization are evident in these markets. Small factories are erected to supply the domestic market with such items as batteries, tires, footwear, clothing, building materials, and packaged foods. The proportion of the population engaged in agricultural activities declines and the degree of urbanization increases. The available educational effort expands and literacy rises.

In addition to expanding consumer markets because of rising incomes, industrial markets develop because of the industrialization process. The range and quantity of products demanded in these countries in both consumer and industrial products markets is limited. Their total income in 1973 was $332 billion, roughly the same as West Germany's during that year.

Semideveloped Countries

The semideveloped markets are those whose 1973 GNP per capita ranged from $500 to $1,999. There were fifty-six countries and territories in this category. In most of these markets more than 33 percent of the population is engaged in agriculture, and less than 30 percent of the population is urban. However, in a majority of these markets at least 50 percent of the population is literate. The semideveloped countries often have highly developed industrial sectors that provide a market opportunity for the industrial products company. Consumer markets in the semideveloped countries are also of significant size on a per capita basis. Some of the larger semideveloped countries, such as Brazil, have cities and regions with all the characteristics of developed countries. For marketing purposes, these markets within a market should be treated as if they were developed country market regions or districts. All the countries in this category are significant markets on a per capita basis for consumer products, including major consumer durables such as the automobile.

Industrialized Countries

Industrialized countries are those whose 1973 GNP per capita ranged from $2,000 to $4,779. There were twenty-eight countries in this category. In these countries the population engaged in agriculture drops substantially. The degree of urbanization increases, and the literacy rate rises to very high levels, in most cases exceeding 85 percent. Wage levels rise sharply, and ownership of every type of consumer durable, transportation, leisure time, and housing product rises sharply. The need for labor-saving methods creates new industrial product markets in existing industries, and development creates entirely new industries. Advertising expenditures rise sharply. Self-service distribution expands.

The difference between the industrialized and the post-industrial country is one of degree rather than of kind. Product saturation levels are a good illustration of this point. In the industrialized country the norm for automobile ownership will be moving toward one car per household, whereas in the post-industrial country the norm will be moving from one to two cars per household.

In 1973 twelve countries had a GNP per capita of $5,000 and over. Of this number, six countries—Canada, Denmark, Germany, the United States, Sweden, and Switzerland—have reached their present income level through a process of organic internal development. These six countries are classified as post-industrial societies. The other six countries in this income category were similar to the six countries classified as post-industrial in income only. Their income level has been achieved from a single economic sector such as mineral production or tourism and does not, therefore, reflect an underlying organic development.

Daniel Bell, a professor of sociology at Harvard University, is a leading proponent of the concept of a post-industrial society. He suggests that the main difference between the industrial and the post-industrial society is that the sources of innovation in a post-industrial society are derived increasingly from the codification of theoretical knowledge, rather than from "random" inventions. Other characteristics, summarized in Table 3-9, are: the importance of the service sector (more than 50 percent of GNP); the crucial importance of information processing and exchange; and the ascendancy of knowledge over capital as the key strategic resource, of intellectual technology over machine technology, of scientists and professionals over engineers and semiskilled workers, and of theory and models over empiricism.

Other aspects of the post-industrial society are an orientation toward the future and the importance of interpersonal and intragroup relationships in the functioning of society.

The United States and Sweden are examples of post-industrial societies. Japan is a particularly interesting case of a rapidly emerging post-industrial society. The Japanese in many respects are uniquely suited in their basic cultural orientation to adapt to the basic requirements of a post-industrial society. Cooperation and harmonious interaction, for example, are important keystones of the Japanese culture. This is in a marked contrast to Britain, which is stuck in the industrial stage of development largely because of the inability of labor and management to find mutually acceptable ways of adapting to the adjustments required by technological, organizational, and managerial modernization.

The Japan Computer Usage Development Institute has prepared a document called "The Plan for Information Society—A National Goal toward Year 2,000," which is a conscious statement of the qualities and goals of a post-industrial society. The introduction to the report states:

> During almost a century, since the Imperial Restoration, Japan endeavored to build a modernized industrial society, and has almost reached this goal. However Japan is now confronting multitudes of social and economic problems that include pollution problems, excessively dense population problems in urban areas, economic depression resulting from industrial and economic structures, increases in aged population, etc.
>
> In the advanced countries, de-industrialization is now under way, and the world is generally and steadily shifting from the industrialized society to the

TABLE 3-9. The Post-Industrial Society: A Comparative Schema

Modes / *Mode of Production*	*Pre-Industrial* / Extractive	*Industrial* / Fabrication	*Post-Industrial* / Processing, Recycling Services
Economic sector	Primary Agriculture Mining Fishing Timber Oil and gas	Secondary Goods producing Manufacturing Durables Non-durables Heavy construction	Tertiary Transportation Utilities Quaternary Trade Finance Insurance Real estate Quinary Health Research Education Government Recreation
Transforming resource	Natural Power Wind, water, draft animals, human muscle	Created Energy Electricity—oil, gas, coal Nuclear power	Information Computer and data-transmission systems
Strategic resource	Raw materials	Financial capital	Knowledge
Technology	Craft	Machine technology	Intellectual technology
Skill base	Artisan, manual worker, farmer	Engineer, semiskilled worker	Scientist, technical and professional occupations
Methodology	Common sense, trial and error, experience	Empiricism, experimentation	Abstract theory: models, simulations, decision theory, systems analysis
Time perspective	Orientation to the past	Ad hoc adaptiveness, experimentation	Future orientation, forecasting and planning
Design	Game against nature	Game against fabricated nature	Game between persons
Axial principle	Traditionalism	Economic growth	Codification of theoretical knowledge

Source: Physics Today, February 1976, p. 47.

information society. Therefore, this committee proposes the establishment of a new national target, "Realization of the Information Society."

The ultimate goal of the information society is the realization of a "society that brings about a general flourishing state of human intellectual creativity." Intellectual creativity may be defined as a process of exploring into future possibilities by fully employing information and knowledge with the aim of materializing such possibilities.

Product and market opportunities in the post-industrial society are more heavily dependent upon new products and innovations than in industrial societies. All the basic products are already owned. Household saturation levels are extremely high, and a marketer seeking to expand his business must either expand his share of existing markets, which is always difficult, or create a new market. This situation explains the very high incidence of new-product development and innovation that takes place in the post-industrial society.

MARKET STAGES BASED ON THE DEVELOPMENT OF THE MIDDLE CLASS

Ernest Dichter has proposed that it is the extent of development of a large middle class that makes the difference between a backward and a modern country both economically and psychologically. He chose the automobile as the most important symbol of middle-class values and contrasted attitudes toward automobiles in five country groupings, which are based on the size and development of the middle class:[7]

> Group one: the almost classless society, contented countries. This group includes the Scandinavian countries. The middle class comprises almost the entire population spectrum, with very few people who are considered really poor or really rich. In this society attitudes toward cars are sober and conservative. Cars are strictly utilitarian.
>
> Group two: the affluent countries, Dichter places the United States, West Germany, Switzerland, Holland, and Canada in this category. In these countries, people want greater individuality in their products. The status value of cars declines substantially and shifts to such things as swimming pools, travel, and education. According to Dichter, the average American considers his car more an appliance than a status symbol. There is attention to functional value and integration in car design and cars are not pampered; they are expected to do their job.
>
> Group three: countries in transition. These countries still have a large working class in the nineteenth-century sense. This class aspires to break out of its boundaries and join the comfortable middle class. The upper classes in the transitional countries still live on a lavish scale, with personal servants and vast estates. The living standards of the working classes are lower than those in the affluent countries. Cars in these countries are pampered. They are an extension of one's personality. They represent major investments and are outward symbols of success.

[7]The following is drawn from Dichter's "The World Customer," *Harvard Business Review,* (July-August 1962).

Group four: revolutionary countries (industrializing countries). Automobiles in these countries are available only to a relatively small group of people. They are expensive and are considered a luxury. They are taxed so heavily that they are beyond the reach of most people. As the middle class develops in these countries, they will become major markets for automobiles.

Group five: primitive countries (pre-industrial countries). In these countries, the few cars that are sold are primarily for government bureaucracy. There is no real car market as such.

Dichter's method of classifying the countries of the world using the criterion of middle-class development is an interesting attempt. Unfortunately, this criterion is difficult to develop, and its application to the automobile example is hardly a guide to managerial marketing planning. For example, Dichter has grouped the United States and Holland in the same category, which is not very useful. The range of automobile products sold in the United States is much broader than that offered in Holland because of enormous differences in the physical characteristics of the two countries. Economic and social differences have created a more segmented market in the United States, with a wider range of product categories. Size is also a factor that makes it possible for small, but very healthy, market segments to exist in the United States. The most popular cars in the United States are not sold at all in Holland, but not vice versa.

Dichter's lack of success in using a single criterion to group the markets of the world underlines the multidimensional character of markets and the need to rely upon multiple dimensions in analyzing market potential. The best single criterion for analyzing markets is undoubtedly national income, but even this criterion can mislead an analyst concerned with opportunity for a particular product.

NATIONAL CONTROLS OF INTERNATIONAL TRANSFERS

The nation-states of the world exercise control over a broad range of international transfers. Items transferred include not only goods and services but also money, people, technology, and rights. All of these elements are important aspects of the multinational marketing mix, particularly goods, money, and people.

There are several motives for controlling international transfers. A major motive is to accomplish economic goals. The earliest economic goal of controls over international transfers was revenue production. Today, only in the less-developed countries is the revenue motive a principal factor guiding national policy in this area. More common motives today are protection of local industry and the corollary of fostering the development of local enterprise. In less-developed countries these three motives work together. A country can increase national revenues by increasing tariffs and duties on transfers of goods and at the same time can provide protection for local infant industries or for local enterprise that has obtained political influence.

Employment is a major economic goal influencing controls over international transfers. When the free play of economic forces results in heavy competitive pressure which in turn creates domestic unemployment, political forces activated by management, as well as workers in the affected industry, are often capable of bringing pressure to control international transfer. The controls may be in the form of higher tariffs or import quotas which place an absolute quantity limit on the quantity by weight, value, or volume of goods that may enter the country. For example, in 1975 the rate of unemployment in the U.S. specialty steel industry was as high as 40 percent, in part because of foreign inroads into this steel market. The specialty steel industry, with the full support of labor, appealed for government protection. In June 1976 President Ford stated that he would impose quotas upon specialty steels. He made the announcement in Middletown, Ohio, home of Armco Steel Corporation, one of the leading U.S. specialty steel makers.

Although economic goals are the prime cause of the imposition of controls on international transfers, political goals are extremely important. Proof of this is the fact that although 13 percent of global income is located in Eastern Europe, the region accounted for only 4 percent of world trade and almost no foreign production in 1974. Political barriers to business involvement have been erected between East and West, which includes all of Soviet Europe, Mainland China, such Asian regions as Vietnam, and Cuba in the Americas. These barriers are very real; they exist because of differences between the East and the West. These political differences were formerly expressed in part by the development of a planned or controlled economic system in the East as opposed to the market system in the West. As political relations, expressed in the general policies of detente, have improved, possibilities for increased trade and investment have also improved. Unfortunately, the underlying differences between planned and market economic systems present formidable barriers to expanded trade and investment. Although trade and investment between East and West are growing, the difficulties of doing business in the East have dampened the initial enthusiasm that accompanied the policy of detente. For example, one large American company, after signing a trade agreement with Poland, set up a special office in Brussels to coordinate purchases from Poland under the agreement. The company discovered that it was much easier to sell to Poland than it was to buy. In spite of the frequent speeches by government officials in Poland underlining the need to expand exports to the West, this company found that it could not even get Polish companies to respond to requests for quotation. An investigation of this problem revealed that Polish companies were well organized to purchase from the West, but they had almost no organization, staff, or experience in selling.

Within the West the emergence of economic nationalism has been a factor affecting the expansion of international business. However, the political forces that have arisen have not had a substantial impact on the nature of expansion in international business. For example, when France was under Gaullist leadership the government took a series of steps designed to discourage foreign investment in France and to encourage a national control over all major economic sectors. The government's efforts toward this end were thwarted by underlying economic realities. After de Gaulle's retirement from office, succeeding French governments adopted a more reasonable policy that was consistent with basic economic realities and, as a result, the penetration of international enterprise in the French economy is now moving at a pace close to that of countries of similar size and income. Many nations, particularly those with large military establishments such as the United States, have cited national security as a basis for controlling international business activity. A number of intended moves by U.S. companies have been affected by U.S. government policy regarding national security. For example, the U.S. government has taken the position that U.S. companies must avoid any transactions with hostile Communist countries (defined by law) that would in any way encourage the economic development of these countries, and therefore their underlying military capability. As a result, several years ago when Ford of Canada took steps to negotiate the sale of trucks to Mainland China, pressure was brought to bear by the U.S. government on Ford headquarters in this country, which in turn directed Ford of Canada not to make the sale. This expression of national political policy by the U.S. had the unfortunate consequence of countering the national policy of Canada which was to expand exports, and in Canadian eyes Mainland China was a major customer. Fortunately, examples of extraterritorial influence are on the decline as governments increasingly adopt a restrained position on the legitimate scope of their influence.

Why Identify Control Motives?

The identification of motives for controlling international transfers is important because this is the first step in the formation of a behavioral model of nation-states in the economic policy area. Admittedly any behavioral model of a nation will be an extremely rough approximation of the reality it attempts to describe. Nevertheless, moves by nations have as great an impact on the success of international marketing programs as do moves of individual competitors. It is essential that the international marketing planner account for and attempt to forecast possible moves by nation-states that would affect marketing programs being designed.

The current Japanese situation is a good example of how motives influence national controls over international transfers. The Japanese have established a worldwide reputation for the stringency of their barriers to direct entry into the Japanese economy and market. In general, it was impossible for most enterprises to obtain permission to begin independent direct operations in Japan. Every company wishing to enter the Japanese economy had to obtain the approval of the National Planning Authority, and all applications were carefully scrutinized and considered in the light of the national plan for Japanese economic development. In most cases the Japanese have permitted entry of foreign firms only on a joint-venture basis. In many industries, automobiles for example, the Japanese have resisted any form of foreign entry until their own industry established a strong base both in Japan and in the international economy.

The major controlling factor that has forced the Japanese to admit foreign companies into the Japanese economy has been the fact that Japan has a major stake in markets in the industrial countries of the world. Because the Japanese are committed to developing a position in international markets, they are responsive to the positions of the national governments who control access to these markets. In a real sense, then, Japan has been a hostage to its own market position in other countries when companies based in these countries have sought permission to enter the Japanese market. Concurrently, the Japanese position has led to a substantial balance-of-payments surplus and the accumulation of large reserves that have created further pressure for allowing greater access to the Japanese markets both of imported goods and of direct operations by foreign companies. The consequence of these pressures has been a major liberalization of the Japanese investment law, which today permits 100 percent foreign ownership in all but four industry areas.

In taking this example one step further, there is considerable pressure today in some sectors in the United States for restrictive measures to reduce the quantity of Japanese goods imported into the United States. As the U.S. market position, both in terms of direct operations and in terms of export markets, develops in Japan, the companies that hold these markets in Japan will naturally be anxious to preserve them. It is likely, then, that these interests will bring pressure upon the U.S. government to maintain amicable relations with Japan, and if their judgment is that the restriction of Japanese imports in the United States would harm United States–Japanese relationships they would protest these restrictions. In this example the United States would, in a real sense, be a hostage to its interests in Japan.

The hostage framework applies very well to industrial countries because all industrial countries today are involved in symmetrical relationships with other industrial countries. They are at the same time both importers and exporters of manufactured goods, both recipients of direct investments and foreign operations, and both direct investors and foreign operators. The relationships between industrial countries and less-developed countries, on the other hand, are not nearly so symmetrical. In general, less-developed countries export raw materials to the industrial countries and import manufactures from them. Moreover the flow of direct investment and foreign operations is one way—from the industrialized countries to the less-developed countries. As a result, the companies from industrial countries have an economic stake in the less-developed countries that is not reciprocated. This lack of symmetry in the relationship between industrialized countries and less-developed countries creates a less stable economic and political environment in the underdeveloped country because there is no hostage motive controlling pressures to restrict or constrain the operations of foreign investors and foreign-based exporters. Without the constraint of hostage investments and market positions, the behavior of less-developed countries responds to a matrix of economic, social, political, cultural, and security motives that must be established and forecast by the marketing planner to estimate the general level of environmental conditions that will exist in the less-developed country over the company's planning horizon. In general, if a country is economically successful, as defined by sustained real growth and the absence of balance-of-payments pressures, the business environment will typically remain favorable. If a country gets into difficulty, pressures will develop to deal with problems. These pressures may take the form of restricting the operations and access of all companies to foreign exchange, making it difficult, expensive, or impossible to import components or repatriate dividends and capital. Another form of response to local frustration may be the requirement that foreign companies localize management and ownership.

Marketing and Economic Development

An important concern in marketing is whether or not it has any relevance to the process of economic development. It is widely asserted that marketing is a field that is relevant only to the conditions that apply in wealthy, industrialized countries where the major problem is one of directing society's resources into everchanging output or production to satisfy a dynamic marketplace. In the less-developed country, it is argued, the major problem is the allocation of scarce resources into obvious production needs. The important focus in the less-developed countries is on production and how to increase output, not on customer needs and wants.

It can also be argued that the marketing process of focusing an organization's resources on environmental opportunities is a process that has no relevance in the less-developed country, that the needs and wants in less-developed countries so far exceed the productive capability of these societies that it is superfluous to focus societal resources on considering these needs. If the existing stock of goods and services available in the world is fixed, this argument has merit. On the other hand, if the existing stock of goods and services is not considered fixed, this argument can be challenged on the grounds that it does not allow for the possibilities of dynamic response to needs within less-developed countries. The application of the marketing process to the less-developed country would involve an appraisal of the list of wants and needs in the country and an appraisal of the productive capabilities of the society. Combined with the creative application of the marketing process, this would lead to the formulation of new products that matched the wants and needs with the true productive capabilities of the society. Indeed the possibilities for the application of the marketing process to market conditions in less-developed countries are unlimited. For example, less-developed countries have a need for washing and cleaning. Because of the low-income levels, this washing is done by hand. It is not feasible for less-developed countries to engage in the production and sale of automatic electrically operated washing machines because the expense and the complexity of these devices far exceed the economic and productive capabilities of these societies. The application of the marketing process under these conditions should lead to the development of a washing device that is appropriate to the economic capability of the society. The possibilities for the development of an inexpensive hand-operated washing machine are considerable.

The economics literature places a great deal of emphasis on the role of "marketing" in economic development when marketing is defined as distribution. In his book *West African Trade*,[8] P. T. Bauer considered the question concerning the number of traders and their productivity. The number and variety of traders in

[8] Peter T. Bauer, *West African Trade* (London: Routledge and K. Paul, 1963).

West Africa had been much criticized by both official and unofficial observers. Traders were condemned as wasteful and were said to be responsible for wide distributive margins both in the sale of merchandise and in the purchase of produce. Bauer examined these criticisms and concluded that they stemmed from a misunderstanding. He argued that the West African system economized in capital and used resources that were largely redundant, such as labor, and therefore that it was a productive system by rational economic criteria.

A simple example illustrates Bauer's point. A trader buys a package of twenty cigarettes for one shilling and resells them one at a time for two cents each, or for a total of two shillings. Has this man exploited his fellow man to the extent of one shilling, or has he provided a useful service? In a society where consumers can afford to smoke only one cigarette at a time, the man has provided a useful service in substituting labor for capital. In this case, capital would be the accumulation of an inventory of cigarettes by a consumer. The first obstacle to this accumulation, which is the possession of a shilling, is paramount. However, even if a consumer were able to accumulate a shilling, his standard of living would not allow him to smoke the twenty cigarettes at a rate that would allow them to be consumed in a fresh condition. Thus even if he were able to save and accumulate a shilling, he would end up with a package of spoiled cigarettes. The trader in this case, by breaking bulk, serves the useful function of making available a product in a quantity that a consumer can afford an in a condition that is attractive. As income levels rise, Nigerians will smoke more frequently and will be able to buy an entire package of cigarettes. In the process, the amount of Nigerian resources consumed by distribution will decline and the standard of living will have risen. Meanwhile, in the less-developed condition where labor is redundant and cheap and where capital is scarce, the availability of this distributive function is a useful one and a rational application of society's resources.

Another function of distribution in economic development, which Peter Drucker identifies, is the important business experience provided by distribution.[9] Both Bauer and Drucker argue that experience in the distributive sector is valuable because it generates a pool of entrepreneurial talent in a society where alternatives for such training are scarce. Adam Smith in *The Wealth of Nations* observed, "The habits besides, of order, economy, and attention, to which mercantile business naturally forms a merchant, render him much fitter to execute with profit and success, any project of improvement."

Product, price, and communications are also marketing decision areas that can be crucial in the process of economic development. This is well illustrated by the role that these decision areas in marketing have played in the economic integration and development of the Central American Common Market (CACM). Local manufacturers of paint in Central America applying the marketing concept and focusing on the needs of the customer decided to offer a medium-quality paint at a price that was 40 to 50 percent lower than that of the formerly available high-

[9] Peter Drucker, "Marketing and Economic Development," *Journal of Marketing* (Chicago: American Marketing Association, January 1958), pp. 252–59.

quality imported paint. This product proved to be much more oriented toward the true needs of the Central American consumer, as demonstrated by the tremendous response of the market to the product. The local companies with their lower-priced paint quickly gained over 80 percent of the market.

A more controversial aspect of marketing is its ability to stimulate and direct demand through merchandising and advertising programs. Until recently marketers in industrialized countries were given complete license to employ marketing to promote any legal product—even products such as cigarettes, which had been known for some time to be harmful to the health or welfare of consumers. Less-developed countries have not been sympathetic to the expenditure of societal resources on stimulating and directing demand, again because of the general position that demand and wants so far exceed the availability of resources that stimulation or direction is unnecessary. In recent years both the license of the industrialized countries and the rejection of the less-developed countries have come into question. In the industrialized countries it is now recognized that complete license to merchandise products is an excess. The most notable example of this revised thinking concerns cigarette advertising, which was banned from television in the United States as of January 1, 1971. In less-developed countries the usefulness of merchandising and advertising to stimulate and promote desired behavior has been recognized in at least some circles. For example, the widely heralded high-protein foods that became available in the latter half of the 1960s were not quickly adopted by the inhabitants of the less-developed countries. This came as a great surprise to many people, since the nutritional value of these foods was clearly superior to that of the traditional diet. Unfortunately, high-protein foods were not what the consumers had accustomed themselves to and developed preferences for, and therefore they needed to be carefully formulated, recognizing taste and texture preferences, and skillfully promoted and merchandised. The use of marketing communications and marketing skills to shift consumer food consumption into more nutritional types of food is an example of an extremely useful application of marketing to the needs of less-developed countries.

BIBLIOGRAPHY

Felix, Fremont, *World Markets of Tomorrow*. London: Harper & Row, Pub., 1972.

Jaffe, Eugene D., *Grouping: A Strategy for International Marketing*. New York: American Management Association, 1974.

Kravis, Irving B., et al., *A System of International Comparisons of Gross Product and Purchasing Power*. Washington, D.C.: International Bank for Reconstruction and Development, 1975.

McHale, John, *The President Directory 1978*. Tokyo, Japan: President Inc., 1978.

——, *World Facts and Trends*. New York: Macmillan, 1972.

Renner, John C., "Trade Barriers, Negotiations, and Rules," *Columbia Journal of World Business,* 8(Fall 1973), 51–58.

LAUNDROWASH S.p.A. (B)

In August 1961, Mr. Mario Paino reviewed his first few months of operation and was concerned about what he could do to increase sales in his new laundry.[1] Mr. Paino had, three months earlier, opened in Turin what he believed to be the first American-style coin-operated automatic laundry in Italy. Initial results were extremely disappointing.

Mr. Paino had equipped the Turin laundry with 16 Speed Wash 4-kilo washers, one 11-kilo washer, six dryers, one water extractor, and a soap and bleach dispenser. The laundry opened on May 9, 1961. Prices were L.200 for the 4-kilo washers, L.400 for the 11-kilo washer, L.50 for each five-minute dryer cycle, and L.50 per packet for the soap and bleach. The water extractor, which was equipped with a L.50 coin meter, was not used due to mechanical difficulties.[2] Hours of operation were from 8:00 to 12:00, and from 15:00 to 19:00, Monday through Saturday. Local regulations made it illegal to operate on Sunday.

ADVERTISING AND PROMOTION

Pre-opening advertising and promotion consisted of movie slides announcing Laundrowash, two pamphlets describing the new laundry, and free wash coupons which were inserted with the two pamphlets into 1,000 mail boxes in the Via Roselli area. Several days after the laundry opened, the slides were discontinued, and no more free wash coupons were distributed.

One of the pamphlets opened to three pages printed on both sides. An English translation of this pamphlet is reproduced in Appendix 1. The second pamphlet was larger and opened to two pages printed on both sides. In addition to a large two-colour picture of the interior of the laundry, it repeated most of the text of the three-page booklet.

There were 86 redemptions of free wash coupons during the first week of business. In the second week this number fell to 20, and in successive weeks it dropped to 10, six, and one. The last coupon was redeemed in July, bringing the total redemption to 123.

OPERATING RESULTS

Laundrowash sales, including free washes, for the first 13 weeks are shown in Exhibit 1. Although complete expense reports were not available, preliminary

---

[1] See Laundrowash S.p.A. (A)

[2] As of mid-August, Mr. Paino had not been able to locate a mechanic who could repair the machine.

EXHIBIT 1. Laundrowash Sales

1961, Week Ending	Washing Operations			Income			Total	
	Paid	Free	Total	Washers Lire	Dryers Lire	Soap Lire	Lire	U.S.$ Equivalent*
May 14	51	86	137	10,200	3,700	3,400	17,300	28.00
May 21	124	20	144	24,800	5,650	10,000	40,450	65.00
May 28	133		133	26,600	6,450	12,350	45,400	73.00
June 4	159	10	169	31,800	6,450	13,800	52,050	84.00
June 11	171	6	177	34,200	7,200	15,200	56,600	91.00
June 18	217	1	218	43,400	6,200	19,200	68,800	110.00
June 25	217		217	43,400	7,350	17,600	68,350	109.00
July 2	216	1	217	43,200	6,850	19,100	69,150	111.00
July 9	232		232	46,400	4,150	19,800	70,350	113.00
July 16	176		176	35,600	4,400	14,250	54,250	88.00
July 23	162		162	32,400	5,000	13,300	50,700	82.00
July 30	226		226	45,200	6,700	14,300	66,200	107.00
August 6	225		225	45,000	7,300	14,750	67,050	108.00

*One U.S. $ = L.620.
Source: Company records.

EXHIBIT 2. Break-Even Calculation for Laundrowash S.p.A.*

Break-even : the point at which fixed plus variable expenses
= total revenue.
Assumption : Each wash load L.200 ($0.32) is matched with
10 minutes drying time L.100 ($0.16) producing
a total revenue of $0.48 per "load".
Let X = the number of break-even "loads" per month.
(Revenue per load × No. of loads = Fixed Costs + variable costs)
$0.48(X) = $925 + $0.07(X)
$0.41X = $925
X = 2256
No. of break-even "loads" per month = 2256
Break-even revenue per month   = $1083 (L.676,800)

---

*Excluding soap, bleach, water extractor, and 11-kilo washer sales.
Source: Mr. Paino's records.

data indicated that fixed expenses were as expected ($925 per month, including $500 for depreciation), while variable expenses were around $0.04 per twenty-minute washer cycle and $0.015 per five-minute dryer cycle.

Mr. Paino was extremely discouraged by the laundry's performance. He estimated that for the month ending August 6th, 1961, his "out-of-pocket" expenses exceeded income by almost $100, and that including depreciation, operating losses were at least $600.

As a rough estimate, Mr. Paino calculated that sales would have to increase to L.640,000 per month in order for the store to break even.[3] His break-even calculation, which is reproduced in Exhibit 2, was figured on the basis of washer and dryer operation only.

Mr. Paino was puzzled by the laundry's failure to achieve a profitable sales level. Although he was unhappy about the continuing losses, he remained firm in his belief that coin-ops could be profitable in Italy. He felt that a major problem was educating people to accept coin-ops. For example, women were observed entering Laundrowash with their laundry concealed in suitcases because they were afraid of being seen on the street with dirty laundry.

Mr. Paino wondered if an advertising and promotion campaign was needed to overcome the public's resistance to coin-ops. One promotion possibility was a formal opening ceremony with the dignitaries from the U.S. Consulate and Italian Foreign Trade Department as guests of honour.

APPENDIX 1 / TEXT OF LAUNDROWASH PAMPHLET

(Translation from the Italian by Miss G. Schori.)

Page 1: Announcing a shop for Automatic Laundry equipped with commercial laundry machines.

---

[3] Break even: the point at which fixed plus variable cost equals total revenue.

Welcome neighbors!! to your Speed Wash automatic laundry, open every day of the week.

Page 2: Welcome neighbors!
To your Speed Wash self service laundry, designed and furnished only for you, yes, it is your shop, and you should feel right at home.

Now you can do your own laundry just as you do at home, with the assurance that there are plenty of machines, big dryers, and unlimited hot and soft water. You can save 50 percent doing your laundry this way.

Finished are the days when you have to do laundry in small loads. Now you can use as many washing machines as you need, and you will be through with your laundry in less than an hour.

The cost is so little that it would be more expensive to do it at home even if you had a free washing and drying machine. We can save you money, because we do not need to pay personnel. We offer you this saving and reduce the cost of your laundry.

Page 3: The 4 ingredients of a good wash:
A really good wash requires:
—a good plant
—a good detergent
—plenty of hot water
—soft water

Our laundry is furnished with the best equipment available, constructed with the utmost care by Speed Wash. The Speed Wash washer does not have an agitator that damages your laundry, and dirty water is removed so that it does not go through your laundry as it does in conventional machines. You need 77 litres of water at 80°C to wash 4 kilograms dry weight. The heaters you have in your house have a capacity ranging from 80–120 litres of which only 45 to 50 litres are warm enough to provide a good wash. You would need at least 6 hours to wash a weekly laundry of 20 kilos because you would have to wait for your boiler to heat the water. The Speed Wash laundry has enough water to provide continuous washing for each machine in the laundry.

Page 4: To dry your laundry at home you need many hours. Instead your speed wash laundry has big commercial dryers which circulate your laundry in a big cylinder drying it quickly and giving a soft dry wash. The water used on the Speed Wash automatic laundry is as filtered and soft as rain water. We use soft water because hard water minerals make the soap less efficient and leave deposits. The Speed Wash machine NEEDS LESS THAN ONE CUP OF DETERGENT.

The reason this is so is that with soft water you get a better wash with less soap. This is another saving for you.

DO NOT USE TOO MUCH DETERGENT: you will only get too many bubbles.

Your Speed Wash automatic laundry was created to lighten your work and lessen your fatigue, from the boring days you spent doing laundry. Remember that this is your neighborhood washing place. Cooperate with your neighbors to make it and keep it a nice and gay place where you can do your weekly laundry.

Page 5: You will obtain a whiter and cleaner wash using the Speed Wash commercial laundry. This laundry uses purified soft water that is as soft as rain.

Page 6: The woman who wants the best of everything uses the Speed Wash Laundrowash.
  * You will get a better wash than you get at home.

* You can do your entire weekly wash in an hour by using several machines.
* You will get scientifically clean, deodorized clothes with machines that are frequently sterilized.
* You can dry your clothes cheaply and quickly.
* You can do the laundry yourself with all the advantages, and none of the disadvantages of home.
* You will reduce the cost of your wash by 50 percent and do your wash in a pleasant atmosphere with your friends and neighbors.

QUESTIONS

1. What changes, if any, would you make in Laundrowash based upon operating results in the (B) case?
2. What is Laundrowash's break-even point as a percentage of the potential market?
3. Would you continue to operate if you were Mr. Paino? What changes, if any, would you make in marketing policies?

social and cultural elements of the world market environment

> Love between man and woman . . . consumes energy and
> wastes time. On the other hand, love of the party and of
> the chairman, Mao Tse-Tung, takes no time at all and is
> in itself a powerful tonic.
>
> *People's Daily (Peking)*

INTRODUCTION

This chapter focuses on the social and cultural forces that shape and affect individual behavior in the world market environment. Every person represents the interaction of his own personality with the collective forces of the culture and milieu in which he has developed and experienced life. The approach of this chapter expresses the conceptual orientation of this book, which is based on the assumption that both individuals and cultures in the world are characterized not only by their differences but also by their similarities. The task of the international marketer is to recognize both the similarities and the differences and incorporate this recognition into the marketing planning process so that products, programs, and strategies can be adapted to significant and important differences. The other side of this coin is that relevant similarities are also recognized so that unnecessary and costly adaptations can be avoided. The aim of this chapter, then, is to provide an orientation or standpoint to culture, to apply analytical approaches to understanding cultural dynamics in the marketplace, and, finally, to suggest ways in which cultural factors operate in international marketing practice.

The popular definition of *culture* is, "What I've got and you haven't." My taste in clothing, music, food, and so forth is cultured, and yours, of course, is not. This is confusing taste with nature. For the anthropologist, culture is: The ways of living built up by a group of human beings which are transmitted from one generation to another. Culture includes both conscious and unconscious values, ideas, attitudes, and symbols which shape human behavior, and which are transmitted from one generation to the next. In this sense, culture does not refer to the instinctive responses of people, nor does it include one-time solutions to unique problems.

BASIC ASPECTS OF CULTURE

Anthropologists agree on three characteristics of culture: (1) it is not innate, but learned; (2) the various facets of culture are interrelated—touch a culture in one place and everything else is affected; (3) it is shared by the members of a group and defines the boundaries between different groups.[1]

Because culture has such an important influence on customer behavior, it is useful to outline some of the major assumptions concerning the nature of culture. The following assumptions are drawn from recent anthropological literature and have fairly general acceptance among anthropologists.

Culture consists of learned responses to recurring situations. The earlier these responses are learned, the more difficult they are to change. Many aspects of culture influence the marketing environment. Taste, for example, is a learned response that is highly variable from culture to culture and has a major impact on the market environment. Preference for such things as colors and styles is culturally influenced. Attitudes toward whole classes of products can be a function of culture. For example, in the United States there is a high cultural predisposition to be interested and intrigued by product innovations that have a "gadgety" quality. Thus the electric knife, the electric toothbrush, the Water-Pik (a tooth-cleaning appliance that cleans teeth with a pulsating stream of water under high pressure), and a host of appliances find a ready and very quick market in the United States even though many of these products are often purchased, used for a period of time, and then quietly put away and never used again. There is unquestionably a smaller predisposition to purchase such products in other developed country markets such as Europe. A reasonable hypothesis is that this difference is partially a result of cultural differences. Nevertheless, because incomes in other industrial country markets and the United States are different, the influence of income on behavior and attitudes is also at work. Indeed the basic question that must be answered by marketers seeking to understand or predict behavior is, to what extent do cultural factors influence behavior independent of income levels? The profusion of automobiles, convenience foods, disposable packages, and other articles in Europe and Japan suggests that many or perhaps even most consumer products have universal appeal and will be purchased in any country, regardless of cultural differences, when consumer disposable income reaches a high enough level.

THE SEARCH FOR CULTURAL UNIVERSALS

For the international marketer the search for cultural universals provides a valuable orientation. A *universal* is a mode of behavior existing in all cultures. To the extent

[1] Edward T. Hall, *Beyond Culture* (New York: Anchor Books, 1977), p. 16.

that aspects of the cultural environment are universal as opposed to unique, it is possible for the international marketer to standardize such aspects of his marketing program as product design and communications, which are two of the major elements of a marketing program. Fortunately for the international marketer, much of the apparent cultural diversity in the world turns out to be different ways of accomplishing the same thing.

A partial list of cultural universals was developed by George P. Murdock and includes the following: "Age grading, athletic sports, bodily adornment, calendar, cleanliness training, community organization, cooking, co-operative labor, cosmology, courtship, dancing, decorative art, divination, division of labor, dream interpretation, education, ethics, etiquette, family feasting, firemaking, folklore, food taboos, inheritance rules, joking, kin groups, kinship, language, law, magic, marriage, mealtime, medicine, modesty concerning natural functions, mourning music, nomenclature, obstetrics, penal sanctions, personal names, population policy, postnatal care, pregnancy usage, property rights, propitiation of supernatural beings, puberty customs, religious rituals, residence rules, sexual restrictions, soul concepts, status differentiation, superstition, surgery, toolmaking, trade, visiting, weaning, and weather control."[2]

Let us consider music as an example of how these universals apply to marketing decision making. Music as an art form is part of all cultures; thus the musical song-type commercial is universally feasible. Although music is culturally universal, its style is not internationally uniform. Therefore the type of music that is appropriate in one part of the world may not be acceptable or effective in another part. A campaign might utilize a bossa nova rhythm or "cha-cha-cha" beat for Latin America, a rock rhythm for North America, a "high life" for Africa, and so on. In this way the universal forms can be adapted to cultural styles in each region.

With increasing travel and communications many of the national attitudes toward style in clothing, color, music, and food and drink are becoming international and even universal. This internationalization of culture has been significantly accelerated by multinational companies that have recognized an opportunity to extend their product/communications strategies into international markets. Coke and Pepsi, Levi Straus, and Kentucky Fried Chicken are just a few examples of U.S. companies breaking down cultural distinctiveness by their expansion into new international markets.

The Anthropologist's Standpoint

As Ruth Benedict points out in her classic *The Chrysanthemum and the Sword,* no matter how bizarre his act or opinion, the way a person thinks, feels, and acts has some relation to his experience. The successful international marketer must adopt this assumption if he is to understand the dynamics of a foreign market.

Any systematic study of a foreign market requires a combination of tough-mindedness and generosity. The appreciation of another way of life cannot develop

[2]George P. Murdock, "The Common Denominator of Culture," in *The Science of Man in the World Crisis.* ed. Ralph Linton (New York: Columbia University Press, 1945), p. 145.

when one is defensive about his own way of life; it is necessary to be secure in one's own convictions and traditions. In addition, generosity is required if one is to appreciate the integrity and value of other ways of life and points of view. The international marketer needs to develop an objective standpoint that recognizes diversity, seeks to understand its origins, and avoids the pitfalls of both rejection and identification. There are many paths to the same end in life—the international marketer knows this and rejoices in life's rich diversity.

ANALYTICAL APPROACHES TO CULTURAL FACTORS

One of the problems with cultural factors in the international market environment is the way in which they are hidden from view. *Culture* is learned behavior passed on from generation to generation and is exceedingly difficult for an outsider to fathom. We are bound by our own cultural assumptions and behaviors to such an extent that we frequently do not see differences even when we are in the midst of that different culture.

To transcend this cultural myopia we must recognize that in order to understand other cultures, we must make explicit the rules by which our own culture operates. This requires an approach to ourselves and to others that must take into account the following facts:

1. The beginning of wisdom is to accept that we will never fully understand ourselves or others—people are far too complex to be "understood." As Carl Jung pointed out, "There are no misunderstandings in nature . . . misunderstandings are found only in the realm of what we call 'understanding'"[3]
2. Our perceptual systems are extremely limited. We "see" almost nothing. Our nervous systems are organized on the principle of negative feedback, i.e., our nervous system operates so smoothly that the only time our control system is brought into play is when input signals deviate from what we expect.
3. We spend most of our energy managing perceptual inputs.
4. When we experience or perceive bizarre behavior, there is something behind this behavior, i.e., a cultural system of beliefs and values that we do not understand.
5. If we want to be effective in a foreign culture, we must attempt to understand beliefs, motives, and values. This requires an open attitude, one that transcends our own culture.

The Need Hierarchy

In the search for cultural universals an extremely useful theory of human motivation was developed by the late A. H. Maslow.[4]

[3]C. G. Jung, *Critique of Psychoanalysis,* Bollingen Series XX (Princeton, N.J.: Princeton University Press, 1975), par. 776, p. 228.
[4]A. H. Maslow, "A Theory of Human Motivation," in *Readings in Managerial Psychology,* eds. Harold J. Leavitt and Louis R. Pondy (Chicago: University of Chicago Press, 1964), pp. 6–24.

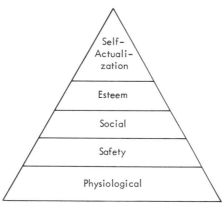

FIGURE 4-1. Maslow's Hierarchy of Needs

Maslow hypothesized that man's desires can be arranged into a hierarchy of needs of relative potency. As soon as the "lower" needs are filled, other and higher needs emerge immediately to dominate the individual. When these higher needs are in turn satisfied, new and still higher needs emerge. Figure 4-1 illustrates the hierarchy identifying the major needs formulated by Maslow.

Physiological needs are at the bottom of the hierarchy because they are most fundamental. They include food, water, air, protection from the elements, comfort, sex, and so on. For the man who is extremely hungry, no other interest except food exists. He thinks only about food, wants only food, and has little interest in writing poetry, reading a good book, acquiring a new automobile or anything other than satisfying his overwhelming need for food. Once these physiological needs are gratified, a new set of needs emerges that Maslow categorizes as safety needs. Safety, in general, refers to a feeling of well-being and a sense that danger is not present in the environment. A person whose physiological and safety needs are satisfied will feel the need for friendships and love relationships and will strive to gratify these needs, which Maslow called social needs.

Once these "lower" needs have been satisfied, two higher needs emerge. First is a need for esteem. This is the desire for self-respect, self-esteem, and the esteem of others and is a powerful drive creating demand for status-improving goods. The status symbol exists across the spectrum of stages of development. In developing East Africa women who owned bras always wore them with straps exposed to show the world that they owned a bra. In the United States a more expensive automobile was for decades a standard form of status improvement.

The final stage in the need hierarchy is self-actualization. When all of the needs for sex, safety, security, friendship, and the esteem of others are satisfied, discontent and restlessness will develop unless one is doing what one is fitted for. A musician must make music, an artist must paint, a poet must write, a builder must build, and so on. As Albert Einstein said when asked how he withstood the acclaim he received for his accomplishments and the peril of corruption by praise: "One is tempted to stop and listen to it. The only thing is to turn away and go on working. Work, there is nothing else."[5] There is a possibility that demand for material goods declines at this point.

The hierarchy of needs proposed by Maslow is of course a simplification of the complexity of need feelings in people. A person's needs do not progress neatly from one stage of a hierarchy to another. A person who is fulfilling self-actualization needs is also in need of love, sex, and food. One may be restless and dissatisfied before approaching self-actualization. Nevertheless, the hierarchy does suggest a hypothesis for relating higher levels of consumption to basic psychological drives.

The usefulness of the need hierarchy hypothesis to the international marketer is its universality. The more highly developed a market, the greater the proportion of goods and products that will be filling social and esteem needs as opposed to physiological. As countries continue to develop, it appears that self-actualization needs begin to affect consumer behavior. In the United States, for example, the automobile is no longer a universal status symbol, and many younger consumers are turning away from material possessions. As countries progress through the stages of economic development, more and more members of a society are operating at the esteem need level and higher, having satisfied physiological safety, and social needs.[6] The expression of these higher needs takes some surprising forms. In Los Angeles, for example, there is a company called Rent A Wreck. This company has discovered a thriving market among affluent Hollywood types who are reacting to what they consider to be a low-brow esteem for expensive cars and who assert their cultural values by driving "wrecks." This is an example of a growing tendency in the United States to reject material objects as "status symbols." This mass rejection of materialism is not so advanced in other leading industrialized countries. For example, in Germany today, the automobile remains a supreme status symbol. Germans give their automobiles loving care, even going so far as to travel to distant locations on weekends to wash their cars in spring water.

Although there are abundant sources of stereotypes that suggest enormous differences in the basic nature of different nationalities and races, increasing evidence is accumulating to dispute these stereotypes. In a study of twenty-five overseas operations of a large manufacturing company, Sirota and Greenwood found considerable similarity in the work goals of employees:

> The implications of our study may be considered at a number of different levels . . .
> Perhaps most relevant to the managers of international organizations, is the considerable similarity we have found in the goals of employees around the world. This finding has an extremely important policy implication: since the goals of employees are similar internationally, corporate policy decisions, to the extent that they are based on assumptions about employee goals, can also be international in scope.
> It is not only Americans who want money, or Frenchmen who want auton-

[5] Ronald W. Clark, *Einstein: The Life and Times* (New York: World Publishing, 1971).

[6] An anomaly of modern times is the emergence of need in the safety area in the United States, the richest country in the world. Indeed, the safety need in the United States may be higher than this need in some of the poorest countries in the world.

omy, or Germans who want their work skills utilized and improved. A management whose policies and practices reflect these stereotypes (for example, providing few advancement opportunities in some countries or using certain countries as dumping grounds for routine, unchallenging work) should be prepared to suffer the consequences of managing a frustrated and uncommitted work force.

In this respect, it would be interesting to determine how much of the difficulty experienced in managing employees in other countries is due not to cultural differences at all but, rather, to the automatic and psychologically self-serving assumption of differences that, in reality, may be minor or even nonexistent.[7]

The Self-Reference Criterion

A way of systematically reducing the extent to which our perception of market needs is blocked by our own cultural experience was developed by James Lee. Lee terms the unconscious reference to one's own cultural values the _self-reference criterion,_ or SRC. He addresses this problem and proposes a systematic four-step framework for eliminating this form of myopia:[8]

1. Define the problem or goal in terms of home country cultural traits, habits, and norms.
2. Define the problem or goal in terms of the foreign culture, traits, habits, and norms.
3. Isolate the SRC influence in the problem and examine it carefully to see how it complicates the problem.
4. Redefine the problem without the SRC influence and solve for the foreign market situation.

Lee provides the following example of an application of this analytical approach. In 1963 the European division of an American automobile manufacturer withdrew its assembly operation from Karachi under government pressure to manufacture automobiles or to sell out. Taking this pressure as the beginning of a product design problem, how might the company have proceeded at the time of its entry into the Pakistani market in the late 1950s?

Step 1. _Define the business problem or goal in terms of domestic cultural traits, habits, or norms._ Western countries in the 1950s were characterized by transportation needs geared to speed, promptness, comfort, and style. European and U.S. highways demanded a cruising speed of sixty to seventy miles an hour and eighty to one hundred octane gasoline was available. Manufacturing techniques were very sophisticated; foreign exchange was not a businessman's problem.

Step 2. _Define the business problem or goal in terms of the foreign cultural_

[7]David Sirota and Michael J. Greenwood, "Understand Your Overseas Workforce," _Harvard Business Review,_ January-February 1971, p. 60.

[8]James A. Lee, "Cultural Analysis in Overseas Operations," _Harvard Business Review,_ March-April 1966, pp. 106–14.

traits, habits, or norms. Make no value judgments. Pakistan was a culture characterized by a strong desire to be mobile but with an extremely low technological skill level. Sixty-octane gasoline was available, and there was extreme pressure on foreign exchange. Consumer credit was a future hope, the national speed limit was thirty-five miles an hour, and the total number of automobiles registered was less than 50,000.

Step 3. *Isolate the SRC influence in the problem and examine it carefully to see how it complicates the problem.* The significant differences between steps one and two suggest strongly that the needs upon which the European and U.S. model were originally based did not exist in Pakistan and that a modification of these models was needed by the market.

Step 4. *Redefine the problem without the SRC influence and solve for the foreign market situation.* This would require the design of a car to fit Pakistan's cultural and economic specifications. Lee maintains that such a car existed in the United States and proposes the King Midget manufactured by Midget Motors of Athens, Ohio. The Midget sells for $680 if made of angle, channel, and strap iron. The capital investment for a plant with a capacity of 1,200 per year in Pakistan would be about $100,000 in hard currency and in the equivalent amount in the local currency. The car would sell for approximately $1,000, would have a cruising speed of forty miles an hour, and would travel eighty miles on a gallon of low-octane gasoline.

Diffusion Theory

Since the late 1930s hundreds of studies have been directed toward achieving and understanding the process through which an individual adopts a new idea.[9] In his book *Diffusion of Innovations,* Everett Rogers reports on 506 diffusion studies that suggest some remarkably similar findings. This enormous body of research has suggested concepts and patterns that are extremely useful to the international marketer because he is involved in introducing innovations in the form of his products into markets.

An *innovation* is something new or different, either in an absolute sense or in a situational sense. In an absolute sense, once a product has been introduced anywhere in the world, it is no longer an innovation because it is no longer new to the world. However, a product introduced in one market may be an innovation in another market because it is a new and different product for the new market. Thus, in international marketing, companies are in the position of marketing products that may be simultaneously new-product innovations in some markets and mature, post-mature, or declining products in other markets. Thus the findings from studies of the diffusion of innovations have great relevance to the various circumstances in which the international marketer finds himself.

[9] This section is drawn from Everett M. Rogers, *Diffusion of Innovations* (New York: Free Press, 1962).

The Adoption Process

One of the basic elements of the theory of the diffusion of innovations is the concept of an adoption process—the mental process through which an individual passes from the time of his first knowledge of an innovation to the time of adoption or purchase of the innovation. Research suggests that an individual passes through five different stages as he proceeds from his first knowledge of a product to the final adoption or purchase of that product. These stages are as follows:

1. *Awareness.* At this stage the customer becomes aware for the first time of the product or innovation. Studies have shown that at this stage impersonal sources of information such as advertising are most important. Frequently one of the major objectives of advertising in international marketing is to create product awareness where the product is an innovation in the new market.

2. *Interest.* During this stage the customer knows of the product and, because of an interest in the product, seeks additional information. In his information gathering he has shifted from a viewing position to a monitoring position. He will incorporate any information on the product in question if information on it should come into his possession. Additionally, because of his interest in the product, he will engage in research activities in order to acquire additional information.

3. *Evaluation.* In this stage the individual mentally applies the product or innovation to his present and anticipated future situation and decides whether or not to try the product.

4. *Trial.* After learning of the product, obtaining information about it, and mentally deciding whether or not to try the product, the next stage is trial or actual purchase depending on the cost of the product. If the product is expensive, then a customer will not purchase it without trial, although the trial may be mental or theoretical rather than actual. A good example of an actual trial that does not involve purchase would be the automobile demonstration ride. For the inexpensive product, trial often involves purchase, but can also involve a free sample. In inexpensive products, adoption is defined as repeat purchase as opposed to a single purchase that is defined as trial.

5. *Adoption.* In this stage the individual either purchases the more expensive product that has been tried without purchase or continues to purchase (repeat purchase) the less-expensive product, such as a razor blade. As a person moves from the evaluation to the trial to the adoption stage, studies show that personal sources of information are more important than impersonal sources. It is during these stages that the salesman, and, perhaps even more important, word of mouth, come into play as major persuasive forces affecting the decision to buy.

Characteristics of Innovations

One of the major factors affecting the rate of adoption of an innovation is the characteristics of the innovation itself. Rogers suggests five characteristics that have a major influence on the rate of adoption of an innovation. They are as follows:

1. *Relative advantage.* How does a new product compare with existing products or methods in the eyes of customers? The perceived relative advantage of a new product versus existing products is a major influence on the rate of adoption. An example of a product with a high perceived relative advantage is the transistor radio vis-à-vis the tube-type radio. If a product has a substantial relative advantage vis-à-vis the competition, it is at a great advantage in the market.

2. *Compatibility.* This is the extent to which a product is consistent with existing values and past experiences of adopters. The history of product failures in international marketing is replete with examples that were caused by the lack of compatibility of the new products in the target market. The fluffy frosted cake mixes were introduced by U.S. companies into the United Kingdom where cake was eaten at teatime with the fingers rather than as a dessert with a fork. The result was lack of sales and failure. The Renault Dauphine was introduced into the United States in 1959 to a market that subjected automobiles to driving conditions far more rigorous than those encountered in France. The result was product breakdowns and failure. The Jolly Green Giant attempted to market corn in Europe where the prevailing attitude is that corn is a grain that is fed to hogs and not to people. The result was a lack of sales and severe losses on investments in European corn production. These products did not succeed in international markets because of the lack of compatibility with existing values and patterns of behavior.

3. *Complexity.* This is the degree to which an innovation or new product is difficult to understand and use. If a product has a high coefficient of complexity, then this is a factor that can slow down the rate of adoption, particularly in developing country markets with low rates of literacy.

4. *Divisibility.* This is the degree or extent to which a product may be tried and used on a limited basis. In the international market wide discrepancies in income levels result in major differences in acceptable levels of divisibility. Hellmann's mayonnaise, a product of CPC International, was simply not selling in U.S.-size jars in Latin America. The company then placed the mayonnaise in small plastic packets and immediately sales developed. The plastic packets were within the food budgets of the local consumers, and they required no refrigeration, which is another plus.

5. *Communicability.* This is the degree to which results of an innovation or the value of a product may be communicated to a potential market.

The major dimensions of the product that determine the rate of its adoption or penetration of international markets are its relative advantage vis-à-vis other products, its compatibility with existing values and patters of behavior, and the price of the product relative to the price of competing or substitute products. A fourth major factor is the availability of the product. Finally, the communicability and the effectiveness of communications concerning the product are a major influence affecting the rate of adoption.

Adopter Categories

Adopter categories are classifications of individuals within a market on the basis of their innovativeness. The hundreds of studies of the diffusion of innovation demonstrate that adoption is a social phenomenon and therefore is characterized by the normal distributions. If the number of adopters is plotted on the *Y* axis and time on the *X* axis, the adopters of an innovation are those shown in Figure 4-2.

Five categories have been assigned to the segments of this normal distribution. The first 2.5 percent of people to purchase a product are defined as *innovators*. The next 13.5 percent are defined as *early adopters,* the next 34 percent as the *early majority,* the next 34 percent as the *late majority,* and the final 16 percent as *laggards.* Studies show that innovators tend to be venturesome, more cosmopolite in their social relationships, and wealthier than those who adopt later. Earlier adopters are the most influential people in their communities, even more than the innovators. Thus the early adopters are a critical group in the adoption process, and they have a great influence on the majority who make up the bulk of the adopters of any product. Several characteristics of early adopters stand out. First of all they tend to be younger, have higher social status, and are in a more favorable financial position than later adopters. They must be responsive to mass-media information sources and must learn about innovations from these sources because they cannot simply copy the behavior of earlier adopters.

One of the major reasons for the normal distribution of adopter categories is the so-called interaction effect. This is the process through which individuals in a social system who have adopted an innovation influence those who have not yet adopted. Adoption of a new idea or product is the result of human interaction. If the first adopter of an innovation or new product discusses it with two other people, and each of these two adopters passes the new idea along to two other people, and so on, the resulting distribution follows a binomial expansion. This mathematical function follows a normal shape when plotted.

From the point of view of the marketing manager, steps taken to persuade innovators and early adopters to purchase a product are critical because these inno-

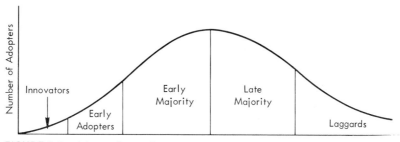

FIGURE 4-2. Adopter Categories

vators must make the first move and are the basis for the eventual penetration of a product into a new market because the majority copy their behavior.

High- and Low-Context Cultures

Edward T. Hall has suggested the concept of high and low context as a way of understanding different cultural orientations.[10] In a low-context culture, messages are explicit; words carry most of the information in communication. In a high-context culture, less information is contained in the verbal part of a message, since much more information is in the context of communication, which includes the background, associations, and basic values of the communicators. Who you are—that is, your values and position or place in society—is crucial in the high-context culture, such as in Japan or the Arab countries. In these cultures, a bank loan is more likely to be based upon who you are than upon formal analysis of pro forma profit-and-loss statements and balance sheets. In a low-context culture, deals are made with much less information about the character and background and values of the participants, and much more reliance upon the words and numbers in the loan application. Examples of low-context cultures would be the United States or, perhaps even more distinctly, the Swiss-Germans.

In general, high-context cultures get along with much less legal paperwork than is deemed essential in low-context cultures such as the United States. In a high-context culture, a man's word is his bond. There is less need to anticipate contingencies and provide for external legal sanctions in a culture that emphasizes obligations and trust as important values. In these cultures, shared feelings of obligation and honor take the place of impersonal legal sanctions—thus the importance of long and protracted negotiations that never seem to get to the point. Part of the purpose of negotiating for a person from a high-context culture is to get to know the potential partner.

For example, insisting on competitive bidding can cause complications in low-context cultures. In a high-context culture, the job is given to the man who will do the best work and whom you can trust and control. In a low-context culture, one tries to make the specifications so precise that a builder is forced by the threat of legal sanction to do a good job. According to Hall, a builder in Japan is likely to say, "What has that piece of paper got to do with the situation? If we can't trust each other enough to go ahead without it, why bother?"

Although countries can be classified as high or low context in their overall tendency, there are of course exceptions to the general tendency. These exceptions are found in subcultures. The United States, for example, is a low-context culture with subcultures that operate in the high-context mode.

Charles A. Coombs, senior vice-president of the Federal Reserve Bank of New

---

[10]See Edward T. Hall, *Beyond Culture* (Garden City, N.Y.: Anchor Press/Doubleday, 1976); and "How Cultures Collide," *Psychology Today,* July 1976, pp. 66–97.

York in charge of the Fed's foreign exchange operations, provides such an example in his book *The Arena of International Finance.* The world of the central banker, as he describes it, is a gentlemen's world, that is, a high-context culture. Even during the most hectic days in the foreign exchange markets, a central banker's word is sufficient for him to borrow millions of dollars. During the rioting and political upheavals in France in 1968, the confidence of central bankers in one another was dramatically demonstrated. Except for telephones, all communications between France and the United States were cut off. Consequently the New York Fed agreed that it would follow instructions received by telephone from the Bank of France for intervening on its behalf in support of the franc. Within eight days the New York Fed had bought more than $50 million of francs without a single written confirmation for any part of the purchase. The Fed was far out on a limb. A couple of weeks later the daughter of the governor of the Bank of France came to New York on personal business. She brought written confirmations with her. "Our legal department heaved a sigh of relief," Coombs remembers. The legal department was operating in a low-context culture with all of the assumptions that go with this culture (everything must be spelled out and confirmed in writing—you can't trust anyone), but the central bankers, who were obviously much more relaxed about the matter, were operating within a high-context culture (a man's word is his bond). Another U.S. high-context subculture is the Mafia, which has imported the high-context culture of Sicily to the United States and has maintained this culture with language, ritual, separation, and a strong sense of distinct identity.

Table 4-1 summarizes some of the ways in which high- and low-context cultures differ.

TABLE 4-1. High- and Low-Context Cultures

Factors/Dimensions	High Context	Low Context
Lawyers	Less important	Very important
A man's word	Is his bond	Is not to be relied upon—"get it in writing"
Responsibility for organizational error	Taken by highest level	Pushed to lowest level
Space	People breathe on each other	People carry a bubble of private space with them and resent intrusions
Time	Polychronic—everything in life must be dealt with in terms of its own time	Monochronic—time is money. Linear—one thing at a time
Negotiations	Are lengthy—a major purpose is to allow the parties to get to know each other	Proceed quickly
Competitive bidding	Infrequent	Common
Country/Regional examples	Japan, Middle East	U.S.A., Northern Europe

CULTURAL FACTORS IN MARKETING

Industrial Products

Without question the impact of culture on international markets is greater for consumer than for industrial products. The reason for this is the strong impact of universal technology and science on product design and standards. Nevertheless, cultural factors are important influences on the marketing of industrial products and must be recognized in formulating an international marketing plan. Different conventions regarding specifications are an important variable internationally. For example, United States specifications typically contain a margin of error so that a buyer will obtain the specifications plus some margin of error that varies from industry to industry. For example, in the United States if you need a metal bar to carry 20,000 pounds with an occasional load of 25,000 pounds, then you can specify 20,000 pounds and get a bar that will have a sufficient safety factor built in to cover overload situations. In Europe specifications are exact. Typically, in Europe if you buy a bar to carry 20,000 pounds, this is the maximum weight that the bar can carry. If you want a safety factor up to 25,000 pounds, you must buy a bar with specifications of that point.

Much has been written about specific cultural differences in various regions of the world. The cultural variety of the world is so great that it is neither feasible nor prudent to attempt to capture these differences in a single volume. The following actual case suggests, however, the way in which cultural differences influenced the marketing of an industrial product in Latin America.

A Latin American republic had decided to modernize one of its communication networks to the tune of several million dollars. Because of its reputation for quality it approached American company "Y."

The company, having been sounded out informally, considered the size of the order and decided to bypass its regular Latin American representative and send instead its sales manager. The following describes what took place.

> The sales manager arrived and checked into the leading hotel. He immediately had some difficulty pinning down just who it was he had to see about his business. After several days without results, he called at the American Embassy where he found that the commercial attaché had the up-to-the-minute information he needed. The commercial attaché listened to his story. Realizing that the sales manager had already made a number of mistakes, but figuring that the Latins were used to American blundering, the attaché reasoned that all was not lost. He informed the sales manager that the Minister of Communications was the key man and that whoever got the nod from him would get the contract. He also briefed the sales manager on methods of conducting business in Latin America and offered some pointers about dealing with the minister.
>
> The attaché's advice ran somewhat as follows:
>
> 1. You don't do business here the way you do in the States; it is

necessary to spend much more time. You have to get to know your man and vice versa.

2. You must meet with him several times before you talk business. I will tell you at what point you can bring up the subject. Take your cues from me. (Our American sales manager at this point made a few observations to himself about "cookie pushers" and wondered how many payrolls had been met by the commercial attaché.)

3. Take that price list and put it in your pocket. Don't get it out until I tell you to. Down here price is only one of the many things taken into account before closing a deal. In the United States, your past experience will prompt you to act according to a certain set of principles, but many of these principles will not work here. Every time you feel the urge to act or to say something, look at me. Suppress the urge and take your cues from me. This is very important.

4. Down here people like to do business with men who are somebody. In order to be somebody, it is well to have written a book, to have lectured at a university, or to have developed your intellect in some way. The man you are going to see is a poet. He has published several volumes of poetry. Like many Latin Americans, he prizes poetry highly. You will find that he will spend a good deal of business time quoting his poetry to you, and he will take great pleasure in this.

5. You will also note that the people here are very proud of their past and of their Spanish blood, but they are also exceedingly proud of their liberation from Spain and their independence. The fact that they are a democracy, that they are free, and also that they are no longer a colony is very, very important to them. They are warm and friendly and enthusiastic if they like you. If they don't, they are cold and withdrawn.

6. And another thing, time down here means something different. It works in a different way. You know how it is back in the States when a certain type blurts out whatever is on his mind without waiting to see if the situation is right. He is considered an impatient bore and somewhat egocentric. Well, down here you have to wait much, much longer, and I really mean much, much longer, before you can begin to talk about the reason for your visit.

7. There is another point I want to caution you about. At home, the man who sells takes the initiative. Here, they tell you when they are ready to do business. But most of all, don't discuss price until you are asked and don't rush things.

The Pitch

The next day the commercial attaché introduced the sales manager to the Minister of Communications. First, there was a long wait in the outer office while people kept coming in and out. The sales manager looked at his watch, fidgeted, and finally asked whether the Minister was really expecting him. The reply he received was scarcely reassuring, "Oh yes, he is expecting you but several things have come up that require his attention. Besides, one gets used to waiting down here." The sales manager irritably replied, "But doesn't he know I flew all the way down here from the United States to see him, and I have spent over a week already of my valuable time trying to find him?"

"Yes, I know," was the answer, "but things just move much more slowly here."

At the end of about thirty minutes, the minister emerged from the office, greeted the commercial attaché with a *doble abrazo,* throwing his arms around him and patting him on the back as though they were long-lost brothers. Now, turning and smiling, the minister extended his hand to the sales manager, who, by this time, was feeling rather miffed because he had been kept in the outer office so long.

After what seemed to be an all too short chat, the minister rose, suggesting a well-known café where they might meet for dinner the next evening. The sales manager expected, of course, that, considering the nature of their business and the size of the order, he might be taken to the minister's home, not realizing that the Latin home is reserved for family and very close friends.

Until now, nothing at all had been said about the reason for the sales manager's visit, a fact which bothered him somewhat. The whole setup seemed wrong; nor did he like the idea of wasting another day in town. He told the home office before he left that he would be gone for a week or ten days at most, and made a mental note that he would clean this order up in three days and enjoy a few days in Acapulco or Mexico City. Now the week had already gone and he would be lucky if he made it home in ten days.

Voicing his misgivings to the commercial attaché, he wanted to know if the minister really meant business, and if he did, why could they not get together and talk about it? The commercial attaché by now was beginning to show the strain of constantly having to reassure the sales manager. Nevertheless, he tried again:

"What you don't realize is that part of the time we were waiting, the minister was rearranging a very tight schedule so that he could spend tomorrow night with you. You see, down here they don't delegate responsibility the way we do in the States. They exercise much tighter control that we do. As a consequence, this man spends up to 15 hours a day at his desk. It may not look like it to you, but I assure you he really means business. He wants to give your company the order; if you play your cards right, you will get it."

The next evening provided more of the same. Much conversation about food and music, about many people the sales manager had never heard of. They went to a night club, where the sales manager brightened up and began to think that perhaps he and the minister might have something in common after all. It bothered him, however, that the principal reason for his visit was not even alluded to tangentially. But every time he started to talk about electronics, the commercial attaché would nudge him and proceed to change the subject.

The next meeting was for morning coffee at a café. By now the sales manager was having difficulty hiding his impatience. To make matters worse the minister had a mannerism that he did not like. When they talked he was likely to put his hand on him; he would take hold of his arm and get so close that he almost "spat" in his face. As a consequence, the sales manager was kept busy trying to dodge and back up.

Following coffee, there was a walk in a nearby park. The minister expounded on the shrubs, the birds, and the beauties of nature, and at one spot he stopped to point at a statue and said: "There is a statue of the world's greatest hero, the liberator of mankind!" At this point, the worst happened, for the sales manager asked who the statue was of and, being given the name of a famous Latin American patriot, said, "I never heard of him," and walked on.

The Failure

It is quite clear from this that the sales manager did not get the order, which went to a Swedish concern. The American, moreover, was never able to see the minister again. Why did the minister feel the way he did? His reasoning went somewhat as follows:

"I like the American's equipment and it makes sense to deal with North Americans who are near us and whose price is right. But I could never be friends with this man. He is not my kind of human being and we have nothing in common. He is not simpático. If I can't be friends and he is not simpatico, I can't depend on him to treat me right. I tried everything, every conceivable situation, and only once did we seem to understand each other. If we could be friends, he would feel obligated to me and this obligation would give me some control. Without control, how do I know he will deliver what he says he will at the price he quotes?"

Of course, what the minister did not know was that the price was quite firm, and that quality control was a matter of company policy. He did not realize that the sales manager was a member of an organization, and that the man is always subordinate to the organization in the United States. Next year maybe the sales manager would not even be representing the company, but would be replaced. Further, if he wanted someone to depend on, his best bet would be to hire a good American lawyer to represent him and write a binding contract.

In this instance, both sides suffered. The American felt he was being slighted and put off, and did not see how there could possibly be any connection between poetry and doing business or why it should all take so long. He interpreted the delay as a form of polite brush-off. Even if things had gone differently and there had been a contract, it is doubtful that the minister would have trusted the contract as much as he would a man whom he considered his friend. Throughout Latin America, the law is made livable and contracts workable by having friends and relatives operating from the inside. Lacking a friend, someone who would look out for his interests, the minister did not want to take a chance. He stated this simply and directly.[11]

Consumer Products

Consumer products are probably more sensitive to cultural difference than industrial products, and among consumer products food is probably the most sensitive of all. In West Germany Campbell's reportedly lost over $10 million trying to change the wet-soup habits of the German consumer from dehydrated soup to a canned soup concentrate. In the United States CPC International faced the same problem in reverse in trying unsuccessfully to significantly penetrate the U.S. soup market (90 percent canned) with Knorr dehydrated soups. Knorr was a Swiss company acquired by CPC that had a major share of the European prepared soup market where bouillon and dehydrated soups accounted for 80 percent of commercial soup sales.

A major cultural factor in food marketing is the attitude and practice of

[11] Edward T. Hall, "The Silent Language in Overseas Business," *Harvard Business Review,* May-June 1960, pp. 93–96.

housewives toward food preparation. Campbell Soup discovered in a study conducted in Italy that Italian housewives were spending approximately 4.5 hours per day in food preparation in contrast to the less than sixty minutes a day spent in food preparation by U.S. housewives. These differences in time spent in food preparation reflect not only a cultural pattern but also the different income levels in the two countries.

Indeed Campbell's discovered how strong the feeling toward convenience food in Italy was by asking a random sample of Italian housewives the following question: "Would you want your son to marry a canned soup user?" The response to this question was sobering. Ninety-nine and six-tenths percent of the respondents answered, "No!" Rising incomes will affect Italian attitudes toward time and convenience and will have a major effect on the market for convenience foods. Meanwhile the habits and customs of people continue to affect food markets independently of income levels.

Thirst is a universal physiological need. What people drink, however, is very much culturally determined. The market for coffee presents an interesting demonstration of the effect of culture on drinking habits. In the United Kingdom instant coffee has 90 percent of the total coffee market as compared with only 15 percent in Sweden. The other countries in the Atlantic community fall between these two extreme points. Instant coffee's large share of the British market can be traced to the fact that in hot beverage consumption Britain has been a tea-drinking market. Only in recent times have the British been persuaded to take up coffee drinking. Instant coffee is more like tea than regular coffee in its preparation, and so it was natural that when the British did begin to drink coffee they should adopt instant rather than regular coffee. Another reason for the popularity of instant coffee in Britain is the practice of drinking coffee with a large quantity of milk, so that the coffee flavor is masked. Differences in the coffee flavor are thus hidden, so that a "better cup" of coffee is not really important. Sweden, on the other hand, is a coffee-drinking country. Coffee is the leading hot beverage. The product tends to be consumed without large quantities of milk, and therefore the coffee flavor is not masked.

A study of consumption patterns of soft drinks in Western Europe and the United States demonstrated, however, that there are conspicuous differences in the demand for soft drinks in Western Europe and the United States.[12] Although the population of the United States in 1965 was only 20 percent greater than the combined population of France, Germany, and Italy, sales of soft drinks in the United States were approximately four times greater than the combined sales of these three countries. The average American drinks about five times as many soft drinks as the average Frenchman, three times as many as the average Italian, and two and one-half times as many as the average German.

The differences in soft-drink consumption are associated with much higher per capita consumption of other kinds of beverages in Europe. In France and Italy,

---

[12] In Mogomi and R. Hamamoto, "Comparative Study on Consumption Patterns of Soft Drinks in Western Europe and the United States" (Student report, Columbia University, 1969).

for example, thirty to forty times as much wine is consumed as in America on a per capita basis. The French prefer mineral water to soft drinks, whereas few Americans have tasted mineral water. German per capita consumption of beer exceeds by far the equivalent figure in the United States. Why the difference then between the popularity of soft drinks in Western Europe and the United States? The following factors are responsible for the differences:

C = F (A, B, C, D, E, F, G) where C equals consumption of soft drinks, and
F = function of, and:
A = influences of other beverages' relative prices, quality and taste.
B = advertising expenditure and effectiveness, all beverage categories.
C = availability of products in distribution channels.
D = cultural elements, tradition, custom, habit.
E = availability of raw materials (particularly of water).
F = climatic conditions, temperature, and relative humidity.
G = income levels.

Culture is an important element in determining the demand for soft drinks. But it is important to recognize that it is only one of seven factors, and therefore an influencing rather than a determining factor. If aggressive marketing programs (including lower prices, more intensive distribution, and heavy advertising) were placed behind soft drinks, the consumption of this product would increase more rapidly than it would otherwise. However, it is also clear that any effort to increase the consumption of soft drinks in Western Europe would be pitted against cultural tradition and custom and the competition of widely available alternative beverages. Culture in this case is a restraining force, but because culture is changing so rapidly, there are many opportunities to accelerate changes that favor a company's product.

Eating habits are changing all over the world in response to rising incomes. The basic trends in a country with rising incomes are toward the increasing consumption of packaged, convenience foods that save time for the housewife and add variety to menus. This is the basic and unmistakable trend, but companies have discovered that specific discrete changes are not always easy to accomplish. In the early 1960s General Mills decided to be one of the first companies to profit from the increasing sales of dry breakfast cereals in Japan. By the time General Mills had organized to move into this market the cereal boom had leveled off. General Mills discovered that not enough Japanese families were willing to order the extra milk that dry cereals require—and even when they did increase the quantities of milk they purchased, they preferred to drink the extra amount without cereal.

NATIONALISM

We live in an age in which the currents of nationalism seem to be running in two directions. Among the industrialized countries, there is an unmistakable tendency and direction toward the affirmation of a world community and interdependence.

Indeed, in Sweden, one of the most advanced social democracies in Europe, there is even a conscious expression of the national goal of strengthening the sense of community within the nation and affirming through international cooperation and support the role of Sweden in the world community. Although these goals may not be as clearly articulated in other industrial nations, the implicit national objectives are clear. When difficulties develop in the economic relations between industrialized countries, negotiations since the end of World War II have always led to a resolution of the problem. This occurs because the negotiations take place within the framework of a shared commitment to cooperation and interdependence.

For example, in 1977 the Japanese color television industry succeeded in obtaining over 40 percent of the U.S. color television market. U.S. manufacturers hastily assembled an organization called COMPACT (Committee to Preserve American Color Television) and began an intensive lobbying program to erect tariff barriers or other devices to protect the industry from Japanese competition. In an earlier era, this type of situation could easily have led to the erection of tariff barriers, Japanese retaliation, American counterretaliation, and a rapidly escalating trade war leading to a withdrawal from interdependence and an increasing autarchy. In 1977, unlike the 1930s, this did not happen. Within the framework of an implicit commitment to international economic, social, and military interdependence, representatives of the two countries met, negotiated, and worked out an agreement which resulted in a program of voluntary restraint on the part of the Japanese and provided some relief for the American industry.

The same implicit commitment to interdependence does not exist among the less-developed countries, nor does it exist between the less-developed and the industrialized countries. In this sphere, the problem is asymmetry. The interdependence of the industrialized countries is based upon a perception of mutual advantage and relative equality of participation. Although individual sectors within nations may strongly disagree with national policy, the general community of the industrialized states recognizes that each nation gains more than it gives up in the act of international cooperation. This is not true in the relations between the industrialized and the developing countries. If an industrialized country nationalizes or if it treats foreign-based enterprise in a discriminating way, it leaves itself exposed to similar treatment of its own enterprise in the home country of the restricted enterprise. If a developing country nationalizes, expropriates, or treats foreign enterprise in a discriminating way, in most situations there is no comparable exposure of the less-developed state in the home country of the foreign enterprise.

As a consequence, investors in companies operating in less-developed countries must be prepared to justify on a continuing basis the contribution they are making to the perceived welfare of the less-developed state. Since most companies are unable to demonstrate a continuing unique advantage over local enterprise, this typically requires a very flexible attitude and willingness to adjust the terms and conditions of participation in the developing country. Only enterprises that have a unique advantage technologically or in some other way are able to resist efforts on the part of less-developed states to appropriate equity and management participation in their operations. India provides a good example. Until recently, the only exception made by the Indian government in implementing its requirement of local participation in all foreign enterprise was IBM, a company that had a unique position of technology leadership and was therefore able to maintain its position that it would only operate in India with a wholly controlled and owned local subsidiary. Coca-Cola attempted to take a similar position with regard to the sale of its concentrate in India, but the Indian government judged that Coca-Cola was a nonessential product and that continued operation in India would only be allowed if local investors were allowed to participate in the manufacture and sale of concentrate as well as bottling operations. The Indian government decided to apply its local participation law to IBM, suggesting that it no longer felt IBM's contribution was unique. IBM in response decided to terminate its Indian operations.

CONCLUSION

Culture has both a pervasive and a changing influence on each national market environment. International marketers must recognize the influence of culture and must be prepared to either respond to it or change it. International marketers have played an important and even a leading role in influencing the rate of cultural change around the world. This is particularly true of food but includes virtually every industry, particularly in consumer products. Soap and detergent manufacturers have changed washing habits, the electronics industry has changed entertainment patterns, clothing marketers have changed styles, and so on.

In industrial products culture does affect product characteristics and demand but is more important as an influence on the marketing process, particularly in the way business is done. International marketers have learned to rely upon people who know and understand local customs and attitudes for marketing expertise. Often, but not always, these are local nationals.

BIBLIOGRAPHY

Benedict, Ruth, *The Chrysanthemum and the Sword.* Rutland, Vt.: Charles E. Tuttle, 1972.

——, *Patterns of Culture.* Boston: Houghton Mifflin, 1959.

Davis, Stanley M., *Comparative Management, Organizational and Cultural Perspectives.* Englewood Cliffs, N.J.: Prentice-Hall, 1971. (Readings and cases.)

——, "U.S. versus Latin America: Business & Culture," *Harvard Business Review,* November-December 1969, pp. 88–98.

Dichter, Ernst, "The World Customer," *Harvard Business Review,* July-August 1962, pp. 113–22.

Engel, J. F., D. T. Kollat, and R. D. Blackwell, *Consumer Behavior.* New York: Holt, Rinehart & Winston, 1968.

Farmer, Richard N., and Barry M. Richman, *Comparative Management and Economic Progress.* Homewood, Ill.: Richard D. Irwin, 1965.

Fayerweather, John, *International Marketing* (2nd ed.). Englewood Cliffs, N.J.: Prentice-Hall, 1970.

Hagen, E., *On the Theory of Social Change.* Homewood, Ill.: Dorsey Press, 1962.

Hall, Edward T., *Beyond Culture.* Garden City, N.Y.: Anchor Press/Doubleday, 1976.

Kroeber, Alfred L., and Clyde Kluckhohn, "Culture: A Critical Review of Concepts and Definitions," Vol. 47. Papers of the Peabody Museum, 1952.

Lee, James A., "Cultural Analysis in Overseas Operations," *Harvard Business Review,* March-April 1966, pp. 106–14.

McClelland, D., *The Achieving Society.* New York: Van Nostrand, 1961.

Skinner, Wickham, *American Industry in Developing Economics.* New York: John Wiley, 1968.

Sommers, Montrose S., and Jerome B. Kernan, *Comparative Marketing Systems: A Cultural Approach.* New York: Appleton-Century-Crofts, 1968. (Readings.)

CHOUFONT-SALVA, INC.

On January 10, 1966, the marketing committee[1] of Choufont-Salva, Inc., the Philippine subsidiary of A. L. Choufont et Fils, S.A., decided to add to the company's product line an oral contraceptive developed by the laboratories of the parent company. Choufont-Salva's marketing division (see Exhibit 1) now was faced with the task of designing a marketing plan that would effectively sell this product.

THE COMPANY

Choufont-Salva, Inc. was founded in 1948 by Mr. Lorenzo J. Salva. The company was known as the L. J. Salva Drug Company until 1959 when the company became a subsidiary of A. L. Choufont et Fils, S.A., of Belgium, the second largest drug company in Europe and a company with operations in thirty-nine countries including the Philippines. Many of the subsidiaries of A. L. Choufont et Fils, S.A., marketed both ethical[2] and proprietary[3] drugs. Choufont-Salva, however, had

---

[1] The marketing committee was composed of the general manager, the marketing manager, the sales manager, and the manager of marketing services.

[2] Ethical drugs were promoted directly to the medical profession whose members in turn recommended or prescribed the drugs to the ultimate consumers. Ethical drugs could be divided further into two groups: (1) prescription pharmaceuticals which were ethical products that legally were available only by prescription; and (2) over-the-counter drugs which were ethical products that could be purchased legally without prescription though physicians frequently

EXHIBIT 1. Organizational Chart of the Marketing Division

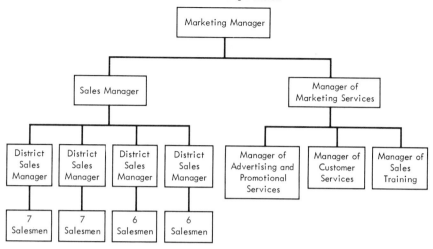

followed the policy established by Mr. Salva when he founded the company of dealing only in ethical drugs.

In 1965 Choufont-Salva marketed sixty-seven different drug products and had sales of approximately ₱6,900,000.[4] Penicillin accounted for forty-seven percent of the sales; and streptomycin, sixteen percent. Thirteen other products were responsible for an additional twenty-one percent of the company's income.

For all products, Choufont-Salva had three prices: the retail price,[5] the semi-wholesale price which was five percent less than the retail price, and the wholesale price which was ten percent less than the retail price. Because of the difficulty in determining whether a purchaser was functioning primarily as a wholesaler or a retailer, Choufont-Salva used the volume of business done annually with the company as the basis for determining which of the price lists was applicable to the customer. Approximately thirty percent of the company's sales were retail; ten percent, semi-wholesale; and sixty percent, wholesale.

In 1965 Choufont-Salva realized an average gross profit of fifty-nine centavos on every peso of sales. Five centavos of this gross profit was paid out in commissions;[6] nine and one-half centavos was spent on advertising and promotions; and

---

did write prescriptions for these drugs. Over-the-counter products typically were manufactured by firms that specialized in prescription pharmaceuticals.

[3] Proprietary drugs were promoted directly to the consumers; the manufacturers of proprietary products usually engaged in heavy consumer advertising and promotions, including extensive in-store display advertising.

[4] Peso = $0.256 (U.S.)

[5] Retail price, as used by Choufont-Salva and other drug companies, referred to the price charged to retail drug outlets and similar purchasers—not to the price paid by the ultimate consumers. The price paid by the ultimate consumers generally was about ten percent higher than this retail price.

[6] Salesmen received commissions of 4 1/2 percent and district sales managers received commissions of 1/2 percent on all sales made in their respective territories.

twenty-one and one-half centavos was expended on other marketing and administrative expenses. However, the gross profit that the company received on sales of a particular product and the expenditures made in promoting the sale of a product frequently varied greatly from this average.

SALES ACTIVITIES

Choufont-Salva had divided the Philippines into twenty-six sales territories. In each territory, there were between one hundred and fifty and three hundred doctors in private practice on whom the salesman assigned to the territory called once per month.

Since Choufont-Salva dealt only in ethical drugs, management believed that the doctor was the most important person to reach in the company's marketing activities. Salesmen in the provinces spent approximately seventy percent of their time calling on physicians. Salesmen in Manila and other large cities devoted an estimated eighty percent of their time to this activity.

Because of the busy schedules of the doctors, most visits with physicians did not last longer than fifteen minutes. During this time a salesman normally made two product presentations. During each presentation, the salesman described how the drug being discussed had been developed, noted the benefits of the product, pointed out how this drug differed from comparable products on the market, and presented clinical evidence attesting to the effectiveness of the drug. At the close of the visit, the salesman left samples of the two products he had discussed and also of two or three other drugs that the company marketed.

Approximately forty percent of the doctors on whom Choufont-Salva salesmen called dispensed their own drugs. During visits to these doctors, the salesman also took orders and made collections for previous purchases.[7] Approximately ten percent of Choufont-Salva's sales in 1965 were made to this group of doctors, most of whom were located in the provinces.

A salesman who had a territory in Manila or another large city and devoted his day exclusively to calling on doctors could make fifteen to eighteen calls if the doctors had their offices at a hospital and twelve to fifteen calls if the doctors had private offices away from a hospital. A provincial salesman calling only on doctors could average ten to twelve calls per day.

Choufont-Salva salesmen called on an estimated twenty-five percent of the doctors in the Philippines. Management believed, however, that these doctors were the ones with the highest professional standing and with the largest and most important practices.

In addition to the doctors, Choufont-Salva salesmen called monthly on fifteen hundred of the estimated five thousand drug stores in the Philippines. Approximately eighty-five percent of the company's sales were made to these pharmaceutical outlets. When calling on drug stores, the salesmen answered any

[7]Commissions on a sale were not paid until the company had received payment.

EXHIBIT 2. Journals in which Choufont-Salva Advertised

Journal	Frequency of Publication	Circulation	Cost per Page*
Family Physician	quarterly	3,000	₱225
The Philippine Journal of Surgeons	quarterly	3,000	₱225
The PMA Journal	monthly	7,000	₱675

*The journals accepted only full-page advertisements.

questions that the personnel had about different products, discussed with the employees new or improved products that the company was introducing, took back old stocks of drugs, accepted orders, and made collections.

Drug stores in the Philippines were free to dispense pharmaceutical products without prescriptions. According to one expert in the field, the Philippines probably had the least restrictive drug laws of any major country in the world. It was not uncommon for anti-biotics and similar drugs to be promoted directly to the consumer through media advertising, posters, and point-of-purchase displays.

The salesmen also called each month on approximately fifty clinics. Sales to these clinics, which were either government health centers or industrial clinics attached to large manufacturing facilities, were responsible for five percent of Choufont-Salva's sales. During the visits to the clinics, the salesmen promoted Choufont-Salva products, left samples, took orders, and received payments for previous orders.

Choufont-Salva supported the activities of its salesmen with advertising and promotional efforts. The company spent ₱8,000 on advertising in 1965. Since Choufont-Salva dealt only in ethical drugs, the entire advertising expenditure was for ads placed in the three leading professional medical journals—*The PMA*[8] *Journal, Family Physician,* and *The Philippine Journal of Surgeons* (see Exhibit 2).

In 1965 Choufont-Salva also spent ₱650,000 on promotional activities. Of this amount ₱550,000 was invested in samples given to physicians. This reflected management's belief that samples were the most effective way of promoting the company's drugs. When samples of drugs were left with a doctor, it reminded him of the products and encouraged him to prescribe them to his patients. Also, the company believed that a doctor liked samples because samples enabled him occasionally to give away medicine free to patients, thus generating goodwill among the recipients.

The remaining ₱100,000 spent on promotions in 1965 was used to print cards, folders, and booklets about various drugs sold by Choufont-Salva. These printed materials were used by the salesmen in discussing the products with the doctors and were left with the doctor at the close of the call.

[8] Philippine Medical Association.

When Choufont-Salva decided to enter the contraceptive market in 1966, the population of the Philippines was approximately 33,000,000. The country had an estimated 5,600,000 households, eighty-five percent of which were located in rural areas. According to government statistics, the population was increasing at the rate of 3 2/10 percent per year, one of the highest population growth rates in the world. If this rate of population growth continued, the country would have 53,000,000 inhabitants by 1980.[9]

In early 1965 the Family Planning Association of the Philippines, Inc. (FPAP) was organized by a group of Catholic laymen. Though three small Protestant family planning groups already were in existence, the FPAP was the first nationwide family planning movement in the Philippines, a country in which eighty-four percent of the population was Catholic.[10]

By the time that Choufont-Salva decided to enter the market in 1966, the management of the company estimated that there were approximately one hundred government or private clinics from which persons could receive information on family planning and, if they desired, birth control products. The majority of these centers were affiliated with either the FPAP or the Planned Parenthood Movement of the Philippines. Birth control products were also available at most drug outlets.

The management of Choufont-Salva estimated that in 1965 Filipinos spent ₱5,000,000 on contraceptive products. Approximately seventy percent of these products were dispensed through drug stores, twenty-five percent through clinics, and five percent directly by doctors. Management predicted that in 1966 the market for contraceptives would be ₱7,500,000 and that the market would continue to grow at least fifty percent per year for the next three years.

In 1965 an estimated ₱4,000,000 was spent on oral contraceptives in the Philippines. The popularity of this method of birth control was attributed to the fact that oral contraceptives were virtually one hundred percent effective and extremely easy to use. Although there were fifteen brands of oral contraceptives on the Philippine market, five brands controlled seventy-five percent of the market (see Exhibit 7).

The second most popular contraceptive product in the Philippines was the intra-uterine contraceptive device (I.U.C.D.). Filipinos in 1965 spent an estimated ₱750,000 on I.U.C.D.'s including fees paid to doctors for inserting the devices. The charges made by private doctors for this service ranged from a low of five pesos to a high of one hundred pesos per patient. Planned parenthood clinics, on the other hand, had a policy of inserting I.U.C.D's completely free or at a charge of five pesos or less.

I.U.C.D.'s were in strong favor with governmental and private agencies in the

---

[9] See Exhibits 3, 4, and 5 for selected demographic data based on the 1960 Census and Exhibit 6 for a summary of the results of a Family Limitation Survey taken by the Bureau of the Census and Statistics in 1965.

[10] See Appendix A for a statement of the position of the Roman Catholic Church concerning family planning; and Appendix B for additional information on the FPAP.

EXHIBIT 3. Population by Marital Status, 1960
(10 years and Over)

Individuals 10 Years Old and Over	Total Philippines		Greater Manila Only	
	Population	Percent	Population	Percent
Single	8,323,157	45.9	452,040	54.6
Married	8,918,739	49.2	339,061	41.0
Widowed	822,412	4.5	33,032	4.0
Divorced or Separated	81,175	0.4	3,022	0.4
Total	18,145,483	100.0	827,155	100.0

Rate of Marriages Per 1,000 Persons: 13.56.

Source: Based on data from the Bureau of Census and Statistics.

EXHIBIT 4. Female Population in the Philippines, 10 Years and Over
(in 000's)

Age	Last Census (1960)		Current
	Total No. of Women	No. of Ever Married Women*	Estimated No. of Women
10–14 years	1,705	2	2,146
15–19	1,401	174	1,802
20–24	1,158	689	1,472
25–29	959	792	1,208
30–34	796	691	996
35–39	675	664	822
40–44	580	497	689
45–49	489	464	585
50–54	384	312	493
55–59	288	218	389
60–64	214	180	284
65 years & over	409	334	462
Total	9,058	5,017	11,348

*Women who currently were married or had been married at one time. Choufont-Salva executives believed that common law marriages were included in these data.

Source: Bureau of Census and Statistics.

Philippines who promoted planned parenthood to low income groups. This method of birth control was inexpensive and did not require instructions that women had to remember. Yet, I.U.C.D.'s had a major drawback. Approximately twenty percent of all women were unable to retain I.U.C.D.'s. This method of birth control, however, was ninety-eight percent effective in preventing pregnancy among the other eighty percent of the women.

Condoms, diaphragms, and spermicidal jellies and creams were not very widely used in the Philippines. In 1965 these products together accounted for only an estimated ₱250,000 of the total contraceptive market.

EXHIBIT 5. Distribution of Households by Income
1960

Annual Income	Percent of Families		
	Greater Manila	Other Metropolitan Areas	Rural Areas
Under ₱500	0.9%	11.3%	21.2%
₱500 to ₱999	4.6	20.0	36.0
₱1,000 to ₱1,499	13.2	16.8	18.0
₱1,500 to ₱1,999	12.2	15.7	10.5
₱2,000 to ₱2,499	10.8	8.8	5.4
₱2,500 to ₱2,999	8.1	6.2	2.8
₱3,000 to ₱3,999	13.3	7.8	2.8
₱4,000 to ₱4,999	7.8	4.4	0.9
₱5,000 to ₱5,999	6.8	2.9	0.7
₱6,000 to ₱7,999	9.4	2.9	0.6
₱8,000 to ₱9,999	4.0	1.0	0.1
₱10,000 & Over	8.7	2.3	0.2
Number of families	361,000	1,444,000	2,921,000
Total number of families: 4,726,000			

Source: Based on data from the Bureau of Census and Statistics.

EXHIBIT 6. Summary of Family Limitation Survey[1]

A total of 4,207 women representing approximately 59 percent of the 7,148 ever-married women[2] in the Philippines covered in the inquiry indicated not wanting more children than what they had in 1965. A significant 39 percent of the total knew how to go about limiting the number of children. In fact, 31 percent of such women had already done something[3] about the matter. The survey further indicated that of women aged below 45 years and who did not know anything about children limitation, 24 percent welcomed the idea of learning possible means of limiting their number of offspring. These indications were revealed by the sample survey conducted in May 1965, covering 7,148 ever-married women from 6,646 sample households throughout the country.

In terms of the level of education attained by the ever-married women included in the inquiry, 32.0 percent belonged to the primary level; 29.5 percent, intermediate; 13.6 percent, high school; 7.0 percent, college; and no grade completed, 16.7 percent. Those whose level of education was not stated represented only 1.2 percent.

According to religious affiliation, on the other hand, 86.5 percent comprised Roman Catholics; 3.4 percent, Aglipayans; 1.2 percent, Iglesia ni Kristo; 2.5 percent, Protestants; and "Others" representing Moslems, Buddhists as well as those not reporting any religion at all, 6.4 percent.[4]

Among the questions asked of the women were: "If all of your children are living, do you think you would like to have more?" "Do you know or have you heard of certain ways by which the number of children in the family may be limited?" "Have you and your husband done anything to limit the number of your children?" And for women aged below 45 years only, the question, "Are you willing to learn any means to limit the number of your children?", was asked. Less than one-half percent did not give answers to any of the four questions.

[1] This summary was prepared by the Bureau of Census and Statistics and based on a survey of conducted by the Bureau in May 1965.
[2] Includes common-law marriages.
[3] Includes both artificial and natural methods of birth control.
[4] The Aglipayan and Iglesia ni Kristo religions were both relatively minor religious sects indigenous to the Philippines. Neither sect objected to artificial means of birth control on theological grounds.

EXHIBIT 6. (Cont.)

Answers to the inquiries showed that in all the sectors of the ever-married women there was widespread refusal to have a bigger size of family and that a sizeable portion were practicing means of limiting their number of children.

To the first question, an appreciable 60 percent of the women in the urban areas did not want more children than what they had at the time of the survey; meanwhile, 57.4 percent of the rural ever-married women included in the inquiry were of the same opinion. The desire to have more children was concentrated among women of ages below 30 years—a common finding to both the urban and rural sectors. It seems that the desire for more children among these young ever-married women is geared towards acquiring a family—to them, the number of children is rather uncertain.

By religious affiliation, 66.7 and 62.9 percent of the Aglipayan respondents in the urban and rural communities, respectively, did not want to have more children. This indication was followed by the Roman Catholic group with 61.0 and 59.3 percent and the Iglesia ni Kristo group with 56.9 and 50.0 percent for the urban and rural sectors, in that order.

It is interesting to note that the desire not to have more children than what they actually have is inversely related to the level of education and this holds true to both the urban and rural ever-married women.

In the urban sector, 72.4 percent, 64.1 percent, 60.1 percent, 55.8 percent and 43.5 percent of the ever-married women with corresponding level of education of no grade completed, primary, intermediate, high school and college, respectively, expressed not wanting more children as compared to the rural ever-married women with 65.0 percent, 61.1 percent, 49.6 percent, 46.9 percent and 33.8 percent, in the same order of level of education.

The survey further revealed that 45.1 and 31.6 percent of the urban and rural ever-married women, respectively, knew or have heard ways of family limitation. Some 45.4 percent of the Roman Catholic group, 45.6 percent of Aglipayan, 44.8 percent of Iglesia ni Kristo and 45.3 percent of Protestant ever-married women in the urban areas knew ways of limiting family sizes as compared to the women in the same order of religion in the rural areas with only 32.4 percent, 32.6 percent, 20.8 percent and 25.3 percent, respectively. It was noted that the Aglipayan women in both urban and rural areas alike proved to be most apprised regarding ways of family limitation than women belonging to the other religious affiliations. This observation was followed by the Roman Catholic, Protestant and Iglesia ni Kristo groups.

The survey also showed that the higher the level of education, the greater is the number of women knowing about family limitation. And this pattern is common in both urban and rural areas. However, in the urban areas, women with high school educations exercised the least family limitation practice, while in the rural areas it was found that the women with no grade completed manifested the same attitude.

It was observed from the answers to the inquiries that a sizeable portion among those who knew means of limiting their number of children were actually practicing or doing something to limit their family size. Some 32.5 percent[5] in the urban areas were practicing family limitation compared to 27.1 percent represented by the rural sector. From among the four major religious groups, 38.5 percent for both Aglipayan and Iglesia ni Kristo groups in the urban centers were noted doing something about family limitation. In the rural areas, however, 38.1 percent of the Protestant women practiced family limitation followed by the Roman Catholic with 27.9 percent, Iglesia ni Kristo with 20.0 percent and Aglipayan with 18.6 percent.

Finally, among those women aged below 45 years who did not know ways of family limitation, many signified intentions of learning about it. This number represented 24.3 percent among the urban women and 23.2 percent from the rural group.

$$* \quad * \quad * \quad * \quad *$$

Special Note to Readers from the Bureau: Readers should bear in mind that these data were gathered from a sample survey conducted simultaneously last year with the annual labor force survey made by the Bureau of Census and Statistics. This being a sample survey, it should, therefore, be treated with certain limitations in mind.

---

[5] I.e., 32.5 percent of those women who knew about family limitation.

EXHIBIT 7. Five Leading Brands of Oral Contraceptives

Brand	Usual Progestin Strengths	Est. Market Share	Retail Price*&**	Comments
Brand A	2.5 mg. or 5.0 mg.	35%	₱3.25	Company concentrated on drug outlets for promotion and distribution
Brand B	4.0 mg.	17%	3.00	Company concentrated on family planning centers for distribution
Brand C	2.0 mg or 10.0 mg.	10%	4.50	
Brand D	3.0 mg.	8%	5.50	An improved version of Brand B; made by same company
Brand E	10.0 mg.	5%	8.00	

*Price per course of medication.
**Retail price referred to the price charged by the drug firms to retail drug outlets and similar purchasers. The prices to the ultimate consumer generally were ten percent higher than these prices.

CHOUFONT-SALVA'S ORAL CONTRACEPTIVE

Choufont-Salva's oral contraceptive was developed in the A. L. Choufont laboratories in Belgium. In early 1965 the product was first introduced on the market in Canada. By 1966 it was being marketed in fourteen countries. The parent company had not yet published for its subsidiaries any detailed information on the market performance of the contraceptive. The bits of data that had been received from the company's Brussels headquarters indicated that the acceptance of the new contraceptive by the market had ranged from fair in Brazil to excellent in Mexico and Denmark.

Oral contraceptives were manufactured in the form of tablets which were taken by women for twenty to twenty-two days during each menstrual cycle. Most oral contraceptive tablets were a combination of a progestin and an estrogen, and tablets containing these two hormonal products were virtually one hundred percent effective as contraceptives.

Oral contraceptives, however, produced in one out of every five women undesirable side effects, such as weight gain, nausea, and headaches. In general the incidence of these side effects were related to the dose of the progestin in the oral contraceptive. As a result, pharmaceutical companies had been trying to develop new progestational agents that could be given in dosages of one milligram or less but still would be effective in controlling fertility.

A. L. Choufont et Fils, S.A., was the first to achieve this breakthrough in steroid research. The company in its laboratories developed a new, totally synthesized and extremely potent progestational hormone. By using this new progestational agent, Choufont et Fils was able to produce a new oral contraceptive that combined in each daily dose only one milligram of progestin with one-tenth of a milligram of an estrogenic agent.

There was only one oral contraceptive compound available in the Philippines that contained as little as one and one-half milligrams of progestin per daily dose. This was a new contraceptive that had been on the market for less than three months. The strength of the progestin in the other compounds on the market varied from two to ten milligrams per tablet.

The low dosage of progestin in the Choufont-Salva contraceptive lessened the chance that a patient would experience undesirable side effects from taking the medication. Clinical data compiled by A. L. Choufont et Fils, S.A., indicated that in only four percent of the patients taking the oral contraceptive developed by the company did the patient experience nausea, headaches, or similar unpleasantness. No other oral contraceptive had such a low incidence of side effects.

The Choufont-Salva oral contraceptive consisted of twenty-one tablets per course of medication. The woman was to take the first tablet on the fifth day of her menstrual cycle and take one tablet daily for twenty-one days. She was then to stop taking tablets for seven days. On the eighth day she was to start the next twenty-one day series of tablets. This meant that each new course of medication started on exactly the same day of the week as the initial course. Always starting the medication on the same day of the week lessened the chance of a woman forgetting to begin the cycle anew. Choufont-Salva felt that this attribute would give the product a slight competitive advantage over most of the other oral contraceptives on the market. Only two other contraceptives on the market had dosages of twenty-one tablets per twenty-eight day period.

Because of the heavy financial investment in equipment required for producing oral contraceptives, Choufont-Salva had signed a contract with Companie Nationale de Pharmacie, S.A., the French subsidiary of A. L. Choufont et Fils, S.A. According to the contract, the French company would supply Choufont-Salva with the contraceptive tablets at a cost equivalent to ₱0.71 per course of medication. This price included shipping to Manila but did not include packaging.

DEVELOPING A MARKETING PLAN

In 1965 sixty-three percent of Choufont-Salva's revenue came from the sales of penicillin and streptomycin. Management wanted to lessen the company's dependence on these two products and felt that its new oral contraceptive had the potential of developing into a major drug in the company's product line. The marketing manager said that to help achieve this goal, the salesmen would devote at least fifteen percent of their time to promoting the contraceptive during the first eighteen months that it was on the market.

The task of developing a marketing plan that would effectively promote Choufont-Salva's oral contraceptive was the responsibility of the company's marketing committee. Deciding on a name for the tablets, selecting the packaging that would be used, determining the price that would be charged, and deciding on what advertising and promotional activities to employ were among the decisions facing the committee.

NAME

The oral contraceptive developed by A. L. Choufont et Fils, S.A., was marketed by the company's Canadian subsidiary under the brand name Controva. This name was formed by combining the prefix *contra*, which makes up the first half of the word *contraceptive* and means against, with *ova*, the plural of *ovum* which means egg. Since entering the market in Canada, the product had been introduced in three other English-speaking countries—Great Britain, the United States, and Australia. In all three of these countries the product was also being sold under the name Controva.

Because *contraceptive* and *ovum* were not words commonly used by Filipinos, some in the marketing organization at Choufont-Salva felt that the company should select another brand name for the product. These persons felt that the name should be easy to remember, be suggestive of a characteristic of the product, and sound western. Two names had been suggested: Combitabs, which was formed from the words *combination* and *tablets* and suggested that the tablets were a combination of progestin and estrogen, and Periodez, which suggested that the tablets were taken during a definite period in the menstrual cycle.

PACKAGING

Management was considering four packaging possibilities for the oral contraceptive: a glass bottle, a simple aluminum strip, a comb case, and a compact case (see Exhibit 8). The company was also faced with the question of what color combinations to use on the packaging. Three combinations had been suggested: black and white, gold and white, and light pink and pale green. An advocate of the pastel colors claimed that they were "feminine and inviting to the woman."

PRICE

Primarily because of its lower progestin content, the progestin-estrogen compound developed by Choufont et Fils cost less to manufacture than did other oral contraceptives. Since the tablets were costing Choufont-Salva only ₱0.71 plus packaging for each dosage of twenty-one tablets, management was considering making the company's retail price for the medication ₱2.50 or ₱2.75 per bottle or package. This would give the company a competitive advantage in price since the retail price[11] of other oral contraceptives on the market ranged from ₱3.00 to ₱10.00 per course of medication.

[11] Price charged to retail drug outlets and similar purchasers.

EXHIBIT 8. Kinds of Packaging Being Considered

Description of the Package*	Estimated Cost**	Major Advantages	Major Disadvantages
Glass Bottle with label on the outside.	₱0.13	Very low cost Adequate protection to the tablets	Not attractive Little room on label for product description or instructions on usage Impossible to mark the package; the woman cannot easily ascertain the number of pills she has taken
Aluminum Strip 5" long & 1-3/4" wide to which the tablets would be affixed by being encased in thin plastic; strip would be packaged in aluminum foil.	₱0.22	Relatively low cost Permits instructions on a separate sheet to be enclosed with the strip Strip can be marked with the days of the week so the woman can easily ascertain the number of pills she has taken	Inadequate protection to the tablets—would have some breakage
Comb Case. Tablets would be affixed (by being encased in plastic) to an aluminum strip 5" long & 1-3/4" wide; the strip would be placed in a comb carrying case 5-1/2" long & 2-1/4" wide. The aluminum strip and carrying case would be packaged in a cardboard container 6" × 2-3/4" × 1/2".	₱0.29	Excellent protection to the tablets Relatively attractive carrying case Permits ample room for instructions to be enclosed separately and/or printed on the package Aluminum strip can be marked so woman can easily ascertain the number of pills she has taken	Relatively high cost
Compact Case. Tablets would be affixed (by being encased in plastic) to an aluminum disc 2-3/4" in diameter; disc would be placed in a compact 3-1/4" in diameter; perforated holes in the bottom of the compact would permit the woman to push the tablet through the bottom of the compact, separating the tablet from the aluminum disc; compact would be packaged in a cardboard container 3-3/4" × 3-3/4" × 3/4".	₱0.76	Very attractive carrying case Excellent protection to the tablets Permits ample room for instructions to be enclosed separately and/or printed on the package Aluminum disc can be marked so woman can easily ascertain how many pills she has taken	Very high cost

*Each package would contain twenty-one tablets.
**This estimated cost includes the price of the container and the cost of labor and other expenses involved in packaging the tablets.

ADVERTISING AND PROMOTIONAL ACTIVITIES

Choufont-Salva did not engage in consumer advertising. The company had the policy of advertising only in medical journals because management wanted Choufont-Salva to have the image of being a responsible pharmaceutical organization that worked closely with and through the medical profession. Some members of management, however, felt that the company should advertise its oral contraceptive directly to the general public. The decision made regarding this matter would influence the theme of the advertising campaign as well as the size of the advertising budget for the product.

Management also was undecided about how to promote Choufont-Salva's oral contraceptive. (A memo from the company's advertising and promotional staff containing suggestions regarding promotional activities is reproduced in Exhibit 9; representative consumer-oriented media costs are shown in Exhibit 10.)

EXHIBIT 9. Memo on Possible Promotional Activities

DATE: February 16, 1966

TO: Mr. Jose J. Lim, Manager of Marketing Services
FROM: Mr. Manuel D. Pineda, Manager of Advertising and Promotional Activities
RE: Possible Promotional Activities for the Oral Contraceptive Product

The sales promotional staff submits the following sales promotional ideas for consideration in the formulation of the marketing plan for the new oral contraceptive product.

I. Sampling. The sales promotion staff suggests that the following sampling activities be considered:
   A. Comprehensive sampling of all the doctors upon whom Choufont-Salva salesmen call. Almost every doctor in the Philippines has patients who are potential customers for our oral contraceptive. Extensive sampling will give broad coverage to our product.

   To get the desired penetration and to develop brand loyalty among doctors, it might be desirable for the company to engage in heavy sampling for at least six months. This could be accomplished:
      1. By giving to gynecologists, obstetricians, and general practitioners with clientele likely to use contraceptives from one to four dozen sample packets per month, depending upon the doctor's location and practice. (We estimate that this group of doctors constitutes no more than one-fourth of the doctors on whom our salesmen call.)
      2. By giving to all other doctors upon whom our salesmen call four sample packets of our oral contraceptive during the product's introductory month and two packets per month for the next five months.

   B. That the approximately one hundred government and private clinics disseminating birth control information and products be heavily sampled. Most of these clinics recommend—and often insert either free or for a very nominal charge—I.U.C.D.'s. For example, at one Manila family planning clinic last year, only two percent of the couples that came to the clinic decided to take oral contraceptives. The others are using I.U.C.D.'s. To help alter this situation, the company might give one to four dozen samples monthly to each of the clinics, the number of samples depending upon the size of the clinic.

II. The printing of both brochures and posters that will be used by the salesmen in describing to physicians our oral contraceptives and will be left with the physicians at the end of the

EXHIBIT 9. (Cont.)

visit. A five-color, eight-page brochure measuring 8" × 11" will cost approximately ₱590.00 per 1,000 with a minimum order of 5,000 required. A five-color 12" × 15" poster will cost approximately ₱500.00 per 1,000 with a minimum order of 5,000 required.

III. Mailing to all physicians on whom our salesmen do not call the eight-page brochure mentioned above. The cost of printing a cover letter and mailing the brochure would be approximately ₱0.20 per physician, not counting the cost of the brochure.

IV. Engaging in outlet promotions. Because of the nature of the product and the large number of potential consumers, the company might consider altering its policy against outlet promotions and engage in the following subtle promotional activities:

    A. Encourage the salesgirls in drugstores to recommend our oral contraceptive to contraceptive customers. This could be accomplished: (1) by the salesmen discussing with the girls both the characteristics of the product and its advantages over similar products on the market and (2) by giving the girls a sample packet of our contraceptive.

    B. Print small booklets on family planning and have them displayed on the sales counter in an attractive heavy cardboard rack. The booklet would define family planning, discuss the various methods of birth control, give the answers to the questions people most frequently ask about family planning and contain semi-humorous illustrations. Printing a three-color, thirty-page booklet that would be 5" × 3-1/2" in size would cost approximately ₱250.00 per 1,000 with a minimum order of 5,000 required. Each display rack would cost approximately ₱5.00. Consideration might also be given to placing these racks in the offices of doctors. Both the booklets and the display racks would carry the name and trademark of Choufont-Salva.

EXHIBIT 10. Consumer-Oriented Media Costs

	Print		
Publication	Circulation	Percent of Copies to Households Earning ₱15,000 & Above	Rates Per Column Inch
Newspapers:			
Evening News	29,000	N.A.*	₱ 8.00
Manila *Chronicle*	72,000	22%	11.00
Manila *Daily Bulletin*	59,000	71	9.50
Manila *Times*	120,000	31	19.00
Mirror	24,000	N.A.	6.00
Philippine Herald	47,000	18	8.50
The Sunday Times	155,000	48	21.00
Weekly Magazines:			
Free Press	86,000	42%	₱15.00
Graphic	88,000	55	12.00
Weekly Women's Magazine	93,000	65	14.00
Woman & the Home	81,000	22	13.00

*N.A. = not available.

(continued)

EXHIBIT 10. (Cont.)

Radio

Class A Time: 6 : 00 AM–9 : 00 AM

Units	60 Sec.	30 Sec.	5–10 Sec.
1– 12	₱12.50/spot	₱9.37/spot	₱3.12/spot
13– 25	11.88	8.91	2.97
26– 38	11.25	8.44	2.81
39– 51	10.63	7.97	2.66
52–103	10.00	7.50	2.50
104–259	9.30	7.03	2.34
260–Up	8.75	6.56	2.19

Class B Time: 5 : 00 AM–6 : 00 AM
9 : 00 AM–2 : 00 PM & 5 : 00 PM–6 : 00 PM

Units	60 Sec.	30 Sec.	5–10 Sec.
1– 12	₱7.50/spot	₱5.62/spot	₱2.28/spot
13– 25	7.13	5.35	1.87
26– 38	6.75	5.06	1.69
39– 51	6.38	4.78	1.59
52–103	6.00	4.50	1.50
104–259	5.63	4.23	1.41
260 & Up	5.25	3.89	1.31

Class C Time: 2 : 00 PM–5 : 00 PM
6 : 00 PM–12 : 00 MN & 4 : 00 AM–5 : 00 AM

Units	60 Sec.	30 Sec.	5–10 Sec.
1– 12	₱4.50/spot	₱3.37/spot	₱1.12/spot
13– 25	4.28	3.21	1.07
26– 38	4.05	3.04	1.01
39– 51	3.83	2.87	0.96
52–103	3.60	2.70	0.90
104–259	3.38	2.53	0.85
260–Up	3.15	2.36	0.79

Class D Time: 12 : 00 MN–4 : 00 AM

Units	60 Sec.	30 Sec.	5–10 Sec.
1– 12	₱3.00/spot	₱2.25/spot	₱0.75/spot
13– 25	2.85	2.14	0.71
26– 38	2.70	2.03	0.67
39– 51	2.55	1.91	0.64
52–103	2.40	1.80	0.60
104–259	2.25	1.69	0.56
260 & Up	2.10	1.57	0.52

EXHIBIT 10. (Cont.)

Production Costs. The estimated costs* of producing a radio ad are as follows:

Length	Estimated Costs
60 seconds	₱500
30 seconds	500
10 seconds	400
5 seconds	400

Television

1. Rates
   a. The rates for TV advertising spots are approximately the following:

Mid-Program Breaks	Prime Time (6:30 PM till 10:00 PM)	Class B Time (All Other Hours)
60 Seconds	₱500/spot	₱250/spot
30 Seconds	250	125
10 Seconds	125	65
5 Seconds	65	35
Station Breaks (Between Programs)		
60 Seconds	₱400/spot	₱200/spot
30 Seconds	200	100
10 Seconds	100	50
5 Seconds	50	25

2. Production Costs
   a. A 30-second film commercial would cost approximately ₱5000 to produce.
   b. The estimated costs of producing a TV slide commercial are as follows:

Length	Estimated Costs
60 Seconds	₱350
30 Seconds	325
10 Seconds	310
5 Seconds	305

*In estimating costs, it was assumed that (a) two announcers would be used in producing a 30 or 60 second ad and that only one announcer would be used in producing a 5 or 10 second ad and (b) a combo would furnish simple background music for the ads. The estimated costs also include the studio fees, the costs of tapes, and similar expenses.

NEW COMPETITION

A week after Choufont-Salva decided to enter the oral contraceptive market, the company learned that within a year a competing Philippine drug company probably would be marketing an oral contraceptive containing only one-half a milligram of progestin. North American Drugs, Inc., the American parent company of the Philippine company, had just developed the new oral contraceptive in its laboratories. The American company planned to test market the product in the United States. If the test marketing was successful, North American Drugs would then release the product to its subsidiaries. Because of the test marketing, Choufont-Salva's management felt that it would be at least nine months and probably twelve months before North American Drug's oral contraceptive would appear on the Philippine market.

APPENDIX A / POSITION OF THE ROMAN CATHOLIC CHURCH CONCERNING CONTRACEPTION

At the present time (1966), the Church holds the position stated by Pope Pius XI in *Casti Connubii,* an encyclical issued in 1930. This excerpt is a summary of it:

Any use whatsoever of matrimony exercised in such a way that the act is deliberately frustrated in its natural power to generate life is an offense against the law of God and nature, and those who indulge in such are branded with the guilt of a great sin. (Para. 56)

The only methods of family limitation which meet with the approval of the Church are continence and periodic continence, or the rhythm method. The Catholic Church does, however, permit the use of artificial contraception for medical (as distinct from birth control) reasons.

APPENDIX B / EXCERPTS FROM "THE FAMILY PLANNING ASSOCIATION OF THE PHILIPPINES—ITS PERFORMANCE AND PROGRAM OF ACTIVITIES."[1]

The present status of the family planning movement in the Philippines has been very favorable and progressing in spite of its predominantly Catholic population, about 84 percent of the total population. Because of this strong religious affiliation, before the year 1965 although there were about three Protestant family planning groups already existing, the mere mention of birth control was strongly tabooed and no public forum on the subject was allowed even by a private organization. Any press publication on family planning and birth control materials were censured and not permitted to enter the country and transmitted through mails (old custom and postal laws).

In the early part of 1965, the Family Planning Association of the Philippines, Inc. (FPAP), organized by progressive Catholic leaders, launched a nation-wide family planning movement which was never done before. Since this concept was very new to the general public, the FPAP's intensified and relentless efforts have been concentrated on dissemination of informative

[1] Published by the FPAP, May 1967.

knowledge of family planning methods and motivation program to change the attitude and behavior of the people through continuing series of lectures and speaking tours in public meetings and forums all over the country, and through extensive use of mass media communications, such as endless publication of articles and news in newspapers, magazines, medical journals, nationwide distribution of pamphlets, handouts, brochures, and lately the use of TV and radio. Note that the first article in the Graphic-Kislap magazine was censured, but the favorable public opinion changed the attitude of authorities which later just ignored the old law, and which was recently repealed "by implication" by the Republic Act No. 4729 of June, 1966.

Training seminars to create man-power are being conducted locally for physicians, nurses, and health educators. Family planning leaders and workers, including those of other allied organizations (PPMP, RPA, PFPA, Manila Health Dept., Municipal Health Officers) were sent through the FPAP under IPPF and other foreign grants to attend training seminars, international conferences, university studies, and observation tours of family planning programs in other countries. To date, the FPAP has 162 assisted clinics and 3 fully supported and maintained clinics in different areas of the country. Including the Manila Health Department, PPMP, RPA, and the Pathfinder Fund to which the FPAP is closely associated, there are now about 300 family planning clinics all over the country. The strongly conservative Catholic sector is starting to establish rhythm clinics, and there are strong indications that other institutions, especially the educational, may follow soon.

The present population of the Philippines is about 33 million, with an annual rate of growth of 3.2 percent, the highest in Asia. The annual birth rate is 45 to 46 per thousand and the annual death rate is 12 to 14 per thousand. The average family size is 6.7. The land area is 115,700 sq. miles. The population density is 280 persons per sq. mile which is already five times the world average. The city of Manila has 80,000 persons per sq. mile. The country cannot feed its population adequately, therefore, if it is overpopulated. Food supply and increasing unemployment are two very serious major problems. The annual net income per capita is only ₱390.-. or about $100.-. Two-thirds of the population are in poverty and medically indigent, and depend very much on government agencies which, at this time, cannot give family planning services. In spite of FPAP efforts in creating more public demand for family planning services and in participation of private medical sectors, without the participation of government health agencies, it would be far from its goal—the promotion of the well-being of the Filipino family and helping in the socioeconomic development of this country.

There is at present increasing awareness and demand from government health officers and agencies relative to the knowledge and methods of family planning. Cognizant of this, the Family Planning Association of the Philippines, Inc. is also exerting its efforts to offer its help to introduce a family planning program in the Maternal and Child Health agencies of the government.

regional market characteristics

This is the place!

Brigham Young, 1801–77
(on first seeing the Valley of the Great Salt Lake, July 24, 1847)

INTRODUCTION

This chapter focuses on the economic, social, political, and regulatory characteristics of the major regional markets in the world. The first half of the chapter outlines economic cooperation and preferential trade arrangements. The second half describes the characteristics of the major regional markets in the world, concluding with an in-depth study of one of these markets.

ECONOMIC COOPERATION AND PREFERENTIAL TRADE ARRANGEMENTS

Since World War II there has been a tremendous interest in economic cooperation. The enthusiasm for international cooperation has been stimulated by the success of the European Common Market, which was itself inspired by the success of the U.S. economy. There are many degrees of economic cooperation, ranging from the agreement of two or more nations to reductions of barriers to trade, to the full-scale economic integration of two or more national economies. In the nineteenth century the German Zollverein and the British imperial preference system were the two most important agreements leading to the reduction of internal tariff barriers in Germany and international barriers in the British Empire.

The best-known preferential arrangement of this century was the British Commonwealth preference system, known as the imperial preference system before World War II. This system was important in trade between such countries as the United Kingdom, Canada, Australia, New Zealand, India, and certain other former

British colonies in Africa, Asia, and the Middle East. The decision by the United Kingdom to join the European Economic Community resulted in the demise of this system. This development illustrates the constantly changing nature of international economic cooperation.

Free Trade Area

A free trade area is a group of countries that have agreed to abolish all internal barriers to trade between the member countries. Country members of a free trade area can and do maintain independent trade policies vis-à-vis third countries. To avoid trade diversion in favor of low-tariff members (for example, importing goods in the member country with the lowest tariff for shipment to countries within the area with higher external tariffs), a system of certificates of origin is used. The most important free trade area during the 1960s was the European Free Trade Association (EFTA). Today the most important may be the Latin American Free Trade Association (LAFTA).

EUROPEAN FREE TRADE ASSOCIATION (EFTA)

The European Free Trade Association was established by the Stockholm convention of 1959. The original seven members were Austria, Denmark, Norway, Portugal, Sweden, Switzerland, and the United Kingdom. Finland became an associate member in 1961 and Iceland a full member in 1970. Internal EFTA tariffs on industrial products were removed by successive cuts between 1960 and 1966; the final 20 percent was abolished December 31, 1966.

The European Free Trade Association does not maintain a common external tariff; instead each member country retains its own tariff structure applicable to non-EFTA countries. In order to prevent the import of non-EFTA goods into one EFTA country by way of another with a lower external tariff, a system of declaration of origin is in operation by which goods can be shown to be EFTA origin and therefore entitled to the tariff reductions.

Between 1959 and 1965 the total foreign trade of EFTA countries rose about 60 percent. Trade between the eight member countries, however, more than doubled to a total $6.8 million. Among the four Nordic countries of EFTA, trade in 1965 was two and one-half times as great as that in 1959. In 1973 the United Kingdom withdrew its membership from EFTA and became one of the European Economic Community (EEC) member nations, thus bringing an end to the EFTA's significant role as a trading group. Subsequently the remaining EFTA countries (Austria, Denmark, Norway, Portugal, Sweden, Switzerland, Iceland and Finland) were granted free trade area treatment, without membership, from the EEC.

LATIN AMERICAN FREE TRADE ASSOCIATION (LAFTA)

Argentina, Brazil, Chile, Colombia, Ecuador, Mexico, Paraguay, Peru, Uruguay, and Venezuela agreed in the Treaty of Montevideo in June 1961 to form LAFTA. The treaty provides for the gradual elimination of all customs duties, surcharges, deposits, and other obstacles to trade between LAFTA members in annual installments of 8 percent by value of member countries' tariff items. The objective of the treaty was to complete these reductions by June 1973. Considerable difficulties have been experienced with regard to this basic timetable. In 1969 delegates to the ninth annual conference of LAFTA at Caracas voted to postpone the trade deadline from 1973 to 1980. This move reflected a frank admission of failure to fulfill the relatively meek requirements of the Montevideo Treaty, a failure that was further demonstrated by the very small number of tariff concessions authorized at the Caracas conference. In 1976 President Pinochet of Chile, while admitting LAFTA's lack of success, urged its continued existence.

CARIBBEAN FREE TRADE ASSOCIATION (CARIFTA)

In February 1968 Antigua, Dominica, Grenada, Trinidad and Tobago, Barbados and Guyana, and the associated West Indies states, together with Montserrat, St. Kitts-Nevis-Anguilla, St. Lucia, and St. Vincent, signed an agreement setting up the Caribbean Free Trade Association. Jamaica joined the other members in August 1968. The agreement provides for the progressive elimination of customs duties and quotas between the member countries over a period of five years for the more developed members and over a ten-year period for the other countries.

Customs Union

The customs union is the logical evolution of the free trade area. In addition to eliminating the internal barriers to trade, members of a customs union agree to the establishment of common external trade barriers. Today there is no significant form of customs union in operation, although a union is a logical stage of development in the transition from a free trade area to a common market. Belgium, Luxembourg, and the Netherlands, for example, were participants in a customs union that dates to 1921 before becoming members of the EEC.

Economic Union

The economic union builds upon the elimination of the internal tariff barriers and the establishment of common external barriers. It also seeks to coordinate economic and social policy within the union to allow free flow of capital and labor from country to country. Thus an economic union is a common marketplace not only for goods but also for services and capital. The full evolution of an economic union would involve the creation of a unified central bank, the use of a single currency, and common policies on agriculture, social services and welfare, regional development, transport, taxation, competition, and mergers. A fully developed economic union requires extensive political unity, which makes it similar to a nation. The further integration of nations that were members of fully developed economic unions would be the formation of a central government that would bring together independent political states into a single political framework. The best-known and most successful example of an economic union is the European Economic Community.

THE EUROPEAN ECONOMIC COMMUNITY (EEC)

Germany, France, Italy, Belgium, Luxembourg, the Netherlands, the United Kingdom, Ireland, and Denmark are being welded into an economic union within the framework of the European Economic Community. The EEC was established by the Treaty of Rome, which came into force on January 1, 1958. A step-by-step reduction of internal customs duties on industrial goods resulted in their complete removal by July 1, 1968. Simultaneously the duties applied to imports from third countries were gradually aligned, and the common external tariff within the EEC also came into force on July 1, 1968. A common agricultural policy has been adopted. The removal of internal agricultural duties has been completed. The external customs duties for the majority of agricultural products, which are subject to EEC regulations, were suspended and replaced by variable import levies designed to bring the price of products imported from third countries in line with those prevailing inside the community. The community has made progress in abolishing restrictions on the movement of capital, in the alignment of taxes, in developing a community policy on competition, restrictive practices such as price fixing, and company mergers. In addition, EEC companies have achieved freedom for workers from member countries to obtain employment anywhere in the community and freedom for firms to establish and operate anywhere in the community.

Association with the community is open to all countries under the Rome Treaty. Greece and Turkey became associate members of the community in 1962 and 1963, respectively. Under these agreements, upon the completion of the customs union between the two countries and the community, it is expected that they will move toward full economic union with the other countries in the EEC.

The Rome Treaty also provided for links between the European community and the colonies and other dependencies in Africa and elsewhere of France, Belgium, the Netherlands, and Italy. The first association agreement signed in 1963 known as the Yaounde Convention, which was renewed in July 1969, specifies duty-free entry for industrial goods to the common market and also specifies that agricultural products subject to EEC market regulations and some tropical products will enjoy a slightly improved preferential treatment in the EEC. The associated African States may reimpose duties or other restrictions on imports for the EEC if it is necessary for their economic development.

In 1975 the EEC entered into a new trade and economic cooperation agreement with forty-six African, Carribbean, and Pacific countries (ACP). The agreement, known as the Lomé Convention, allows the EEC duty-free access to all the industrial goods and 96 percent of the agricultural products of the ACP. Included in this agreement is an Export Revenue Stabilization Plan through which the EEC provides development assistance to the ACP countries.

ANDEAN COMMON MARKET (ANCOM)

To counterbalance the influence of Argentina, Brazil, and Mexico within LAFTA, five smaller Latin American nations signed an economic agreement in 1961. Chile, Colombia, Bolivia, Ecuador, and Peru were joined by Venezuela in 1973 to form a common market covering 2 million square miles and 55 million people, with a GNP in 1976 of $25 billion, or 70 percent of that of Mexico. ANCOM's plans include redirection of intra-ANCOM tariffs (down 60 percent since the agreement was signed), growth of trade between the members (up 217 percent in the first six years), gradual lowering of tariffs on goods produced outside the region, and strict regulation of foreign investment. ANCOM calls for the closing of such areas as public utilities, banking, and the media to new foreign investment, and the gradual transformation ("fade-out") of present foreign-owned enterprises into mixed enterprises having at least 51 percent local equity and control. One of ANCOM's most interesting achievements for the multinational marketer has been the development of programs to institute regional economic planning schemes with each country assigned a specific area of expertise and production, resulting in some cases in the creation of regional multinational companies.

CENTRAL AMERICAN COMMON MARKET (CACM)

Costa Rica, El Salvador, Guatemala, Honduras, and Nicaragua signed an agreement in 1961 that provided for the dismantlement of internal tariffs and the adoption of a common external tariff. Both of these objectives were virtually completed (over 90 percent) in 1967. In June 1968, however, member countries introduced a temporary surcharge of 30 percent to be levied on top of the external tariff for a period of five years.

In 1969 a war between Honduras and El Salvador stopped further progress of CACM. By late 1970 an agreement was made among the five CACM central banks covering the organization of a monetary stabilization fund. From this, member banks could borrow on a short-term basis to ease temporary difficulties with their balance of payments.

At the end of 1974 a draft treaty concerned with the creation of a Central American Economic and Social Community was submitted to the governing committee. This draft treaty called for common treatment of foreign investment and technology; foreign acquisition of existing domestic firms; rules covering repatriation of profits and reinvestment; and the creation of multinational Central-American companies. Adoption of this treaty was projected to occur after the normalization of relations between Honduras and El Salvador and the return of Honduras as a member of CACM.

ARAB COMMON MARKET

The Arab Common Market was established on January 1, 1964, between the UAR, Iraq, Jordan, and Syria. Sudan and Yemen joined later. The agreement provides for the gradual dismantlement of tariffs and quantitative restrictions on trade between the member countries.

REGIONAL MARKET CHARACTERISTICS

There are innumerable ways of dividing the countries of the world into different regional markets. In effect, defining regional markets is an exercise in clustering countries where, it is hoped, both within-cluster similarities and between-cluster differences will be maximized. Clustering can be accomplished with the use of mathematical programs that determine the spatial relationship of objects (countries) defined by variables (market measures), or by judgmental analysis on the basis of both explicit and implicit criteria. In the section that follows, national markets are clustered judgmentally on the basis of geographic proximity. A brief survey of each region is presented. Japan in examined in greater detail as an example of a more in-depth analysis.

Western Europe

Europe is the second smallest of the world's continents; only Australia is smaller. All Europe, including the USSR, accounts for only 7 percent of the land surface of the earth. In Western Europe, the countries of the common market and EFTA, together with Ireland, Finland, and Spain, could be fitted into Australia or more than twice over into Brazil. This small area in 1975 generated 30 percent of global income.

The sixteen countries and 404 million people of Western Europe are distinguished by a wide range of different customs, tastes, and traditions. Their populations range from more than 62 million poeple in West Germany to less than 300,000 people in Luxembourg. The biggest country in area, France, is more than twice the size of the United Kingdom or Germany but has fewer people than either of these countries. The most densely populated country, the Netherlands, has more than thirty times as many people per square kilometer as Norway, the least crowded country.

There are eleven major languages spoken in Europe, a fact that presents a special challenge to the international marketer.

The countries of Europe are among the most prosperous in the world, although their income is unevenly distributed. The average per capita annual income in Portugal is only $1,628 as compared with $9,349 in Switzerland. Both Sweden and Switzerland had per capita incomes over $9,000 in 1976. In the judgment of many observers, each of these countries is richer in terms of standard of living or quality of life than the United States. The different levels of prosperity across Europe are the basis for many other differences, such as the different proportions of ownership of various consumer durable goods, and the different ways the housewives do their work. These income differences also reflect radically different societies. For example, in Portugal 29 percent of the population is still employed on the land as compared with 7 percent of Sweden's population and less than 2 percent of Britain's.

Eastern Europe

Eastern Europe includes Bulgaria, Czechoslovakia, East Germany, Hungary, Poland, Rumania, and the USSR. The region has been dominated economically and militarily by the USSR, which accounts for two-thirds of the region's net national product. Even though Eastern Europe accounted for 13 percent of global income in 1975, it accounted for only 4 percent of exports to the world. The discrepancy between the share of world income and participation in world trade is due to a number of factors. The political hostility between East and West, for example, is reflected in the denial of most-favored-nation status to most East European countries by the United States. This means, in effect, that U.S. tariff barriers are roughly double those applying to MFN countries. The fundamental reason, however, is that the Eastern European economy is not fully compatible with the Western market economic system. For many years the USSR, and to a lesser extent the other East European countries, were basically committed to self-sufficiency and a centrally planned economic organization. In recent years Russia, and especially the smaller East European countries, have made substantial moves toward economic decentralization and a shift from the control of resources at the state plan level to control at the enterprise level, with increasing reliance on the market as a mechanism both for establishing production priorities and for allocating resources. Nevertheless, the ability of East European enterprise to compete in world markets remains limited. The discipline of competitive markets revealed the limitations of state planning and state control of the resource allocation and resource management process. The simple fact is that the East Europeans, especially the Russians, must employ controls to ensure that their purchases from the West do not exceed their sales and credit receipts. There is no free exchange or convertibility of East European currency because this would violate their decision to rely upon state planning instead of the market as a resource allocation mechanism.

Marketing is undoubtedly the key to expanded participation of the East European economies in the international economic order, as well as the key to the standard-of-living aspirations of the East Europeans. Without improved marketing performance, East European enterprises will continue to turn in lackluster performance in the competitive market economies of the West. This will result in continued shortages of foreign exchange, which will of course put limits on the ability of East Europeans to import and purchase products and services from the West. Thus it is no exaggeration to conclude that the key to expanded economic cooperation between East and West is marketing. To the extent that economic cooperation and exchange promote understanding and create conditions that support world peace, it follows that marketing in this part of the world is contributing to world peace.

The various economic reforms (Hungary, 1968; Poland, 1970s; Rumania, 1978) and an increasing involvement in international trade by the countries in Eastern Europe have resulted in East European markets that are quite different from one another.

The potential for close economic ties between multinational corporations and East European socialist economies is substantial.[1] The markets are there and the skilled labor is available. A major limiting factor is the East European countries' position on foreign ownership. Most companies are reluctant to undertake long-term commitments involving a substantial transfer of technology, know-how, and skill unless they can have a major ownership and control. Opposed to this, most of the East European socialist economies have difficulties in permitting even minority equity ownership by capitalist corporations.

The trend in Eastern Europe is toward increased contact and closer relations with the West. In the view of many experts, multinational corporations will play a major role in the transfer of technology and know-how to East European countries. Rumania and Hungary, for example, now permit 49 percent equity ownership by foreigners, which is a gesture of encouragement to companies who are concerned about control and equity participation in a profit stream as an incentive to invest in any country.

The political and economic stability of the East European countries is relatively high due to the permanence of the governments and the general tightness of the political situation. The quality of the labor force in East Europe is high, literacy is high, and production costs are relatively low.

TRADING WITH THE USSR [2]

The first step in trading with the Russians is to understand the Soviet economic planning process, and how it affects their approach to foreign trade. Every fifteen years the Supreme Soviet adopts a plan for the national economy. The fifteen-year plan is transmitted to the central planning committee of the Soviet Union, "Gosplan," for disaggregation into five- and one-year plans.

All imports are ultimately coordinated with the production goals established by Soviet plans. The following example illustrates how the process works.

Assume that Gosplan calls for a 10 percent increase in oil production in a particular year. The ensuing sequence of events would be as follows:

1. Gosplan would send production figures to the Ministry of Petroleum. The Ministry would give the figures to various technical institutes and production organizations under its jurisdiction. They would return these figures to the Ministry with indications of requirements in order to achieve the targeted production increases and percent.

---

[1] This section is adapted from Geza P. Lauter and Paul M. Dickie, *Multinational Corporations and East European Socialist Economies* (New York: Praeger, 1975).

[2] I am indebted to Mr. Carl Longley of Satra Consultant Corporation, New York, N.Y., for the account that follows.

2. The Ministry would then determine the equipment needed to fulfill the goal, and how much equipment would be available from Soviet sources.

3. If necessary equipment was not available from Soviet sources, the Ministry of Petroleum would then contact internal production organizations and institutes as well as the State Committee for Science and Technology to determine the availability and the quality rating of equipment available in foreign countries.

4. After its plan and budget incorporating a project were approved by Gosplan, the Ministry of Petroleum would then send a processed order for foreign equipment in its budget to the Ministry of Foreign Trade, which has a monopoly for conducting all foreign trade in the Soviet Union.

5. The Ministry of Foreign Trade would purchase the needed equipment from foreign sources through its own staff.

6. Money needed for the equipment would be dispersed by Gosbank, the Soviet central bank under the authorization of Gosplan. These funds would then be transferred to the bank for foreign trade of the Soviet Union, and then to the suppliers' bank through a variety of possible banking channels.

The example above underlines the importance of pursuing a sales program in the Soviet Union on many levels. It is not enough to sell only the foreign trade organization. An effective sales program necessarily involves contact with the State Committee for Science and Technology, appropriate internal Ministries, and organization under Ministry control. In addition, any transaction large enough to require special financial arrangement, such as barters or switch financing, will require special coordinated negotiations with finance sections of the Minsitry of Foreign Trade, Gosplan, and the Bank for Foreign Trade of the Union of Soviet Socialist Republics.

MARKETING WITHIN THE SOVIET STRUCTURE [3]

One approach that a Western supplier can follow is to contact Russian institutions in his home country. In the United States, Amtorg, the all-union Chamber of Commerce, arranges exhibits and represents Gosplan and the Russian Embassy. Unfortunately, working through Amtorg can be a very time consuming process.

A second approach is to exhibit at annual trade exhibitions sponsored by the all-union Chamber of Commerce. It is important that the exhibition be planned and coordinated with marketing contacts within the Soviet trade structure. Larger companies have found that direct contacts with state agencies—often through subsidiary companies in key European countries, such as Finland and Germany, that have extensive contacts in Eastern Europe—have been extremely successful.

One way of facilitating the process of directly contacting Soviet decision makers is to rely on the services of agencies specializing in Russian trade. In New

---

[3] The account that follows is adapted from Lyman E. Ostlund and Kjell M. Halvorsen, "The Russian Decision Process Governing Trade," *Journal of Marketing,* April 1972, pp. 3–11.

York Satra has been very active in working with U.S. corporations interested in specific trade sectors in the Soviet economy.

There are many hazards and problems facing the company that is trying to expand its trade with the Soviet Union. Researching the marketplace is extremely difficult and in effect requires contact with relevant decision-making bodies. Information regarding national production goals, specific production plans, and priority lists is not published and is not available to foreign enterprise. The Russians are extremely tough bargainers on price, often beyond any point of reason. Realizing the preoccupation with price in the Soviet Union, many Western countries often quote inflated prices so that after concessions they still have a price that allows for comfortable business transactions.

In spite of all of the obstacles and problems, the enormous size of the Eastern European economic system makes it an irresistible area of interest for any company that pretends to operate on a global scale. The relaxation and reduction of old political and ideological barriers between the East and the West gives promise that the political climate will be improving, thereby providing an opportunity for creative businessmen to work out arrangements for trade and investments that are mutually beneficial to the East and the West.

North America

The North American market is a distinctive world regional market. In the United States there is a concentration of wealth and income within the framework of a single national economic and political environment that presents unique marketing characteristics. Per capita GNP in the united States in 1975 was $7060, which is $820 less than that of Sweden, which ranked highest in the world.

The distinctive characteristic of the U.S. market is the unique combination of high per capita income, large population, vast space, and plentiful natural resources.

High product ownership levels are associated with a high income and relatively high receptivity to innovations and new ideas both in consumer and industrial products.

The U.S. industrial product market is particularly receptive to innovations and products that reduce labor. The intensive application of computers and automated equipment in the United States reflects the high cost of labor, which creates an incentive to manufacture, process, and control as much activity as possible with machines. In general, U.S. industry is the most automated and efficient in the world, although there are notable exceptions. The U.S. steel industry, for example, is believed by many experts to be at least fifteen years behind the industry in other parts of the world, especially Japan.

The United States presents a unique foreign market opportunity for companies based outside the United States. It is in a single national market an opportunity as large as that presented by almost all the countries of Western Europe. Indeed the size of the U.S. market is so great that most foreign companies wisely enter the U.S. market with regional strategies where they focus their program on target regions and eventually go national.

The United States was formerly a unique market also in terms of product saturation levels for consumer products, receptiveness to consumer product innovation, and receptiveness to innovative industrial products. Although these are no longer unique U.S. market qualities, the United States is still a market that is receptive to innovative ideas, especially in the consumer products area.

Another distinctive feature of the U.S. market is that because of the size of the United States, there is to an unusual degree an arm's-length—even an adversary—relationship between business and government. This relationship grows out of a long and complex history, which we do not have time or space to go into in this book. However, for the non-U.S.-based marketer, the arm's-length relationship provides greater opportunities for competing as a foreign firm than is true in most countries of the world, where closer partnership between government and business often excludes foreign suppliers from major product categories, especially industrial products. For example, the United States is one of the few industrial countries in the world where foreign manufacturers can bid on and obtain orders for power generation equipment. In almost every other country with a major power generation industry, either formal or informal collaboration between power generation companies and national equipment manufacturers excludes foreign competitors.

Canada, with a population of 23.3 million and per capita income of $5,838, only $1,222 below that of the United States, shows many similar marketing characteristics. Canada also maintains the closest trading ties with the United States: 68 percent of the $34.6 billion worth of goods imported by Canada in 1975 came from the United States, 66 percent of Canada's $32 billion exports went to the United States, and U.S. investment in Canada is already $30 billion. This creates strains as well as advantages. In 1974 Canada instituted a Foreign Investment Review Act, with important implications for multinational marketing, to prevent foreign domination of important economic sectors and to ensure that foreign investment in Canada is in that nation's best interests.

Asia

The seventeen-country Asian market is a colossus, with 53 percent of the world's population. The region accounted for 13 percent of global income in 1975 and 43 percent of this was concentrated in Japan, which has only 5 percent of the region's population. Many of the smaller countries in the region—South Korea, Taiwan, Hong Kong—are developing rapidly, and no company can afford to ignore China, a country with 850 million potential customers. Last year China exported $700 million worth of oil and was the world's third largest coal producer. The United States is anxious to import oil-producing equipment, telecommunications equipment, and other high-technology products. Politics permitting, the United States is well positioned to supply many imports in Asia. However, there are many political and cultural constraints operating in this most dynamic market area of the world. Let us examine Japan in greater detail to demonstrate the benefits of an in-depth regional analysis.

The success of the Japanese economy has resulted in a growing interest in the underlying factors, forces, and methods that have enabled the Japanese to perform so impressively in raising their own standard of living and in competing worldwide across a broad range of products. Marketing has been a key factor in the Japanese success. It creates as well as fills needs in a society.

One of the most striking aspects of the Japanese marketing system as compared with the U.S. system, particularly in view of the cultural differences, is the remarkable similarity of the processes of change in the two countries. Japanese food retailing today has been dominated by small establishments. These small establishments have been threatened by larger chains, and each year the total number of food stores is declining. The reduction parallels that which started almost forty years ago in the United States.

In addition to rising incomes there is a process of diffusion of wealth that is reducing inequalities in income distribution. For example, in 1958 the average cash wage of a blue-collar worker with a secondary education was 64 percent of that paid a white-collar worker. By 1968 the difference was narrowed to 74 percent. This current prosperity and diffusion of wealth is more remarkable when viewed in the light of the great disparity in income distribution that existed in prewar Japan. As late as 1930 nearly 90 percent of Japanese families earned less than $150 annually. Collectively they received only half the total national income.

One of the major marketing implications of the rapidly rising income level of Japanese consumers has been the "Shohi Kakumai," or consumption revolution. Every aspect of daily life has been affected. Per capita calorie intake has increased from 2,097 in 1949 to 2,450 in 1967. In terms of diet per capita, consumption of rice is declining, whereas that of meat, eggs, and fish is rising. Per capita consumption of clothing is steadily increasing. By the mid-1960s the average Japanese woman owned 6.5 dresses and suits, 1.6 coats, and 15.6 kimonos.

In 1977, refrigerators, washing machines, color television sets, and electric vacuum cleaners all had a diffusion or household ownership rate of more than 90 percent. The saturation or diffusion of stereo sets was over 50 percent, dining room sets about 50 percent, automobiles and beds about 45 percent, air conditioners 25 percent, and golf sets about 15 percent.

The large number of kimonos reflects both the rising income and wealth of Japanese consumers as well as the love of the traditional Japanese culture. Japanese dress, Professor Yoshino maintains, reflects in many ways the national response to the difficult choice between modernization (efficiency) and traditional (inefficient) practices. The Japanese prefer Western dress for business because it is more efficient, but they prefer the traditional dress for social and family occasions because they feel it reflects the style and elegance of traditional Japanese culture.

Japanese firms widely accept the critical importance of marketing. One of the major reasons for the frequent reorganization of Japanese firms is to improve their marketing capability. The product division has been widely adopted to allow full implementation of a marketing orientation.

In distribution, modern merchandising with emphasis on self-service, lower gross margins and prices, and rapid turnover has been introduced by a pioneering group of new entrepreneurs who have carefully studied the U.S. model. They have built successful and rapidly growing chains in Japan. There are only a handful of suburban shopping centers in Japan, but they are expected to grow rapidly in the coming years. Interestingly, the primary mode of transportation to the existing centers is public transportation. For example, one major center conducted a study and estimated that only 30 percent of its shoppers travel to the center by automobile.

The traditional retail and wholesale system in Japan is by and large not responsive to the dynamic changes that are taking place in distribution. Studies profile a large group of small family businesses that will not survive the retirement of the owners. Efforts by the more adaptive small retailers take the form of various cooperative arrangements or voluntary chains.

Three hundred major trading firms are responsible for 80 percent of Japanese imports and exports. The two leading firms, Mitsui & Co. and Mitsubishi Corporation, have sales exceeding $11 billion. A dozen large firms account for 60 percent of total trading company volume.

There are two types of Japanese trading companies. One type handles diversified merchandise lines; the other specializes on a product basis. The trading companies act as both purchasing and sales agents for the companies they represent. For example, a company might purchase iron ore and coal as agent for a steel mill and sell its finished product. Recently, trading companies have been moving into mass merchandising in Japan. With their resources some observers predict that they will emerge as a dominant force in this field.

The most striking thing about Japan is the similarity of the impact of wealth and mass consumption on both the society and marketing system in Japan and the United States. The U.S. influence on Japanese marketing has been profound, not directly but through Japanese borrowings and adaptations of U.S. practices. The Japanese have not merely copied, but the major environmental differences have required systematic adaptation. Nevertheless the Japanese experience suggests that wealth and mass consumption have a similar impact on societies of fundamentally different cultural traditions. Japan exemplifies the fact that as the world grows richer, it becomes more homogeneous in its consumption patterns.

Perhaps the best illustration of this point is the growing appetite in Japan for U.S. fast foods. In 1978 there were more than eleven hundred pizza parlors, hamburger stands, fish and chips shops, coffee shops, doughnut shops, and the like, in Tokyo alone. The American fast-food craze in Japan began around 1970. It is a response to the basic changes in Japanese life that parallel those in the United States. Automobile ownership has reached about 45 percent saturation of households, disposable incomes are up, television promotions are aimed at small children who lead the family to the hamburgers and milkshakes. In short, Japanese families in circumstances that are in many respects similar to those in the United States are responding similarly to the availability of the fast-food-away-from-home alternative. Even pizza has caught on in the Japanese market. According to Pizza Hut Inc. vice-president, David A. Seavey, "The pizza market here is about where it was 20

TABLE 5-1. Contrasts in Culture, Tradition, and Behavior

United States	*Japan*
1. Individualistic	1. Collective
2. Independent	2. Dependent
3. Authoritative decision making	3. Participative decision making
4. Competitive	4. Cooperative
5. Style: Confrontation	5. Style: Compromise
6. Quick decision making but slow implementation	6. Slow (due to consensus) decision making but quick implementation
7. Direct	7. Indirect
8. Short-term view	8. Long-term view
9. Communications are one way and secretive	9. Communications are interactive and open
10. Efficiency oriented	10. Effectiveness oriented
11. Management is control oriented	11. Management is customer oriented
12. High job mobility and low loyalty	12. Life employment and high loyalty
13. Incompetence is fatal	13. Shame is fatal
14. Heterogeneous society: dynamic melting pot	14. Homogeneous society: gradual screening process
15. Relaxed and casual in attitude	15. Tense and formal in attitude
16. Enjoyable	16. Serious
17. Specialist is valued	17. Generalist is valued
18. Freedom and equality	18. Reliance upon order and hierarchy

Adapted from a list prepared by Chikara Higashi, World Bank.

years ago in the U.S. The only difference I can see is that the Japanese like a crispier crust and the cheese goes on first."[4]

U.S.-JAPANESE CONTRAST

Table 5-1 summarizes the major contrasts in U.S. and Japanese cultural values and orientation. At the top of the table is the overall orientation in the two societies. The United States is oriented by the ideal of individualism, whereas Japan is oriented by the ideal of the collective. Of course, each society recognizes the importance of both the individual and the collective, but a very fundamental difference between the two countries is the fact that the United States is oriented by the myth of the importance of the individual, whereas Japan is oriented by the myth of the importance of the collective.

In the United States the ideal is independence, whereas in Japan there is an affirmative attitude toward dependence.[5] The U.S. traditional culture prefers authoritative decision making, whereas the Japanese culture prefers participative decision making. The United States emphasizes competition and Japan values and celebrates cooperation. There is in the U.S. culture a style preference for confrontation as opposed to the very definite preference in Japan for compromise.

Americans are quick in decision making but slow and hesitating in implementation, whereas the Japanese are very slow due to the consensus process in decision

[4] *Business Week*, April 17, 1978, p. 53.

[5] See, for example, T. Doi, *The Anatomy of Dependence* (Tokyo: Kodansha International Ltd., 1973).

making but quick and steady in implementation. The U.S. cultural style is direct, whereas the Japanese favor the indirect.

In the eyes of many observers, the United States is more short-term oriented than Japan where the more interactive and participative style of decision making, because it is so deliberate and incorporates so many inputs, is necessarily more long-term.

A review of the eighteen contrasting items in Table 5-1 demonstrates that the United States and Japan are fundamentally different cultures. And yet, as we have already observed, the Japanese consumer exhibits behavior that is remarkably similar to that of the U.S. consumer when income levels are similar. Thus the ultimate paradox of the Japanese market is the striking and fundamental dissimilarity of the Japanese and U.S. cultures, and at the same time the rather remarkable similarity in customer behavior. The international marketer needs to be responsive both to the widespread requirements for adaptation in Japan and to the widespread opportunity of supplying needs that express cultural universals.

For example, American fast-food franchisers have found Japan to be a remarkably fertile market opportunity. On the other hand, American manufacturers of doormats have had no success at all in Japan.[6]

NEGOTIATING IN JAPAN[7]

The success or failure of a foreign businessman's efforts in Japan will be largely determined by a myriad of negotiations with Japanese businessmen and government officials. These negotiations involve a number of important steps and actions.

Planning the talks. Once a company has decided to negotiate in Japan, it should prepare its representatives for a long stay and arm them with thorough and exhaustive explanations of what the company has to offer and what the company is seeking. Experienced negotiators in Japan report that on the average it takes six times longer and is three times more difficult to reach an agreement in Japan than in the United States. There are many reasons for this including the need for interpreters and the fact that neither the Japanese nor the Westerners understand very much about each other's thinking processes.

Because interpreters are used, it is wise to follow some basic rules when dealing with them:

1. Brief the interpreter in advance and provide him or her with a copy of the material to be discussed.

---

[6] A Japanese purchasing delegation visiting the U.S. had to politely explain to a doormat manufacturer that the Japanese remove their shoes before entering their houses and that there was no market for doormats.

[7] Adapted from Howard F. Van Zandt, "How to Negotiate in Japan," *Harvard Business Review*, November–December 1970.

2. Speak clearly and avoid the use of unusual or rare words.
3. Assume that all numbers over 10,000 will be mistranslated. Write them down for all to see and repeat them carefully. Avoid using the number billion because it means one with twelve zeros in Europe, and one with nine zeros in the United States.
4. Avoid the use of slang terms, such as "right on." Say "very good" or "good."
5. Do not expect an interpreter to work more than an hour or two without a rest. If nonstop discussions are planned over a day, arrange for two interpreters.
6. Be understanding if it develops that the interpreter has made a mistake, because these are difficult to avoid given the great dissimilarities between European languages and the Japanese language.

Personal relations. The Japanese go to great lengths to establish a warm personal relationship as the basis for business activities. Entertainment is a very important part of the process of establishing a relationship. Gift giving is customary and a definite factor in business relations. Gifts need not be expensive. Foreigners visiting Japan are advised to bring souvenirs from their country to give to Japanese contacts. The cost of these items should not be excessive because it is the sentiment rather than the value that is important.

Making a presentation. The Japanese, like businessmen everywhere, are looking for sincerity and honesty in potential partners, customers, or suppliers. One useful way to obtain credibility in Japan is to show information in print that supports a presentation. The Japanese feel that when a person is willing to put his case in print where all may challenge what has been said, it is likely that he will be as accurate as possible in order not to lose face. Material appearing in a respected technical or trade publication is especially valuable.

Closing discussions. The final stage of negotiotions should include the joint drawing up of a contract that reaches agreement on points at issue. It is important for foreigners, particularly Americans, to recognize that the Japanese have a custom of being silent for what seems to Westerners as an excessively long time. The Westerner should not become excited and feel a compulsion to speak during these periods of silence, because it often results in a concession on a disputed point by the Westerner when he simply tries to keep the conversation going. It is common for the Japanese to insist that negotiations end by gathering large amounts of data to justify the action being taken. Some of the data will be needed for internal company use, and a considerable amount of data will be required to satisfy the Japanese government. Besides the need to satisfy government requirements, one of the reasons for requiring supporting data is that, should the venture fail, no one in the Japanese company can be rebuked for having proceeded on a project without sufficient evidence to justify the action. In America this kind of documentation is called alibi paper.

Latin America

Latin America, with 4 percent of the world's wealth and 7 percent of its population, is a developing region, richer than Asia, Africa, or the Middle East, but with an average per capita income half that of the world average. It is a region of great contrasts. Argentina, one of the richest countries in the world at the turn of the century, had a per capita income of only $1,600 in 1977, far behind the $6,000–$9,000 range of today's top-income countries. This relatively low income reflects the years of industrial conflict that arrested the country's growth. Today, in Argentina, business and the middle class are happy; labor is not. The road back is expected by many observers to be a sucessful but also a very long one.

Brazil, Argentina's very near neighbor, is one of the most rapidly developing countries in the world, with real growth in most recent years running at 8–9 percent per annum. In contrast to Argentina, Brazil has demonstrated its capability to adjust to adversity and in very unorthodox ways to manage the process of economic growth successfully. The distinctive characteristics of Brazil are its vast territory and resources, a diversity of racial background in the population that is perhaps unique in the world, and the country's almost unique ability to utilize the inputs of foreign investors (including almost every multinational company in the world) in a way that does not sap the national esprit de corps or the sense of identity. Many observers believe that Brazil's enormous resources and capacity to adjust to adversity indicate acceptable risks for foreign investors over the long pull.

A striking fact about Latin America is that over half of its 322 million people live under some form of military rule, including the populations of Argentina, Bolivia, Brazil, Chile, Ecuador, Peru, and Paraguay. This form of governance is a reflection of the very volatile political climate of this region. For many decades the combined problems of poverty, maldistribution of income, underemployment, low productivity, and inability of the societies to create a viable democratic political process have made Latin America a very volatile and risky region.

Today most Latin American countries have made significant progress in coping with balance-of-payments problems and sustaining the industrialization process. Restrictive policies and administrative practices with respect to foreign enterprises are gradually being liberalized. Markets are growing. For these reasons, many observers consider the countries less risky now than they were a decade ago.

Although the Latin American countries have made substantial efforts to create a more regionally integrated economy, these countries are highly differentiated and this very pronounced diversity (geographic, economic, and social) encourages both nationalism and what appears to be a trend toward more independent actions. Realistically, international marketers should approach Latin American integration efforts as more aspiration than fact.

Africa

It is not really possible to treat Africa as a single economic unit. The continent is divided into three distinct areas: the Republic of South Africa, North

Africa, and, between the Sahara Desert in the north and the Zambezi River in the south, Black Africa. The economy of the Republic of South Africa is rapidly developing, with a well-diversified manufacturing base and with a demand for goods and services that is much more comparable to the poorer countries in Western Europe or the richer countries in Latin America than it is to other African nations. In North Africa the 78 million Arabs are differentiated politically and economically. They are richer and more developed, with many of the states benefiting from large oil resources. The Arab states have been independent for a longer period than the Black African nations.

Black Africa has been characterized in the past twenty years by symptoms common to areas faced with the dual task of creating a nation *and* developing the economy. Unrealistic expectations, an absence of training and experience, lack of capital, organizational problems, and a host of other difficulties have plagued these nations. Tanzania provides a good example of the difficult challenge in creating a nation and developing a country simultaneously. In 1964 the Tanzania army mutinied because of dissatisfaction with pay and conditions of service. What started out as a complaint against pay and conditions of service became within a week a coup d'etat as dissident labor leaders seized the opportunity to combine with the dissatisfied military. Much to the embarrassment of President Nyerere it was necessary to call in British forces to put down the rebellion. The fact that a British Commando unit of twenty-six men put down a rebellious army of nine hundred men who had overthrown the government of a nation of 12 million people gives some idea of the vulnerability and instability that characterizes nations at their early stage of development.

Nigeria offers an example of a more successfully developing nation of Black Africa, with an economy growing at 9 percent a year and annual oil revenues of $9 billion. The sixth-largest producer of crude oil in the world, Nigeria has recently replaced Venezuela as the second largest oil exporter to the United States. On the other hand, over $500 million worth of food must be imported by Nigeria annually, and per capita income is only $320.

Although many of the nations in Black Africa are poor and underdeveloped both politically and economically, the expectations of the people are very high. President Nyerere of Tanzania has said that the standard of living in the United States is part of Tanzania. Although he regrets that this is the case, modern communications and information have created a situation in the world where nearly everyone knows how other people live. The expectations of Tanzanians are based partly on what they know about the rest of the world.

The challenge to marketing in this type of market is not to stimulate demand for products but to identify the most important needs of the society and to develop products that fit these needs. There is much opportunity for creativity in developing unique products that fit the needs of the people in developing countries rather than merely giving copies of products that have been developed for richer countries and therefore may not be the most suitable product for a poorer country.

During the 1960s the average growth in gross domestic product for Black

Africa was 4 percent. Most disappointing, however, was the fact that per capita income increased an annual average of only 1 percent because of population growth.

Oceania

Australia and New Zealand are island economies in the Asian region that have been settled by Europeans. The combined population of these countries is only 17 million, or less than 0.5 percent of the world total. The income level in both countries is relatively high at approximately $4,958 per capita, which means the region accounts for over 2 percent of global income. The real rate of growth in Australia, which has been stimulated by the enormous mineral resources of the continent, has exceeded 5 percent per annum. Australia is actually more important to the international economy as a source of mineral wealth than as a market.

Middle East[8]

The Middle East has been going through a sudden and dramatic transformation since the energy crisis of 1973. As a result, it is estimated that over $100 billion will be added to the reserves of countries such as Saudi Arabia and Kuwait within the next five years. One does not have to be a shrewd marketer to see the opportunities underlying such accumulation of buying power.

The Middle East includes fifteen countries: Bahrain, Egypt, Iraq, Iran, Israel, Jordan, Kuwait, Lebanon, Oman, Qatar, Syria, Saudi Arabia, the United Arab Emirates, and the two Republics of Yemen.

In a total population of approximately 112 million the majority, 68.0 percent, are Arabs, with 28.8 percent Persians, and 2.9 percent Israelis. However, Persians and Arabs share the same religion, beliefs, and Islamic traditions, making the population 95 percent Muslim and 5 percent Christian and Jewish. Despite this apparent homogeneity, heterogeneity exists within each country and within religious groups. The differences are deeply rooted and are as ancient as the history of the area itself.

Seven of the countries have high oil revenue: Bahrain, Iraq, Iran, Kuwait, Oman, Qatar, and Saudi Arabia hold more than 75 percent of free world oil reserves. Recent increases in oil revenue have widened the gap between poor and rich nations of the Middle East, and income disparities are an urgent problem that contribute to political and social instability in the area. Shantytowns stand side by side with plush palacelike buildings and fancy villas in most Middle Eastern cities. At one extreme, Saudi Arabia, Israel, Kuwait, and the UAE with 10.9 percent of the population share 40.0 percent of the area's wealth. At the other extreme, Egypt, Oman, and the Arab Republic of Yemen with 49.4 percent of the population have only 14.2 percent of the area's income. These disparities are expected to increase as income rises with the demand for Middle Eastern crude.

[8] I am indebted to Michel I. DeBakey for the account that follows.

The markets of these countries are changing rapidly. Demand for consumer products has risen as anticipated, but purchases of industrial goods have exceeded expectations due to ambitious plans for developing an industrial base.

Until late 1974, industrial and consumer goods were chaneled through Lebanese and Jordanian ports. Lebanon and Jordan have been, for the last twenty years, the Middle Eastern headquarters of many MNCs. For instance, it was not uncommon for a foreign business executive to travel all the way from Riyadh (Saudi Arabian capital) to Beirut (Lebanese capital) to make a phone call to his European headquarters or to the United States. Also, most banking activities for the gulf states were handled through the Lebanese capital. Nowadays there are definite signs of change; with growing national pride and as a result of the Lebanese troubles, entrepreneurs who were the backbone of the Lebanese economic infra-structure have spread all over the petrodollar area and especially to Saudi Arabia, Kuwait, the UAE, and Qatar.

Iran and Egypt were expected to replace Lebanon as a base for MNCs in the Middle East. The former is understandably excluded because of the language barrier. The latter is most likely to play such a role, due to its location on the Mediterranean as a natural link between three continents—Africa, Asia, and Europe —and its prestige as a leader among Arab and African nations. The population of Egypt is by far the largest among the nations of the area (32 percent of the area's total population), and the country is rich in natural resources (water and minerals) awaiting exploitation.

The Palestinian dilemma has had serious repercussions on the economy of the region. Communication, the lifeline of economic activity, does not exist between Israel and its Arab neighbors. The negative effect of such a situation on business and economic activities is obvious and influences the daily life of most foreign businessmen operating in the region.

Most local Middle Eastern markets are still primitive and fragmented. Marketers cannot apply the latest schemes and techniques of marketing. On one hand, market surveys and studies are costly; on the other hand, necessary data are totally lacking. In addition, impulsive buying is very common and market behavior is often unpredictable. There does not exist a societal type with a typical belief, behavior, and tradition; each capital and major city in the Middle East has a variety of social groups differentiated by their religion, social classes, educational fields, degree of wealth, and so forth. In general, however, Middle Easterners are warm, friendly, and clannish. Tribal pride and generosity toward guests are basic beliefs. Decision making is by consensus, and seniority has more weight than educational expertise. Life of the individual centers on the family. Leadership emanates from the clan, and the bigger the clan, the stronger the leadership. Ideological revolution never existed; rather, clannish uprise is more frequent in the Middle East. Authority is acquired by aging, and power is related to family size and seniority. Marrying a leader's daughter makes one a leader, and the more powerful her family, the more powerful the leadership.

Important decisions in the Middle East are often made quickly on the basis of feeling or intuition, and management is politic, in its broad sense, and family oriented. Honor is put above all, and a good reputation is a Middle Easterner's most valuable asset.

According to a Business International report, the success of the Japanese in penetrating Middle Eastern markets is based on:

1. Realizing that technical competence and good reputation count more than money.
2. Being prepared for hard bargaining and bargaining hard in return.
3. Being flexible in trading off short-term profits for a longer-term but steadier flow of profit.
4. Taking time in negotiations and use of same social and traditional methods by applying the informal personal approach rather than the formal organizational approach. Put another way, the Japanese emphasize "feeling" connections in their business dealings.

These matters are of great importance when dealing in the Middle East. Business is typically mixed with pleasure, and time is viewed as well spent when shared with people who are valued and trusted. For the typical Western businessman, it is especially important to realize that the Western (especially the U.S.) view of time and approach to life is in a fundamental sense a shared value. The difference lies in the Middle Eastern belief that you should do business with those you trust and their need to take time to develop rapport and trust. Thus, in both cultures, time is money.

MARKETING IN LESS-DEVELOPED COUNTRIES

Does marketing have a role in less-developed countries? Many government officials and planners have asked this question and have concluded that it does not. They point out that a shortage of goods and services is the central problem of developing countries, and that the most pressing need is to expand production. Needs are well known, almost anything produced can be sold, and marketing with its focus on identifying needs and wants is really quite out of place in an environment characterized by scarcity.

Certainly, marketing that focuses on creating new needs and wants, which is very important in a developed, mass-consumption economy, is out of place in a poor developing country. But dynamic, modern marketing is more than a search for new needs and wants. It is, fundamentally, a system of concepts, tools, and skills that enables managers to match the capability of organizations to the needs of society. As such, marketing science can be directed toward the needs of the less-developed country[9] as well as the needs of the nonprofit organization.[10]

[9] Peter F. Drucker, "Marketing and Economic Development," *Journal of Marketing,* January 1958.
[10] See, for example, the July 1971 issue of the *Journal of Marketing,* which is devoted entirely to "Marketing's Changing Social/Environmental Role." Articles include "Social Marketing: An

For example, there is a need in every developing society for laundry. The human desire for cleanliness is universal. However, the automatic electric washing machine, which is the ideal solution to the problem of dirty clothes in a developed country, is not going to be the appropriate solution in an underdeveloped country. Between the extremes of washing clothes in a stream of running water, or on a rock, and using a fully automatic electric washing machine lie many possibilities. For example, a small plastic washing machine that is handpowered has been developed with the conditions of developed countries as a constraint, and the result has been a handpowered washing machine that is most efficient.[11]

Another example of the importance of marketing to a developing country is in the communications or persuasion area. Marketers have long been associated with their skill in stimulating or even creating demands for products. There are many products or items whose use should be encouraged in underdeveloped countries. For example, in many African countries there are plentiful supplies of fish from lakes and the sea. Fish is an extremely nutritious and desirable food from a health point of view. However, Africans are not accustomed to eating fish and do not consume it in any significant quantity. A program of persuading Africans to consume fish would be highly beneficial to the health and welfare of the African people. Marketers with skills in the advertising and promotion area clearly have a contribution to make in this kind of program.

The important role of marketing in the less-developed countries is to focus societal resources in organizations on the creation and delivery of products that best serve the needs of the people. The conditions of scarcity in less-developed countries make it imperative that products designed for developed country markets are not automatically copied. Basic marketing concepts can and should be applied to design a product that fits the needs and ability to buy of the less-developed country market. These concepts must also be applied to educate the taste and preferences of the people to accept these products. Marketing in the dynamic sense can relate resources to opportunity and satisfy needs on the consumer's terms.

BIBLIOGRAPHY

BOOKS

Benedict, Ruth, *The Chrysanthemum and the Sword*. Rutland, Vt.: Charles E. Tuttle, 1972 (first published in 1946).

Delassus, Jean-Francois, *The Japanese*. New York: Hart Publishing, 1972.

Doing Business with the USSR – A Guide for Western Corporations. Geneva: Business International, 1972.

Approach to Planned Social Change,'' by Philip Kotler and Gerald Zaltman; and ''Marketing's Application to Fund Raising,'' by William A. Mindak and Malcolm Byber.

[11] See Chapter 11 for a fuller description of this adaptation.

Granick, David, *Enterprise Guidance in Eastern Europe: A Comparison of Four Socialist Economies.* Princeton, N.J.: Princeton University Press, 1975.

Michener, James A., *Iberia.* New York: Random House, 1968.

Nakane, Chie, *Japanese Society.* Berkeley: University of California Press, 1972.

Yoshino, M. Y., *Japan's Managerial System.* Cambridge, Mass.: M.I.T. Press, 1968.

ARTICLES

Bent, F. T., E. Cracco, and R. Vuerings, "The Belgian Environment for Multinational Business: Conflicting Perspectives," *Columbia Journal of World Business,* 10 (Fall 1975), 119–31.

Brunner, James A., and George M. Taoka, "Marketing and Negotiating in the People's Republic of China: Perceptions of American Businessmen Who Attended the 1975 Canton Fair," *Journal of International Business Studies,* Fall/Winter 1977, pp. 69–82.

Cunningham, William H., Russell M. Moore, and Isabella Cunningham, "Urban Markets in Industrializing Countries: The Sao Paulo Experience," *Journal of Marketing,* 38, No. 2 (April 1974), 2–12.

Dufey, Gunter, "Financing East-West Business," *Columbia Journal of World Business,* 9 (Spring 1974), 37–41.

Glazer, Herbert, "Japan's Marketing Structure," *Sophia University Socio-Economic Bulletin,* No. 23. Tokyo: Sophia University, 1970.

Goldman, Marshall I., "Who Profits More from U.S.-Soviet Trade?" *Harvard Business Review,* November-December 1973, pp. 79–87.

Green, Robert T., and Eric Langeard, "A Cross-National Comparison of Consumer Habits and Innovator Characteristics," *Journal of Marketing,* 39, No. 3 (July 1975), 34–41.

Hayden, Eric W., and Henry R. Nau, "East-West Technology Transfer," *Columbia Journal of World Business,* 10 (Fall 1975), 70–82.

Hertzfeld, Jeffery M., "New Directions in East-West Trade," *Harvard Business Review,* May-June 1977, pp. 93–99.

——, "Setting Up Shop in Moscow," *Harvard Business Review,* September-October 1974, pp. 137–42.

Holt, John B., "Industrial Cooperation in Eastern Europe: Strategies of U.S. Agricultural and Construction Equipment Companies," *Columbia Journal of World Business,* 12 (Spring 1977), 80–89.

——, "New Roles for Western Multinationals in Eastern Europe," *Columbia Journal of World Business,* 8 (Fall 1973), 131–39.

Lange, Irene, and James S. Elliott, "U.S. Role in East-West Trade," *Journal of International Business Studies,* Fall/Winter 1977, pp. 5–16.

Lauter, G. Peter, "The Changing Role of Marketing in the Eastern European Socialist Economies," *Journal of Marketing,* October 1971, pp. 16–21.

Lauter, G. Peter, and Paul M. Dickie, "Multinational Corporations in Eastern European Socialist Economies," *Journal of Marketing,* October 1975, pp. 40–46.

Nazarevsky, Valentin A., "A Soviet Economist Looks at U.S. Business," *Harvard Business Review,* May-June 1974, pp. 49–57.

Ozawa, Terutomo, Moyes Puciennik, and K. Nagaraja Rao, "Japanese Direct Investment in Brazil," *Columbia Journal of World Business,* 11 (Fall 1976), 107–16.

Rushing, Francis W., and Anne R. Lieberman, "The Role of U.S. Imports in the Soviet Growth Strategy for the Seventies," *Journal of International Business Studies,* Fall/Winter 1977, pp. 31–48.

Sood, James H., "Marketing in Finland: An Entree to the East," *Columbia Journal of World Business,* 10 (Fall 1975), 93–100.

Sorenson, Ralph Z., II, "U.S. Marketers Can Learn from European Innovators," *Harvard Business Review,* September-October 1972, pp. 89–99.

Van Zandt, Howard F., "How to Negotiate in Japan," *Harvard Business Review,* November-December 1970.

——, "Learning to Do Business with 'Japan, Inc.'," *Harvard Business Review,* July-August 1972, pp. 83–92.

Walters, J. Hart, Jr., "Marketing in Poland in the 1970's," *Journal of Marketing,* October 1975, pp. 47–51.

GULF OIL CORPORATION
(Corporate Conduct/Business Ethics)

In December 1975 the Special Review Committee of the Board of Directors of Gulf Oil Corporation submitted its report to the United States District Court for the District of Columbia and the Securities and Exchange Commission.[1] This report was prepared by a special review committee which was established after a number of inquiries and proceedings had led to the public disclosure of substantial and illegal political contributions or payments from Gulf's corporate funds.

Part Three of the report is devoted to Gulf's foreign political contributions. At the outset of its investigation, the committee was informed that Gulf, in response to demands on the part of political figures in South Korea, had made a $1 million contribution to the Korean Democratic Republican Party (DRP) in 1966 and another contribution of $3 million in 1970. These payments were authorized by Bob Dorsey, chairman of the board and chief executive officer of the Gulf Oil Corporation. The committee in its report of the background of these payments made the following comment about the circumstances under which the demands and the payments were made.

(a) The Korean Evolution from Agrarian Autocracy to Industrial Democracy

It is difficult to conceive of a country anywhere in the world whose rule in the last century has been more disturbed than that of Korea. It is an Asian country wedged in between the mass of China and the Soviet Union on the north

---

[1] Civil Action No. 75-0324 in the United States District Court for the District of Columbia, Report of the Special Review Committee of the Board of Directors of the Gulf Oil Corporation, John J. McCloy, Chairman, December 30, 1975 (hereafter referred to as "Report").

and the power and strength of Japan to the east. The peninsula in the earlier part of the century was under a long dictatorial rule and, so far as its industrial and political development was concerned, a repressive foreign occupation, resulting in a largely agricultural and authoritarian society. More recently, due to the failure of the Soviet Union and the United States to agree on a plan for the reconstitution of the government of the whole country following the defeat of Japan in World War II, it was arbitrarily torn apart and divided. Thereafter, the southern half of the country was invaded by forces from the north and the country was ravaged by what turned out to be, in terms of the number of casualties and devastation suffered, one of the greatest wars in history. The war was marked by the steadfastness and fighting qualities of a rapidly organized ROK Army which, in conjunction with strong American forces aided by important United Nations contingents, fought off the invasion and finally restored the territorial integrity of South Korea.

Military rule in South Korea was followed by attempts to install democratic processes in an area where the traditions and the experience of representational government were largely non-existent. Following the war, American advisors, educated in traditional American constitutional doctrine and procedures, helped the South Koreans set up what was to them a relatively novel form of government. At the same time, the Korean government undertook an ambitious and serious attempt to expand greatly the country's industrial base. Theretofore, such industrialization and economic strength as the country had enjoyed was in the north. In spite of many vicissitudes, limited funds and sparse natural resources, South Korea did succeed in creating an imposing political and economic post-war development. The Korean development was not accomplished without strong and resolute leaders at the top. In the course of it, the security of South Korea became a significant commitment in American foreign policy.

It was with this background that Gulf in 1963 and 1964 made its first, rather heavy, investments in the petroleum industry of South Korea, where the need and demand for energy was becoming very great. Gulf, in seeking an outlet for some of its Kuwait crude at a time when crude was in long supply, saw an opportunity in Korea where this industrial development, based on a limited supply of petroleum and petroleum products, was taking place. According to Gulf officials who took part in the Korean venture, the idea of developing the industry of Korea appealed greatly to Whiteford, then Chairman of Gulf. He saw it not only as an immediate outlet for a part of Gulf's Kuwait crude, but he also became actively interested in the efforts being made to expand Korean industry. Other foreign interests began to see the possibilities of Korean development, but the Gulf investment was undoubtedly the most significant private investment by any foreign company in Korea at the time. Certainly it was the most important private United States investment.

A refinery at Ulsan (known as the "Pittsburgh of Korea") was started in 1963 and completed and inaugurated in 1964. It was later expanded. In this period Gulf made its original investment of $25,000,000 in the Korean Oil Company ("KOCO"), which was and is jointly owned with the Korean government. What turned out to be successful plastic and fertilizer plants were built by Gulf on a joint venture basis with the Korean Government, and altogether Gulf officials estimate the company's Korean exposure grew in a few years to some $200,000,000 if not more. In the meantime, Gulf was steadily increasing the daily flow of oil into the refinery until it reached as much as 150,000 to 200,000 barrels of oil a day. In the Committee's interviews with Mr. Herbert Goodman, now the head of Gulf's shipping interests and in the mid-sixties an important factor among Gulf executives operating in the Far East, including Korea, he stressed that Gulf had not only an interest in what was becoming a very profitable venture but also a sense of commitment to Korea as an active partner in its industrial development.

While this industrial expansion was occurring, political developments were also moving forward. Operatives from United States Government agencies then functioning in Korea were, according to Goodman, constantly pressing the then Korean leaders for the creation and maintenance of an electoral system which could serve as a base for a stable form of representative government for the future. Efforts were made by United States Government personnel to instruct the Koreans in election forms, such as registration and election procedures, and in how to create the other machinery of an elective system. Goodman and others referred to the fact that the Korean Government was poor and had little, if any, money to carry on the usual electoral processes associated with representative government. It was emphasized that it took a great bit of money on the part of the Koreans to establish these procedures and the mechanics by means of which an electoral system could be made to function.

The driving force of the new Korean development was President Park Chung Hee, the former leader of the Revolutionary Council which had ousted Syngman Rhee. As President, he became intensely interested in the economic development of the country. He himself directed much of the effort being made toward Korea's industrial expansion. Gulf officials and President Park and his representatives at times, according to Goodman, jointly participated in planning for the expansion of the country's industry. Other American companies entered the country—some, according to Dorsey, with the encouragement of Gulf—and they also became a part of the industrial development.[2]

The committee's report on the two contributions is duplicated in its entirety in the following section.

(b) The 1966 Contribution

The Committee's investigation showed that in 1966, with this background of national development but otherwise out of a clear sky, a substantial political contribution was requested of Gulf to help meet the expenses of a coming election campaign. Goodman was approached by a high official of President Park's Secretariat, who told him that the government felt a contribution should be made by Gulf to the Democratic Republican Party ("DRP") in the amount of $1,000,000 for the coming election campaign. Goodman promptly reported the matter to Messrs. E. D. Loughney, a Gulf Vice President, and Dorsey, in Pittsburgh. Goodman did not suggest in his interview with the Committee that the request was in the nature of a threat, and Loughney's recollection is consistent with Goodman's in this respect. Loughney told the Committee that Goodman did not report that any specific reprisal would occur if no contribution were made. Loughney does recall that Goodman said that most other companies had been or would be asked to make a contribution.[3] Loughney was aware that an election in Korea could be expensive, that

---

[2] Source: Report, pp. 95–98.

[3] Goodman did not state that he had knowledge that any other companies had in fact made contributions, but he felt certain that others had been approached and had complied.

the Koreans were poor, and that the DRP had to depend largely on industry and business for political contributions.

There was no question in the minds of the Gulf officers then on the ground of the identity of the government with those officials who were making the request.

There is another element which recurs in the Committee's examination of the atmosphere in which the first Korean contribution was made by Gulf, and that is the persistent encouragement, if not pressure, on the part of American government officials on the Korean Government toward the institution of American-style elections. The Koreans who approached Gulf for the contribution believed that to respond to this "encouragement" or policy would involve heavy expenses which they could not meet, and it was thought natural on their part to turn to the foreign investors, particularly the Americans, as a source of funds for the purpose. The Gulf representatives involved viewed the 1966 contribution as supportive of the developing democratic process in Korea, and they communicated this attitude to Pittsburgh.

In regard to the 1966 payment, Dorsey testified before the Senate Foreign Relations Subcommittee on Multinational Corporations as follows:

> "Our investigation indicates that the demand was made by high party officials and was accompanied by pressure which left little to the imagination as to what would occur if the company would choose to turn its back on the request. At that time the company had already made a huge investment in Korea. We were expanding and were faced with a myriad of problems which often confront American corporations in foreign countries. I carefully weighed the demand for a contribution in that light, and my decision to make the contribution of $1 million was based upon what I sincerely considered to be in the best interests of the company and its shareholders."

Dorsey also stated to the Review Committee his recollection of the 1966 request. He recalled obtaining information about the request only from Goodman saying:

> ". . . it was a very strong approach, indeed; not threatening, but with implications that if you really want to do well and if you really want to survive, we appreciate what you have done, but now—now, it's time that friends stand together. It's a critical situation with us. We are trying to adopt democratic processes after two thousand years of autocracy.
>
> "Your government is encouraging us in this. We need money to do it, and you have fared well here. And in addition, in kind of an oblique way, made it rather apparent—rather clear to him that our—his continued well-being and our continued well-being depended on our doing what they wanted us to do, which was to give them a million dollars.
>
> "He (Goodman) came to Pittsburgh and talked to me about it and we made it rather apparent—rather clear to him that our—his continued well-being and our continued well-being depended on our doing what they wanted us to do, which was to give them a million dollars.
>
> "He (Goodman) came to Pittsburgh and talked to me about it and we ultimately agreed—I ultimately agreed to give them the million dollars as a contribution to that party under the pressure—there was great pressure that existed to do it.

"I thought it was the correct thing to do. It was in the best interests of the corporation, so I did it."

Later in his interview, Dorsey again implied that a certain amount of coercion was involved in the 1966 request:

"But certainly, I was told by him (Goodman) that there were veiled threats of what—you know—threats that if you want to survive and do well—if you want to continue in the role you're in and prosper in this country, you had best do this.

"Now, the other side of that coin, obviously, if you don't do it, you don't prosper and stay here very long. But nothing more specific than that."

The Committee is satisfied that the documentation shown to its accountants in connection with the 1966 transfer of $1,004,000 charged against Bahamas Ex. related to the $1,000,000 contribution to the Korean DRP in 1966 and that the payment constituted a political contribution within the meaning of the Undertaking.

(c) The 1970 Contribution

In 1970 there came another demand in the face of a heavier political challenge to the DRP. This time it was $10,000,000 and it was attended by a much more blunt approach. Mr. S. K. Sim, who is now deceased, made the demand. He was a sort of party head, close to the administration and a man of great determination and vigor. Gulf officials who knew him speak of him as a rough customer. Kim made his demand by summoning to his office a Mr. Nam, a Vice President in charge of government relations of Korean Gulf Oil Company ("KORGOC," a wholly-owned Gulf subsidiary). Kim indicated that other concerns operating in Korea were being faced with similar demands. This demand also was immediately conveyed to Pittsburgh, but no action was taken on it pending Dorsey's visit to Korea which had been scheduled prior to receipt of the demand. When Dorsey arrived, he met with Kim. It turned out to be an unpleasant encounter, resulting in Dorsey's refusal to meet the demand for $10,000,000 and his departure from the meeting in anger. Subsequently, after temperatures had subsided, Dorsey agreed to pay the sum of $3,000,000 which he justified on the basis of the need for the continued goodwill and cooperation of the Korean Government on which, in the newly-organized society, it was necessary for a foreign company to rely.

Dorsey described for the Committee his first encounter with Kim as follows:

"He (Kim) dived right into the matter and told me that we were doing exceedingly well out there and that basically, our continued prosperity depended on our coming up with a ten million (dollar) political contribution to the party.

"And I, politely as I could, demurred and told him I thought we had been helpful before; we had been pleased to, because we believed in it— believed in his country; we knew the necessity for election, and there was no—almost no way of raising popular funds in Korea for these things, and we had done it out of a sense of obligation before. But the question of ten million dollars, there was no way I could do anything like that; that it was almost preposterous. And at that point, he became exceedingly angry with me and exceedingly irritated and talked to me just about as roughly as he could; in effect, saying, you know, 'I'm not here to debate matters. You are either going to put up the goddamned money or suffer the consequences,' although he said it substantially more roughly than that.

"I was very angry. I was very upset, and I told him that I was not going to be talked to that way. And that was the end of the conversation. I walked out of his house and he made no attempt to restrain me or apologize or anything else."

The figure of $3,000,000 was reached in the following manner:

"So, in effect, we then sort of negotiated the matter down. He had impressed on me that the needs were infinitely greater; this was a serious campaign; real opposition and a real need for getting out the votes and talking to people.

"So, somehow or other, we arrived at the amount of three million dollars and I was agreeable."

Dorsey summarized his reasons for making the payment as follows:

"So you really are there at the mercy of the government and you are there at the sufferance of the government; if you're going to prosper and do well, you need the government on your side. You need that kind of an environment, unlike any Western country.

"Mr. Jackson (for the Committee): Did you fear that if you didn't make the contribution there might be nationalization of assets of your company?

"Mr. Dorsey: No. I don't think I—I don't think I thought that, at all.

"I just thought that the opportunity to continue a profitable business, without unwarranted and inhibiting government interference, required it.

"I think that I felt that there were further opportunities to—or, for further investment to expand and to do other things there.

"And that our ability to do, then, again depended on ministers and government officials that really made the decisions in the end."

(d) Motivations and Mechanics of the Two Contributions

Whatever the nuance behind the "requests" in terms of pressure may have been, it is quite clear that Gulf was in no sense a volunteer seeking to suborn favors by means of largesse. Neither the first nor second payment was in any sense initiated by Gulf or treated by Gulf as anything other than a distasteful effort on the part of the government or the party to obtain a contribution which Gulf had no desire to make.

Dorsey, after thoughtful consideration, ordered the payments made, and according to him he took no part in arranging the details involved in carrying them out. Such arrangements were made by the Comptroller's and Treasurer's offices which used Gulf funds in the United States, booked them to Bahamas Ex. and transferred them to a Swiss bank account.[4] Goodman recalls that

---

[4] For example, in regard to the 1970 payment, the committee reviewed accounting documents dated July 20 and 31, 1970, supporting a disbursement (including a check request from Mr.

Henry, Executive Vice President, advised him that the employment of such methods of payment was due to a desire to avoid any handling of the matter in Korea by Gulf personnel stationed there. Although there was some discrepancy between Henry's and Goodman's recollections as to what took place in connection with the routing of the money to Switzerland for payment, this discrepancy does not appear to be significant.

In testifying before Senator Church's Subcommittee, as previously noted, Dorsey unsuccessfully endeavored to withhold the identity of the country involved through agreeing to disclose the fact of the payments. This, he later stated to the Committee, was due to his desire to avoid any embarrassment to the South Korean Government or its leaders at a time when sharp political attacks were being made on the administration of President Park.

The Committee has found it most difficult to arrive at a satisfactory conclusion in regard to the legality or illegality under then existing Korean law of the political contributions made by Gulf to the DRP in the 1966 and 1970 campaigns. The opinions of Korean counsel which the Committee has been able to obtain cannot be said to be conclusive of the question in the circumstances of this case under Korean law. Neither Dorsey nor Goodman seemed to have given any thought at the time as to whether the contributions were legal or illegal under Korean law. They seemed to have treated it as either a request or a demand from the Korean Government to be acceded to or not as the interests of the company appeared. Dorsey met the request for the first payment which only led to a more peremptory demand for an even greater sum of a few years later. He stated that he acted reluctantly but with the conviction that what he did, considering all the circumstances, was in the best interests of the company and its stockholders.

The reason given by Dorsey for the failure to disclose the payments or the demands therefor to the Gulf Board of Directors at or about the time of the payments is best stated in his own words:

> "First, I didn't need the authorization of the Board to make the—to make the payments. So it was clearly within my authority to do it.
>
> "As to why I didn't—and it is very difficult to go back and reconstruct one's mental processes that far back—but I suppose in a sense, my reasoning was that—my reasoning grew out of a deep conviction—personal conviction that what I was doing was in the best interest of the corporation—something I believe in as strongly now as I believed in then.
>
> "That being true, and the matter being rather delicate, and recognizing that any revelation of this would be both embarrassing to Gulf and embarrassing to the party to whom the payment was made, that I simply decided that the better course was not to tell them.

* * * * *

W. H. Burkhiser, assistant treasurer, to Deering, the comptroller), and an advice from the Mellon Bank indicating that a transfer of funds in the amount of $3 million was made from a Gulf account to the Union Bank of Switzerland, attention of Mr. Robert Strebel. Documentation was reviewed which indicated that $3 million was disbursed from the Swiss bank, pursuant to instructions from Goodman, in the following manner:

9 checks of $200,000 each	$1,800,000
Cash aggregating	1,199,790
Bank commission	210
	$3,000,000

"If there was any risk being run, I was quite willing to assume that risk myself. It was just my judgment that I should not involve these other people, because there was a potential risk of this being revealed and there being substantial embarrassment all the way around.

"That is about as near as I can come to my reasoning at the time."[5]

QUESTIONS

1. Do you agree with Bob Dorsey's conviction that the payments he authorized to the Korean DRP were in the best interests of the Gulf Oil Corporation? Why? Why not?
2. In what alternative ways might Dorsey have responded to the Korean "requests"?
3. Formulate a corporate code of conduct that provides explicit guidance on how to respond to "requests" for political contributions.

[5]Source: Report, pp. 98–105.

legal
dimensions

> When you are at Rome live in the Roman style; when you
> are elsewhere live as they live elsewhere.
>
> *St. Ambrose, A.D. 340–397*
> *(advice to St. Augustine)*

INTRODUCTION

The field of international law is complex and fascinating, but far beyond the scope
of this book. This chapter (1) examines the development of international law as it
relates to multinational marketing and (2) considers the most pressing current issues
and the rules and organizations now in existence to deal with them.

LEGAL ENVIRONMENT

International law as it exists today dates from the late sixteenth century. Early
international law was concerned with the waging of war, the establishment of
peace, and other such political issues as diplomatic recognition of new national
entities and governments. Thus, while elaborate international rules gradually
emerged—covering, for example, the status of neutral nations—the creation in the
nineteenth century of laws governing commerce was done on a state-by-state basis.
This perpetuated the major split in legal systems between those areas under English
influence founded on common law (such as Great Britain, the U.S., and Canada)
and those under the influence of the old Roman law and, later, the Napoleonic
Code based on civil or code law. Under civil law, the judicial system is divided into
civil, commercial, and criminal law. Thus, commercial law has its own administrative structure, and property rights, for example, are established by a formal registration of the property. Under common law, on the other hand, the law is established

by the creation of precedents from previous rulings, and commercial law until recently was not recognized as a special entity. Property rights, under common law, are based on ownership established by use. A significant recent development is the Uniform Commercial Code, now recognized by forty-nine (49) U.S. states, which brings together a body of specifically designed rules covering commercial conduct.

International law has the function of upholding order. While at first, as we have noted, this referred to preventing war or dealing with problems arising from war, with the growing trade among nations, order in commercial affairs came to assume increasing importance. While the law had originally dealt only with nations as entities, a growing body of law rejected the idea that only states can be subjects of international law. *Reparation for Injuries Suffered in the Service of the United Nations* (International Court of Justice Reports, 1949, p. 179), for example, recognized the claims of an individual. The Nuremberg International Tribunal in its trial of Nazi war criminals reiterated this concept:

> It was submitted that international law is concerned with the actions of sovereign states, and provides no punishment for individuals; and further that where the act in question is an act of state, those who carry it out are not personally responsible, but are protected by the doctrine of the sovereignty of the state. In the opinion of the Tribunal, both these submissions must be rejected. Crimes against international law are committed by men, not by abstract entities, and only by punishing individuals who commit such crimes can the provisions of international law be enforced.

International law may be defined as the rules and principles that states and nations consider binding upon themselves. This raises the first of two unique characteristics of international law: those areas in which law has been written are those that have always belonged to individual states or nations—property, trade, immigration, and so on—and the law now exists only to the extent that individual states are willing to relinquish their rights in these areas. Even today there is very little one nation can do if another refuses to submit to arbitration or to recognize an unfavorable judgment against it. This deficiency is increased by the second characteristic of international law: the lack of an adequate international judicial and administrative framework or a body of law that would form the basis of a truly comprehensive international legal system.

In this situation the multinational marketer will be faced by a multitude of legal environments. He will discover that simply finding out what the law is, or whose law prevails, in a given situation is a difficult task. First, laws of various states, rulings, and local customs must be identified and classified. Then it must be decided whether enough states have actually followed a rule over sufficient time so that it may be considered binding. The twentieth century has seen an increase in international judiciary organizations paralleled by a growing body of international case law. The complex background of this new body of law was aptly summed up in a 1900 fishing case:

> . . . where there is no treaty and no controlling executive or legislative act or

judicial decision, resort must be had to the customs and usages of civilized nations, and, as evidence of these, to the work of jurists and commentators who by years of labor, research, and experience have made themselves peculiarly well acquainted with the subjects of which they treat.

The court goes on to rule that

By the general consent of civilized nations of the world, and independently of any express treaty or other public act, it is an established rule of international law, founded on considerations of humanity.[1]

Notice the important precedent emphasized here; there *is* an established rule of international law per se. Thus, while the law was at first an amalgam of treaties, covenants, codes, and agreements, there is an increasing codification of law starting with the formation by the United States in 1947 of the International Law Commission. To this may be added the rulings of the Permanent Court of International Justice (1920-45); the International Court of Justice, founded in 1946; and the results of various other organizations and conferences—e.g., the Geneva Conference on the Law of the Sea, which began in 1958 and is still meeting regularly.

RELEVANT BUSINESS ISSUES

While it becomes clear in such a situation that the best course to follow is to get expert legal help, an astute marketer, by being aware of the complexity of the legal environment, may do a great deal to avoid situations in which a conflict might arise. Most issues center on the following major questions.

Establishment

Under what conditions am I allowed to establish trade? In order to transact business, citizens of one country must be assured that they will be treated fairly in another country. Treaties of friendship, commerce, and navigation give U.S. citizens the right to nondiscriminatory treatment in trade, the reciprocal right to establish a business, and particularly to invest in the forty-three countries with which the United States has signed these agreements. There are, however, important exceptions: the Coelso Doctrine in Latin America, for example, insists that foreigners, by entering Latin America, agree to being treated as nationals. This can create problems for businessmen who may still be under the jurisdiction of their own laws even when they are out of their native country. U.S. citizens, for example, are forbidden by the Foreign Corrupt Practices Act to bribe an official of a foreign government or political party, even if bribes or "payments" are customary and almost essential for conducting business elsewhere.

[1] Gerard F. Mangor, *The Elements of International Law* (Homewood, Ill.: Dorsey, 1967), p. 14.

Patents and Trademarks

Will my patents and trademarks be protected? There is no international patent. Patents and trademarks that are protected in one country are not necessarily protected in another, so international marketers must ensure that every product is registered in each country they intend to trade in. There are a number of separate patent agreements, the most important of which is the International Convention for the Protection of Industrial Property, first signed in 1883 and now honored by forty-five countries. This gives nationals of each country the same privileges as other nationals are given by their country in patent, trademark, and related areas. It also gives patent coverage for a year in all signatory countries after the patent is applied for in one country, thus ensuring that the product will not be quickly pirated elsewhere. A 1910 Inter-American Convention covered basically the same concerns for Latin American countries, while sixteen European countries made plans in 1973 for a European patent office to open in Munich in 1978.

Recourse

Lawsuits in other countries may be long, costly, and aggravating and may create an unfavorable public image, while at the same time subjecting a company to a court that is unfamiliar with international law or unfavorably disposed toward foreign companies. For these reasons, most businessmen prefer to arbitrate disputes. Arbitration generally involves efforts at conciliation, a hearing of all parties before a three-member panel, and a judgment which the parties agree in advance to abide by. The decades since World War II have seen an increase in the numbers and scope of arbitration groups. Some of the most widely used and respected of these are the International Chamber of Commerce, the American Arbitration Association, the London Court of Arbitration, and the Inter-American Commercial Arbitration Committee.

Lawyers advise that arbitration clauses should be written into all contracts. They also advise that all contracts should contain a clause that establishes jurisdictional rules in the event of a conflict. Jurisdiction is generally established on the basis of (1) a jurisdictional clause, (2) where a contract was entered into, and (3) where the provisions of a contract are to be performed.

Still another consideration should be the site of incorporation, with its implications for taxes and other economic and legal issues. Some countries consider incorporation to be the location of main business activity, others look at the location of the central management, while still others, including the United States, decide on the basis of place of incorporation.

A final concern, lawyers advise, is the need for extreme care in the writing of all contracts, and in having them translated with infinite pains so that all parties are absolutely clear on their obligations.

Taxes

What taxes will my company face abroad? Taxes are an area in which states fiercely retain their national rights. U.S. companies pay taxes to the country in which the income is earned and receive tax credits in the United States on taxes paid abroad. Credits in the United States are limited by a ceiling determined by the ratio of foreign profits to total profits. Because of differing tax rates, it is often advantageous for a company to have as much income taxed abroad as possible. In 1974 and 1975 the U.S. government considered changing accounting rules to cut these tax credits by requiring multinational companies to apply a larger proportion of their indirect costs, such as R & D, to foreign revenue.[2]

By 1976 the United States had twenty-five treaties on taxes, but many complex tax issues remain to be considered by each individual company: Should a foreign subsidiary use multiple corporate entities to reduce the tax burden? How should the company handle transfer pricing in transactions between various divisions of the company?

Expropriation

The ultimate threat of the nation-state is expropriation. The incidence of manufacturing company expropriations is widely exaggerated by the business community, especially among those without international experience. In fact, the total expropriation loss to American companies during this century not only is trivial compared with the total amount of American foreign direct investment but is concentrated entirely outside of the Western industrialized states.

Franklin Root identified 187 U.S. companies that had experienced expropriation since the end of World War I.[3] These companies were involved in 240 separate acts of expropriation—171 in Communist countries and 69 in non-Communist countries. Cuba alone accounted for 137 seizures of American business property. As can be seen in Table 6-1, the total value of major expropriations of U.S. business property by foreign governments from 1917 to 1965 was less than $2.5 billion, or only 5 percent of the total U.S. foreign direct investment base of $49 billion in 1965.[4]

Although the risk of expropriation may be exaggerated it is still quite real, especially in certain industries. As can be seen in Table 6-2, between 1960 and 1974, 12 percent of all U.S. oil properties and 18 percent of all U.S. mining concessions were expropriated. Other sectors with relatively high rates of expropriation were utilities and transportation, which experienced a 4 percent rate of expropria-

[2] *Wall Street Journal*, August 13, 1974, p. 1.
[3] Franklin R. Root, "The Expropriation Experience of American Companies," *Business Horizons*, April 1968, pp. 69–74.
[4] *Survey of Current Business*, 45, No. 9 (September 1966), 39.

TABLE 6-1. Major Expropriation of U.S. Business Property by Foreign Governments

Country	Date	Estimated Amount of U.S. Assets Expropriated (millions of dollars)
Soviet Union	1917–1920	$ 175
Mexico	1938	120
Eastern Europe	1945–1948	240
Cuba	1959–1960	1,400
Argentina	1963	237
Indonesia	1965	160
		$2,332

Root, "Expropriation Experience of American Companies," p. 71.

TABLE 6-2. Expropriation by Industry Group, 1960–1974

Industry	Number of Expropriations	Percent of Total
Oil	84	12.0
Extraction	38	18.0
Utilities and transportation	17	4.0
Insurance and banking	33	4.0
Manufacturing	30	1.2
Agriculture	19	*
Sales and service	16	*
Land, property, and construction	23	*

*Data unavailable.

Source: Bradley, "Managing against Expropriation," p. 79.

tion. By contrast, only 1.2 percent of U.S. manufacturing properties have been expropriated since 1960.

A regional analysis of expropriation between 1960 and 1976 revealed that Latin American countries were responsible for 49 percent of all U.S. expropriations, the Arab states for 27 percent, the Black African states for 13 percent, and the Asian states for 11 percent.[5]

When governments that are frustrated by economic development progress expropriate foreign property, they are taking a step that conflicts directly with the property and income concerns of the highly developed nations of Western Europe and the United States. Industrial countries are committed to "prompt, adequate, and effective compensation" and support the establishment of an international consultation procedure in cases of expropriation. Nevertheless, there are bars to action to reclaim a national's property based on the Act of State Doctrine, which assumes that the acts of foreign states are legal. As U.S. Chief Justice Fuller said in 1897, "Every sovereign state is bound to respect the independence of every other

[5] David G. Bradley, "Managing against Expropriation," *Harvard Business Review,* July-August 1977.

sovereign state, and the courts in one country will not sit in judgement on the acts of government of another done within its territory" (*Underhill* v. *Hernandez,* 168 U.S. 250 [1897]). This policy has been upheld as recently as the reversal of *Banco Nacional de Cuba* vs. *Sabbatino* (U.S. Supreme Court, 1964, 376 U.S. 398). The expropriation of the copper companies in Chile shows most clearly, perhaps, the impact that companies can have on their own fate. Companies that strenuously resisted government efforts to introduce nationals into the company management were expropriated outright while other companies that made genuine efforts to follow Chilean guidelines were allowed to remain under joint Chilean–U.S. management.

Expropriated companies may have recourse to arbitration at, for example, the World Bank Investment Dispute Settlement Center. They may also seek protection by buying expropriation insurance, offered both by private companies and, to an extent limited to new investment in needy countries, by the U.S. government's Overseas Private Investment Corporation (OPIC).

Antitrust

Antitrust laws, a legacy of the nineteenth-century U.S. "trust-busting" era, are intended to maintain free competition by limiting the concentration of economic power. Long a part of the U.S. legal environment, they are taking on increasing importance outside the United States as well. In 1973 the European Community Commission began work on a proposal to control multinational mergers. It proposed a ninety-day notice period for mergers between companies with total sales of over $1.2 billion. In that same year the European Community Court of Justice ruled against Continental Can in a merger decision, and in 1974 moved against IBM in Europe, demanding that it obey the same standards of fair competition demanded of it in the United States.

These moves were made under Articles 85 and 86 of the Treaty of Rome, which prohibits agreements and practices that prevent, restrict, and distort competition. The interstate trade clause of the treaty includes trade with third countries, so that a company must be aware of the conduct of its affiliates.

The international marketer should be aware that the European Community Commission also exempts large categories of "good" cartels from Articles 85 and 86 in an effort to encourage the growth of certain businesses so they can compete on an equal footing with Japanese and U.S. companies and also permits selective distribution in some cases.[6]

Bribery

As Walter Guzzardi points out, history does not record a burst of international outrage when Charles M. Schwab presented a $200,000 diamond and pearl

---

[6]Robert T. Jones, "Executive's Guide to Antitrust in Europe," *Harvard Business Review,* May-June 1976, pp. 106–18.

necklace to the mistress of Czar Alexander's nephew, although in return for that consideration, Bethlehem Steel won the contract to supply the rails for the Trans-Siberian railroad.[7] Today, far less crass sales inducements are quickly and universally denounced when used by U.S. companies doing business abroad. We now are living in a post-Watergate age which requires continuous investigation, discovery, and condemnation.

The recent discussion of payments by international companies has demonstrated that there is an enormous difference across the globe in judgments about what is right and what is wrong. What emerges from this discussion is that even in the remotest cultures there are rights and wrongs on the extremes. This is not really a problem. The problem arises in the question of how you judge the gray areas—where most companies work.

In a report made by the SEC (Securities and Exchange Commission) to the Senate Committee on Banking, Housing and Urban Affairs, the commission recognized the difference between payments made to government officials "to procure special and unjustified favors" and those made "to persuade low-level government officials to perform functions that they are obliged to perform as part of their governmental responsibilities but which they may refuse or delay unless compensated." These SEC efforts at making practical distinctions in the type of payments involved in foreign operations are certainly a step in the right direction.

In 1977 the U.S. government passed a law called the Foreign Corrupt Practices Act, which makes it a crime for U.S. corporations to bribe an official of a foreign government or political party in order to obtain or retain business in a foreign country. The law requires publicly held companies to institute internal accounting controls and makes it a crime to make payments to any person when the company has reason to believe that part of the money will go to a foreign official. The law excludes government employees who are essentially ministerial or clerical and therefore permits payments to expedite shipments through customs or to secure permits. It is unclear as to whether the law permits the bribery of tax officials.[8]

When companies operate abroad, in the absence of home country legal constraints they face a continuum of choices concerning company ethics. At one extreme they can maintain home country ethics worldwide with absolutely no adjustment or adaptation to local practice. At the other extreme they can abandon any attempt to maintain company ethics and adapt entirely to local conditions and circumstances as they are perceived by company managers in each local environment. Between these extremes companies may select varying degrees of extension of home country ethics, or alternatively they may adapt in varying degrees to local customs and practices. For companies that are headquartered outside the United States, this theoretical range of choice is indeed the actual choice because with the

---

[7]Walter Guzzardi, Jr., "An Unscandalized View of Those 'Bribes' Abroad," *Fortune,* July 1976, pp. 118ff.

[8]"The Antibribery Bill Backfires," *Business Week,* April 17, 1978, p. 143.

exception of the United States no major industrial country attempts to establish the extraterritorial sovereignty of its laws. The United States has—either happily or regrettably depending on your point of view—an imperial tendency to impose U.S. laws and therefore U.S. values and mores on American companies and citizens worldwide. Most observers feel that while this tendency is not without substantial merit, when it is rigidly applied without any recognition of actual beliefs and competitive practices it often puts American companies in an impossible position vis-à-vis foreign competitors.

Jacoby, Nehmenkis, and Eells conclude that payments interfere with the workings of efficient markets and that companies should therefore avoid payoffs where they can.[9] But they feel that governments, not companies, have the most to do in rectifying this situation.

A recent article that focuses on the long tradition of close relations between powerful politicians and businessmen in the Philippines concludes:

> Is it fruitful to deal with a ministry and its technocrats when final decisions are made in the Presidential palace? Is it possible to play the local national sport without hiring local people who know the rules of the game, and who in fact are usually related to the referee?
>
> As long as authoritarian regimes are the rule in the Third World, and favoritism is part of it, foreign companies will continue to face decisions that may not agree with business ethics in their home countries.[10]

Congress should take a close look at the code of conduct recently adopted by the Organization for Economic Co-operation and Development (see the Appendix to this chapter). What is needed is legislation that will be clear about what is legal and what is not — legislation that will have useful applications in actual situations. Then marketers will be able to judge with some degree of certainty what is right and what is wrong. When this is done, marketers will be relieved of the burdens now imposed by standards that are clouded in a foggy morality.

CONCLUSION

Astute marketers use their awareness of the complexity of the legal environment to avoid situations that might result in conflict, misunderstanding, or outright violation of national laws. Clearly, there is no substitute for competent legal advice. This is especially true when operations extend internationally because it is less possible to rely on knowledge of law gained from personal experience.

---

[9] Neil H. Jacoby, Peter Nehmenkis, and Richard Eells, *Bribery and Extortion in World Business* (New York: Macmillan, 1966).

[10] "Payments for Foreign Contracts . . .," *Wall Street Journal,* January 27, 1978, p. 8.

BIBLIOGRAPHY

BOOKS

Jacoby, Neil H., Peter Nehemkis, and Richard Eells, *Bribery and Extortion in World Business*. New York: Macmillan, 1977.

Mangone, Gerard J., *The Elements of International Law*. Homewood, Ill.: Dorsey, 1967.

ARTICLES

Behrman, Jack N., "International Divestment: Panacea or Pitfall," *Looking Ahead*, National Planning Association, Vol. 18, No. 9, November-December 1970.

Bennet, Peter D., and Robert T. Green, "Political Instability as a Determinant of Direct Foreign Investment in Marketing," *Journal of Marketing Research*, 9, No. 2 (May 1972), 182-86.

Boddewyn, Jean, and Etienne F. Cracco, "The Political Game in World Business," *Columbia Journal of World Business*, January-February 1972, pp. 45-56.

Bradley, David G., "Managing against Expropriation," *Harvard Business Review*, July-August 1977.

deVries, Henry P., "Transnational Legal Trends," *Columbia Journal of World Business*, July-August 1969, pp. 79-80; and November-December 1969, pp. 81-82.

"Economic Implications of Proposed Changes in the Taxation of U.S. Investments Abroad," National Foreign Trade Council. New York, 1972.

Hawkins, Robert B., Norman Mintz, and Michael Provissiero, "Government Takeovers of U.S. Foreign Affiliates," *Journal of International Business Studies*, Spring 1976.

Holtzman, Howard, "Long-Term Multinational Disputes: A Challenge to Arbitration," *Arbitration Journal*, January 1970, pp. 234-38.

Howard, Fred, "Overview of International Taxation," *Columbia Journal of World Business*, 10, No. 2 (Summer 1975), 5-11.

——, "U.S. Income Tax Treaties," *Columbia Journal of World Business*, 10, No. 2 (Summer 1975), 21-28.

Jones, Robert T., "Executive's Guide to Antitrust in Europe," *Harvard Business Review*, May-June 1976, pp. 106-18.

Kalish, Richard II., and John Patrick Casey, "The Dilemma of the International Tax Executive," *Columbia Journal of World Business*, 10, No. 2 (Summer 1975), 62-73.

——, "The Tax Planning Process and the International Tax Executive," *Management Controls*, June 1976, pp. 91-100.

Kohlhagen, Steven W., "Host Country Policies and MNCs—The Pattern of Foreign Investment," *Columbia Journal of World Business*, 12, No. 1 (Spring 1977), 49-58.

Marshall, Byron K., "Japanese Business Ideology and Labor Policy," *Columbia Journal of World Business*, 12, No. 1 (Spring 1977), 22-29.

Peters, J. Irwin, "The New Industrial Property Laws in Mexico and Brazil—Implications for MNCs," *Columbia Journal of World Business,* 12, No. 1 (Spring 1977), 70–79.

Rapp, William V., "Japan: Its Industrial Policies and Corporate Behavior," *Columbia Journal of World Business,* 12, No. 1 (Spring 1977), 38–48.

Rummel, R. J., and David A. Heenan, "How Multinationals Analyze Political Risk," *Harvard Business Review,* January-February 1978, pp. 67–76.

Simons, W. W., "Government-Industry Partnership in the Third World: A United Nations Experiment Begins to Pay Off," *Columbia Journal of World Business,* 10, No. 3 (Fall 1975), 15–28.

Straus, Donald B., "Arbitration of Disputes between Multinational Corporations," *Arbitration Journal,* January 1970, pp. 228–34.

Summa, Donald J., "Remittances by U.S. Owned Foreign Corporations—Some Tax Considerations," *Columbia Journal of World Business,* 10, No. 2 (Summer 1975), 40–45.

Walters, Kenneth D., and R. Joseph Monsen, "The Nationalized Firm: The Politicians' Free Lunch?" *Columbia Journal of World Business,* 12, No. 1 (Spring 1977), 90–102.

WORLD ELECTRIC
(Business Ethics)

TO: Officers, General Managers and
Managers at Department Level and Higher

At our recent Division General Managers meeting, I called attention once again to the need for all Company employees to comply with the standards of proper business practices set forth in Policy Number 40.0.

In summary, that policy provides that no employee of World Electric or of any of its subsidiaries will arrange or make payments in the nature of kickbacks or bribes, nor will the Company and its subsidiaries use intermediate parties such as sales representatives for such purposes.

The wisdom of following such a policy has been borne out in the recent headlines and by the investigations conducted by various governmental agencies.

As in the case of other fundamental Company policies, such as those governing employee conflicts of interest and compliance with the antitrust laws, each of you has a dual responsibility, first, to comply personally with the policy, and, second, to promote full compliance by Company and subsidiary employees.

This latter responsibility entails a broad teaching function plus effective monitoring of the component for which you are responsible. In the execution of these functions it is, I believe, essential that your associates know that you stand unequivocally in support of the policy, and further that you are available to assist them in maintaining full compliance. We shall emphasize this subject in connection with annual strategic planning reviews.

Justin Balance
President

WORLD ELECTRIC
Policy Number 40.0

Subject: Business Ethics; Payments to Sales Representatives

NEED FOR A POLICY

It is the policy of World Electric Company to conduct its business affairs in strict compliance with all applicable laws. In particular, this policy requires a constant awareness and vigilance on the part of every employee to avoid violations of said laws arising out of a transfer directly or indirectly through commission payments or otherwise of anything of value (in the form of compensation, gift, contribution, or otherwise) to any employee, representative, person or organization in any way connected with or designated by any customer, private or governmental. Because of the severe penalties and severe consequences to the Company which participation in any such practice could produce under the laws of the United States and foreign countries, it is deemed necessary to single out such activity for clear and detailed prohibition by way of a Division Policy.

POLICY

1. No employee of the Division or an affiliate company acting on behalf of the Division shall offer, or commit to the making of, or make a transfer of anything of value (in the form of compensation, gift, contribution or otherwise) to any employee, representative, person or organization in any way connected with any customer, private or governmental. No such offer or commitment made by such employee will be honored, and the employee making the offer or commitment will be removed from his position and subject to further disciplinary action, including possible discharge.

2. No employee of the Division or an affiliate company acting on behalf of the Division shall make any offer or commitment for, or concur in the payment of, or pay any sales commission where the fact is made known to such employee that all, or some part, of such commission will be transferred to any employee, representative, person or organization in any way connected with any customer, private or governmental. Such offer or commitment will not be honored and any employee making such offer, commitment or concurrence shall be removed from his position and subject to further disciplinary action, including possible discharge.

3. Where any employee is requested to make, authorize or concur in any commitment or payment contrary to this Policy, the employee shall promptly report to his manager full details of such request.

4. The provisions of the foregoing paragraphs 1, 2 and 3 are not intended to apply to (i) reasonable business entertainment or to personal gifts of nominal value, provided such business entertainment or nominal value gifts are of the type customary in the particular commercial environment and do not violate any applicable law or regulation, or (ii) financial support or payments provided in accordance with Company Policy.

5. The contents of this Policy shall be communicated to all applicable personnel by operation, section and/or unit managers in meetings conducted to explain and clarify the intent of this Policy, and to answer any questions that may arise. These managers shall advise the Manager–Financial Operation by memorandum when their communications program is complete.

RESPONSIBILITY AND COUNSELING

Each Manager is responsible for the compliance of his personnel with this Policy. The Financial Operation shall be responsible for auditing compliance by all employees with this Policy. The Division Counsel will counsel on application and interpretation of this Policy.

QUESTIONS

1. Do you agree with Justin Balance concerning the wisdom of Policy Number 40.0? Why? Why not?

APPENDIX

ORGANIZATION FOR ECONOMIC CO-OPERATION AND DEVELOPMENT (OECD)

Guidelines for Multinational Enterprises

Member countries set forth the following guidelines for multinational enterprises with the understanding that Member countries will fulfil their responsibilities to treat enterprises equitably and in accordance with inter-

Organization for Economic Co-operation and Development, "Declaration by the Governments of OECD Member Countries and Decisions of the OECD Council on Guidelines for Multinational Enterprises," 1976.

national law and international agreements, as well as contractual obligations to which they have subscribed:

GENERAL POLICIES

Enterprises should

1. Take fully into account established general policy objectives of the Member countries in which they operate;
2. In particular, give due consideration to those countries' aims and priorities with regard to economic and social progress, including industrial and regional development, the protection of the environment, the creation of employment opportunities, the promotion of innovation and the transfer of technology;
3. While observing their legal obligations concerning information, supply their entities with supplementary information the latter may need in order to meet requests by the authorities of the countries in which those entities are located for information relevant to the activities of those entities, taking into account legitimate requirements of business confidentiality;
4. Favour close co-operation with the local community and business interests;
5. Allow their component entities freedom to develop their activities and to exploit their competitive advantage in domestic and foreign markets, consistent with the need for specialisation and sound commercial practice;
6. When filling responsible posts in each country of operation, take due account of individual qualifications without discrimination as to nationality, subject to particular national requirements in this respect;
7. Not render—and they should not be solicited or expected to render—any bribe or other improper benefit, direct or indirect, to any public servant or holder of public office;
8. Unless legally permissible, not make contributions to candidates for public office or to political parties or other political organisations;
9. Abstain from any improper involvement in local political activities.

DISCLOSURE OF INFORMATION

Enterprises should, having due regard to their nature and relative size in the economic context of their operations and to requirements of business confidentiality and to cost, publish in a form suited to improve public understanding a sufficient body of factual information on the structure, activities and policies of the enterprise as a whole, as a supplement, in so far as necessary for this purpose, to information to be disclosed under the national law of the individual countries in which they operate. To this end, they should publish within reasonable time limits, on a regular basis, but at least annually, financial statements and other pertinent information relating to the enterprise as a whole, comprising in particular:
   i. The structure of the enterprise, showing the name and location of the parent company, its main affiliates, its percentage ownership, direct and indirect, in these affiliates, including shareholdings between them;

ii. The geographical areas[1] where operations are carried out and the principal activities carried on therein by the parent company and the main affiliates;

iii. The operating results and sales by geographical area and the sales in the major lines of business for the enterprise as a whole;

iv. Significant new capital investment by geographical area and, as far as practicable, by major lines of business for the enterprise as a whole;

v. A statement of the sources and uses of funds by the enterprise as a whole;

vi. The average number of employees in each geographical area;

vii. Research and development expenditure for the enterprise as a whole;

viii. The policies followed in respect of intra-group pricing;

ix. The accounting policies, including those on consolidation, observed in compiling the published information.

COMPETITION

Enterprises should, while conforming to official competition rules and established policies of the countries in which they operate,

1. Refrain from actions which would adversely affect competition in the relevant market by abusing a dominant position of market power, by means of, for example,
   a. Anti-competitive acquisitions,
   b. Predatory behavior toward competitors,
   c. Unreasonable refusal to deal,
   d. Anti-competitive abuse of industrial property rights,
   e. Discriminatory (i.e. unreasonably differentiated) pricing and using such pricing transactions between affiliated enterprises as a means of affecting adversely competition outside these enterprises;

2. Allow purchasers, distributors and licensees freedom to resell, export, purchase and develop their operations consistent with law, trade conditions, the need for specialisation and sound commercial practice;

3. Refrain from participating in or otherwise purposely strengthening the restrictive effects of international or domestic cartels or restrictive agreements which adversely affect or eliminate competition and which are not generally or specifically accepted under applicable national or international legislation;

4. Be ready to consult and co-operate, including the provision of information, with competent authorities of countries whose interests are directly affected in regard to competition issues or investigations. Provision of

---

[1] For the purposes of the guideline on disclosure of information the term "geographical area" means groups of countries or individual countries as each enterprise determines is appropriate in its particular circumstances. While no single method of grouping is appropriate for all enterprises or for all purposes, the factors to be considered by an enterprise would include the significance of operations carried out in individual countries or areas as well as the effects on its competitiveness, geographic proximity, economic affinity, similarities in business environments and the nature, scale and degree of interrelationship of the enterprises' operations in the various countries.

information should be in accordance with safeguards normally applicable in this field.

FINANCING

Enterprises should, in managing the financial and commercial operations of their activities, and especially their liquid foreign assets and liabilities, take into consideration the established objectives of the countries in which they operate regarding balance of payments and credit policies.

TAXATION

Enterprises should

1. Upon request of the taxation authorities of the countries in which they operate, provide, in accordance with the safeguards and relevant procedures of the national laws of these countries, the information necessary to determine correctly the taxes to be assessed in connection with their operations in other countries:
2. Refrain from making use of the particular facilities available to them, such as transfer pricing which does not conform to an arm's length standard, for modifying in ways contrary to national laws the tax base on which members of the group are assessed.

EMPLOYMENT AND INDUSTRIAL RELATIONS

Enterprises should, within the framework of law, regulations and prevailing labour relations and employment practices, in each of the countries in which they operate,

1. Respect the right of their employees, to be represented by trade unions and other bona fide organisations of employees, and engage in constructive negotiations, either individually or through employers' associations, with such employee organisations with a view to reaching agreements on employment conditions, which should include provisions for dealing with disputes arising over the interpretation of such agreements, and for ensuring mutually respected rights and responsibilities;
2. a. Provide such facilities to representatives of the employees as may be necessary to assist in the development of effective collective agreements,
   b. Provide to representatives of employees information which is needed for meaningful negotiations on conditions of employment;
3. Provide to representatives of employees where this accords with local law and practice, information which enables them to obtain a true and fair view of the performance of the entity or, where appropriate, the enterprise as a whole;
4. Observe standards of employment and industrial relations not less favourable than those observed by comparable employers in the host country;
5. In their operations, to the greatest extent practicable, utilise, train and

prepare for upgrading members of the local labour force in co-operation with representatives of their employees and, where appropriate, the relevant governmental authorities;

6. In considering changes in their operations which would have major effects upon the livelihood of their employees, in particular in the case of the closure of an entity involving collective lay-offs or dismissals, provide reasonable notice of such changes to representatives of their employees, and where appropriate to the relevant governmental authorities, and co-operate with the employee representatives and appropriate governmental authorities so as to mitigate to the maximum extent practicable adverse effects;

7. Implement their employment policies including hiring, discharge, pay, promotion and training without discrimination unless selectivity in respect of employee characteristics is in furtherance of established governmental policies which specifically promote greater equality of employment opportunity;

8. In the context of bona fide negotiations[2] with representatives of employees on conditions of employment, or while employees are exercising a right to organise, not threaten to utilise a capacity to transfer the whole or part of an operating unit from the country concerned in order to influence unfairly those negotiations or to hinder the exercise of a right to organise;

9. Enable authorised representatives of their employees to conduct negotiations on collective bargaining or labour management relations issues with representatives of management who are authorised to take decisions on the matters under negotiation.

SCIENCE AND TECHNOLOGY

Enterprises should

1. Endeavour to ensure that their activities fit satisfactorily into the scientific and technological policies and plans of the countries in which they operate, and contribute to the development of national scientific and technological capacities, including as far as appropriate the establishment and improvement in host countries of their capacity to innovate;

2. To the fullest extent practicable, adopt in the course of their business activities practices which permit the rapid diffusion of technologies with due regard to the protection of industrial and intellectual property rights;

3. When granting licences for the use of industrial property rights or when otherwise transferring technology do so on reasonable terms and conditions.

[2] Bona fide negotiations may include labour disputes as part of the process of negotiation. Whether or not labour disputes are so included will be determined by the law and prevailing employment practices of particular countries.

the financial framework

Though mothers and fathers give us life, it is money alone
which preserves it.

Ihara Saikaku, 1642–93

(The Japanese Family Storehouse;
or The Millionaires' Gospel, Book One)

INTRODUCTION

The multinational marketer is exposed to foreign exchange risk whenever his business involves either payments or receipts in foreign currencies or the ownership of assets valued in foreign currencies. This chapter focuses on the major factors that affect foreign exchange rates. The chapter begins with a description of the foreign exchange market where currency values are established, and continues with a section on balance of payments, the accounting tool that provides a summary of the economic transactions between a country and the rest of the world. The concept of balance-of-payments disequilibrium is explained, and typical government responses to balance-of-payments disequilibrium are described. The chapter then examines the international monetary system as it has evolved over the past century and concludes with a discussion of future prospects in the international financial area and a brief section on forecasting foreign exchange rates.

CURRENCY SUPPLY AND DEMAND

Exhibit 7-1 shows a supply curve of U.S. dollars and two demand schedules for dollars by holders of German deutsche marks. In the example, demand moves from D1 to D2, with a resultant increase in the price of dollars from 2.5 to 5.0 deutsche marks. In this example, we assume that the supply of dollars is constant and that

EXHIBIT 7-1.

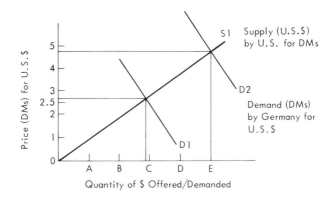

THE FOREIGN EXCHANGE MARKET

DM = Deutschmarks

Quantity of $ Offered/Demanded

C = Equilibrium of supply and demand for U.S. $

D1 = 2.5 DMs = $1.00
D2 = 5.0 DMs = $1.00

EXCHANGE RISKS AND GAINS IN FOREIGN TRANSACTION

Foreign Exchange Rates	$1M Contract		DM 4M Contract	
	U.S. Seller Receives	Germany Buyer Pays	U.S. Seller Receives	Germany Buyer Pays
DM 4 = $1	$1M	DM4	$1M	DM4
DM 3 = $1	$1M	DM3	$1.33M	DM4
DM 2 = $1	$1M	DM2	$2M	DM4

for various reasons the demand for dollars by holders of deutsche marks increases from quantity C to quantity E. Such an increase in demand could result from a multiplicity of factors; for example, a major shift in German consumer automobile preferences from domestic and other foreign cars to cars imported from the United States. In such a hypothetical case—assuming that all other things were equal and unchanging—there would indeed be an increase in demand by Germany for dollars and the price of dollars would rise. This would result in an increase in the price of DMs of U.S. dollars or, put another way, a devaluation of the deutsche mark and a revaluation of the U.S. dollar.

The point of this illustration is simply to indicate that the price of one currency in any other currency is a result of forces of supply and demand as expressed in the foreign exchange market. The foreign exchange market itself consists of traders operating principally by telephone and teletype engaging in transactions to meet customer requirements with their counterparts in banks and foreign exchange trading houses around the world. These foreign exchange traders are operating during normal business hours in every world time zone, with the result that foreign exchange trading activity is being conducted on a twenty-four-hour basis every day of the year. When the traders on one side of the world conclude their work at the end of their working day, the basis of prices for their trading on the following working day will be established on the other side of the world while they are sleeping.

The purchases and sales in the foreign exchange market represent supply and demand of each of the world's traded currencies deriving from actual trade in goods and services, as well as short- and long-term capital flows and speculative purchases and sales. To the extent that a country sells more than it buys, there will be a greater demand for its currency and a tendency for it to appreciate in value. If the foreign exchange market were influenced only by purchases and sales to support actual trade in goods and services, it would be a rather simple matter to forecast foreign exchange rates. Unfortunately, there are many other forces and motives for buying and selling currencies. Short- and long-term capital flows and speculative purchases and sales are a major source of supply and demand for foreign exchange. Short-term capital is sensitive to interest rates, long-term capital to return expectations, and both are sensitive to perceptions of risk.

Governments intervene regularly in the foreign exchange market to either support or depress the price of their own or other currencies. This is considered a legitimate government function and is normally aimed at either dampening the fluctuations in foreign exchange rates or attempting to influence over the short and medium term the actual exchange rate. For example, many governments are reluctant to see the value of their currency appreciate because their exporters fear the effects that rising exchange value will have on their price competitiveness in foreign markets. In response to this basic domestic pressure, governments have been known to engage in extensive trading to stem the rise in their own currency value. A good example of this in the 1970s was the government of Japan, which acquired foreign currency reserves in excess of $30 billion in an attempt to stem the rise of the Japanese yen.

While government efforts in the long run will not prevail against underlying factors, they can have a profound effect on exchange values in the short and medium run.

Another major factor influencing the foreign exchange market is expectations concerning future developments. Expectations will have a major influence on speculative decisions to purchase or sell any currency.

The foreign exchange market deals in two basic types of transactions: a so-called spot transaction, which is a sale or purchase for immediate delivery; and a future or forward transaction, which is a commitment to take or deliver a currency at a specified future date. Depending on expectations for a currency, it will sell at either a premium or a discount vis-à-vis the dollar or any other currency in the futures market.

Thus the foreign exchange market consists literally of a buyer's and a seller's market where currencies are traded for both spot and future delivery on a continuous basis. As such, this market represents one example of a true market where prices are based on the combination of forces of supply and demand that come into play at the moment of any transaction. A currency in this market is worth what people are willing to pay for it or, put another way, it is worth what people are prepared to sell it for.

BALANCE OF PAYMENTS

A major and invaluable tool for understanding the forces affecting the foreign exchange market is the balance of payments. This device is an accountant's construction for reporting all the economic transactions between a country and the rest of the world. Exhibit 7-2 is a simplified listing of balance-of-payments accounts. Above the line there are three headings. The first is the *current account,* which is the account for all transactions that are on a recurring basis, such as merchandise trade, travel, income received on investments abroad, dividends paid to foreign investors, military expenditures and receipts, and foreign aid (either gifts or receipts). The second heading is the *capital account,* which is divided into short term and long term. Short-term capital is any financial instrument with a maturity of less than one year. The major category of short-term capital transactions is, of course, demand deposits. Long-term capital is divided into two categories: direct investment and portfolio investment. Direct investment is any investment in which the holding of the investor is 20 percent or more of the total equity of the company or enterprise in question. Any holding of less than 20 percent is in most countries treated as a so-called portfolio investment.

The third heading above the line is *errors and omissions,* which is an account that enables the balance-of-payments statistician to balance the balance of payments by plugging in a figure that will make the entire balance of payments come out to zero. (More about this in a subsequent paragraph).

Below the line in Exhibit 7-2 the heading is *official reserves* and includes

EXHIBIT 7-2. Balance of Payments—
A Simplified Statement of Accounts

Current Account
  Merchandise trade
  Travel
  Income on investments
  Military expenditure
  Aid and gifts
Capital Account
  Short term
  Long term
    Direct investment
    Portfolio investment
Errors and Omissions

Official Reserves
  Foreign exchange
  Gold
  SDRs
  IMF position

---

foreign exchange, gold, SDRs, and IMF position. The official reserves are exactly equal to the net amount of the above-the-line surplus or deficit with the opposite sign. For example, if above the line there is an overall surplus of, say, $1 billion, below-the-line official reserves will increase by $1 billion. The above-the-line surplus will be shown with a plus sign, and the below-the-line increase will be referenced with a minus sign. This is a confusing accounting convention, and the student of the balance of payments must simply remember that below the line a minus sign indicates an increase, whereas a plus sign indicates a decrease. This is necessary in order to make the sum of the above- and below-the-line totals add to zero.

Applying this to another example, assume that above the line there is an overall deficit of $1 billion. This will be offset by a decline in official reserves of $1 billion, which will be represented by a plus sign in the balance-of-payments report. These examples illustrate the function of reserves. They provide a buffer that enables a country to have both surpluses and deficits, and they release countries from the necessity of operating on an exact balance with the rest of the world on a year-to-year basis.

Theoretically reserves should simply offset temporary periods of surplus or decline. Any secular or long-term tendency toward surplus or deficit should be recognized by an adjustment in the country's actual exchange rate. In practice, countries have a tendency to get into secular or long-term positions of surplus and deficit vis-à-vis the rest of the world. Japan and Germany are two countries who have for more than two decades been in a surplus position vis-à-vis the rest of the world. The United States is an example of a country that is in a deficit position. The reason for the United States being in a secular deficit position is that the U.S. dollar is a major official reserve currency. Thus, if the United States spends more than it receives in revenues, it pays for its surplus of expenditure with dollars that end up in the reserve asset portfolio of the central banks of surplus countries such as Japan and Germany. Many observers believe that the ability of the United States to operate with persistent deficits vis-à-vis the rest of the world undermines the strength of the U.S. economy and simultaneously weakens the international economic order by contributing to worldwide inflation.

ALTERNATIVE GOVERNMENT RESPONSES
TO BALANCE-OF-PAYMENTS DISEQUILIBRIUM

The first response to balance-of-payments disequilibrium is to do nothing. If a country has accumulated reserves, it is in the position of being able to do absolutely nothing in response to a balance-of-payments deficit. Alternatively, if a country is in a surplus position, it can accumulate reserves. Obviously a country has much more freedom to accumulate reserves than it does to give them up because when reserves go to zero, the ability to give up reserves is exhausted. On the other hand, there is no theoretical limit to the amount of reserves that a country might choose to accumulate.

When a country has exhausted its reserves or, alternatively, has decided that it does not wish to accumulate further reserves (or more likely has submitted to pressure from trading partners to put limits on or to end the accumulation of reserves), a second line of response is to interfere with transactions. The most publicized forms of interference are in the current account of the balance of payments and consist of import and export controls, subsidies and taxes on imports and exports, dividend restrictions, and travel restrictions. A deficit country will seek to encourage exports and limit imports with controls, administrative "guidance," and subsidies and taxes. Dividend restrictions and travel restrictions are other examples of ways of limiting current account balance-of-payments outflows.

The capital accounts provide another major area of interference. Governments have at their disposal various ways of limiting or encouraging foreign direct and portfolio investments and short-term capital flows. The Swiss, for example, have from time to time required foreign demand deposit holders to pay interest on Swiss franc deposits to discourage the inflow of foreign deposits.

A third major line of government response is to adjust the country's basic economic policies. This might take the form of an adjustment in interest rates, government spending, programs to restrain inflation, programs to restrict and limit domestic demand (particularly demand for foreign goods), and, finally, programs to improve productivity and international competitiveness. The last-mentioned government program should be the first employed to deal with the balance-of-payments disequilibrium, but unfortunately it is often the last.

A fourth major way of responding to a balance-of-payments disequilibrium is to devalue, revalue, or let the currency simply float and to rely on the foreign exchange market to bring about equilibrium.

THE INTERNATIONAL MONETARY SYSTEM

Today's international monetary system is a descendant of the system established in 1944 at Bretton Woods, New Hampshire, by the Allied powers. The Bretton Woods system aimed to create a world of fixed stable exchange rates to encourage trade and investment and international economic integration. There was a feeling at the conference that World War II had in part been the result of the breakdown of international economic cooperation in the 1930s when countries increasingly retreated into economic autarchy behind barriers of high tariffs and exchange control. The major aim of the Bretton Woods conference was to create an international monetary system that would ensure (1) currency convertibility and (2) fixed exchange rates. The Allied powers believed that such a system would promote trade and investment and contribute to international economic cooperation, which was seen as a cornerstone of broader cooperation between various nations of the world.

The five major elements of the system designed at Bretton Woods were as follows:

1. Fixed or pegged exchange values. All currencies were defined in terms of

their value vis-à-vis the U.S. dollar, and the U.S. dollar was defined in terms of its value vis-à-vis gold. Thus, in effect, all currencies had an official gold exchange value.

2. Each country committed itself to maintain its currency values within plus or minus 1 percent of the pegged or fixed value. If a currency fluctuated in exchange markets outside of the pegged limits, central banks were committed to intervene by purchasing or selling their own currency and other currencies in order to maintain the pegged or fixed value.

3. The U.S. dollar was valued at 1 troy ounce of gold equal to 35 U.S. dollars. This was the official value of the U.S. dollar and the United States government unilaterally committed itself to exchange official dollars, that is to say, dollars held by central banks of member countries of the International Monetary Fund, for gold at the rate of 1 troy ounce for each 35 official dollars. This commitment did not apply to privately held dollars. This was known as the Gold Exchange Value of the U.S. dollar and was limited to officially held dollars.

4. The reserves under the system were gold, foreign exchange, and the International Fund position. The principal foreign exchange reserve was the U.S. dollar, and in 1944 the secondary reserve currency was the pound sterling. Over the years the pound sterling declined in importance as a reserve currency while the U.S. dollar increased in importance. The IMF position is a small and technical element of the country reserves and has never been significant as part of the total world reserves.

5. The last element of the Bretton Woods system was the provision for adjustment in fixed exchange values in the event of a persistent disequilibrium in balance of payments between a country and the rest of the world. In such cases a country was permitted to devalue its currency or was expected to revalue its currencies in accordance with procedures spelled out by the International Monetary Fund.

The expectation of the architects of the Bretton Woods system was that these adjustments would be taken promptly and that they would reflect the actual value of a currency and restore equilibrium in the system. In practice such adjustments were infrequent, typically rather large in amount, and often adopted too late to restore equilibrium.

In 1971, because of the persistent deficits of the United States in balance of payments, other countries had accumulated over 50 billion U.S. dollars in their official reserve accounts and private holders overseas had accumulated over 150 billion U.S. dollars. It was clear in 1971 that the U.S. gold reserve position of roughly $10 billion was only one-fifth of the total dollar reserves held directly by foreign governments and only one-twentieth of all foreign-held dollars. For many years the world had simply chosen to ignore the fact that the gold exchange value of the U.S. dollar was indeed a mere fiction because the U.S. government would be unable to redeem all central bank official dollars for gold at the official price of 1 troy ounce equal to 35 U.S. dollars. By 1971 the tension surrounding this gap between the original intention and the actuality resulted in a decision by

President Nixon to unilaterally terminate the U.S. government commitment to exchange gold for official dollars at the price of 35 dollars to the ounce. The first move was a "devaluation" of the U.S. dollar by increasing its gold exchange value, which very quickly gave way to a decision by the U.S. government to allow the U.S. dollar to "float" against other currencies—that is, to allow the dollar to find its exchange value vis-à-vis other currencies in the foreign exchange markets of the world without central bank support. Since 1971 the international monetary system has evolved into what could best be described as a managed dirty float with SDRs (special drawing rights). "Managed" and "dirty" refer to the fact that central banks regularly seek to control or influence exchange markets by buying and selling to support or reduce currency values. Thus values reflect market forces *and* regulatory forces.

The SDR

In 1968 members of the IMF agreed on a scheme to provide systematic and controlled additions to world liquidity through the creation of so-called special drawing rights. As reserve assets, SDRs are created and allocated by the members of the IMF to the participating governments as credit on their books at the IMF in Washington. Member countries agree that within certain constraints SDRs will be transferable among central banks in exchange for convertible currencies needed for settlement of payments imbalances. Initially the SDR was defined in terms of a fixed quantity of gold. The initial allocations began in 1970 and lapsed after 1972, reflecting a widespread view that world reserves were more than adequate following a massive official deficit incurred by the United States in the final years of the Bretton Woods era of fixed exchange rates. In 1974, as part of an effort at continuing reform of the international monetary system, a new valuation mechanism was adopted for the SDR, which dropped all connections with gold or artificial currency conversion rates. The SDR was defined at this time as a basket of currencies, with each component of the basket and hence the basket itself to be valued at prevailing spot market exchange rates. Table 7-1 shows the agreed composition of the basket in terms of the units of each currency. The IMF calculates daily an official value of the SDR first in terms of the dollar and then in terms of other currencies.

The weights adopted for the sixteen currencies included in the SDR basket are based upon the country of issue's share of world merchandise trade and of world gross domestic product.

As a unit of value reflecting the average of the currencies in the SDR basket, the SDR presents many attractive qualities. It is an average and therefore will always reflect less upward and downward appreciation than currencies at the extreme points in the basket.

Although the total quantity of SDRs created is small in comparison with total world reserves, the significance of this addition to world liquidity lies in the potential expansion in its use rather than its actual importance today. The existence of a created and managed international reserve asset is a major act of economic

TABLE 7-1. The IMF SDR Currency Basket

Currencies of:	Units of Each Currency
United States	0.40
Germany	0.38
United Kingdom	0.045
France	0.44
Japan	26.0
Canada	0.071
Italy	47.0
Netherlands	0.14
Belgium	1.60
Sweden	0.13
Australia	0.012
Denmark	0.11
Norway	0.099
Spain	1.1
Austria	0.22
South Africa	0.0082

Source: Morgan Guaranty Trust Co., "World Financial Markets," August 19, 1975, p. 1.

cooperation and could indeed be the forerunner of a world currency. For the present the SDR is more of a symbol than an actual working international reserve.

FORECASTING FOREIGN EXCHANGE RATES

One of the most valuable tools for forecasting long-term foreign exchange rates is the so-called purchasing power parity theory. Table 7-2 illustrates the basis of this theory with actual data from Argentina and Brazil over the 1954-67 period. In Table 7-2 the reader will note that there is no year-to-year relationship between the dollar exchange rate and the cost of living for either Argentina or Brazil. The two columns' depreciation or devaluation of the Argentine peso and the Brazilian cruzeiro and an increase in the cost of living in each of the countries seem to fluctuate without any relationship to each other. However, if you glance at the averages at the bottom of the table, you will see that there is a remarkable similarity between the dollar depreciation of the peso and the cruzeiro and the increase in cost of living. This similarity reflects the so-called purchasing power parity value of the peso and the cruzeiro. According to purchasing power parity, the value of a country's currency will decline or increase vis-à-vis other currencies to the extent that inflation in the country is greater or less than the average rate of inflation in the rest of the world. In Argentina in the period reviewed, the cost of living increased 29 percent between 1954 and 1967 and the value of the peso declined 31 percent. In the 1961-67 period the cost of living increased 25 percent, whereas the value of the peso declined 25 percent. In the 1964-67 period the cost of living increased 28 percent as compared with a 28 percent depreciation in the value of the peso. In other words, as the cost of living increased the exchange value of the peso declined. This illustrates the purchasing power parity principle.

TABLE 7-2. Percentage Annual Increases in Dollar Rates of National Currencies and Cost of Living in Two Latin American Countries, 1954–67.

	Argentina			Brazil	
Year	Dollar %*	COL%†		Dollar %*	COL%†
1954	0	4		38	19
1956	3	13		1	22
1958	89	32		53	15
1960	0	27		0	35
1962	61	28		49	52
1964	14	22		198	86
1966	31	32		0	46
1967	42	28		22	30
Averages					
1954–67	31	29		39	39
1961–67	25	25		54	55
1964–67	28	28		60	58

*Percentage of devaluation of Argentine peso or Brazilian cruzeiro.
†Percentage increase in cost of living.

The purchasing power parity theory proposes that over the long run, currencies are valued for what they will buy at home. Here is how the theory works: Assume that a unit of currency A will purchase four times as many goods in country A as a unit of currency B does in country B. Then the equilibrium purchasing/ power parity exchange rate of A for B is 4. If the market exchange rate is higher than 4, A is overvalued. If it is lower than 4, it is undervalued. If A were overvalued at, say 4 1/2, this would result in people buying more from B because things would be cheaper there, and people in B would buy less from A because things would be more expensive there. This imbalance will push A's exchange rate down toward 4, and the converse forces will push to adjust the undervalued B currency.

The purchasing power parity theory will forecast exchange rates in the long run. In the short and medium run many forces other than the purchasing power of a currency operate to influence exchange value. Exhibit 7–3 lists sixteen different factors that must be taken into account in any effort to forecast currency value changes. The balance of payments is, as we have already pointed out, an analytical presentation which records a country's economic relationship with the rest of the world. While it is not within the scope of this book to explore balance-of-payments accounting in depth and the use of the balance of payments as a forecasting tool, it is evident that certain accounts in the balance of payments, especially the merchandise trade account, are excellent indicators of the economic strength of the country vis-à-vis the rest of the world. If a country is in a trade surplus, this is an indication that at current price levels the world buys more from that country than the country buys from the world. This means that not only price levels but also the general attractiveness of the goods and services that the country offers are competitive in world markets. It also means that they are competitive not only in the eyes of foreigners but also in the eyes of domestic purchasers.

Many other financial factors must be taken into account in forecasting cur-

EXHIBIT 7-3. Elements in Forecasting Currency Value Changes

Economic Factors
 1. Balance of payments
 2. Monetary reserves of the government
 3. Extent of foreign indebtedness and willingness of foreigners to retain it
 4. Present and anticipated economic strength of trading partners
 5. Monetary and fiscal policies of the government
 6. Trade, exchange, capital controls/incentives

Relational Factors
 7. Domestic inflation relative to world average rate of inflation
 8. Importance of currency
 9. Importance of country in total world commerce or certain items of trade
10. Elasticities of supply/demand for goods, services, and capital

Political Factors
11. History of past changes
12. Personal philosophies of government officials
13. Party philosophies
14. Proximity of elections

Expectational Factors
15. Opinions of bankers and businessmen and government officials and experts
16. Forward market rates/black market

Significance of Factors
  I. Factors 1–4 determine whether a currency ought to devalue under existing conditions.
 II. Factors 5 and 6 determine the possibility of relieving pressure on the currency through policy measures. Will it be effective?
III. Factors 8–10 determine results of currency value change on balance of payments. How much should it be?
 IV. Factors 11–14 are political considerations for estimating government intentions. These factors are less important with floating rates. With fixed rates, they are critical for estimating timing and amounts of devaluations/revaluations.
  V. Factors 15–16 can be seen as leading indicators.

rency values. Monetary reserves of a government indicate the extent to which a government is capable of intervening to support its currency value in exchange markets. A government with reserves has the freedom to use those reserves to intervene in exchange markets, whereas a government without reserves lacks this freedom. The extent of foreign indebtedness and the willingness of foreigners to retain the country's debt are important measures of a country's ability to borrow. A country that has, for example, exhausted its reserves can borrow if foreigners are willing to lend. The United States is in a unique position vis-à-vis this factor inasmuch as the U.S. dollar is a major reserve currency held by foreign central banks as part of their reserve assets and also a widely accepted currency in financial markets all over the world.

The strength of a country's economic trading partners must be taken into account in forecasting. This estimation, of course, is relative. A country may be doing rather well economically, but if its trading partners are doing even better this will result in a relative decline in the country's currency value. Monetary and fiscal policies of government are a major factor affecting the exchange rate. If government policies permit or encourage inflation, or if they permit or encourage balance-of-payments deficits, this must be taken into account in any forecasting of future currency values.

The last item on the list of economic factors—trade, exchange, and capital controls incentives—can of course have a major short-term effect on currency value, but in the longer run they cannot increase the attractiveness of a country's competitive offering.

Three relational factors must be taken into account in forecasting. If a currency is a major reserve currency, it holds a very different position in the world economy than does a currency that is used only as a national currency. Elasticities of supply and demand for a country's goods, services, and capital are very important. If, for example, a country's major export product is a commodity, the demand for this commodity will be critical to any realistic forecast of the country's currency value. In some cases, a country's major export products have been displaced by substitute materials having a major impact on the currency value because of the decline in value of the country's major export commodity. This happened to Tanzania with sisal, a fiber whose major application was in the manufacture of baler twine. The increasing use of synthetic materials and wire-tied balers has reduced the total demand for sisal and has depressed prices. Another example is the manufactured goods offered by a country like Britain, whose companies have not been able to remain competitive with companies in countries like Japan. The latter are much more sensitive to market preferences and do a much better job of meeting market demand.

In addition to these economic factors, political factors must be taken into account to assess the possible directions of government policy which, as we have already seen, can have a major effect on currencies' short- and medium-term value. Finally, expectational factors must be taken into account. In the world there are facts, and one of the facts that must be recognized is that which people believe is a "fact." If people believe that something is going to happen they will act accordingly, and if they are wrong the actual development will have caused an adjustment, but until actual development demonstrates the error of their belief the belief will operate as the major determining fact. Therefore in forecasting exchange values or any other value, we must take into account the expectations that exist among those who are in a position to buy and sell currencies.

RESPONDING TO EXPECTED DEVALUATION
OR EXCHANGE RATE RESTRICTIONS

If it is concluded that a currency will devalue, there are many appropriate defensive steps that may be taken to ensure that a company's assets and financial position will be preserved and protected. Exhibit 7–4 lists ten of the most frequently employed defensive moves, which seek to ensure that to the extent possible, purchases and remittances are transacted at the best possible foreign exchange rate, payments are delayed when due from stronger currency sources, cash holdings in weak currencies are minimized, forward contracts are used to confirm exchange rates for

EXHIBIT 7-4. Summary of Various Methods of Responding to Expected Adversity from Devaluation or Exchange Restrictions

---

(Relative attractiveness depends on their availability and cost-benefit analysis)
1. Prearrange suitable sources of domestic and foreign exchange financing.
2. Speed up timing and/or increase size of remittances from local affiliate
    —Dividends
    —Best repayment; interest
    —Intercompany account
3. Negotiate in advance permissible FX remittances.
4. Lag payment of foreign receivables of weak currency affiliate.
5. Minimize holdings of local currency cash and near-cash assets.
6. Incur indebtedness in local currency rather than stronger foreign currency.
7. Alter transfer prices on international sales and purchases.
8. Enter into forward currency contracts.
9. Build up stock of imported supplies and equipment.
10. Establish terms of payment for corporate sales to be in strong currency.

---

future receipts and obligations, inventories are built up at pre-devaluation prices, and whenever possible sales are booked in stronger currencies. If a currency is expected to appreciate in value, the appropriate policy move would be to simply reverse the action indicated for expected devaluation. For example, if devaluation is expected, purchases of foreign exchange should be made at current rates. If revaluation or appreciation is expected, purchases of foreign currency should be delayed as long as possible.

CONCLUSION

Foreign exchange risk is a fact of life for the international marketer. This chapter has described the evolving international financial framework and the forces and factors that determine foreign exchange rates. The principal analytic tool for identifying factors that affect foreign exchange rates is the balance of payments, a systematic record of all the economic transactions between a country and the rest of the world. Whenever a country is in a surplus or deficit position on its balance of payments, it is said to be in a state of disequilibrium. If the disequilibrium is perceived as a fundamental disequilibrium rather than a temporary fluctuation, this perception will be reflected in either appreciation or depreciation of the national currency in the foreign exchange markets of the world.

Forecasting foreign exchange rates requires a skillful combination of art and science. The *science* is required to identify and quantify the fundamental economic factors that are at work, and the *art* is required to evaluate intentions of political leaders and businessmen as well as the expectations of market participants. Foreign exchange rate forecasting is no job for an amateur. The purpose of this chapter has not been to create international financial experts or foreign exchange rate forecasters but rather to provide a basic background of understanding that will enable international marketers to use international finance specialists more effectively and creatively.

BIBLIOGRAPHY

Ankrom, Robert K., "Top Level Approach to the Foreign Exchange Problem," *Harvard Business Review,* July-August 1974, pp. 79–90.

Bennett, Jack F., "A Free Dollar Makes Sense," *Foreign Policy,* Winter 1975–76, pp. 63–75.

Bergsten, C. Fred, "New Urgency for Monetary Reform," *Foreign Policy,* Summer 1975, pp. 79–93.

Burns, Arthur F., "The Need for Order in International Finance," *Columbia Journal of World Business,* 12 (Spring 1977), 5–13.

Evans, Michael K., and John F. Norris, "International Business and Forecasting," *Columbia Journal of World Business,* 11(Winter 1976), 28–35.

Folks, William R., Jr., and Stanley R. Stansell, "The Use of Discriminant Analysis in Forecasting Exchange Rate Movement," *Journal of International Business Studies,* Spring 1975, pp. 33–50.

Giddy, Ian H., and Gunter Dufey, "The Random Behavior of the Flexible Exchange Rates: Implications for Forecasting," *Journal of International Business Studies,* Spring 1975, pp. 1–32.

Gull, Don S., "Composite Foreign Exchange Risk," *Columbia Journal of World Business,* 10(Fall 1975), 51–69.

Hagemann, Helmut, "Anticipate Your Long-Term Foreign Exchange Risks," *Harvard Business Review,* March-April 1977, pp. 81–89.

Kaikati, Jack G., "The Reincarnation of Barter Trade as a Marketing Tool," *Journal of Marketing,* April 1976, pp. 17–24.

Karchere, Alvin J., "Economic Forecasting in International Business," *Columbia Journal of World Business,* 11(Winter 1976), 62–69.

Kohlhagen, Steven W., "The Performance of the Foreign Exchange Markets 1971–1974," *Journal of International Business Studies,* Fall 1975, pp. 33–40.

Labys, Walter C., "International Commodity Markets, Models and Forecasts," *Columbia Journal of World Business,* 11(Winter 1976), 36–45.

Ness, Walter L., Jr., "U.S. Corporate Income Taxation and the Dividend Remission Policy of Multinational Corporations," *Journal of International Business Studies,* Spring 1975, pp. 67–78.

Oppenheim, V. H., "Whose World Bank?" *Foreign Policy,* Summer 1975, pp. 99–108.

Rippe, Richard D., "The Integration of Corporate Forecasting and Planning," *Columbia Journal of World Business,* 11(Winter 1976), 54–61.

Rogalski, Richard J., and Joseph D. Vinso, "Price Level Variations as Predictors of Flexible Exchange Rates," *Journal of International Business Studies,* Spring/Summer 1977, pp. 71–82.

Shapiro, Alan C., "Evaluating Financing Costs for Multinational Subsidiaries," *Journal of International Business Studies,* Fall 1975, pp. 25–32.

Teck, Alan, "Control Your Exposure to Foreign Exchange," *Harvard Business Review,* January-February 1974, pp. 66–75.

Weigand, Robert E., "International Trade without Money," *Harvard Business Review,* November-December 1977, pp. 28–56.

HOW TO READ INTERNATIONAL FINANCIAL STATISTICS

Exhibit 1 shows sections of the United States pages from *International Financial Statistics* of May 1978, published by the International Monetary Fund. This section indicates the kind of data that can be extracted from this valuable source. *International Financial Statistics* is published monthly and is available in every library or on a subscription basis for your own personal or company library. Line 1ad on pages 396 and 397 shows that U.S. gold reserves declined from $22 billion in 1953 to $11.8 billion in 1977. Interestingly, total U.S. reserves were less in 1977 than they were in 1953. Meanwhile, line 4d shows that U.S. external liabilities increased from $11.3 billion to $192 billion. Thus the international reserve position of the United States was immeasurably weaker in 1977 than it was in 1953 when the dollar was, as they say in Texas, real money. On pages 398–99, interest prices and production data show what happened to price levels, wages, and production over a twenty-five-year period. Consumer prices, for example, in 1977 on an index were at 112.7 as compared with 100 in 1975 and 49.7 in 1953. These data come from line 64. What this means is that in twenty-five years consumer prices increased 2.27 times or, put another way, consumer prices in 1977 were 226 percent of prices in 1953.

The international transaction beginning with line 70 tells a great deal about the position of the United States in the world economy. As can be seen on line 70,

EXHIBIT 1. Sections of the United States Pages—*International Financial Statistics*

	1953	1954	1955	1956	1957	1958	1959	1960	1961	1962	1963	1964	1965	1966	1967
											End of Period (sa and sc) Period Averages (sb and sd)				
sa	1.00000	1.00000	1.00000	1.00000	1.00000	1.00000	1.00000	1.00000	1.00000	1.00000	1.00000	1.00000	1.00000	1.00000	1.00000
sb	1.00000	1.00000	1.00000	1.00000	1.00000	1.00000	1.00000	1.00000	1.00000	1.00000	1.00000	1.00000	1.00000	1.00000	1.00000
sc	1.00000	1.00000	1.00000	1.00000	1.00000	1.00000	1.00000	1.00000	1.00000	1.00000	1.00000	1.00000	1.00000	1.00000	1.00000
sd	1.00000	1.00000	1.00000	1.00000	1.00000	1.00000	1.00000	1.00000	1.00000	1.00000	1.00000	1.00000	1.00000	1.00000	1.00000
														Par Value in May	
am x	....	....	....	....	....	....	....	....	....	....	....	....	....	....	....
														Billions of US Dollars:	
1..d	23.46	22.98	22.80	23.67	24.83	22.54	21.51	19.36	18.75	17.22	16.84	16.67	15.45	14.88	14.83
1a.d	22.09	21.79	21.75	22.06	22.86	20.58	19.51	17.80	16.95	16.06	15.60	15.47	14.07	13.24	12.07
1b.d	—	—	—	—	—	—	—	—	—	—	—	—	—	—	—
1c.d	1.37	1.19	1.04	1.61	1.98	1.96	2.00	1.55	1.69	1.06	1.04	.77	.60	.33	.42
1ca d	—	—	—	—	—	—	—	—	—	—	—	—	—	—	—
1d.d	—	—	—	—	—	—	—	—	.12	.10	.21	.43	.78	1.32	2.35
2dc d	-.65	-.46	-.32	-.88	-1.24	-1.22	-.92	-.49	-.64	-.03	-.02	.23	.38	.90	.79
2f.d	2.75	2.75	2.75	2.75	2.75	2.75	4.13	4.13	4.13	4.13	4.13	4.13	4.13	5.16	5.16
4..d	11.36	12.45	13.52	15.29	15.82	16.84	19.43	21.03	22.94	24.27	26.39	29.36	29.57	31.02	35.67
4a.d	....	....	....	....	....	....	10.12	11.09	11.83	12.91	14.43	15.78	15.82	14.89	18.19
4aa d	....	....	....	....	....	....	....	....	....	....	1.79	1.81	1.70	1.33	1.31
4ab d	....	....	....	....	....	....	....	....	....	....	8.51	9.32	8.83	7.77	10.32
4ac d	....	....	....	....	....	....	....	....	....	....	1.06	1.28	1.55	1.31	1.58
4ad d	....	....	....	....	....	....	....	....	....	....	2.74	3.03	3.31	3.95	4.43
4ae d	....	....	....	....	....	....	....	....	....	....	.15	.16	.19	.28	.25
4af d	....	....	....	....	....	....	....	....	....	....	.18	.18	.24	.25	.30
4b.d	4.35	4.37	4.76	5.44	5.72	5.95	7.62	7.60	8.35	8.36	9.21	11.05	11.48	14.21	15.76
4ba d	2.57	2.57	2.98	3.41	3.47	3.52	4.68	4.82	5.48	5.35	5.82	7.30	7.42	9.94	11.08
4c.d	.53	.56	.50	.70	.96	1.25	1.69	2.34	2.75	2.99	2.76	2.52	2.26	1.92	1.71
4d.d	10.55	11.71	12.22	13.99	14.40	15.66	17.42	18.80	20.73	22.07	23.29	25.62	25.50	27.12	29.91
4e.d	....	....	....	....	....	....	1.51	1.43	1.41	1.20	1.52	1.50	1.58	1.39	1.47
4f.d	—	—	—	—	—	—	—	—	—	—	.70	1.08	1.20	.26	.71
4g.d	....	....	....	.20	.20	.20	.50	.80	.80	.80	.80	.80	.83	1.01	1.03
4h.d	....	....	....	....	....	....	—	—	—	.20	.07	.36	.45	1.24	2.55
6..d	1.22	1.83	2.22	2.79	3.37	3.90	4.16	5.31	6.85	7.32	9.00	12.24	12.25	12.03	12.53
6a.d	.90	1.39	1.55	1.95	2.20	2.54	2.62	3.61	4.82	5.16	5.97	7.96	7.73	7.85	8.61
6b.d	.32	.44	.67	.84	1.26	1.54				2.16	3.03	4.28	4.52	4.18	3.92

396

exports increased from $12 to $120 billion; but, as can be seen on line 71, imports increased from $15 to $156 billion. Thus the United States had a trade deficit of $36.5 billion in 1977. The source of this deficit can be attributed entirely to a single item—petroleum. As can be seen on line 71a, U.S. imports of petroleum were $506 million in 1953 and had increased to $41 billion in 1977. If U.S. petroleum imports had remained constant, the United States would have had a $4 billion surplus in 1977 on its trade account.

Line 77ad, goods and services, shows a U.S. deficit of $8.7 billion. This line takes into account all of the current account transactions, including not only merchandise but services as well. The trade balance on an FOB basis was minus $31.2 billion. This is smaller than the balance calculated by subtracting line 70 from line 71 because those lines used CIF, or cost insurance in freight, as a basis for valuation of imports adding additional value to the import total. Line 77hhd shows that the U.S. military expenditures and sales were net positive $1.4 billion for 1977. This line is net of all expenses for maintaining U.S. bases and operations overseas, as well as the revenues from the sale of military equipment and services to foreigners. Line 77rd shows an income of $21.1 billion for other services. A major portion of this income is dividends to U.S. multinational companies paid by their overseas subsidiaries and affiliates. Line 77tad shows a $1 billion private transfer deficit, indicating that U.S. residents sent $1 billion more abroad than was received by U.S. residents from foreign residents. Line 77tgd shows that U.S. government

EXHIBIT 1. (Cont.)

1968	1969	1970	1971	1972	1973	1974	1975	1976	1977		United States 111
End of Period (sa and sc) Period Averages (sb and sd)											**Exchange Rates**
1.00000	1.00000	1.00000	1.08571	1.08571	1.20635	1.22435	1.17066	1.16183	1.21471		US Dollar/SDR Rate............aa=......**sa**
1.00000	1.00000	1.00000	1.00298	1.08571	1.19213	1.20264	1.21415	1.15452	1.16752		US Dollar/SDR Rate.............................**sb**
1.00000	1.00000	1.00000	.92105	.92105	.82895	.81676	.85422	.86071	.82324		SDR/US Dollar Rate............ac=......**sc**
1.00000	1.00000	1.00000	.99702	.92105	.83883	.83150	.82362	.86616	.85652		SDR/US Dollar Rate ....**sd**
1970=100											
....	....	99.3	96.8	89.8	82.3	84.2	83.5	87.7	86.7		Effective Exchange Rate: MERM..... **am** x
End of Period											**International Liquidity**
15.71	16.96	14.49	13.19	13.15	14.38	16.06	15.88	18.32	19.39		International Reserves....................... 1..d
10.89	11.86	11.07	11.08	10.49	11.65	11.83	11.26	11.17	11.80		Gold (See country notes)............ 1a.d
—	—	.85	1.19	1.96	2.17	2.37	2.33	2.39	2.63		SDRs... 1b.d
1.29	2.32	1.94	.63	.46	.55	1.85	2.21	4.43	4.95		Reserve Position in the Fund....... 1c.d
—	—	—	—	—	—	—	—	—	.70		of which: GAB Lending.............. 1cad
3.53	2.78	.63	.28	.24	.01	.01	.08	.32	.02		Foreign Exchange 1d.d
											Fund Position
—	-1.05	-.30	1.17	1.38	1.54	-.04	-1.32	-3.79	-3.64		Net Draw/Fund Sales(-) to Date 2dc d
5.16	5.16	6.70	7.27	7.27	8.08	8.20	7.84	7.78	8.14		Quota 2f.d
38.47	45.91	46.96	67.81	82.86	92.49	119.16	126.55	151.36	192.28		External Liabilities .... 4..d
17.34	15.99	23.77	50.64	61.53	66.85	76.83	80.71	91.98	126.04		Central Banks & Governments..... 4a.d
1.87	1.62	2.95	3.98	4.28	3.85	3.66	3.13	3.41	2.33		Canada 4aad
8.06	7.07	13.61	30.13	34.20	45.76	44.33	45.70	45.88	70.71		Western Europe.......................... 4abd
1.86	1.91	1.68	1.43	1.73	2.54	4.42	4.45	4.91	4.63		Latin America............................ 4acd
5.00	4.55	4.71	13.82	17.58	10.89	18.63	22.55	34.11	45.69		Asia 4add
.25	.55	.41	.41	.78	.79	3.16	2.98	1.89	1.74		Africa 4aed
.30	.29	.41	.87	2.96	3.02	2.63	1.90	1.78	.94		Other.. 4afd
19.38	28.23	21.77	15.09	19.71	23.62	39.02	40.22	50.90	58.59		Other Banks & Other Foreigners. 4b.d
14.47	23.64	17.17	10.95	14.67	17.69	30.11	29.52	37.33	42.50		of which: Short-Term to Bks ... 4bad
1.75	1.68	1.41	2.07	1.63	2.00	3.32	5.62	8.48	7.65		International Agencies.................. 4c.d
30.96	39.45	41.39	55.18	60.70	69.07	94.77	94.34	108.99	124.26		By Type: Short-Term.................... 4d.d
.93	.87	.86	2.40	5.87	6.16	5.71	7.70	15.80	38.62		Long-Term Marketable 4e.d
.70	.55	3.45	9.53	15.75	15.56	16.34	19.98	20.65	20.44		Nonmarketable 4f.d
1.03	1.02	.57	.54	—	—	—	—	—	—		Fund Gold Dep. & Invest.. 4g.d
4.86	4.02	.70	.14	.54	1.67	2.35	4.54	5.92	8.96		Other Readily Marketable. 4h.d
12.28	12.93	13.87	16.94	20.43	26.58	46.07	59.77	81.14	92.60		External Claims.............................. 6..d
8.71	9.68	10.80	13.28	15.51	20.72	38.91	50.23	69.24	79.96		Short-Term.................................. 6a.d
3.57	3.25	3.07	3.66	4.92	5.86	7.16	9.54	11.90	12.64		Long-Term................................... 6b.d

397

transfers or aid was $4.1 billion. Line 78afd shows a capital outflow of $18.4 billion. Line 79add shows how the U.S. financed its balance of payments. The total deficit amounted to $35.3 billion, which was financed almost entirely by increasing the liabilities to foreign central banks, as shown on line 79rpd where liabilities increased by $35.5 billion. There was also an outflow of foreign exchange of $303 million shown on line 79cad, an increase in the fund gold position (a technical part of reserves) of $293 million shown on line 79bdd, an increase in SDR holdings of $120 million shown on line 79bbd, and an increase in monetary gold of $118 million shown on line 79bad.

EXHIBIT 1. (Cont.)

	1953	1954	1955	1956	1957	1958	1959	1960	1961	1962	1963	1964	1965	1966	1967
													Per Cent or Index Numbers (1975=100):		
60	2.00	1.50	2.50	3.00	3.00	2.50	4.00	3.00	3.00	3.00	3.50	4.00	4.50	4.50	4.50
60c	1.94	.95	1.74	2.66	3.26	1.84	3.42	2.94	2.38	2.78	3.16	3.55	3.95	4.88	4.33
61a	2.42	1.60	2.42	3.13	I 3.69	2.84	4.46	3.98	3.54	3.47	3.67	4.03	4.22	5.23	5.03
61	2.92	2.52	2.80	3.06	I 3.54	3.48	4.13	4.06	3.92	4.00	4.05	4.19	4.27	4.77	5.01
62	25.7	31.3	43.9	51.6	49.3	51.1	63.7	61.6	72.5	67.9	76.0	89.3	96.9	94.4	102.8
63	50.0	50.1	50.2	51.9	53.3	54.1	54.2	54.3	54.1	54.2	54.0	54.1	55.2	57.1	57.2
63a	49.4	49.6	50.7	52.9	54.4	54.6	55.6	55.6	55.3	55.3	55.2	55.5	56.2	57.5	58.3
63b	52.0	52.2	52.3	53.8	55.8	57.0	56.9	57.4	57.3	57.5	57.4	57.6	58.5	60.2	61.2
63ba	54.5	54.5	54.1	54.9	56.5	57.7	57.2	57.8	57.6	57.8	57.5	57.6	58.7	60.8	61.1
63bb	45.3	45.8	47.2	50.7	53.9	55.2	56.3	56.4	56.6	56.7	56.9	57.4	58.2	59.6	61.5
64	49.7	49.9	49.8	50.5	52.3	53.7	54.2	55.0	55.6	56.2	56.9	57.6	58.6	60.4	62.0
65m	36.2	37.0	38.7	40.5	42.6	43.9	45.5	47.0	48.2	49.7	51.1	52.6	54.3	56.5	58.8
66..c	46.5	44.1	49.7	51.9	52.5	49.2	55.0	56.2	56.6	61.3	64.9	69.4	76.2	83.0	84.9
66aa	....	....	....	....	....	....	....	....	....	....	92.2	93.4	97.1	101.8	107.8
67..c	65.2	63.6	65.7	68.0	68.6	66.7	69.2	70.4	70.2	72.1	73.6	75.7	78.9	83.0	85.5
													Millions of US Dollars		
70.x	12,271	12,860	14,302	17,345	19,518	16,370	16,415	19,651	20,227	20,986	22,467	25,831	26,751	29,490	31,030
70	15,782	15,114	15,558	19,102	20,873	17,920	17,643	20,601	21,037	21,714	23,387	26,650	27,530	30,430	31,622
71	11,846	11,140	12,489	13,987	14,620	14,616	17,006	16,367	15,939	17,779	18,616	20,304	23,185	27,744	28,744
71a	....	....	....	....	1,551	1,628	1,533	1,533	1,609	1,733	2,573	1,873	2,093	2,126	3,592
71aa	506	561	678	841	986	996	932	951	1,006	1,070	1,088	1,080	1,142	1,141	1,079
71.v	11,009	10,372	11,564	12,903	13,413	13,385	15,688	15,071	14,758	16,462	17,205	18,748	21,428	25,618	26,889
														1975=100	
72	26.5	28.1	31.0	36.2	39.4	33.4	33.3	39.6	40.0	41.7	44.8	51.1	51.2	54.5	56.6
73	28.1	26.2	29.2	32.1	32.9	34.5	40.7	39.1	38.7	43.8	45.6	48.6	55.2	64.3	66.9
74	43.4	42.8	43.3	44.9	46.4	46.0	46.0	46.3	47.2	46.9	46.8	47.3	48.8	50.3	51.3
75	40.0	40.8	40.8	41.2	42.0	39.9	39.2	39.8	39.2	38.3	38.6	39.6	40.0	41.1	41.5
													Millions of US Dollars:		
77a.d	980	1,749	1,881	4,823	7,162	3,209	1,179	5,240	6,618	6,234	7,322	9,824	8,383	6,046	5,683
77ab d	1,291	2,460	2,748	4,574	6,099	3,313	988	4,892	5,571	4,521	5,224	6,801	4,951	3,817	3,800
77ba d	12,254	12,814	14,264	17,350	19,390	16,265	16,298	19,650	20,108	20,781	22,272	25,501	26,461	29,310	30,666
77ca d	-10,963	-10,354	-11,516	-12,776	-13,291	-12,952	-15,310	-14,758	-14,537	-16,260	-17,048	-18,700	-21,510	-25,493	-26,866
77hh d	-2,423	-2,603	-2,804	-2,797	-2,793	-3,116	-2,807	-2,752	-2,596	-2,449	-2,304	-2,133	-2,122	-2,935	-3,226
77r.d	2,112	1,892	1,937	3,046	3,856	3,012	2,998	3,100	3,643	4,162	4,402	5,156	5,554	5,164	5,109
77ta d	-476	-486	-456	-530	-543	-540	-575	-423	-434	-477	-575	-614	-677	-655	-879
77tg d	-1,866	-1,675	-1,895	-1,934	-1,881	-1,900	-1,963	-1,994	-2,363	-2,369	-2,333	-2,403	-2,271	-2,409	-2,376
78af d	-391	-1,281	-1,082	-2,217	-3,154	-3,171	-405	-5,209	-4,179	-4,917	-5,990	-7,434	-6,267	-3,391	-5,642
78cg d	—	—	—	—	—	—	434	54	695	680	326	123	221	428	6
78ch d	-229	201	33	-66	-334	-632	-431	-411	-1,319	-1,368	-1,113	-1,487	-1,745	-1,594	-2,556
78ci d	11	-108	-343	-563	-624	-339	-356	-528	-261	-245	-447	-19	-16	-265	209
78d.d	-577	-543	-626	-1,719	-2,287	-1,083	-1,134	-2,625	-2,341	-2,506	-3,252	-3,423	-4,595	-4,939	-3,949
78ed d	255	-170	-48	-242	-615	-1,469	-455	-567	-656	-1,085	-1,391	-2,178	-1,166	759	-95
78eg d	167	-635	-191	-517	-276	-311	-77	-1,349	-1,556	-546	-786	-2,147	754	-414	-1,228
78mg d	-59	1	410	428	60	48	1,158	140	586	-138	470	1,454	116	2,697	1,272
78mh d	41	-27	-317	462	922	615	456	77	673	291	203	243	164	-63	699
78w.d	—	—	—	—	—	—	—	—	—	—	—	—	—	—	—
79ad d	2,120	1,542	1,056	105	-1,414	2,815	2,283	3,402	1,347	2,651	1,935	1,534	1,289	-219	3,418
79ba d	1,161	298	41	-306	-798	2,275	1,075	1,702	857	890	461	125	1,665	571	1,170
79bb d	—	—	—	—	—	—	—	—	—	—	—	—	—	—	—
79bd d	95	182	141	-563	-367	17	-40	442	-135	626	29	266	-94	537	-94
79ca d	—	—	—	—	—	—	—	—	-116	17	-113	-220	-349	-540	-1,024
79rp d	864	1,062	874	974	-249	523	1,248	1,258	741	1,118	1,558	1,363	67	-787	3,26c
79w.d	-367	151	496	-247	-170	-413	-519	-1,016	-989	-1,122	-359	-907			

Line 79wd, net errors and omissions, is minus $2.9 billion, indicating that unrecorded and reported items accounted for this amount of the overall balance-of-payments deficit. This item is assumed to be largely short-term capital flows, which are not picked up by the present reporting system.

Exhibit 2 shows the world interest rates table that appears in *International Finance,* issued biweekly by the Economics Group of the Chase Manhattan Bank. At the bottom of this table there is a line entitled "Forward Exchange Cover." The numbers on this line indicate whether or not a country's currency is selling at

EXHIBIT 1. (Cont.)

United States
111

1968	1969	1970	1971	1972	1973	1974	1975	1976	1977	
Period Averages										**Interest,Prices,Production**
5.50	6.00	5.50	4.50	4.50	7.50	7.75	6.00	5.25	6.00	Discount Rate *(End of Period)*......... **60**
5.35	6.69	6.44	4.34	4.07	7.03	7.87	5.82	4.99	5.27	Treasury Bill Rate............................. **60c**
5.69	7.02	7.29	5.66	5.72	6.95	7.82	7.49	6.77	6.69	Govt. Bond Yield: Med.-Term......... **61a**
5.46	6.33	6.86	6.12	6.01	7.12	8.06	8.19	7.87	7.67	Long-Term............ **61**
111.4	110.1	94.6	112.3	126.2	124.8	96.3	100.0	118.5	112.3	Industrial Share Prices..................... **62**
58.6	60.9	63.1	65.2	68.1	77.0	91.5	100.0	104.6	111.0	Wholesale Prices.............................. **63**
59.8	61.8	64.1	66.5	68.7	73.4	89.7	100.0	106.4	113.8	Industrial Goods **63a**
62.9	65.3	67.5	69.5	71.7	78.2	90.2	100.0	104.1	110.5	Finished Goods.............................. **63b**
62.8	65.2	67.2	69.0	71.3	78.9	92.8	100.0	103.3	109.4	Consumer **63ba**
63.7	65.8	68.9	71.8	73.6	76.0	86.8	100.0	106.6	114.2	Producer **63bb**
64.6	68.1	72.1	75.2	77.7	82.6	91.6	100.0	105.8	112.7	Consumer Prices.............................. **64**
62.6	66.3	69.9	74.2	79.2	84.8	91.7	100.0	107.7	117.0	Wages: Hourly Earnings **65m**
90.2	94.3	91.5	93.0	101.6	110.2	109.8	100.0	110.2	116.4	Industrial Production, Seas. Adj... **66..c**
111.5	112.7	117.8	115.7	115.8	112.3	107.2	100.0	99.6	....	Crude Petroleum Production **66aa**
88.2	91.5	92.1	92.4	95.6	99.8	101.8	100.0	103.1	106.6	Nonagr Employment, Seas.Adj. .... **67..c**
Millions of US Dollars										**International Transactions**
34,063	37,332	42,659	43,549	49,199	70,823	97,908	107,130	114,802	120,101	Exports: Excluding Military Aid **70.x**
34,636	38,006	43,224	44,130	49,758	71,339	98,507	107,592	114,992	120,164	Including Military Aid.......... **70**
35,319	38,314	42,429	48,342	58,862	73,575	107,996	103,389	129,565	156,695	Imports, cif.................................... **71**
2,343	2,560	2,764	3,323	4,300	7,674	24,329	25,027	31,390	41,026	Petroleum..................................... **71a**
1,208	1,321	1,283	1,704	2,383	4,239	15,335	18,374	25,480	33,582	Crude Petroleum **71aa**
33,226	36,043	39,952	45,563	55,583	69,476	100,251	96,116	120,678	146,819	Imports, fob................................... **71.v**
1975=100										
61.3	64.9	70.1	69.3	76.0	93.7	102.2	100.0	103.4	102.8	Volume of Exports........................... **72**
81.7	85.7	89.0	96.6	109.7	116.5	112.6	100.0	121.9	136.7	Volume of Imports........................... **73**
52.0	53.7	56.7	58.6	60.3	70.4	89.4	100.0	103.6	108.6	Unit Value of Exports........................ **74**
41.9	43.2	46.3	48.7	52.3	61.6	92.6	100.0	103.2	111.6	Unit Value of Imports........................ **75**
Minus Sign Indicates Debit										**Balance of Payments (Source R)**
3,438	3,305	5,799	2,448	-1,941	10,999	8,599	22,550	10,052	-8,702	Goods and Services **77a.d**
635	607	2,603	-2,267	-6,418	916	-5,362	8,997	-9,320	-31,239	Trade Balance, fob **77abd**
33,626	36,414	42,469	43,312	49,380	71,410	98,307	107,090	114,693	120,476	Exports, fob.............................. **77bad**
-32,991	-35,807	-39,866	-45,579	-55,797	-70,493	-103,670	-98,094	-124,011	-151,713	Imports, fob.............................. **77cad**
-3,143	-3,328	-3,354	-2,895	-3,622	-2,285	-2,083	-877	367	1,433	Military Expenditures - Sales ... **77hhd**
5,946	6,026	6,550	7,608	8,098	12,369	16,045	14,429	19,004	21,102	Other Services.............................. **77r.d**
-836	-939	-1,096	-1,118	-1,103	-1,249	-1,017	-902	-946	-1,035	Transfers: Private **77tad**
-2,245	-2,186	-2,346	-2,740	-2,945	-2,858	-6,415	-3,964	-4,398	-4,168	Government.................. **77tgd**
845	4,075	-12,821	-19,228	-3,121	-9,521	-8,434	-28,032	-25,051	-18,431	Capital, Excluding Reserves........ **78afd**
269	-87	244	228	138	—	—	—	—	—	US Govt:Advance Repayments.. **78cgd**
-2,620	-1,880	-2,283	-2,572	-2,058	-749	376	-1,528	3,545	195	Other Long-Term.......... **78chd**
62	-50	76	-85	701	-955	1,409	2,355	-42	-1,361	Other Short-Term.......... **78cid**
-4,223	-4,471	-6,125	-7,237	-6,798	-8,555	-3,867	-11,014	-8,547	-9,799	Direct Investment................... **78d.d**
3,750	2,315	1,818	541	3,081	2,568	-3,213	-6,469	-10,370	-2,901	Other Private Long-Term......... **78edd**
-1,087	-569	-1,132	-3,438	-3,009	-7,035	-21,079	-12,191	-20,774	-11,401	US Private Short-Term Assets. **78egd**
3,387	9,176	-6,502	-5,622	3,716	3,022	12,399	-697	8,077	5,251	Foreign Commercial Banks...... **78mgd**
1,307	-359	1,083	203	1,075	2,183	5,542	1,508	3,060	1,584	Other Foreign Short-Term....... **78mhd**
—	—	867	717	771	—	—	—	—	—	Allocation of SDRs....................... **78w.d**
-1,641	-2,739	9,840	29,739	10,313	5,356	8,822	4,711	10,468	35,314	Foreign Exchange......................... **79add**
1,173	-967	787	864	547	—	53	—	—	-118	Monetary Gold............................. **79bad**
—	—	-851	-249	-763	10	-172	-66	-77	-120	SDR Holdings................................ **79bbd**
-870	-1,034	389	1,351	171	-34	-1,266	-461	-2,219	-293	Fund Gold Tranche Position..... **79bdd**
-1,183	814	2,152	380	36	234	3	-75	-240	303	Foreign Exchange **79cad**
-761	-1,552	7,363	27,393	10,325	5,147	10,256	5,260	13,004	35,543	Liabilities to Foreign Official...... **79rpd**
439	-1,516	-243	-9,818	-1,974	-2,728	-1,554	5,637	9,875	-2,976	Net Errors and Omissions........... **79w.d**

EXHIBIT 2. World Interest Rates

market rates as of June 7, 1978; bond yields as of June 2, 1978

in percent per annum	U.S.	Canada	Britain	Belgium	France	Germany	Italy	Netherlands	Switzerland	Japan
Central Bank Discount Rate	7.00	8.50	10.00	5.50	9.50	3.00	11.50* penalty rate 14.50	4.00	1.00	3.50
Day-to-Day Money	7.50 June 8	8.75	8.25	3.25	7.50	3.50	11.50*	4.50	0.50	3.75
Treasury Bills 91-day, Middle Rates	6.63	8.20	8.6875	5.75 120-day	n. a.	n. a.	10.999*	no dealing	no market	3.375 2-month
Commercial Paper prime, 3-month, asked	7.45 finance paper	8.40 finance paper 15% tax w/h	10.125 H. P. on discount basis	5.10 Certified	7.9375 Interbank	no market	no market	no market	no market	not traded
Bankers' Acceptances 3-month, asked	7.40	8.30 15% tax w/h	9.0625	5.25 Certified	not traded	4.65	no market	no market	3.25 not traded	no market
Government Bonds Long-term, new and old issues, average yield	8.50	9.50	12.56	8.14 20% tax w/h	8.98	5.56	12.99*	7.70	3.45	6.17
Industrial Bonds prime, long-term, new and old issues, average yield	8.90 Aa Industrials	9.85	12.96	8.51 20% tax w/h	11.52	5.55	13.33*	7.76	4.34	7.05
Bank Short-Term Rate to Best Borrowers (prime rate)	8.50	9.25	10.00	8.00	10.10	6.25	16.50*	6.50	5.75	3.75
Bank Sight Deposits	zero	zero	zero	0.50	zero	0.50	8.25-* 9.25	1.00-3.00 large deposits	0.50 residents only	zero
Bank Time Deposits 3-month	7.375 Cert. of Dep.	8.35 Cert. of Dep.	9.875 Cert. of Dep.	5.80	8.0625	3.65	8.50-* 9.50	4.875 large deposits	1.00 residents only	2.50 15% tax w/h
Exchange Rates—in U.S.$ rates floating against the $	--	.8921	1.8220	.030600	.2169	.4781	.001160	.4464	.5225	.004526
Forward Exchange Cover 3-month, in percent p.a. D = discount, P = premium	--	.25 D	3.50 D	2.50 P	2.25 D	4.625 P	4.88 D	3.25 P	6.75 P	5.00 P

Eurodollar Deposits		International Arbitrage		Eurobonds		Gold Price
(London, interbank, bid) June 8		(3-month, hedged)	*+ in favor of U.S. dollars*	Straight debt of U.S. subsidiaries average yield on seasoned issues	n. a.	London afternoon fixing
7-day	7.625	U.S.-U.K. Treasury Bills	+1.56	Convertible debt of U.S. subsidiaries		
1-month	7.6875	U.S.-Canada Treasury Bills	−1.03	representative terms of most recent issues		
3-month	8.00	U.S.-Canada Finance Co. Paper	− .58	coupon:	7.00	182.95
6-month	8.4375	Eurodollars-U.K. Local Auth. Deposits	+2.37	conversion premium:	5.00	(per fine ounce)

The above interest rate quotations refer to the past week and may not be construed as offers by The Chase Manhattan Bank. The quotations for Bank Short-Term Rate to Best Customers, while including customary commissions, reflect neither possible other fees nor varying compensating balance requirements.
* Market rates as of May 31, 1978; bond yields as of May 26, 1978.

Source: International Finance, The Chase Manhattan Bank, June 12, 1978.

a discount or a premium in three-months' futures contracts. The percentages are in percent per annum. Reading down the column for Britain, we find the number 3.50 *D*. This means that sterling, the British currency, is selling at an annual discount of 3.5 percent. A three-month forward exchange contract would therefore be discounted by 0.875 percent as compared with the spot or current price. Looking down the column for Germany, we see the number 4.62 *P*. This means that the German deutsche mark is selling at a premium of 4.625 percent on an annual basis for three-month forward exchange contracts. A three-month futures contract in deutsche marks would sell at a premium of 1.16 percent over the spot or current exchange rate.

The existence of the foreign exchange markets and foreign exchange rate fluctuation adds a major element of risk and uncertainty to doing business internationally. It is possible to eliminate uncertainty and risk by using forward contracts where they are available, but (1) they are available for major currencies only, and (2) use of these contracts carries with it a cost in the form of a risk reward, which goes to the financial intermediaries who make the contracts. The international marketer faces a choice: eliminate risk and uncertainty through the use of forward contracts at a price or increase long-term marketing margins with associated risk and uncertainty in the short term. It has been demonstrated for portfolio investing that an internationally diversified portfolio is less risky than a national portfolio—an international portfolio offsets business cycles and fluctuations in a number of countries against each other, reducing the total amount of fluctuation and market risk as a result of the diversification. The same risk reduction occurs when a company diversifies its investments and operations internationally. This is contrary to the almost instinctual belief that international diversification increases risk exposure. In fact, for the new investor or marketer, international diversification extends operations into areas that are *less well known* but not necessarily riskier.

In general, we believe that it is wiser to absorb risks of exchange fluctuation than it is to attempt to contract these risks to financial intermediaries. Unfortunately, as a result of the Financial Accounting Standards Board (FASB) ruling it is no longer possible for a company to create a reserve for charging foreign exchange gains and losses. Under the current FASB rules, foreign exchange gains and losses must be reported on a quarterly and annual basis. Many argue that fluctuating exchange gains and losses will destroy investor confidence in the stability of company earnings and depress stock values. This may be true in the short run, but it is our position that investors are capable of expanding their own understanding and sophistication concerning the realities of the foreign exchange market. Companies should simply report gains and losses and give the financial and investor community time to learn that international diversification paradoxically reduces rather than increases risk.

part three

IDENTIFYING
GLOBAL OPPORTUNITIES
AND THREATS

marketing information systems

> Knowledge is of two kinds. We know a subject ourselves, or we
> know where we can find information upon it.
>
> *Samuel Johnson, 1709–84*
> *(from Boswell, Life of Johnson, 1763)*

INTRODUCTION

Information, or useful data, is the raw material of executive action. The multinational marketer is faced with a dual problem in acquiring the information he needs for decision making. In the industrialized or developed countries the amount of information available far exceeds the absorptive capacity of an individual or an organization. The problem is superabundance, not scarcity. While industrialized countries all over the world are enduring an information explosion, there is relatively little information available on the marketing characteristics of less-developed countries. Thus the multinational marketer is faced with the problem of information abundance and information scarcity. The multinational marketer must know where to go to obtain information, the subject areas that should be covered, and the different ways that information can be acquired. We shall refer to this process of information acquisition as *scanning*. The section that follows presents a scanning model for multinational marketing.

ELEMENTS OF AN INTERNATIONAL INFORMATION SYSTEM

Information Subject Agenda

A subject agenda, or list of subjects for which information is desired, is a basic element of an international marketing information system. Because each company's subject agenda should be developed and tailored to the specific needs and objectives of the company, it is not possible to suggest an ideal or standard agenda. Therefore any framework such as that proposed in Table 8-1 is only a starting point in the construction of a specific agenda for any particular organization.

The general framework suggested in Table 8-1 consists of five broad informa-

TABLE 8-1. Twenty-five Categories for a Global Business Intelligence System

Category	Coverage
I. Market Information	
1. Market potential	Information indicating potential demand for products, including the status and prospects of existing company products in existing markets.
2. Consumer/customer attitudes & behavior	Information and attitudes, behavior, and needs of consumers and customers of existing and potential company products. Also included in this category are attitudes of investors toward a company's investment merit.
3. Channels of distribution	Availability, effectiveness, attitudes, and preferences of channel agents in company's system, a competitor's system or of independent distributors, wholesalers, retailers, and so on.
4. Communications media	Media availability, effectiveness, and cost.
5. Market sources	Availability, quality, and cost.
6. New products	Nontechnical information concerning new products for a company (this includes products that are already marketed by other countries), ideas, and market potential.
7. Competitive sales	Sales performance of competitive products.
8. Competitive marketing programs & plans	Marketing programs and plans (sales promotions, advertising, area coverage, etc.) for existing and for new products.
9. Competitive products	Prices and features for existing and proposed products.
10. Competitive operations	Information relating to a competitor's operating capability. Employee morale, transfers, production efficiency, and so on.
11. Competitive investments	Information concerning competitive investments, expansion plans, or moves. New capacity, investment proposals, indications of manufacturing resource commitments.
II. Prescriptive Information	
12. Foreign exchanges	Information concerning changes or expected changes in foreign exchange rates by exchange control authorities and immediate influences upon these authorities.
13. Foreign taxes	Information concerning decisions, intentions, and attitudes of foreign authorities regarding taxes upon earnings, dividends, and interest.

TABLE 8-1. (Cont.)

Category	Coverage
14. Other foreign prescriptions	All information concerning local, regional, or international authority guidelines, rulings, laws, decrees other than foreign exchange and tax matters affecting the operations, assets, or investments of a company.
15. U.S. government prescriptions	U.S. government incentives, controls, regulations, restraints, etc., affecting a company.

III. Resource Information

16. Manpower	Availability of individuals and groups. Employment candidates, sources, strikes, etc.
17. Money	Availability and cost of money for company uses.
18. Raw material	Availability and cost.
19. Acquisitions and mergers	Leads or other information concerning potential acquisitions, mergers, or joint ventures.

IV. General Conditions

20. Economic factors	Macroeconomic information dealing with broad factors, such as capital movements, rates of growth, economic structure, and economic geography.
21. Social factors	Social structure of society, customs, attitudes, and preferences.
22. Political factors	"Investment climate," meaning of elections, political change.
23. Scientific technological factors	Major developments with broad but relatively untested implications.
24. Management and administrative practices	Management and administrative practices and procedures concerning such matters as employee compensation, report procedure.
25. Other information	Information not assignable to another category.

5. 2

tion areas with twenty-five information categories. The framework satisfies two essential criteria. First, it is exhaustive; it accepts all the subject areas of information encountered by a company with global operations. Second, the categories in the framework are mutually exclusive; any kind of information encompassed by the framework can be correctly placed in one and only one category.

The most important of the five areas is market information. This includes information on market potential, consumer and customer attitudes and behavior, channels, communication and market services, new products, and every other aspect of competitive sales and operations.

The second area encompasses prescriptive information, that is, information that will lay the foundation for rules for action in the foreign market. This category incorporates information from guidelines to regulations, rulings, and laws by public and private groups and authorities. The framework in Table 8–1 is a starting point for a U.S.-based company, and therefore it includes U.S. government prescriptions as a separate category. A company based in a different country would need to identify a special category for the home base country because prescriptions of the base country are of great importance and have an impact on the operations of an international company.

Resource information includes all information on resources that a company requires to carry out its programs. Included are four categories: manpower, money, raw materials (the basic factor inputs of the firm), and acquisitions and mergers.

Information Collection

Once the subject agenda has been determined, the next step in formulating a systematic information-gathering system in the organization is the actual collection of information. There are two important modes or orientations in information collection or scanning: surveillance and search.

In *surveillance* the scanner is oriented toward acquiring relevant information that is contained in messages that cross his scanning attention field. In *search* the scanner is deliberately seeking information, either informally or by means of an organized research project. The two orientations and their components are briefly described in Table 8–2.

The significance of determining scanning mode is the measure it offers (1) of the extent that a scanner actively seeks out information, as contrasted with the

TABLE 8-2. Scanning Modes

Modes	Coverage
Surveillance Orientation	
Viewing	General exposure to external information where the viewer has no specific purpose in mind other than exploration.
Monitoring	Focused attention, not involving active search, to a clearly defined area or type of external information.
Search Orientation	
Investigation	A relatively limited and informal seeking out of specific information.
Research	A formally organized effort to acquire specific information usually for a specific purpose.

TABLE 8-3. Relative Importance of Scanning Modes in Acquiring
International Information (Percent of Responses)

		Overall Sample
Surveillance		73
Viewing	13	
Monitoring	60	
Search		27
Investigation	23	
Research	4	
Total		100
Number of instances		139

Source: Keegan, "Scanning the International Business Environment."

more passive acquisition of information, and (2) of the scanner's attention state at the time of acquiring information.

Table 8-3 shows that the bulk of information acquired by headquarters executives of major U.S. multinational firms is gained through surveillance as opposed to search (73 percent versus 27 percent).[1] However, viewing (general exposure), the least oriented of the surveillance modes, generates only 13 percent of important external information acquired, where monitoring generates 60 percent.

This paucity of information generated by viewing is the result of two factors. One is the extent to which executives are exposed to information that is not included in a clearly defined subject agenda. The other is their receptiveness to information outside of this agenda. Both factors operate to limit the relative importance of viewing as a scanning mode. Every executive limits his exposure to information that will not have a high probability of being relevant to his job or company. This is a rational and necessary response to the basic mental limitations of man. A person can handle only a minute fraction of the data available to him. Because exposure absorbs limited mental resources, exposure must be selective.

Nevertheless, receptiveness by the organization as a whole to information not explicitly recognized as important is vital. The effective scanning system must ensure that the organization is viewing areas where developments that could be important to the company might occur. This may require the creation of a full-time scanning unit that would have explicit responsibility for acquiring and disseminating information on subjects of importance to the organization.

Information Media

The medium is the channel through which information is transmitted. Any marketing information system is based on three basic media. These media are the human voice for transmitting words and numbers, printed words and numbers, and

[1] Warren J. Keegan, "Scanning the International Business Environment: A Study of the Information Acquisition Process" (Unpublished doctoral dissertation, Harvard Business School, 1967).

TABLE 8-4. Basic International Marketing Information System Media

Basic Information Media	Setting/Format	Important International Electronic and Travel Extensions of Basic Media
Human voice	Face-to-face/One-to-one	Television
		Radio/Telephone
	Talks to groups	Jet aircraft
Printed words & numbers	Letters	Teletype
	Reports	Cable
	Publications	Jet aircraft
	Information services	
Direct perception	Direct observation	Teletype
	via country visits	Television
Sight		Radio
Hearing		Jet aircraft
Smell		
Taste		
Touch		

direct perception through the senses of sight, hearing, smell, taste, and touch. Each of these basic information system media has been extended in recent years by important innovations in electronic and travel technologies. Of particular importance to the marketing information system have been the impressive developments in telephone, teletype, and transportation via jet aircraft. The basic media of an international marketing information system are summarized in Table 8–4.

The teletype and telephone, plus the more-long-standing cable, are important media for the transmission of information internationally: 67 percent of all important international information acquired by international executives comes from human sources, and 81 percent of this information is transmitted by voice.[2] Moreover, of the human information transmitted by voice, 94 percent is communicated in face-to-face conversation. This finding underlines the importance of the jet aircraft as a communications device because a large proportion of the important information transmitted in international marketing is accomplished by people who have come together in a face-to-face situation as a result of the high-speed travel of jet aircraft.

The importance of language

Information Matching

The final stage in the operation of a scanning system is the matching of information acquired with information needs of sytem users. When a person acquires information for his own use matching presents no problem. It becomes a problem when people acquire information that is not relevant to their job but could be of considerable value to the company if it were communicated to the right person. It is also a problem when information is acquired by a full-time scanning unit. In each case the need is to get the information to the person or persons who can use it. This

[2]Ibid.

requires knowledge of information needs, and the motivation to take the trouble to pass information on.

When the exchange of information is between individuals, the best way to communicate information needs is in face-to-face conversation. When an organized full-time scanning unit is involved, a survey of system users will be required to determine information needs. The need categories should be defined by subject and in terms of whether they can best be scanned by viewing, monitoring, investigation, search, or some combination of these modes.

Scanning is too important to the success of a global company to be left to chance. A systematic approach is needed to ensure that a company gets the information it needs from abroad to seize opportunities and avoid threats that exist in the international business environment. A simplified model of the proposed system is illustrated in Figure 8-1. After determining the information subject requirements and collection approaches, it is necessary to go to specific sources. As a framework

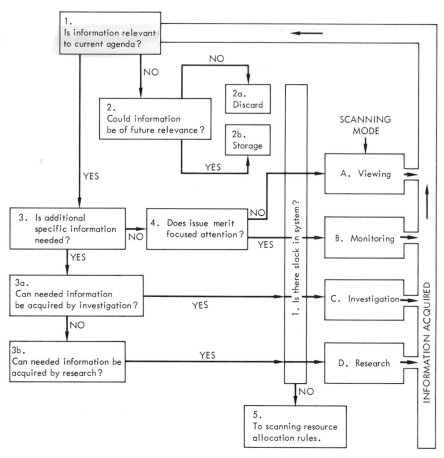

FIGURE 8-1. Mode Assignment

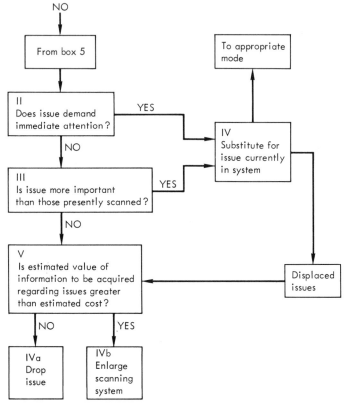

FIGURE 8-1 (cont.). Scanning Resource Allocation

for thinking about sources of information for multinational marketing, it is useful to know where executives responsible for managing multinational business operations obtain environmental information.

Human Sources[3]

As can be seen in Table 8-5, human beings are the most important source of information for headquarters executives of multinational companies. The most important human source of external information is company executives based abroad in company subsidiaries, affiliates, and branches. The importance of executives abroad as a source of information about the world environment is one of the most striking features of the modern international corporation. The general view of headquarters executives is that company executives overseas are the people who

---

[3]The following is drawn from Keegan, "Scanning the International Business Environment." Respondents in this study were international headquarters executives on a sample of U.S. multinational companies.

TABLE 8-5. Sources of Information (in percent)

Location of Sources		Types of Sources	
Inside organization	34	Human	67
Outside organization	66	Documentary	27
		Physical phenomena	6

know best what is going on in their areas. Typical comments of headquarters executives are:

> Our principal sources are internal. We have a very well informed and able overseas establishment. The local people have a double advantage. They know the local scene and they know our business. Therefore, they are an excellent source. They know what we are interested in learning, and because of their local knowledge they are able to effectively cover available information from all sources.
>
> Our principal sources of information are our country managers. Take India, for example. Our manager there has his own staff which includes, in addition to the usual business functions, a man in government affairs. The manager himself regularly sees people in government, the trade, other companies, and, of course, the physical setting. Of course, it is quite different when you don't have operations in a country. In fact, I could say there are two distinct positions for an international company as far as information is concerned. One is when a company is operating with its own staff in an area and the other is when it is thinking of entering an area. There is an enormous difference in the information potential of these two situations.

For the most part, company executives abroad are in the same functional area as the headquarters executive acquiring information. The international division head tends to get information from the head of operating companies abroad, the headquarters marketing executive from the overseas company's top marketing executive, and so on. There is a notable absence of information gained from lower-level employees, such as salesmen whose work brings them into everyday contact with the environment. (This pattern is by no means unique to international operations. Domestic business operations have been analyzed and there is little or no direct information flow from lower-level field sales people to headquarters marketing executives, product engineers, etc.). One of the major untapped information sources for international marketing is lower-level employees, particularly salesmen, who are in daily contact with customers and competitors.

The presence of an information network abroad in the form of company people is a major strength of the international company. It may also be a weakness in the scanning posture of a company that has only partially extended the limits of its geographical operations because inside sources abroad tend to scan only information about their own countries or region. Although there may be more attractive opportunities outside existing areas of operation, the chances of their being noticed by inside sources in a domestic company are very low because the horizons of domestic executives tend to end at national borders. In his book on foreign trade,

Kindleberger identifies the impact of horizons upon trade patterns:

> A man may be perfectly rational, but only within a limited horizon. As a consumer, he will normally restrict his expenditures to those goods offered to him through customary channels. As a producer, he will sell his goods typically in a given ambit. Over his horizon there may be brilliant opportunities to improve his welfare as a consumer or his income as a producer, but unless he is made aware of them, they will avail him nothing.[4]

Service organization staff are almost as important a source of information as the company's own executives abroad. Included in this category are all staff members of organizations that sell a service to manufacturing corporations. They are principally bankers, lawyers, and public accountants, but also include other specialists such as advertising and public relations executives.

Executives rely on the service organization group for three types of information. One type is the monitoring of rulings, expected rulings, and decisions of various foreign and domestic public authorities who control the conditions of market entry and participation: tariff and quota regulations, exchange controls, and so on. Another important type of information provided by service organizations is general investment climate information for a country or area. The major city banks in New York, Chicago, and Boston are particularly competent at providing this kind of information because of their worldwide network of personnel and the bank officers' practice of making periodic visits to various parts of the world, partly for the purpose of reporting back to client companies regarding business conditions, investment climate, and so on.

The third type of information acquired from service organizations is competitive intelligence. Advertising agencies and public relations executives are particularly valuable as sources of marketing information. Agency people talk about their clients' experience and plans. They are not malicious and certainly seek to do no harm to a company; they just tend to talk more than company people. Agencies know a lot about their clients, and they are not so security conscious as company employees. Public relations people are good sources of competitive information because they hear so much. Even if they are not directly involved, they are on the grapevine.

Another important human source of information for international executives is competitors. There appears to be a much greater willingness and openness in exchanging information with competitors among international U.S. executives than among domestic executives. The exchange of information is particularly apparent among those representing other U.S. international companies. There is a feeling among international executives that "we are all in this boat together." Overseas U.S. executives often face well-developed patterns of cooperation among established national firms. At home many international executives are still engaged in a struggle to gain recognition, support, and understanding of international operations

---

[4]Charles P. Kindleberger, *Foreign Trade and the National Economy* (New Haven: Yale University Press, 1962), p. 16.

TABLE 8-6. Comparison of Personal and Impersonal Human Sources
(In Percent)

Source Relationship	Inside Sources	Outside Sources	All Human Sources
Personal sources	97	80	86
Impersonal sources	3	20	14
Total	100	100	100
Number of instances	33	60	93

Live in isolation / dream world

from corporate management. In addition, international U.S. companies that are intensely competitive in the United States are often less competitive abroad, particularly in the lower- and middle-income areas of the globe. All of these factors *True* plus the social factor of common experiences, language, and attitudes serve to create a climate of relatively free information exchange among U.S. international executives. *Common bond : language - social contacts*

Distributors, consumers, customers, suppliers, and government officials are also important information sources. Information from these sources is largely obtained by country operating personnel as opposed to headquarters staff. Other sources are friends, acquaintances, professional colleagues, "free-lance" university consultants, and even candidates for employment, particularly if they have worked for competitors. As shown in Table 8-6, personal human sources of information far exceed impersonal sources in importance.[5] Eighty-six percent of the human sources utilized by respondents were personal. Interestingly, when human sources inside and outside the company are compared, 97 percent of sources inside the company were personal. The comparison suggests that lack of acquaintanceship is a barrier to the flow of information in an organization, thus underlining the importance of travel and contact.

Significantly, three-quarters of the information acquired from human sources is gained in face-to-face conversation. Why is face-to-face communication so important? There are many factors involved. Some information is too sensitive to transmit in any other way. Political information from government sources, for example, could be damaging to the source if it were known that the source was transmitting certain information. In such cases word of mouth is the most secure way of transmitting information. Information that includes estimates of future developments or even appraisals of the significance of current happenings is often considered too uncertain to commit to writing. One executive in commenting upon this point said:

> People are reluctant to commit themselves in writing to highly "iffy" things. They are not cowards or overly cautious; they simply know that you are bound to be wrong in trying to predict the future, and they prefer to not have their names associated with documents that will someday look foolish.

[5]*Personal* is defined as either a friend or an acquaintance, and *impersonal* as a person not known.

Other information does not have to be passed on immediately to be of value. For example, a division president said:

> Information of relevance to my job [strategic planning] is not the kind of information which must be received immediately. Timeliness is not essential; what is more important is that I eventually get the information.

The great importance of face-to-face communication lies in the dynamics of personal interaction. Personal contact provides an occasion for executives to get together for a long enough time to permit communication in some depth. Face-to-face discussion also exposes highly significant forms of communication, such as the tone of voice, the expression of a person's eyes, movements, and many other forms of communication that cannot be expressed in writing. One executive expressed the value of face-to-face contact in these terms:

> If you really want to find out about an area, you must see people personally. There is no comparison between written reports and actually sitting down with a man and talking. A personal meeting is worth four thousand written reports.

The greatest technological contribution to face-to-face communication of information has been the jet aircraft, which has made it possible for executives in a far-flung organization to maintain personal contact with one another. A measure of the importance of travel in international operations is provided by the size of travel budgets. The average travel budget of international executives (area directors, department heads, and key executives) is in excess of $15,000 per annum. It is not unusual to find executives whose travel budgets exceed $35,000 per annum, and a few hardy executives manage to spend over $50,000 per annum.

Documentary Sources

Of all the changes in recent years affecting the availability of information, perhaps none is more apparent than the outpouring of documentary information. The outpouring has created a major problem, the so-called information explosion. The problem is particularly acute for international marketers who must be informed about numerous national markets.

Although executives are overwhelmed with documentary information, only a handful of companies employ a formal system for monitoring documentary information. The absence of formal monitoring systems has resulted in a considerable amount of duplication. A typical form of duplication is the common practice of an entire management group reading one publication covering a particular subject area when several excellent publications covering the same area are available.

The best way to identify unnecessary duplication is to carry out an audit of reading activity by asking each person involved to list the publications he reads regularly. A consolidation of the lists will reveal the reading attention of the group.

In a surprisingly large number of instances, the reading attention of the group will be limited to a handful of publications to the exclusion of other publications of considerable merit. An elaboration of this procedure could involve consultation with experts outside the company regarding the availability and quality of publications in relevant fields.

External documentary sources are a valuable source of information for part of every company's international information requirement, and they are also a particularly valuable source of information for the student who typically does not have the human and written sources available to a long-time professional working in the field.

Appendix I of this book is a guide to major external sources of documentary information. Appendix II explains how to look up trade, tariff, and production data; Appendix III explains how to use the information resources of the U.S. Department of Commerce field offices; and Population, GNP at market prices and GNP per Capita (1974–76) is in Appendix IV.

Perception Sources

Direct perception is the source of a very limited proportion of the information acquired by executives as measured by message volume. However, it provides a vital background for the information that comes from human and documentary sources. There are three types of direct perception. One type is information easily available from other sources, but it requires sensory perception of the actual phenomena to register the information in the respondent's mind. An example is the case of the executive who realized that his flight from Australia to New Zealand took three hours.

Another type of direct perception is information not readily available from alternative sources. An example is the information that a company is erecting a plant in a country capable of producing a competitive product. Local executives in the country drove by the new plant every day on their way to their offices but were unaware of the product X potential of the plant under construction. The company erecting the plant had announced that it was for product Y, and local executives accepted this announcement. The headquarters executive realized immediately as he was being driven by the plant that it was potentially capable of producing product X. He possessed technical knowledge that enabled him to perceive information in a physical object (the plant) that his local executives were unable to perceive.

These two types of direct perception account for the messages obtained from this source. The third type of direct perception is perhaps the most important. This is the background information that one gets from observing a situation. It is one thing to receive a report or hear a description of, say, a new type of retail outlet such as the European hypermarché. It is another thing to actually visit such an outlet. Of course, in multinational marketing direct perception requires travel. Thus the independent variable in the use of this source is travel. Travel should be seen not only as tool for management control of existing operations but also as a vital and indispensable tool in information scanning.

MARKETING RESEARCH

A major source of information on international markets is marketing research, or the systematic collection of data. There are two basic ways to conduct marketing research. One is to design and implement a study with in-house staff. Too many companies overlook the tremendous potential of their own employees as sources of information. Salesmen, for example, are frequently the most knowledgeable people in an organization concerning competition and customer needs, and too frequently they are never consulted by management. The second source is firms specializing in marketing research. Each country has its own directory of market research firms, and there are also firms such as International Research Associates (IRA) in New York that specialize in international studies. International Research Associates has in recent years prepared studies of Europe and the Far East on a multicountry basis using a standardized questionnaire and a research design that provides comparable results.

COMPARABILITY OF INTERNATIONAL DATA

International statistics are subject to more than the usual number of caveats and qualifications concerning comparability. An absence of standard data-gathering techniques is the basis for some of the lack of comparability in international statistics. In Germany, for example, consumer expenditures are estimated largely on the basis of turnover tax receipts, whereas in the United Kingdom consumer expenditures are estimated on the basis of data supplied not only by tax receipts but also from household surveys and production sources.

Even with standard data-gathering techniques, definitional differences would still remain internationally. In some cases these differences are minor, in others they are quite significant. Germany, for example, classifies the purchase of a television set as an expenditure for "recreation and entertainment," whereas the same expenditure falls into the "furniture, furnishing, and household equipment" classification in the United States.

Survey data are subject to perhaps even more comparability problems. When Pepsico International, a typical user of international research, reviewed its data it found a considerable lack of comparability in a number of major areas. Table 8-7 shows how age categories were developed in seven countries surveyed by Pepsico.

TABLE 8-7. Age Classifications from Consumer Surveys, Major Markets— Pepsico International

	Mexico	*Venezuela*	*Argentina*	*Germany*	*Spain*	*Italy*	*Philippines*
Age	14–18	10–14	14–18	14–19	15–24	13–20	14–18
	19–25	15–24	19–24	20–29	25–34	21–25	19–25
	26–35	25–34	25–34	30–39	35–44	26–35	26–35
	36–45	35–44	35–44	40–49	45–54	36–45	36–50
	46 & Over	45 & Over	45–65	50 & Over	55–64	46–60	
					65 & Over		

TABLE 8–8. Definition of Consumption Used by Pepsico Market Researcher

Mexico	Count of number of occasions product was consumed on day prior to interview.
Venezuela	Count of number of occasions product was consumed on day prior to interview.
Argentina	Count of number of drinks consumed on day prior to interview.
Germany	Count of number of respondents consuming 'daily or almost daily.'
Spain	Count of number of drinks consumed, 'at least once a week.'
Italy	Count of number of respondents consuming product on day prior to interview.
Philippines	Count of number of glasses of product consumed on day prior to interview.

While flexibility may have the advantage of providing groupings for local analysis that are more pertinent (fourteen to nineteen, for example, might be a more pertinent "youth" classification in one country, whereas fourteen to twenty-four might be a more useful definition of the same segment in another country), Pepsico's headquarters marketing research group pointed out that if data were reported to the company's headquarters in standard five-year intervals, it would be possible to compare findings in one country with those in another. Without this standardization, such comparability was not possible. The company's headquarters marketing research group recommended, therefore, that standard five-year intervals be required in all reporting to headquarters, but that any other intervals that were deemed useful for local purposes be perfectly allowable. Pepsico also found that local market definitions of consumption differed so greatly that it was unable to make intermarket comparisons of brand share figures. Representative definitions of consumption are shown in Table 8–8.

One important qualification about comparability in multicountry survey work is that comparability does not necessarily result from sameness of method. A survey asking the same question and using the same methods will not necessarily yield results that are comparable from country to country. For example, if the data were recorded by household the definition of *household* in each of these countries could vary. The point is that comparability of results has to be established directly; it does not simply follow from the sameness of method. Establishing that results will be comparable depends upon either knowing that methods will produce identical measurements or knowing how to correct any biases that may exist.

SUMMARY

The first step in identifying international market opportunities is obtaining information about the location of market potential and competition. Once a company has established operations in different countries, the information required to manage these operations on an international scale covers a broad range of categories.

The skillful international marketer systematically not only exploits documentary or printed sources of information but also recognizes the tremendous importance of personal or human sources and the value of direct observation. The fully developed multinational marketing information system integrates information from each source category to ensure the best possible data base for analysis and decision making.

BIBLIOGRAPHY

BOOKS

Aguilar, Francis J., *Scanning the Business Environment.* New York: Macmillan, 1967.

Daniells, Lorna M., *Business Information Sources.* Berkeley: University of California Press, 1976.

Greene, Richard M., *Business Intelligence and Espionage.* Homewood, Ill.: Dow-Jones Irwin, 1966.

Le Breton, Preston P., *Administrative Intelligence-Information Systems.* Boston: Houghton Mifflin, 1969.

ARTICLES

American Management Association, "International Management Information Systems," Management Bulletin No. 103. New York, 1967.

Heskett, James L., and Peter F. Mathias, "The Management of Logistics in MNC," *Columbia Journal of World Business,* 11 (Spring 1976), pp. 52–62.

Keegan, Warren J., "Acquisition of Global Business Information," *Columbia Journal of World Business,* March-April 1968.

——, "Global Intelligence: A Framework for Action," *Worldwide P. & I. Planning,* July-August 1968.

——, "Multinational Scanning: A Study of the Information Sources Utilized by Headquarters Executives in Multinational Companies," *Administrative Science Quarterly,* September 1974, pp. 411–18.

——, "Scanning the International Business Environment: A Study of the Information Acquisition Process." Unpublished Doctor of Business Administration dissertation, Harvard University, 1967.

Kilmann, Ralph, and Kyung-Il Ghymn, "The MAPS Design Technology: Designing Strategic Intelligence Systems for MNCs," *Columbia Journal of World Business,* Summer 1976.

King, Williams R., and David I. Cleland, "Environmental Information Systems for Strategic Marketing Planning," *Journal of Marketing,* October 1974, pp. 35–40.

QUAKER OATS COMPANY (A)

The Quaker Oats Company, a large producer and marketer of food products and animal feeds, has long been interested in foods to help solve the serious malnutrition problems which exist in many countries of the world. Such a product is Incaparina, a bland flour which can be used as an ingredient in drinks (similar to low-calorie diet products which are sold in large volume in the United States), soups, sauces, pancakes, muffins, cookies, cake, and bread. Quaker Oats is considering whether or not they should market Incaparina in developing countries. The company is concerned about the impact of such products on long-range growth and profitability.

GENERAL BACKGROUND ON THE QUAKER OATS COMPANY

The Quaker Oats Company was founded in the United States in 1901 to produce oat meal for human consumption, and oat by-products for animal feeds. The company's first plant, and still the largest, was established at Cedar Rapids, Iowa. Today, over thirty manufacturing facilities are located in sixteen states; sales offices are located in principal cities throughout the United States and Canada.

The company also operates country elevators in Iowa, Kansas, Mississippi, and South Dakota, research laboratories in Barrington, Illinois, and experimental farms in Barrington and Libertyville, Illinois.

Foreign subsidiaries are located in Canada (nine plants), Latin America (plants in Argentina, Brazil, Colombia, Mexico, and Venezuela), Australia, and Europe (plants in Denmark (2), England (3), Germany, Italy, and the Netherlands (2)).

Over the years the company's product line has been broadened to include: (1) a variety of *food products* (e.g., Cap'n Crunch and Life cereals, Aunt Jemima mixes, and frozen foods, Ken-L-Ration dog food, and Puss-n-Boots cat food, (2) an extensive line of *animal feeds* (e.g., Ful-O-Pep Feeds), and (3) *chemicals* (e.g., QO Furfural, derivatives of furfural, and chemicals for uses in various plastic industries). Company sales exceed $450 million. Of this amount, sales outside the United States account for more than $100 million, primarily in Europe, Latin America, and Canada.

In the United States Quaker Oats products are sold through food retailers and wholesalers. Company representatives handle promotional activities with the trade, especially to obtain adequate shelf space and to assist retailers in promoting and advertising Quaker Oats Products. Consumer products are widely advertised, especially on network television.

The chief executive officer of Quaker Oats is the Chairman of the Board. The Vice Chairman, President, and two Executive Vice-Presidents report directly to the Chairman. Top management responsibility and authority is divided among these four.

The Vice Chairman has general responsibility for the Chemicals Division and several corporate staff functions—legal, purchasing, planning, and finance.

The President has general responsibility for the marketing activities of the Burry Biscuit Division, the Grocery Products Division, and the corporate staff functions of sales, advertising, and research and development.

The Executive Vice-President, Operations, has general responsibility for the Feed Division, and the remaining corporate staff functions, including production, traffic, personnel and public relations.

The Executive Vice-President, International Division, has basic responsibility for exporting and for manufacturing and marketing outside the United States. The world is divided into areas, headed by a general manager (Australia), a President (Canada), or a corporate vice-president (Europe and Latin America).

Although the Vice Chairman, President, and Executive Vice-President, Operations, have primarily domestic authority and responsibilities, they are gradually working toward "internationalizing" by fostering the idea among domestic officers and operating personnel that they should "think international" and be concerned about the types of problems and activities which are being handled in the international division. Close cooperation with international operations is encouraged.

LATIN AMERICAN AND PACIFIC ORGANIZATION AND OPERATIONS

Both the Vice-President and the General Manager for Latin American and Pacific Operations are located in New York City. These two officers have the general responsibility for exports, including sales, advertising, and physical distribution: also, line authority extends through them to the General Managers of Subsidiaries located in Argentina, Brazil, Colombia, Mexico, and Venezuela.

The Export Sales Manager and the Far East Sales Director are concerned primarily with exports. Foreign subsidiaries each have their own sales manager and sales force. The Production Manager, the Advertising and New Products Manager, and the Manager of Administrative Services, have responsibilities for coordinating and guiding subsidiaries.

The Production Manager has responsibility for directing the production and engineering activities of subsidiaries. He maintains continued liaison with domestic production, engineering, and research and development activities, makes or disseminates policies to guide subsidiary manufacturing, and provides assistance and direction in solving subsidiary manufacturing and engineering problems.

The Office Manager and Manager of Administrative Services for Subsidiaries has responsibilities similar to those of a financial officer, working to implement the policies of the domestic controller with regard to accounting and credit policies. He serves as the link between the domestic controller and subsidiary controllers. He also supervises those who are responsible for the preparation of documents for exports.

The Advertising and New Product Manager (A & NP Manager) has dual responsibilities, as his title suggests. With regard to advertising, he has responsibility of two kinds:

1. Export Advertising. The A & NP Manager works with an export advertising agency in much the same way that domestic advertising managers work with domestic agencies. After products are selected to be advertised, after countries are chosen in which the selected products are to be advertised, and after budget limitations are determined, the advertising agency prepares advertisements and makes media recommendations for review and approval by the A & NP Manager. The recommendations of the advertising agency often include (1) selection of foreign media, i.e., local media such as foreign newspapers, radio, cinema, and outdoor, and (2) selection of international media, i.e., media that circulates in a number of countries, for example, *Selecciones, Hablemos, Life en Español*.

2. Subsidiary Advertising. Subsidiaries have basic responsibility for planning and preparing their own advertising budgets and campaigns, but there are submitted to the A & NP Manager in the New York office for final approval. A substantial degree of local independence is felt to be necessary because market and competitive conditions differ from country to country, and people on the scene have the needed detailed knowledge to handle advertising properly. Likewise, subsidiaries usually have the freedom to employ whichever local advertising agency they feel is the best available to meet their needs. They are under no pressure to choose any one agency over another.

Subsidiaries prepare their proposed advertising budgets and programs and submit them to New York for approval, comments, and advice. Budgets which are out-of-line with established percent of sales guidelines, or which are based on unrealistic estimates, could be rejected or revised. The New York Advertising Manager also reviews materials (e.g., television story boards) sent in by the subsidiary's advertising agency and can exercise some influence if he feels his advice is warranted.

The A & NP Manager also is responsible for the exchange of advertising information and ideas between domestic and subsidiary operations, and among subsidiaries. He handles requests for assitance from subsidiaries and forwards successful materials and ideas to any location where he thinks they might be useful.

With regard to new products, the A & NP Manager performs a coordinating function. Although subsidiaries have their own product planning personnel and laboratory facilities, many new ideas come from the corporate research facility in Barrington, Illinois. The A & NP Manager attends a meeting every two months with research personnel in Barrington to learn about their new product projects. He sends ideas or samples of new products to any subsidiaries that could have an interest.

Every month subsidiaries prepare a New Product Progress Report in which they report on the status of new products which are being developed by subsidiaries. Other divisions in the company also prepare such a report. These reports are than circulated to all General Managers and research personnel, domestically and in

Europe, Canada, and Australia. By this method Quaker Oats personnel throughout the company are kept informed of activities elsewhere in the company. The report sometimes leads to direct exchange of detailed information and to cooperation among interested parties from several countries in the development of new products.

The A & NP Manager, working with the General Manager of Latin American and Pacific Operations, also influences priorities which subsidiaries give to the development of products. Occasionally, the priority accorded to a new product by a subsidiary (based on local considerations) is different from the priority which corporate considerations require.

The Corporate Staff uses all available sources of information on competitors' new products, both within the company (e.g., subsidiaries) and outside the company (e.g., newspapers, trade publications). Any division or subsidiary, domestic or foreign, can query Chicago for information and samples of competitors' products.

Since the company has unparalleled experience in oat products, the company capitalizes on this strength to sell oat products wherever they can be sold. Thus, in all South American subsidiaries, the basic product is rolled oats.

In addition, subsidiaries examine local foods which are widely used and seek to "instantize" them. The policy is to take a well-established food and to add "convenience."

Thus, in Mexico, in addition to rolled oats, the company produces and sells such products as Aunt Jemima Pancake Mix, Chocavena (an oat-based powder used to prepare a chocolate flavored drink), and Atolvena (a powdered drink preparation which is stirred into milk or water). Atolvena is an instant *atole* (the Spanish word for thin gruel).

In Colombia a major product is Frescavena (a powdered formula of oat flour, sugar, and various ingredients). Frescavena is a quick version of a popular drink which consumers formerly made by grinding oats into oat flour and adding sugar. The drink is popular in restaurants, as well as in the home, and is considered to be a refreshing, cooling drink.

Another major product in Colombia is Areparina, a pre-cooked corn flour. Arepas are a stapel in the Colombian diet, much as bread is a staple in the United States and Europe. Arepas are long and tedious to prepare and Areparina, an "instant version" of Arepa, has met with considerable success. Other major products sold in Colombia include animal feeds, oat flour in tins, Chocavena.

The major products in other South American countries are:

1. Argentina—Magica, a pre-cooked corn meal,
2. Venezuela—rolled oats, oat flour, and Frescavena,
3. Brazil—Vitavena (a version of Frescavena), a line of soups, Polentina (similar to Magica), and Milharina (similar to Polentina but prepared somewhat differently in order to meet the preferences of a substantial segment of the Brazilian market which desires this variation.

MALNUTRITION IN THE WORLD

It has been estimated that between one-half and two-thirds of the world's population suffers from malnutrition or undernutrition. In many Latin American countries the net food supply per person in terms of calories per day is less than 2/3 of the food supply available to U.S. residents. Even more importantly, high nutrition foods are in short supply. One of the most serious nutritional problems is lack of protein. The supply of meat and milk in many Latin American countries is about 1/3 of the supply in the United States. Moreover, the traditional sources of protein —meat, eggs, fish, milk, and dairy products—are too expensive for impoverished consumers in low-income nations; per capita income in most Latin American countries ranges between 1/5 and 1/3 of the U.S. level.

Due mainly to the synergism of malnutrition and infection, mortality rates are twenty to forty times higher for pre-school children in less developed areas compared to those of more favored countries.[1] Since pre-school malnutrition may retard irreversibly the mental and physical development of the survivors, the adult population of some areas probably has less vigor and enterprise and therefore is unable to contribute as fully as they might to economic, industrial, and social development. Some countries are finding it difficult to break out of the vicious circle of population explosion—malnutrition—slow economic development.

However, essential proteins are contained not only in expensive foods; they are readily available in legumes, fish, and in oilseed residues such as soy, cottonseed, or peanut meal. Since the technology exists to prepare foods from such sources at a cost which can be afforded by low-income consumers, one solution to the malnutrition problem may be to interest public or private organizations, with the manufacturing know-how and marketing capabilities, in producing and marketing such products.

INCAP

In 1949 the Institute of Nutrition of Central America and Panama (INCAP) was established in Guatemala City by the governments of Costa Rica, El Salvador, Guatemala, Honduras, Nicaragua, and Panama. The purpose of INCAP was to establish a cooperative effort to study nutritional problems and to find ways of solving them.

After determining that protein malnutrition was a critical problem, INCAP set about developing vegetable protein mixtures that could be made from local resources at low cost. After a few years the results of INCAP's work began appearing in the nutrition literature. Through papers presented at nutrition and food technology conferences and through continual publication in the literature, INCAP

[1] G. E. Belden et al., *The Protein Paradox* (Boston: M. R. Management Reports, 1964), p. v.

efforts received considerable attention. After more than a decade of research, INCAP, with a substantial reputation in the international medical and scientific community, took steps to arrange for commercialization of the products that had been developed.

INCAP had developed a number of vegetable mixture formulas based on raw materials which were available locally in Central and South American countries. The formulas contained corn flour or sorghum flour as a base, sesame, cottonseed or soy meal as a source of concentrated protein, calcium carbonate, yeast, and several vitamins, especially vitamin A.

INCAP had tested its formulas with normal children, comparing it with milk, and found no significant difference in nutritional value. Tests were also made with children suffering from protein malnutrition to compare recovery by the use of the formula and by the use of milk. In all tests the INCAP product resulted in satisfactory progress toward recovery. When tested as a cure of Kwashiorkor, the malnutrition disease that is a major child killer in tropical and subtropical areas of the world, the formula again was judged as satisfactory. Babies in advanced stages of Kwashiorkor recover rapidly when they receive an adequate quantity of the formula. They often show signs of recovery within three or four weeks and substantial improvement in six to eight weeks.

But, since INCAP intended its formula for foods rather than medicines, additional testing was necessary to establish its acceptability. In Guatemala acceptability trials were conducted in four villages. Mothers who attended regularly the health centers in these villages, were given a mixture to feed to their children as an *atole*. *Atole* (gruel) made with this mixture is prepared by adding water and boiling for 15 minutes. It is consumed hot. Over the 16-week test period 75 percent of the children drank two or three glasses of the new *atole* every day, and parents showed great interest in the product.[2]

At this point INCAP selected a trade name for the product. The combination of INCAP and harina, the spanish word for flour, led to Incaparina, the registered trademark for INCAP-developed mixtures containing 25 percent or more of proteins comparable in quality to those of animal origin and which have proved suitable for feeding young children.

Before making arrangements for commercialization, INCAP undertook a pilot test to see how the product was accepted when offered for sale. With the assistance and cooperation of the Ministry of Health and some interested commercial firms, a three-month sales test was carried out in a town of 3,600 near Guatemala City. The product was sold in 75 gram polyethylene bags, enough to prepare three glasses of *atole,* or one day's supply for a child. The retail price was set of $0.03 (U.S.) per bag. About 750 pounds of Incaparina were sold during the first four weeks. INCAP considered the test a success and made arrangements for a larger test to be conducted over a 7-month period in Guatemala City and other urban areas. Sales during this test amounted to 120,000 pounds, convincing INCAP that commercial introduction was feasible.

[2]Ibid., p. 32.

INCAP felt that the most effective way to make the fruits of its research available to the greatest number of people would be through commercial production and distribution, rather than relying on public organizations.

Since INCAP wished to protect its reputation as a scientific research institute, it felt that only responsible firms should be permitted to manufacture and market the product. In addition, INCAP wished to maintain some degree of control over product quality, advertising, promotion, and price.

Therefore, INCAP prepared a resolution which set forth the basic policies for licensing Incaparina. Commercial firms are required to:

(1) get the approval of the local government; (2) meet the general requirements of INCAP (see next paragraph); (3) submit samples to INCAP for analysis and approval prior to distribution; (4) maintain the specified quality and submit production samples required on a regular basis; (5) get INCAP approval of all packaging and descriptive matter relating to the product; and (6) pay the cost of analyses and other services in accordance with a schedule of fees.[3]

In explanation of the second requirement, i.e., the "general requirements of INCAP," it was decided that a commercial firm must:

(1) present proof of financial capacity; (2) describe the facilities to be used including laboratory equipment and machinery; (3) report the background of the technical and laboratory personnel involved; (4) describe the methods of distribution, storage, and transportation; (5) describe the arrangements for promotion, publicity, and advertising; (6) report on the sources of raw material supply to insure uninterrupted production throughout the year; and (7) present production estimates and request specific authorization for retail prices and special reduced prices to public and private charitable institutions.[4]

INCAP's policies with regard to consumer advertising are worth special mention. Some of the highlights of the policies are:

1. All advertising claims and other promotion should be based on well-established facts which have been substantiated by the scientific method . . .
2. The product should be advertised as a balanced vegetable mixture of high nutritive value. The protein content of 27 percent, while very important, should not be overstressed to the extent that the other valuable dietary elements . . . are overlooked.
3. The product should be promoted as a suitable supplement to the daily diet . . . Advertising based solely on the approach that Incaparina is a substitute for other recognized protein-containing foods should be avoided.
4. Incaparina is a food which has been found to be beneficial to all age groups . . . Nevertheless, because of high nutritive value, its use by pregnant and lactating mothers and growing children is recommended.

[3] Ibid., p. 35
[4] Ibid.

5. Any claims implying properties to the product which it does not contain must be avoided in the interest of ethical advertising and the protection of the consumer.
6. The following are a few of the descriptive phrases which must not be used in connection with the product: "Miracle Food," "High Energy Food," "Complete Diet," etc.[5]

In essence INCAP's restrictions on advertising prohibit a firm from advertising Incaparina as "better than milk." The restrictions also prohibit the licensee from engaging in "unethical" practices or from using exaggerated or unfounded claims. In some areas where Incaparina might be sold, standards or government controls on labels, advertising, and claims are non-existent, and INCAP felt that the product, consumer, and producer need protection.

LICENSING OF INCAPARINA TO PRODUCTOS QUAKER, S.A.

INCAP decided to license the production and sale of Incaparina in countries where suitable licensees could be found. When Quaker Oats learned that INCAP was ready to license Incaparina, inquiries were made to determine if such a venture would be desirable for the company.

The Quaker Oats Company has long been interested in the development of foods to solve nutritional deficiencies of large numbers of low-income people in underdeveloped areas of the world. The Company has been interested not only in selling such products profitably, but also in helping low-income undernourished people to obtain an adequate diet at a cost which they can afford. Moreover, Quaker Oats realized that to market a product such as Incaparina involves considerable risk and very likely a relatively long payout period. Since margins must be low, profits must depend on high sales volume, and this takes time to develop.

Quaker Oats had devoted laboratory efforts to developing a low-cost high-protein food since World War II. In fact, Quaker Oats had developed products that were as good or better than Incaparina, but had not marketed them. The company had planned to enter the market with its own brand, but INCAP had gained such a tremendous amount of favorable publicity that consideration was given to exploiting it by licensing Incaparina. It would have been costly and time consuming for Quaker to put its own product through extensive clinical testing and to achieve acceptance from health, hospital, and medical authorities, such as that enjoyed in Incaparina. It was felt that a basic advantage of affiliating with INCAP was that it would facilitate obtaining the support of the medical profession and public health authorities quickly. Such support was considered essential.

The INCAP license was considered desirable for additional reasons. INCAP licenses were granted on an exclusive basis in each country. Thus, Quaker Oats need not fear that INCAP would license a competitor in the same market. Moreover, if

[5] Ibid., p. 36.

Quaker Oats found this arrangement satisfactory in Colombia, there was a good possibility that Quaker Oats would be able to obtain an exclusive license from INCAP in other countries in which Quaker Oats had subsidiaries.

Preliminary planning was initiated. It was decided that if Quaker Oats entered into a licensing arrangement, a major commitment in personnel and facilities must be made. Quaker Oats had a strong, well-established subsidiary in Colombia, "Productos Quaker, S.A." The Colombian subsidiary, with more than 200 employees, was of sufficient size, with the necessary organization structure and financial resources, to handle a product like Incaparina.

Although Productos Quaker had experience with products such as Quaker Rolled Oats, Frescavena, Chocavena, and Areparina, local personnel had no manufacturing or marketing experience with a product such as Incaparina. Therefore, it was felt that the product should be given its own full-time sales manager and a dietician, as well as the part-time services of a chemical engineer, a chemist, a nutritional chemist, and a bacteriologist. For a General Manager, it was considered essential to obtain a young, dynamic, enthusiastic supporter of the entire concept of Incaparina as a "business venture to solve a pressing social need." Company officials had in mind such a man, who was currently employed with the Quaker Oats Company. This man already had indicated a strong interest in such a post.

Productos Quaker planned to distribute the product through normal wholesale and retail channels, which required a markup of approximately 5 percent and 10 percent respectively. After initial promotional efforts to obtain retail distribution in the introductory stage, it was planned to use the company's existing sales force to reach approximately 120 wholesalers throughout Colombia. These wholesalers sell to about 30,000 retailers.

A major reason for selecting Colombia as a potential market for Incaparina was the availability of suitable raw materials, at low cost, to make the product in accordance with INCAP specifications.

There were two factions in the company with fairly strong opinions about the project. One side felt that Quaker Oats should not go into the planned venture. They argued that the payout period would be too long, that the task of educating the people to use the product would be too difficult, and that the high degree of risk made a product of doubtful potential profitability an undesirable venture. Moreover, they argued, even if the product should achieve sufficient volume to yield a satisfactory profit, foreign governments might impose price controls.

Some of those who felt the product could not be sold on a profitable basis argued that governments should be responsible for producing and distributing such products. They argued that such products must be sold at such low prices that a government subsidy is needed.

On the other side were those who argued that Quaker Oats has a public and social responsibility to explore such ventures and enter into them whenever there seems to be a chance to do more than break even. It was argued that such activities provide a base for future profitability; enhancement of the company's reputation would facilitate the sale of other products and encourage foreign governments to treat the company fairly and with respect. Further, it was felt that governments would be reasonable in permitting a price which would yield adequate profits. Moreover, although the payout period may be long, it was argued that as economies develop in the future there will be opportunities to up-grade the product to the point where it can be sold at a reasonable profit. Advocates of private enterprise to introduce such products argued further that a nonprofit, give-away approach would provide only temporary distribution, rather than continuing distribution; they felt that a long-term commitment to distributing the product requires motivated people with managerial talent, and only private enterprise can get them. This is in accordance with the INCAP concept of producing and marketing the product.

QUESTIONS

1. Should Quaker Oats become involved in marketing low-cost, protein-rich foods to solve malnutrition problems in developing countries?
2. If not, what conditions must be changed before Quaker Oats becomes involved?
3. If so, what form should the initial commitment take, and what major factors should be considered in implementing this commitment?

information analysis

Given for one instant an intelligence which could comprehend
all the forces by which nature is animated and the respective
position of the beings which compose it, if moreover this
intelligence were vast enough to submit these data to analysis,
it would embrace in the same formula both the movement of the
largest bodies in the universe and those of the lightest atom; to
it nothing would be uncertain, and the future as the past would
be present to its eyes.

Pierre Simon de Laplace, 1749–1827

(Oeuvres, Vol. VII,
Theorie Analytique des Probabilitiés)

INTRODUCTION

The basic objective of international market analysis is to identify opportunity.
There are three basic types of opportunity to consider: those in existing markets,
latent markets, and incipient markets. Existing markets are those in which customer needs are serviced by existing products. Existing markets can be measured
directly by estimating the consumption rate of products in the market, or by
measuring the rate of local production of the products in question plus imports
and minus exports. Latent markets have potential customers, but because no one
has offered a product to fill the latent need there is no existing market. Incipient
markets do not exist in the present. However, conditions and trends can be identified that point toward the emergence of *future* needs and preferences for products
and services that will create a latent market, which if supplied will become an existing market.[1]

[1] I am indebted to H. Igor Ansoff for suggesting the terms *existing, latent,* and *incipient demand*
in his *Corporate Strategy* (New York: McGraw-Hill, 1965), p. 191.

Assessing opportunity requires a measure of both the overall size of a market and the competitive conditions in the market. It is the combination of total size and competitive conditions that determines profit and sales opportunity. In international marketing, companies focusing on existing markets must first estimate the size of these markets and then assess their company's overall competitiveness as compared with that of the competitors in the market by measuring product appeal, price, distribution, advertising, and promotional effectiveness and coverage. Cameras are a good case in point. The Japanese offered a superior design (they were the first to develop the single-lens reflex design in the 35-mm camera). While the overall quality and design of Japanese cameras was high, prices were relatively low (aided by an undervalued currency and lower wages), distribution was intensive, and communications were at least as good as those of the competition (mainly German companies). The results of this Japanese tour de force are shown in a comparison of the export data in Figure 9-1. In 1960 Germany exported $42 million and Japan $16 million. By 1970 Japanese exports had increased from 75 percent to 270 percent of German exports during this period.

A second market objective in international marketing is to identify and exploit latent markets. These markets present a very different challenge from those presented by existing markets, where the main challenge is the competition. The major challenge in successfully exploiting latent markets is the identification of market opportunity. Initial success will not be competitiveness, but rather ability to identify opportunity and launch a marketing program to supply the latent demand. Of course, if there are other companies producing the same or equivalent products, it is important to assess the likelihood and expected timing of competitive entry into latent markets. An example of a latent market was the

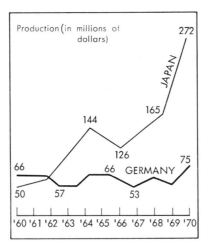
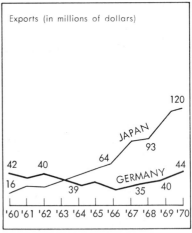

FIGURE 9-1. Japanese and German Camera Production and Exports, 1960–1970

demand for the very small refrigerators that developed in the United States because of the emergence of the vacation trailer or caravan. European and Japanese companies were producing small refrigerators for the household market and their smallest models were well suited to the needs of the U.S. camper. The same type of U.S. market developed for the subcompact car. People wanted small inexpensive transportation, and Detroit would not offer a U.S. model of this type. Volkswagen and other foreign companies exploited an existing latent market and positioned themselves in an emerging incipient market. Because of their leadership in exploiting this market, foreign manufacturers held roughly 20 percent of the U.S. market in 1977.

The British and Japanese motorcycle industries provide an example of different approaches to market demand. The British industry was well established before World War I and had attained a leading position in world markets. In 1969 the British industry sold 30,000 motorcycles (more than 450 cc.) in the United States as compared with Japanese sales of 27,000. In 1973, British sales remained at 30,000 units while Japanese sales had increased to 218,000 units. The Japanese had, in the short space of four years, opened up entirely new markets with products that attracted an entirely new segment of the population to motorcycle riding. Japanese machines were cheaper and more reliable than British machines. The combination of product design, quality, price, and aggressive advertising and promotion resulted in a 430 percent increase in market size, which was entirely captured by the Japanese. In 1969 the British industry held a 49 percent share of the U.S. market for motorcycles in the 450–749 cc.-size class. Four of eight available models were British. In 1973 the British share of this market was down to 9 percent, and only two of ten available models were British.

The basis of the Japanese success was a combination of marketing and manufacturing strategy. The Japanese identified the latent demand for motorcycles in the United States and then developed, manufactured, and marketed products that appealed to this market. Their strategy required major investments. A study by the Boston Consulting Group revealed that in 1973 net fixed investment per worker at Norton in the United Kingdom was only £1,300 as compared with £5,000 for Honda in Japan. Japanese value added per worker was £18,000 in 1975, as compared with £5,000 in Britain. In addition to illustrating the rewards to companies who identify and respond to latent demand, this example also illustrates the hazards to companies who rest on the sidelines while competitors move ahead. The British had experienced a false sense of security in their steady exports to the United States when Japanese sales were dramatically rising. Instead of focusing on absolute sales, they should have been sensitive to the implications of loss of market share. Their failure to respond quickly resulted initially in the loss of foreign markets and subsequently in the loss of their domestic markets as well. The Japanese have an absolute superiority in cost position and in resources available for engineering, manufacturing, design, and marketing.

Incipient international markets are those that will emerge as a consequence of known conditions and trends. Internationally these are important for planning purposes. In the United States, because of high wages there is a ready market for any product that saves labor and thereby reduces costs. Because domestic labor is scarce and incomes are high, there is also a ready market for household labor-saving devices. The same pressures or forces operate throughout the world. Companies marketing labor-saving products can predict with reasonable accuracy when demand will emerge in a country as wages and incomes rise, and can plan to deploy their resources to tap these markets as they emerge.

SPECIAL PROBLEMS IN INTERNATIONAL MARKETING ANALYSIS

The objectives outlined above are not unique to international marketing. However, international market researchers do face special problems and conditions that differentiate their task from that of the domestic market researcher. First, instead of analyzing a single national market, the international market researcher must analyze many national markets if the company investigates every nation in the world with a population of one million or more. Each of these markets has unique characteristics that must be recognized in analysis. And for many of these 146 markets the availability of data is limited. This limitation is particularly true of less-developed countries where statistical and research services are relatively primitive.

The small markets around the world pose a special problem for the international researcher. The relatively low profit potential in smaller markets permits only a modest marketing research expenditure. Therefore the international researcher must devise techniques and methods that relate the expenditures on research to the profit potential of markets. The smaller markets put a premium on discovering economic and demographic relationships that permit demand estimation from a minimum of information, and on inexpensive survey research that sacrifices some elegance in order to achieve results within the constraints of the smaller market research budget.

The marketing literature is replete with complaints concerning the difficulties of researching less-developed country markets. One of the most frequently repeated complaints is the lack of statistics and information on national economies. The criticism is somewhat empty because it is the nature of marketing research everywhere that only a small amount of data in the typical study is obtained from public sources. The great bulk of data for a study of a specific product or market segment must be obtained by the researcher in the market in both high-income and in developing country markets.

Another frequently encountered problem in developing countries is that data may be inflated or deflated for political expediency. For example, a Middle Eastern country revised its balance of trade in a chemical product by adding one thousand tons to its consumption statistics. It did this to encourage foreign investors to install domestic production facilities. Consumer research is inhibited by a greater reluctance on the part of people to talk to strangers, greater difficulty in locating people, and an absence of telephones. Both industrial and consumer research services are less developed, although the cost of these services is much lower in a high-wage country.

RESEARCHING INTERNATIONAL MARKETS

Survey Research

When data are not available through published statistics or studies, direct collection is necessary. One of the most important means of collecting market data is via survey research. Survey research involves interviewing a target group, for example potential customers, in order to obtain the desired information. Normally a questionnaire is essential in order to ensure a successful survey. There are many good textbooks that suggest how to design and administer questionnaires. The following is not intended to be a complete guide to questionnaires, but a summary of design with particular reference to conditions in developing countries.

A good questionnaire has three main characteristics:

1. It is simple.
2. It is easy for respondents to answer and easy for the interviewer to record.
3. It keeps the interview to the point and obtains desired information.

To achieve this, the following principles should be observed:

1. Single-element questions. An apparently simple question may have many elements. Questions should focus on a single element.

2. Expected replies. Wherever possible, expected replies should be listed on the questionnaire where the interviewer can check the answer. This eliminates a difficult coding task of trying to decide what people meant by replies that are written out on the questionnaire.

3. Ambiguity in questions. Carelessly worded questions can be ambiguous, as can questions with words that are not understood by respondents. Therefore questionnaires must be carefully stated in language that even the least educated respondents will understand.

4. Leading questions. Leading questions suggest answers and should be avoided. For example, "Do you prefer brand X because of its high quality?" is an assertion that provides its own answer.

5. Personal and embarrassing questions. This is a difficult area to deal with. One rule is to rely upon local managers and experts who are familiar with local customs and mores. It is important to ensure, however, that the local adviser is not excessively conservative in his judgments about what can be asked. Therefore the use of several judges is advisable to ensure that a single bias is not determining the questionnaire design.

6. Pretesting. A pretest is invaluable in determining whether or not a questionnaire accomplishes what is desired. No matter how much thought and effort go into questionnaire design, there are always unanticipated problems or ambiguities that are often identified in a pretest.

Sampling

Sampling is the selection of a subset or group from a population that is representative of the entire population. The two basic sampling methods in use today are probability and quota sampling. *Probability sampling* is a calculated method of selecting units for investigation. In a random probability sample each unit chosen has an equal chance of being included in the sample. In a nonrandom probability sample each unit selected has a known probability of being selected. Because the size of the universe in the probability sample is known, findings from the sample, if it is large enough, can be projected to the entire population from which the sample is drawn.

Quota sampling is the selection from the universe with specified proportions of various types of cases that are known to exist in the universe in the same proportions as they occur in the universe. Since the units selected for a quota sample do not have an equal or even a known chance of being selected, the results of a quota sample cannot be projected with any statistical reliability to the universe. However, if there are no reasons to expect that the quota is significantly different from the universe, then it is assumed that the sample will be representative of other characteristics. Thus only the probability sample produces results of statistically measurable accuracy. This is the major advantage of a probability sample. The disadvantage of a probability sample is the difficulty of selecting elements from the universe on a random or probability basis. The quota sample does not require selection on a probability basis and is therefore much easier to implement. Its main disadvantage is the possible bias that may exist in the sample because of inaccurate prior assumptions concerning population or because of unknown bias in selection of cases by field-workers.

Three key characteristics of a probability sample determine the sample size:

1. The permissible sampling error that can be allowed, (e).
2. The desired confidence in the sample results. In a statistical sense the confidence is expressed in terms of the number of chances in 100 tries that the results obtained could be due to chance. Confidence is usually desired at the 99 percent level and is expressed as three standard errors, (t).
3. The amount of variation in the characteristic being measured. This is known as the standard deviation, (s).

The formula for sample size is:

where n = sample size

t = confidence limit expressed in standard errors (three standard errors = 99 percent confidence)

s = standard deviation

e = error limit

$$n = \frac{(t^2)\,(s^2)}{e^2}$$

The important characteristic of this formula from the point of view of international marketers is that the sample size (n) is not a function of the size of the universe. Thus a probability sample in Tanzania requires the same sample size as one in the United States if the standard deviation in the two populations is the same. This is one of the basic reasons for scale economies of marketing research in larger markets.

A quota sample is designed by taking known characteristics of the universe and including respondents in the sample in the same proportion as they occur in the known characteristic universe. For example, population may be divided in six categories according to income as follows:

| Percent of population: | 10% | 15% | 25% | 25% | 15% | 10% |
| Earnings/month: | 0–10 | 10–20 | 20–40 | 40–60 | 60–70 | 70–100 |

If it is assumed that income is the characteristic that adequately differentiates the population for study purposes, then a quota sample would include respondents of different income levels in the same proportion as they occurred in the population, that is, 15 percent with monthly earnings from 10–20, and so on.

ANALYTICAL TECHNIQUES FOR RESEARCHING INTERNATIONAL MARKETS

Demand Pattern Analysis

Industrial growth patterns provide an insight into market demand.[2] Production patterns, because they generally reveal consumption patterns, are helpful in assessing market opportunities. Additionally, trends in manufacturing production indicate potential markets for inputs to the manufacturing processes. Figure 9-2 illustrates patterns of growth in large industry categories. It relates the percentage of total manufacturing production accounted for by major industrial groups to gross domestic product per capita. At the early stages of growth in a country, when per capita incomes are low, manufacturing centers on necessities: food, beverages, textiles, and light manufacturing. As incomes grow, these industries decline relatively and are replaced in importance by heavy industries.

Income Elasticity Measurements

Income elasticity describes the relationship between demand for a good and changes in income. Symbolically it can be expressed as:

$$\frac{\frac{\Delta QA}{QA}}{\frac{\Delta Y}{Y}} = \text{Income elasticity of demand for product } A$$

[2] This section is adapted from Reed Moyer, "International Market Analysis," *Journal of Marketing Research* (Chicago: American Marketing Association, November 1968).

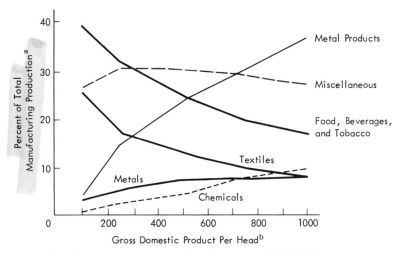

FIGURE 9-2. Typical Patterns of Growth in Manufacturing Industries

[a]Based on time series analysis for selected years, 1899–1957, for seven to ten countries depending on commodity.

[b]Dollars at 1955 prices.

where Q represents the quantity demanded, and Y represents income. When the elasticity coefficient is > 1, it is said to be inelastic. If a 10 percent increase in Y results in a 20 percent increase in the quantity A demanded or consumed, the income elasticity coefficient is 2.0. In this relationship A is said to be income elastic, because the coefficient is > 1. If a 10 percent increase in Y results in only a 5 percent increase in quantity A demanded or consumed, the income elasticity coefficient is 0.5. Since it is less than 1, the coefficient of elasticity is said to be inelastic.

Income elasticity studies covering both consumer and industrial products show that necessities such as food and clothing tend to be income inelastic, that is, expenditures on products in this category increase but at a slower percentage rate than increases in income. This is the corollary of Engel's law, which states that as incomes rise, smaller proportions of total income are spent on basic necessities such as food and clothing. Demand for durable consumer goods such as furniture, appliances, and metals tends to be income elastic, increasing relatively faster than increases in income.

Regional Lead-Lags

A regional lead-lag analysis assumes that demand patterns in a leading country are predictive of those that will occur in a country under consideration. The positing of a lead-lag relationship requires that economic, social, and cultural conditions in the two countries be analogous and separated only by time. There is empirical evidence to support the hypothesis that regional lead-lags exist. Two examples are television sets and automobiles.

Figures 9–3 and 9–4 show the diffusion of television sets in the United States, England, and Germany from 1946 to 1970.

Television was introduced into the United Kingdom and the United States at approximately the same time and into the German market about six years later. The yearly increase in penetration (Figure 9–3) in the United States was much greater than that in the United Kingdom. Thus, although there was no lag in the initial introduction of the product in the two countries, the initial market development of the product was quite different. The U.S. penetration levels have been approached by the United Kingdom with a time lag and with a less rapid growth pattern.

Comparing the ownership and growth data for England and West Germany shows the initial German imitation lag of six years remained almost constant during the complete pattern, and that German sales patterns have almost duplicated United Kingdom patterns in every way except in time. This constant time lag allows the forecasting of future development in Germany by simply taking the percentage figures for England six years earlier and multiplying them by the number of households.

On the basis of the data, it is clear that market forces influencing television demand are similar in England and Germany but different in the United States. The usefulness of this lead-lag analysis using the United Kingdom as a predictor for Germany exists because the time series of data for the two markets is long enough to allow formulation of a lead-lag hypothesis. Lead-lag analysis is analytic strategy appropriate for comparing markets that have developed over some period of time.

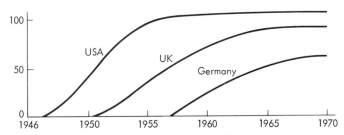

FIGURE 9–3. Percent of Households owning TV sets

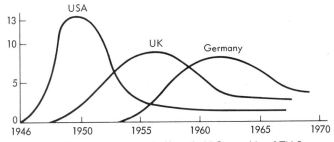

FIGURE 9–4. Yearly Increase in Household Ownership of TV Sets

Estimation By Analogy

Estimating market size with available data presents challenging analytic tasks. When data are unavailable, as is frequently the case in both less-developed and industrialized countries, resourceful techniques are required. One resourceful technique is estimation by analogy. There are two ways to use this technique. One way is to make cross-section comparisons, and the other is to displace a time series in time. The first method, cross-section comparisons, amounts simply to positing the assumption that there is an analogy between the relationship of a factor and demand for a particular product or commodity in two countries. This can best be explained as follows:

Let X_a = demand for product X in country A
Let Y_a = factor that correlates with demand
for product X in country A, data from
country A
Let X_b = demand for product X in country B
Let Y_b = factor that correlates with demand for
product X in country A, data from
country B

If we assume that $\dfrac{X_a}{Y_a} = \dfrac{X_b}{Y_b}$

And if X_a, Y_a, and Y_b are known, we can solve for X_b as follows:

$$X_b = \frac{(X_a)(Y_b)}{Y_a}$$

Basically, estimation by analogy amounts to the use of a single factor index with a correlation value obtained from one country applied to a target market. This is a very simple method of analysis, but in many cases an extremely useful, rough estimating device whenever data are available in at least one potentially analogous market for product sales of consumption and a single correlation factor. Some researchers have been quite creative in identifying analogous products. A major U.S. chemical company, for example, found that soup consumption was the only reliable index forecasting chemical sales in Asia.

Displacing time is a useful method of market analysis when data are available for two markets at different levels of development. This method is based on the assumption that an analogy between markets exists in different time periods or, put another way, that the markets in question are going through the same stages of market development. The method amounts to assuming that the demand level for product X in country A in time period one was at the same stage as demand for product X in time period two in country B. This can be illustrated as follows:

Let X_a1 = demand for product X in country A during
time period 1

Let Y_a1 = factor associated with demand for product
X in country A during time period 1

Let X_b2 = demand for product X in country B
during time period 2

Let Y_b2 = factor or factors correlating with demand
for product X in country A: data from
country B for time period 2

$$\text{Assume } \frac{Xa1}{Y_a1} = \frac{Xb2}{Y_b2}$$

If X_a1, Y_a1, and Y_b2 are known, we can solve for

X_b2 as follows: $X_b2 = \dfrac{(Xa1)\,(Yb2)}{Ya1}$

The use of the method of displacing time involves arriving at an estimate of when two markets were at similar stages of development. One might assume on the basis of analyzing factors associated with demand that the market for product X in Mexico in 1971 was comparable to the markets for the same product in the United States in 1936. If this assumption were valid, by obtaining data on the factors associated with demand for product X in the United States in 1936 and in Mexico in 1971, as well as actual U.S. demand in 1936, one could solve for the unknown, that is, potential demand for product X in Mexico in 1971.

Any technique as simple as estimation by analogy is subject to substantial limitations. The following factors should be kept in mind in using this technique:

1. Are the two countries for which the analogy is posited really similar either in cross section or in displaced time? To answer this question, the analyst must understand the similarities and differences in the cultural systems in the two countries if a consumer product is under investigation, and in the technological systems if an industrial product is being considered.

2. Have technical and social developments resulted in a situation where demand for a particular product or commodity will leapfrog previous patterns, skipping entire growth patterns that occurred in more developed countries? For example, it is clear that washing machine sales in Europe leapfrogged the pattern of sales in the United States. In the United States the consumer went from hand-washing machine methods to nonautomatic washing machines, and then, when they were finally available and reliable, to semiautomatic and fully automatic machines. In Europe many consumers are skipping the entire progression from nonautomatic to semiautomatic machines and are moving from hand washing to fully automatic equipment. Thus it is clear that the simple analogy between the growth in sales for nonautomatic, semiautomatic, and automatic machines does not

exist between the United States and Europe. Nevertheless, the analyst might conclude that one could lump together the nonautomatic and semiautomatic equipment in the United States market and use this growth pattern as the basis for estimation by analogy of potential demand in Europe.

3. The distinction between potential demand for a product based on underlying factors, and actual sales based on the combination of potential demand, and the offering conditions of a product should be kept clearly in mind. If there are differences between the availability, price, quality, and other factors associated with the product in two markets, potential demand in a target market will not develop into actual sales of a product because the offer conditions are not comparable.

Comparative Analysis

One of the unique opportunities in international marketing analysis is to comparatively analyze market potential and marketing performance. Three basic categories of comparison can be drawn in international marketing. The first are national comparisons, both intracompany and intercompany. These comparisons are a basis for much analysis in domestic marketing and also are applicable in single-country situations in international marketing. A second major form of comparative analysis is the intracompany cross-national comparison. This comparison is based upon the assumption that there is enough similarity between two or more countries to justify cross-national comparison of performance and potential. For example, if the general market conditions in country X on such matters as income, stage of industrialization, and other relevant factors are similar to those in country Y, it is valuable to raise the question of why any discrepancy between per capita sales in the two countries might exist. There may be good explanations for discrepancies or there may not be. Comparative cross-national analysis raises questions and suggests areas for investigation and is therefore a valuable analytical tool.

A third form of comparative analysis is based on national-subnational markets. Table 9-1 is a 1975 comparison between France, a national market, and California, a subnational market. The two markets are substantially different in terms of total population and total income. France's population was more than twice that of California, although it was growing much more slowly. French gross national product is double that of California. Although these differences in the microeconomic dimensions of the two markets exist, there are striking similarities in the area of specific products. Indeed, for many products, such as microwave ovens and dishwashers, California is a bigger market than France. As the data available within company management information systems become increasingly available on a worldwide basis, the possibility of analyzing marketing expenditure effectiveness on a market basis that cuts across national boundaries becomes a reality. Companies can then decide where they are achieving the greatest marginal effectiveness for their marketing expenditures and can adjust expenditures accordingly.

TABLE 9-1. National-Subnational Market Comparisons, 1975

National Accounts Data	France	California
GNP	$346 billion	$170 billion
GNP per capita	$5,950	$8,024
Rate of growth	3.4% approx.	

Demographic Data		
Pop.	53,100,000	21,185,000
Pop. growth	0.8%	7.8% (1970–76)
Pop. density	252.8	135.5/sq. mile
Urban/rural dist.	71.0/29.0	90.9/9.1
Principal city	Paris	Los Angeles
Pop. (Met. area)	9,863,400 (1975)	6,944,900
No. of city(ies) over 100K	14	21

Selected Statistics		
Road mileage	490,658	169,616
Railroad mileage	22,940	29,240
Automobiles (total)	15,000,000	11,311,000
Telephones per 100 people	26.2	77.0
Radios (total)	17,000,000	10,595,800
TV (total)	12,335,000	7,748,100
Number of radio & TV stations	91	280
Newspapers	103 dailies	122 dailies
Total area	211,152 sq. miles	158,693 sq. miles

Total Employment Sectors of the Economy		
Manufacturing	30%	22%
Trade/services	49%	39%
Agriculture	11%	16%
Government	12%	18%
Construction	9%	5%

Sources: United Nations, *Statistical Yearbook and Statistical Analysis of the United States, 1976; World Bank Atlas, 1977;* and *Statistical Abstract of the United States, 1977.*

Cluster Analysis

The objective of cluster analysis is to group variables into clusters that maximize within-group similarities and between-group differences. This objective is well suited to international marketing research because the national markets of the world are made up of similarities as well as differences that are clustered within regions and across income levels or stages of economic development. A number of computer programs are available for cluster analysis. One such program developed by Tryon and Bailey[3] was used to cluster data for ninety-one countries and twenty-

[3] Robert C. Tryon, and Daniel E. Bailey, *Cluster Analysis* (New York: McGraw-Hill, 1970).

nine political, social, and economic variables for 1966.[4] The analysis produced four clusters of variables: (1) aggregate production and transportation, (2) personal consumption, (3) trade, and (4) health and education. The ninety-one countries were grouped into seven clusters and one unique object, the United States.

Multiple Factor Indexes

A multiple factor index measures potential demand indirectly by using as proxies variables that either intuition or statistical analysis suggests can be closely correlated with the potential demand for the product under review.

Gross indicators such as GNP, net national income, or total population are useful in constructing an index, but wherever possible the analyst should restrict the use of factors to variables that are closely related to product demand. For example, an analyst interested in the potential demand for small electrical appliances might conclude on the basis of cross-national analysis and the time series analysis within single countries that personal disposable income was the best proxy measure of expenditures on small appliances. If the analyst is attempting to measure demand for coffee-making appliances of all types, an essential additional proxy would be the number of coffee drinkers in the country and the type of coffee preferred.

Ordinarily, market indexes are constructed not to measure total potential but to rank submarkets or to assign potential shares of the total market to each submarket. Erickson constructed such an index for Brazil using population, domestic income, and retail store sales, all expressed as percentages of national figures.[5] This gave him a measure of the potential for consumer goods for each of Brazil's twenty-one states.

An index of this kind can be used to establish sales quotas or evaluate sales performance. The Brazilian index assigns a potential to the state of Sao Paulo of 30 percent of the nation's total. If sales of the company's product fall below 30 percent, and the product sales are related to the three-factor index, management would have reason to question the performance in that submarket. Obviously such a tool must be used with great care. Full investigation may show that the sales performance in Sao Paulo is satisfactory, but that the index is an inaccurate measure of potential.

Regression Analysis

Regression analysis can be a powerful tool for predicting demand in international markets. If the researcher elects to use multiple regression tactics, which is the use of independent or predictor variables to estimate a dependent variable, there are computer programs available today that follow a stepwise procedure. The

[4] See S. Prakash Sethi, "Comparative Cluster Analysis for World Markets," *FMR* (August 1971), pp. 348–54.
[5] Leo G. Erickson, "Analyzing Brazilian Consumer Markets," *Business Topics,* Summer 1963, p. 23.

procedure selects the independent variable that accounts for the most variance in the dependent variable, and then the variable that accounts for most of the remaining variance, and so on until the user decides to stop. Using these tactics the analyst can select from a set of potential predictor variables those variables that explain the greatest amount of variance in the independent variable under investigation.

Table 9-2 summarizes regression results that relate consumption of various commodities to a single microeconomic indicator, GNP per capita. A linear simple regression model of the form $Y = A + BX$ was used, where Y is the amount of product in use per thousand population, and X is GNP per capita. As can be seen from the unadjusted R^2 in Table 9-2, this single microeconomic variable explains from 50 to 78 percent of the variation in the dependent variables.

The results in Table 9-2 can be interpreted as follows: An increase in $100 per capita GNP will result on the average in an increase of ten automobiles, ten refrigerators, nine washing machines, seven television sets, and twenty-seven radio sets per thousand population.

The variance in the dependent variable under investigation could be reduced by adding variables that are related to demand. For example, in the case of automobiles, in addition to looking at income, data could be obtained on the road system availability, on the price of automobiles, on the availability of public transportation, on the cost of keeping and operating an automobile, and on other relevant factors that could affect the sale of automobiles. With these additional variables it is possible to follow a stepwise progression analysis strategy and select that combination of variables that explains the greatest amount of variance in automobile sales consistent with an acceptable level of statistical significance. The demand for automobiles in New York City, for example, is far less than the income variable would suggest because of the negative influence on automobile sales of high insurance rates, lack of availability, high cost of parking, and the availability of extensive public transportation systems.

Many products do not lend themselves to simple single variable regression analysis. Moyer, for example, found a very poor fit for a regression of cement consumption per capita on gross disposable product per capita. Fortunately, however, the consumption of many products can be estimated reasonably ac-

TABLE 9-2. Regression of Amount of Product in Use per 1000 Population on Gross National Product

Product	Number of Observations	Regression Equation	Unadjusted R^2
Autos	37	$-21.071 + .101x$	.759
Radio sets	42	$8.325 + .275x$	.784
Television sets	31	$-16.501 + .074x$	.503
Refrigerators	24	$-21.330 + .102x$	.743
Washing machines	22	$-15.623 + .094x$	.736

Source: Reed Moyer, "International Market Analysis," *JMR*, November 1968.

curately by a knowledge only of income for GNP per capita in the market under investigation.

To use regression to estimate demand, analysts must first compute the regression using those "predictor" variables that are expected to explain variation in the dependent variable. If the unexplained variation is reasonably low, the analyst may use the results of these calculations to estimate current demand in countries for which no demand data are available. Getting the estimate of demand requires that the data on the predictive or independent variable be available. Assume, for example, that we want to estimate the ownership of refrigerators in country X where data on ownership are unavailable. We have through regression analysis of twenty-four countries the equation $Y = -21.330 + .102X$, $R^2 = .743$, which is statistically significant at the .01 level where Y equals refrigerators in use per thousand population, and X equals GNP per capita. GNP per capita in country X is \$1,000. Using the above equation we calculate the number of refrigerators in use to be 80.67 per thousand population. If we expect GNP per capita in country X to grow to, say, \$1,300 during the next five years, and if our regression equation is valid over this range of incomes, using the same equation the number of refrigerators per thousand population in five years in country X will be roughly 111.

HEADQUARTERS CONTROL OF INTERNATIONAL MARKETING RESEARCH

In the multinational company an important issue is where to locate the organization's research capability. If the company has, in addition to country subsidiaries, regional and international headquarters, then there are three possible locations for a research capability. Virtually every multinational company has allowed subsidiaries, if they are large enough, to develop their own research capability. This may create serious problems. Often, subsidiary marketing research is uncoordinated and unreviewed by headquarters, or, if there is review, it does not extend beyond the regional headquarters. In general, the worldwide marketing research efforts of multinational companies today are characterized by relatively autonomous country research efforts.[6] As a result there is much unnecessary research duplication and insufficient standardization. The unnecessary duplication can occur when a research unit asks a question without first determining whether other subsidiaries in similar countries have already asked the same question. Often the findings of a study in a country will be transferable to similar countries. Insufficient standardization occurs when countries managing autonomous research efforts produce results that cannot be compared on an international basis.

Comparability requires that scales, questions, and research methodology be standardized. To achieve this, the company must inject a level of control and review of marketing research at the global level. The director of worldwide market-

[6] A study of ten large U.S.-based multinational companies revealed that only one was making any effort to direct country research efforts. See "Multinational Marketing Management" by Warren J. Keegan (Marketing Science Institute Working Paper, January 1970), p. 20.

TABLE 9-3. Worldwide Marketing Research Plan

Research Objective	Country Cluster A	Country Cluster B	Country Cluster C
Identify market potential			X
Appraise competitive intentions		X	
Evaluate product appeal	X	X	X
Study market response to price	X		
Appraise distribution channels	X	X	X

ing research must respond to local conditions as he searches for a research program that will be implementable on a global basis. It is most likely that he will end up with a number of programs tailored to clusters of countries that exhibit within-group similarities. The agenda of a coordinated worldwide research program might look like Table 9-3.

The director of worldwide research should not simply "direct" the efforts of country research managers. His job is to ensure that the corporation achieves maximum results *worldwide* from the total allocation of its research resources. To achieve this, the director will need to ensure that each country is aware of research being carried out in the rest of the world and that each country is involved in influencing the design of its own country as well as the overall research program. Although each subsidiary will influence the country and the overall program, the director of worldwide research must be responsible for the overall research design and program. His job is to take inputs from the entire world and produce a coordinated research strategy, that generates the information needed by managers to achieve global sales and profit objectives.

BIBLIOGRAPHY

BOOKS

AMA Management Report No. 53, *Market Research in International Operations.* New York: American Management Association, 1960.

AMA Research Study No. 95, *Researching the European Markets.* New York: American Management Association, 1969.

Jaffe, Eugene D., *Grouping: A Strategy for International Marketing.* New York: American Management Association, 1974.

Kraemar, John Z., *Marketing Research in the Developing Countries.* New York: Praeger, 1971.

Kravis, Irving B., Zoltan Kenessey, Alan Heston, and Robert Summers, *A System of International Comparisons of Gross Product and Purchasing Power.* Baltimore: Johns Hopkins University Press, 1975.

Liander, Bertil, Vern Terpstra, Michael Y. Yoshino, and A. A. Sherbini, *Comparative Analysis for International Marketing.* Boston: Allyn & Bacon, 1967.

Armstrong, J. Scott, "An Application of Econometric Methods to International Marketing," *Journal of Marketing Research*, May 1970.

Boddewyn, J., "A Construct for Comparative Marketing Research," *Journal of Marketing Research*, May 1966.

Boyd, Harper W., Jr., Ronald E. Frank, William F. Massy, and Mostafa Zoheir, "On the Use of Marketing Research in the Emerging Economies," *Journal of Marketing Research*, November 1964, pp. 20–25.

Crosby, Richard W., "Attitude Measurement in a Bilingual Culture," *Journal of Marketing Research*, November 1969.

Green, Robert T., and Eric Langeard, "A Cross-National Comparison of Consumer Habits and Innovator Characteristics," *Journal of Marketing*, July 1975, pp. 34–41.

Green, R. T., and P. D. White, "Methodological Considerations in Cross-National Consumer Research," *Journal of International Business Studies*, Fall/Winter 1976, pp. 81–88.

Hodgson, Raphael W., and Hugo E. R. Uyterhoeven, "Analyzing Foreign Opportunities," *Harvard Business Review*, March-April 1962.

Holton, Richard H., "Marketing Policies in Multinational Corporations," *Journal of International Business Studies*, Summer 1970, pp. 1–20.

Moyer, Reed, "International Market Analysis," *Journal of Marketing Research*, November 1968.

Samli, A. Coskun, "An Approach for Estimating Market Potential in East Europe," *Journal of International Business Studies*, Fall/Winter 1977, pp. 49–55.

Sethi, S. Prakash, "Comparative Cluster Analysis for World Markets," *Journal of Marketing Research*, 8 (August 1971), 350.

Stobaugh, Robert B., Jr., "How to Analyze Foreign Investment Climates," *Harvard Business Review*, September-October 1969, pp. 100–108.

Vogel, R. H., "Uses of Managerial Perceptions in Clustering Countries," *Journal of International Business Studies*, Spring 1976, pp. 91–100.

Wilson, Aubrey, "Industrial Market Research in Britain," *Journal of Marketing Research*, February 1969.

QUAKER OATS COMPANY (B)

The Quaker Oats Company received from INCAP the exclusive right to produce and market Incaparina through its subsidiary, Productos Quaker, S.A., in Colombia. Terms of the licensing agreement were in accordance with the established policies of INCAP, as specified in Case (A). Although INCAP agreed to provide technical assistance in accordance with a schedule of modest fees, Quaker Oats paid no royalties.

Prior to making a final determination of whether or not to go ahead with the commercial introduction of Incaparina in Colombia, and prior to making final decisions on such matters as the precise nature of the product, package, marketing channels, promotional program, and the price, Productos Quaker decided to engage in extensive product and consumer testing.

Within a period of eleven months (from three months before, to eight months after, the date of Productos Quaker's licensing agreement) INCAP licensed other producers of Incaparina in El Salvador, Guatemala, Mexico, and Nicaragua.

COMMERCIAL SALE OF INCAPARINA IN GUATEMALA

Three months before the licensing agreement with Quaker, INCAP had negotiated a licensing agreement with Cerveceria Centro Americana, S.A., a locally owned company with 75 years of experience in the production and marketing of soft drinks, beer, and other food products. It took the firm six months after the date of the licensing agreement to take over the pilot facilities previously used by INCAP for testing Incaparina, and to begin its commercial sales efforts.

The retail price of the product was $.04 (U.S.) for a 75 gram package, with the wholesaler and retailer getting approximately 14 percent and 13 percent margins respectively.

Since Incaparina was already well known in Guatemala because of testing done by INCAP, the initial response of the trade strained production capacity. Sales within two months peaked at 23,000 pounds per month. Thereafter sales declined somewhat to an average of between 15,000 and 20,000 pounds per month for the next five months, which concluded the calendar year.

Sales in the first months of the next calendar year averaged about 17,000 pounds per month, and peaked in October when sales hit 30,000 pounds. However, sales in the last part of the year dropped off sharply as the supplier of cottonseed flour ran out of stock. Total sales for the year were about 238,000 pounds, a monthly average of nearly 20,000 pounds.

In cooperation with INCAP, the Guatemalan company developed during the first year a promotional campaign centered around public hospitals and health centers operated by the Guatemalan Ministry of Health to serve large urban and rural low-income populations.

Before the campaign, a sales supervisor and demonstrator had been trained in INCAP. During the campaign they were employed to promote Incaparina in rural areas. They used a panel truck especially equipped with a generating unit, a motion picture projector, and a tape recorder and loud speakers to demonstrate the preparation and use of the product. Efforts were made to inform church officials, physicians, charitable organizations, school teachers, and other influential people about Incaparina and to request that they advise people to purchase it.

Typically, the sales supervisor called first on the doctor in charge of the local medical center to inform him about Incaparina and to distribute technical information and samples. Then, a series of demonstrations were arranged for the medical center staff, teachers, mothers' clubs, church groups, etc., at which an *atole* or some other application was prepared and samples given to the audience. Several movies dealing with nutrition were shown in the public square or in auditoriums. The movies presented information on malnutrition and the development and use of Incaparina. Since movies are a rare and special event for rural areas, they tended to be well attended.

Following the film some of the product was sold from the mobile van. The sales supervisor then contacted as many local retailers as possible to gain distribution or to obtain reorders if Incaparina had been stocked previously. The mobile van campaign made it easy to get rural merchants to carry Incaparina.

The sales supervisor was also charged with the task of assisting and promoting local "Healthy Baby Contests." These contests are part of the regular efforts of most of the governmental medical centers to encourage better child care. The sales supervisor helped to organize and publicize the contests, to solicit prizes from local businessmen, and to demonstrate Incaparina in connection with the award ceremony.

TABLE 1. Sales of Incaparina in Guatemala

Year	*Pounds*
First (8 months)	153,000
Second	238,000

During the third year of sales in Guatemala, a researcher from Productos Quaker, S.A., in Colombia interviewed 86 retailers and 139 consumers in Guatemala City. He found that 56 percent of the retailers carried Incaparina, and that the product had a good reputation among consumers. Sales appeared to be better in small stores in poor neighborhoods than in other types of stores. Retailers, however, complained that they were not visited often enough by the distributor, a wholly-owned subsidiary of the producer, and that more and better consumer advertising was required. Subsequently, at the suggestion of INCAP, the producer opened up the sales of Incaparina to regular food wholesalers. This greatly improved retail distribution and sales increased to a monthly rate of 80,000 pounds; the trend continued and not long thereafter the increased volume and concomitant economies of scale permitted a reduction of over 20 percent in the retail price.

About 43 percent of consumers interviewed had purchased Incaparina. Usage was about evenly split between adults and children. The main application was in the form of the *atole,* although frequently consumers mentioned that they used Incaparina in soups. Consumers had a generally favorable attitude toward the product, price and package. They reported that they had learned of the product primarily through demonstrations at medical centers and to a lesser degree from friends, stores, doctors, and the mobile unit. Average consumption appeared to be about 2.5 packages per family per week, a rather small amount.

COMMERCIAL SALE OF INCAPARINA IN EL SALVADOR

Two months after the licensing agreement between INCAP and Productos Quaker was established, INCAP authorized the firm of Productos Alimenticios, S.A., to produce and sell Incaparina in El Salvador. This company was a major processor of food products in El Salvador and had some experience with packaged foods.

Governmental health officials and the local medical profession were strong supporters of Incaparina and offered to help in any way they could. For example, the Nutrition Section of the Ministry of Health provided training in nutrition to persons who were to be used as field demonstrators.

A formula for the product was selected (from among those that had been developed by INCAP) which utilized locally available grains. Productos Alimenticios, confident of success, purchased and installed the best production equipment they could find. Several hundred thousand packages were ordered in advance, as well as several thousand pamphlets and descriptive materials.

Introduction of the product was delayed a few months until a supply of cottonseed meal could be obtained from the only Central American producer of this material (another firm in El Salvador).

Once production began, Productos Alimenticios put the full weight of its sales organization behind the product. Heavy advertising was initiated, using local health centers as much as possible. No consumer acceptability or market tests were done by the producer prior to launching the product nationally.

Almost immediately it was clear that the program was not successful. The taste of the product was not palatable to the El Salvador consumer; apparently the product needed to be sweetened and flavored. Also the El Salvadorian preferred to let the boiled mixture cool before drinking; unfortunately when it cooled the mixture became too thick to drink. Moreover, the package was not considered attractive. Finally, it seemed that promotion had been directed too strongly to the "pharmaceutical characteristics" of the product, and that an approach was needed which concentrated on telling the consumer, in terms that he could understand, what Incaparina could do for him.

To correct the situation Productos Alimenticios added sugar and cinnamon to the product to improve the taste, and an enzyme suggested by INCAP to help keep the product liquid after it cooled. A new package was designed, slightly larger to accommodate the sugar, with a price per package increase of 50 percent. All of the previous promotion materials were scrapped and new materials were prepared.

However, rather than launching another national campaign, Productos Alimenticios decided to test market the product in Zacatecoula, a small agricultural town which was considered by the producer to be representative of the population of El Salvador.

The new product, named "Campeon," was introduced, and for two months the company made an intensive selling effort in the test market. Leaflets and samples were distributed, and up to 100 announcements per day were made on the local radio station. A truck equipped with a loud speaker and movie projection equipment was utilized also.

In spite of this effort, no "real demand" for the product developed. Thus, after two years, the license agreement was terminated.

INCAP, after reviewing the situation, felt that some preliminary consumer research and better use of carefully controlled market tests might have led to more effective packaging and promotion. Productos Alimenticios felt, however, that the *atole* concept was not suited at all to El Salvador. In Guatemala consumers were familiar with the use of an *atole;* but El Salvadorians were not. Also, the company felt that the Guatemalan effort might have been helped by the publicity surrounding INCAP's research and development work.

COMMERCIAL SALE OF INCAPARINA IN NICARAGUA

Six months after the agreement between INCAP and Productos Quaker in Colombia, INCAP licensed the newly-established firm of Alimen-Infantiles in Nicaragua to manufacture and distribute Incaparina. The firm was founded by a group of physicians who were interested in having a local supply of an inexpensive, nutritious food. Their primary motive was humanitarian rather than commercial.

Since the Nicaraguan government was interested in the project, the laboratory of the Ministry of Health was made available for product testing and development of facilities to meet INCAP requirements for product quality.

Production was started eight months after licensing. Since the Guatemalan tests had indicated the product was acceptable (to Guatemalans) they used basically the same product formula as had been used in Guatemala. Also, since the product was acceptable, they anticipated that sales would develop with relatively little promotional effort. Therefore, no consumer or market testing was done in Nicaragua.

However, sales did not go well; at the end of the first seven months of production only 4,000 pounds had been sold. At this point the company decided to dispose of its equipment and dissolve the enterprise.

TESTING CONSUMER ACCEPTANCE OF INCAPARINA IN MEXICO

In contrast with the above-mentioned ventures, INCAP licensed, at the request of the Mexican Government, the production and sale of Incaparina in Mexico to a nonprofit government-owned corporation, Compania Distribuidora de Subsistencias Populares, S.A. (CONASUPO). CONASUPO was licensed in Mexico eight months after Productos Quaker was licensed in Colombia.

CONASUPO is a part of the Mexican Government's social welfare program and, among other things, distributes food, clothing, and other basic necessities to low-income Mexican families at low cost. The company operates retail stores throughout Mexico in which are sold a complete line of basic consumer products such as clothing, food, and household utensils. Prices are below prevailing retail prices.

Since corn is more abundant locally than sorghum, CONASUPO selected an INCAP formula based on corn. Efforts were initiated to develop a local source of cottonseed flour, but until a local source was available, it had to be imported from El Salvador.

For some time CONASUPO had marketed successfully to low-income families an *atole* which is packaged in attractive, multi-colored, heavy-gauge, polyethylene bags. "Atole Popular CONASUPO," regular variety, which sold for 35 centavos ($0.028 U.S.) for a 100 gram bag; "Atole con chocolate CONASUPO," the flavored variety, sold at 70 centavos ($0.056 U.S.) for a 140 gram bag.

The experience of CONASUPO indicated that a flavored product might be best for Mexico, therefore a formula containing Incaparina, natural chocolate, a sweetener, and an enzyme was developed that had the consistency and taste of the chocolate drink which CONASUPO had previously marketed successfully to low-income families. Tentatively, it was planned to package and price the Incaparina chocolate drink similar to the *atole* already on the market.

Within sixteen months after the licensing agreement with INCAP, CONASUPO had developed several flavors of Incaparina *atoles*—cinnamon, rum and coconut, vanilla, rice, and chocolate.

For testing the consumer acceptance of the product CONASUPO incorporated the product into a mass feeding program, to provide food for people living in an area ravaged by drought. The program utilized a field headquarters, a grain and basic food packaging plant, 33 retail stores, and pilot centers in five towns. Each center consisted of one retail store, a tortilla factory, a sewing center, and a public kitchen and restaurant.

In the public restaurant in each of the five towns, the daily menu consisted of a rice dish with fish, a bean dish, and an Incaparina *atole*. The flavors of the *atole* were varied from day to day. Two serving lines were used, one inside and one facing outside for those who wanted to take the food home. The price of the meal was 50 centavos (about $0.04 U.S.).

Between 2,000 and 3,000 persons visited each of the five restaurants each day. The Incaparina *atole* apparently was well accepted and it was noted that considerable numbers of pre-school children and lactating mothers consumed Incaparina in the dining hall or took it home.

In addition, CONASUPO decided to test Incaparina in five field kitchens which it operated for 10,000 workers on an irrigation project. At each of the five field kitchens as many as 2,000 workers were fed each day. The Incaparina *atole* was well received, and there were frequent requests for second helpings. Many workers who were not familiar with atoles prior to the program liked them as part of their meals.

It has been estimated that about 12,000 people out of the 500,000 in the drought area used Incaparina regularly. At this rate, extending usage to the entire Mexican population would result in a total market potential of about 25 tons per day. CONASUPO felt that these tests indicated that the product had been well accepted and that, with proper promotion and advertising, the potential for the product would be even higher.

PLANNING AND DEVELOPMENT OF INCAPARINA FOR SALE IN COLOMBIA

Productos Quaker, recognizing the many possible pitfalls in entering into the production and marketing of Incaparina, concerned itself first with the development of an adequate and reliable supply of cottonseed flour, suitable for human consumption. Negotiations with Grasas, S.A., a principal oilseed processor in the area, led to a modification of the production process which provided cottonseed flour meeting specifications. Modification of the production process was necessary in order to eliminate a toxic ingredient which was present. A year after the licensing agreement, the first satisfactory batch of cottonseed flour finally was produced successfully.

Although Productos Quaker had done considerable laboratory and survey work during the first 12 months, the assurance of an adequate supply of cottonseed flour permitted the company to begin broader field testing.

During the next year, Productos Quaker conducted product acceptability tests at four hospitals and medical centers in order to demonstrate the nutritive value of the product. Although INCAP had already done such tests in Guatemala, it was felt that local work would provide greater impact with the Colombian medical profession, as well as give an indication of the acceptance and tolerance of Incaparina by children under Colombian conditions. The tests were completely successful.

Before making a decision on the product formula, Productos Quaker conducted a consumer survey among 150 low-income families in Cali and the surrounding area. Since the interviews showed a preference for corn, it was decided to develop a product with a corn base.

In May, two years after the licensing agreement was signed, Productos Quaker held a series of conferences with public officials in order to acquaint them with the product and the work that had been done to date. Leading public officials of the national and local government, including the National Institute of Nutrition, the medical and public health professions, and others, participated in the conferences. They reacted favorably to the proposed plans for production, quality control, promotion and advertising, and distribution of Incaparina, and they indicated their support.

In July, two years and four months after licensing, a comparison test was run to see if the consumer preferred a formula with cottonseed as the prime source, or a formula which substituted toasted soy flour for half of the cottonseed flour. The sample included 400 housewives, children and other persons. No significant preference was found.

A few months later Productos Quaker, convinced that it had an acceptable product, began a large-scale, 12-month test marketing program in Cali, a city with a population of about 700,000, representing about 5 percent of the population of Colombia. The objective of the test was to determine how well the product would move through regular retail and wholesale channels.

After obtaining placement of Incaparina in retail outlets, a promotional program was begun. The basic promotional approach was to use a "shock theme." A poster was prepared which compared sickly, emaciated-looking children suffering from malnutrition with healthy, smiling pictures of the same child a few months later after having been fed on an Incaparina-based diet. The "before and after" approach was used as the basis for the message that Incaparina was a matter of life and death. Additionally a five-minute movie was prepared, dramatizing the devastating effects of Kwashiorkor in an infant. This promotional approach was not inconsistent with INCAP advertising guidelines.

The reason for this severe, dramatic theme was that there was already a large number of other products being advertised as "good foods." It was felt that Incaparina's special characteristics must be stated in a way to clearly separate the product from others.

For a slogan, Productos Quaker coined "Es Mucho Alimento Y Cuesta Menos," which means, "a great deal of nourishment at a low price." The slogan has more "punch" in Spanish than when it is translated into English.

In the development of the promotional campaign full advantage was taken of the fact that the product had the active support of public health officials, social welfare groups, the medical professions, and others interested in supporting the basic social welfare objectives of the product. Much free publicity and advertising time and space were donated by advertising media.

In addition, the following media were utilized in the test campaign:

1. Radio. Four major radio stations each carried 360 commercial spots per month. The content of these spots was developed from information obtained during the Cali consumer survey. The messages dealt with concepts regarding nutrition as well as presenting facts about Incaparina, especially its nutritive value.

2. Newspapers. Because of the widespread community interest in the product, newspapers carried a number of news releases and feature stories on Incaparina, reporting on the reaction of various public officials and physicians. Newspapers were used only for publicity; it was felt that no paid advertising was required.

3. Point-of-Purchase and sales aids. Posters for use in stores, institutions and other public places were distributed widely. A special folder containing the basic facts about Incaparina in graphic form was utilized by salesmen in presenting the product to retailers.

4. Television and Cinema. The five-minute film (mentioned above) was shown in movie theaters and on television.

5. Demonstrations before Groups. One of the key aspects of the promotional program was the practical demonstration before a wide variety of groups of how Incaparina is prepared in the home. These demonstrations were given at schools, mothers' clubs, parochial centers, and other organiza-

tions. The same movie that was prepared for television and cinema was also used in these presentations. Additional visual aids were also used.

6. Seminars and Conferences. Meetings with physicians, nurses, teachers, and social workers were conducted on a regular basis to inform them of the views of prominent Colombian and foreign doctors and scientists. Special tape recordings of their views were presented.

In view of the need to make Incaparina available to low-income families, the basic pricing policy was to set the price as low as possible, based on estimated potential sales volume which could be obtained in the national market, and consistent with raw material, manufacturing and marketing costs plus a reasonable return on investment.

Since the price had to bear a reasonable relationship to basic food staples, if Incaparina were to be used as a staple food, and since the prime market was the 80 percent of the Colombian market that was not in the habit of purchasing any packaged foods in significant quantity, Productos Quaker felt that at a maximum, the price could be set at only a very small premium over staples.

No studies were made to determine price elasticity. The company relied on the price of other food products and the judgment of executives in estimating demand at the planned price. After taking all factors into consideration the retail price was set at 1.3 Colombian pesos for a 500 gram package ($0.13 U.S. on the basis of a 10:1 exchange rate).

Wholesalers and retailers were allowed a 5 percent and 10 percent markup respectively, which were normal margins for such products in Colombia. Institutions were quoted the wholesale price ($0.105 per 500 grams) when they bought in 35 kilogram quantities.

At that price a consumer could prepare a glass of Incaparina "*colada*" (a popular drink in Colombia similar to the Guatemalan *atole*) containing protein and other nutritive elements found in a glass of milk, at less than 1/5 the price of a glass of milk. In terms of protein per peso, Incaparina compared favorably to other products, as shown in Table 2.

In view of the need to keep the price low, inexpensive packages were required. Producers of Incaparina in other countries had used relatively expensive 75 gram bags. But, in Colombia it was noted that grocery retailers often bought products like Areparina in bulk, and then repackaged it into small brown bags. Therefore, it was decided to sell Incaparina in 12 and 35 kilogram bags and include,

TABLE 2. Protein Which Can Be Purchased Per Peso

Product	Protein Per Peso (in Grams)
Incaparina	114.5
Eggs	14.0
Powdered Milk	10.7
Corn Flour	7.0
Plantain Flour	6.8

separately from the product, sufficient empty 500-gram paper bags for repackaging at the sales point. The small bags were printed in attractive red and black. On the back of each package were four suggested recipes for home preparation. The recipes were for *colada,* soups, baby foods, and meals.

Although the repackaging method was not normal trade practice for Quaker products, retailers were approached with the observation that in order to sell at prices their customers could pay, many retailers were buying other products (e.g., Areparina) in large quantities and repackaging them in small bags. Since retailers had to buy the bags themselves, and Productos Quaker provided the bags free, they took the approach: "This is what we are going to do for you." Retailers were quite pleased and did not resist doing the packaging job.

RESULTS OF THE FIRST THREE MONTHS OF THE TEST IN CALI

In the initial placement (the first month of the test) 40,000 pounds of Incaparina were distributed to 984 stores and 16 health centers. Of the stores contacted about 70 percent accepted the product on the first offering.

All subsequent orders from retail outlets were turned over to four wholesalers. In the second month of the test wholesalers moved 32,000 pounds to retailers and institutions. An additional 23,600 pounds were ordered for delivery in the third month.

In addition to factory sales figures, Productos Quaker made a weekly audit of sales of Incaparina and similar products in a sample of 25 retail stores. The audit revealed, tentatively, that Incaparina sales appeared to be cutting into the sales of other flour products and tinned powdered milk.

Contacts with wholesalers and retailers indicated also that purchases being made in the third month were largely repurchases, indicating a favorable level of acceptance beyond the "curiosity sales volume" which might be expected for this kind of new product.

ESTIMATED INVESTMENT AND PRODUCTION COSTS

During the first two and one-half years of development work leading up to the test market, total costs were between $30,000 and $40,000 (U.S. dollars). This included staff time, materials, laboratory work on ingredient improvement, production facilities needed to produce pilot quantities of Incaparina, and the services rendered by the company's U.S. research facilities.

The installed production equipment needed to produce Incaparina in adequate volume to reach and exceed the point where it will become profitable is estimated to cost about $60,000. In addition, since the break-even volume of about 2000 tons per year is about two years away, the operation will operate at a loss of about $20,000 (including the net loss on the test market project). Thus, if the forecasted volume is achieved, four and one-half years after the licensing agreement was signed Productos Quaker would have an investment in Incaparina of approxi-

TABLE 3. Production Costs

Nature of the Cost	Cost in Pesos
Package material	5.95 per 35 kilo sack
	2.57 per 12 kilo sack
Grain and other ingredients	40.00 per 35 kilo sack
	13.75 per 12 kilo sack
Direct manufacturing, packaging, and other variable costs	30.00* per 35 kilo sack

*This figure is fictitious. Since the actual costs are confidential and cannot be released, this figure may be used for purposes of case analysis.

mately $120,000. But, if volume does not increase as rapidly as planned, the loss could be as high as $30,000 or $40,000 per year; these additional "sunk costs" which would have to be amortized could increase the break-even volume to as high as 3,000 tons per year.

QUESTIONS

1. Should Quaker Oats make the final commitment to produce and sell Incaparina in the Colombian national market?
2. If not, what conditions must be changed before Quaker Oats makes such a commitment?
3. If so, what should be Quaker Oats' marketing policies, especially with regard to branding, packaging, and advertising and promotional activites?

part four

FORMING
THE MULTINATIONAL
MARKETING PROGRAM

strategy alternatives for entry and expansion

The best Strategy is *always to be very strong,* first generally
then at the decisive point . . . there is no more imperative
and no simpler law for Strategy than to keep *the forces
concentrated.*

Karl von Clausewitz, 1780–1831

*(Vom Kriege (1833), Book III, Chapter XI,
"Assembly of Forces in Space")*

INTRODUCTION

When a firm decides to go international, it has a choice of alternative strategies or
tools for achieving its international objectives. In far too many cases, firms expanding internationally for the first time fail to realize the range of alternative
strategies open to them and instead, often to their disadvantage, fall into a single
strategy. In this chapter we identify the strategy alternatives for international
operations and suggest a framework for relating strategy alternatives to a company's
situation.

EXPORTING

Exporting is the most traditional and well established form of operating internationally. It is often identified as a low-investment alternative, but this perception in
our view is a gross and unfortunate misconception. Exporting does indeed require
no investment in manufacturing operations abroad, but if it is done effectively and
well it typically requires significant investments in marketing.

The advantages of exporting are that it allows the manufacturing operations
to be concentrated in a single location. Many companies in a variety of industries

have concluded that concentrated manufacturing operations give them cost and quality advantages over the alternative of decentralized manufacturing.

Part of the export versus global manufacture decision is an exercise in cost analysis and forecasting, which can be facilitated by advanced management science techniques in linear programming. Indeed a number of companies have developed sourcing models that take into account all cost factors and compute the lowest-cost source for supplying markets. Another part of the export versus local manufacture decision is estimating political risk and conditions affecting the access to target markets. For example, many companies have decided to invest in foreign market manufacturing facilities even though they could more cheaply supply target markets from home country manufacturing operations because their access to the target markets is blocked by formal or informal trade barriers or the threat of such barriers.

The decision to export or manufacture should not change the basic marketing program for the product in a market. Indeed it is essential to clearly differentiate the sourcing plan and the marketing plan so that each is given full attention regardless of the source of product supply for a market. Serious exporters invest in marketing in target markets. This investment begins with intensive market study leading to the development of a country marketing strategy. The hallmarks of this strategy are products that have been adapted to customer needs and preferences in the market (or in some cases left unchanged if this fits the strategy) and price, distribution, and communication policies that are an integrated part of the country marketing strategy. Each marketing strategy is of course unique so it is impossible to generalize, but the following examples illustrate the principles of export marketing.

Japanese automobiles. The spectacular penetration of the U.S. auto market by Japanese manufacturers is no accident. The Japanese product is a design that is targeted on the mass market in Japan and the compact and subcompact segment in the United States. The Japanese automobile was designed as much for the U.S. compact and subcompact segment as it was for the overall Japanese market. Japanese prices have been a major competitive advantage, which has enabled the industry to gain its market position. Japanese manufacturers have invested heavily in distribution to create an effective and extensive dealer network. Finally, they have invested in advertising and promotion. Indeed the distribution and communications strategies have been largely created by the U.S. marketing subsidiary of the Japanese manufacturers and are totally focused on the U.S. market.

Perrier water. After years of limited sales in the U.S. market, Perrier decided to create a U.S. marketing subsidiary. Based on a study and knowledge of the U.S. market, the president of Perrier U.S.A. decided to formulate a strategy for Perrier in the U.S. market. The major elements of this strategy involved the positioning of Perrier not as bottled water as it is in France but rather as a no-cal beverage. As part of this positioning, the product was moved from the gourmet or specialty food section of supermarkets to the beverage section, which has much greater traffic and turnover than the specialty food section. A second element of the strategy was to reduce the price from $1.39 to $0.79 a bottle. A third element was to create a substantial advertising budget to support and pull the product through the channels. This marketing strategy resulted in a spectacular increase in Perrier sales, underlining once again the necessity and value of a marketing strategy.

Historically the position of various countries in the world as export market locations has shifted. In the late 1940s and early 1950s the United States was a major exporter of manufactured goods. As the war-torn countries got back on their feet, the United States became increasingly uncompetitive in world markets, and as a result U.S. companies increasingly shifted their sourcing to offshore production facilities as opposed to exporting U.S.-manufactured products. This trend was reversed in the 1970s as a result of the devaluation of the U.S. dollar and the general factor cost inflation among industrialized countries in Europe and in Asia, which tended to equalize factor costs in the high-income industrialized countries.

Today factor costs in manufacturing are actually in three tiers. The first tier consists of the industrialized countries where factor costs are tending to equalize. The second tier consists of the industrializing countries which offer significant factor costs savings as well as an increasingly developed infrastructure and political stability, making them extremely attractive manufacturing locations. The third tier consists of those countries that have not yet become significant locations for manufacturing activity and which present the combination of lower factor costs (especially wages) offset by limited infrastructure development and greater political uncertainty.

LICENSING

Licensing is an alternative strategy that has an extremely seductive appeal. A company with technology and know-how can, through licensing agreements, attractively supplement its bottom-line profitability with no investment and very limited expenses. Indeed, licensing offers an infinite return on investment. The only cost is the cost of signing the agreements and of policing their implementation. Of course, anything so easily attained has its disadvantages. The principal disadvantage of licensing is that it is a very limited form of participation. All of the potential returns from marketing and manufacturing are precluded by licensing. In addition, a license agreement is often an asset with a short-lived maturity as licensees develop their own know-how and capability to stay abreast of technology in the licensed product area.

Even more distressingly, licensees have a troublesome way of often turning themselves into competitors. Thus many companies have found that the up-front easy money obtained from licensing turns out to be a very expensive source of revenue. One way of avoiding the danger of strengthening a competitor through a licensing agreement is to ensure that all licensing agreements provide for a cross-technology exchange between licenser and licensee.

For companies who do decide to license, agreements should anticipate the possibility of extending market participation and, insofar as is possible, keep options and paths open for expanded market participation. One path is joint venture with the licensee.

JOINT VENTURES

A more extensive form of participation in foreign markets than either exporting or licensing is a joint venture with a local partner. The advantages of this strategy are the sharing of risk and the ability to combine strength in a joint venture. Thus a company with in-depth knowledge of a local market might combine with a foreign partner who lacks market knowledge but has considerable know-how in the area of technology and process applications.

The disadvantages of joint venturing are not insignificant. Of course, a joint venture requires the sharing of rewards as well as risks. The main disadvantage of this form of international expansion is that there are very significant costs of control and coordination associated with working with a partner. These difficulties have actually become so great that more than one-third of the eleven hundred joint ventures of 170 multinational firms studied by Franko were unstable, ending in "divorce" or a significant increase in the U.S. firm's power over its partner.[1]

OWNERSHIP

The most extensive form of participation in international markets is 100 percent ownership. This form of participation requires the greatest commitment of capital and managerial effort and offers the fullest means of participating in a market. In addition, there is the not insignificant advantage of avoiding through 100 percent ownership any of the potential problems of communication and conflict of interest which may arise with a joint venture or coproduction partner.

One hundred percent ownership may be attained by either direct expansion or acquisition. Direct expansion is expensive and involves a major commitment of managerial time and energy. Alternatively, the acquisition route creates an instant position in a market but presents a demanding and challenging task of integrating the acquired company into the worldwide organization.

The four alternatives—exporting, licensing, joint ventures, and ownership—are in fact points along a continuum of alternative strategies or tools for international expansion and operation. There are an infinite number of possible combinations of these four basic alternatives. For example, a firm may decide to enter into a joint venture or coproduction agreement for purposes of manufacturing and may either market the products manufactured under this agreement in a wholly owned marketing subsidiary or sell the products from the coproduction facility to an outside

[1] Lawrence G. Franko, "Joint Venture Divorce in the Multinational Company," *Columbia Journal of World Business,* May-June 1971, pp. 13–22.

marketing organization. Joint ventures may be fifty-fifty partnerships or minority or majority partnerships. Ownership may range anywhere from 51 percent to 100 percent. There may be in addition combinations of exporting, licensing, joint ventures, and ownership in the overall design of the international strategy and in relationships with particular foreign enterprises.

INTERNATIONAL COMPETITION

A critical aspect of industry competitiveness is production cost.[2] The Boston Consulting Group and other researchers have demonstrated that for a wide variety of manufactured products, total cost per unit in constant dollars will decline characteristically by 20–30 percent each time accumulated production experience (the total amount ever produced) doubles. Although the precise reasons for this relationship are not entirely known, it appears to be a combination of learning by doing, management experience, working smarter, and scale economies in manufacturing as well as marketing and general management.

Given this relationship between cost and volume, a firm's cost position within an industry depends on its growth relative to the entire industry, that is to say, on its market share. Conversely, an industry's ability to lower prices for a given amount of production depends on the market shares of the individual producers or, put another way, on the industry's concentration. In the past a company's competitive strength was measured in a national framework. Today a company's competitive strength in an increasing number of industries must be measured on world scale.

The Case of Color Television *Worker Coop ?* *Subsidized by domestic industry?*

Japanese television producers offer a pointed illustration of an industry that took advantage of greater accumulated experience to obtain a large cost-price advantage over U.S. competitors. Between 1962 and 1970 the Japanese producers accumulated experience at 170 percent per year while that of the U.S. producers was only 56 percent. This differential growth rate was inevitable because it was based on domestic market growth. Exports did not begin until Japanese domestic prices were below U.S. prices, and penetration of the U.S. market did not occur until the price differential was substantial and also until third-country export experience had been acquired in black-and-white sets.

The mistake of the U.S. manufacturers who had once had a leading position was in believing themselves to be solidly established in the U.S. market. This was an expensive illusion because, as they eventually learned, they were competing not in a national market but in a world market. The lower-cost position of the more concentrated higher-volume Japanese producers has been a continuing undermining threat to U.S. manufacturers. By the end of 1977 Japanese imports accounted for

[2]This section is adapted from William V. Rapp, "Strategy Formulation and International Competition," *Columbia Journal of World Business,* Summer 1973, pp. 98–111.

over 2 million of the roughly 9 million sets sold in the United States. Also in that same year over 1 million Japanese sets were manufactured in production facilities in the United States. By ignoring the accumulation of experience in the Japanese domestic market, U.S. manufacturers permitted Japanese competitors to obtain the volume/cost position that has allowed them to make massive inroads into the U.S. market.

Market Position—A Strategic Guide

Although an increasing number of firms in the U.S. see the importance of domestic market dominance, few perceive the importance of worldwide market share. For U.S. companies, exports are still considered a fringe or an incremental production market. But since production experience effects are independent of where a product is sold, overseas markets are as important as domestic markets.

The pricing implications of experience theory are profound indeed. First of all, companies should vary their prices depending on the location and characteristics of market segments. Low export prices enable a firm to penetrate foreign markets rapidly and keep foreign competitors from gaining a foothold outside the domestic market because they frustrate the foreign competitors' ability to gain experience and lower costs. At the same time a dominant producer profits from a large but slow-growing domestic market by maintaining profit margins at a level that stabilizes market shares.

This strategy perserves the dominant domestic position by frustrating potential foreign and domestic competition and by preserving the domestic base. It enables the company to fund overseas growth from domestic sales. An export pricing policy of "domestic price plus freight and insurance" is inappropriate and dangerous from this perspective.

If a foreign competitor penetrates a firm's domestic market, the domestic firm should lower its domestic prices. In the United States this could be a problem for a dominant producer if such a price cut damaged smaller U.S. producers and invited government antitrust action. This consideration makes an aggressive export pricing policy an even more desirable strategy for U.S. competitors.

An example of the integrated use of this strategy on a multinational basis is the U.S. semiconductor industry where experience curve analysis has been well understood and widely applied. In this industry, current generation semiconductors and integrated circuits are produced in the United States and older established products are produced abroad. By following this strategy American producers have successfully encircled potential Japanese competition.

The recommended strategic program for the single-product, single-plant firm is investment in process as well as product improvement and the maintenance of world market dominance from the single source by developing and dominating new segments of markets and keeping cost competitive in old ones. Exports are absolutely critical to the single-plant firm's continued competitiveness. Thus the single-plant firm needs an overseas marketing system and strategy. It must seek to reduce overseas marketing costs through integrated logistical systems, and it must invest in country marketing programs to ensure that it reaches customers with an integrated marketing mix.

MARKETING STRATEGIES OF U.S., EUROPEAN, AND JAPANESE MULTINATIONAL SUBSIDIARIES

Brandt and Hulbert found distinct national influences in subsidiary strategies in management practices in their study of subsidiaries of multinational companies in Brazil.[3] The American subsidiaries in their sample were characterized as mature, established firms operating within a well-defined management system under the watchful eye of the home office. In contrast to the European and Japanese, the American procedures for planning, reporting, and control and evaluation were much more formalized and clearly defined.

According to Brandt and Hulbert, American subsidiaries rely on product innovation as the key to continued growth. European strategies, they found, were much more defensive. European subsidiaries, for example, demonstrated a strong preference for penetration of existing or closely related markets rather than entry via new products into new markets. The Japanese companies adopted a strategy of low-cost, high-volume production in limited product lines, which enabled them to use price as a major competitive tool for achieving the number one goal which was sales growth. The Japanese concern is with sales volume. One manager described this as a "profit neglecting selling strategy" and pointed out that his company profits resulted as much from concern over production efficiencies as from profit margins. According to Brandt and Hulbert, Japanese companies seemed to operate with less overhead. Their offices were typically spartan and organizational structures were lean.

THE EPRG FRAMEWORK

The EPRG schema (ethnocentrism, polycentrism, regiocentrism, geocentrism) identifies four types of attitudes or orientations toward internationalization that are associated with successive stages in the evolution of international operations. *Ethnocentrism* is associated with a home country orientation, *polycentrism* with a host country orientation, *regiocentrism* with a regional orientation, and *geocentrism* with a world orientation.[4]

In the ethnocentric company, overseas operations are viewed as being secondary to domestic and primarily as a means of disposing of surplus domestic production. Plans for overseas markets are developed in the home office utilizing policies

---

[3]William K. Brandt and James M. Hulbert, "Marketing Strategies of American, European and Japanese Multinational Subsidiaries" (Paper presented at the Academy of International Business Meeting, Fontainebleau, France, July 7–9, 1975).

[4]Yoram Wind, Susan P. Douglas, and Howard V. Perlmutter, "Guidelines for Developing International Marketing Strategy," *Journal of Marketing,* 37 (April 1973), 14–23.

and procedures identical to those employed at home. There is no systematic marketing research conducted overseas, there are no major modifications to products, there is no real attention to customer needs in foreign markets.

In the polycentric stage, subsidiaries are established in overseas markets. Each subsidiary operates independently of the others and establishes its own marketing objectives and plans. Marketing is organized on a country-by-country basis, with each country having its own unique marketing policy.

In the regiocentric and geocentric phases, the company views the region or entire world as a market and seeks to develop integrated regional or world market strategies. The ethnocentric company is centralized in its marketing management, the polycentric company is decentralized, the regiocentric and geocentric companies are integrated.

A crucial difference between the orientations is in the underlying assumption for each orientation. The ethnocentric orientation is based on a belief in home country superiority. This leads to an extension of home country products, policies, and programs. The underlying assumption of the polycentric approach is that there are so many differences in cultural, economic, and market conditions in each of the countries of the world that it is impossible to attempt to introduce any product, policy, or program from outside or to integrate any country's program in a regional or world context.

The regiocentric and geocentric assumptions hold that it is possible to identify both similarities and differences and to formulate an integrated regional or world marketing strategy on the basis of actual as opposed to imagined similarities and differences. While there can be no question that the geocentric orientation most accurately captures market reality, it does not follow that the geocentric orientation requires an integrated world structure and strategy. In order to implement the geocentric orientation, experienced international management and a great deal of commitment are required. For companies with limited experience it may be wiser to adopt either a centralized or a decentralized strategy and wait until experience accumulates before attempting to design and implement integrated marketing programs.

To underline this point, the case of a basically ethnocentric U.S. company is instructive. Several years ago this company, after reviewing the international business literature, decided that its ethnocentric corporate international division structure was not the most advanced way of operating internationally. Management decided therefore to abandon or dissolve the corporate international division and establish each of the company's product divisions as worldwide product divisions. This was implemented by top-management edict, and overnight each of the formerly domestic product divisions was responsible for its products on a worldwide basis. The consequences of this move were disastrous. In one typical division, managers acquired a European company and neglected to retain the seller as general manager. The seller proceeded to go to Switzerland for a ski holiday and the American company proceeded to run the acquired company into the ground. Eighteen months after the acquisition the seller publicly announced his willingness to repurchase his own company at one-half the price the American company had paid for it. To add insult to injury he also publicly announced that each day the American company waited the price would go down. The American company accepted the offer! This case illustrates the disastrous consequences of adopting a design or approach without giving full consideration to the capabilities of existing management.

Table 10-1 suggests three basic alternative international business strategies: stage 1 and stage 2 international strategies correspond with ethnocentric and poly-centric orientations, respectively; the multinational stage 3 strategy corresponds with the geocentric orientation. The basic design of the stage 1, or ethnocentric, strategy is extension. Companies following this approach seek either consciously or unconsciously to extend their products and programs as much as possible. The basic design of stage 2 is decentralization where insofar as possible responsibilities for local operations are delegated to subsidiary management. The stage 3 design is an integration model, which seeks to synthesize inputs from world and regional head-quarters and the country organization.

As can be seen from Table 10-1, there is an evolution from stage 1 to stage 3 in all the major elements that make up the overall organization and its approach to international business. Structurally the evolution is from an international division to a regional organization to the matrix. The planning process is top down in stage 1, bottom up in stage 2, and interactive in stage 3. Decision-making and marketing programs evolve from standardized or centralized in stage 1, to unique and decen-tralized in stage 2, to an interactive and circumstantial process in stage 3. The marketing process itself tends to be ad hoc in stages 1 and 2 and standardized in stage 3. In this area a major hallmark of evolution is the adoption not of stan-

TABLE 10-1. International Business Strategy: Three Alternatives

Strategic Focus	International		Multinational
	Stage 1	Stage 2	Stage 3
Management assumptions	Ethnocentric	Polycentric	Geocentric
Design	Extension	Decentralization	Integration
Structure	International division	Regional division	Matrix/grid
Planning process	Top down	Bottom up	Interactive
Decision making	Centralized	Decentralized	Circumstantial/ interactive
Marketing process	Ad hoc	Ad hoc	Standardized
Marketing programs	Standardized	Unique	Circumstantial/ interactive
Product sourcing	Export	Local manufacture	Circumstantial
Human resources			
Key job nationality			
Country management	Home country	Host country	Best person
H.Q. management	Home country	Home country	Best person
R&D—Product development	Home country	Decentralized, fragmented	Circumstantial/ integrated
Control/measurement	Home country standards	Decentralized	Circumstantial

dardized marketing programs but of a standardized marketing vocabulary and approach.

In stage 1 the typical product sourcing plan is an export arrangement where, as in stage 2, the most frequent or preferred sourcing arrangement is local manufacture. In stage 3, product sourcing is based on a sourcing plan that takes into account cost, delivery, and all other factors affecting competitiveness and profitability and produces a sourcing plan that maximizes both competitive effectiveness and profitability. In stage 1, companies' key jobs go to home country nationals in both the subsidiaries and the headquarters. In stage 2, key jobs in host countries go to country nationals, whereas headquarters management positions are usually held by some country nationals. In stage 3 the best person is selected for all management positions regardless of nationality. Research and development in stage 1 is conducted in the home country and in stage 2 becomes decentralized and fragmented. In stage 3, research is part of an integrated worldwide research and development plan and is typically decentralized taking advantage of resources, as well as responding to local aspirations to produce a worldwide decentralized research and development program.

Control and measurement standards are usually in stage 1 based on home country experience, whereas in stage 2 they become highly decentralized. In stage 3, control and measurement standards are circumstantial and take into account both local conditions and international experience.

This scheme is of course a simplification of actual behavior. No company exactly fits the stages outlined. Nevertheless, the strategy alternatives model of Table 10-1 suggests evolutionary patterns and can be a useful guide to developing a more effective multinational company.

CONCLUSION

Companies face a wide range of alternative ways of participating in international markets. Those who have had experience in international marketing realize that it is necessary to practice marketing regardless of sourcing arrangements. Companies committed to marketing study the foreign customer and in effect become so knowledgeable about the "foreign" market that it is no longer foreign but rather a market in a geographical location as are all other markets. This is a fundamental application of the marketing concept and if applied leads to the formulation of a unique and adapted marketing strategy that integrates product, price, distribution, and communication elements in an appropriate way consistent with corporate and product strengths and weaknesses as well as competitive reality.

Companies who have developed an appropriate marketing strategy are then able to reach a decision about the most effective sourcing arrangements. Sourcing plans must again take into account organizational resources, strengths and weaknesses, factor costs, transportation costs, conditions of market access and entry, and realistic assessments of political risk and of future conditions at entry, as well as security of investment position in the target market. Obviously the choice of an appropriate strategy is complex and is one that always involves an element of risk and uncertainty. In this chapter we have outlined the major alternative tools and highlighted factors and conditions that should influence the choice of these tools.

BIBLIOGRAPHY

Barnett, John S., "Corporate Foreign Exposure Strategy Formulations," *Columbia Journal of World Business,* 11, No. 4 (Winter 1976), 87–97.

David, H. L., G. D. Eppen, and L. G. Mattsson, "Critical Factors in Worldwide Purchasing," *Harvard Business Review,* November-December 1974, pp. 81–90.

Franko, Lawrence G., "Patterns in the Multinational Spread of Continental European Enterprise," *Journal of International Business Studies,* Fall 1975, pp. 41–54.

Gregory, Gene, "Japan's New Multinationalism: The Canon Giessen Experience," *Columbia Journal of World Business,* 11, No. 1 (Spring 1976), 122–29.

Gullander, Steffan, "Joint Ventures and Corporate Strategy," *Columbia Journal of World Business,* 11, No. 1 (Spring 1976), 104–14.

Hawkins, R. G., N. Mintz, and M. Provissiero, "Government Takeovers of U.S. Foreign Affiliates," *Journal of International Business Studies,* Spring 1976, pp. 3–16.

Kitching, John, "Winning and Losing with European Acquisitions," *Harvard Business Review,* March-April 1974, pp. 124–36.

Lamont, Douglas F., "Joining Forces with Foreign State Enterprises," *Harvard Business Review,* July-August 1973, pp. 68–79.

McClain, David, "European Economic Forecasting: The State of the Art," *Columbia Journal of World Business,* 11, No. 4 (Winter 1976), 20–27.

McIntyre, David R., "Multinational Positioning Strategy," *Columbia Journal of World Business,* 10, No. 3 (Fall 1975), 106–10.

Mazzolini, Renato, "European Corporate Strategies," *Columbia Journal of World Business,* 10, No. 1 (Spring 1975), 98–108.

Perlmutter, Howard V., and David A. Heenan, "How Multinational Should Your Top Managers Be?" *Harvard Business Review,* November-December 1974, pp. 121–32.

Peterson, Richard B., and Hermann F. Schwind, "A Comparative Study of Personnel Problems in International Companies and Joint Ventures in Japan," *Journal of International Business Studies,* Spring/Summer 1977, pp. 45–56.

Phahalad, C. K., "Strategic Choices in Diversified MNC's," *Harvard Business Review,* July-August 1976, pp. 67–78.

Rugman, A., "Risk Reduction by International Diversification," *Journal of International Business Studies,* Fall/Winter 1976, pp. 74–80.

Shearer, John C., "The External and Internal Manpower Resources of Multinational Corporations," *Columbia Journal of World Business,* 9, No. 2 (Summer 1974), 9–17.

Stopford, J. M., "Changing Perspectives on Investment by British Manufacturing Multinationals," *Journal of International Business Studies,* Fall/Winter 1976, pp. 15–28.

van Cise, Jerrold G., "Antitrust Guides to Foreign Acquisitions," *Harvard Business Review,* November-December 1972, pp. 82–88.

Welles, John G., "Multinationals Need New Environmental Strategies," *Columbia Journal of World Business,* 8, No. 2 (Summer 1973), 11–18.

Wells, Louis T., Jr., "Negotiating with Third World Governments," *Harvard Business Review,* January-February 1977, pp. 72–80.

——, "Social Cost/Benefit Analysis for MNC's," *Harvard Business Review,* March-April 1975, pp. 40–50.

Wind, Yoram, Susan P. Douglas, and Howard V. Perlmutter, "Guidelines for Developing International Marketing Strategies," *Journal of Marketing,* April 1973, pp. 14–23.

Zeira, Yoram, "Overlooked Personnel Problems of Multinational Corporations," *Columbia Journal of World Business,* 10, No. 2 (Summer 1975), 96–103.

ODYSSEUS, INC.

> She faced him, waiting. And Odysseus came, debating inwardly what he should do: embrace this beauty's knees in supplication? or stand apart, and, using honeyed speech, inquire the way to town, and beg some clothing? In his swift reckoning, he thought it best to trust in words to please her—and keep away: he might anger the girl, touching her knees.
>
> Homer, *The Odyssey*
> Book Six, *The Princess at the River*
> (*Robert Fitzgerald translation*)

In early 1971, Mr. Donald R. Odysseus,[1] president of the Odysseus Manufacturing Company of Kansas City, Kansas, was actively considering the possibilities of major expansion of the firm's currently limited international activities, and the form and scale such expansion might take.

Odysseus was founded in 1906 by Edward Odysseus as a small machine shop. By 1971, the head office and production facilities of the company were located in a 500,000 square-foot modern factory on a 30-acre site near the original location. Odysseus products were sold throughout the United States and Canada. In 1970, net sales were over $26,000,000 while after-tax profits were about $1,500,000. In early 1971, Odysseus employed just over a thousand people, and its stock was held by 1,000 shareholders. (The company's 1970 income statement and balance sheet are given in Exhibits 1 and 2.)

Odysseus produced a line of couplings and clutches including flange, compression, gear type, flex pin, and flexible disc couplings, and overrunning and

---

[1] All names and places have been disguised.

EXHIBIT 1. Odysseus Manufacturing Company
Consolidated Income Statement, Year Ending December 31, 1970
(In Thousands of Dollars)

Income		
Net sales	$26,276	
Royalties, interest, and other income	54	
		$26,330
Costs and Expenses		
Cost of goods sold	$16,758	
Depreciation	550	
Selling, administrative, and general expense	5,846	
Interest on long-term debt	68	
		$23,222
Income before income taxes		3,108
Federal taxes on income (estimated)		1,600
Net income		$ 1,508

(Price/Earnings Ratio, 1971: 10.5)

EXHIBIT 2. Odysseus Manufacturing Company
Balance Sheet, December 31, 1970
(In Thousands of Dollars)

Assets		
Cash	$1,758	
Marketable securities	1,144	
Accounts receivable	1,985	
Inventories	7,935	
Total current assets		$12,822
Investments and other assets		419
Property, plant, and equipment (net)		7,190
Total assets		$20,431
Liabilities		
Accounts payable	$ 625	
Dividends payable	231	
Accruals	1,053	
Federal income tax liability (estimated)	1,164	
Installment on long-term debt	86	
Total current liabilities		$ 3,159
Long-term debt (20-year 6 7/8% notes: final maturity 1987)		1,567
Preferred stock		1,976
Common stock and retained earnings		13,729
Total liabilities		$20,431

multiple disc clutches. In all, the company manufactured about 600 different sizes and types of its eight standard items. The company's single most important product was the Odysseus Flexible Coupling which its research department had developed in 1965 and which, produced in about 70 different sizes and combinations, now accounted for one-third of Odysseus' sales. Odysseus held patents throughout the world on its flexible coupling as well as several other devices. By 1971, Odysseus had carved itself a secure niche in the clutch and couplings market, despite the competition in this market of larger firms with widely diversified product lines.

Odysseus was not dependent on any single customer or industry. Sales were made through distributors to original equipment manufacturers for use in small motor drives for a wide range of products including machine tools, test gear, conveyors, farm implements, mining equipment, hoisting equipment, cranes, shovels, etc. No more than 10% of its output went to any single industry; its largest single customer took less than 4% of production. Speaking generally, Odysseus couplings and clutches were used more by small and medium-sized producers of general purpose equipment than by large manufacturers of highly automated machines. Odysseus' sales manager believed that demand for the company's couplings and clutches would benefit from continuation of a long-term trend toward increased installation of labor-saving equipment in medium-sized enterprises. This trend and the breadth of its market had provided some protection against cyclical fluctuations in business activity. During the period 1957 to 1970, sales had increased from $10 million to $26 million; the largest annual decline during the period had been 8%, while in the most recent recession year sales had actually increased by 5%.

The company's commercial objective was to operate as a specialist in a product field in which its patents and distinctive skills would give it a strong competitive position. In the past the company had experimented with various products outside its coupling and clutch line; it had tried to make components for egg candling machinery, among other things. The investment in these products was initially considered a means of more efficiently utilizing the company's forging and machining capacity, but they had not been particularly successful. The Odysseus management had come to the conclusion that they should concentrate their efforts on their line of couplings and clutches; and in 1971, Mr. Odysseus stated the company's corporate objectives explicitly as being a coupling and clutch manufacturer. New investments were made to develop better products within this field, and to open new markets for Odysseus products.

Odysseus' production and assembly facilities were located in its modern factory near Kansas City, Kansas. The site offered ample room for expansion and was well located for both rail and highway transportation. The company maintained warehousing facilities in Boston, Jersey City, Atlanta, Columbus, Ohio and Oakland, California. The scale economies stemming from concentrating production in one factory can be seen from the following examples. One of the company's largest selling items, product K-2A (a flexible coupling component) produced in lots of 750, cost $1.61 each; in lots of 1,200, $1.31 each. The incremental 450 units produced after the initial 750, therefore, cost only $.81 each. Put differently, on this particular product, a 50% cost saving could be realized on the marginal production from the 750 unit level to the 1,200 unit level. Though specific cost savings from higher volume varied among its products, a fundamental characteristic of Odysseus' cost structure was that marginal cost typically was significantly less than average cost, and that important economies of scale could be obtained by achieving larger lot sizes and longer production runs.

Odysseus' cost structure was, of course, dictated by its manufacturing process. In the first of three major steps in the manufacture of couplings or clutches, steel bars or tubing were cut and forged. Apart from the unit cost reductions stemming from more complete utilization of the existing forging facilities, economies of scale in this department were limited. Second, the forged steel pieces were machined to close tolerances in the machine shop. Here costs varied significantly with lot sizes. For most products, the choice among two or three alternative methods of production depended on the lot size. If a large lot size were indicated, special purpose automatic machines with large setup costs and lower variable unit costs were used. Smaller lot sizes were produced on general purpose turret and engine lathes where setup time was less but unit costs were higher. Typically, production of smaller lot sizes was more labor-intensive than the larger runs. For example, one operator running three automatic machines could perform all the boring and cutting operations on 300, 2 1/2-inch coupling flange units in an hour. The same output on general purpose lathes and boring machines would require about six man-hours. To set up the automatic machines required a day and a half, however, while the lathes could be set up in about two hours. Furthermore, the burden charge on the automatics was considerably higher. On the other hand, the cost of the third step, assembly, did not vary under different lot sizes. (Exhibit 3 presents a breakdown of the costs of some representative components.)

Mr. Odysseus regarded Odysseus' U.S. and Canadian market position as a strong one. The patented Odysseus Flexible Coupling possessed unique characteristics which no other coupling device duplicated, and many other Odysseus products served special functions not performed by competitive devices. Of course, other coupling and clutch systems competed with Odysseus, but no single company could be said to compete directly by producing an identical product line. Mr. Odysseus estimated that Odysseus accounted for roughly 10% of total sales of its products in the American market, and that there was ample room for Odysseus to expand its sales in this domestic market as the total market grew and through an increase in its share of industry sales. Odysseus products were sold by distributors who generally, but not always, carried the entire line of Odysseus couplings and clutches. These distributor organizations were complemented by a 45-man Odysseus sales force.

In 1970, export sales were $420,000 on which the company made a $50,000 operating profit. Although export sales had never been actively solicited, a small but steady stream of orders for export trickled into the Kansas City sales office. These orders were always filled expeditiously, but the active exploitation of export markets was considered too difficult in view of the barriers of language, custom, and currency. Furthermore, although he recognized that foreign wages were in-

EXHIBIT 3. Odysseus Manufacturing Company
Typical Variation of Production Costs with Lot Sizes
Product N–15C1

Operation	Lots of 150	Lots of 400
I. Foundry	$16.03	$16.03
II. Machine shop		
1. Boring	17.27	10.14
2. Turning	4.39	3.55
3. Facing	6.14	5.04
4. Drilling	10.00	8.16
5. Turning	5.88	4.78
6. Facing	6.19	4.58
7. Finishing	5.82	5.82
8. Finishing	5.57	5.66
III. Assembly	2.47	2.47
	$79.76	$66.23

Product L-36G:

Lots of 3: $67.40 each
Lots of 4: $56.20 each

---

creasing more rapidly than those in the U.S., Mr. Odysseus had always believed that Odysseus could not compete in export markets because its costs in Kansas City were too high. Also, tariffs imposed on Odysseus products by foreign governments were typically 10% *ad valorem*[2] or higher.

Odysseus sold all products on flat price basis (f.o.b. warehouse) to all customers. In competing with other suppliers of similar products, Odysseus stressed delivery time, quality, service, and merchandising, but not price.

In its management's view, improvements in its products or in delivery or service promised more than temporary competitive advantage. Price cutting moves, in contrast, would likely be matched by competitors the same day. No added sales would be gained, and total revenues would be cut. The company's export pricing policy was identical to its domestic policy. This meant that the foreign importer paid the United States f.o.b. price plus freight and import duties.

Along with filling orders, Odysseus' activities outside the United States and Canada consisted of a licensing agreement with an English coupling manufacturer. In 1965, on a vacation trip in England, where Odysseus' vice president in charge of engineering had spent his youth, he met the chairman of Siren Ltd. of Manchester. Siren, a manufacturer of related equipment with sales of $3.5 million in 1964, was anxious to diversify by adding other power transmission products. Consequently, Siren became interested in several Odysseus patents, particularly those on the

---

[2] Duties may be *specific, ad valorem* or *compound. Specific* duties are assessed on the weight or quantity of an article without reference to its monetary value or market price. *Ad valorem* duties are expressed as a percent of the dutiable value of an article without reference to weight or quantity. *Compound* duties combine both *specific* and *ad valorem* valuations; for example, in 1976, the U.S. duty on polyethylene resins amounted to 1.3% per pound plus 10% *ad valorem.* The U.S. tariff on clutches and couplings was 9.5% *ad valorem.*

Odysseus Flexible Coupling. In late 1965, Odysseus granted the English concern an exclusive 15 year license to manufacture and sell all present and future Odysseus products in the United Kingdom. The licensing arrangement specifically defined the United Kingdom to include England, Scotland, Wales and Northern Ireland. Siren was granted also a nonexclusive license to sell products produced from Odysseus patents in all other countries except the United States, Canada, Mexico and France. The terms of the license agreement stipulated a 1 1/2% royalty on the ex-factory sales price of all products in which devices manufactured from Odysseus patents were incorporated. The 1970 royalty income from Siren amounted to $40,000 and was expected to rise to $50,000 in 1971.

Mr. Odysseus had noted Siren's success with considerable interest. The royalty payments were a welcome addition to Odysseus income, especially since they had not necessitated any additional investment. Mr. Odysseus felt that the licensee was receiving very generous profits from this deal; as Siren had almost tripled its sales (which by 1970 were equivalent of $11 million) during its five year association with Odysseus, and its equity had appreciated many times the total royalties of about $150,000 which Odysseus had received.

During the five years Odysseus and Siren had worked together, however, the English firm had made it understood that in general it considered its territory to be the Eastern Hemisphere, while Odysseus' was the Western Hemisphere. Siren was especially interested in the German market for couplings and clutches and was a licensee of a German brakeshoe manufacturer.

In addition, Odysseus had a licensing agreement on the same terms (1 1/2% royalty) with Scylla, S.A. Scylla was a medium-sized French manufacturer of clutches and complementary lines, located near Paris. The company was financially sound and was headed by a young and aggressive management team. Scylla had been granted an exclusive license in France and a nonexclusive license in Belgium to sell products incorporating Odysseus-patented devices. Odysseus had entered the agreement during 1969 for an initial period of 10 years. Royalty income in 1970, the first full year of operation in France, had totaled roughly $10,000. Mr. Odysseus expected a doubling of this figure in 1971.

In February 1971, M. Scylla, the president of the French firm, had proposed to Mr. Odysseus a closer association of their two companies. M. Scylla was anxious to expand his operations and needed capital to do this. He, therefore, proposed that Odysseus form a joint venture with Scylla. According to the terms of the proposal Odysseus would bring $200,000 into the joint venture, paid in cash, while Scylla would provide a 40,000-square-foot plant, equipment, a national distribution system and managerial personnel. Scylla S.A. would cease to exist as a corporate entity; its expanded organization and plant would become Scylla Odysseus S.A. (SOSA). The original owners of Scylla S.A. (the Scylla family) would own 60% of SOSA and their return would be in the form of dividends plus salaries of members of the Scylla family employed by SOSA. Odysseus would own 40% of SOSA and, for tax reasons, would receive fees and royalties rather than dividends totaling 5% of the ex-factory price of all products incorporating Odysseus patents.

Mr. Odysseus thought that he should give this proposal serious attention. The

French market for couplings looked very attractive. Moreover, the geographical location of SOSA and the formation of the European Economic Community would make it theoretically possible to supply the even larger German market from the SOSA plant near Paris. M. Scylla had indicated that he considered Germany as a primary target for future expansion.

So far, Odysseus had not actively pursued business leads in Germany, in spite of several inquiries about licensing from German companies. Odysseus even had the possibility of acquiring an existing German manufacturer of couplings, Charybdis Metallfabrik GmbH (CMF) of Kassel. Mr. Odysseus had learned that CMF's aging owner-managers were anxious to sell their equity interest in the company, but would stay on in a managerial capacity. Odysseus' British licensee, Siren, had made it clear, however, that although they had no sizable business in Germany, they considered this market to be in Siren's sales territory, and a move into Germany by Odysseus without Siren an "unfriendly act." In the light of Odysseus' growing royalty income from Siren, Mr. Odysseus did not want to antagonize the British licensee.

Mr. Odysseus had no ready means of precisely quantifying the market potential for clutches and couplings in Germany and in France. He knew, however, that the total market for Odysseus' "type L" couplings in the United States was $22.5 million a year. Odysseus' United States sales of type L couplings were $3.2 million in 1970, or 14% of the United States market. Odysseus assumed that the coupling market in France was correlated with sales of durable equipment in France which were 12% of the United States total. The French type L coupling market, therefore, would be $2.7 million a year of which SOSA should expect to capture 14%, or $378,000. Similarly in Germany, durable equipment sales were 20% of those in the United States. The type L coupling market could therefore be expected to be about $4.5 million, of which a company using Odysseus patents and know-how should obtain between 10% and 15%. Sales of comparable lines by both Scylla S.A. and CMF appeared to justify these estimates; Scylla had sold $280,000 of a device closely comparable to the type L coupling, or 10% of the assumed French market; and CMF had sold $375,000 of virtually the same device, or 8% of the assumed German market.

In 1971, the European market with its accelerating pace of industrial development and mechanization appeared to offer great opportunities for Odysseus. Mr. Odysseus, therefore, was most anxious to capitalize on these opportunities, presumably by manufacturing in Europe in cooperation with a European firm. He saw three reasons why Odysseus should expand its foreign operations.

First, the corporate objectives of focusing on a single line of products sold in as large a market as possible—the policy of area instead of product diversification—dictated expansion into markets outside the United States and Canada. The nature of the demand for Odysseus' products appeared to limit near term sales potential in less developed areas; but in Europe, especially, Odysseus couplings and clutches appeared to find ready acceptance. Proof of this seemed to be contained in Siren's success in the United Kingdom.

Second, an important improvement on Odysseus' multiple disc clutch had been the result of European research. Mr. Odysseus felt that by becoming an active participant in the European market, the company could obtain valuable recent innovations which would be important to its competitive position in the United States. There was considerable activity in the clutch and coupling field in Europe, and Mr. Odysseus wanted to be in touch with the latest developments in the industry.

Third, Mr. Odysseus was seriously worried about the trend of costs in his Kansas City plant. He knew that a French firm could sell its gear-type coupling in Kansas City, Kansas, cheaper than Odysseus' current list price. How could Odysseus, paying its workers $3.65 an hour, compete with French firms paying $.99 an hour? Ultimately Odysseus might have to follow the lead of United States watch and bicycle firms and perform much of its manufacturing abroad and import parts, or even finished products, into the United States. At the present time, Mr. Odysseus felt that there was some reluctance on the part of American manufacturers to buy foreign couplings and clutches, and foreign competition was virtually nil in this market in 1970. But Mr. Odysseus was worried about the future and wanted to preserve Odysseus' competitive position by assuring a foreign source of supply. Also, the company would be in a better position to withstand exorbitant demands from the local labor union if it possessed alternative manufacturing facilities.

Before definitely deciding whether Odysseus should become more deeply involved in foreign operations, Mr. Odysseus wanted to review the ways this might be done. First, Odysseus could establish foreign markets by expanding export sales. Mr. Odysseus believed, however, that Odysseus' costs might be too high for it to compete successfully on this basis. Second, the company could enter into additional licensing agreements. This it had done with Siren in England and Scylla in France, but there was a definite ceiling on the possible profit potential from exclusive use of this method. Third, the company could enter "joint ventures" with a firm already established in foreign markets. Presumably, Odysseus would supply capital and know-how and the foreign firms would supply personnel (both local managerial skill and a labor force), market outlets, and familiarity with the local business climate. This approach appeared particularly promising to Mr. Odysseus. Finally, the company could establish wholly-owned foreign subsidiaries. Mr. Odysseus saw formidable barriers to such action, since Odysseus lacked managerial skill in foreign operations. They were unfamiliar with foreign markets and business practices. They did not have executives to spare from the Kansas City operations who might learn the intricacies of foreign business and the development of wholly-owned operations from scratch would require significant investment of time and money.

Mr. Odysseus recognized that certain deep-seated ideas of his tended to make him predisposed toward active development of overseas business. These included a view that his business should not shrink from difficult tasks—organizations, he believed, couldn't stand still—the choice was one of moving forward or falling backward. He considered "taking the plunge" into less familiar areas and learning from the experience was generally preferable to long-extended and expensive inquiry before taking action. Nonetheless, he wanted to be sure that the most basic issues related to expansion overseas by Odysseus were thought through before firm decisions were made.

QUESTIONS

1. Should Odysseus expand international business operations?

2. Rightly or wrongly, Odysseus management has decided in the affirmative. What *form* should these operations take? What *scope* will be required for Odysseus' international activities in order to achieve success? (Possible forms, which in turn may be combined, include (1) exporting; (2) licensing; (3) joint ventures; and (4) wholly owned subsidiaries, either by starting them from scratch or by acquiring one or more existing companies.) This decision should take into account *Odysseus' capabilities* (as determined, for example, by its products, its capital and manpower strength, and its marketing and research needs) as well as the industry's *competitive requirements* and *foreign conditions,* such as trade and business barriers, the number and sizes of countries to be covered, and political and business risks.

3. Evaluate the arrangement with Siren, particularly the following questions:
   a. What assumptions were in Mr. Odysseus' mind when he concluded the licensing arrangement with Siren?
   b. Do you consider it a success?
   c. How does the timing of this arrangement fit into Odysseus' overall business strategy?

4. Evaluate the Scylla, S.A., proposal and the Charybdis possibility.

5. Recommend an international strategic plan to Mr. Odysseus.

APPENDIX

ODYSSEUS MANUFACTURING COMPANY

	National Income ($ billion)	1971 Population (million)	National Income ($)	Exports ($ million)	Imports ($ million)	Avg. Hourly Earnings in Mfg. 1971	% of World National Income
United States	851.1	207.0	4,111	44,137	48,520	3.56	30%
Western Europe	768.8	394.0	1,951	157,132	169,549		27%
France	148.2	51.3	2,889	20,743	21,268	.95	5%
Germany	194.4	61.3	3,171	38,942	34,256	2.10	7%
United Kingdom	105.1	55.6	1,890	22,340	24,000	1.76	
Eastern Europe	465.3*	348.8	1,334	33,956	32,826		17%
Japan	199.3	105.6	1,888	24,040	19,727	1.29	7%
Oceania & Canada	108.2	37.4	2,893	24,884	23,431	(Australia) 2.35	4%
Latin America	137.8†	285.3	483	17,084‡	20,813‡	(Brazil) 0.89	5%
Asia (excluding Japan)	179.9	1,826.2	99	18,194	22,107	(Hong Kong) 0.40	6%
Middle East	32.9	103.2	319	8,802§	7,265§	(Egypt) 0.39	1%
Africa	58.73	307.7	191	11,865§	13,834§	(Ghana) 0.45	2%
Global Total	2,802.03	3,415.2	820	340,094	358,072		99%

*Net material product.
†Estimate, data missing for parts of Caribbean.
‡Totals do not include missing country data for Caribbean.
§Totals do not include missing country data.

Data source: Business International, "Indicators of Market Size for 131 Countries," December 1972 (& 1973 for wage data).

product
decisions

The prospects for American car manufacturers in Europe would appear to be good if they will meet the conditions and requirements of these various countries but to attempt to do so on the lines on which business is done in American would make it a fruitless task.

Statement by James Couzens, 1907,
officer of the Ford Motor Company

INTRODUCTION

The focus of this chapter is the product, probably the most crucial element of a marketing program. To a very important degree a company's products define its business. Pricing, communication, and distribution policies must fit the product. A firm's customers and competitors are determined by the products it offers. Its research and development requirements will depend upon the technologies of its products. Indeed, every aspect of the enterprise is heavily influenced by the firm's product offering.

In the past, product decisions in international marketing have been neglected by managers who have fallen into two types of errors, often simultaneously. One error has been to ignore product decisions taken by subsidiary or affiliate managers and in effect abandon any effort to influence or control product policy outside the home country market. The other error has been to impose product policy upon all affiliate companies on the assumption that what is right for customers in the home market must also be right for customers everywhere. In most cases neither of these extreme positions can be justified by profit maximization criteria. The challenge facing a company with international horizons is to develop a product policy and strategy that is sensitive to market needs, competition, and company resources on a global scale. This requires a product policy that strikes a balance between the need and payoff for adapting to local market preferences and the competitive advantages that come from concentrating company resources on a limited number of products.

This chapter examines the major dimensions of international product decisions. First, basic concepts are explored. The diversity of preferences and needs in international markets is then underlined by an examination of product saturation levels. Product design criteria are identified and attitudes toward foreign products are explored. The next section outlines strategic alternatives available to international marketers, and the chapter concludes with an examination of new products in international marketing.

BASIC CONCEPTS

As an introduction to international product decisions it is worthwhile to begin by briefly reviewing basic marketing concepts of a product. In addition to these concepts, which have full application to international marketing, there are also product concepts that apply specifically to international marketing.

Definition of a Product

What is a product? At first glance this is a simple question. A product is defined by its physical attributes—weight, dimensions, and material. Thus an automobile could be defined as 4,000 lbs of metal, mainly iron, and is 210″ long, 75″ wide, and 59″ high. This description could be expanded to include color, texture, density, shape, contour, and so on, but any description that is limited to physical attributes will remain inadequate as a full description because it says nothing about the needs a product fills. The automobile, for example, is a product that fulfills many needs. The most obvious is transportation, but the marketer cannot ignore the important recreation, status, and power needs satisfied by this product. Indeed, major segments of the automobile market are developed around these consumer desires.

The most basic contribution of marketing thought in the product decision area has been to shift the emphasis from the product itself to the needs and desires of the customer. This shift in emphasis applies with equal weight to consumer and industrial products. This new concept of marketing is still lost on many marketers more than twenty years after it was brilliantly expounded by J. B. McKitterick[1] and then expanded by Theodore H. Levitt in his article "Marketing Myopia."[2] We shall define a product, then, as a collection of physical, service, and symbolic attributes which yield satisfaction, or benefits, to a user or buyer. Product management is concerned with the decisions that affect the customer's perception of the firm's product offering.

[1] "What Is the Marketing Management Concept?" a speech given to the American Marketing Association (Philadelphia, December 27, 1957). Reprinted by Intercollegiate Case Clearinghouse, ICHDCIM 64.
[2] *Harvard Business Review,* July-August 1960.

Product Characteristics

Products have been characterized in a number of ways. The oldest classification has been the consumer industrial goods distinction between users. Consumer goods have been distinguished on the basis of how they are purchased (convenience, shopping, and specialty goods), and according to their life span (durable and non-durable). These and other classification frameworks developed for domestic marketing are fully applicable to international marketing.

LOCAL VS. INTERNATIONAL PRODUCTS

By a process of both acquisition and expansion of existing businesses, many international companies have products that they offer in a single national market. A typical example of this situation is the case of General Foods, which is in the chewing gum business in France, the ice cream business in Brazil, and the pasta business in Italy. While each of these unrelated businesses in isolation was quite profitable, the scale of each was too small to justify international headquarters marketing, production, financial management, or heavy expenditures on R & D. Indeed, if such headquarters systems were developed, it would in the case of a single-country business amount to one-over-one management. An important question regarding any product is whether it has the potential for expansion into other markets. The answer to this question will depend upon the company's goals and objectives, and upon perceptions of opportunity. In any event, companies will develop multimarket programs for a finite number of products. The two product categories that arise because of this limit are:

> Local products: In the context of a particular company, any product that is perceived as having potential only in a single national market.
> International products: Products that are perceived as having potential for extension into a number of national markets.

The local product may be quite profitable, but the existence of a single national business does not provide an opportunity to develop international leverage from headquarters services in such areas as marketing, R & D, and production, and from the transfer and application of experience gained in one market to other markets. One of the major tools available to the multicountry marketer is comparative analysis, which is unavailable to the single-country marketer. Another shortcoming of a single-country product business is the lack of transferability of managerial expertise acquired in the single-product area. A manager who gains experience in this single-product area can utilize his product experience in the company only in the single market where the product is sold. Similarly, any manager coming from outside the market area where the single product is sold will not have had any experience in the single-product business. Therefore, while attractive profit opportunities in unrelated product areas may present themselves from time to time to the international company, there is a substantial opportunity cost of moving into the single-product area.

It is critically important for the international company to evaluate proposed new products in terms of their local-international potential. All other things being equal, the product with profitable international extension potential is more attractive than the product whose potential for any reason is basically local. In general, a company should not add a purely local product to its line when an attractive international product addition is available.

Another way of looking at a product is to consider its characteristics. John Fayerweather suggests five important characteristics that are relevant to international marketing consideration: primary functional purpose, secondary purpose, durability and quality, method of operation, and maintenance.[3]

Primary function is illustrated by the example of the refrigerator as used in the United States and in Europe. The primary function of the refrigerator in the United States is (1) to store frozen foods for a week or more, (2) to preserve perishable food (vegetables, milk, and meat) between car trips to the supermarket, (3) to store products like margarine not requiring refrigeration, and (4) to keep bottled drinks cold for short-notice consumption.

In lower-income countries, frozen foods are not widely used. Housewives shop on a daily basis rather than a weekly basis, and because of lower incomes people are reluctant to pay for the third and fourth American uses of the refrigerator. These are luxury uses that require high-income levels to support. The function of the refrigerator in a lower-income country is merely (1) to store small quantities of perishable food for one day, and (2) to store leftovers for slightly longer periods. Because the needs fulfilled by the refrigerators are limited in these countries as compared with the United States, a much smaller refrigerator is quite adequate.

In Mexico refrigerators have, according to Fayerweather, an important secondary purpose. They fulfill a need for prestige. Therefore, in spite of the fact that Mexican incomes are slightly below European incomes, the only demand for refrigerators in Mexico is for the largest models, which are prominently displayed in the living room rather than hidden in the kitchen.

Durability and quality are important product characteristics that must be appropriate for the proposed market. The durability and quality of an appliance, for example, must be suited to the availability of service within a market. In lower-income markets, appliances are more likely to be repairable (a repairable appliance is a quality product in these markets) than in the United States, where the cost of labor makes it prohibitively expensive to repair appliances costing under $20. In the United States appliances are constructed without the additional "quality" that would allow a repairman to take the appliance apart and repair it. In the American market context, since the availability of repair is either nonexistent or prohibitively expensive, to build repairability into appliances would add nothing of value for the consumer. However, the American product in a low-income market is a lower-quality product because of its lack of repairability.

Two other important characteristics are method of operation and mainte-

[3] John Fayerweather, *International Marketing,* 2nd ed. (Englewood Cliffs, N.J.: Prentice-Hall, 1970), p. 51.

nance. For example, the voltage and cycle requirements for an electrical appliance or the driving conditions for an automobile are important method-of-operation considerations in determining the product design and characteristics. The same principle is true of maintenance. Standards and conditions of use vary considerably, and the level of maintenance available is highly variable; this should be incorporated into considering the appropriate characteristics of a product for a market.

International Trade Product Life Cycle

An approach to international trade that offers promise to business executives concerned with formulating a long-range product strategy is closely related to the product life cycle concept in marketing.[4] The trade cycle model suggests that many products go through a cycle during which high-income mass-consumption countries are initially exporters, then lose their export markets, and finally become importers of the product. At the same time other advanced countries shift from the position of importers to exporters later in time, and still later, less-developed countries shift from the position of being importers to being exporters of a product. These shifts correspond to the three stages in the product life cycle—introduction, growth and maturity, and decline. These stages are represented graphically in Figure 11–1.

The pattern from the point of view of the high-income country is as follows: phase 1—export strength; phase 2—foreign production begins; phase 3—foreign production becomes competitive in export markets; and phase 4—import competition begins. The model suggests that new products are initially introduced in high-income markets. There are two main reasons for this. First, high-income markets offer the greatest potential demand for new products, both consumer and industrial. Second, it is useful to locate production facilities close to the product's markets because of the need in the early stages of a product's life to respond quickly and fully to the customer in adjusting and adapting the design and performance of the product. Thus it is typical for products to initially be produced in the market where they will be sold. The first manufacturers of the new product have a virtual monopoly in world markets. Foreigners who want the new product must order it from companies in the high-income country. At this point unsolicited orders begin to appear from overseas; high-income-country exports begin to grow from a trickle to a steady stream as active export programs are established. Markets for the new product exist not only in the high-income country but also in foreign countries that are supplied by high-income-country exports.

In the relatively high income foreign countries, entrepreneurs are quick to note the growing markets in the new product and are relatively swift in taking advantage of lower labor costs and factor costs in many foreign markets. Production is then initiated abroad in the new product. In the second stage of the cycle, foreign and high-income-country production supply the same export markets. As foreign producers gain experience and expand, competition from the lower-cost

<hr/>

[4]This section draws from "A Product Life Cycle for International Trade?" by Louis T. Wells, Jr., *Journal of Marketing,* July 1968, pp. 1–6.

FIGURE 11-1
A Trade
Cycle Model

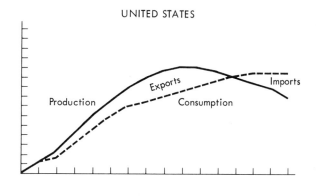

UNITED STATES

Production

Exports

Consumption

Imports

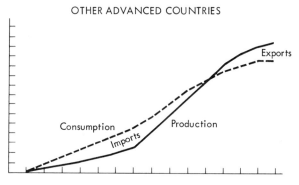

OTHER ADVANCED COUNTRIES

Exports

Consumption

Production

Imports

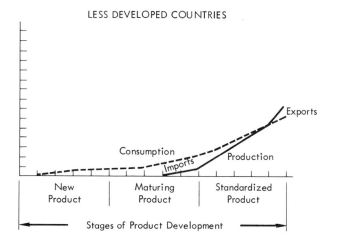

LESS DEVELOPED COUNTRIES

Exports

Consumption

Production

Imports

| New Product | Maturing Product | Standardized Product |

◄──────── Stages of Product Development ────────►

foreign production increasingly displaces the high-income-country export production source for the product. At this point high-income-country companies often decide to invest in foreign markets in order to retain market shares acquired via export sourcing.

As foreign manufacturers expand production to supply home markets, their growing economies of scale make them a competitive source for third-country markets where they compete with high-income-country export marketers.

The final phase of this cycle occurs when the foreign manufacturer achieves mass production based on home and export markets, and due to lower factor costs is able to produce at a lower cost than his American counterpart. The foreign manufacturer then begins to export to the high-income-country market. The cycle is now complete, and high-income-country companies that once had a virtual monopoly in the product find themselves facing foreign competition in their home market.

The cycle continues as the production capability in the product extends from the other advanced countries to less-developed countries of the world who eventually displace the other advanced countries first at home, then in international trade, and finally in the other advanced countries' home market. Textiles are an example of a product that has gone through the complete cycle for the investing country (Britain), other industrialized countries, and finally for less-developed countries.

PRODUCT SATURATION LEVELS IN INTERNATIONAL MARKETS

Many factors determine market potential. Income is clearly a necessary enabling factor, but availability, price levels, need, and custom all act as important codetermining influences.

Complementarity can be an important determinant of demand that will not be revealed by examination of income and general cultural data. The differences within Europe in saturation levels for electric vacuum cleaners is due to the type of floor coverings used in the different countries. Virtually all the homes in the Netherlands have rugs on the floor, whereas French and Italian homes tend not to have rugs as floor covering. Thus, in addition to attitudes toward cleanliness, the complementarity factor operates very significantly for electric vacuum cleaners. If the French had more carpets on the floor, then the saturation level for vacuum cleaners would be higher.

Some products have achieved high saturation levels in one market and little acceptance elsewhere, which raises the question of whether or not their success can be extended. The electric coffee percolator has a high saturation level in the United States but very low saturation levels elsewhere. The United States is a major coffee-consuming country, and is at the same time a major market for electrical appliances of all kinds. U.S. taste has become accustomed to percolated coffee, and U.S. consumers have experimented with and found the electric coffee percolator acceptable. The product is widely available in the United States and at relatively low prices. In other countries the coffee-drinking habits are not the same as those in the United States, and the standards of taste and preference have developed differently.

Moreover, availability is much less extensive, and the relative and absolute price of the electric coffee percolator is much higher outside the United States than within.

Is there a major opportunity abroad for the U.S. manufacturer and marketer of electric coffee percolators? Clearly, the electric coffee percolator marketer does not face high saturation levels for his product outside the United States. At home his marketing objective probably involves obtaining a share of the replacement and initial purchase market in competition with numerous other companies. In international markets the replacement market does not exist; therefore the ultimate measure of success will be the extent to which the marketer is able to persuade consumers to make initial purchases of an electric coffee percolator. This could be an enormously difficult and unprofitable effort. On the other hand, a well-designed marketing program executed at the right place and at the right time could lead to impressive and profitable results.

The existence of wide disparities in the demand for a product from one market to the next is an interesting suggestion of the possible potential for that product in the low-saturation-level market. However, study of the obstacles and incentives that would affect the success of the product under consideration in the proposed market is required before any program can be launched.

PRODUCT DESIGN

Product design is a key factor determining success in international marketing. Should a company adapt product design or offer a single design in international markets? It depends upon (1) the extent to which a design change will increase sales, and (2) the cost of changing a product's design and testing it in the market. The impact of design upon sales will depend largely upon the factors discussed below.

Preferences. There are marked and important differences in preferences around the world for factors such as color and taste. The marketer who ignores preferences does so at his peril. In the 1960s the Olivetti Corporation discovered that its award-winning modern consumer typewriter designs (Olivetti typewriters have been placed on display in New York's Museum of Modern Art) were quite successful in Europe, but not successful in the United States. The U.S. consumer wanted a heavy bulky typewriter that was "ugly" by modern European design standards. Bulk and weight were considered prima facie evidence of quality by American consumers and Olivetti was therefore forced to adapt its award-winning design in the United States.

However, this can work in reverse. European and Japanese companies were able to seize and hold 15 to 20 percent of the U.S. market by concentrating on the functionally designed small car, which appeals to a segment of the U.S. market that was until recently ignored by U.S. manufacturers, who had concentrated on the traditional U.S. preference for big cars.

Cost. When product design is determined, cost factors must be considered broadly. The cost of the product will place a floor under pricing alternatives. The cost of associated inputs must also be considered. The cost of labor, for example, varies quite substantially around the world. One example of how labor cost affected product design in a high-technology area is the approach to design of aircraft by the British and the Americans. The British approach, which resulted in the Comet, was to place the engines inside the wing. This produced an aircraft that had lower wind resistance and therefore greater fuel economy, with the disadvantage of an engine that was less accessible than an externally mounted engine and therefore more time consuming to maintain and repair. The American approach to this question of engine location was to hang the engine from the wings at the expense of efficiency and fuel economy in order to gain a more accessible engine, and therefore to reduce the amount of time required for engine maintenance and repair. Both approaches to engine location were rational. The British approach took into account the relatively lower cost of the labor required for engine repair, and the American approach took into account the relatively high cost of labor for engine repair in the United States.

Prescriptions. Prescriptions are laws and regulations that have a major impact upon product design in international marketing. Taxes on automobiles based upon engine displacement are a good example of a prescription. The engine displacement tax, which is found in almost every country in the world outside the United States and Canada, makes the car equipped with a U.S. engine more expensive to buy abroad than in the United States. Taxes on gasoline are much higher abroad than in the United States. The higher taxes make the larger U.S. engine more expensive to operate abroad and much more expensive to operate than the smaller displacement engines on foreign cars. These two cost differences have limited the market potential abroad for U.S. engine designs to a small wealthy and novelty-oriented segment of the foreign car market.

An important class of prescriptions for the marketer sourcing across national boundaries is the so-called nontariff barriers to trade. These barriers are assorted requirements and rulings that purport to be impartial regulations, but in some cases serve only to restrict or eliminate foreign competition. Florida tomato growers, for example, succeeded in persuading the U.S. Department of Agriculture to issue regulations establishing a minimum size for tomatoes marketed in the United States. The effect of this regulation was to eliminate the large Mexican tomato industry, which raised a tomato that just happened to fall below the minimum size specified.

Other prescriptions levied may be labeled as nontariff barriers when they are in fact quite legitimate efforts to promote the public welfare. The U.S. automobile safety regulations have, for example, been objected to by some foreign manufacturers as a trade barrier. The intention behind the prescription is important. If a country has a prescription that is designed to reduce or eliminate foreign competition, any effort to comply with the prescription would probably be met with additional legislation or rulings that reiterated the original objective. A good test of a country's intention when prescriptions affect a product is to determine whether the prescription affects all companies or just foreign companies. If the effect of the prescription is universal, as have been U.S. safety and pollution laws, this is a priori evidence that they were not motivated by an effort to restrict foreign-based competition.

Compatibility. A product must be compatible with the environment in which it is used. Power systems must be compatible with their environment, particularly electrical power, which varies in voltage and cycles around the world. Most European and Japanese companies as a matter of course offer appliances and small electrical devices with multipurpose plugs and converters that adapt their products to all major power systems in use today. The multipurpose plugs and converters give these companies an important advantage over U.S. companies whose regular production is entirely in the 60 cycle–120 volt U.S. electrical mode.

Climate is an environmental characteristic that often demands compatibility. Many products require tropicalization to withstand humidity, whereas other products must withstand extreme cold. Many European automobiles are not suited to extremely cold conditions of parts of North America, particularly those cars coming from Britain and Italy, which do not have extreme winters.

Measuring systems do not demand compatibility, but the absence of compatibility in measuring systems can create product resistance. The lack of compatibility is a particular danger for the United States, which is the only nonmetric country in the world. Products calibrated in inches and pounds are at a competitive disadvantage in metric markets. When companies integrate their worldwide manufacturing and design activity, the metric-English measuring system conflict requires expensive conversion and harmonization efforts.

ATTITUDES TOWARD FOREIGN PRODUCTS

One of the factors in international marketing that must be faced is the existence of stereotyped attitudes toward foreign products. Stereotyped attitudes may either favor or hinder the marketer's efforts. No country has a monopoly on a favorable foreign reputation for its products or a universally inferior reputation. There are marked differences in general country attitudes toward foreign products. One new enterprise in Brazil, which supplied a sensitive scientific instrument to the oil-drilling industry, discovered the impact of attitudes toward foreign products when it attempted to market its product to an oil-drilling company in Mexico and found that its Mexican customers would not accept scientific instruments manufactured in Brazil. In order to overcome the prejudice in Mexico against instruments from Brazil, the company was forced to export the components for its instruments to Switzerland where they were assembled and the finished product stamped "made in Switzerland." The company then obtained a very satisfactory sales result for its product in Mexico.

The reputation of a country as a manufacturer of products varies from country to country. Indeed the attitudes of countries toward foreign products vary quite considerably around the world. For example, the Germans have a very high regard for products manufactured in Germany. In a recent survey of the reputation of nine countries as manufacturers, Germans rated their own products for quality with an index number of 54 as compared with 24 for Dutch, 30 for British, 16 for French, 8 for Belgium, and 2 for Italian products. The Italians, on the other hand, rated German products with an index number of 37, Dutch products 25, British 10, Italian 24, French -1, and Belgium -2.[5]

An experimental study by Curtis C. Reierson tests various communications to determine their impact on attitudes toward foreign products.[6] Reierson found that if prejudice toward foreign products is not too intense, consumer attitudes may be improved by exposure to communication and promotion devices. However, if there are strong unfavorable attitudes toward a nation's products, such attitudes cannot be changed without substantial efforts. If a marketer is willing to engage in substantial and sustained communications efforts, then even a nation with strong unfavorable attitudes can expect a cumulative effect of communications efforts to change attitudes toward its products.

A very interesting finding of the Reierson study is that association with a prestige retailer is beneficial to the image of a nation's products. Thus an international marketer should consider as an alternative to mass communications to improve its product image the strategy of obtaining distribution through a prestige retailer. When the budget for a marketing effort is limited, the latter strategy may be the only economically feasible method open to the international marketer.

In some cases foreign products have a substantial advantage over their domestic counterparts simply because they are foreign. For example, this appears to be the case with beer in the United States. In one study, subjects were asked to indicate preference gradings for domestic and foreign beer. The preference ratings were obtained in a blind test in which the labels from the beers being rated were removed. Subjects in this test indicated a preference for the domestic beers. The same subjects were asked to indicate preference ratings for beers with labels attached. In this test, the same subjects preferred imported beer.[7]

When foreign origin has a positive influence on perceptions of quality, this is a happy situation for the international marketer. One way to reinforce foreign preference is by charging a premium price for the foreign product to take advantage of the widespread tendency to associate price and quality.[8] Such a doubly reinforced quality image can put a product in a commanding position in the so-called quality segment of the market. Certainly imported beer in the U.S. market is an excellent example of this segmentation strategy.

There are numerous examples of a negative association between perception

[5]The European Common Market in Britain Basic Report, A Market Survey sponsored by Readers' Digest, Copyright 1963, Table 52.

[6]Curtis C. Reierson, "Attitude Changes toward Foreign Products," Journal of Marketing Research, November 1967.

[7]David T. Meinertz, Michael Nadelberg, William Pelicot, and Michael R. Sullivan, "The 'Imported' Label and Consumer Choice" (Unpublished Columbia Business School student report, January 8, 1968).

[8]The positive correlation between price and perception of quality is well documented in the marketing literature. See, for example, J. Douglas McConnell, "The Price-Quality Relationship in an Experimental Setting," Journal of Marketing Research, August 1968.

of quality and foreign origin. The perception varies from product group to product group and from source and market country to source and market country. When the international marketer does find that his product is in the position of having a negative quality association because of its foreign source, he has two alternatives. One is to attempt to hide or disguise the foreign origin of his product. Package and product design can minimize evidence of foreign sourcing. A brand policy of using local names or of using well-known local brand names will contribute to a domestic identity. Sophisticated U.S. companies with major consumer brand franchises are using foreign sourcing and are therefore following this strategy. The other alternative is to continue the foreign identification of the product and attempt to change consumer or customer attitudes toward the product.

GEOGRAPHIC EXPANSION—STRATEGIC ALTERNATIVES

International companies can grow in three different ways.[9] The traditional methods of market expansion—further penetration of existing markets to increase market share, and extension of the product line into new product market areas in a single national market—are both available. In addition the international company can expand by extending its existing operations into new countries and areas of the world. The latter method, geographical expansion, is one of the major opportunities of international marketing. In order to effectively pursue geographic expansion, a framework for considering alternatives is required. Given any geographic product market base within a multicountry system, five strategic alternatives are available to the company seeking to extend this base into other geographic markets.

STRATEGY ONE: PRODUCT-COMMUNICATIONS EXTENSION

Many companies in extending their operations internationally employ product extension, which is the easiest and in many cases the most profitable marketing strategy. In every country in which they operate, these companies sell exactly the same product with the same advertising and promotional themes and appeals they use in the United States. One of the leading practitioners of this approach is Pepsico, whose outstanding international performance is a persuasive justification of this practice.

Unfortunately, Pepsico's approach does not work for all products. When Campbell Soup tried to sell its U.S. tomato soup formulation to the British, it discovered after considerable losses that the English prefer a more bitter taste. Another U.S. company spent several million dollars in an unsuccessful effort to capture the British cake mix market. It offered U.S.-style fancy frosting covered cake mixes only to discover that Britons consume their cake at teatime, and that the cake they prefer is dry, spongy, and suitable for being picked up with the left hand while the right manages a cup of tea. Another U.S. company, which turned

---

[9]This section is adapted from Warren J. Keegan, "Multinational Product Planning: Strategic Alternatives," *Journal of Marketing*, January 1969.

to a panel of housewives and asked them to bake their favorite cake, discovered this about the British and has since acquired a major share of the British market with a dry, spongy cake mix.

Closer to home, Philip Morris attempted to take advantage of U.S. television advertising campaigns that have a sizable Canadian audience in border areas. The Canadian cigarette market is a Virginia or straight tobacco market in contrast to the U.S. market, which is a blended tobacco market. Philip Morris officials decided that they would ignore market research evidence, which indicated that Canadians would not accept a blended cigarette, and go ahead with programs that would achieve retail distribution of U.S. blended brands in the Canadian border areas served by U.S. television. Unfortunately, the Canadian preference for the straight cigarette remained unchanged. American-style cigarettes sold right up to the border but no farther. Philip Morris had to withdraw its U.S. brands.

The experience of discovering consumer preferences that do not favor a product is not confined to U.S. products in foreign markets. CPC International discovered this in an abortive attempt to popularize Knorr dry soups in the United States. Dry soups dominate the soup market in Europe and Corn Products tried to transfer some of this success to the United States. However, a faulty marketing research design led to erroneous conclusions concerning market potential for this product. CPC International based its decision to push ahead with Knorr on reports of taste panel comparisons of Knorr dry soups with popular wet soups. The results of these panel tests strongly favored the Knorr product. Unfortunately, these taste panel tests did not simulate the actual market environment for soup, which includes not only eating but also preparation. Dry soups require fifteen to twenty minutes cooking, whereas wet soups are ready to serve as soon as heated. The preparation difference is apparently a critical factor in influencing the kind of soup purchased, and it resulted in another failure of the extension strategy.

The product–communications extension strategy has an enormous appeal to most multinational companies because of the cost savings that are associated with this approach. Two sources of savings, manufacturing economies of scale and elimination of product R & D costs, are well known and understood. Less well known but still important sources of savings are the substantial economies associated with standardization of marketing communications. For a company with worldwide operations, the cost of preparing separate print and TV-cinema films for each market would be enormous. Although these cost savings are important, they should not distract executives from the more important objective of maximum profit performance, which may require the use of an adjustment or invention strategy. As we have seen above, product extension in spite of its immediate cost savings may in fact prove to be a financially disastrous undertaking.

STRATEGY TWO: PRODUCT EXTENSION– COMMUNICATIONS ADAPTATION

When a product fills a different need or serves a different function under use conditions that are the same or similar to those in the domestic market, the only adjustment required is in marketing communications. Bicycles and motor scooters are illustrations of products that often fit this approach. They satisfy needs mainly for recreation in the United States and for basic transportation in many foreign countries. Outboard motors are usually sold to a recreation market in the United States, while the same motors in many foreign countries are sold mainly to fishing and transportation fleets.

When the approach to products fulfilling different needs is pursued (or, as is often the case, when it is stumbled upon by accident) a product transformation occurs. The same physical product ends up serving a different function or use than that for which it was originally designed. An example of a very successful transformation is provided by the U.S. farm machinery company that decided to market its U.S. line of suburban lawn and garden power equipment in less-developed countries as agricultural implements. The company's line of garden equipment was ideally suited to the farming task in many less-developed countries, and most importantly it was priced at almost a third less than competing equipment offered by various foreign manufacturers and especially designed for small acreage farming.

There are many examples of food product transformation. Many dry soup powders, for example, are sold mainly as soups in Europe and as sauces or cocktail dips in the United States. The products are identical; the only change is in marketing communications. In the soup case the main communications adjustment is in the labeling of the powder. In Europe the label illustrates and describes how to make soup out of the powder. In the United States the label illustrates and describes how to make sauce and dip as well as soup.

The appeal of the product extension–communications adaptation strategy is its relatively low cost of implementation. Since the product in this strategy is unchanged, R & D, tooling, manufacturing setup, and inventory costs associated with additions to the product line are avoided. The only costs of this approach are in identifying different product functions and reformulating marketing communications (advertising, sales promotion, point-of-sale material, etc.) around the newly identified function.

STRATEGY THREE: PRODUCT ADAPTATION–COMMUNICATIONS EXTENSION

A third approach to international product planning is to extend without change the basic communications strategy developed for the United States or home market, and to adapt the United States or home product to local use conditions. The product adaptation–communications extension strategy assumes that the product will serve the same function in foreign markets under different use conditions.

Exxon (then Esso) followed this approach when it adapted its gasoline formulations to meet the weather conditions prevailing in market areas, and employed without change its basic communications appeal, "Put a Tiger in Your Tank." There are many other examples of products that have been adjusted to perform the same function internationally under different environmental conditions. International soap and detergent manufacturers have adjusted their product formulations to meet local water conditions and the characteristics of washing equipment with no change in their basic communications approach. Agricultural chemicals have been adjusted to meet different soil conditions and different types and levels of insect resistance. Household appliances have been scaled to sizes appropriate to different use environments, and clothing has been adapted to meet fashion criteria.

STRATEGY FOUR: DUAL ADAPTATION

Market conditions indicate a strategy of adaptation of both the product and communications when there are differences in environmental conditions of use and in the function that a product serves. In essence, this is a combination of the market conditions of strategies two and three. U.S. greeting card manufacturers have faced this set of circumstances in Europe, where the function of a greeting card is to provide a space for the sender to write his own message in contrast to the U.S. card, which contains a prepared message, or what is known in the greeting card industry as "sentiment." The conditions under which greeting cards are purchased in Europe are also different from those in the United States. Cards are handled frequently by customers, a practice that makes it necessary to package the greeting card in European markets in cellophane. American manufacturers pursuing an adjustment strategy have changed both their product and their marketing communications in response to this set of environmental differences.

STRATEGY FIVE: PRODUCT INVENTION

The adaptation and adjustment strategies are effective approaches to international marketing when potential customers have the ability, or purchasing power, to buy the product. Unfortunately, this is not always the case, particularly in the less-developed countries of the world, which contain three-quarters of the world's population. When potential customers cannot afford a product, the strategy indicated is invention, or the development of an entirely new product designed to satisfy the identified need or function at a price that is within reach of the potential customer. This is a demanding but, if product development costs are not excessive, a potentially rewarding product strategy for the mass markets in the middle and less-developed countries of the world.

Although potential opportunities for the utilization of the invention strategy in international marketing are legion, the number of instances where companies have responded is small. For example, there are an estimated six hundred million women in the world who still scrub their clothes by hand. These women have been served by multinational soap and detergent companies for decades, yet until recently not one of these companies had attempted to develop an inexpensive manual washing device.

How To Choose a Strategy

Most companies seek a product strategy that optimizes company profits over the long term, or more precisely one that maximizes the present value of cash flows associated with business operations. Which strategy for international markets best achieves this goal? There is, unfortunately, no general answer to this question. Rather the answer depends upon the specific product-market-company mix.

Some products demand adaptation, others lend themselves to adaptation, and others are best left unchanged. The same is true of markets. Some are so closely similar to those in the United States as to require little adaptation. Other markets are moderately different and lend themselves to adaptation, and still others are so different as to require adaptation of the majority of products. Finally, companies differ not only in their manufacturing costs but also in their capability to identify and produce profitable product adaptions.

PRODUCT-MARKET ANALYSIS

The first step in formulating international product policy is to identify the product-market relationship of each product in question. Who uses the product, when is it used, for what, and how is it used? Does it require power sources, linkage to other systems, maintenance, preparation, style matching, and so on? Examples of almost mandatory adaptation situations are products designed for 60-cycle power going into 50-cycle markets; products calibrated in inches going to metric markets; products that require maintenance going into markets where maintenance standards and practices differ from those of the original design market; and products that might be used under different conditions than those for which they were originally designed. Renault discovered this latter factor too late with the ill-fated Dauphine, which acquired a notorious reputation for breakdown frequency in the United Staes. Renault executives attribute the frequent mechanical failure of the Dauphine to the high-speed turnpike driving and relatively infrequent U.S. maintenance. The driving and maintenance turned out to be critical differences for a product that was designed for the roads of France and the almost daily maintenance that a Frenchman lavishes upon his car.

Even more difficult are the product adaptations that are clearly not mandatory but are of critical importance in determining whether the product will appeal to a narrow market segment rather than a broad mass market. The most frequent offender in this category is price. Too often, U.S. companies believe they have adequately adapted their international product offering when they make mandatory adaptations to the physical features of a product (for example, converting 120 volts to 220 volts) but extend its U.S. price. The effect of such practice in markets where average incomes are lower than those in the United States is to put the U.S. product in a specialty market for the relatively wealthy consumers rather than in the mass market.[10] When price constraints are considered in international marketing, the result can range from margin reduction and feature elimination to an "inventing backwards" approach that starts with price and specifications and works back to a product.

Even if product-market analysis indicates an adaption opportunity, each com-

---

[10]The extreme case of this occurs when the product for the foreign market is exported from the United States and undergoes the often substantial price escalation that occurs when products are sold via multilayer export channels and exposed to import duties.

pany must examine its own product/communication development and manufacturing costs. Clearly any product or communication adaption strategy must survive the test of profit effectiveness. The often repeated exhortation that in international marketing a company should always adapt its products, advertising, and promotion is clearly superficial because it does not take into account the cost of adjusting or adapting products and communications programs.

Adaptation costs fall under two broad categories—development and production. Development costs will vary depending on the cost effectiveness of product/communications development groups within the company. The range in costs from company to company and product to product is great. Frequently the company with international product development facilities has a strategic cost advantage. The vice-president of a leading U.S. machinery company told recently of an example of this kind of advantage:

> We have a machinery development group both here in the States and also in Europe. I tried to get our U.S. group to develop a machine for making the elliptical cigars that dominate the European market. At first they said "who would want an elliptical cigar machine?" Then they grudgingly admitted that they could produce such a machine for $500,000. I went to our Italian product development group with the same proposal and they developed the machine I wanted for $50,000. The differences were partly relative wage costs but very importantly they were psychological. The Europeans see elliptical cigars every day, and they do not find the elliptical cigar unusual. Our American engineers were negative on elliptical cigars at the outset and I think this affected their overall response.[11]

Analysis of a company's manufacturing costs is essentially a matter of identifying potential opportunity losses. If a company is reaping economies of scale from large-scale production of a single product, then any shift to variations of the single product will raise manufacturing costs. In general, the more decentralized a company's manufacturing setup, the smaller the manufacturing cost of producing different versions of the basic product. In the company with local manufacturing facilities for each international market, the addition to marginal *manufacturing* cost of producing an adapted product for each market is relatively low.

A more fundamental form of company analysis occurs when a firm is considering whether or not to explicitly pursue a strategy of product adaptation. At this level, analysis must focus not only on the manufacturing cost structure of the firm but also on the basic capability of the firm to identify product adaptation opportunities and to convert these perceptions into profitable products. The ability to identify preferences will depend to an important degree on the creativity of people in the organization and the effectiveness of information systems in the organization. The existence of salesmen, for example, who are creative in identifying profitable product adaption opportunities is no assurance that their ideas will be translated into reality by the organization. Information in the form of their ideas and perceptions must move through the organization to those who are involved

[11] Interview with a vice-president of a large U.S. manufacturing company.

in the product development decision-making process, and this movement is not automatic.

To sum up, the choice of product and communications strategy in international marketing is a function of three key factors: (1) the product itself defined in terms of the function or need it serves; (2) the market defined in terms of the conditions under which the product is used, the preferences of potential customers, and the ability to buy the products in question; and (3) the costs of adaptation and manufacture to the company considering these product-communications approaches. Only after analysis of the product-market fit and of company capabilities and costs can executives choose the most profitable international strategy. The alternatives are outlined in Table 11-1.

NEW PRODUCTS IN MULTINATIONAL MARKETING

Managers in dynamic economies are realizing that the key to growth and survival is the continuous development and introduction of new products. In spite of the major efforts behind new-product management in the United States, where it is a highly developed activity, the failure rate of new products introduced in the United States is extremely high. Estimates of this rate vary from a Booz, Allen & Hamilton estimate of 33 percent to a 90 percent estimate by a New York industrial design firm.[12] Unfortunately, a study of the international new-product failure rate does not exist, but the large number of known failures of international new products suggests that the rate is very high.

What is a new product? There are many degrees of newness. A product may be an entirely new invention or innovation, or it may be a slight to major modification of an existing product. Newness may be organizational, which is the case when an existing product is new to a company. Finally, an existing product that is not new to a company may be new to a particular market. Table 11-2 illustrates these four degrees of product newness.

Any of the degrees of newness in Table 11-2 may apply to an international new product, but the most characteristic type of newness is category IV, an existing product already marketed by a company that is introduced for the first time to a particular national market. When this type of new product is introduced, the performance of the product in one or more markets is known, and an important question facing the international marketer is the extent to which the record of the product in existing markets is relevant to the proposed new international market.

Timing is a critical factor in appraising the relevance of previous market experience. Typically, entirely new products are first introduced in high-income markets. The extension of such products to less-affluent markets must often wait until the general development of the economies in these markets has progressed enough to create income and sociocultural conditions that create a demand for the product.

[12] Booz, Allen & Hamilton, *Management of New Products,* 4th ed. (New York, 1965), p. 9.

TABLE 11-1. Multinational Product-Communications Mix: Strategic Alternatives

Strategy	Product Function or Need Satisfied	Conditions of Product Use	Ability to Buy Product	Recommended Product Strategy	Recommended Communications Strategy	Relative Cost of Adjustments	Product Examples
1	Same	Same	Yes	Extension	Extension	1	Soft drinks
2	Different	Same	Yes	Extension	Adaptation	2	Bicycles, motor scooters
3	Same	Different	Yes	Adaptation	Extension	3	Gasoline, Detergents
4	Different	Different	Yes	Adaptation	Adaptation	4	Clothing, Greeting cards
5	Same	—	No	Invention	Develop new communications	5	Hand-powered washing machine

TABLE 11-2. Degrees of Product Newness

	I	II	III	IV
Degrees of newness	Entirely new inventions and innovations	Modification of existing products	Existing products, new to company but not to market	Existing product, not new to company, that is new to a national market

There are degrees of difficulty in new-product introduction. The most difficult situation in which a company can become involved occurs when it attempts to market an entirely new product in a market where the company has little experience. This situation is avoided by all companies. Another difficult situation occurs when a company introduces an existing product that is new to the company and market. Again, most companies avoid attempting this kind of introduction. A third dgree of difficulty occurs when a company takes a product, which is new to the company, and introduces it into an existing market. An example of this kind of introduction is CPC International's attempt, which was previously mentioned, to extend the success of Knorr soup products acquisition from Europe to the United States. The marketing plan for Knorr soups was based on the assumption that there would be a substantial increase in the market share of dry soups at the expense of wet soups. Unfortunately, Corn Products' inexperience in dry soups in the United States led to an underestimation of the difficulty of converting the U.S. wet-soup user to the dry-soup product. As a result the sales goals of the original plan proved to be quite unrealistically high. This was costly to Corn Products because the original sales targets had been the basis for a massive marketing program and for investment in a large dry-soup manufacturing facility.

Identifying New-Product Ideas

The starting point for an effective world-wide new-product program is an information system that seeks new-product ideas from all potentially useful sources and channels these ideas to relevant screening and decision centers within the organization. The major sources of new-product ideas are customers, suppliers, competitors, company salesmen, distributors and agents, subsidiary executives, headquarters executives, documentary sources such as information service reports and publications, and, finally, the actual observation of the physical market environment. The potential of many of the sources suggested above is often overlooked. For example, companies will frequently engage outside consultants and "experts" to suggest new-product ideas when the company's own salesmen are a rich potential source of ideas on the subject. In many companies, salesmen learn that there is no channel or means for them to communicate their ideas on products within the organization. This is an unfortunate waste of organizational talent. One way to overcome this problem is to provide opportunities for salesmen and product planning and design people to meet together to review the perceptions and ideas of field salesmen.

The International New-Product Department

One approach to dealing with the problem of the high volume of information flow required to adequately scan new-product opportunities and to subsequently screen these opportunities to identify candidates for investigation is a headquarters new-product department. Although few companies have organized such departments, there may be a trend in this direction.[13] In the multiproduct, multicountry company, the enormous number of possibilities for new-product extension combined with the massive potential flow of information dealing with new-product ideas requires that a full-time organizational unit be established to oversee this whole area. The function of such a department would be fourfold: (1) to ensure that all relevant information sources are continuously tapped for new-product ideas; (2) to screen these ideas to identify candidates for investigation; (3) to investigate and analyze selected new-product ideas; and (4) to ensure that the organization commits resources to the most likely new-product candidate and is continuously involved on a worldwide basis in an orderly program of new-product introduction and development.

With the enormous number of possible new products, most companies establish screening grids in order to focus on those ideas that are most appropriate for investigation. The following questions are relevant to this task: (1) How big is the market for this product at various prices? (2) What are the likely competitive moves in response to our activity with this product? (3) Can we market the product through our existing structure? If not, what changes and what costs will be required to make the changes? (4) Given estimates of potential demand for this product at specified prices with estimated levels of competition, can we source the product at a cost that will yield an adequate profit? (5) Does this product fit our strategic development plan? (a) Is the product consistent with our overall goals and objectives? (b) Is the product consistent with our available resources? (c) Is the product consistent with our management structure? (d) Does the product have adequate international potential?

Introducing New Products in National Markets

The major lesson of new-product introduction in foreign markets has been that whenever a product interacts with human, mechanical, or chemical elements, there is the potential for a surprising and unexpected incompatibility. Since every product is involved with one or more of these interactions, it is important whenever any significant investment of money or manpower is involved to test a product under actual market conditions before proceeding with full-scale introduction. A test does not necessarily involve a full-scale test-marketing effort. It may simply involve the actual use of the product in the proposed market. A typical example of the kind of problem that can emerge if this is not done is the case of the Singer sewing machine sold in African markets. This machine, which was manufactured in

[13] See, for example, "Introducing a New Product in a Foreign Market," Management Monograph No. 33 (New York: Business International 1966), p. 7.

Scotland by Singer, was slightly redesigned by Scottish engineers. A small bolt was relocated at the base of the machine, which had no effect on the functional performance of the machine but did save a few pennies per machine in manufacturing costs. Unfortunately, when the modified machine reached African markets, it was discovered that this small change was disastrous for the product. The Scottish engineers had not realized that in Africa the Singer sewing machine was transported on the heads of women, and their relocated bolt was placed at the exact point where women were accustomed to setting the machines on their heads!

COMPARATIVE ANALYSIS

One of the most useful techniques for aiding the new-product decision in international marketing is comparative analysis. Comparative analysis is always possible when an experience record for a product exists in one or more markets at the time of introduction of the product into a new market. The secret to effective comparative analysis is finding market comparability. There are two ways to obtain comparability. One way is to find an example of a market that is basically similar in terms of economic and social structural development to that of the target market and to compare the position of the product under study in the two markets. If such comparability exists, for example in Colombia and Mexico, one can take the experience in one market, Colombia, and make estimates of performance for another market, Mexico, on the experience accumulated in the first market.

Another means of achieving comparability is to displace time periods and find points of comparability at different time periods for markets that are not comparable in the same time period. If, for example, one seeks to apply the experience gained on a product in the United States to a marketing problem in Mexico, it is clear that in most cases U.S. experience will not be applicable to current Mexican circumstances. However, it is possible that U.S. experience in 1948–58 would be applicable in certain situations to the current marketing situation in Mexico.

If this analogy exists, the time displacement device can be an effective instrument for obtaining comparability. An interesting example of the time displacement device is the history of efforts to market Kleenex facial tissues in Germany. The first effort to market this product in Germany centered on a program that promoted Kleenex as a substitute for handkerchiefs. The result of this effort was unsuccessful because Germany had a four-ply heavy paper towel that was stronger than Kleenex and in their judgment a better substitute for a handkerchief. When this effort failed, Kleenex turned to a second advertising program, which promoted Kleenex as an all-purpose tissue. Again the effort achieved no success. German consumers were confused by the multiple uses identified in this promotion and concluded that Kleenex had no purposes. A third effort promoted the tissue as a woman's facial tissue. This promotion proved to be very successful. Interestingly, the third approach to marketing the Kleenex tissue was identical to the approach utilized to introduce it to the U.S. markets in the 1930s.[14]

[14] This example is taken from Richard Alymer, "Marketing Decisions in the Multinational Firm" (Unpublished doctoral dissertation, Harvard Business School, 1968).

SUMMARY

The product is the most important element of a marketing program. At any point in time a company is largely defined by the products it offers. Multinational marketers face the challenge of formulating a coherent global product strategy for their companies. Product strategy requires an evaluation of the basic needs and conditions of use in the company's existing and proposed markets, together with an evaluation and appraisal of the company's basic strengths and weaknesses. Full recognition must be given to the importance in the multinational company of establishing a viable and economic headquarters organization that can develop leverage (that is, the application of useful experience developed in one market to the formulation of a program for another market and the ability to avoid repeating mistakes within the multinational system). In order to develop leverage, the organization must have at the supranational level an organization that can accumulate and transfer knowledge concerning successful and unsuccessful practices. Another important dimension of the supranational organization's activity is the application of comparative analysis between comparable national markets to further enhance the effectiveness of marketing planning and marketing programs within the multinational system.

BIBLIOGRAPHY

BOOKS

Alymer, Richard, "Marketing Decisions in the Multinational Firm." Unpublished doctoral dissertation, Graduate School of Business Administration, Harvard University, 1968.

Business International, "Introducing a New Product in a Foreign Market," Management Monograph No. 33. New York: Business International, 1966.

Wells, Louis T., Jr., ed., *The Product Life Cycle and International Trade.* Boston: Division of Research, Graduate School of Business Administration, Harvard University, 1972.

ARTICLES

Buzzell, Robert D., "Can You Standardize Multinational Marketing?" *Harvard Business Review,* November-December 1968.

Keegan, Warren J., "Multinational Product Planning: Strategic Alternatives," *Journal of Marketing,* January 1969, pp. 58–62.

Nagashima, Akira, "A Comparison of Japanese and U.S. Attitudes toward Foreign Products," *Journal of Marketing,* January 1970, pp. 68–74.

Schooler, Robert D., "Product Bias in the Central American Market," *Journal of Marketing Research,* November 1956, pp. 394–97.

Sommers, Montrose, and Jerome Kernan, "Why Products Flourish Here, Fizzle There," *Columbia Journal of World Business,* March-April 1967, pp. 89–97.

Vernon, Raymond, "International Investment and International Trade in the Product Cycle," *Quarterly Journal of Economics,* May 1966, pp. 190–207.

Wortzel, Lawrence H., "Product Policy and the United States Multinational Corporation: Some Emerging Generalizations," *Marketing and the New Science of Planning,* 1968 Fall Conference Proceedings Series, No. 28, American Marketing Association.

INTERNATIONAL FOODS INCORPORATED (A)

INTERNATIONAL PRODUCT EXTENSION—EUROPE TO THE UNITED STATES

In early 1972, International Foods Incorporated (IFI) was evaluating its plan for Boor Concentrated Soups in the U.S. market. IFI had marketing subsidiaries in 112 countries, and manufacturing plants in 30 countries. Over half of the company's sales of $1 billion came from outside the United States. Consumer sales accounted for over 60 percent of worldwide sales, up from 25 percent only 10 years earlier. Forty percent of the company's sales were of refined corn products sold in bulk form to a wide range of industries. The company was pursuing an aggressive program of taking successful products from a single national market to its international markets. Many U.S. companies had launched U.S. products abroad, but IFI was determined to extend products in all directions, including from foreign markets to the United States.

In 1964, IFI acquired the H. C. Boor Company, the largest European producer of dehydrated dry packaged soups. This acquisition extended IFI's product line into soups for the first time. Boor produced soups in twenty countries, and held a major share of the market for dehydrated soups in most of these markets. The European market for soup in which Boor participated was characterized by a level of per capita consumption that was four times higher than that in the United States. There were four types of soup consumed in the European market: Homemade, which accounted for 45 percent of all soup consumption, bouillon, dehydrated, and canned. Bouillon soup, which accounted for 30 percent of soup consumption, was the main commercially produced soup in Europe. It was a concentrated extract cube which dissolved into bouillon when dropped into boiling water. Dehydrated soups which accounted for 15 percent of soup consumption were the second most important commercially produced soups in Europe. These were made from dehydrated vegetables, noodles, and other ingredients. A user made soup by adding the dehydrated powder to water and boiling for approximately 10 minutes. Canned soups in both concentrated and ready-to-serve form accounted for only 10 percent of European soup consumption. Canned concentrate soups were prepared by mixing the contents of the can with an equal quantity of water and heating. Ready-to-serve canned soup was prepared by simply heating the

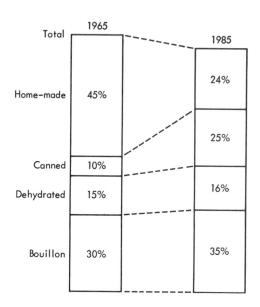

FIGURE 1. European Soup Consumption
1965 Market Share and Estimated
Market Shares in 1985

contents of the can. The 1965 European market share and expected growth by
1985 are shown in Figure 1. Overall, as shown in Figure 1, total soup consumption
was expected to decline in Europe. Homemade soups were expected to drop to
25 percent of the total market while canned soups were expected to increase to 25
percent of the market. This was part of a general convenience foods revolution
expected to occur in Europe as a result of rising income levels.

THE U.S. SOUP MARKET

Prior to the introduction of Boor in 1971 by IFI, the U.S. soup market totalled
about $500 million in annual sales, almost double the size of the market in 1946.
Wet or canned soups accounted for over 90 percent of the market. Compbell was
the major supplier in the wet-soup area with close to 90 percent of the market. The
dry-soup market was a more-or-less static $35–40 million, about 8 percent of the
overall market. The major factors in the industry were as follows:

Campbell's, by far the leader in the household market with almost 90 percent
of the canned soup market.

H. H. Heinz, a distant second in the canned wet-soup field with a 7–10
percent market share. Heinz was, however, the leader in institutional sales.

Thomas J. Lipton, Inc., a division of Unilever, the biggest and oldest maker of
dehydrated soups. Lipton dominated the dry-soup market with almost 95
percent of sales.

Wyler Co., a division of Borden Co., a Chicago-based manufacturer of dry-soup mixes.

By 1971, the domestic per capita consumption of canned soups had climbed from 10 to 15 pounds annually since 1950, although this was still only about one-fourth that of European consumption. It was estimated that 25 percent of the nation's families served canned soup on an average day. The sales of soup accounted for roughly one or two percent of food store sales.

Before 1971 Boor was sold in the United States as an imported European soup. Sales were very low and represented an insignificant factor in the U.S. soup market. Carried by a few specialty stores and delicatessens, Boor was perceived as a gourmet's food. Prior to International Foods Incorporated's introduction of Boor soups, the 1971 MRCA figures for the total soup sales in the United States were as follows:

		Millions of Cases	Millions of Dollars
Canned soups		100.7	382.8
Dehydrated soups		8.7	32.4
	Total:	109.4	415.2

Dehydrated soup sales made up about 8 percent of total sales by volume and 7.8 percent of the total dollar sales.

DECISION TO INTRODUCE BOOR

In 1970 a virtually autonomous team was established to manage Boor's soups in the United States. This new product development team was to create and introduce a new line of Americanized Boor soups. This concept of management, it was felt, would be a stimulus to hard work and initiative and would encourage the team to operate like an aggressive new company.

Market Research

Boor's soups were European products tailored to suit continental tastes. The new soups had to be adapted to fit American tastes and images. International Foods Incorporated undertook this task of translating its recipes very carefully through extensive product development and product tasting tests. Psychological studies were conducted to determine the image American women held of soup. The American housewife was found to have a somewhat vague and negative attitude towards dehydrated soups. Particular findings of importance regarding dehydrated soups were:

1. Not as convenient
2. Made thin soups
3. Only limited flavors available
4. Were less fresh
5. Were economical
6. Were easy to carry

IFI was anxious to convince the consumer that Boor soups were easy to make and that they were of the highest quality available at the grocery store or supermarket. The product development task was basically to create recipes which were similar in processing to Boor's other soups but which were, in flavor and body, typically attractive to Americans.

Product Testing and Adoption

Nearly two years were spent (1970–71) in developing recipes for the new Boor soup line. A Swiss master chef sent sample after sample to the International Foods Incorporated Home Service Department for evaluation. Every sample was tested by four panels of twenty to thirty people. According to their feedback replies, the master chef altered his soup formulae to suit their tastes. An outside research firm was hired to test family preferences and responses to the more nearly final forms. This research was conducted in homes throughout the country. Ten thousand home consumer tests were used to perfect the taste to American standards. The results of all these efforts was a seven-product line of which only one was totally new to American consumers (leek soup). Every one of the Boor soups had, however, at least one ingredient feature not found in other American manufacturers' version of that particular flavor. The product offering was to be as follows: beef and noodle, golden onion, cream of mushroom, chicken and noodles, smoky green pea, garden vegetable, and cream of leek.

Package Design

Package development and research was carried out with much care and awareness of current marketing techniques. Basically the International Foods Incorporated marketing team required that the package express all the following characteristics of Boor soups:

1. The ideal image as defined by the team:
   a. Uniqueness; not a "me-too" product.
   b. Broad appeal; all customers, families, and gourmets.
   c. Convenience; easy to carry, store, prepare.
   d. Value; best quality ingredients.
2. Serve as an advertisement.
3. Stack easily.
4. Lend itself to various types of external and internal promotions.

Extensive in-depth studies were conducted to appraise the two most popular of the many package designs developed. One used an ingredient motif and illustrated only the ingredients which went into the soup. The other showed a large bowl of soup superimposed against a European landscape background. The study's results indicated to the development team the ingredient design was superior to the European landscape background. The study's results indicated to the development team the ingredient design was superior to the European design in meeting the requirements. They felt that it said:

> This is a soup.
> This is a modern product from Europe designed for American tastes and preferences.
> This soup is made from the best and freshest ingredients.
> This is a light soup with a rich body.
> This is a high-quality soup, easy to prepare.
> This soup satisfies the discriminating consumer.

After the ingredient design was chosen for the outer box, a design was needed for the individual packets which held the soup itself, inside the box (two to a carton). The inner packets were designed to follow the European motif and to represent the seven countries associated with the different flavors. The packets said, for example, "take a kettle cruise to Sweden with Boor smoky green pea soup . . . smaklig." Following the determination of the product offering and the package design the necessary equipment was ordered for limited production and four test markets were selected.

TEST MARKETING AND RESULTS

Starting in January 1971 the new Boor soups were testmarketed in 4 cities: Syracuse, N.Y., Providence, R.I., and Columbus and Dayton, Ohio. The combined population of these cities was 3.5 million, or approximately 1.5 percent of total U.S. population. Prices were made competitive and the usual channels of distribution for soups were selected. In Columbus and Providence, IFI undertook an enormous free-sampling program in which pouches of soup were mailed to 57 percent of the local families. Included with each sample was a certificate which, when coupled with a store-bought box top from a Boor carton, was redeemable for a free soup carton.

Backing the sampling efforts were TV spots and color spreads in local Sunday newspaper supplements. In Syracuse and Dayton International Foods Incorporated decided to concentrate on pre-print color advertisements in newspapers. In these cities there was no free-sample program but the newspaper advertisements carried coupons similar to those used in the mailings. Expenses for the four test markets ran close to $500,000. Surprisingly, the sales resulting from the promotions in the four cities ran proportionately about the same, the free samples notwithstanding.

Results from the test markets showed that the volume of dry-soup sales doubled after the new Boor soups got to the stores. Data further revealed that Boor's promotional efforts did not cause a decrease in total sales by Lipton, Heinz, and Campbell's, although the market share percentages changed. All the companies benefited from the increased market activity of dehydrated soups resulting from the promotion. The test markets were continued for a full year. By the end of 1971 the company was convinced that an attempt at achieving greatly increased nation-wide distribution was in order.

PRODUCTION DECISION

After the decision to begin a new sales effort was reached, IFI built a modern new manufacturing and packaging plant with an annual one-shift capacity of 5.8 million cases in Centrallia, Kansas. Construction of the plant was completed on October 25, 1971. The technology and machinery employed were the most modern available but were so specialized that they were not transferable to alternative uses. The plant and equipment investment in the Centrallia plant amounted to $10 million.

NATIONAL ADVERTISING CAMPAIGN

IFI's introductory magazine advertising campaign for Boor soups was described as "the largest single grocery advertisement in history." The main vehicle for the introduction was the use of seven-page spreads in magazines conveying the theme of the campaign: "Take a kettle cruise to Europe." A full page was devoted to each of the seven flavors with an accompanying national motif. Approximately $375,000 was allotted for each of these seven-page spreads. Another 60 percent of the advertising budget was spent on television advertisements. The budget for the first six months of 1972 was to be $5 million. This was considered to be the advertising cost of "launching" the new Boor soups.

TOTAL COMPANY COMMITMENT

Fifteen million dollars was committed to the new investment in Boor soups in an effort to capture a 30 percent share of the dehydrated soup market which was expected to triple over the next two years (from $32 million to $96 million).

IFI hoped that by the time Campbell's Soup Co. made a countermove in dry soup, the Boor line would be firmly entrenched on the grocers' shelves and in the consumers' memory.

National distribution was achieved by the beginning of 1972. IFI hoped to reach their proposed break-even point by October of 1972 and to achieve pay-back by 1974. Projected sales by the end of 1972 were $32 million.

QUESTIONS

1. What are the major assumptions that underline IFI's decision to introduce Boor soups in the United States?
2. Evaluate these assumptions—which are well grounded in evidence and which are doubtful?
3. In what ways would you adjust IFI's program for Boor soups in the United States based on assumptions that you believe are reasonable?

INTERNATIONAL FOODS INCORPORATED (B)

INTERNATIONAL PRODUCT EXTENSION—EUROPE TO THE UNITED STATES

In July 1975 a special committee presented a report to top management of International Foods Incorporated (IFI) on possible courses of action for Boor Soups. In 1964, IFI had acquired the A. C. Boor Company, a leading European producer and marketer of dehydrated dry-packaged soups. In 1971, IFI introduced Boor soups to the U.S. market with the largest single grocery-advertising campaign in history. Backing up heavy advertising and promotional budgets was an intensive product-testing program and an investment in a modern fully automated manufacturing facility in Centrallia, Kansas. (See International Foods Incorporated (A) for a full description of the planning for Boor's introduction to the U.S. market.)

In late 1971, Boor was joined in the dehydrated soup market by Red Kettle, a new dehydrated soup developed by Campbell, the country's largest producer of canned concentrate soups.

During 1972 the dry soup industry achieved sales of 12.2 million cases, an increase of 40 percent over the 1971 level. (See Exhibits 1 and 2.) This was short of the tripled market that International Foods Incorporated had expected. In addition, as the year progressed it became apparent that there was not enough room in the dehydrated soup market for two new entrants.

Furthermore, as can be seen in Exhibits 1 and 2, Boor sales failed to maintain the new expanded levels projected for the following years. Sales achieved through extensive promotional activities in 1972 were not repeated in 1973 and 1974 when volume fell back to 125 percent of the 1971 sales level from 140 percent. Of added significance is the fact that this lagging performance of the dry soups in the marketplace occurred during a general expansion of total soup sales (see Exhibit 2).

During these circumstances each brand performed in a particular manner, each of which will be described here and in Exhibits 3, 4, and 5. Lipton's market share rapidly yielded to the Boor attack on the market (see Exhibit 5, 3rd and 4th

EXHIBIT 1. Total Soup Market Trends (1968–1974)
Sales Volume in Millions of Cases

	Canned	Dry	Total	Dry as Percent of Total
1968	101.4	7.9	109.3	7.2
1969	98.7	8.2	106.9	7.6
1970	104.4	8.3	112.7	7.5
1971	100.7	8.7	109.4	8.0
1972	102.5	12.2	114.7	10.6
1973	103.2	11.5	114.7	10.0
1974	105.2	10.9	116.1	9.4

Sales Volume in Millions of Dollars
(at retail level)

	Canned	Dry	Total	Dry as Percent of Total
1968	385.3	29.2	414.6	7.1
1969	375.0	30.4	405.5	7.5
1970	389.2	30.6	419.8	7.3
1971	382.8	32.4	415.2	7.8
1972	390.1	46.8	436.9	10.7
1973	388.1	41.6	430.0	9.1
1974	390.0	40.0	430.0	9.3

Source: MRCA.

quarters, 1971). Following this initial decline, Lipton successfully protected its market share against new efforts from both Boor and Red Kettle. It is of interest to note that Lipton's sales were not permanently harmed by Red Kettle's record performance through the second to fourth quarters of 1972. In fact, during the first half of 1973, Lipton soup sales rebounded and returned to the level from which they had so rapidly fallen during the end of 1972. In absolute terms, Lipton's decline in 1972 is not nearly as dramatic as is indicated by the market share analysis; the reason being that this decline occurred in a market which had expanded by 140 percent. One Lipton executive had this to say about the events of 1972 and 1973:

> "We developed a strategy and we stuck to it. If a company has a good franchise to start with, which we always have had, it's able to withstand the onslaughts of competition.
>
> "You've got to start with the basic product. A housewife doesn't remember promises about a glorious trip to Moscow or Finland. We offered them an excellent value and taste sensation the other products just didn't have."

The introduction of Red Kettle dehydrated soups by the Campbell Soup Co. was purely defensive. An International Foods Incorporated executive described Red Kettle as "a bad product, with bad packaging, promoted by excessively high advertising." This quick move was aimed to put Campbell's in a market that some

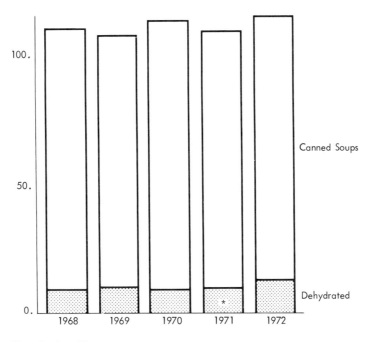

EXHIBIT 2. Total Soup Market in the U.S.:
Sales Volume in Millions of Cases

Canned Soups

Dehydrated

*Introduction of Boor.

EXHIBIT 3. Brand Shares in the Dry Soup Market

Quarter		Boor	Lipton	Red Kettle	Wyler	Others
1971	3°	8.3%	67.1%	— %	9.9%	14.7%
	4°	29.0	49.3	1.1	8.9	11.7
1972	1°	34.6	40.8	6.3	8.7	9.6
	2°	29.4	39.6	9.8	10.9	10.3
	3°	26.4	42.1	14.3	8.7	8.5
	4°	21.7	36.6	22.6	10.7	8.4
1973	1°	20.5	40.9	18.2	10.8	9.6
	2°	n.a.	—	—	—	—
	3°	n.a.	—	—	—	—
	4°	16.3	43.5	17.5	15.7	7.0
1974	1°	21.5	43.4	12.7	15.7	6.7
	2°	18.4	44.7	10.5	17.0	9.4
	3°	15.6	51.0	9.0	16.4	7.9
	4°	15.9	47.0	10.4	17.5	9.2
1975	1°	19.1	42.4	12.8	17.0	8.7

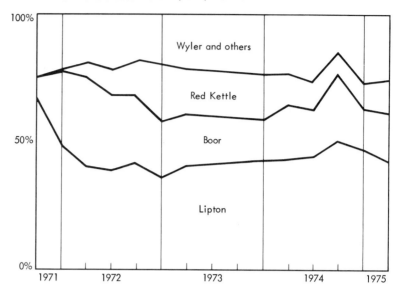

EXHIBIT 4. Brand Shares in the Dry Soup Market

Source: Quarterly publication of MRCA.

feared would be the future supplier of soup for American housewives. Red Kettle was developed and marketed with such speed that it reached the national market-place at the same time as Boor. In fact, more advertising dollars were spent in 1971 on Red Kettle than on Boor.

When sales of Red Kettle developed in the second quarter of 1972, they cut mainly Boor's growing market share. This relationship is shown quite clearly in Exhibit 4. Red Kettle so effectively squeezed Boor soup sales that by the end of 1972 Boor had fallen below them in share of market figures. Red Kettle's soups had a year of declining sales in 1974. Campbell's eventually decided to discontinue the Red Kettle brand when it became obvious that there was no real future for them in the dry soup market.

Boor soups began 1972 with a promising increase in sales but their breakeven point was never reached. Their sales peak was attained in the first quarter of 1972. This was followed by a steady decline during the rest of 1972 after which Boor saw their market share settle between 15 percent and 20 percent.

Advertising expenditures, with a peak of $5.2 million in 1962, *did* success-fully introduce the product and create awareness but repeat purchases failed to materialize as the successive quarters of 1972 progressed. Promotions during the following years continued to emphasize the foreign appeal of Boor. During 1973 a box-top from any of the nine Boor soups was exchangeable for a cash refund in coinage from any of the following countries: France, Italy, England, Holland, Denmark, Sweden, Switzerland, Austria and Norway. Color-page spreads in maga-zines supported this premium promotion. In October 1973 they undertook another premium promotion, this time offering dolls representing the nine nations.

EXHIBIT 5. Advertising and Measurable Media Expenses in Millions of Dollars

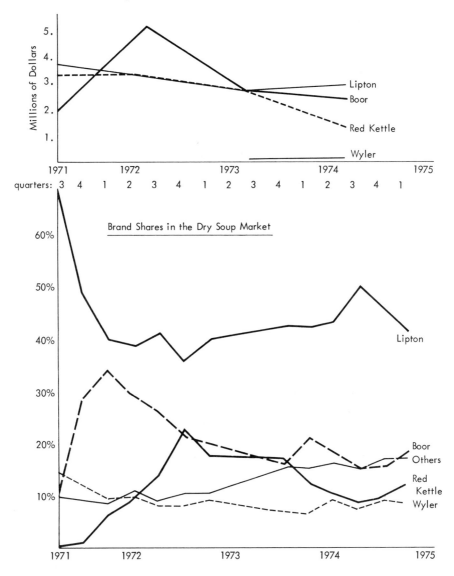

At an interview an International Foods Incorporated executive summed up the events of these three years with three points:

1. The market only achieved half of the expected volume.
2. Advertising expenses were much higher than originally expected.
3. Boor achieved a higher than expected market share. In their Annual Report for 1973 IFI had this to say about the venture:

EXHIBIT 6. Advertising and Measurable Media Expenses in Millions of Dollars

Brand	1971	1972	1973	1974
Boor	1.9	5.2	2.8	2.6
Lipton	3.8	3.4	2.8	3.1
Red Kettle	3.4	3.4	2.7	1.4
Wyler	n.a.	n.a.	0.2	0.3
Total Dry Soup	9.1	12.0	8.5	7.4
Campbell's	13.4	15.2	14.3	15.0
Total Soup	22.5	27.2	22.8	22.4

> "Despite the general trend to increased sophistication in consumer tastes, strongly ingrained habits have not been overcome in the dehydrated soup market. Although the company's Boor Soups are increasingly popular in overseas markets, U.S. sales of Boor soup and the entire dried-soup market have not yet met expectations."

The company Chairman admitted that "International Foods Incorporated had stubbed its toe on the introduction of Boor soups." Following a review by top level management it was decided that, in the future, advertising expenditures would be pulled back, a new policy of retrenchment would be practiced and the Boor soups would be allowed to seek their own level of sales.

THE DISINVESTMENT DECISION

In July of 1975, a special committee presented a report to top management of IFI on possible courses of action with regard to Boor Soups. The report considered the merits of two alternatives—complete disinvestment or continuing in the business of producing and marketing Boor Soups in the United States.

1. *Disinvestment.* This involved ceasing production, ending the sale of the products, liquidating the finished goods inventory, and selling surplus equipment for realizable value. A conservative estimate of the cash gain resulting from such disinvestment was $2.6 million resulting from $1.3 million of nontaxable income and a $1.3 million tax credit.

2. *Continuation in the business.* The decision to continue Boor operations in the United States was compared to the cash gain of $2.6 million from disinvestment. Top management felt that since International Foods Incorporated had already been badly burned in the attempt to sell Boor to U.S. housewives, the decision to continue in the business at this time would have to be accompanied by the development of major new marketing and product strategies.

The committee presented a sales forecast for the next eight years (1976–1983) based on the following assumptions:

1. Average total soup market would be between 124 and 127 million cases per year.

EXHIBIT 7. Pro Forma Cash Flow Statement

		(000 omitted)
Sales (cases)	2,000	
Gross sales (dollars)		$ 7,200
Freight	$ 220	
Cash discount	132	
Breakage & spoilage	200	552
Net sales		$ 6,648
Raw materials	$2,400	
Packaging	940	
Other direct mfg.	1,020	4,360
Gross margin		$ 2,288
Factory overhead	$ 125	
Factor margin		$ 2,163
Advertisement and promot.	$2,500	
Marketing (other)	40	
Brokerage & warehousing	200	
General & administr. exp.	50	
Marketing & selling (est.)	100	-2,890
Net cash flow		$ -727

2. The dry-soup market would average between 9.4 percent and 10.6 percent of the average total soup market.
3. The Boor share of the dry-soup market would range between 15 percent and 20 percent.

Using these assumptions, the committee predicted the most likely sales volume for Boor would be 2.2 million cases per year with a 10 percent probability that 1.7 million cases would be sold (the minimum) and a 10 percent probability that 2.7 million cases would be sold (the maximum). Top management was known to favor staying in business even if the return on investment was as low as 5 percent per year after taxes (10 percent pretax). Cash flows of at least $400,000 per year would thus be required in order to make staying in business at least as attractive as disinvestment (the present value, assuming a 5 percent discount rate, of $400,000 a year for eight years is approximately $2.6 million).

As Exhibit 7 indicates, even if two million cases could be sold in 1976, the Boor operation would run a cash flow loss of something over $700,000, or more than $1 million below the required cash flow. From this it was clear that the chances were minimal that staying in business could ever be as profitable as disinvestment.

QUESTIONS

1. What were the major reasons for Boor's failure in the U.S. market?
2. Could these reasons have been predicted on the basis of IFI's market research prior to launching Boor? If not, what additional research would have been needed?
3. What are the major lessons to be learned from IFI's experience with Boor?

pricing
decisions

The subject of price determination has baffled teacher and
students alike.

Alfred R. Oxenfeldt
(Pricing for Marketing Executives, 1961)

INTRODUCTION

Pricing, as one expert on the subject has observed, is a subject that has baffled
the teacher and student alike. In any single market three basic factors determine
the boundaries of the pricing decision. The price floor, or minimum price, is
bounded by product cost. The price ceiling, or maximum price, is bounded by
competitive prices for comparable products and the ability of customers to pay.
Between the floor and ceiling for every product there is an optimum price, which
is a function of the demand for the product and the cost of supplying the product.
The international executive must develop a pricing system and pricing policies
that address these fundamental factors in each of the national markets in which
his company operates.

The system must also be consistent with a number of uniquely international
constraints. In addition to the diversity of national markets in all three basic
dimensions—cost, competition, and demand—the international executive is also
confronted by conflicting governmental tax policies and claims as well as governmental controls such as dumping legislation, resale price maintenance legislation,
price ceilings and general review of price levels. Other factors affecting the
international pricing decisions are the often surprisingly high international transportation costs, middlemen in elongated international channels of distribution,
and multinational accounts demanding equal price treatment regardless of location.

Pricing decisions have a major impact on a number of societal groups: consumers, customers, employees, stockholders, the public interest, and, of course,

the competition. These interest groups are affected by pricing decisions, which in turn constrain the international executive. For example, IBM, in response to U.S. antitrust pressure, offered its equipment on a purchase as well as on a lease basis. In the process of developing the purchase price schedule the company raised its lease prices. The British government calculated that this price increase would cost Britain several million dollars per annum, and that this cost exceeded the government's price guidelines. The company was forced to roll back its price increase for the United Kingdom market but was successful in obtaining the increase in most other markets.

A widespread effect of international business is to lower prices. Indeed, one of the major arguments favoring international business is the favorable impact of foreign competition upon national price levels and upon a country's rate of inflation. The reason for this effect will be discussed later in this chapter.

Within the corporation there are many interest groups and frequently conflicting price objectives. The divisional vice-president is concerned about profitability at the divisional level. Regional executives are concerned about profitability at the regional level, and country managers are concerned about profitability at the country level. The direction of international marketing seeks competitive prices in world markets. The controller and financial vice-president are concerned about profits. The manufacturing vice-president seeks long runs for maximum manufacturing efficiency. The tax manager is concerned about compliance with government transfer pricing legislation, and company counsel is concerned about the antitrust implications of international pricing practices.

With such a large number of divergent and often conflicting interests combined with the limitations of our existing measures of demand, it is premature to expect that we should be able to determine "optimal" prices in international marketing. A more feasible objective for the international executive is to formulate international pricing strategy and policy that will contribute rather than detract from company sales and profit objectives worldwide. In order to effectively manage the pricing function in international marketing, the international executive needs a knowledge of the factors affecting the pricing decision and a framework for approaching the pricing decision. The purpose of this chapter is to provide the knowledge and the framework required.

EXPORT PRICING

The United States is not an exporting nation. Less than 7 percent of the total gross national product of the United States is accounted for by exports of manufacturers, and only a relatively small proportion of firms are involved in exporting at all. One observer has estimated that more than 90 percent of U.S. manufacturers have never developed export markets.[1] Part of the reason for the limited export performance by U.S. firms lies in pricing policies. The most frequently encountered

[1] Eugene M. Lang, "Small Businesses Venture Abroad," *Columbia Journal of World Business,* November-December 1968, p. 87.

export pricing policy by U.S. companies is a cost-plus method. The typical cost-plus formula involves the following: manufacturing cost plus administrative, R & D, and overhead cost plus freight forwarding, and customs charges plus distributor margins plus profit allowance. The typical effect of this cost-plus pricing approach in export marketing is a final price that is completely out of line with competitive conditions in export markets around the world.

Cost-plus pricing has a number of serious disadvantages. First of all, it completely ignores demand and competitive conditions in target markets. Second, it is often based upon distorted measurements or appraisal of costs. Third, it involves a circular form of reasoning because prices influence cost through their effect on sales volume. Cost-plus pricing is justified only if the cost of information about demand and the administrative cost of applying a demand-based pricing policy exceed the profit contribution obtained by applying these approaches. The alternative to the cost-plus pricing approach, which makes price a fixed or static factor in the marketing mix, is to view pricing as a major strategic variable that can contribute toward achieving marketing objectives.

Costs are important, but an effective export pricing strategy must recognize competitive prices as a second constraint on the pricing decision. Competitive prices can only be determined by examining the price levels of competitive and substitute products in the target market locations. Once these price levels have been established, the base price, or price that the buyer will pay for the product, can be determined. Three steps are involved in determining a base price.[2] Step 1: Estimate the relevant demand schedules (quantities that would be purchased at various prices) over the planning period. Step 2: Estimate incremental and full manufacturing and marketing costs to achieve projected sales volumes. Step 3: Select the price that offers the highest profit contribution, that is, sales revenue net of all costs. The final determination of a base price for a product can only be made after other elements of the marketing mix have been established. These include the distribution strategy and product strategy. The nature and length of channels utilized in the marketing program will affect margins, thus the final price of the product, and product adaptation costs will affect the cost base for a marketing program.

The three steps outlined above may sound simple, but they are in fact so difficult that it is not really possible to reach definitive and precise answers to the questions posed. Estimating demand, for example, must take into account product appeal if a product is differentiated from competitive products. Product appeal can be measured in experimental settings and in test markets, but these measures are costly and subject to error. In many export markets the size of the potential market is often too small to justify even minimum expenditures on formal market research involving testing and data collection from potential consumers or customers. Under these circumstances, potential demand estimates must be based

---

[2] For a fuller description of a marginal analysis base price method for export marketing, see Franklin R. Root, "Planning Export Pricing Strategy," in *Strategic Planning for Export Marketing* (Scranton, Pa.: International Text Book Company, 1966), pp. 55–71.

upon judgmental estimates of company and trade executives. One way of improving the potential demand estimates, if a company has experience with a product in markets, is to extrapolate potential demand estimates for target markets from actual sales in markets judged to be similar to target markets in terms of the basic factors affecting demand.

Estimates of full manufacturing costs are normally available in any company that has installed a cost accounting system. Incremental costs, however, are normally not available in standard management reports. In order to get incremental costs it is necessary to analyze manufacturing division cost data to identify costs, which, over a relevant range, are fixed and variable costs. If production can be expanded without expanding fixed costs, the only additional cost of obtaining additional output is variable costs.

Clearly, selection of the profit-maximizing price depends upon the time period for which the profit estimates are based. If the time horizon extends beyond the short term, then the pricing decision must be based upon all costs that will be incurred over the planning period. The pricing decision must also recognize the competitive and governmental responses that might be encountered. In practice, the complexity of these variables leads companies to pursue secondary objectives rather than the ultimate optimum profit maximization goal. Three of the most frequently encountered objectives are market penetration market skimming, and market holding.

Penetration pricing is the use of low prices to stimulate market growth and obtain the largest possible share of the market developed. Penetration pricing as a strategy in international pricing has perhaps been most effectively practiced by the Japanese. In Latin America, for example, the Japanese managed to move from a minor position to a 40 percent share of the market for telecommunications equipment in five years. In doing this they reduced the price level of telecommunications equipment in Latin America by roughly 50 percent. Their earnings on their sales in Latin America during this period are not known, but their market position has clearly been established.

Market skimming is a deliberate attempt to reach a segment of the market that is willing to pay a premium price because the product has a high value to them. U.S. companies are widespread practitioners of this kind of export pricing, although their practice is based not upon a conscious selection of this approach but is the result of their cost-plus approach to pricing.

Market holding pricing is the attempt to set a price that will maintain a company's share of the market. This pricing approach is frequently adopted by companies that have a major market share, which they want to retain. For example, in the late 1960s and throughout the 1970s, Volkswagenwerk AG raised its export prices to the United States less than it did export prices to other markets and less than domestic prices in an effort to hold its U.S. market position.

Although price is an important factor in the marketing mix, it is not in itself a conclusive factor. This principle is true even of products that have commodity characteristics. Steel is a good example. For more than a decade foreign steel has sold for 15 to 30 percent less per ton than the U.S. product. Why under these pricing circumstances didn't foreign companies gain more than a 10 to 15 percent share of the U.S. market? An examination of the structure of steel markets in the United States provides an answer to this question. Forty percent of steel used in the United States is mill ordered, that is, orders are placed directly with the steel producers and shipped directly to the user without any market intermediary. For most mill order customers, delivery according to a prearranged schedule is a critical factor in determining where their business will be placed. These are large customers for whom movements in the published *list* prices in products do not necessarily reflect actual market prices. However, even if moderate differences favoring imports exist for such buyers, the importance of reliable delivery is so critical that they are reluctant to transfer any significant portion of their purchases overseas.

Price Escalation

Price escalation is the frequently remarkable increase in a foreign sourced product's price as transportation, duty, and distributor margins are added to the product's former factory price. Table 12-1 is a typical example of the kind of price escalation that can occur. The reader will note that a shipment, in this case ordinary household chemicals such as insecticides and cleaners, that cost $10,090 in Kansas City ends up having a total retail price of $21,390 in Encarnación, Paraguay. This is double the FOB Kansas City price.

Let us examine this shipment to see what happened. First of all, there is the total shipping charge of $2,862, which is 28 percent of the FOB Kansas City price. The principal component of this shipping charge is the $1,897 freight charge for ocean freight from New Orleans to Buenos Aires, Argentina, and a river boat from Buenos Aires to Encarnación. In addition there is a $434 "port charge" and an insurance charge of $383, which is necessitated by the heavy pilferage and breakage that occurs in ocean shipping. Many observers feel that the freight and other charges involved in ocean shipments are completely out of line with what charges might be if the whole ocean freight industry were organized more efficiently. At this point, the international marketer can only appraise the extent and nature of these charges and either factor them into his pricing equation or seek alternative methods of transportation, such as air freight. For the future the modernization of the ocean freight industry and the introduction of jumbo jets, together with developments in the containerization and materials-handling areas, should substantially reduce existing transporation charges. This will make it possible to consider a number of heretofore excluded sourcing alternatives in international marketing.

The duty on the household chemical shipment in Table 12-1 is 20 percent of the CIF[3] value ($2,590), which is 26 percent of the FOB[4] Kansas City price, because the duty is levied not only on the FOB price but on the insurance and freight charges as well. A distributor markup of 10 percent ($1,553) is 15 percent of the FOB Kansas City price, again because it is a markup not only on the FOB

---

[3] CIF = cost + insurance + freight.
[4] FOB = Free on Board, or delivered to the ship, aircraft, or truck at a specific location.

TABLE 12-1. Price Escalation in International Marketing
A Shipment of 1,908 Cases of Assorted Household Chemicals,
Wt. 35,000 lbs., 40 cu. ft.

Item			As Percent of FOB Price
FOB Kansas City		$10,090	100%
Freight to New Orleans	$ 110		
Freight to Encarnación, Paraguay	1,897		
Counselor invoices	21		
Port toulaye	6		
Forwarding fee	8		
Insurance ($19,000 value)	383		
Port charge	434		
Documentation	3		
Total shipping charges		2,862	28
CIF value		$12,952	
Duty (20% on CIF value)		2,590	26
Distributor markup (10%)		1,553	15
Dealer markup (25%)		4,295	43
Total retail price		$21,390	212%

This shipment was sent by truck to New Orleans, by ocean freighter to Buenos Aires, Argentina, and by river steamer to Encarnación, Paraguay. Total transit time for K.C. to distributor is six to ten weeks.

price but on freight and duty as well. Finally, a dealer markup of 25 percent, which is quite low in percentage terms, adds up to $4,295, or 43 percent of the FOB Kansas City price, again because it is added on to everything else. The net effect of this add-on accumulating process is a total retail price in Paraguay of $21,390 or 212 percent of the FOB Kansas City price. This is price escalation.

The reader should recognize that the situation described above is by no means an extreme case. Indeed, if longer distribution channels or channels that required a higher operating margin were utilized, and they typically are in export marketing, the markups in Paraguay could easily exceed 50 percent of the CIF value.

The international marketer has two options in addressing the problem of price escalation. The first is to search the international manufacturing system of the company to identify a potential lower-cost source of merchandise. This source could include local manufacture but, alternatively, could involve sourcing at other points in the world to take advantage of lower freight and duty charges. The second weapon available is a thorough audit of the distribution structure in the target markets. In some cases distribution channels include intermediaries who perform no real function or make no contribution to the total marketing program and who therefore unnecessarily add to the price of the product in the marketplace. When this situation exists, a rationalization of the distribution structure by selecting new intermediaries, assigning new responsibilities to old intermediaries, or by establishing direct marketing operations can substantially reduce the total markups required to accomplish distribution programs in the target market.

International Dumping Regulations

The U.S. antidumping act of 1921, which is enforced by the U.S. Treasury, did not define dumping specifically but instead referred to unfair competition. However, the Congress has defined *dumping* as "unfair trade practices—unfair price cutting having for its objective the injury, destruction, or prevention of the establishment of American industry." Under this definition, dumping in the United States embraces every form of price differential resulting from sales of imports on the U.S. market at prices either below those of comparable domestic goods or below those prevailing in the producing country.[5] The General Agreement on Tariffs and Trade (GATT), on the other hand, defines *dumping* as the difference between the normal domestic price and the price at which a product leaves the exporting country. The GATT definition is more constrained than the U.S. definition because it refers only to prices that differ from those in the producing country.

Dumping legislation may either be a legitimate device to protect local enterprise from predatory pricing practices by foreign companies or a device for limiting foreign competition in a market. The rationale for dumping legislation is that "dumping" is harmful to the orderly development of enterprise within an economy. Few economists would object to long-run or continuous dumping. If this were done, it would be an opportunity for a country to take advantage of a low-cost source of a particular good and to specialize in other areas. However, continuous dumping only rarely occurs (the sale of U.S. wheat abroad at international prices with U.S. farmers receiving subsidized higher prices is an example of continuous "dumping" of sorts). The common type of dumping practiced by companies is a sporadic variety that is unpredictable and does not provide a reliable basis for national economic planning but may result in injury and harm to domestic enterprise.

Over the past twenty years the U.S. government has instituted an increasing number of dumping proceedings. Less than one-third of the cases were found to have a foundation, but the cost of this potential administrative harassment is one that must be considered by world marketers. Several cases have become national issues as domestic manufacturers of TV sets, shoes, steel, and even golf carts have charged that their industries are being threatened by unfairly priced foreign goods.

Several different approaches to solutions of the dumping issue have been taken. When, for example, the Japanese share of the color TV market in the U.S. jumped from 11 percent to 29 percent in the first six months of 1976, U.S. manufacturers filed complaints with the International Trade Commission (formerly the Tariff Commission) and brought suit against the Japanese companies for dumping and illegal price fixing. U.S. labor unions formed committees to petition the commission for TV tariffs and quotas.

[5] *Columbia Law Review,* February, 1965, pp. 185–231.

In 1976 the U.S. Treasury Department, after an investigation of foreign-car pricing practices, concluded that twenty-three out of twenty-eight foreign automakers had been dumping cars in the United States and demanded an increase in prices by 1977. Volkswagen, for example, was forced to raise its 1977 car prices an average of 2.5 percent. In a similar case that same year, the International Trade Commission ruled that Japanese steelmakers were engaged in unfair competition, ordered them to stop "predatory" pricing of their estimated $20 million steel exports to the United States, and forced the steel companies to provide detailed production and pricing figures. Citing the 1974 Trade Act provision that calls for the establishment of reference prices below which importers will be charged with dumping, the Treasury Department then set minimum steel import price levels.

Antitrust limitations, while vague, are very real. They are immediately brought into play if a foreign company's activities result in excessive competition by pricing in one market far below the prices it uses in another market or if it makes agreements with competitors that result in lessened competition. The Robinson-Patman Act deals with price discrimination and fair value, which, since 1975, have been determined as the production cost of the U.S. manufacturer plus a ten percent allowance for overhead and 8 percent for profit. The difficulty of establishing the actual costs of production has been the roadblock to proving dumping—many foreign manufacturers have simply refused to reveal their costs.

The 1974 Trade Act does not permit the use of production costs in a Communist-run country as a basis for determining fair costs but requires, instead, the use of reference prices of comparable goods from free-market countries. The difficulties that can arise from the reference price provision are best illustrated in the Polish golf cart case, which raised the question of what constitutes a fair price for imports into the U.S. from state-run economies. When a Polish aircraft company, Melex, began making golf carts for export to the United States (Poland has only one golf course), a U.S. manufacturer charged that it was being hurt by dumping. Melex at first raised its prices and paid duties based on price comparisons with a Canadian manufacturer's product, but when the Canadian firm stopped production, antidumping duties were also halted. The Treasury Department then sought to "construct" a fair value for the carts by estimating what production costs would be in a free-market country whose state of economic development was comparable to that of Poland. Spain and Mexico, neither of which makes golf carts, were selected for the constructed price decision. The constructed price approach attempts to identify what prices would have been if the products were manufactured in a market economy at a similar stage of development. While this appeals to many as "fair," it has also been attacked by the Federal Trade Commission as protectionist and harmful to the U.S. economy because it encourages the creation of de facto minimum prices and thus impedes free competition. It also presents the problem of almost insurmountable and unmanageable costs of implementation.

In order for a positive finding of dumping to occur in the United States, both price discrimination and injury must be present. The existence of either one without the other is an insufficient condition to constitute dumping. Companies that are concerned with running afoul of antidumping legislation have developed a number of approaches for avoiding the dumping laws. One approach is to differentiate the product sold from that in the home market. An example of this is an auto accessory that one company packaged with a wrench and an instruction book, changing the "accessory" in the process to a "tool." The tariff rate in the foreign market happened to be lower on tools, and the company also acquired immunity from antidumping laws because the package was not comparable to competing goods in the target market. Another approach is to make nonprice competitive adjustments in arrangements with affiliates and distributors. For example, credit can be extended and, to a point, have the same effect as a price reduction.

Reverse dumping, or the charging of a *higher* price in foreign markets than in home markets, is less frequently encountered but not unknown. One case involved a finding by a Canadian Royal Commission that wholesale prices of tractors made in Britain were from 35 percent to 40 percent lower in Britain than in Canada. The report called for direct government action to reduce British tractor prices in Canada.[6]

Devaluation and Revaluation

Devaluation is the reduction and *revaluation* an increase in the value of one currency vis-à-vis other currencies. Prior to 1971, under the fixed exchange rate system, devaluation was a reluctantly and infrequently used government economic policy measure designed to restore equilibrium in the balance of payments of a country that had been plagued by persistent deficits. In the long run, markets determined exchange values, but in the short and medium run, governments under the fixed rate system determined the foreign exchange rate. Since 1971, under the floating exchange rate system, devaluation and revaluation take place when currency values adjust in the foreign exchange markets in response to supply and demand pressure. One of the last major currency devaluations under the old fixed exchange rate system occurred in 1967 when the British dropped the price of the pound from $2.80 to $2.40. Since 1971, under the floating exchange rate system, the pound has fallen as low as $1.70.

If a devaluing country's domestic prices were unaffected by a currency devaluation, the prices of all goods to the foreigner would decline by the amount of the devaluation. In practice the rise in the cost of imported goods as a result of devaluation raises costs and prices in the devaluing country, so that part of the price reduction intended by devaluation is taken up by devaluation-induced price increases. Any price adjustments subsequent to devaluation should anticipate this source of price inflation, which is related to the size of the import component of a country's total national product. In the United Kingdom, where imports account for almost 20 percent of GNP, the internal price effect of devaluation is immediately felt by those purchasers of that component of Britain's GNP that is imported.

In practice the businessman sourcing in a country that has devalued its currency must first evaluate the price elasticity of demand for his product and

[6] "Pricing of Tractors in Canada Decried," *New York Times,* January 17, 1970, p. 43.

his basic marketing position. In the case of the British devaluation, consider the position of two exporters. One exporter is marketing Scotch whiskey and the other is marketing sports cars which sell for $5,000 in the United States. Would the demand for Scotch be buoyed by an across-the-board reduction in price? Sales might increase, but probably by less than the amount of price reduction, so that total revenue after the reduction would be less than before (demand is price inelastic). This was apparently the estimate of the British Scotch Whiskey Association, which recommended a price increase of 11.5 percent shortly after the 14.3 percent November 1967 devaluation. The sports car manufacturer, on the other hand, may estimate that in his market a price reduction of $500, or 10 percent, would have an appreciable effect upon sales, that is, it would increase sales by more than 10 percent. Thus he might decide to use devaluation as a device to lower foreign market prices. Another possibility would be to take the increase in revenue that would result if his foreign prices were unchanged and, instead of letting it fall through to the bottom of the P and L account, use the additional revenues to increase advertising and promotion efforts, to strengthen the distribution system, or perhaps adapt or change the product to better fit the market. Thus devaluation provides an opportunity for an exporter to increase profits immediately by (1) raising gross margins without increasing expenses, (2) reducing prices in foreign markets, and, it is hoped, increasing profits as sales expand, or (3) increasing marketing efforts either in communication, distribution or product design, again in the expectation of increasing profits.

Revaluation is an increase in the value of a currency vis-à-vis other currencies. The effect of revaluation on an exporter or a marketer sourcing in a revaluing country is the opposite of devaluation. The price of goods in foreign currencies goes up by the amount of revaluation, and the international marketer must decide whether to (1) pass the price increase on to his customers, (2) absorb the price increase and reduce operating or marketing expenses in an effort to maintain profit levels, (3) absorb the price increase in foreign currencies by reducing the price in the home country currently, or (4) maintain operating and marketing expense levels and thus accept lower operating margins on business.

When the underlying reason for a country's surplus has been a more attractive national product, a slight revaluation has little effect upon export performance. In many cases price increases are passed on to foreign customers by individual firms with no significant effect upon volume. In more competitive market situations, companies in the revaluing country will often absorb the price increase by maintaining foreign currency prices at pre-revaluation levels. Under these circumstances, revaluation does not eliminate a balance-of-payments surplus, as Germany and Japan have demonstrated for the past two decades.

PRICING IN AN INFLATIONARY ENVIRONMENT

Inflation, or a persistent upward change in price levels, is a worldwide phenomenon. Thus the existence of inflation is not a unique variable facing the international marketer. The unique international aspects of inflation are the differential rates of

TABLE 12-2. World Purchasing Power

	Industrialized Countries and Other Europe						Less-Developed Countries				
	Indexes of Value of Money (1965=100)		Annual Rate of Depreciation of Money				Indexes of Value of Money (1965=100)		Annual Rate of Depreciation of Money		
	1970	1975	'65-70	'70-'75	1976†		1970	1975	'65-70*	'70-75*	1976†
Switzerland	85	58	3.3%	7.1%	2.2%	India	72	42	6.4%	10.4%	+11.7%#
West Germany	88	65	2.8	5.8	4.9	Singapore	94	57	1.2	9.1	+ 1.3#
United States	81	59	4.1	6.3	5.8	Panama	92	65	1.6	6.7	1.2
Denmark	73	47	6.2	8.5	6.5	Malaysia	94	66	1.3	6.8	1.7
Austria	85	60	3.2	6.8	7.0	China (Taiwan)	81	45	4.2	10.9	3.7
Canada	83	58	3.7	6.8	7.9	Philippines	75	37	5.6	13.2	3.8
Netherlands	79	52	4.6	7.9	8.4	Honduras	92	68	1.7	5.9	4.2
France	81	53	4.2	8.1	8.7	Iran	93	59	1.4	8.6	4.9
Japan	77	45	5.2	10.2	8.7	Thailand	88	58	2.5	8.0	5.2
Norway	79	53	4.7	7.7	9.0	Bolivia	75	32	5.6	15.8	5.6
Belgium	84	56	3.4	7.7	9.0	Venezuela	92	70	1.6	5.4	6.1
Luxembourg	86	61	3.0	6.7	9.6	Paraguay	94	54	1.3	10.3	6.9
Sweden	80	55	4.4	7.3	9.9	Ecuador	79	42	4.5	10.2	7.7
South Africa	85	55	3.2	8.5	10.2	Jamaica	77	39	5.0	12.9	8.6
Australia	86	53	3.0	9.3	11.8	Trinidad/Tobago	83	45	3.7	11.6	9.2
Greece	88	49	2.4	11.0	12.2	Colombia	62	26	9.2	16.0	9.7
Yugoslavia	59	24	10.0	16.1	12.4	Mexico	84	47	3.5	10.8	13.1
Italy	86	50	2.9	10.2	12.7	Kenya	91	54	1.8	9.9	14.3
Spain	78	44	4.8	10.8	13.0	S. Korea	58	29	10.2	13.1	17.9
Finland	64	37	8.5	10.4	13.8	Israel	82	32	3.9	17.3	19.4
Ireland	77	41	5.0	11.7	13.9	Peru	63	35	8.9	11.2	21.1
Turkey	67	29	7.6	15.7	14.3	Brazil	30	11	21.5	17.4	27.8
New Zealand	79	48	4.7	9.3	14.7	Zaire	36	15	18.5	15.7	43.0
Britain	80	43	4.4	11.5	15.3	Chile	31	‡	20.9	67.5	72.3
Portugal	74	36	6.0	13.1	17.4	Argentina	41	‡	16.2	39.2	84.0
Median rates			4.4	8.5	9.9	Median rates			4.2	10.3	7.7

*Compounded monthly.
† Based on average monthly data available for 1976 compared with corresponding period of 1975.
‡ Less than 1.
# Appreciation.

Source: Citibank, *Monthly Economic Letter,* September 1976, p. 14.

inflation that are encountered in the world today. Table 12-2 shows the decline of money purchasing power around the world for the 1965-75 period. With 1965 as a base point of 100, 1975 indexes of the value of money ranged from West Germany's high of 65 to Chile's low of less than one.

Obviously, inflation requires periodic price adjustments. These adjustments are necessitated by rising costs that must be covered by increased selling prices. An essential requirement of pricing in an inflationary environment is the maintenance of operating profit margins. Regardless of cost accounting practices, if a company maintains its margins, it has effectively protected itself from the effects of inflation. It is not within the scope of this text to examine the many issues and conventions employed in accounting to deal with price adjustments. However, it is worth noting that the traditional Fifo costing method (first in, first out) is hardly appropriate for an inflationary situation. A more appropriate accounting practice under conditions of rising prices is the Lifo (last in, first out) method, which takes the most recent raw-material acquisition price and uses it as the basis for costing the finished product. For very rapidly inflating environments, perhaps the most appropriate costing method is Nifo (next in, first out). This method involves an estimate of the price that will be paid for raw and component materials and the use of these prices in order to arrive at a costing of final product or finished product.

Regardless of the accounting methods used, an essential requirement under inflationary conditions of any costing system is that it maintain gross and operating profit margins. Managerial actions can maintain these margins subject to the following constraints:

Government controls. If government action limits the freedom of management to adjust prices, the maintenance of margins is definitely compromised. Under certain conditions government action is a real threat to the profitability of a subsidiary operation. A country that is undergoing severe financial difficulties and is in the midst of a financial crisis (for example, a foreign exchange shortage caused in part by runaway inflation) is under pressure to take some type of action. In some cases governments, rather than getting at the underlying causes of inflation and foreign exchange shortages, will take expedient steps, such as the wholesale use of price controls or, more likely, selective use of price controls. When selective controls are imposed, foreign companies are more vulnerable to control than local enterprise, particularly if they lack the political influence over government decision making possessed by local businessmen.

Competitive behavior. A second constraint on the flexibility of management to maintain its gross and operating profit margins is the behavior of competition. If competition, both local and international, does not adjust its prices in response to rising costs, a management with a sophisticated awareness of the effect of rising costs on its operating margins will be severely constrained in its ability to reflect that awareness in price adjustments. Clearly, as in all pricing situations, decisions are bounded not only by cost but by demand and competitive action.

Market demand. A final constraint on the ability of a manufacturer to adjust prices is the market itself. A company should be alert to the effect of price adjustments upon demand for its products. The objective of a business is not merely to maintain any specific gross or operating margin but to survive and, it is hoped, operate as profitably as possible. In some situations, a reduction in margins can lead to more profitable results than the maintenance of margins. Management should be alert to this possibility.

One of the consequences of rapid inflation is an increase in marketing costs. Consider, for example, marketing of packaged goods through self-service outlets where the goods are priced on the shelf. This pricing is a significant cost to any retailer, but in the normal or typical North American and European environment the turnover of goods is sufficiently rapid to make it unnecessary to reprice goods at any point during their shelf life. This, however, is not the case in certain rapidly inflating Latin American economies. In Brazil, for example, at some periods of very rapid inflation supermarket operators have found it necessary to reprice their goods three times a month. The cost of this triple marking is obviously three times that of a single marking. The international marketer should be aware of this possible additional marketing cost that is caused by rapid inflation.

TRANSFER PRICING

As companies have expanded by creating decentralized operations, the concept of the corporate profit center has become increasingly popular. Ideally, the decentralized profit center is a device for measuring and evaluating performance and motivating divisional management to achieve corporate goals. To achieve these goals, a rational system of transfer pricing is required. In domestic operations the aim in developing transfer pricing systems has been to devise methods that would simultaneously (1) motivate divisional management to achieve subsystem goals, (2) provide sufficient flexibility to enable divisional management to achieve goals, and (3) at the same time further corporate profit goals. When a company with such a transfer pricing system extends its operations across national boundaries, new and complicating dimensions to the transfer pricing problem are added.

Taxes, particularly income, duties, and tariffs, have received much attention in discussions of transfer pricing in international operations. In addition, however, a number of other environmental factors must be considered, including market conditions, the ability of potential customers to pay for a company's product, the competitive circumstances of different markets' profit transfer rules, the sometimes conflicting objectives of international partners in joint ventures, and government requirements such as deposit requirements on foreign imports.

There are at least four major alternative approaches to transfer pricing. Each approach has advantages and disadvantages, which vary with the nature of the firm, products, markets, and the historical circumstances of each case. The alternatives are (1) transfer at direct cost; (2) transfer at direct cost plus additional expenses; (3) transfer at a price derived from end market prices; and (4) transfer at an "arm's-length" price, or the price that unrelated parties would have reached on the same transaction.

A few companies employ the transfer-at-cost pricing method, recognizing that sales of foreign affiliates contribute to corporate profitability by generating scale economies in domestic manufacturing operations. Most companies follow the cost-plus pricing method, however, taking the position that foreign affiliate sales must earn a profit at every stage of their movement through the corporate system. This policy has resulted in a considerable lack of market orientation in the pricing practices of international U.S.-based companies because it often results in a price that is completely unrelated to competition and the ability to buy in foreign markets.

A market-based transfer price is derived from the price required to be competitive in the foreign market. The constraint on this price is cost. However, there is a considerable degree of variation in how costs are defined, and since costs generally decline with volume, there is a question as to whether to price on the basis of current or planned volume levels.

One overlooked and potentially valuable strategy is to use market-based transfer prices and foreign sourcing as a device to enter a new market that is too small to support local manufacturing. This enables a company to establish its name or franchise in the market and to develop a cadre of people with experience. With its own experienced people a company is in a much better position to appraise the potential of the market and to develop and implement appropriate and effective strategies.

A fourth approach to transfer pricing is to adopt a system that attempts to set transfer prices at the "arms-length" (the price that would have been reached by unrelated parties in a similar transaction) level. The problem with this approach is the extreme difficulty in identifying a point "arm's-length" price for all but the commodity type of products, and since few companies are dealing in commodities this is a very real limitation. The "arm's-length" price can be a useful target if it is viewed not as a point but rather as a range of prices. The important thing to remember is that pricing at "arm's length" in differentiated products results not in pre-determinable specific prices but in prices that fall within a predeterminable range.

In a world characterized by differential rates of income taxation, there is an incentive for a multicountry organization to seek to maximize system income in the lowest tax environments and to minimize income in high tax environments. For example, the U.S. corporate income tax rate is currently 46 percent. If a U.S. company is transferring goods into a foreign country with a tax rate of 25 percent, there is a tax incentive for the U.S. company to minimize its transfer prices to the hypothetical country because the lower the price charged to the affiliated company in the hypothetical country, the lower the profits will be in the United States and the higher they will be in the hypothetical country. If the corporate objective is to minimize taxes, this is accomplished by shifting earnings whenever possible to low-tax environments. Governments, naturally, have been aware of the possibilities of tax minimization efforts on the part of international companies. During recent years there has been a considerable effort on the part of a number of governments to maximize their tax revenues.

Section 482

As governments pursue their tax maximization objectives, it is becoming increasingly necessary for companies to comply with government prescriptions in this area. Since the U.S. Treasury transfer price review program is perhaps the most advanced in the world today, it is valuable to examine the nature of this program and its implications for management.

Treasury review of transfer pricing includes the sale of tangible property ranging all the way from raw materials to intermediate and finished goods; the pricing of money (loans), services (research and development, consulting, managerial assistance); the use of tangible property (equipment, buildings); and the transfer or use of intangible property (patents, copyrights, trademarks, procedures, forecasts, estimates, customer lists). In addition to the normal internal control problems posed by such transfers in a domestic environment, when a corporation spans national boundaries and tax jurisdictions, such transfers are subject to review and must be accepted by frequently inscrutable national tax authorities. Interest in the transfer and approaches to taxation are potentially in conflict. When the transfer involves tangible property, for example, the customs authorities must accept the transfer price. Their interest in a high import price to maximize duties is in direct conflict with the income tax authority's interest in a low price, which raises local company income and thereby raises income tax revenues.

For the U.S.-based multinational corporation, Section 482 is one of the most important single provisions of the U.S. tax law affecting international pricing practice.

Section 482, Internal Revenue Code, 1954:

> In any case of two or more organizations, trades, or businesses (whether or not incorporated, whether or not organized in the United States, and whether or not affiliated) owned or controlled directly or indirectly by the same interests, the Secretary or his delegate may distribute, apportion, or allocate gross income, deductions, credits, or allowances between or among such organizations, trades, or businesses, if he determines that such distribution, apportionment or allocation is necessary in order to prevent evasion of taxes or clearly to reflect the income of any of such organizations, trades, or businesses.

This section of the code is relevant to international business principally as it has developed during the past two decades. In earlier years the great bulk of international transactions were in the form of trade between U.S. companies and independent foreign purchasers. Since the parties in these transactions were unrelated, the prices they set were by definition "arm's length." In the past two decades, U.S. participation in the international economy has been increasingly dominated by direct marketing and direct manufacturing abroad by the subsidiaries of U.S. companies.

Internationally, the possibility of deferring U.S. taxes exists wherever there are foreign tax jurisdictions with tax rates lower than those in the United States because the shareholder of a controlled foreign corporation is not taxed on his share of that company's income until it is returned to the United States in the form of dividends *if* more than 70 percent of the income derives from manufacturing operations within the foreign country as opposed to nonmanufacturing income such as rents, royalties, licensing fees and dividends, or income from services performed for related persons outside the foreign country, or income from sales of property to related persons outside the foreign country.

The second basic justification for Section 482 applies even when the tax deferral escape is not a factor, as is the case when a U.S. company has income in foreign jurisdictions that tax income at rates equal to or greater than U.S. rates. From the viewpoint of the U.S. Treasury, Section 482 is still needed to ensure that the U.S. government gets it fair share of the taxes on income earned by a multinational corporate system. In order to get its fair share, the U.S. tax authority must ensure that multinational corporate systems fully account for all income earned in the United States. To provide this accounting, U.S. companies in such systems must fully price all transfers to foreign affiliates. When transfers are not fully priced, the income of the company's foreign affiliates will be artificially inflated, and taxes on this income will go to the foreign tax jurisdiction. As long as the United States allows a credit against the U.S. tax liability of foreign taxes paid, any exaggeration of the true income of foreign subsidiaries owned by U.S. companies will increase the tax revenues of foreign tax jurisdictions at the expense of the U.S. Treasury.

The question facing the international marketer and his advisers is, What can a company do in the international pricing area in the light of current tax law? The U.S. Treasury promulgated regulations in 1968 that spell out approaches to international pricing in considerable detail.[7] The IRS is bound to follow these approaches in its enforcement efforts. It is important to note, however, that Treasury regulations do not have the weight of law until they are accepted by the courts. Thus it is important to examine the regulations carefully, not because they are the present tax law but because they will guide the IRS review of transactions between related business organizations during the coming years.[8]

Sales of Tangible Property

Section 482 of the Treasury regulations is of particular interest to international marketers because it deals with controlled intracompany transfers (for example, transfer pricing) of raw materials, finished, and intermediate goods. The general rule that applies to sales of tangible property is again the "arm's-length" formula. Three methods are spelled out in the regulations for establishing its existence. They are, in order of preference, the "comparable uncontrolled price method," the "resale price method," and the "cost-plus method."

---

[7]"Allocation of Income and Reduction among Taxpayers: Determination of Source Income" (Section 482, Internal Revenue Code), Washington, D.C.: *Federal Register,* April 16, 1968.
[8]For a detailed review of Section 482, see James Eustice, *Tax Law Review,* Spring 1968.

Comparable uncontrolled price method. Uncontrolled (where buyer and seller are unrelated) sales are considered comparable to controlled sales (sales between related parties) if the physical property and circumstances involved are identical or nearly identical to the physical property and circumstances of controlled sales. The precision of this method is impressive, but unfortunately in practice it will have little applicability except in cases of companies dealing in such standard items as number 2 winder grade wheat or number 16 nails.

Resale price method. Of the other two methods the resale price method is given preference in the regulations. It provides that an arm's-length price can be established by reducing the applicable resale price by an appropriate markup and making adjustments to reflect any differences between uncontrolled sales used as the basis for establishing the appropriate markup percentage and the resale of property involved in the controlled sale. The applicable resale price is the price at which property purchased in a controlled sale is resold by the buyer in an uncontrolled sale. This method must be used if all of the following circumstances exist: there are no comparable uncontrolled sales, an applicable resale price is available, and the buyer has not added more than an insubstantial amount of the value of the property.

What is an appropriate markup? According to the regulations, it is the gross profit as a percentage of sales earned by the reseller or another party on the resale of property that is both purchased and resold in an uncontrolled transaction most similar to the resale of property involved in the controlled sale. The regulations permit markup percentages to be obtained from resales by other resellers in the foreign market if these are available, and then markup percentages earned by U.S. resellers performing comparable functions may be used.

The resale price method in Section 482 enforcement is an innovation of major significance. Already it appears to be the cornerstone of a major enforcement effort by the IRS. In 1967, for example, IRS examiners allocated almost $2 million of income from Pittsburgh Plate Glass Company International (PPGI), first incorporated in Cuba and later in Puerto Rico, to Pittsburgh Plate Glass Company (PPG) for tax years 1960 and 1961. The basis for the allocation was the IRS conclusion that the PPG pricing formula for sales to PPGI (cost plus 10 percent) resulted in a net profit as a percentage of sales (8 percent) for PPGI that was too high, considering the functions performed by PPGI. This move follows the traditional approach to enforcement of Section 482. The IRS examines the distribution of income, and if it does not appear to be in line, allocates income to achieve the desired distribution.

PPG went to court to challenge the IRS allocation. In court the IRS made a rough attempt to apply the resale price method by arguing that PPGI was comparable to a combination export manager (CEM) in terms of functions performed. Government economists had estimated that CEMs in general earned about 2 percent net on sales, and the government had evidence that a CEM dealing in products comparable to those sold by PPGI was earning approximately the same amount. With the argument of comparability of function the government asserted that the 2 percent net return was in fact the appropriate return for PPGI.

Although the new Section 482 regulations were available during the PPG case, the IRS continued to focus on net profit results rather than arm's-length prices and gross profit percentages to reach its income allocation decisions. It appears that the IRS will continue to look at results rather than at the actual prices and gross margins of operations. The new element is likely to be a partial application of the regulations with an emphasis on rates of return in allegedly comparable business organizations.

In defense of its pricing decisions, PPG referred to the new Section 482 regulations. The company argued that PPGI was not comparable to a combination export manager, and that PPG's prices in the disputed years were reasonable in comparison to prices charged by an unrelated company for comparable products sold to PPGI.

Cost-plus method. The third and lowest-priority method of establishing the existence of an arm's-length price is the cost-plus method. Note that this method is easily the most relied upon method currently in use by U.S. corporations to establish transfer prices.

The regulations specify that cost must be determined by following standard accounting practices that neither favor nor burden controlled sales in comparison to similar uncontrolled sales. The allowable gross profit percentage is the figure that is equal to the gross profit earned by the seller on uncontrolled sales that are most similar to the controlled sale in question. The regulations specify that wherever possible, gross profit percentages should be derived from uncontrolled sales made by the seller involved in the controlled sale and that, in the absence of such sales, evidence may be obtained either from uncontrolled sales of other sellers who perform a similar function or, failing this, from the prevailing gross profit percentages in the particular industry involved. Since the comparable uncontrolled price and the resale price are likely to find little application in practice, the "cost-plus" method could eventually be the most applicable section of the regulations dealing with tangible property.

Competitive Pricing

A businessman examining the Section 482 regulations will quickly begin to wonder, with all the emphasis on an arm's-length price, whether it is possible under the spirit of these regulations to continue to price with regard to market and competitive factors. Clearly, if only the arm's-length standard is applied, it does not necessarily permit a company to respond to competitive factors that exist in every market, domestic and foreign. Fortunately, the regulations may provide an opening for the multinational company that seeks to be price competitive or to price aggressively in its foreign marketing of U.S.-sourced products. It appears that drafters of the Treasury regulations intended to leave a wide opening for companies that wish to respond to competitive factors or any other price factors, that may exist in foreign markets. The applicable passage in Section 482 reads:

One of the circumstances which may affect the price of property is the fact that the seller may desire to make sales at less than a normal profit for the primary purpose of establishing or maintaining a market for his products. Thus, a seller may be willing to reduce the price of his product, for a time, in order to introduce his product into an area or in order to meet competition. However, controlled sales may be priced in such a manner only if such price would have been charged in an uncontrolled sale under comparable circumstances. Such fact may be demonstrated by showing that the buyer in the controlled sale made corresponding reduction in the resale price to uncontrolled purchasers, or that such buyer engaged in substantially greater sales-promotion activities with respect to the product involved in the controlled sale than with respect to other products.

The key provision in this section is the third sentence citing "comparable circumstances." This term could be interpreted as a nullification of what is an essential provision in the regulations. A company may properly reduce prices and increase marketing expenditures in a market through a controlled affiliate when it would not do so through an independent distributor. This would be the case when a company lowered its prices in order to gain a market position. The market position is, in effect, an investment and an asset. A company would invest in such an asset only if it controlled the reseller. If the third sentence applies, there is extremely limited endorsement of competitive or marginal cost pricing. If the last sentence applies, and it should, the regulations will permit a company to lower its transfer price for the purpose of entering a new market or meeting competition in an existing market either by price reductions or by increased marketing efforts in the target markets. Companies must have and use this latitude in making price decisions if they are to achieve any success in foreign markets with U.S.-sourced goods.

Importance of Section 482 Regulations

The immediate significance of these regulations and of recent enforcement efforts by the IRS is that companies can expect that the arm's-length standard established in the regulations will be tested by attempts to identify comparable uncontrolled prices, gross margins, and, most important, rates of return. International marketers concerned with intercorporate pricing should be aware of this probability. In those few cases where a comparable arm's-length price or margin from a comparable business-product relationship exists, companies that use these prices and margins will presumably not find their prices challenged. In the vast majority of cases, companies will not have comparable arm's-length prices or business-product situations and will have to rely upon either standards of reasonableness and cost-plus methods of defending their transfer pricing decisions or, in the case of competitive or marginal cost pricing, upon evidence that the prices charged were the basis for market price reductions or marketing expenditures.

Whatever the pricing rationale, it is important that executives involved in the pricing policy decisions of multinational companies familiarize themselves with the Section 482 regulations, and that the pricing rationale utilized by the company conform with the intention of these regulations. In practice this will not result in a massive adoption of the Treasury's arm's-length pricing standard, but companies should be prepared to demonstrate that their pricing methods were not the result of oversight but of informed choice. There is ample evidence that regardless of the sometimes perplexing inscrutability of Treasury regulations and IRS enforcement policy, there is no intention on the part of the government to do anything other than seek to prevent tax avoidance and to ensure that the income from the operations of multinational companies is fairly distributed. The company that makes a conscientious effort to comply with the new regulations and documents this effort should have no difficulty with IRS deficiencies. In the event that there are deficiencies, it should be able to make a strong case for its decisions in court.

The regulations call for a much more rigorous standard of review of intracompany transfer pricing. However, assuming that the IRS and the courts do not use the third sentence of the section dealing with competitive pricing to nullify the entire section, the regulations offer a specific opening to permit price reductions to support lower market pricing or more intensive marketing efforts. Without the competitive pricing section, the regulations put a straitjacket on intracompany transfer prices and effectively erect a major new barrier to U.S. exports.

Other Constraints on International Pricing

Company controls. Transfer pricing to minimize tax liabilities can lead to unexpected and undesired distortions. One interesting case of distortion occurred in a major U.S. company a few years ago. The company, a decentralized profit-centered organization, had promoted and given substantial salary increases as frequently as twice a year to its divisional manager in Switzerland. The reason for the manager's rapid rise was his outstanding profit performance record, which was picked up by the company's performance appraisal control system, which in turn triggered the salary and promotion actions. The problem in this very large company was that the control system, which rewarded managers for profit performance, had not been adjusted to recognize that in this company a Swiss "tax haven" profit center had been created, and that the manager's "profits" were simply the result of artificially low transfer pricing into the tax haven operations and artificially high transfer pricing out of the Swiss tax haven to operating subsidiaries. It took a team of outside consultants to discover the situation. In this case the company's profit-and-loss records were a gross distortion of true operating results. The company had to adapt its control sytem to realistically evaluate tax haven manager performance.

Duty and tariff constraints. Corporate costs and profits are also affected by the rates of import duty applied by a country. The higher the duty rate, the more desirable a lower transfer price. A country's customs duties and tax rates do not always create the same pressure on transfer prices. For example, consider a country with a high import duty and a low income tax rate. The high duty creates an incentive to reduce transfer prices to minimize the customs duty. The low income tax rate, however, creates a pressure to raise the transfer price to locate income in the low tax environment. These two factors are of course pulling in the opposite direction. Notwithstanding the importance of tax and duty considerations, many companies tend to minimize the influence of taxes on pricing policies or ignore them altogether. There are a number of reasons for such approaches. Some companies consider tax savings to be trivial in comparison to the earnings that can be obtained by concentrating on effective systems of motivation and corporate resource allocation. Other companies consider any effort at systematic tax minimization to be morally improper. Other companies argue that a simple, consistent, and straightforward pricing policy minimizes the tax investigation problems that can develop if sharper pricing policies are pursued, and that the savings in executive time and the costs of outside counsel compensate for any additional taxes that might be paid by such an approach. Other companies have analyzed the worldwide trend toward harmonization of tax rates and have concluded that any set of policies appropriate to a world characterized by wide differentials in tax rates would soon become obsolete, and they have therefore concentrated on developing pricing policies that are appropriate for a world that is very rapidly evolving toward relatively similar tax rates, at least in the major industrial countries.

Government controls. There are a number of government requirements that can influence the pricing decision. One of these is the frequently encountered cash deposit requirement imposed on importers. This is a requirement that a company has to tie up funds in the form of a non-interest-bearing deposit for a specified period of time, frequently six months or more, if it wishes to import foreign products. Where such requirements exist, there is clearly an incentive to minimize the price of the imported product. Other government requirements that affect the pricing decision are profit transfer rules that restrict the conditions under which profits can be transferred out of a country. Under such rules the transfer price paid for imported goods by an affiliated company can be a device for transferring profits out of a country.

Other government controls go directly to market pricing in a country. The United Kingdom has in recent years investigated and caused changes in the pricing practices in two industries with heavy U.S. participation, photographic film and pharmaceuticals. The pharmaceutical makers case illustrates the kind of review companies can expect when the government is a major customer. In 1967 subsidiaries of U.S. companies had annual sales in the United Kingdom of $180 million, which was one-quarter of the total industry sales in Britain. More important, these companies supplied about one-half of all the drugs paid for by the National Health Service. A Labor government appointed a committee to look into prices charged on brand-name drugs. To reduce drug prices, the committee proposed among other things: (1) abandonment of brand names for all new drugs and the use of generic names instead, and (2) a required standard cost report for all new drugs. The government's arguments centered on the investigating committee's profit findings, which showed that three companies earned 50 percent before taxes on net assets in the 1963–65 period and the average return on sales was 231 percent.[9]

[9] "Britain Prescribes a Bitter Pill," *Business Week,* October 7, 1967.

In February 1973 the British Monopolies and Mergers Commission forced the Swiss-based F. Hoffman–La Roche & Company to reduce the price of Librium by 60 percent and Valium by 75 percent, and to refund $27.5 million for overcharging. In a nutshell, the government's case was based on the argument that the company was spending too much on research.[10]

Joint Ventures

Joint ventures present an incentive to transfer price goods at a higher rate than one that would have been used in transfer pricing goods to their own wholly owned affiliates because a company's share of the joint venture earnings is less than 100 percent. Any profits that occur in the joint venture must be shared, whereas profits taken in wholly owned subs or at headquarters are not shared. Because of this potential conflict it is important for companies with joint ventures to work out in advance a pricing agreement that is acceptable. The increasing frequency of tax authority audits is an important reason for working out an agreement that will also be acceptable to the tax authorities. The tax authorities' criteria of "arm's-length" prices is probably most appropriate for most joint ventures.

MULTICOUNTRY PRICING—THREE POLICY ALTERNATIVES

What worldwide pricing policy should a multicountry company pursue? Viewed broadly there are three alternative positions a company can take toward worldwide pricing. The first can be called an *ethnocentric* pricing policy. This policy would require that the price of an item be the same around the world and that the customer absorb freight and import duties. This approach has the advantage of extreme simplicity because no information on competitive or market conditions is required for implementation. The disadvantage of this approach is obvious. It does not respond to the competitive and market conditions of each national market and therefore does not maximize the company's profits in each national market.

The second pricing policy can be termed *polycentric*. This is a policy of permitting subsidiary or affiliate companies to establish whatever price they feel is most desirable in their circumstances. Under such an approach, there is no control or fixed requirement that prices be in any way coordinated from one country to the next. The only constraint on this approach is in setting transfer prices within the corporate system. Such an approach is sensitive to local conditions, but it does present problems of product arbitrage opportunities in cases where disparities in local market prices exceed the transportation and duty cost separating markets. When such a condition exists, there is an opportunity for the enterprising businessman to take advantage of these price disparities by buying in the lower price market and selling in the more expensive market. There is also the problem that under such a policy, valuable knowledge and experience within the corporate system concern-

[10]"A Drug Giant's Pricing under International Attack," *Business Week,* June 16, 1975, p. 50.

ing effective pricing strategies is not applied to each local pricing problem. The strategies are not applied because the local managers are free to price in the way they feel is most desirable, and they may not be fully informed about company experience when they make their decision.

The third approach to international pricing can be termed *geocentric*. Under this approach a company neither fixes a single price worldwide nor remains aloof from subsidiary pricing decisions, but instead strikes an intermediate position. A company pursuing this approach works on the assumption that there are unique local market factors that should be recognized in arriving at a pricing decision. These factors are principally local costs, income levels, competition, and the local marketing strategy. Local costs plus a return on invested capital and manpower fix the price floor for the long term. However, for the short term, a company might decide to pursue a market penetration objective and price at less than the cost-plus return figure using export sourcing in order to establish a market. Another short-term objective might be to estimate the size of a market at a price that would be profitable given local sourcing and a certain scale of output. Instead of building facilities, first supply the target market from existing higher-cost external supply sources. If the price and product are accepted by the market, the company can then build a local manufacturing facility to exploit the identified market profitably. If the market does not materialize, the company can experiment with the product at other prices because it is not committed by existing local manufacturing facilities to a fixed sales volume.

Selecting a price that recognizes local competition is essential. Many international marketing efforts have floundered on this point. A major U.S. appliance manufacturer introduced its line of household appliances in Germany and, using U.S. sourcing, set price by simply marking up every item in its line by 28.5 percent. The result of this pricing method was a line that contained a mixture of under-priced and overpriced products. The overpriced products did not sell because better values were offered by local companies. The underpriced product sold very well, but it would have yielded greater profits at a higher price. What was needed was product *line* pricing, which took lower than normal margins in some products and higher margins in others to maximize the profitability of the full line.

For consumer products, local income levels are critical in the pricing decision. If the product is normally priced well above full manufacturing costs, the international marketer has the latitude to price below prevailing levels in higher-income markets and, as a result, reduce the gross margin on the product. While no business-man enjoys reducing margins, they are merely a guide to the ultimate objective, which is profitability, and in some markets income conditions may dictate that the maximum profitability will be obtained by sacrificing "normal" margins. The important point here is that in international marketing there is no such thing as a "normal" margin.

The final factor bearing on the price decision is the local marketing strategy and mix. Price must fit the other elements of the marketing program. For example, when it is decided to pursue a "pull" strategy that uses mass-media advertising and intensive distribution, the price selected must be consistent not only with income levels and competition but also with the costs and heavy advertising programs.

In addition to these local factors, the geocentric approach recognizes that headquarters price coordination is necessary in dealing with international accounts and product arbitrage. Finally, the geocentric approach consciously and systematically seeks to ensure that accumulated national pricing experience is applied wherever relevant.

BIBLIOGRAPHY

BOOKS

Business International, *Solving International Pricing Problems.* New York: Business International, 1965.

Duerr, Michael G., *Tax Allocations and International Business.* New York: The Conference Board, 1972.

ARTICLES

Barrett, M. Edgar, "Case of the Tangled Transfer Price," *Harvard Business Review,* May-June 1977, pp. 20–39.

Feinschreiber, Robert, "The U.S. Law Privides Two Export Incentives," *Columbia Journal of World Business,* Summer 1975, pp. 46–49.

Fieleke, Norman S., "The Tariff Structure for Manufacturing Industries," *Columbia Journal of World Business,* Winter 1976, pp. 98–104.

Howard, Fred, "Overview of International Taxation," *Columbia Journal of World Business,* Summer 1975, pp. 5–11.

Keegan, Warren J., "How Far Is Arm's Length?" *Columbia Journal of World Business,* May-June 1969, pp. 57–66.

Leff, Nathaniel H., "Multinational Corporate Pricing Policy in the Developing Countries," *Journal of International Business Studies,* Fall 1975, pp. 55–64.

Miller, Robert R., "Price Stability, Market Control and Imports in the Steel Industry," *Journal of Marketing,* April 1968.

Monroe, Kent B., "Buyer's Subjective Perceptions of Price," *Journal of Marketing Research,* February 1973, pp. 70–80.

Ravenscroft, Donald R., "Foreign Investment, Exchange Rates, Taxable Income, and Real Values," *Columbia Journal of World Business,* Summer 1975, pp. 50–61.

Russo, J. Edward, "The Value of Unit Price Information," *Journal of Marketing Research,* May 1977, pp. 193-201.

Shulman, James, "When the Price Is Wrong—By Design," *Columbia Journal of World Business,* May-June 1967, pp. 69–76.

Wheatley, John J., and John S. Y. Chiu, "The Effects of Price, Store Image, and Product and Respondent Characteristics on Perceptions of Quality," *Journal of Marketing Research,* May 1977, pp. 181–86.

MALLORY BATTERIES LIMITED

U.S. DEAF-AID FIRM GETS PRICE REBUKE

> On the advice of the Prices and Incomes Board, the government yesterday invited Mallory Batteries Limited, of Crawley, makers of mercury batteries for hearing aids, to withdraw price increases, which they introduced on January 1.

So read the headline and lead paragraph in the *London Times* on May 14, 1968. "That's our problem in a nutshell," said Mr. John D. Buchanan, managing director of Mallory Batteries Limited and of the several other European subsidiaries of P.R. Mallory & Company, their U.S. parent. "We needed the price increase to protect our export markets, and the Ministry of Technology did not object to it. Now the Prices and Incomes Board[1] has published a report which says we should roll back the prices. How can we ever hope to further our own exports and to hold up our end in a worldwide pricing policy for the parent company's battery division if our factory price to our U.K. wholesalers is only about 60 percent of the price our distributors in other countries charge to wholesalers handling our batteries elsewhere?"

Even before devaluation of the British pound (which occurred November 18, 1967) had made the price gap as wide as it was, Mallory Limited had discovered that some of its U.K. distribution channels had found that they could make a profit by shipping to Mallory's outlets in Europe, thus undercutting legitimate European distributors, some of which were company-owned.

PRODUCTS, MARKETS, AND MARKET SHARES

In discussing the troublesome gap which had arisen between U.K. and export prices on mercury batteries for hearing aids, Mr. Buchanan pointed out that this particular line of products was Mallory Limited's most important one, contributing 45 percent of the subsidiary's $10 million total dollar sales and 53 percent of its 47 million unit volume. Exports, moreover, accounted for the major part of Mallory Limited's hearing aid business: about 67 percent in dollars and 60 percent in units (see Exhibit 1).

In explaining this sales breakdown for hearing aid batteries, Mr. Buchanan pointed out that the U.K. or "domestic" market was limited by the fact that mercury batteries could not be used with the bulky type of hearing aid furnished to

---

[1]Under the British system of voluntary income and price controls in effect during 1968, the Ministry of Technology passed initial judgment on company proposals for a price increase while the National Board for Prices and Incomes reviewed their judgments on such cases as might be referrred to it by the government.

EXHIBIT 1. Mallory Batteries Limited, U.K., Export, and Total Sales of Batteries by Product Type 1967 (figures in thousands)

Batteries by Product Type	U.K. Sales		Export Sales		Total Sales	
	U.S. Dollars	Units	U.S. Dollars	Units	U.S. Dollars	Units
Hearing aids	$1,500	10,000	$3,000	15,000	$4,500	25,000
Photographic	1,200		3,000		4,200	
Electronic	200	6,500	600	15,500	800	22,000
Government	250		250		500	
Total	$3,150	16,500	$6,850	30,500	$10,000	47,000

Source: Company records.

some 600,000 hard-of-hearing Britons who obtained their equipment free through the socialized National Health Plan. Mercury batteries were used, however, by another estimated 200,000 people who bought their own equipment as private patients, and who preferred a small, behind-the-ear type of aid for reasons of appearance, bulk, and weight.

For these 200,000 private patients and the manufacturers who produced their aids (at a price of up to $180 each), Mallory was the sole U.K. supplier. Although another well-known brand name accounted for about 10 percent of the market, the batteries sold under this name were actually made by Mallory Limited.

The U.K. company's export market had been assigned to it by its U.S. parent. Although the latter had a number of partly or wholly owned sales and manufacturing subsidiaries on the European continent, including one in Belgium that could conceivably produce batteries for hearing aids,[2] all of Europe and parts of the Far East had been put in Mallory Limited's sales territory, so far as batteries for hearing aids were concerned. Responsibility for selling this line in other parts of the world-wide market had been given to P.R. Mallory plants in the United States, Canada, Mexico, and Japan.

As explained by Mr. Buchanan, the parent company's decision to have product specialization in most of the firm's plants had resulted in a relatively high percentage of export sales on a worldwide basis. This, in turn, had led management to adopt a policy whereby all P.R. Mallory battery plants would, for a given product, quote identical export prices stated in U.S. dollars. Mr. Buchanan also indicated that, beyond being responsible for a major portion of the parent's export sales, Mallory Limited had a significant role to play in the formulation of a pricing strategy for the parent company's battery division.

On an overall basis, Mr. Buchanan said that in 1967 Mallory Limited supplied about 13 percent of the total company's worldwide business in batteries and about 10 percent of its worldwide business in batteries for hearing aids. Regarded as a

[2]If hearing aid batteries were to be produced in Belgium, they could be imported back to England by U.K. customers. However, given duty, taxes, and Belgian production costs, the U.K. retail price of the imported Belgian batteries would be even higher (by about 30 percent) than the new U.K. prices that the Prices and Incomes Board wanted Mallory to roll back.

source of Europe's supply, Mallory Limited accounted for 10 percent of European dry battery business and 30 percent of European hearing aid battery business. Historically, Mallory Limited had been quite profitable. Company-wide pretax earnings in 1967 had been 20 percent on sales and 40 percent on net assets.

BACKGROUND OF THE PRICE-GAP PROBLEM

The initial gap between U.K. and export factory prices on mercury batteries for hearing aids had started to develop back in 1958, Mr. Buchanan explained, owing to a prior management's decision not to raise U.K. prices when the company's export prices were raised. Two reasons were given for this decision. The first was the resistance to a price increase offered by Britain's traditionally strong hearing aid producers, who absorbed 25 percent of sales (at 50 percent off retail list, mostly for new equipment, but including an unknown portion which was resold for replacements). Second was the absence of strong financial pressure: even without increasing U.K. prices, Mallory Limited had been quite profitable.

Since 1958, successive increases in export prices had continually widened the differential between the U.K. and export prices. By 1966, which was the year when Mr. Buchanan had been promoted to his present post after 11 years with the U.S. parent, it was discovered that some of Mallory's U.K. wholesalers (who purchased at 40 percent off the U.K. retail list) and even some of its retailers (who purchased at 25 percent to 30 percent off list) were shipping batteries to Mallory's customers in Europe. For example, the Swiss market of about 400,000 units was 50 percent supplied by a Mallory U.K. wholesaler who sold to a Swiss hearing aid manufacturer. Besides putting the batteries in new equipment, this manufacturer also sold them to wholesalers in the replacement market for 10 percent less than Mallory's official Swiss distributor's price. Normally, in contrast, Mallory's foreign distributor would service his whole national market, with 50 percent to 55 percent of his sales going to local manufacturers who supplied consumers directly, the rest going to local wholesalers who supplied druggists and hearing aid retailers.

How many batteries were sold abroad through illicit U.K. channels Mr. Buchanan said he did not know, though an effort at a rough computation had been made. Thus it was determined that total U.K. unit sales divided by the estimated number of users implied a per capita consumption of 50 batteries a year. Given an average battery life of approximately 70 hours, Mallory executives thought this figure, although not impossible, was high. Actual average use, they believed, was more likely to be from 43 to 45 units a year, which meant that illegal exports had been running at 10 percent to 15 percent.

EFFECTING THE PRICE INCREASE

On taking over his European duties in February 1966, Mr. Buchanan had decided that an increase must be made in the U.K. price for domestic hearing aid battery sales in order to protect both export market income and the marketing arrangements of profitable foreign distributors.

Before this decision was put into effect, however, Britain's Labor Government took steps which not only delayed a price adjustment but made the price-gap problem more acute. In the interest of stemming rising inflation and improving a worsening balance of trade, the government (1) urged a voluntary standstill on prices and incomes for the last six months of 1966; (2) later converted this voluntary standstill into a program of much more severe restraints amounting, in effect, to a price freeze for the first six months of 1967; and (3) devalued the pound on November 18, 1967, from $2.80 to $2.40.

After devaluation, the gap between Mallory's "frozen" U.K. prices and its export prices increased. For example, the most popular hearing aid battery (RM 675), which accounted for over 50 percent of its product group's unit sales, now retailed in Britain for $0.22, which was only a fraction of a cent higher than the foreign distributor's price to the wholesaler. The resulting European price at retail was at least 70 percent as high again as the U.K. retail price, and in most important markets it was over twice as much. Nor was this difference an atypical one (see Exhibit 2). Channels and discount structures were such that a British channel buying at discounted U.K. prices might be strongly tempted to seek out Mallory customers abroad, whom he might well be able to supply at a lower price than the customers would pay by using Mallory's official local channels. (For an example based on battery Model RM 675 and the Swiss market, see Exhibit 3.)

By the time devaluation had widened the price gap to a point where the British wholesaler was paying roughly 60 percent of what the foreign wholesaler was paying (Exhibit 3), the Labor Government had also relaxed the very stringent program of price controls that was in effect during the first half of 1967. New criteria had been established against which requests for a price rise would be judged (Exhibit 4), and a new procedure had been laid down whereby a manufacturer could give an "early warning" of a planned increase and get an official reaction to it (Exhibit 5). Should the reaction prove unfavorable, the company could still go ahead. But if voluntary restraints did not work and if rising prices touched off a cycle of rising wage demands, the Labor Government might feel itself compelled, however reluctantly, to sponsor legislation for imposing compulsory restraints.

Acting under this "Early Warning System" in November 1967, Mallory Limited asked for an across-the-board price increase which would average about 35 percent, and for an increase on batteries for hearing aids which would average 45 percent. On the highest volume hearing aid model (RM 675), the one that accounted for more than half of unit sales, the proposed increase was 50 percent.

In requesting approval for these raises. Mallory applied to the Ministry of Technology with an argument that mentioned increased costs, but emphasized primarily the price-gap problem and its attendant threats to export business. According to the company's plea, (1) raw materials costs had risen 100 percent since 1958 and costs overall had risen 14.4 percent in the 12 months prior to 1968,[3] (2) the price increase requested would only narrow the price gap, not close it,

---

[3] The 12-month 14.4 percent rise was attributed in part to an increase in the cost of raw materials, 90 percent of which were imported and thus directly affected by the November 1968 devaluation and in part to increased spending on R & D and on marketing.

EXHIBIT 2. Mallory Batteries Limited, Retail List Prices (in U.S. cents)[1]

Type	Germany	France	Italy	Belgium	Holland	Switz.	Sweden	Denmark	Austria	Spain	Greece	Norway	U.S.A.	U.K. (Before Price Increase)	U.K. (After Price Increase)	Percent Change in U.K. Price
RM13GH	36.25	36.45	36.00	38.00	38.67	31.18	29.00	26.31	32.31	37.14	40.00	33.60	25	24	23	(4.2)%
RM312H	36.25	36.45	36.00	38.00	33.15	32.34	31.90	26.31	40.39	27.14	40.00	38.51	30	19	25	31.6
RM401H	76.25	77.97	76.80	82.00	69.06	66.99	63.79	56.66	70.39	58.57	83.33	72.11	60	28	50	78.6
RM575H	41.25	41.52	41.60	44.00	37.29	35.80	33.83	30.35	38.08	31.43	46.67	39.21	35	22	30	36.4
RM625H	62.50	62.78	62.40	66.00	56.63	54.28	51.23	46.54	56.54	47.14	70.00	58.11	50	24	42	75.0
RM675H*	48.75	51.65	50.40	54.00	45.58	43.89	40.60	37.10	46.15	38.57	56.67	48.31	40	22*	33*	50.0
PX13	86.25	91.14	88.80	94.00	73.20	76.23	73.46	65.43	80.77	66.43	96.67	84.71	75	28	58	71.5
PX23	98.75	117.47	116.00	116.00	103.59	99.33	94.72	84.99	105.00	86.43	126.67	108.52	85	48	73	52.0
PX825	48.75	62.78	54.40	66.00	56.63	56.59	55.09	55.31	70.39	46.43	70.00	68.61	50	30	40	33.3
Mn1500	48.75	62.78	54.50	66.00	56.63	54.28	51.23	46.54	56.54	47.14	70.00	59.51	50	33	40	21.2
Mn2400	48.75	59.75	54.40	66.00	54.49	54.28	51.23	46.54	56.54	47.14	70.00	59.51	50	27	40	48.2
ZM-9	123.75	130.63	127.20	136.00	107.73	109.72	104.39	93.76	115.39	95.00	140.00	119.72	95	66	79	19.7
RM312	45.00	45.57	44.80	48.00	35.91	40.42	39.63	39.80	50.77	32.86	50.00	47.61	35	19	28	47.4
RM401	88.75	91.14	88.80	94.00	73.20	76.23	73.46	65.43	80.77	66.43	96.67	84.01	75	28	58	107.0

[1] £1.00 = 20 shillings—240 pence = $2.40.

*The most popular hearing aid battery, accounting for over 50 percent of hearing aid battery sales.

Source: Company records.

EXHIBIT 3. Mallory Batteries Limited, Legitimate Channels, Discounts, and Prices for Hearing Aid Battery Model RM675,* U.K. and Switzerland (in U.S. cents)

United Kingdom	*Switzerland*
(Prior to price increase)	Factory price to distributor 16.17 Add: Shipping and handling (3%) +.49 Add: Sales tax (5.4%) +.90 Landed cost to distributor (at 40% of retail list) 17.56
Factory price to wholesaler (At 60% or retail list) 13.2	Distributor's price to wholesaler (At 50% of retail list) 21.94
Wholesaler's price to retailer (At 70%–75% of retail list) 15.4 – 16.0	Wholesaler's price to retailer (At 60.7% of retail list) 26.60
Retailer's list (At markup of 27%–30%) 22.0	Retailer's list (At markup of 39.9%) 43.89

*The most popular hearing aid battery, accounting for over 50 percent of hearing aid battery sales.

Source: Company records and Exhibit 2.

EXHIBIT 4. Mallory Batteries Limited, Criteria for Requesting Price Increases

Criteria for Price Behaviour

10. ... Price increases should take place only where they can be fully justified against these criteria and every effort should be made to absorb increases in costs. The criteria are:
   (i) if output per employee cannot be increased sufficiently to allow wages and salaries to increase at a rate consistent with the criteria for incomes without some increase in prices, and no offsetting reductions can be made in non-labour costs per unit of output or in the return sought on investment;
   (ii) if there are unavoidable increases in non-labour costs such as materials, fuel, services or marketing costs per unit of output which cannot be offset by reductions in labor or capital costs per unit of output or in the return sought on investment;
   (iii) if there are unavoidable increases in capital costs per unit of output which cannot be offset by reductions in non-capital costs per unit of output or in the return sought on investment;
   (iv) if, after every effort has been made to reduce costs, the enterprise is unable to secure the capital required to meet home and overseas demand.

Source: These paragraphs are copies verbatim from *Prices and Incomes Policy After 30th June 1967* (London, Her Majesty's Stationery Office, November 1965), pp. 4, 5.

Types of Prices Covered

---

8. The arrangements will apply primarily to manufacturers' prices and only to manufacturers' prices for the home market. . . . It is not normally intended to cover prices which are fixed by individual contract or some similar process.

Action to be Taken by Manufacturers, etc.

---

9. Any enterprise which plans to increase the price of any of the goods and services listed in Part A of the Appendix* is asked to inform the appropriate Government Department not less than four weeks before the date from which the price increase is to take effect. In general the following information should be provided together with a brief assessment of the justification for the proposed increase . . . a description of the goods or services concerned, including any changes being made in the product or in the service offered; the present price and the proposed price and the price trend over the previous three years; the annual sales value of the goods or services concerned; the reason for the price increase; and, where this is due to cost increases, an explanation of these together with a statement of the part played in total costs by e.g., labour, raw materials and other costs.

---

*An Appendix to this document listed some 27 products or product groups, including batteries, to which these regulations applied.

Source: These paragraphs are exerpted from *Prices and Incomes Policy: An "Early Warning" System* (London, Her Majesty's Stationery Office, November 1965), pp. 4, 5.

since the new U.K. retail prices would still be lower than the prices quoted anywhere else, including the United States (Exhibit 2); (3) the new prices would, however, be high enough to protect the company's export markets around the world; and (4) such protection was necessary in view of the fact that Mallory Limited exported 68 percent of its overall dollar volume and hence was extremely vulnerable.

REACTION TO THE PRICE INCREASE

On December 19, 1967, the Ministry of Technology answered Mallory's "Early Warning" about its projected price increases. "No objections will be raised to their implementation," was the verdict from this official source. Accordingly, the price increase went into effect on January 1, 1968.

No sooner was this move announced than the price increase became a political issue. A record number of user complaints (460) poured into the Prices and Incomes Board from customers for hearing aid batteries. Newspaper comment brought out the fact that an increase of 50 percent, as made on Mallory's biggest selling hearing aid unit, was the highest ever requested. In discussing the motivation for it, the press stressed protection of Mallory Limited's U.S. parent's interests rather than Mallory Limited's point that British export income was decreased when batteries moved out through illicit channels. Radio and TV joined in adverse publicity, and in the House of Commons questions were put to the Minister of Technology, asking that the matter be referred to the National Board for Prices and Incomes.

On February 6, after renewed questions in the Commons, the Minister of Technology agreed to submit the issue to the Board, and on May 6, 1968, the Board gave its answer. As earlier noted, the PIB invited the company to withdraw its price increases and to enter into conversations with the Government on the basis of the preexisting prices.

The following is a summary of salient excerpts from the PIB report:

1. With respect to Mallory's contention that the price increase was justified in part by the need to absorb increased costs, the PIB did not contest the validity of Mallory's cost figures, but the report went on to say:

> "The crucial question is whether the estimated rate of return without any price increase was sufficient to allow the company both to absorb increased costs and provide for investment requirements. It was certainly higher than that of most companies operating in the U.K. In our view it was high enough —and it must be remembered that in the U.K. the company had no direct competition—to allow both for the absorption of increased costs and future investment needs."

2. With respect to Mallory's second and more important argument that the price increase was needed to preserve the integrity of its export markets, the PIB concluded:

> "We consider that the company acted both in their own and in the national interest in seeking to protect their export revenue. Their manner of doing so, however, drew attention to the glaring contrast between the limited increases in earnings allowed by national policy and the sharp increases sometimes sought in prices and thus did damage to the national attempt to contain costs. We consider that the company would have been more prudent to have continued to sell to wholesalers at the existing U.K. price while placing on them a restrictive covenant designed to prevent selling, directly or indirectly, at prices undercutting Mallory overseas.

3. Finally, the report called attention to the fact that in the U.K., Mallory recommended resale prices and that the increases in question applied not only to factory prices but to retail prices as well. The increases, therefore, also resulted in a 45 percent rise in the cash margins realized by the distributive trade. The PIB then concluded that:

> "Since the main purpose of the increase was to bring up the U.K. price to the export price, we see no justification for its full reflection in the price charged in the shops through an unchanged percentage margin for the distributor. We recommend that in the future the margin for the distributor allowed for in the recommended price be expressed in cash rather than percentage terms."

THE DILEMMA

Thus, Mr. Buchanan's dilemma in May 1968 was to decide what steps to take in response to the report and recommendations of the Prices and Income Board. He knew there were a variety of alternative actions that could be taken, but his problem was to decide which of these was the wisest in terms of the overall well-being of the company.

QUESTIONS

1. What is the problem?
2. Why did this problem occur?
3. What alternatives are open to Mallory?
4. What would you do if you were Mr. Buchanan?

channel decisions

Wherever the Roman conquers, there he dwells.

Lucius Annaeus Seneca, 8 B.C.–A.D. 65

(Moral Essays to Helvia on Consolation)

INTRODUCTION

According to marketing definitions of the American Marketing Association, a *channel of distribution* is "the structure of intracompany organization units and extracompany agents and dealers, wholesale and retail, through which a commodity, product, or service is marketed."[1] This definition of the channel of distribution purposely includes both the internal company marketing organization and the external independent organization because the marketing manager must combine these systems in order to achieve product distribution. Distribution is the physical flow of goods through channels, and channels are the internal and external organizational units that perform functions that add utility to a product or service. The major sources of utility created by channels are: place, or the availability of a product or service in a location that is convenient to a potential customer; time, or the availability of a product or service at a time that fills a customer need; and information that answers questions and communicates useful product and applications knowledge to potential customers. Since these main utilities are a basic source of competitive advantage and "product" value, one of the key policy decisions marketing management must make at the policy level is what channel strategy to adopt.

The distribution channels in markets around the world are among the most highly differentiated aspects of national marketing systems. For this reason, chan-

---

[1] *Marketing Definitions: A Glossary of Marketing Terms* (Chicago: American Marketing Association, 1960), p. 10.

nel strategy is one of the most challenging and difficult components of an international marketing program. Smaller companies are often blocked by their inability to establish effective channel arrangements. In larger multinational companies, operating via country subsidiaries, channel strategy is the element of the marketing mix that is least understood and controlled by headquarters. To a large extent, channels are an aspect of the marketing program that is left to the control and discretion of the local marketing management group. Nevertheless, it is important for managers concerned with world marketing programs to understand the nature of international distribution channels. Distribution is an integral part of the total marketing program and must either fit or be fitted to product design, price, and communications aspects of the total marketing program. Another important reason for placing channel decisions on the agenda of international marketing managers is that channel decisions typically involve outside agents and organizations and long-term legal commitments and obligations to other firms and individuals, which are often extremely expensive to terminate or change. Even in cases where there is no legal obligation, commitments may be backed by good faith and feelings of obligation, which are equally difficult and painful to adjust.

From the viewpoint of the marketer concerned with a single-country program, international channel arrangements are a valuable source of information and insight into possible new approaches to more effective channel strategies. For example, self-service discount pricing of food and hard and soft goods in the United States was studied by retailers from Europe and Asia who then introduced the self-service concept in their own countries. The Japanese trading company is being examined with great interest by governments and businessmen all over the world who are anxious to imitate the success of these Japanese organizations.

This chapter will examine international channel systems by focusing on (1) what the multinational marketer should know about channels in order to contribute to channel planning and control, and (2) what the marketer concerned with a single country should know in order to exploit channel innovations that have been tried in other countries.

CHANNEL OBJECTIVES AND CONSTRAINTS

The starting point in selecting the most effective channel arrangement is a clear determination of the market target for the company's marketing effort, and a determination of the needs and preferences of the target market. Where are the potential customers located? What are their information requirements? What are their preferences for service? How sensitive are they to price? Each of the dimensions of customer preference must be carefully determined because there is as much danger to the success of a marketing program in giving too much service, credit, and so forth, as there is in giving too little. Moreover, each market must be analyzed to determine the cost of providing service. What is appropriate in one country may not be effective in another.

An example of giving too much service is the case of the international manufacturer of construction products who emphasized the speedy service provided by his salesmen in radio-equipped station wagons. The company prided itself on the fact that the maximum elapsed time between the receipt of an on-site customer order and the actual delivery by a salesman was under two hours. While its service record was outstanding, the company discovered that in the United States the cost of this service, which was included in the price the company charged for its products, placed it at a serious competitive price disadvantage vis-à-vis its major competition. Customers had praised the company for its service, but their preference in terms of actual buying behavior was for the offering of the competitor whose costs were much lower because he did not offer the immediate delivery service and who passed on his cost savings to customers in the form of lower prices. This finding for the United States did not apply to European markets where competition and custom made delivery necessary.

Channel strategy in an international marketing program must fit the company's competitive position and overall marketing objectives in each national market. If a company wants to enter a competitive market, it must either provide incentives to independent channel agents, which will induce them to promote the company's product, or it must establish company-owned or franchised outlets. The process of shaping international channels to fit overall company objectives is constrained by the following factors, each of which will be discussed briefly.

Customer Characteristics

The characteristics of customers are an important influence on channel design. Their number, geographical distribution, income, shopping habits, and reaction to different selling methods all vary from country to country and therefore require different channel approaches.

In general, the larger the number of customers, the greater the need for channel agents regardless of the stage of market development. For example, if there are only ten customers for an industrial product, in each national market these ten customers must be directly contacted by either the manufacturer or an agent. If a product is sold to millions of customers, retail distribution outlets or mail-order distribution is required. If there are a large number of low-volume retailers, it is usually cheaper to reach them via wholesalers. For large-volume retailers, it may be more cost effective to sell direct. These generalizations apply to all countries, regardless of stage of development.

Product Characteristics

Certain product attributes such as degree of standardization, perishability, bulk, service requirements, and unit price have an important influence on channel design. Products with high unit price, for example, are often sold through a direct company sales force because the selling cost of this "expensive" distribution method is a small part of the total sale price. Moreover, the high cost of such products is usually associated with complexity or with product features that must be explained in some detail, and this can be done most effectively by a controlled sales force. A good example of this type of product is a computer, which is expensive, complicated, and requires both explanation and applications analysis focused on the customer's needs. A controlled and trained salesman or "sales engineer" is tailor-made for this task.

Some products require margins to cover the costs of expensive sales engineering. Others require margins to provide a large monetary incentive to a direct sales force. Encyclopedias are an excellent example of this latter type of product. The function of the encyclopedia salesman is to call on potential customers and to create an awareness of the value of an encyclopedia and to evoke in the customer a feeling of need for this value. The sales activity must be paid for. Companies using direct distribution for consumer products rely upon wide gross selling margins to generate the necessary compensation revenue for salesmen.

Perishable products usually require more direct marketing to ensure that the condition of products in channels is satisfactory for purchase by the ultimate customer. In developed countries, vegetables, bread, dairy products, and many perishable food products are distributed by controlled sales forces, and stock is checked by these sales-distributor organizations to ensure that it is fresh and ready for distribution. In less-developed countries, producers typically sell these products in public marketplaces. Bulky products usually require channel arrangements that minimize the shipping distances and the number of times products are turned over in the channels before they reach the ultimate customer. Soft drinks and beer are examples of bulky products whose widespread availability is an important aspect of an effective marketing strategy, and which are typically handled by a bottler or brewer sales-distribution organization whenever a bottler or brewer is large enough to support direct distribution.

Middleman Characteristics

Channel strategy must recognize the characteristics of existing middlemen. Middlemen are in business to maximize their own profit and not that of the manufacturer. They are notorious for their "cherry picking," which refers to the practice of taking orders for products, brands, and manufacturers that are in demand and avoiding any real selling effort for a manufacturer's products that may require "push." This is a rational response by the middleman, but it can present a serious obstacle to the manufacturer attempting to break into a market with a new product. The "cherry picker" is not interested in building a market for a new product. This is a problem for the expanding international company. Frequently, this practice forces a manufacturer with a new product or a product with a limited market share to set up some arrangement for bypassing the "cherry-picking" segment of the channel. In some cases manufacturers will set up an expensive direct distribution organization in order to obtain a share of the market. When they finally obtain a share of the target market, they may abandon the direct distribution system for a more cost-effective intermediary system. The move does not mean that intermediaries are "better" than direct distribution. It is simply a response by a manufacturer to the altered attractiveness of his product to independent distributors.

Another method of dealing with the "cherry-picking" problem without setting up an expensive direct sales force is to subsidize the entire cost of salesmen who are assigned by a distributor to the products of the subsidizing company. The advantage of this method is that it eliminates the cost of sales management and physical distribution by tying the missionary and support selling in with the distributor's sales management and physical distribution. Using this method it is possible to place managed direct selling support and distribution support behind a product at the expense of only one salesman per selling area. The distributor's incentive for cooperating in this kind of arrangement is that he obtains a "free" salesman for a new product that promises to be a profitable addition to his line. This cooperative arrangement is ideally suited to getting a new export-sourced product into distribution in a market.

Environmental Characteristics

The general characteristics of the total environment are a major consideration in channel design. Because of the enormous variety of economic, social, and political environments internationally, there is a tremendous need to delegate a large degree of independence to local operating managements or agents. It is useful to compare food distribution in countries at different stages of development because it illustrates how channels reflect and respond to underlying market conditions in a country. For example, in the United States high incomes, high wages, large-capacity refrigerators with large freezer units, intensive automobile ownership (two persons per car), convenience food acceptance, and availability and attitudes toward food preparation combine to make the supermarket or the self-service one-stop food store the basic food retailing unit. The American housewife wants to purchase in one trip enough food to last for a week. She has the money, the refrigerated storage capacity, and the hauling capacity of the car to move this large quantity of food from the store to her home. The supermarket, because it is efficient, can fill the food shoppers' need at lower prices than that of traditional service food stores. Additionally, supermarkets can offer more variety and a greater selection of merchandise than smaller food stores, which is appealing to higher-income-level consumers.

Europe is in transition today. Twenty years ago European housewives relied upon daily, twice-a-day, or even three-times-a-day food shopping. Specialized small food shops supplied the various requirements: in France, for example, bread from the boulangerie; beef from the boucherie; pork from the charcuterie; fish and fowl from another shop; fruit, vegetables, and general supplies from the épicerie; and milk, cream, butter, and cheese from the crémerie. Incomes were lower, few households had refrigerators, automobile ownership was minimal, and housewives were accustomed to spending several hours per day in purchasing food and preparing meals. A combination of necessity and habit comprised the underpinnings of continental shopping habits. Cold storage, transport capacity, and funds for food were limited. Daily shopping was therefore a necessity. Today the increase in incomes on the Continent has resulted in widespread ownership of refrigerators, which have increased in size over the years. Automobile ownership has risen and attitudes and habits are changing. Today all over Europe one finds self-service one-stop food stores competing with the traditional specialized shops. The average money amount of food purchases is increasing, and the frequency of shopping is declining. A larger and larger proportion of Europe's total food dollar is being spent in self-service one-stop food stores that are more efficient (they require a smaller gross margin than traditional stores) retailing units. The basic cultural tradition of food shopping in specialized stores will continue to act as a countervailing force, but the underlying factors favor the growth of large self-service food stores at the expense of the traditional specialized service store.

In less-developed countries food stores do not exist outside the cities. Food is grown on farms for personal consumption. Small amounts of food are sold by the producers in public markets. Small stores that stock a few dozen supplemental items such as salt, matches, some canned items, and seasoning serve the very small market for nonlocally produced food. The less-developed country system combines a large subsistence economy with a very small cash economy and, as a result, is not significantly a commercial food economy.

CHANNEL TERMINOLOGY

Channel terminology can be misleading to the international marketer. The same designation is used around the world, but the same meaning cannot always be associated with a designation. The term *supermarket* is a good illustration of this fact. What is a supermarket? It all depends upon where you are. Since the term originated in the United States, the U.S. definition will be used as a standard.

Supermarket—U.S. Version

There are four main elements of a U.S. supermarket. The first is self-service, which is an essential and enduring characteristic. When supermarkets were introduced in the United States in the 1930s, they originated the self-service concept in the merchandising of food. Today this is a characteristic of all supermarkets.

The second element is gross margins. When supermarkets were introduced the average margin on food sold at retail was over 30 percent. Supermarkets, which initially were very low cost operations in converted warehouses, began operating on gross margins of 18 percent and less, clearly offering a substantial price discount to the shopper. Over a period of time these gross margins have tended to increase as supermarkets have added such services as the carryout of food items, check cashing, lighting, Muzak, and expensive promotional devices, such as trading stamps. Today the average gross margin of a U.S. supermarket is roughly 22-24 percent. The gradual increase in average gross margins sometimes leads to the offering of a new mix of services in the supermarket that reduces the frills and brings gross margins back to a lower level with the associated price reduction. The constant swing from low service, low gross margins, and low prices to additional service, rising margins, and rising prices was labeled by the late Malcolm P. McNair as the "wheel of retailing." That is, there is a cycle of moving from additional service and higher prices back to reduced service and lower prices.

Number of items is the third element of a U.S. supermarket. This number ranges from less than two hundred in the small superette to several thousand items in the full-scale market. The number of items is one of the product features of this type of retail outlet. It offers the shopper a wide selection of merchandise. In expanding the selection of merchandise supermarket operators typically add non-food items, thus offering a "scrambled" product line.

A fourth element is the annual monetary volume of business. In the United States a store doing $1 million or more of annual business is regarded as a supermarket.

Supermarkets Outside the U.S.

How do "supermarkets" outside the United States compare with the super markets described above? In less-developed countries a food retailing store called a supermarket has the following characteristics. The first is self-service. Food items are stacked on shelves and the shopper selects the item and carries it to a checkout counter. In this important aspect the store is identical to the U.S. supermarket. The second is gross margin. In many less-developed countries "supermarkets'" average gross margins are in excess of 25 percent. The prices in these "supermarkets" are higher than prices in alternative traditional retail outlets where gross margins might be as low as 10 or 12 percent. Third is the number and selection of items. The less-developed country's supermarket is similar to the smaller U.S. supermarket in number of items stocked. Their selection, however, offers a range of merchandise not normally found in traditional retail outlets. There is a heavy emphasis on specialty food items and imported food items for the elite and wealthy foreign community in the country, who can afford imported foods at higher prices.

In Europe the first "supermarkets" in the 1950s were located in the high-density, high-cost shopping areas and were in effect a large specialty food store operating on a self-service basis. They were not typically used by the housewife for ordinary day-to-day food items. With rising incomes, refrigeration, and so on supermarkets in Europe are beginning to look more like their U.S. counterparts.

Today the Europeans have shown themselves capable of telescoping time and leapfrogging a number of intermediate stages of retailing development by intro-ducing a number of retailing concepts that are more advanced than anything in the United States. European mass merchandising provides a good example. The two best examples are the "hypermarché" in France and the "verbrauchermarkt" in Germany. These are enormous self-service combination food and general mer-chandise stores that occupy as much as 250,000 square feet of space. All items are under the same roof, and a single set of checkout counters is used for both types of merchandise. Much of the merchandise in these stores is displayed in ship-ping containers in which the goods have been prepriced by the manufacturer. The hypermarchés operate on much lower gross margins than U.S. stores, averaging

TABLE 13-1. Carrefour of France Compared with all U.S. Discount Stores, 1970 (In U.S. Dollars)

	Average Sales per Square Foot	*Average Gross Margin per Square Foot*
Carrefour	$360	$65
All U.S. discount stores	79	24
Newer U.S. discount stores	87	27

Data source: Ralph Z. Sorenson II, "U.S. Marketers Can Learn from European Innovators," *Harvard Business Review*, September-October 1972, pp. 89-99.

TABLE 13-2. Glossary of Channel Terms

AGENT—an independent intermediary, who may act in the name of, and for, a principal. His contract will define these provisions along with territorial rights, exclusively, and sales commission.

BROKER—an independent intermediary between buyer and seller who brings parties together to facilitate the conclusion of sales contracts. The broker does not necessarily have a continuous relationship with his principals, even though they may frequently call on his services. He charges a fee for his assistance and is sometimes called a "selling agent."

DISTRIBUTOR—an independent trader who takes title to the goods of a principal, and who thus buys and sells for his own account and in his name in a specified territory. He may or may not have exclusive sales rights. His compensation consists of his profit margin.

FRANCHISEE—a person or legal entity that is granted the right in a specified territory to conduct business under the trade name, trademarks, and other property for which franchise fees or royalties are paid to the franchisor. (Typical and well-known examples of franchise operations are AMF Bowling Centers, Howard Johnson Restaurants, and Wimpy Bars.) Individual operators are franchised to do business under the trade name of the franchisor, provide services, and/or sell brandname goods, or goods associated with the franchisor's trading name. The franchisee and his employees are generally provided with management and technical training: assisted in locating, equipping, and decorating business premises, and sometimes given financial assistance.

MANUFACTURERS' REPRESENTATIVE—a person—or an unrelated firm—who is paid a commission (usually 5 percent) when he arranges a sale between the manufacturer and an actual buyer. The function of a manufacturers' representative is similar to that of a broker.

WHOLESALER—a person who usually buys for his own accounts. A "full service" wholesaler is expected to provide transport and storage, break up bulk shipments, assemble selling assortments, extend credit to retailers, promote sales, and supply repair facilities and spare parts. However, in less developed markets (for example, in Italy or Spain) wholesalers are traditionally important sources of financing for retailers, but they are generally less effective in sales promotion or after-sales servicing.

Source: Business International, *"Developing Distribution in Europe"* (New York: Business International, August 1969), p. 15.

12 percent on food as compared with over 20 percent for U.S. supermarkets and 15 to 18 percent on a storewide basis.

In 1970 Carrefour, one of France's largest and most successful hypermarché operators, averaged $24 million in sales per store in each of nine outlets. There was an average of 66,000 square feet of selling space per store. As can be seen from Table 13-1, the sales per square foot and gross margin per square foot were far above U.S. averages for discount stores in the same year.

Another example of innovative developments in European retailing is the Migros organization in Switzerland, which gave its customers unit pricing, informational labeling, and nutritional advice long before the consumerism movement got started in the United States.

The only safe practice in international marketing is to never assume you know what a term means. The prudent manager will always investigate to determine precisely what functions are performed by a channel unit and the practices employed by the unit. In this way the manager can ensure that he is relying upon an accurate map of function and practice, which is the purpose of terminology.

Fortunately there is considerable overlap between the use of channel terms in the United States and Europe. Table 13-2 is a glossary of channel terms as they are currently defined in Europe.

CHANNEL STRUCTURE

Consumer Products

Figure 13-1 summarizes channel structure alternatives for consumer products. A consumer products manufacturer can sell directly to his customer either by a door-to-door sales force, through mail-order selling using a catalog or other printed description of his offerings, or through manufacturer-owned stores. Of the three direct alternatives the mail-order business is the most thriving. Indeed, some observers predict that this form of distribution will grow in importance as time, one of the scarcest of modern resources, becomes increasingly scarce as consumers trade off the time cost of in-store shopping versus the demands upon time of leisure activity.

Door-to-door selling, which is an expensive form of distribution that requires high gross margins and results in higher prices to the customer, is a form of selling that is not growing in importance and is possibly declining. Certain items continue to be sold in this manner—namely, encyclopedias, brushes, and vacuum cleaners. A variation on the door-to-door selling method is the consumer party selling arrangement where a representative of a manufacturer arranges an informal semisocial gathering in the home of a cooperating consumer in order to describe and demonstrate the goods he is selling. This "house party" form of selling has been particularly effective for manufacturers of cosmetics and kitchenware. Although the house party method originated in the United States, its viability has been demonstrated in Europe and Asia by successful applications of the method.

Another variant of the door-to-door selling method, which has achieved some success in Europe, is the consignment sale of merchandise to part-time salesmen who take orders for the company's product from a circle of acquaintances and friends. A French company established a major market position in the liquid household cleaner market in France by using this distribution method.

A third direct selling alternative is the manufacturer-owned store. Although in some industries manufacturer-owned stores are a major channel of distribution,

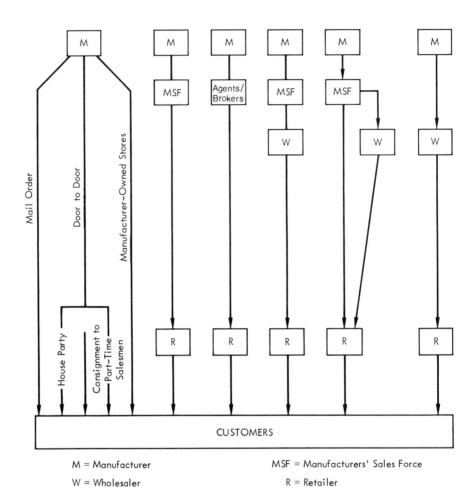

FIGURE 13-1. Marketing Channel Alternatives—Consumer Products

M = Manufacturer   MSF = Manufacturers' Sales Force

W = Wholesaler   R = Retailer

most companies avoid this alternative. They choose instead to establish one or two retail outlets for obtaining marketing intelligence rather than as a distribution strategy. In those areas where a manufacturer's product line is sufficient to support a viable retail outlet, the possibilities for this form of distribution are much more attractive. The shoe store, for example, is a viable retail unit, and shoe manufacturers typically have established their own direct outlets as a major weapon in their distribution strategy. One of the first successful U.S. international companies, Singer, established a worldwide chain of company-owned and -operated outlets to sell and service sewing machines.

The other alternatives for consumer products channel structure are various combinations of a manufacturer's sales force and wholesalers calling upon retail outlets, which in turn sell to customers.

These alternatives usually produce patterns that are characteristic of a product class in a country at a particular time. In Japan, for example, several layers of small wholesalers play an important role in the distribution of food. Attempts to bypass these apparently unnecessary units in the channel have failed because the cost to a manufacturer of providing their service (frequent small deliveries to small grocery outlets) is greater than the margin they require. Channel patterns that appear to be inefficient *may* reflect rational adjustment to costs and preferences in a market, or they may present an opportunity to the innovative international marketer to obtain a competitive advantage by introducing more effective channel arrangements.

International Retailing

International retailing is activity by an organization that reaches across national boundaries. There is an active interest among successful retailers today to extend internationally. However, international retailing is not new. For centuries venturesome merchants have gone abroad both to obtain merchandise and ideas and to operate retail establishments. In 1929 the spread of foreign-owned jewelry shops in New York City led the *New Yorker* to speak of "the invasion of Rue de la Paix houses."[2] The development of trading company operations in Africa and Asia by British, French, Dutch, Belgian, and German retailing organizations progressed extensively during the nineteenth and early twentieth centuries. International trading and retail store operation was one of the economic pillars of the colonial system of the nineteenth and early twentieth centuries. The big change taking place in international retailing today involves the gradual dissolution of the colonial retailing structure, and in its place the creation of international retailing organizations, which operate in the industrialized countries. Sears, for example, currently receives less than 2 percent of its sales from units outside the United States and Canada. The bulk of retail trade everywhere is in the hands of domestic enterprises.

The large number of unsuccessful international retailing ventures suggests that anyone contemplating a move into international retailing should do so with a great deal of caution. The critical question, which the would-be international retailer must answer, is, "What advantages do we have relative to local competition?" The answer to this question, when local laws governing retailing practice are taken into account, in many cases will be "Nothing." In such cases there is no reason to expect highly profitable operations to develop from a venture into international retailing. On the other hand, the answer to this question may indicate positive points. Basically, a retailer has two things to offer the public. One is the selection of goods at a price, and the second is the overall manner in which the goods are offered in the store setting. This includes the store site, parking facilities, in-store setting, customer service, and so on. An excellent example of an international retailer with an advantage over local competition is Sears, which obtains a superior selection of goods and prices in a country by direct contact with local manufac-

---

[2] "On and Off the Avenue," November 23, 1929, p. 95, quoted in Stanley C. Hollander, "The International Storekeepers," *MSU Business Topics,* Spring 1969.

turers and, where necessary, setting up local manufacturers to supply goods for sale through Sears outlets.

Industrial Products

Figure 13-2 summarizes marketing channel alternatives for the industrial product company. Three basic elements are involved: the manufacturer's sales force, distributors or agents, and wholesalers. A manufacturer can reach customers with his own sales force, or a sales force that calls on wholesalers who sell to customers, or a combination of these two arrangements. A manufacturer can sell directly to wholesalers without using a sales force, and wholesalers in turn can supply customers. Finally, a distributor or agent can call on wholesalers or customers for a manufacturer.

Patterns vary from country to country. In order to decide which pattern to use and which wholesalers and agents to select, each country must be studied individually. The larger the market, the more feasible the manufacturer's sales force alternative.

In some countries, channels in certain industries are blocked by vertically

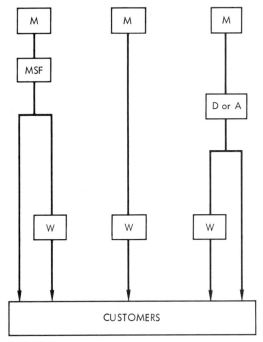

M = Manufacturer   MSF = Manufacturers Sales Force

W = Wholesaler   D or A = Distributor or Agent

FIGURE 13-2. Marketing Channel Alternatives—Industrial Products

integrated manufacturers. The aluminum industry presents an interesting example of how channel arrangements affect the possibilities for market entry. In the United States there are three major primary aluminum producers: Alcoa, Reynolds, and Kaiser. Together they account for roughly 75 percent of the industry's ingot capacity. The aluminum industry is structured in three stages. Primary producers refine ore into aluminum and produce aluminum ingots. Fabricators turn the ingots into a marketable shape, and end users take the marketable shapes and incorporate them into finished products. Fabricators can be dependent or independent. Several fields, such as the production of aluminum castings and aluminum extrusions, are dominated by independent fabricators in the United States. The existence of these independent fabricators provides an opportunity for foreign aluminum products to find a market for ingots in the United States.

In France, however, the situation is different. France has two major fabricators, Cegedur GP and Trefinefaux, both of which belong to the Pechiney group, which includes Pechiney with 80 percent of the ingot market and Eugine with 20 percent. Although there are other fabricators, these are also linked with Pechiney and Eugine. As a result of this integration of production and fabrication, the possibilities for entry of U.S. aluminum producers in the French market are extremely limited. Indeed a foreign country wishing to penetrate the French market would be faced with the need to persuade the integrated producers and fabricators to accept foreign ingot production, or, if this were not possible, the foreign producer would be forced to enter the market with production and fabrication in order to establish himself.[3]

CHANNELS IN LESS-DEVELOPED COUNTRIES

One of the conspicuous features of channels in less-developed countries is the remarkable number of people engaged in selling merchandise usually in very small quantities. The number and variety of intermediaries in the channel have been criticized by official and unofficial observers. B. P. Bauer comments on these criticisms as follows:

> These criticisms rest on a misunderstanding. The system (in LDCs) is a logical adaptation to certain fundamental factors in the West African economies which will persist for many years to come. So far from being wasteful, it is highly economic in saving and salvaging those resources which are particularly scarce in West Africa (above all, real capital) by using the resources which are largely redundant and for which there is very little demand: and thus it is productive by any rational economic criteria.[4]

Another way of looking at the channel arrangements in less-developed countries is to examine the costs of these arrangements to consumers. A study in East Africa revealed that the small "dukas" (a small store typically carrying under one

[3]I am indebted to Mr. Alain V. Setton for this account.
[4]B. P. Bauer, *West African Trade* (Cambridge: Cambridge University Press), p. 22.

hundred items and occupying no more than 50 to 75 sq. ft. of space) indicated that they were operating on average gross margins of approximately 12 percent. This fact the reader will recall is to be compared with the average gross margin in the typical U.S. supermarket of roughly 22 percent. Clearly, by the measure of markup the small East African duka is a lower-cost form of distribution.

Since these dukas operate at lower costs, does it mean that they are more efficient than the supermarket? If a measure of efficiency is the ratio of productivity or output per man-hour, and if in retail trade the measure of productivity is the physical volume or monetary volume of sales per person, the East African duka is a highly inefficient form of distribution compared with the U.S. supermarket. The sales per person in the duka are a fraction of sales per person in the U.S. supermarket. Duka prices and margins are lower because the total income or salary of the duka operator is a fraction of that of even the lowest-level employee of a large American supermarket. By using overabundant resources that are in surplus (labor), the duka employs resources that would otherwise be unemployed and does so at a cost to the consuming public market that is only slightly more than half the cost of U.S. supermarket retailing.

In the early 1960s the Tanganyika government decided that it would contribute to the general welfare of the nation by opening government-managed supermarkets or food distribution outlets that would compete with the small duka. At the time it was mistakenly alleged by the government, and perhaps believed by some of the population, that duka operators were overcharging the public. The government, after establishing its own food distribution outlets, discovered that it was impossible to compete in price with the dukas. The government discovered that the operators of the dukas, or dukawallas as they are known, were earning modest incomes and that in terms of cost to the consumer, the private retail system of East Africa was a lower-cost arrangement than the government-run stores. The main reason for this was that the dukawalla was willing to work from dawn to dusk for the same or less return than the government employee who worked from 9:00 A.M. to 5:00 P.M. with two hours off for lunch.

Bolivian Channels: A Case Example

The channel arrangements in Bolivia are typical of those in less-developed countries.[5] Bolivia in 1967 had a population of 3.8 million, which was growing at an annual rate of 1.4 percent. The country's per capita national income was $168 and GNP was growing at an annual rate of 5.9 percent.

In La Paz, a city of eighty thousand families, food is marketed through a system of small-scale retailing and wholesaling establishments. Two basic channels exist, one handling perishable items and the other almost completely separate

---

[5] This section is drawn from Donald S. Henley and Vincent Farace, "Consumer Buying and Communication Patterns in Bolivian Urban Food Retailing: A Preliminary Report" (Unpublished paper, December 1967).

channel handling dried, canned, and bottled items. Perishable items are sold in large public markets by a corps of vendors who established themselves along the streets. Dried, canned, and bottled items (relatively spoilage free items), which are likely to be used in a normal diet, are sold through an institution called a tienda, which is a small, one-room establishment whose proprietor is also the manager.

A retailer census in La Paz in early 1967 showed 9,806 retailers operating in the city. Twenty-three percent of these retailers were street vendors; 32 percent were retailers in public markets, and the remaining 45 percent were tiendas. There was, on the average, one tienda for every twenty families in La Paz.

Henley and Farace estimated that annual sales of tiendas were somewhere between $1,720 and $6,170, and that they averaged a gross margin of 14 percent and had a net profit of between $615 to a loss of $9. One of the reasons for the relatively low gross margins in tiendas was the relative ease of entry into this kind of business. The mean original capital invested was $108 and the median was $38. Over 53 percent of the tienda operators had been in business for two years or less.

In tiendas the mean customer purchase in La Paz was about 23¢ and the median purchase was 8¢. The following items are typical of what a customer could purchase with 8¢: 5 pieces of bread, 1 pound of sugar, 1 1/2 eggs, 1 pound of rice, or 1/2 pound of shortening.

One of the characteristics of the small shopkeeper is the highly traditional manner in which he operates. In the 1967 census over half of the tienda retailers reported making no changes whatsoever. Among tienda retailers making some additions to inventory, most commented that changes were made to make their shop appear well-stocked even though they knew that many of the new items had very low turnover rates. Indeed, diaries kept by 979 tienda customers showed that nine items (beer, liquor, cigarettes, soft drinks, bread, sugar, shortening, flour, and canned sardines) accounted for almost two-thirds of the total value of purchases recorded.

Another aspect of retailing practice in the La Paz tiendas was the interaction between retailers and consumers. The researchers found that half of the tienda shoppers spend one minute or less in the retail outlet. Only one conversation in fourteen between the retailer and the customer involved any extended social interaction. The researchers concluded:

> Analysis of the extensive conversations uncovered little indication of bargaining between customer and retailer or that either one was trying to influence the other on some aspect of the purchasing situation. Nor was there any evidence that the outlet was serving any social function, e.g., as a gathering spot for discussion and interaction purposes.[6]

This contrasts with the widespread myth of the less-developed country retail store as a bazaar and community center where animated bargaining and continuous social interaction are the main activities.

[6]Ibid., p. 9.

The nature of channels in markets around the world is highly differentiated. At first glance there is little to explain the nature of this differentiation other than culture and the income level that exists in the market. Upon further study, however, four postulates have been formulated that explain the incidence and rate of innovation in channels at the retail level. These postulates are as follows:

1. Innovation takes place only in the most highly developed systems. Channel agents in less-developed systems in general will adapt developments already tried and tested in more highly developed systems.
2. The ability of a system to successfully adapt innovations is directly related to its level of economic development. Certain minimum levels of economic development are necessary to support anything beyond the most simple retailing methods.
3. When the economic environment is favorable to change, the process of adaptation may be either hindered or helped by local demographic-geographic factors, social mores, government action, and competitive pressures.
4. The process of adaptation can be greatly accelerated by the actions of aggressive individual firms.[7]

Self-service, or the provision for customers to handle and select merchandise themselves in a retail channel without supervision, is a major channel innovation of the twentieth century. It provides an excellent illustration of the propositions outlined above. Self-service was first introduced in the United States. The spread of self-service to other countries supports the hypothesis that the ability of a system to accept innovations is directly related to the level of economic development in the system. Self-service was first introduced internationally into the most highly developed systems. It has spread to the countries at middle and lower stages of development but serves very small segments of the total market in these countries.

Noneconomic factors have been an important force in effecting the diffusion of self-service internationally. The intervention of government and private agencies has limited the diffusion of this innovation. For example, the diffusion of self-service discount retailing has been slowed by the resale price maintenance laws that make it illegal to sell merchandise below prices established by the manufacturer.

Finally, if a marketing system has reached a stage of development that will support a channel innovation, it is clear that the action of aggressive individual firms can contribute considerably to the diffusion of the channel innovation. The integration by Sears of the retailing and manufacturing function in Latin America and Europe by the introduction, against enormous opposition, of self-service food merchandising by the Bigros organization under the leadership of Gottlieve Duttweiler is an excellent example of self-service diffusion.

[7]Adapted from Edward W. Cundiff, "Concepts in Comparative Retailing," *Journal of Marketing,* January 1965, pp. 59–63.

A multinational company expanding across national boundaries often finds itself in the position of entering a new market. A major obstacle to establishing a position in a new market can be obtaining distribution. This obstacle is particularly true in the case of entering a competitive market with established brands and supply relationships. There is little immediate incentive for an independent channel agent to take on a new product when established names are accepted in the market and are satisfying current demands. The international company seeking to enter the market must provide some incentive to channel agents or establish its own direct distribution. Each of these alternatives has its disadvantages. If a company decides to provide special incentives to independent channel agents, these incentives can be extremely expensive. They might involve outright payments for sales performance, either a direct cash bonus or some contest award. Another incentive could be the guarantee of a gross margin in highly priced competitive markets. Both incentive payments and margin guarantees are expensive. The incentive payments are directly expensive; the margin guarantees can be indirectly expensive because they affect the price to the consumer and the price competitiveness of a manufacturer's product.

The alternative of establishing direct distribution in a new market has the disadvantage of being expensive. Salesmen and sales management must be hired and trained. The sales organization will inevitably be a heavy loser in its early stage of operation because in a new market it will not have sufficient volume to cover its overhead costs. Therefore any company contemplating the establishment of a direct sales force, even one assigned to distributors, should be prepared to underwrite losses for this sales force for a reasonable period of time.

The expense of a direct sales force acts as a deterrent to establishing direct distribution in a new market. Nevertheless, it is often the most effective method. Indeed, in many instances the only feasible way that a new company can establish itself in a market is via direct distribution. With a sales force the manufacturer can ensure aggressive sales activity and attention to his products. With sufficient resource commitment in sales activity, backed up by appropriate communications programs including advertising, in time a manufacturer with competitive products and prices can expect to obtain a reasonable share of market. When the market share has been obtained, then the manufacturer is in a position to consider the abandonment of the direct sales force and shift to reliance upon independent intermediaries. This shift becomes a possibility when market share and its corollary, market recognition, makes the manufacturer's brand interesting to independent intermediaries.

The Princess Case Example

The experience of a major U.S. appliance manufacturer in attempts to enter the German market illustrates the formidable obstacle posed by saturated or "full" channels. Princess was a leading manufacturer of small electrical appliances in the United States. The company's sales of $150 million represented nearly 15 percent of the total U.S. market for small appliances. Prior to 1964 the company's European operations had consisted of a small, profitable, and rapidly growing export business. Export sales had increased from only $25,000 in 1960 to $300,000 in 1964. The company modified the product sold through export channels to meet European requirements for electrical voltage and frequency. The distribution arrangements used by Princess for this export marketing were an independent distributor who sold to wholesalers, mail-order houses, and large retailers, who in turn sold to retailers and the public.

When the company decided to enter the German market with direct marketing arrangements, a company study team presented management with two basic alternatives. They were as follows:

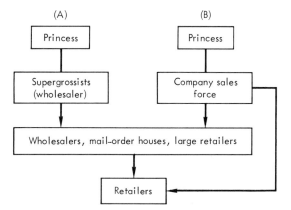

The study team advised management that alternative A, although the least expensive in terms of company cash outlays, would not perform adequately to achieve the company's market share objectives. The problem with supergrossists was that Princess was virtually an unknown brand and these independent intermediaries would "cherry pick" the Princess line by selling only those products that they felt would be an immediate sales success. Cherry-picking supergrossists would not enable Princess to establish itself in the German market. Therefore, the study team recommended that Princess adopt plan B, or the establishment of a company sales force.

The major difficulty with plan B was the problem of recruiting salesmen in Germany. In 1966 Germany was experiencing an extreme shortage of labor, which had pushed up the wages of salesmen and had in general made it difficult to recruit people for selling. Nevertheless, management accepted the recommendation of the study team to establish a company sales force.

The result of this decision was not entirely successful. The sales force was expensive and focused its efforts on the lowest-price, easiest-to-sell company product, which happened to be an electric clock that was sold through specialty clock stores. The product, which had a major price advantage over competing products, sold very well and was profitable, but unfortunately the success of the company's other products was not matched by that of the clocks partly because the sales force did not devote attention to the other products.

One of the reasons the salesmen had difficulty in selling the company's other products was management's decision to use resale price maintenance to maintain retailer gross margins of approximately 25 percent, or roughly 10-15 percent greater margins than retailers were obtaining on comparably branded merchandise. The decision, which was made because management wished to guarantee a wide margin to the retailer in order to obtain initial distribution of its products, resulted in a higher price to the consumer than that which would have prevailed without resale price maintenance.

At the time of the company's effort to break into the German market, a major structural change was taking place. The old system of resale price maintenance in Germany was breaking down, and the overwhelming preference of the German consumer was for obtaining products that were discounted from the recommended selling price. By adopting resale price maintenance as a company policy, Princess went against this trend and against the strong preference of the German consumer for purchasing products such as appliances at a "discount."

Princess's experience illustrates several points. First, the decision to rely on a direct company sales force was taken without consideration of the shortage of salesmen in Germany. Second, the decision to use resale price maintenance as a wedge for obtaining distribution did not adequately consider the impact of the decision on the final selling price of the company's product and on the price sensitivity of the German consumer. Princess traded the advantage of wider margins for the disadvantages of higher final prices to the consumer and the absence of discounts in the trade on Princess products. In retrospect the higher margins were of little value in persuading retailers to adopt the company's products because margins do not guarantee profits. Profits are the result of sales times the margin. Unfortunately, the pricing policy Princess adopted discouraged sales and left the size of the gross margin in percentage terms an academic rather than a real consideration for prospective retailers. The failure to respond to the conditions in the German market was the result of inadequate market study at the outset. Princess looked at Germany through the eyes of U.S. experienced executives.

The initial study needed the insight and judgment of German marketers as well. The only local inputs to the Princess market study were from local advertising agencies who recommended massive advertising!

CASE EXAMPLE: JAPAN

Japan has presented an especially difficult distribution challenge.[8] Distribution in Japan has often been described as complex because of the many fragmented retail outlets and the number of intermediaries needed to service these outlets.

[8] This section is adapted from "Planning for Distribution in Japan," Japan External Trade Organization (JETRO) Marketing Series No. 4, no date.

In the mid-1960s, 88 percent of the retail stores in Japan had four or fewer employees. Since that time, there has been a slight decrease in the ratio, but it is still much higher than in most Western nations.

The categories of wholesalers and retailers in Japan are very finely divided. For example, meat stores in Japan do about 80 percent of their business in meat items. Similar concentrations exist in other speciality stores as well. This kind of concentration is also true at the wholesale level. This very high degree of specialization in Japan is made possible by the clustering of various types of stores at major street intersections or stops along commuter rail lines.

There are, of course, many instances in which overseas firms have entered the Japanese market and have been able to overcome difficulties presented by the distribution system. Unfortunately, problems in coping with and adapting to Japanese distribution have also prevented a number of firms from achieving the success they might have had. Foreign marketers in Japan make two basic mistakes. The first is their attitude that distribution problems can be solved the same way they would be in the West, that is to say, by going as directly as possible to the customer and thus cutting out the middleman. In Japan, because of the very fragmented nature of retailing, it is simply not cost effective to go direct.

The second mistake often made is in treating the Japanese market at arm's length by selling to a trading company which in turn sells to a very limited segment of the market, such as the luxury segment at low volumes. With limited volume, there is usually limited interest on the part of the trading company and the end result is disappointing to everybody involved.

Successful distribution in Japan (and in any other market) requires adaptation to the realities of the marketplace. In the Japanese case this means adaptation to the reality of fragmented distribution. Second, it requires research into the market itself: customer needs, competitive products, and then the development of an overall marketing strategy that positions the product vis-à-vis market segment identified according to need, price, and so forth, and which positions the product against competitors and lays out a marketing plan including a distribution plan for achieving volume and share-of-market objectives.

There are 261 department stores and about 9,000 self-service stores in Japan. Each of these categories handled about 10 percent of Japanese retail sales in 1970. The bulk of retail sales fell into the categories of specialty stores and neighborhood stores. *Specialty stores* are those that handle a single line of goods and base their competitive appeal on offering either more variety than other stores or higher quality than other types of stores. The specialty stores are usually located in urban and suburban shopping centers. *Neighborhood stores* form the bulk of total stores in Japan. They are usually located within ten to fifteen minutes' walking distance of residential areas and are generally grouped together, providing shoppers with a variation on "one-stop shopping." There are about 1.4 million of these neighborhood stores in Japan handling the bulk of national sales and many products.[9]

[9] "Retailing in the Japanese Consumer Market," JETRO Marketing Series No. 5.

SUMMARY

Channel decisions are difficult to manage internationally because of the variety of channel structure from country to country. Nevertheless, certain patterns of change associated with market development offer the international marketer who recognizes this pattern the opportunity to innovate and gain a competitive advantage in the channels.

In retail channels there is a substitution of capital for labor in developed countries in the self-service store, which offers a wide range of articles at relatively low gross margins. Less-developed countries with abundant labor disguise their unemployment in "inefficient" retail and wholesale channels that are suited to the needs of consumers and operate gross margins that are often 50 percent lower than those in more efficient self-service stores in developed countries. An international marketer must be able to tailor his marketing program to these different types of channels and must sense opportunities to draw upon his international experience for ideas on how and when to innovate.

BIBLIOGRAPHY

BOOKS

Bartels, Robert, *Comparative Marketing: Wholesaling in Fifteen Countries.* Homewood, Ill.: Richard D. Irwin, 1963.

Bauer, P. T., *West African Trade.* Cambridge: Cambridge University Press.

Business International, "Developing Distribution in Europe." Geneva: Business International S.A., 1969.

Carson, David, *International Marketing, A Comparative Systems Approach.* New York: John Wiley, 1967.

Deschampsneufs, H., *Marketing Overseas.* London: Pergamon Press, 1967.

Fayerweather, John, *International Marketing* (2nd ed). Englewood Cliffs, N.J.: Prentice-Hall, 1970.

Gunnar, Beeth, *International Management Practice, An Insider's View.* New York: Amacom, 1973.

Hollander, Stanley C., *Multinational Retailing.* East Lansing, Mich.: MSU International Business and Economic Studies, 1970.

Jefferys, James B., and Derek Knee, *Retailing in Europe: Present Structure and Future Trends.* London: Macmillan, 1962.

Moyer, Reed, and Stanley C. Hollander, eds., *Markets and Marketing in Developing Economies.* Homewood, Ill.: Richard D. Irwin, 1968.

Mulvihill, D. F., *Domestic Marketing Systems Abroad—An Annotated Bibliography.* Kent, Ohio: Kent State University Press, 1967.

Riley, Harold, et al., *Food Marketing in the Development of Puerto Rico.* Research Report No. 4, Latin American Studies Center. East Lansing: Michigan State University, 1970.

Ryans, John K., Jr., and James C. Baker, eds., *World Marketing: A Multinational Approach.* New York: John Wiley, 1967.

Stuart, Robert Douglass, *Penetrating the International Market: Effective Overseas Distribution.* New York: American Management Association, 1965.

ARTICLES

Abegglen, James C., and Douglas Norby, "The World's Newest Mass Market," *McKinsey Quarterly,* Winter 1965.

Broehl, Wayne G., "Venture in Venezuela," *MBA,* November 1967.

Cundiff, Edward W., "Concepts in Comparative Retailing," *Journal of Marketing,* January 1965.

David, Michel, "Developments in the Structure of Distribution in France: A Moderate Degree of Concentration," *Journal of Retailing,* Vol. 41, Summer 1965.

"Everything is Mitsui's Business," *Reader's Digest,* October 1966.

Guerin, Joseph R., "Limitations of Supermarkets in Spain," *Journal of Marketing,* October 1964.

Henley, Donald S., and R. Vincent Farace, "Consumer Buying and Communications Patterns in Bolivian Urban Food Retailing: A Preliminary Report." Unpublished paper presented at the American Marketing Association Annual Meeting, Washington, D.C., 1967.

Hollander, Stanley L., "The International Storekeepers," *MSU Business Topics,* Spring 1969.

Hollander, Stanley, ed., *Journal of Retailing,* New York University Institute of Retail Management, Spring 1968.
      S. C. Hollander–"The Internationalization of Retailing: A Forward."
      D. Knee–"European Retail Trade Associations Come of Age."
      C. H. Hochstrasser–"Opportunities and Responsibilities of Retailers around the World."
      Lord Campbell of Esken–"Shopkeeping in Developing Countries."
      A.C.R. Dressmann–"Patterns of Evolution in Retailing."

Lipson, H. A., and D. F. Lamont, "Marketing Policy Decisions Facing International Marketers in the Less-Developed Countries," *Journal of Marketing,* October 1967.

Marino, John A., "Japan's Trading Companies: The Two-Way Bridges of International Trade," *Business Review,* Boston University, Spring 1965.

Sorenson, Ralph Z., II, "U.S. Marketers Can Learn from European Innovators," *Harvard Business Review,* September-October 1972.

RICHARDSON MANUFACTURING COMPANY, INC.

A DOMESTIC COMPANY CONSIDERS INTERNATIONAL MARKETING OPPORTUNITIES

In 1893 Emmit D. Richardson, father of Bob and Ray Richardson, began serving agriculture in Glen Elder, Kansas. In February 1908 he purchased a blacksmith shop in Cawker City, Kansas, a farming community in the North Central part of the state which at that time had a population of 1,064. By 1978 the population of Cawker City had declined to 686, but net sales of the successor to Richardson's original blacksmith shop, the Richardson Manufacturing Company, Inc., were $865,000 and net profit was $79,000. Richardson's 1974–78 profit and loss statement and balance sheet are shown in Exhibits 1 and 2.

The Richardson brothers, both of whom were graduates of Kansas State University, divided between them responsibilities for company operations. Bob, with the title of President, concentrated upon the financial side of the company, and Ray took responsibility for design, engineering, and manufacturing. As sales of the company expanded, the two brothers decided to expand the executive staff of the company by hiring a director of sales. The man selected for this position was George, "Jiggs," Taylor. Before coming to Richardson, Jiggs had been for 15 years the personal pilot to E. C. Riley, Cawker City's most famous entrepreneur whose widespread operations included a 5,000-acre Mexican cotton ranch, apartment buildings and office buildings in widely scattered locations, distributorships for farm implements, domestic and foreign automobiles, cattle feed lots, and, finally, a construction company whose operations consumed the liquid funds of Mr. Riley's operations and forced him into bankruptcy.

PRODUCTS AND U.S. MARKETS

Richardson 1978 sales were accounted for by three principal products:

1. Products 40 and 45, *The Richardson AD-Flex Treader and Mulch Treader*. 45 percent of sales ($407,000). This implement, which had been invented by James Van Sickle, a son-in-law of E. D. Richardson, was priced at $100 per foot at retail, and sold mainly in 11- to 15-foot lengths. It was designed for the ground tillage that follows the initial ground breaking either by the traditional moldboard plow or by one of the more recent approaches to ground breaking, such as the undercutter plow.[1] The treader enabled a farmer to practice what was known as stubble mulch

---

[1] The moldboard plow was a device that cut a furrow into the earth and with a curved board or metal plate turned over the earth from the furrow. The undercutter plow simply cuts under the earth to form a furrow without turning over the earth.

EXHIBIT 1. Profit and Loss Statement

	1974	1975	1976	1977	1978
Sales	601,308.73	613,528.77	733,735.98	848,040.50	910,162.12
Less cash discount given	30,054.88	29,829.60	38,901.82	44,417.43	45,407.80
Net Sales	571,253.85	583,699.17	694,834.16	803,623.07	864,754.36
Beginning inventory	59,597.50	78.160.88	78,381;88	65,631.88	70,138.98
Purchases	283,752.40	276,521.23	296,756.00	339,669.59	311,380.88
Direct mfg labor	59,080.44	56,092.19	69,375.55	78,665.32	81,572.08
Subtotal	402,430.34	410,774.30	444,516.43	483,966.72	463,091.94
Ending inventory	78,160.88	78,384.88	65,631.81	70,138.98	50,369.42
Cost of goods sold	324,269.46	332,389.42	378,884.62	413,827.74	412,722.52
Gross Profit (Loss)					
on Mfg	246,984.39	251,309.75	315,949.54	389,795.33	452,031.84
Indirect mfg exp	62,432.37	61,053.73	81,430.11	93,475.87	102,944.17
Production control exp	2,219.11	1,502.22	3,406.17	2,839.90	3,675.96
Engineering exp	13,600.11	17,398.53	17,238.60	22,647.37	22,018.95
Sales exp	86,016.63	85,228.51	105,226.88	143,836.93	154,232.74
Advertising exp	24,779.01	27,946.61	26,897.99	31,824.46	33,314.75
Admin & off exp	46,760.19	46,781.88	61,873.96	74,766.84	79,658.91
Net Profit (Loss)					
on Mfg	11,176.97	11,398.27	19,875.83	20,403.96	56,186.36
Other Income					
Sales tax collections	374.51	467.66	279.17	317.95	352.06
Parcel post charged tax	11,951.62	13,472.15	16,075.18	15,519.49	16,521.55
Interest income	1,339.86	1,502.68	2,144.44	1,359.87	1,274.14
Rental income	956.00	1,333.42	1,133.00	942.00	912.00
Cash discount on					
purchases	2,055.75	2,359.38	1,676.98	2,711.96	2,925.52
Salvage scrap sales	1,177.76	287.63	758.82	4,500.13	757.04
CO-OP patronage dividend	166.02	175.57	126.20	144.09	143.46
Other Expenses					
Rental expenses	547.90	978.74	923.56	4,533.96	536.18
Net Profit (Loss)					
on Operations	28,650.59	29,958.04	41,146.06	41,365.49	78,535.95

farming, a

system of farming including harvesting, tillage and planting operations which maintains much of the crop residue anchored on the soil surface. The main purpose of this system of farming is to keep enough residue on the surface to protect both the soil and the young crop from damage by water and wind erosion.[2]

2. Product 46, *The Richardson AD-Flex Stubble Mulch Plow.* 40 percent of sales ($364,000). This plow, which was pulled by a tractor, was priced at $100 per foot of length, retail. The average length sold was 15 feet. It was especially designed to prepare a seed in ground that received limited annual rainfall. It was an under-cutter plow which literally cut a straight furrow under the soil instead of turning the soil over as the traditional plow did.

[2] "Use of Stubble Mulch Tillage Tools" by Walter E. Selby, Extension Agricultural Engineer (duplicated) (no date).

EXHIBIT 2. Balance Sheet

	1974	1975	1976	1977	1978
Current assets:					
Cash in register	150.00	150.00	150.00	150.00	150.00
Farmers & Merchants					
State Bank	(18,088.93)	(18,569.52)	(23,128.10)	(24,781.39)	(27,295.83)
Exchange Nat'l Bank	1,000.00	1,159.40	1,306.93	995.89	1,003.29
Accounts receivable	18,635.13	14,299.90	24,486.80	15,511.05	38,858.60
Investments:					
Treasury bills			25,000.00		
Note participation	25,319.25	25,000.00			
Saving & loan	20,971.76	22,267.63	25,970.20	25,636.00	25,100.00
Stamps	61.61	59.43	2.66	2.66	
Inventory	78,160.88	78,384.88	65,631.81	70,138.98	50,369.42
Prepaid insurance:					
Total current assets	126,209.70	122,751.72	119,520.30	87,653.19	88,185.48
Fixed assets:					
Depreciable assets cost					
less accumulated					
depreciation	54,785.70	57,019.66	66,644.48	70,774.82	67,871.04
Investment in Cawker					
City Clinic	80.00				
Deposits	166.91	239.65	365.85	381.10	451.68
Land special assessment					
improvements	7,216.93	7,665.74	9,284.58	9,433.39	9,582.20
Total fixed assets	62,249.54	64,925.05	76,294.91	80,589.31	77,904.92
Total assets	188,459.24	187,676.77	195,815.21	168,242.50	166,090.40
Current liabilities:					
Accounts payable	2,223 32	4,392.05	14,331.73	4,242.50	2,090.40
Accrued property taxes					
Notes payable					
Cash with order	2,486.86	947.30			
Total current liabilities	4,710.18	5,339.35	14,331.73	4,242.50	2,090.40
Net worth:					
Capital	164,000.00	164,000.00	164,000.00	164,000.00	164,000.00
Paid in surplus	1,098.47	1,098.47	1,098.47	1,098.47	
Shareholders undistributed					
taxable income	10,043.50	10,043.50	10,043.50	10,043.50	
Net income (loss) year					
to date	28,650.59	29,958.04			
Net income paid to					
shareholders	20,043.50	29,958.04	41,146.06	58,848.97	78,535.95
Total net worth	183,749.06	182,337.42	181,483.48	164,000.00	164,000.00
Total liabilities &					
net worth	188,459.24	187,676.77	195,815.21	168,242.50	166,090.40

Richardson's principal markets for this plow were wheat farmers in the three-state area of Kansas, Colorado, and Nebraska. The total potential U.S. market for this type of plow was estimated by Bob Richardson to be from $15 to $25 million.

The competition in the undercutter plow market was described by Mr. Taylor as "extreme." There were five major competitors, all of them small specialized manufacturers like Richardson. Deere and Oliver, two full-line implement manufac-

EXHIBIT 3

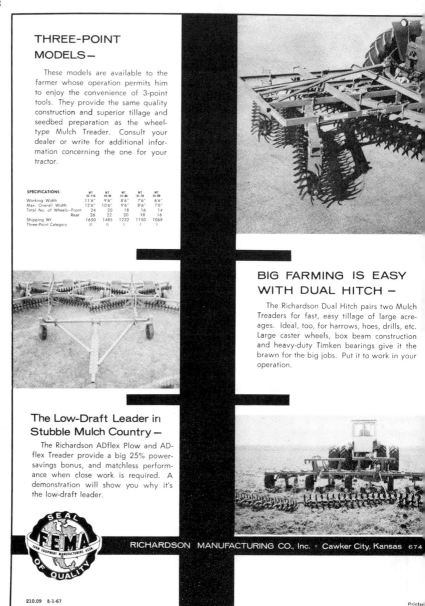

turers, had entered this market and withdrawn according to Mr. Taylor apparently due to production problems and the small size of the market. Richardson's success in this market was attributed by Mr. Taylor to "our dealer organization, service, a good product, and top performance." The main competitive weakness, in Mr. Taylor's view, was the relatively high average price of the Richardson product.

EXHIBIT 3 (cont.)

The Seedbed Comes First...

Give
It
Top
Priority
Treatment
with -

RICHARDSON

Mulch Treader

The AD-Flex Picker Treader and the Mulch Treader were identical in performance and were both tractor-drawn farm implements. The only difference between them was in construction. The AD-Flex Picker Treader was a modular design and was used in tandem with the AD-Flex Stubble mulch plow. The only direct competitor in this product line was by the Williston Co. of Albany, Georgia, who

EXHIBIT 3 (cont.)

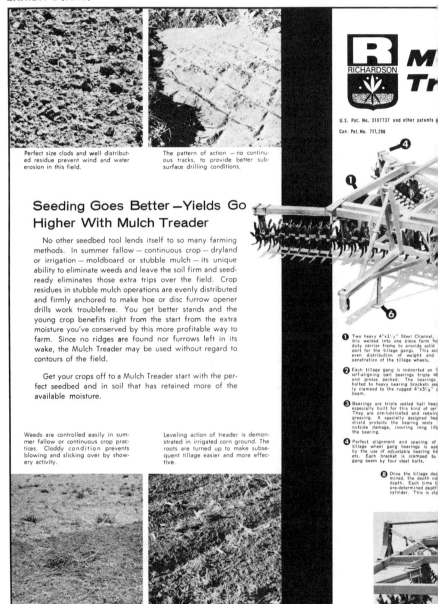

Perfect size clods and well distributed residue prevent wind and water erosion in this field.

The pattern of action — no continuous tracks, to provide better subsurface drilling conditions.

Seeding Goes Better —Yields Go Higher With Mulch Treader

No other seedbed tool lends itself to so many farming methods. In summer fallow — continuous crop — dryland or irrigation — moldboard or stubble mulch — its unique ability to eliminate weeds and leave the soil firm and seedready eliminates those extra trips over the field. Crop residues in stubble mulch operations are evenly distributed and firmly anchored to make hoe or disc furrow opener drills work troublefree. You get better stands and the young crop benefits right from the start from the extra moisture you've conserved by this more profitable way to farm. Since no ridges are found nor furrows left in its wake, the Mulch Treader may be used without regard to contours of the field.

Get your crops off to a Mulch Treader start with the perfect seedbed and in soil that has retained more of the available moisture.

Weeds are controlled easily in summer fallow or continuous crop practices. Cloddy condition prevents blowing and slicking over by showery activity.

Leveling action of treader is demonstrated in irrigated corn ground. The roots are turned up to make subsequent tillage easier and more effective.

RICHARDSON

M
Tr

U.S. Pat. No. 3107737 and other patents

Can. Pat. No. 717,296

❶ Two heavy 4"x1¹⁄₂" Steel Channel, tric welded into one piece form he duty carrier frame to provide solid port for the tillage gangs. This as even distribution of weight and penetration of the tillage wheels.

❷ Each tillage gang is supported on self-aligning ball bearings triple se and grease packed. The bearings bolted to heavy bearing brackets se ly clamped to the rugged 4"x3¹⁄₈" beam.

❸ Bearings are triple sealed ball bea especially built for this kind of ser They are pre-lubricated and require greasing. A specially designed bea shield protects the bearing seals outside damage, insuring long life the bearing.

❹ Perfect alignment and spacing of tillage wheel gang bearings is as by the use of adjustable bearing br ets. Each bracket is clamped to gang beam by four steel bolts.

❽ Once the tillage de mined, the depth co depth. Each time t pre-determined depth cylinder. This is sta

358

EXHIBIT 3 (cont.)

with EXCLUSIVE

Magic Mulch

TOOTH DESIGN

Special high-carbon steel teeth are specially stress relieved to insure long life and ductility. The cross section of the tooth is a half oval. The outer ends are beveled at 45° making a sharp point. Each tooth is curved and twisted. This shape permits easy soil penetration to go in deep and break out a solid clod. At the same time, the side motion of the tooth rips out weeds and leaves them roots-up on the surface.

The wheels are 18 inches in diameter spaced on six-inch centers on the gang bolt. Wheels and teeth are replaceable.

Zero angle adjustment of rear gangs.

Mulch Treader is mounted on four-[in]ch drop center wheels for easier [tr]ansporting from one field to another, [acro]ss hard-surfaced roads, grass water-[way]s and other areas. These wheels are [mou]nted on Timken tapered roller bear-[ings] on a removable stub axle which [faci]litates switching single wheels from [insi]de to outside position, or for easy [addi]tion of duals. See SPECIFICATIONS [for] tread widths obtainable by switching [whe]el positions.

[A p]arking stand is built into the Tread-[er t]o aid in parking and hitching.

[All] models of the Mulch Treader are [equi]pped to use the standard 8-inch [hyd]raulic lift cylinder. The "parallelo-[gra]m" lift mechanism automatically [mai]ntains the level of the Treader in all [posi]tions in or out of the ground. This [ins]ures even penetration of all tillage [whe]els and saves time when changing [the] working depth of the Treader. The [Tre]ader may be raised to clear the [grou]nd 8 inches and lowered to work 8 [inc]hes below the surface.

[Once] operation has been deter-[mined,] set to accommodate this [and] it will return to this [with] a stroke control hydraulic

Built for Your Job and Built to Do It for Years to Come

Heavy-duty construction throughout, and quick, positive adjustments, combine to make the Richardson Mulch Treader a tool that will meet your seedbed preparation requirements for years to come. An almost limitless variety of soil treatment is possible with adjusting depth, angle, and speed of travel. No other tool in a single pass can promise • a soil surface protected from run-off and blowing • the perfect seedbed — firm with fine soil below — clods at top • trouble-free seeding and best possible germination • a more desirable young plant environment.

Specifications

	MTA-83	MTA-93	MTA-103	MTA-113	MTB-123	MTB-133	MTB-143	MTB-153
Working Width	8'3"	9'3"	10'3"	11'3"	12'3"	13'3"	14'3"	15'3"
Number of Tillage Wheels	37	41	45	49	53	57	61	65
Transport Wheels Tread Width (C to C)								
Wheels In	80"	80"	80"	80"	101"	101"	101"	101"
Wheels Out	106"	106"	106"	106"	127"	127"	127"	127"
Weight (Less Tires)	2076	2186	2271	2351	2534	2619	2699	2779

Treader Width	ACRES TREADED PER HOUR AT GIVEN SPEEDS			
	5 mph	6 mph	7 mph	8 mph
8'	4.84	5.81	6.78	7.74
10'	6.05	7.26	8.47	9.68
12'	7.26	8.71	10.16	11.62
14'	8.47	10.16	11.86	13.55

Strippers are available for operating in extremely wet-trashy conditions.

Optional middle buster will work the soil left undisturbed by certain angle settings.

EXHIBIT 3 (cont.)

began production of a product in 1977. The treader was a substitute for the spring tooth harrow, a traditional farm implement with large steel teeth, that was used to break up the soil after plowing.

The advantage of a mulch treader was best realized in geographical areas that were semiarid where the soil was subject to erosion by wind and water. The treader inverted the soil, thus conserving moisture while the spring tooth harrow broke the soil up and exposed moisture in the soil to the air which resulted in evaporation and moisture loss. The retail price of a mulch treader was $100 per foot, and sold mainly in 11- to 15-foot lengths. This was approximately double the retail price of a quality spring tooth harrow. Richardson estimated that the 1978 market for spring tooth harrows was about $20 million.

The Richardson brothers considered the treaders, shown in Exhibit 3, to be

EXHIBIT 4. Product Sales, 1978

Product	Product Description	1978 Jan.-Dec.	1978 Percentage
40	Ad-flex Treader	294,914.06	32.4
41	Dual Hitch	263.48	
42	Flexo Guard	110,179.54	12.1
43	Simflex	2,271.80	.2
44	Sta-Kleen	3,061.48	.3
45	Mulch Treader	112,264.09	12.3
46	Ad-flex Plow	363,555.87	39.9
47	Furrow Opener Wire Winder	17,754.14	2.0
48	Cylinder & Concave Rasp		
49	Miscellaneous	7,507.98	.8

Source: Company records.

the main hope for the company's continued expansion. They held patents on the treaders and were encouraged by their growth in popularity. The treader was first used in 1969 by Kansas wheat farmers and then spread to wheat farmers in Nebraska and Colorado. More recently, its use had spread to corn, soybean, and alfalfa growers in Illinois, Southern Louisiana, Indiana, Utah, California, and to Canada as well.

3. <u>Product 442, *The Richardson Flexo Guard.* 15 percent of sales ($110,000)</u>. The Flexo Guard was an attachment for combines which extended ahead of the cutting sickle to retrieve and deliver grain heads which would otherwise fall back onto the ground. This device was sold at retail for $45 to $50 all over the middle west, in California, and Arizona, and to a limited extent in the East. Richardson faced one competitor in the Flexo Guard market, another small company located in Clay Center, Kansas, a town of 4,613 people only 77 miles east of Cawker City. Richardson, which had manufactured the Flexo Guard for almost 15 years, had a majority of the available market.

The complete 1978 product line and the sales of each product are shown in Exhibit 4.

CUSTOMERS

What kind of farmer bought the Richardson Stubble Mulch Plow and Mulch Treader? According to Mr. Taylor,

> the farmer who buys our product is interested in change as a means of in-increasing his profitability. The man who will switch from the traditional implement to our new design is a farmer who is aggressive, and who understands costs and performance. We can make a strong impression on this kind of farmer. We offer 25 percent less power consumption when our tools are used, and our method leaves the seedbed in much better condition for retaining moisture and therefore in much better condition to produce high crop yields. We're selling lower cost ground preparation, better crop yields, and a soil erosion prevention method of farming.

EXHIBIT 5. Geographical Distribution of Richardson's Sales

	No. of Farms Growing Wheat	Acres of Wheat Harvested 1977	Annual Rainfall	Richardson's 1978 Sales
Kansas	84,171	11,081,000	19–35"	$295,722
North Dakota	n.a.	7,962,000	14–18"	0
Oklahoma	31,200	5,217,000	18–37"	387,797
Montana	15,513	4,734,000	12–18"	0
Texas	29,172	3,326,000	18–33"	48,454
Nebraska	39,712	3,325,000	16–29"	47,948
Colorado	9,600	1,961,000	10–14"	0
Washington	8,755	2,922,000	9–20"	0
Other U.S.A. and Canadian	—	—	—	130,241
Total U.S.A.	366,598	59,004,000		$910,162

Source: Richardson Company records.

U.S. CHANNELS OF DISTRIBUTION

Richardson employed a two phase distribution program. Roughly 75 percent of the company's sales were realized by 88 contract dealers located in the company's three principal territories: Kansas, 38 dealers; Oklahoma and the Texas Panhandle, 32 dealers; and Colorado and Nebraska, 18 dealers. A salesman was assigned to each of these territories, and called upon the dealers in his territory. Each of the contract dealers was located in a geographical trading area, and almost all of the dealers were contract dealers for one of the major implement manufacturers such as John Deere or International Harvester.

The remaining 25 percent of the company's sales were through seven distributors, located in Kansas City, Mo., Dallas and Amarillo, Texas, Evansville, Indiana, Fargo, N.D., Raleigh, N.C., and Stockton, California. The geographical distribution of Richardson sales is shown in Exhibit 5.

The discount schedule was 40 percent off list for distributors, and for dealers, 20 percent + 5 percent 10 days, net 30 days.[3] In addition, dealers could earn up to an additional 7 percent of list through volume discounts which were paid in the form of rebates at the end of the year.

U.S. ADVERTISING AND PROMOTION

Richardson spent $33,314 on advertising in 1978, or roughly 3.75 percent of sales. The entire program was print, and magazines were the principal media, with newspapers and mailed circulars filling out the program. A partial list of the farm trade magazines used was as follows:

Colorado Rancher & Farmer
Dakota Farmer

[3] That is, 25% off list if the bill was paid in 10 days, net amount (20% off list) due in 20 days.

Farmer Stockman (Oklahoma, Kansas, Texas)

Farm Journal (Montana, Wyoming, North and South Dakota and other mid-west states)

High Plain Journal (Colorado, Kansas)

Irrigation Age (Montana, Wyoming, South Dakota, Nebraska, Kansas, Colorado)

Kansas Farmer

Nebraska Farmer

Western Farm Life

Typical advertisements are shown in Exhibit 3. The production and placement of company advertising was handled by the George Eschbaugh Agency in Wilson, Kansas, a town 64 miles south of Cawker City.

In addition to print advertising, Richardson also supported a promotional program at a cost of about $4,000 to $5,000 per year. This program, which was implemented by the three territory managers responsible for direct sales to dealers and for distributors in their areas, consisted mainly of facilitating and arranging demonstrations, and making necessary arrangements to rent space and transport equipment to fairs in the area. Mr. Taylor thought field demonstrations arranged by country agricultural agents were particularly effective because they attracted, as he put it, "people who are really interested, not just the curiosity viewers that you get at the fairs."

EXPORTS

In the late 1960s Richardson had shipped a small order to a company in South America which had seen an advertisement for a Richardson product and placed an order. Since then, Richardson had not made any efforts to achieve foreign sales, and none had materialized. Finally, on June 8, 1977, Richardson received an unsolicited letter from Napier Bros., Limited, an Australian manufacturer and distributor of agricultural implements requesting "your best price C.I.F. Port of Brisbane for the supply of a Mulch Treader equipped with Zero Angle Attachment and 15″ Dual Wheels less tyres and tubes and less hydraulics" (See Exhibit 6). With the press of business Richardson did not get around to answering the letter immediately, and on the first of July, they received a second letter from Napier requesting a reply to the first letter. Meanwhile, Mr. Taylor had requested a freight forwarder in Kansas City to provide him with a quotation on charges for ocean shipment of equipment to Australia. He received a quotation on July 20th and discovered, to his surprise, that an implement that sold for $945.84 in Cawker City would incur shipping and insurance costs of $642.50 just to the port of Brisbane, for a total CIF price of $1,587.34. This did not, of course, include inland transportation in Australia, or the 27 percent F.O.B. *ad valorum* Australian duty on imported implements.[4] He was somewhat taken aback by the cost of shipping abroad,

[4] This duty could be reduced to 7.5 percent if it was shown that no Australian manufacturer was offering for sale a "suitably equivalent good." If neither an Australian nor a U.K. company was supplying the item, the duty could be eliminated.

EXHIBIT 6

NAPIER BROS. LIMITED
(INCORPORATED IN QUEENSLAND)
Manufacturers of Agricultural Implements and General Engineers.
Registered Office: Bunya Street, Dalby, Queensland.

1370/02   5th June, 1977.

Request for Price Quotation

Richardson Manufacturing Co. Inc.,
Cawker City,
KANSAS. . . . . .U.S.A.

Dear Sir,

We refer to correspondence which we had with you some two years ago in regard to the possibility of importation of one of your Mulch Treaders. At that time, we were unable to raise sufficient interest in the machine to warrant its importation but we have now received very definite enquiries and we would appreciate your quoting us your best price C.I.F. Port of Brisbane for the supply of a Mulch Treader equipped with Zero Angle Attachment and 15" Dual Wheels less tyres and tubes and less hydraulics in the following sizes -

10' 3"
12' 3"
14' 3"
15' 3"

With your quotation, which we would appreciate in seven copies for customs purposes, we shall be obliged if you could also forward us twenty copies of your descriptive leaflets.

We would appreciate your forwarding the above information as early as possible and at the same time would you please advise the best delivery available from time of receipt of order.

Yours faithfully,

NAPIER BROS. LIMITED

(N. Coldham-Fussell)

SECRETARY

particularly as he recalled having just made a shipment weighing 3,000 lbs (the same weight as the Australian quotation) to Fresno, California, by truck at a cost of $254.00.

The realization that the Richardson Mulch Treader would cost roughly twice as much in Australia as it did in Kansas dampened considerably Mr. Taylor's hopes that an Australian market for the treader might be opened up. Nevertheless, he forwarded the quotation to Napier Bros. To his surprise, a month later he received an order for the MTBCD-153L (Dual Wheel Unit) Mulch Treader with a CIF Port of Brisbane price of $1,832.55.

By October 5, the Mulch Treader for Napier Bros. was crated and ready to be shipped. Everything seemed to be in order until October 17 when Richardson learned from their forwarding agent in Kansas City that they would be unable to get the Mulch Treader on an ocean vessel until November. As a result, they wrote to Napier Bros. requesting an extension on the letter of credit and also an adjustment on price as the ocean freight turned out to be $30.00 higher than was anticipated. Napier increased and extended their letter of credit as requested, and also expressed concern that the delay in shipment might make it impossible for them to test the Mulch Treader on stubble after the conclusion of the 1977 wheat harvest in mid to late December. When Mr. Taylor learned that the shipment would arrive in Brisbane on the 19th of December, he was hopeful that this would enable Napier to arrange for a test following the December 1977 harvest. If this were not done, the next harvest was a year away, and Richardson would lose an entire year in its effort to penetrate the Australian Market.

In the ensuing months, Taylor heard nothing from Napier. In May 1978, at the suggestion of Ray Richardson, he attended a regional export expansion conference sponsored jointly by Drake University and Iowa export expansion council. Attending the conference reminded Mr. Taylor again of the potential of export markets, and he resolved to follow up the Richardson lead as soon as he returned to Cawker City. The letter he wrote is reproduced below:

May 27, 1978

Napier Brothers Limited
Bunya Street
Dalby,
Queensland, Australia
Attention: N. Coldham-Fussel

Dear Sir:

We thank you for putting one of our Mulch Treaders to work in your country. We have not to date received any word of its success, therefore we are very interested to know many things such as: types of soil the machine was used in, when and where it was used, what crops used on, annual rainfall amounts, whether it satisfied your expectations and any other pertinent information regarding the machine you have available.

Assuming the answers are favorable, can you suggest a preferred way to introduce this tool into general use? Do you distribute your own agricultural implements or work through other distributors? Also do you feel we have a market for our Mulch Treader in your country?

May we hear from you by return airmail.

If we may be of any assistance at any time, please do not hesitate to call on us.

Sincerely yours,

RICHARDSON MANUFACTURING CO., INC.

George A. Taylor
Director of Sales

GAT/mm

Mr. Taylor received an immediate reply from Napier (see Exhibit 7). Six weeks later he received another letter which enclosed the results of a field test of the Richardson treader by an Australian government agricultural extension agent by the name of Tod. The following are excerpts from the agent's report, dated June 6, 1978:

> In general this machine has exceeded our expectations in its ability to handle heavy straw and weeds, and to prepare soil for conventional planting equipment and we are very pleased with its performance.
>
> It would be a tremendous help in saving our soil from erosion, which in this state is a problem of some magnitude. Most of the 5 million acres of cultivated land in this state has a subtropical summer rainfall, most of which falls in high density rainstorms, which, allied with the winter cropping programme, makes it imperative that crop residues be kept standing as long as possible, to help conserve this rain and prevent soil erosion. Most of our machinery is designed for the gentle winter rainfall areas of the southern states, where this type of erosion is not a problem. Therefore it is unsuitable for our conditions.
>
> To sum up, your mulch treader could solve one of our two main problems in the search for suitable stubble mulching machinery, that is, preparing a standing stubble quickly for planting. However, our other pressing need is for a more efficient subsurface tillage implement, with enough tyres to give soil disturbance for weed killing. Neither the present scarifier nor the chisel plough have enough clearance for heavy stubble, and the latter is not an efficient weed killer. We would be interested to hear if your company makes an implement of this type.
>
> We would also be grateful for more information on the adjustment of the treader to get a level surface when using the machine as a cultivator only.
>
> H. H. Tod
Growers Representative
Soil Conservation Committee*

(agricultural extension agent)

Mr. Taylor replied to the two letters and report from Australia. (See page 368.)

EXHIBIT 7

Napier Bros. Limited
Bunya Street
Dalby
Queensland, Australia

31st May, 1978

Richardson Mfg. Co. Inc.
P. O. Box 5
Cawker City
Kansas, 64730, U.S.A.

Attention: Mr. G. A. Taylor, Director of Sales

Dear Sir:

We thank you for your letter of the 27th May, 1978.

In connection with the second paragraph of your letter, I have asked our Design Staff to prepare for you a report to answer the matters which you raised in the second paragraph of your letter. As soon as this is in hand we will forward it to you. We are also endeavoring to obtain a report from the Government Department of Primary Industries who have been particularly interested in this project and we will also forward this to you.

We advise that our Company manufactures and distributes a wide range of agricultural tillage and general purpose equipment. The company has its own subsidiary marketing organisation, i.e., Napier Machinery Sales Pty. Limited which markets through distributors and dealers in the Eastern States of Australia. In addition we manufacture equipment for tractor companies and number amongst our clients, Ford, Fiat, Case, Massey-Ferguson and Chamberlain. In addition we have a substantial export operation working mainly in South America, South-East Asia and East Africa.

As the Mulch Treader only arrived towards the end of the mulching season, it was not possible for a complete testing to be carried out and we had it in mind to wait for the results after this year's harvest in approximately October/December before taking the matter up further with you. If there is sufficient interest in this item we feel that there may be an opportunity to develop substantial business by the following steps:

(a) Initially importing the units,
(b) As volume grows, entering into part manufacture of the implements, and
(c) When volume is sufficient enter into some arrangement to manufacture the units under license.

We would appreciate your thoughts on these types of arrangements and will forward you the reports on the operations of the machine as soon as they come to hand.

Yours faithfully,

NAPIER BROS. LIMITED (N. Coldham-Fussell, Export Manager)

July 22, 1978

Napier Brothers Limited
Bunya Street
Dalby
Queensland, Australia 4405
Attention: Mr. N. Coldham-Fussel

Dear Sir:

We have read with much interest your letter and Mr. Tod's report regarding the use of the Mulch Treader. We are enclosing some literature on our AD-Flex Plow which is a highly successful implement for undercutting stubble and the AD-Flex Picker Treader may be attached for a more effective weed kill.

The undercutting plow is made in five foot sections and may be used by itself leaving the stubble standing or by adding the Picker Treader which somewhat mixes the stubble and mulches the soil, also tearing out the growing vegetation. It would appear to be a highly suitable implement for your stubble mulching program with the Mulch Treader following up to do a more complete job of chopping up the straw and finishing up the seed bed.

We do have a new model plow but the literature and instruction books are not available as yet, although the picker treader is shown mounted on the new model plow.

In Mr. Tod's report, he asked for more information on adjusting the treader so we are enclosing an operators manual which explains adjustments under the heading of OPERATING INSTRUCTIONS.

The middle buster tyne sells for $20.41. This included bracket, bolts and curved shank. A chisel point or small shovel may be attached. We cannot furnish this point.

The steps you outlined in your letter of May 31st certainly look feasible in regards to the distribution of our implements.

I certainly wish it were possible to visit with you personally regarding the operations of the plows and to see the conditions you are confronted with as the farmers in the arid and semi-arid regions of this country have and are adopting these practices and implements. Their farming expenses are being reduced approximately one-third and are conserving more moisture along with eliminating soil erosion by water and wind and many are claiming higher yields per acre over previous practices.

In Mr. Tod's report, he mentions a slasher which we are not sure of. Possibly what we call a stalk cutter or rotary mower. Perhaps you could enlighten us more on this implement.

I presume you will pass along this information to Mr. Tod and if we can be of further assistance, please do not hestitate to let us know.

Twenty sheets of mulch treader literature will be forwarded under separate cover.

Sincerely,

RICHARDSON MANUFACTURING CO., INC.

George A. Taylor
Director of Sales

GAT/mm

Enc: 210.09 81-1-77 Mulch Treader
      210.6 5M/6-1-77 AD-Flex Plow
      410.09 6-10-77 Instruction Booklet

After signing this letter, Mr. Taylor wondered if Richardson was following the right approach to international marketing. One possibility he considered was to sign on with an export merchant. He had recently attended an export expansion conference in Iowa where he had been approached by a Kansas City Export Manager who offered to take on the Richardson line of equipment for export markets if Richardson would give him the distributor discount of 40 percent plus an additional "export bonus" of 15 percent off list. The problem with this offer, according to Mr. Richardson, was that 55 percent off list cut too deeply into Richardson's operating margin. (See Exhibit 8 for company operating ratios.) Also, he wondered how much push an export merchant would give to the Richardson line.

Appendixes A, B, C, D, and E contain data Mr. Taylor kept in a file labeled "International Markets." As he opened this file his thoughts were focused on the question of whether Richardson should take the plunge and go international. It seemed clear that there was a market overseas for Richardson's products, but the

EXHIBIT 8.

True Operating Ratios 1978

	1978
Adjustments necessary to reflect true operating ratios	
(1) Cost of goods sold	412,722.52
Less: Salvage scrap sales	757.04 Cr
Cash discount on purchases	2,925.96 Cr
	409,039.52
(2) 500's engineering expenses	22,018.95
Add: 50% Ray's salary from 602	12,500.00
	34,518.95
(3) 600's sales expenses	154,232.74
Less: 50% Ray's salary to 500's	12,500.00 Cr
Parcel post & freight charged for patronage dividend	16,521.55 Cr
	143.46 Cr
Add: Out freight from 800's (parcel post)	2,670.40
	127,738.13
(4) 800's administrative & office expenses	79,658.91
Less: Out freight to 600's	2,670.40 Cr
Sales tax collections	352.06 Cr
Interest income	1,274.14 Cr
	75,362.31

True Operating Ratios For	*1978*	*1977*
Cash discount/total sales	4.99%	5.23%
Cost of goods sold/total sales	44.95	47.94
Indirect mfg exp & prod control exp/total sales	11.71	11.82
Engineering exp/total sales	3.79	4.14
Selling exp/total sales	14.00	13.64
Advertising exp/total sales	3.66	3.75
Administrative & office exp/total sales	8.28	8.62
Net profit on operations/total sales	8.62	4.86
	100.00%	100.00%

APPENDIX A. Acres of Wheat Harvested in Selected Geographical Areas

Area	Acres Harvested (in Millions)	Yield per Acre (in Bushels)
European Economic Comm.	48.2	33.9
U.S.A.	49.9	26.3
Canada	29.7	27.9
Mexico	1.7	35.0
Argentina	12.9	17.8
India	31.3	12.2
Australia	20.3	23.0

APPENDIX B. Wheat Farm Investments

	U.S.[1]	Australia[2]	Canada[3]	Argentina[4]
# of Farms	366,593	51,000	77,395	
Farm value:				
Land			$20,358–$41,679	
Buildings	$66,397	$76,000–$93,000	$16,774–$26,360	
Livestock			$ 2,799–$ 4,560	
Total:	$66,397	$76,000–$93,000	$39,931–$72,599	
# of Acres/farm	456	1,800	802–1,434	
Value/acres	$122	$42–$52	$50–$51	
# of tractors/farm	2.1	1.62	1.48	.29
Annual rainfall	17–30″	11–20″	20–30″	12–22″

[1] U.S. farm is average one in Kansas in 1964. (*Source:* 1964 U.S. Census of Agriculture.)

[2] Australia farm is a "typical one in Victoria in 1964 (medium and large). The larger acreage is due to the need for grazing area for sheep. (*Source:* Department of Primary Industry, Agriculture Production Branch).

[3] Canadian farm is average of medium and medium-large, in 1958. (*Source:* Handbook of Agriculture Statistics by Canadian Bureau of Statistics.)

[4] In the wheat belt of Argentina, which includes the provinces of Buenos Aires, Cordoba, La Pampa and Santa Fe, there are about 12,500 farms of 400 acres or larger. It is not known how many grow wheat (*Source:* Argentine Commercial Attaché in New York.)

question in Taylor's mind was how to approach these markets. Also, he wondered how much attention and effort he should give to international as opposed to domestic markets.

QUESTIONS

1. Identify the strengths and weaknesses of Richardson in the North American market.
2. Should Richardson go international? Why? Why not?
3. If Richardson decides to go international, what alternative strategies should it consider?
4. Recommend a strategy for Richardson. Identify objectives and develop a marketing, sourcing, staffing, and financial plan for years 1 and 5.

APPENDIX C

File Note—Canada

The climate in the Canadian wheat belt in the province of Saskatchewan is similar to that here in Kansas. All farm implements and equipment manufactured in the United States can be imported into Canada duty free.

File Note—Argentina

The taxes in Argentina are 90 percent *ad valorem* on CIF value, a 5 percent Statistics Tax on CIF value and a charge of 20 Argentine pesos per gross kilo. Also, there is a 10 percent sales tax on retail value in Argentina levied at the time of importation.

File Note—Australia

Australia's wheat belt follows the eastern coast, plus a small section in the west. The particular states and their 1966–67 acreages are listed below:

New South Wales	7,135*	15,300#
Victoria	3,138	6,400
Queensland	1,227	3,400
South Australia	2,960	5,100
Western Australia	6,347	8,100
Total Australia	20,823	31,900
Total U.S.	159,000	145,600

Source: Commonwealth Bureau of Statistics, Canberra.

The wheat belt is typified by a 10–20 inch rainfall, somewhat less than the 17–30 inch annual rainfall in the United States. The Department of the Interior mentioned in their April 1967 publication, "The Northern New South Wales and Queensland wheats rely heavily on the conservation of summer rain moisture in the soil, while spring rains are important for the growth of wheat in Victoria." The bulletin states more explicitly later that rains in all of the regions are very unreliable and the threat of a serious drought is omnipresent. The soil is also less rich than in the United States and Canada, and is particularly deficient in nitrogen and phosphate.

It is difficult to draw conclusions based on the number of farms. In the United States there are 3,400,000 farms, but they differ from the 252,000 Australian farms; many of the Australian farms are devoted to sheep grazing, making the average acres per farm considerably higher than in the United States which considers livestock farms a separate category. Over 51,000 farms grow wheat in Australia, but few grow solely this crop.

The tractor sales in 1964 were a record 25,000 units, whereas the U.S. sales were 143,000 units. Tillage implements sold about 9–11,000 units in Australia, 83,000 units in the United States. Nearly 87 percent of all tractors owned in Australia belong to farmers in the wheat belt states named above.

The farmer has a supported pricing structure for export wheat. The wholesale wheat price in 1966–67 was $1.75 compared to $1.41 in the United States. The government offers the wheat farmer rural credits, preferential interest rates and guarantees to marketing groups for prepayments. Favorable depreciation allowances plus investment credits aid the farmer. Also, farm items which are not available in the country may be imported duty free.

Australia has a climate and soil which are suitable to stubble mulch farming. Both the mulch treader and the AD-Flex Plow could be used to advantage here. It appears from the tractor sales figures that the Australian farmer does tend to be a capital expediture oriented businessman. The figure below substantiates this by demonstrating a consistently high, for the size of the country, tractor sales pattern.

---

* Acres of wheat, in thousands.
\# Acres of total grains, in thousands.
Source: The Australian Financial Review, Nov. 21, 1968.

APPENDIX D. New Tractor (Wheels) Sales in Australia

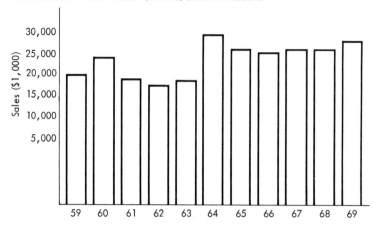

APPENDIX E

NEGOTIATION ASSIGNMENT

Richardson teams: Negotiate an agreement with Napier for penetrating the Australian market with Richardson products.

| *Napier teams:* | Negotiate an agreement with Richardson for penetrating the Australian market. |

Issues (Partial list)

Sourcing—location and responsibility
Marketing—responsibility, plans, budgets
Product adaptation
Pricing
Distribution
Selling, advertising, promotion
Service
Design: Export licensing, joint venture, split ownership
Timing
Plan

Key assumptions

APPENDIX / HOW TO FIND A DISTRIBUTOR

Selling through distributors overseas is an effective method of sales distribution for many companies. An organization of good distributors can be a key to export success. It has been said, "A product line is only as good as its distributors."

A good distributor should have a number of salesmen and several branch offices to cover his territory adequately. He will be familiar with methods of importation, business practices and methods of selling in his territory. The exporter will sell his products to the distributor for resale to customers in the territory. This method will reduce the credit risks that would be involved in selling directly to many customers. A distributor should finance the importation of products, develop sales, maintain a sales and service organization, handle sales promotion, advertising and service as well as maintain the good reputation of the manufacturer.

QUALIFICATIONS

The qualities to look for in a distributor will vary according to the products to be sold and the market area. Special knowledge, skills or facilities may be required.

Here are some basic considerations: Is he honest? Does he operate his company according to good business standards? Is the company financially sound and does it have a record of prompt payment? Does the company have a good reputation in the business community? Is the top management sales-minded, rather than merely order-takers? Does it understand good salesmanship and the need for training a sales organization? Does it maintain a sales organization of adequate size to cover the territory? Does it represent manufacturers

Source: International Trade Forum, Vol IV, No L, August 1968. Reprinted with permission.

of other reputable and well-known products? Is this distributor's organization efficient, hard working, loyal and enthusiastic?

If the answers are yes, appoint him.

Finding Them

There are several sources of names of prospective distributors:

Producers of related types of goods. Check with producers who are exporting products related, but not competitive, to yours, and who use distributors in the markets you wish to enter. These distributors call on customers who may be potential users of your product. In this way it may be possible to locate a network of sales agencies already in operation.

Trade publications. Space advertising in international publications can be helpful in locating names of possible distributors. Editors of publications, as well as advertising agencies, should be able to give you advice and helpful market information. There are directories of publications for every important market. You can find them through local publishers' associations. Several international directories are published. For example, Publishing & Distributing Co., Ltd. (Mitre House, 177 Regent Street, London, W.1) publishes "Overseas Newspapers and Periodicals Guide Book," and supplies a variety of other overseas reference books.

Trade fairs. Specialized fairs in particular draw distributors interested in taking on new lines. Even if you cannot exhibit at important trade fairs, you still can attend them and look for distributors displaying products complementary to your own.

Direct mail. This is a shotgun approach but can be successful in locating a distributor for certain commodities. A simple form letter with sales literature, can be mailed to a list of firms in a certain country or market area. Trade lists are available from chambers of commerce, trade associations, international magazines and a variety of directories. . . .

Trade leads in export publications, such as Commerce Today, published by the U.S. Department of Commerce (Washington, D.C.), and *Moniteur du commerce international,* published by Centre National du Commerce Extérieur (10, Av. d'Iéna, Paris 16e). Many chambers of commerce and trade associations also publish trade leads.

Trade development departments. An increase in trade will result in more business for commercial banks, steamship lines, airlines, port authorities, marine insurance companies, international trade publications and other service organizations. The more progressive of these organizations have active trade development departments.

When asking these agencies for help in locating names of possible distributors, it is important to submit a good business proposal. It should be a clear, concise letter stating the products you wish to sell, what arrangements you desire, whether you will grant exclusive representation and what type of firm is best qualified to transact your business. You may wish to include a report showing the size and financial position of your own company. Be sure to include catalogue pages or sales literature describing your products. Be clear and specific and give only essential information. By making it easy for these agencies to tell your story, you will get better results.

The World-Wide Marketing Service of Pan American World Airways is one such service offered by a commercial enterprise to assist in finding overseas contacts. The first step in using it is to contact the nearest Pan Am office and furnish a business proposal to be sent overseas to the Pan Am representative. A report is furnished you, together with marketing facts and air schedules and rates. Pan Am's "Clipper Cargo Horizons," a publication with world-wide circulation, will give you a free listing of your products. Other publications provide a similar service.

Checking Them Out

The next step is to check on the prospective distributors. You can do this by correspondence or travel. Suppose you have the names of several prospective distributors for Spain. Write a letter to each one asking for information which will help you make a determination (see sample).

On the basis of information received from the overseas firms you can make a careful and complete credit investigation in the following ways:

Commercial banks with International Departments. You can verify information received by writing directly to the bank.

Sample Letter

To Prospective Distributor

Name
Address
Gentlemen :   Re . Representation in Spain

Your name has been suggested as a possible distributor for our line of products described in the enclosed catalogue sheets. We believe that our products have a large potential market in your country and we are anxious to discuss selling arrangements with you.

Please give us the following information on your company and number your replies as follows :

1. A list of the products you now sell.
2. Names and addresses of all the companies you represent.
3. How many salesmen do you have ?
4. How many branch offices ?
5. A list of banking and trade references.
6. The exact territory in which your salesmen make personal calls.
7. Names of the officials of your company.
8. Date your company was started.
9. Can you correspond with us in our language ?
10. Have you had any experience selling products similar to ours ?

Our products are sold outright to the foreign distributor for resale to his customers.

Your letter will have our careful attention and if satisfactory arrangements can be made we will send you our export prices, terms and complete selling information together with our selling arrangement.

Sincerely yours,

Mercantile agency reports supplied by such firms as Dun & Bradstreet, Inc., (466 Lexington Avenue, New York, N.Y. 10017) and the Foreign Credit Interchange Bureau of the National Association of Credit Management (44 East 23rd Street, New York, N.Y. 10010). A nominal fee is charged for these very complete credit reports.

Sample Letter

To Bank

Name
Address
Attention: International Department
        Subject: Name and address of prospective distributor

Gentlemen:
    The subject company has given us your name as a reference. Would you be kind enough to tell us what you know about its reputation, credit rating, and record of payment?
    We understand this information is to be kept confidential and is furnished without any liability on your part.
    Thank you for your cooperation.

                        Sincerely,

Sample Letter

Request for Credit Information

Name
Address
Gentlemen: Re: Name and address of
                    prospective overseas distributor

    The subject firm has given us your name as a reference; it is interested in representing us. Will you please give us the following information, based on your experience with this firm:
Distributor .... Customer ....
Commission representative ....
Sold for ....years Sales territory ....
Highest credit ....
Terms of sales ....
Payment record: Prompt......, 30–90 days slow......, over 90 days......
Do they produce a satisfactory volume of business? ....
Comments ....
....
....
                        Signature

    We understand this information is furnished without any responsibility on your part and assure you it will be held in strict confidence. Please tell us when we can reciprocate. A self-addressed return envelope is enclosed.
    Thank you for your cooperation.

                        Sincerely,

A chamber of commerce or trade association overseas may be able to tell you about the reputation and business standing in the community of the firm you are investigating. Available at consulates.

Request credit and sales information from other suppliers who are selling to the firm you are investigating.

The Agreement

The usual arrangements are for a long term agreement with sales rights for the territory or country, and with a stipulation that the distributor will not handle competitive products. The agreement should set out clearly what your policy is, the sales volume expected, what you will do, and what you expect the distributor to do.

Agreements usually run for one year, after which they can be renewed automatically for additional periods of one year, unless terminated by either party under the cancellation clause. You will need the help of your attorney in writing the agreement with your overseas distributor.

Your relationship with your overseas distributor should be based not only on a written agreement, but on a spirit of mutual confidence, cooperation and friendship aimed at a single purpose—increased sales of your products.

1) $100 × 13 = 1,300

2) 75% × 32% = 24

25% × 40% =

66 × 13 $858.-   474 units in US

407,000

Average Acres K, N, Col 16,367,000

In Australia Queensland   1,227,000   18.%

1,135,000   65 units

3,010,750

communications decisions

> Drawers—Bermudas—and Undies—for woman and little girl.
> Whe shall be most grate ful to send you our samples, that you pay
> on countersign if, you requested them. In this manner, everything
> will be semplified, and we could choose the object of trade without
> difficulty. We hope that we will soon be abble to serve you; so
> your nominative case will be classed among our dear customers.
> Packing is invoiced at cost. Payment is to be made by countersign,
> but we send you a regular confirmation in Italian language with all
> the sale.
>
> *Letter from a manufacturer in*
> *Brenta, Italy*
>
> *"Aw, don't spoil it."*
> *(from* The New Yorker, *May 19, 1975, p. 93)*

INTRODUCTION

Communications is a major decision variable in the marketing mix. As used in this book, *communications* refers to all forms of information transfer and persuasion concerning a product. The principal means of marketing communications are advertising, promotion (point-of-sale displays, skywriting, premium offers, and so on), personal selling, and trademarks. This chapter surveys the major characteristics of the international communications environment and then considers international approaches to this decision variable.

ADVERTISING

Advertising and Stages of Economic Development

Table 14-1 shows advertising as a percentage of GNP and advertising volume per capita for all of the major non-communist countries. The striking fact contained in Table 14-1 is the unmistakable association between advertising volume as a percentage of GNP and the general level or stage of economic development of a country. If correlation were evidence of causation, one could conclude that Morocco, with the lowest advertising expenditures per capita, could increase its per capita national income by increasing its advertising expenditures so that the amounts expended as a percentage of national income would equal those of the United States. Obviously, this would be a naive conclusion based upon the assumption that association implies causation. An equally naive conclusion is that the advertising expenditures of the countries at the top of the list are excessive merely because they are higher than the expenditures of countries with lower levels of GNP per capita. Table 14-1 merely presents the unmistakable association between the proportion of income spent on advertising in a country and the general level of income in that country.

Until recently per capita GNP and advertising as a percentage of GNP were directly correlated, that is, the higher the per capita GNP, the higher the advertising as a percentage of GNP. By the late 1960s this correlation had broken down somewhat. The present data suggest the hypothesis that advertising expenditures as a percentage of GNP increase to a point as an economy industrializes. As a country's income rises, countervailing forces emerge. On one hand, rising incomes create an even larger potential market for goods and services and thus create a greater incentive to engage in advertising. On the other hand, this increasing level of advertising in response to the growing potential and size of the market results in higher intensity of communications messages, which are directed toward customers and reduce the effectiveness of any particular message. Another major factor is the availability of media, television in particular. In many countries, advertising on television is severely restricted or even totally prohibited.

Table 14-2 illustrates the relationship between these variables. The sales/awareness impact of any particular advertising message (A), is a function of the effectiveness of the advertising message and media combination (B), the potential market size (C), and the receptiveness of audiences to additional advertising messages (D). This principle can be written $A = (B)(C)(D)$. As incomes rise, C becomes larger, and D, because of the increasing intensity of advertising in the economy, becomes smaller. Therefore, C and D work in opposite directions as a country moves from lower to higher incomes.

An intriguing question for international marketers that has not yet been empirically studied is the marginal efficiency of advertising expenditures in economics at different stages of economic development. Is a marginal dollar of advertising in Argentina, where the potential market size is smaller than that in the United States but where the receptiveness to additional advertising message is presumably higher than that in the United States, greater than the marginal expenditure of a dollar of advertising in the United States? From the point of view of the international advertising manager attempting to optimize his global expenditure of advertising revenues, this is an important question.

An international company needs to determine the optimum total level of worldwide advertising expenditure as well as the optimum allocation of expenditure among countries. An international company will want to ensure that its country

TABLE 14-1. Advertising Expenditures in Selected Nations, 1974

Country	GNP (Billions U.S. $)	Per Capita GNP (U.S. $)	Advertising Expenditures (Millions U.S. $)	Advertising as a Percent of GNP	Per Capita Advertising Expenditures (U.S. $)
United States	1,294.9	6,108.0	26,780.0	2.07	126.32
Switzerland	50.1	7,707.7	744.2	1.82	114.49
Australia	52.2	3,924.8	864.3	1.66	64.99
Finland	17.1	3,638.3	256.9	1.50	54.66
Canada	118.9	5,308.0	1,703.7	1.43	76.06
South Africa	26.1	1,044.4	356.2	1.37	14.31
Denmark	27.4	5,372.5	355.3	1.30	69.67
Netherlands	59.7	4,389.7	771.8	1.29	56.75
United Kingdom	174.8	3,121.4	2,215.0	1.27	39.55
Spain	60.2	1,710.2	753.1	1.25	21.40
Austria	27.9	3,720.0	342.6	1.23	45.68
Brazil	77.2	734.5	941.9	1.22	8.96
Puerto Rico	6.8	2,266.7	72.3	1.06	24.10
Jamaica	1.7	850.0	17.6	1.04	8.80
Trinidad-Tobago	1.4	1,272.7	14.4	1.03	13.09
New Zealand	11.7	3,900.0	119.4	1.02	39.80
Japan	413.1	3,765.7	4,163.4	1.01	37.95
Sweden	50.1	6,109.8	506.0	1.01	61.71
Singapore	4.3	1,954.5	43.0	1.0	19.55
Taiwan	10.2	641.5	98.5	0.97	6.20
Norway	18.8	4,700.0	178.2	0.95	44.55
Ecuador	2.5	384.6	23.4	0.94	3.60

Lebanon	2.8	1,000.0	26.4	0.94	9.43
Hong Kong	6.0	1,395.3	55.0	0.92	12.79
Argentina	31.4	1,250.0	285.0	0.91	11.36
Turkey	22.0	606.1	186.4	0.85	5.14
Colombia	10.0	416.7	81.7	0.82	3.40
France	255.1	4,859.0	1,981.7	0.78	37.75
Venezuela	16.1	1,387.9	124.3	0.77	10.72
Mexico	48.7	838.2	353.4	0.73	6.08
West Germany	348.2	5,616.1	2,523.1	0.73	40.70
Israel	9.0	2,727.3	65.0	0.72	19.70
South Korea	12.4	370.1	85.9	0.69	2.56
Italy	138.3	2,487.4	942.8	0.68	16.96
Peru	9.1	590.9	59.5	0.65	3.86
Belgium	45.7	4,663.3	276.9	0.61	28.26
Ireland	6.7	2,101.3	7.1	0.60	12.81
Iceland	1.0	5,000.0	5.6	0.56	28.00
Malaysia	6.6	564.1	36.6	0.56	3.13
Luxembourg	1.8	6,000.0	9.3	0.52	31.00
Portugal	11.2	1,287.4	54.7	0.49	6.29
Chile	7.6	730.8	31.2	0.41	3.00
Bolivia	1.0	181.9	3.6	0.36	0.66
Greece	16.3	1,811.1	45.4	0.28	5.04
Morocco	5.0	295.9	7.4	0.15	0.44

Source: World Advertising Expenditures, 1976, Starch Inra Hooper and the International Advertising Association (New York, 1976). Data rearranged by author.

TABLE 14-2. Advertising Payoff: The Major Variables

(A)		(B)	(C)	(D)
Sales/Awareness Impact of Advertising Message	=	Advertising Message/Media Effectiveness	Potential Number of Customers	Receptiveness of Audiences to Additional Advertising

advertising budgets are such that marginal payoff (sales/awareness impact) of its country advertising expenditures are equal. If by shifting expenditure from country O to country P a company finds that its global advertising payoff rises, it has not yet achieved the maximum payoff.

Let A = Advertising sales/awareness effect

Let $E \ldots n$th = Country markets

Let Q = Marginal advertising expenditure

At the Optimum Allocation Point,

$$A = QE = QF \ldots = Qn\text{th}$$

World Advertising Expenditures[1]

Table 14-3 shows the distribution of world advertising expenditures by region. Almost 60 percent of total non-Communist advertising of $49.1 billion in 1974 was spent in the United States and Canada, and 24 percent was spent in

TABLE 14-3. World Advertising Expenditure by Region

Region	Total 1974 Advertising Expenditures (in millions of U.S. $)	Per Capita Expenditures (in reporting countries)	Percent of World's Expenditures Made in Each Region
U.S. and Canada	$28,483.7	$121.51	58%
Europe	12,003.9	35.06	24
Asia	4,765.4	4.18	10
Latin America	2,077.4	7.00	4
Australia and New Zealand	983.7	60.35	2
Middle East and Africa	854.1	2.60	2
Total World*	$49,168.2	$20.86	100%

*Eighty-six countries.

[1] This section is adapted from *World Advertising Expenditures, 1976,* International Advertising Association (New York, 1976).

Europe. Of the remaining 18 percent spent in the rest of the world, almost half was accounted for by Japan.

Distribution of Expenditure by Media

When the distribution of advertising funds among the three major media—print, television, and radio—is examined, it is clear that regional variations exist. These regional differences are not necessarily attributable to preference or choice on the part of advertisers but are influenced materially by media availability; for example, whether TV is available as advertising media.

The proportion of advertising spent on print is relatively low in Latin America and high in the Middle East and Africa area:

Region	Total 1974 Print Expenditures (in millions of U.S. $)	Percent of Region's Total Expenditures in Print	Per Capita Print Expenditures (in U.S. $)
U.S. and Canada	$11,177.5	39%	$47.69
Europe	6,438.7	54	18.84
Asia	1,886.1	40	1.77
Latin America	530.1	28	2.07
Australia and New Zealand	511.2	52	31.36
Middle East and Africa	408.0	50	1.52
Total world*	$20,951.6	43%	$9.58

*Sixty-seven countries.

Television expenditures, as a percentage of all advertising, are notably above average in Asia and are very low in the Middle East and Africa:

Region	Total 1974 Expenditures in TV (in millions of U.S. $)	Percent of Region's Total Expenditures in TV	Per Capita TV Expenditures (in U.S. $)
U.S. and Canada	$5,076.9	18%	$21.66
Europe	1,385.5	12	4.05
Asia	1,517.8	32	1.42
Latin America	559.6	29	2.18
Australia and New Zealand	245.9	7	15.09
Middle East and Africa	59.2	7	0.22
Total world*	$8.844.9	18%	$4.05

*Sixty-seven countries.

Radio receives a higher than average proportion of expenditures in the Middle East and Africa, in Latin America, and in Australia/New Zealand:

Region	Total 1974 Radio Expenditures (in millions of U.S. $)	Percent of Region's Total Expenditures in Radio	Per Capita Radio Expenditures (in U.S. $)
U.S. and Canada	$2,025.7	7%	$8.64
Europe	348.4	3	1.02
Asia	252.6	5	0.24
Latin America	260.1	14	1.01
Australia and New Zealand	97.8	10	6.00
Middle East and Africa	72.2	9	0.27
Total world*	$3,056.8	6%	$1.40

*Sixty-seven countries.

PRINT ADVERTISING

More advertising money was spent in 1974 on print, which includes newspapers and both consumer and trade magazines, than on any other media alternatives. In terms of the absolute amounts spent on print advertising, the leading countries are the United States and Canada, the industrialized nations of Western Europe, Japan, and Australia. The forty countries in which more than $10 million was spent on print advertising are shown in Table 14-4.

A different picture emerges if the use of print media is measured according to the proportion of all advertising dollars expended on it. Where television is unavailable for advertising, available only during limited time periods, or impractical because the proportion of the population having access to sets is low, the percentage of advertising funds devoted to print tends to be very high. In eleven countries, over 75 percent of 1974 advertising expenditures were made in print media:

	Percent of 1974 Advertising Budgets Allocated to Print Media
Denmark	96.0%
Norway	94.4
Sweden	92.6
Israel	84.4
Malaysia	84.3
Netherlands	83.2
Singapore	81.8
Finland	79.6
Egypt	79.3
Switzerland	79.3
West Germany	75.6

The last seven countries listed in this table have commercial television.

As the incidence and popularity of television grows and commercial time becomes increasingly available, it may well be that the importance of television will decline in these countries. In the United Kingdom the use of television depends

TABLE 14-4. 1974 Print Advertising Expenditures in Forty Leading Print-Using Countries

	Reported Advertising Expenditures for All Print Media (in millions of U.S. $)		% Increase	Print as a % of Total 1974 Measured Media Expenditures†	1974 Per Capita Print Expenditures (in U.S. $)
	1972	1974			
United States	$9,288.0	$10,477.0	+13%	59.8‡	$49.42
Japan	1,181.9	1,627.2	+38	50.6‡§	14.83
West Germany	1,533.6	1,565.8	+ 2	75.6	25.26
United Kingdom	1,220.1	1,512.9	+24	71.6	27.02
Canada	495.7	700.5	+41	56.2‡	31.27
France	599.0	698.1	+17	64.4	13.30
Italy	334.4	469.4	+40	61.3	8.44
Netherlands	279.3	462.4	+66	83.2	34.00
Australia	274.2	426.9	+56	49.4	32.10
Spain	237.1	351.8	+48	60.4	9.99
Switzerland	204.5	303.8	+49	79.3	46.74
Sweden	211.0	253.0	+20	92.6	30.85
Brazil	133.5	214.7	+61	38.0	2.04
Denmark	138.0	212.6	+54	96.0	41.69
South Africa	126.3	211.1	+67	74.2	8.48
Belgium	120.0	151.5	+26	74.6	15.46
Norway	107.9	139.1	+29	94.4	34.78
Finland	81.7	136.0	+67	79.6	28.94
Argentina	64.1	124.1	+94	50.7	4.94
Austria	78.3	120.2	+54	61.7	16.03
Mexico	75.5	90.7	+20	26.2	1.56
New Zealand	67.6	84.3	+25	71.4	28.10
India	*	54.0	*	61.8	0.09
Turkey	20.5	51.4	+151	37.1	1.42
Israel	26.7	50.8	+90	84.4	15.39
Venezuela	47.0	48.2	+ 3	38.8	4.16
South Korea	22.4	35.8	+60	44.4	1.07
Singapore	10.6	34.9	+229	81.8	15.86
Taiwan	17.5	33.9	+94	45.5	2.13
Malaysia	17.2	30.8	+79	84.3	2.63
Egypt	25.3	30.3	+20	79.3	0.83
Ireland	18.5	23.6	+28	59.4	7.61
Iran	18.2	20.6	+13	48.5	0.64
Philippines	12.9	19.8	+54	39.3	0.48
Portugal	15.3	19.7	+29	41.1	2.26
Hong Kong	*	19.4	*	38.7	4.51
Indonesia	*	18.5	*	58.7	0.15
Greece	15.4	18.1	+18	39.9	2.01
Colombia	12.7	16.6	+31	25.8	0.69
Nigeria	5.2	11.2	+115	45.3	0.18

*Not available or not dependable.

†Percentages are based upon reported advertising expenditures in print, "outdoor and transportation," cinema, radio and television, where these media are available for advertising.

‡Base for percentage does not include cinema expenditures.

§Base for percentage does not include "outdoor and transportation" expenditures.

upon the relative success of the public noncommercial network (BBC), or upon the private commercial networks. In the major industrial nations, where television coverage is fairly well developed, the proportion of total expenditures allocated to print clusters between 50 and 65 percent—for example: United States, 59.8 percent; Japan, 50.6 percent, Canada, 56.2 percent; France, 64.4 percent.

TELEVISION ADVERTISING

The United States is the world's major user of television advertising by a considerable margin measured either by the total amount spent in the medium or by per capita expenditures. Reports on total expenditures on television during 1974 indicate that spending was above U.S. $100 million in ten countries. Details on the thirty countries reporting more than $10 million in television advertising are given in Table 14-5.

On a per capita basis, advertisers in the United States are clearly the heaviest users of television, with per capita expenditures of $22.88. In Australia, Japan, and Canada spending was also over $10 per capita, and in twelve other countries the levels of television expenditures are over $3 per capita:

	1974 Per Capita Television Expenditures (in U.S. $)
United States	$22.88
Australia	17.35
Japan	12.71
Canada	10.09
United Kingdom	8.66
Austria	6.01
Finland	5.72
Hong Kong	5.09
New Zealand	5.07
Switzerland	4.89
West Germany	4.69
Netherlands	4.24
Spain	3.64
Ireland	3.61
Venezuela	3.55
Mexico	3.09

The television advertising industry has been in a state of flux during the last few years. Generally, expenditures have been increasing, although the rate of increase has varied widely from country to country. Thirteen countries for example, reported that television budgets had risen by more than 50 percent between 1972 and 1974.

In the United States, the United Kingdom, West Germany, and France increases have been less than 20 percent. As television expenditures grow in countries where the medium has only become available for commercial use, changes in the list of "top" television nations in terms of per capita expenditures may occur.

TABLE 14-5. 1974 Television Advertising Expenditures in Thirty Leading Television-Using Countries

	Advertising Expenditures For Television (in millions of U.S. $)		% Increase	Television as a % of Total 1974 Measured Media Expenditurest	1974 Per Capita Television Expenditures (in U.S. $)
	1972	1974	1972-74		
United States	$4,091.0	$4,851.0	+91%	27.7%‡	$22.88
Japan	958.8	1,394.5	+45	43.3‡§	12.71
United Kingdom	431.2	485.2	+13	23.0	8.66
West Germany	248.3	290.6	+17	14.0	4.69
Australia	142.4	230.7	+62	26.7	17.35
Canada	158.1	225.9	+43	18.1‡	10.09
Brazil	128.3	209.1	+63	37.0	1.99
Mexico	96.8	179.4	+85	51.8	3.09
France	128.0	142.1	+11	13.1	2.71
Spain	78.2	128.1	+64	22.0	3.64
Italy	94.6	125.0	+32	16.3	2.25
Netherlands	42.3	57.6	+36	10.3	4.24
Argentina	48.7	56.4	+16	23.1	· 2.25
Austria	29.5	45.1	+53	23.2	6.01
Venezuela	38.7	41.2	+ 6	33.2	3.55
Switzerland	21.3	31.8	+49	8.3	4.89
Turkey	8.0	27.5	+244	19.9	0.76
Peru	21.0	27.3	+30	58.8	1.77
Finland	16.1	26.9	+67	15.7	5.72
South Korea	12.6	25.1	+99	31.1	0.75
Taiwan	14.9	24.9	+67	33.4	1.57
Colombia	14.3	24.4	+71	38.0	1.02
Thailand	16.0	22.0	+38	50.6	0.54
Hong Kong	*	21.9	*	43.7	5.09
Greece	13.9	20.7	+49	45.4	2.30
Portugal	9.8	17.7	+81	36.9	2.03
Philippines	10.5	17.6	+68	35.1	0.42
New Zealand	10.9	15.2	+39	12.9	5.07
Iran	8.4	14.2	+69	33.4	0.44
Ireland	10.0	11.2	+12	28.2	3.61

*Not available or not dependable.

†Percentages are based upon reported advertising expenditures in print, "outdoor and transportation," cinema, radio and television, where these media are available for advertising.

‡Base for percentage does not include cinema expenditures.

§Base for percentage does not include "outdoor and transportation" expenditures.

In considering the proportion of a country's advertising spent in television, it is interesting to note that the 1974 television percentage in countries with a Latin background seems relatively high. In thirteen countries where spending on television is high (over 30 percent) in relation to their total advertising, the percentage is notably higher than in the United States. Of these thirteen countries, seven are Spanish or Portuguese speaking or were once Spanish or Portuguese colonies:

	Percent of 1974 Measured Media Advertising Expenditures Allocated to Television
Peru	58.8%
Mexico	51.8
Thailand	50.6
Greece	45.4
Hong Kong	43.7
Japan	43.3
Colombia	38.0
Brazil	37.0
Portugal	36.9
Philippines	35.1
Iran	33.4
Taiwan	33.4
Venezuela	33.2

RADIO ADVERTISING

Radio advertising expenditures were a relatively modest proportion of most countries' advertising budgets in 1974. Only in the United States (where $1.555 billion was spent) did the funds exceed $600 million. In fact, 1974 radio budgets were above $20 million in only thirteen countries.

	1974 Per Capita Radio Expenditures (in U.S. $)
United States	$8.67
Canada	8.42
Australia	6.29
New Zealand	4.70
Austria	2.40
France	1.87
Venezuela	1.86
Japan	1.80
South Africa	1.55
Argentina	1.47
Italy	1.37
West Germany	1.37

ADVERTISING STRATEGY—FORMULATING OBJECTIVES

A critical and often overlooked aspect of the international advertising decision is the formulation of a strategy and an objective for communications. Too frequently the advertising component of an international marketing plan is assembled without any real analysis of just what communications programs are intended to accomplish and how communications relates to the other basic marketing variables such as product, price, and distribution. For a company entering a market for the first time, an important objective of advertising is the creation of a favorable image for the company, both in the trade and among the public.

A second major objective of advertising is to create awareness and interest and to stimulate an evaluation of the company's products that will lead to their sale. Advertising must communicate appeals that are effective in the target market environment. Because products are frequently at different stages in their life cycle in various international markets, and because of the basic cultural, social, and economic differences that exist in those markets, the most effective appeal for a product may vary from market to market. Therefore it is essential to consider what advertising is intended to accomplish in the particular stage of the marketing plan and in the circumstances of the target market.

For example, the same product may at any point in time be at entirely different stages of the life cycle. In some markets, awareness of the product may be low—advertising should focus on creating awareness and interest in a new product. In other markets, the same product may be mature—advertising should in these markets focus on mature market-selling appeals, such as price. The danger for the international advertiser is that the advertising approach in major markets will be followed or imposed worldwide. This is very often done in a way that ignores the real communications need in target markets that are very different from major markets.

Extend, Adapt, or Invent

Every international advertiser must decide whether or not to extend, adapt, or invent for each national market appeals, illustrations, and copy.[2] The basic differences of economic, social, and cultural dimensions in markets around the world provide the framework for this decision.

The requirements of effective communication and persuasion are fixed and do not vary from country to country. The specific advertising message and media strategy must often be changed from region to region and must frequently be adapted from country to country to correspond with the requirements for effective communication and persuasion in the particular region or country. In international and domestic advertising the advertiser must locate his market segments as precisely as possible and study the backgrounds and motivational influences that operate in the target market before preparing an advertising campaign.

During the 1950s the widespread opinion of advertising professionals was that effective international advertising required delegating the preparation of the campaign to a local agency. In the early 1960s this idea of local delegation was repeatedly challenged, most effectively by Eric Elinder, head of a Swedish advertising agency, who wrote: "Why should three artists in three different countries sit drawing the same electric iron and three copywriters write about what after all is largely the same copy for the same iron?"[3] Elinder argued that consumer differences between countries were diminishing, and that he would more effectively serve a

[2]This section draws heavily upon Gordon E. Miracle, "Management of International Advertising," Michigan International Business Studies Number 5, University of Michigan, 1966.
[3]Eric Elinder, "International Advertisers Must Devise Universal Ads, Dump Separate National Ones, Swedish Ad Man Avers," *Advertising Age,* November 27, 1961, p. 91.

client's interest by putting top specialists to work devising a strong international campaign. The campaign would then be presented with insignificant modifications, which were mainly directed toward translating the advertisement into idiomatic local language.

To the extent that markets are similar, Elinder's point of view has great merit. Within Europe, for example, there is a growing similarity among markets, and the application of his approach is increasingly effective. On the other hand, it is clear that across the world there are still major cultural, social, and economic differences which, for many products, demand more than superficial adaptations to advertising strategy.

The debate between national and multinational advertising is to some extent a straw man—in practice much depends upon the kind of product being sold. Industrial and other capital goods, as well as expensive consumer goods, such as Swiss watches and Scotch whiskey, are well suited to a multinational campaign. The artwork can be identical and the text can be translated with minor adaptations.[4] The reason multinational campaigns work for these products is that buyers' needs are the same regardless of nationality. The same logic applies to services such as banks, airlines, car rental firms, and credit card companies.

While markets are becoming increasingly similar in industrial countries, media situations still vary to a great extent. For example, consider the case of television advertising in Europe: it does not exist in Belgium, Denmark, Sweden, or Norway. The time allowed for advertising each day varies from ten minutes in Holland to more than sixty in Spain, with thirteen, fifteen, twenty, and twenty-seven minutes allowed in France, Switzerland, Germany, and Austria, respectively. Regulations concerning content of commercials vary, and there are waiting periods of up to two years in several countries before an advertiser can obtain broadcast time. Indeed, a media director of a large Paris-based agency recently concluded after surveying the European media situation:

> The media situations differ so much from one country to the next that the same problem may be solved in a different way in each country . . . Continental Europe is comprised of 15 nations whose differences are greater than their similarities.[5]

Three major difficulties can emerge in attempting to communicate internationally:

1. The message may not get through to the intended recipient. This difficulty could be a result of an advertiser's lack of knowledge about media that are appropriate for reaching certain types of audiences. For example, the effectiveness of television as a medium for reaching mass audiences will vary proportionately with the extent to which television viewing occurs within a country.

[4] "Multinational Advertising Takes Off," *Vision,* February 1972, pp. 52–56.
[5] Philippe Chopin, "International Media Planning: The Europe Jigsaw," *International Advertisor,* 13, No. 2, 10–11.

2. The message may reach the target audience but may not be understood or may be misunderstood. This can be the result of an inadequate understanding of the target audience's level of sophistication.

3. The message may reach the target audience and may be understood but still may not induce the recipient to take action desired by the sender. This could result from a lack of cultural knowledge about a target audience.

Appeals

Advertising appeals should be consistent with tastes, wants, and attitudes in a market. The trade literature of marketing is filled with anecdotal conclusions about the basic differences that exist in markets, which make adaptation of appeals necessary. In Belgium, it is said, fashion models would not enhance a product's appeal because they are scarce and their trade is hardly considered honorable. In France the appeal of an effective toothpaste is less cogent than in the United States because Frenchmen are not as inclined as Americans are to be concerned about the number of cavities in their teeth. Nigerian men are openly physique-conscious and products, especially in food and drink areas, can be sold using this approach.

In the face of all these cautionary conclusions, many international marketers are searching for and finding universal appeals for their products. Coca-Cola and Pepsi-Cola have both discovered that slogans have universal appeal.

Perhaps the best-known universal campaign was the Esso "Put a tiger in your tank" campaign, which, after considerable success in the United States, was tested in Europe and Asia. Minor modifications in wording were made in certain countries. For example, in France the word *tank* is *reservoir,* which in the context of the phrase could have been risqué so the word *moteur* was substituted. In Thailand the campaign was modified because the tiger is not a symbol of strength and therefore was misunderstood.

Illustrations and Layouts

Some forms of artwork are universally understood. Revlon, for example, has used a French producer to develop television commercials in English and Spanish for use in international markets. These commercials, which are filmed in Parisian settings, communicate the appeals and advantages of Revlon products in international markets. In France Revlon obtains effective television commercials at a much lower price than it would have to pay for similar-length commercials made in the United States.

Pepsico has used four basic commercials to communicate its theme "Come alive with Pepsi." The basic setting of young people having fun at a party or on a beach has been adapted to reflect the general physical environment and racial characteristics of North America, South America, Europe, Africa and Asia. The music in these commercials has also been adapted to these five regions: rock for North America, bossa nova for Latin America, high life for Africa, and so on.

The international advertiser must make sure that advertisements are not inappropriately extended into markets. An example of such an inappropriate extension would be the advertisement of cheese alongside a foaming glass of beer in France. Such an ad would be perfectly consistent with German eating habits, but in France a more appropriate combination would be cheese and wine.

Copy

Translating copy, or the written text of an advertisement, has been the subject of great debate in advertising circles. There is some agreement that effective translation requires (1) good literary knowledge and command of the technical terminology of both the original and the translated language, (2) a good understanding of technical aspects of the products and any special appeals of the products, and (3) copywriting ability, which can recreate the persuasive tone of the original copy. In effect, there is a need for effective creative translation and not just literary translation. This need is not different from the requirement for literary translation. There is ample evidence that translations can be exceedingly effective when accomplished by a creative individual. For example, some bilingual German-English speakers have concluded that the German translation of Shakespeare is more powerful than the English original. Inept translations can detract from the intended message. There are hundreds of examples of translation bloopers, including the Japanese translation of "As Smooth as a Baby's Bottom" to "As Smooth as a Baby's Ass." One expert on international advertising makes the following suggestion:

> Before deciding whether to prepare new copy for a foreign market, or simply to translate the English copy, an advertiser must consider whether the message as translated can be received and comprehended by the foreign audience to which it is directed. Anyone with a knowledge of foreign languages realizes that it is usually necessary to be able to think in that language in order to communicate accurately. One must understand the connotations of words, phrases, and sentence structures, as well as their translated meaning, in order to be fully aware of whether or not his message will be received and how it will be understood. The same principle applies to advertising—perhaps to an even greater degree. Difficulty of communication in advertising is compounded, because it is essentially one-way communication, with no provision for immediate feedback. The most effective appeals, organization of ideas, and the specific language, especially colloquialisms and idioms, are those developed by a copywriter who thinks in the language and understands the consumer to whom the advertisement is directed. Thinking in a foreign language involves thinking in terms of the foreigner's habits, tastes, abilities, and prejudices: One must assimilate not only words but customs and beliefs.
>
> People the world over have the same needs—such as food, safety, and love. But people differ in the ways in which they satisfy their needs. Just as it is important to provide physical variations in products to meet the varying demands of diverse market segments, it is also important to tailor advertisements to meet the requirements of each market segment. But it is the demands of the market segments which are diverse, not the approach to planning and preparing marketing programs. The principles underlying communication by advertising are the same in all nations. It is only the specific

methods, techniques, and symbols which sometimes must be varied to take account of diverse environmental conditions. Therefore U.S. advertisers may be well advised to export their approach to planning and preparing international advertising; but before making final decisions on copy or media they should be sure to consult personnel who know the foreign market intimately.[6]

INTERNATIONAL ADVERTISING

An advertisement developed specifically for a national market with identifiable national or ethnic models in an obviously national locale may have general success in all countries where that national association provides a positive frame of reference. The same campaign would probably be ineffective if used in a country hostile to the country of origin or in a country so nationalistic that no other country could provide a positive frame of reference.[7]

In a study of international advertising managers in U.S. nondurable goods manufacturing firms, it was found that 90 percent of the responding managers reported that their firms make at least some use of standardized advertising campaigns or individual advertisements. However, only about 17 percent of the respondents estimated that their firms used standardized campaigns of advertisements as much as one-half of the time. Indeed, 75 percent of the firms responding reported that they used common advertising campaigns or advertisements less than one-third of the time.

Most international advertisers believe that their domestic advertising must be adapted to each locale in which it appears. Two-thirds of the responding managers agreed with the statement "Basic human nature is the same everywhere. Therefore, the traditional advertising appeals of economy, comfort, advancement, and social approval are applicable in all markets." The consensus of the managers' poll seems to be that while they recognize basic similarities in the markets, they also believe that their differences were sufficient to require adaptation of at least basic advertising. Thus the universal appeal, such as the "Put a tiger in your tank" slogan, is still distinctly in the minority in terms of the total volume of international advertising.[8]

One study has shown that there is a relationship between managers' views concerning the importance of cultural variables and the approach of their firms to planning and management of international advertising. Respondents in firms having centralized international decision making, and using a U.S.-based agency with international affiliates, agree more frequently than do respondents in companies following a decentralized approach to the management of international advertising with the statement that the only major difference between foreign markets is language and idiom and that an individual approach in each foreign market is unnecessary.

[6]Miracle, "Management of International Advertising," p. 12.

[7]Stephen Schleifer and S. Watson Dunn, "Relative Effectiveness of Advertisements of Foreign and Domestic Origin," *Journal of Marketing Research,* August 1968, pp. 296–99.

[8]John K. Ryans, Jr., and James H. Donnelly, Jr., "Standardized Global Advertising, A Call as Yet Unanswered," *Journal of Marketing,* April 1969, pp. 57ff.

Managers in firms following centralized management of advertising agreed more frequently than those practicing decentralized management with statements about the global applicability of standardized advertising.[9] Thus, basic assumptions about cultural variables are an important influence on advertising practices of international companies.

BIBLIOGRAPHY

BOOKS

American Association of Advertising Agencies, *Advertising Agency Business around the World.* New York, 1964.

Dunn, S. Watson, ed., *International Handbook of Advertising.* New York: McGraw-Hill, 1964.

Miracle, Gordon E., *Management of International Advertising.* Ann Arbor: International Business Studies Number 5, Bureau of Business Research, University of Michigan, 1966.

ARTICLES

Brain, Leroy M., "An Innocent Abroad," *Industrial Marketing,* August 1968, pp. 47–50.

Britt, Steuart Henderson, "Standardizing Advertising for the International Market," *Columbia Journal of World Business,* 9, No. 4 (Winter 1974), 39–45.

Boyd, Harper W., Jr., and Michael L. Ray, "What Big Agency Men in Europe Think of Copy Testing Methods," *Journal of Marketing Research,* 8, No. 2 (May 1971), 219–23.

Cooper, George, "On Your Mark," *Columbia Journal of World Business,* March-April 1970.

"Domesticating Those Intriguing World Markets," *Marketing Communications,* September 1969, pp. 20ff.

Donnelly, James H., "Attitudes toward Culture and Approach to International Advertising," *Journal of Marketing,* July 1970, pp. 60–68.

Dunn, S. Watson, "The Changing Legal Climate for Marketing and Advertising in Europe," *Columbia Journal of World Business,* 9, No. 2 (Summer 1974), 91–98.

—— "Effect of National Identify on Multinational Promotional Strategy in Europe," *Journal of Marketing,* 40, No. 4 (October 1976), 50–57.

Dunn, S. Watson, and David A. Yorke, "European Executives Look at Advertising," *Columbia Journal of World Business,* 9, No. 4 (Winter 1974), 54–60.

Elinder, Erik, "How International Can European Advertising Be?" *Journal of Marketing,* April 1965, pp. 7–11.

Fatt, Arthur C., "The Danger of 'Local' International Advertising," *Journal of Marketing,* January 1967, pp. 60–62.

---

[9]James H. Donnelly, Jr., "Attitudes toward Culture and Approach to International Advertising," *Journal of Marketing,* July 1970.

Josephs, Ray, "A Global Approach to Public Relations," *Columbia Journal of World Business,* 8, No. 3 (Fall 1973), 93–97.

Klippel, R. Eugene, and Robert J. Boewadt, "Attitude Measurement as a Strategy Determinant for Standardization of Multinational Advertising," *Journal of International Business Studies,* Spring 1974, pp. 39–50.

Lambin, Jean-Jacques, "What Is the Real Impact of Advertising?" *Harvard Business Review,* May–June 1975, pp. 139–47.

Liotard-Vogt, Pierre, "Nestle—At Home and Abroad," *Harvard Business Review,* November-December 1976, pp. 80–88.

"Madison Avenue Goes Multinational," *Business Week,* September 12, 1970, pp. 48–58.

Markham, James W., "Is Advertising Important to the Soviet Economy?" *Journal of Marketing,* April 1964, pp. 31–37.

Miracle, Gordon E., "International Advertising: Principles and Strategies," *MSU Business Topics,* Autumn 1968, pp. 29–36.

Nielsen, Richard P., "International Marketing Public Policy: U.S. Penetration of the Canadian Television Program Market," *Columbia Journal of World Business,* 11, No. 1 (Spring 1976), 130–39.

—— "Marketing and Developing in LDC's, *Columbia Journal of World Business,* 9, No. 4 (Winter 1974), 46–49.

Patterson, Jere, "Coordinating International Advertising," *International Advertiser,* December 1967.

Roostal, Filmar, "Standardization of Advertising for Western Europe," *Journal of Marketing,* October 1963, pp. 15–20.

Ryans, John K., "Is It Too Soon to Put a Tiger in Every Tank?" *Columbia Journal of World Business,* March-April 1969, pp. 69–75.

Ryans, John K., Jr., and James H. Donnelly, "Standardized Global Advertising, A Call As Yet Unanswered," *Journal of Marketing,* April 1969, pp. 57–60.

Schleifer, Stephen, and S. Watson Dunn, "Relative Effectiveness of Advertisements of Foreign and Domestic Origin," *Journal of Marketing Research,* August 1968, pp. 296–99.

Sorenson, Ralph Z., and Ulrich E. Weichmann, "How Multinationals View Marketing Standardization," *Harvard Business Review,* May-June 1975, pp. 38–56.

Tsurumi, Yoshi, "East Meets West: China for American Managers," *Columbia Journal of World Business,* 12, No. 1 (Spring 1977), 59–69.

Ward, James J., "How European Firms View Their U.S. Customers," *Columbia Journal of World Business,* 8, No. 2 (Summer 1973), 79–82.

Weichmann, Ulrich E., "Intercultural Communication and the MNC Executive," *Columbia Journal of World Business,* 9, No. 4 (Winter 1974), 23–28.

Weinstein, Arnold K., "Foreign Investments by Service Firms: The Case of the Multinational Advertising Agency," *Journal of International Business Studies,* Spring/Summer 1977, pp. 83–92.

PHILIP MORRIS INTERNATIONAL

INTRODUCTION

In late 1961, executives of Philip Morris International were considering the introduction of a new cigarette brand into the Canadian market through their Canadian
affiliate, Benson and Hedges (Canada) Ltd. Philip Morris had purchased virtually
all of the outstanding common stock of Benson and Hedges (Canada) Ltd. in 1958
and were anxious to increase the business of Benson and Hedges in Canada. The
company was successfully selling Trump cigars, but did not have an effective entry
in Canada's cigarette market. Philip Morris executives were contemplating employing their second most popular U.S. brand, Parliament, using identical blend and
packaging. They reasoned that changes were unnecessary because "awareness"
studies had indicated that Canadians were cognizant of the brand name, Parliament,
through the overlap, through U.S. media, of Parliament advertising into Canada.

THE CANADIAN MARKET

Canada was the second largest country in the world (next to the U.S.S.R.) but was
greatly underpopulated relative to other countries. Population as of June 1960
was 18 million, with approximately 80 percent of this stretched in a thin line
within 100 miles of the Canada-United States border. Officially, the country was
bilingual and bicultural, but most of the French-speaking population was concentrated within the province of Quebec where they constituted about 85 percent of
the province's approximately 5 million persons. Montreal, Canada's largest city, had
a metropolitan area population of just over 2 million and is in Quebec province.
Toronto, the largest city in the province of Ontario, and the second largest in
Canada, had a population of just under 2 million. Other major cities were Van-
couver, on the Pacific coast, at about 0.8 million, and Winnipeg, at 500,000 in the
province of Manitoba. Average per capital GNP in Canada was approximately $U.S.
2,100 as compared with the United States at $3,240.[1]

Canada was usually ranked either second, third, or fourth behind the United
States in terms of income per capita, vying with Sweden and Switzerland.

Canadians were often characterized as a cross between people from the States
and the British, and indeed many institutions, such as government, exhibited
characteristics of both countries. While Canadians displayed many traits similar to
those of U.S. citizens and Britishers, they considered themselves unique, being more
reserved and more conservative than people of the U.S., yet less cautious than the
British and possessing a much more socially mobile society, in the U.S. manner.

[1] Based on 1965 figures compiled by International Bank for Reconstruction and Development,
Washington, D.C.

French-Canadians exhibited many of the characteristics of their European fore-fathers, being more volatile than English-speaking Canadians, yet in many ways quite different from their European counterparts. Both main groups in Canada sought to retain and foster a peculiar identity—the English-speaking against the culturally and economically dominant neighbor to the south; the French against the superior numbers and economic strength of English Canadians within the country.

The cigarette market in Canada exhibited rapid growth after 1920 (see Exhibits 1, 2, 3). Sales of cigarettes increased from about 3 billion in 1920 to over 34 billion in 1960. Consumption per capita rose from 250 cigarettes to just under 2,000 cigarettes over the same period. The most pronounced growth in recent years has been exhibited by the filter and king-size varieties. In the 1957–61 period filter cigarettes share of the total market increased from 29 percent to over 50 percent. After the introduction of king-size cigarettes into Canada in 1957, the market share for this type of cigarette soared from zero to 15 percent by the end of 1960. The rapid acceptance of the filter and king-size cigarettes (see Exhibits 4 and 5) was one

EXHIBIT 1. Tax-Paid Withdrawals of Cigarettes for Consumption in Canada, 1920–1960 (Billions of Cigarettes)

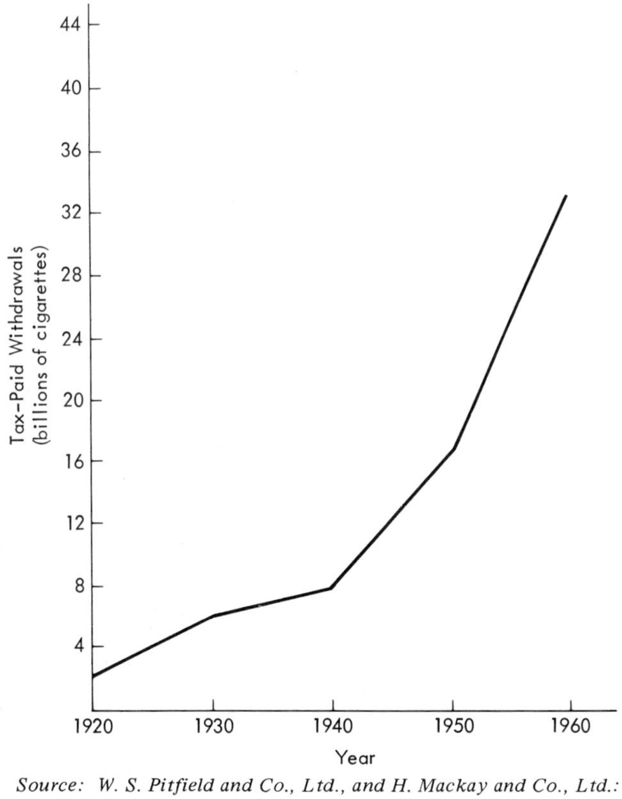

Source: W. S. Pitfield and Co., Ltd., and H. Mackay and Co., Ltd.:
The Canadian Cigarette Industry—Annual Review 1965, p. 16.

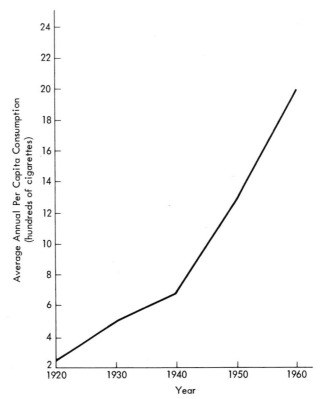

EXHIBIT 2. Average Annual Per Capita Canadian Consumption of Cigarettes, 1920–1960 (Hundreds of Cigarettes)

Source: W. S. Pitfield and Co., Ltd., and H. Mackay and Co., Ltd.: The Canadian Cigarette Industry –Annual Review 1965, p. 16.

of the most significant developments to occur in the Canadian cigarette market in this period.

Distribution of cigarettes in Canada followed much the same pattern as in the U.S. The importance of the chain store in the distribution process was not as great as in the U.S., but outlets of this type already accounted for a substantial proportion of the 16.8 percent figure for combination stores. (See Exhibit 6.) Tobacco stores were still very important, accounting for 14.2 percent of total sales. Distribution followed a sequence virtually identical to that in the U.S. Cigarettes were sold through wholesalers and jobbers to independent retailers and chains as well as directly through larger retailers. It was estimated that tobacco products could be purchased in over 100,000 retail outlets in Canada. Cigarettes were shipped by the case from manufacturing facilities in Ontario and Quebec to manufacturer-owned warehouses throughout Canada, and from there they were shipped as ordered. In general, retailers bought their products from the jobber or whole-

EXHIBIT 3. Average Annual Canadian Per Capita Usage of Cigarettes, 1924–1960

Year	Per Capita Usage of Cigarettes	Year	Per Capita Usage of Cigarettes
1924	275	1944	1036
1925	304	1945	1255
1926	341	1946	1209
1927	392	1947	1207
1928	451	1948	1236
1929	507	1949	1252
1930	493	1950	1252
1931	437	1951	1118
1932	353	1952	1234
1933	404	1953	1415
1934	446	1954	1447
1935	485	1955	1565
1936	508	1956	1679
1937	602	1957	1817
1938	613	1958	1901
1939	630	1959	1939
1940	663	1960	1925
1941	746	1961	2012
1942	879	1962	2083
1943	953	1963	2110

Source: W. S. Pitfield and Co., Ltd., and H. Mackay and Co., Ltd.: The Canadian Cigarette Industry—Annual Review 1965, p. 16.

saler, but some retailers (the foremost of which were the chains such as United Cigar Stores, Ltd.) were able to purchase direct from the manufacturer.

All advertising and sales promotion was provided by the manufacturers themselves. Advertising campaigns were implemented via national advertising media (of which there was a full range of print newspapers, and for segmented markets magazines, many of which were American); and electronic (radio, television, via two national networks) media and various specialized media such as billboards were also available. In addition, the manufacturers' selling organizations promoted distribution by systematically visiting wholesalers and retailers, and encouraged sales by point of sale displays.

THE COMPETITION

The cigarette industry in Canada was a classic case of an oligopoly market. As of 1960, there were only five major firms in the marketplace, with two of them holding a combined 80 percent share. These two firms, Imperial Tobacco Company of Canada, Limited, and MacDonald Tobacco Company, never held less than 70 percent of the market since Imperial was incorporated in 1912. In 1960, Imperial held a 54 percent share and was the acknowledged market leader. MacDonald, with a 27 percent share, seemed to be content with a defensive strategy and spent relatively little on advertising and promotion. (MacDonald's was established in 1857.)

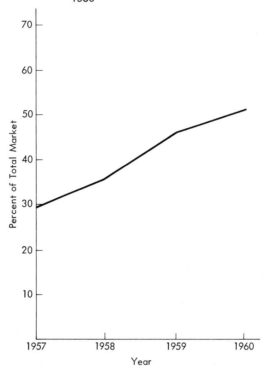

EXHIBIT 4. Filter Cigarettes as a Percentage of the Total Canadian Cigarette Market, 1957–1960

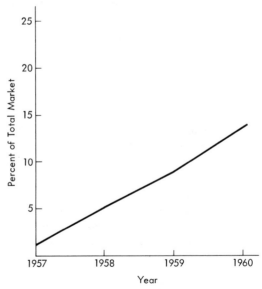

EXHIBIT 5. King Size Cigarettes as a Percentage of the Total Canadian Cigarette Market, 1957–1960

Source: Rothmans of Pall Mall Canada Ltd.: "Annual Report—1961."

EXHIBIT 6. Cigarettes, Cigar, and Tobacco Sales by Type and Number of Outlets, 1960

Type of Outlet	No. in Canada	Sales	Percent
Confectionary stores	—	na	na
Fruit & vegetable stores	—	na	na
Grocery stores (no fresh meat)	21,683	$ 25.4	3.8%
Grocery stores (fresh meat), beer	—	na	na
Variety stores	1,081	18.6	2.8%
Combination stores (groc. & meat)	9,340	109.1	16.8%
Combination stores (with beer)	—	na	na
Eating places	—	na	na
Eating places (with alcoholic beverages)	—	na	na
Eating places (other merchandise)	—	na	na
Department stores	74	21.7	3.4%
General stores	7,739	23.0	3.5%
General merchandise stores	702	25.6	3.9%
Drug stores (no soda fountain)	4,630	44.6	6.8%
Drug stores (soda fountain)	154	2.5	0.4%
Tobacco stores & stands	2,702	92.0	14.2%
New dealers	—	na	na
	44,175	$654.71	100%

Source: Census of Canada, *1961, Volume 6, Retail Trade, Part 6–7.*

The other three companies were Rock City Tobacco Company Ltd., Rothmans of Canada Ltd., and Canadian Tabacofina Company Ltd., with 7.5 percent, 5.5 percent, and 4.5 percent market shares, respectively. The Philip Morris affiliated company, Benson and Hedges (Canada) Ltd., had a negligible market share. Both Canadian Tabacofina and Rock City were considered to be somewhat the weak sisters of the industry with Rock City losing shares since 1956 and Canadian Tabacofina just holding its own since entering the market in 1957. Rothmans was considered the up-and-comer. Since entering the market in 1957, the firm quickly got the reputation as a company in a hurry. Rothmans engaged in marketing practices, according to some observers of the Canadian industry, that the old time companies considered quite rough, tough, and even nasty. They were spending heavily on advertising and promotion and had introduced the first king-size cigarette, Rothmans' King Size, to the Canadian market— it was doing extremely well.

Imperial Tobacco was recognized as being the price leader much as R. J. Reynolds was in the United States. Competition, as in the U.S. market, was not waged on price grounds, but was instead concentrated on advertising, promotion, and packaging. Interestingly, however, it was generally agreed that as late as 1957 the Canadian cigarette market was very badly "underadvertised" by U.S. standards. Canadian manufacturers were spending between 7¢ and 15¢ per 1,000 cigarettes in 1956 while by 1959, this level had jumped to 25¢ to 45¢ per 1,000 cigarettes.[2]

[2] According to *Advertising Age,* Sept. 16, 1968, Philip Morris spent 70¢ per thousand on Parliament advertising in 1959. In 1959 most U.S. brands were between the Canadian figure of 15¢ per thousand and Parliament's high figure of 70¢ per thousand.

Much of this spending change was due to the entry of Rothmans into the market. The new entrant had managed to usurp some of Imperial's leadership functions.

Although the rapid growth of filter and king-size cigarettes underlined the dynamic nature of the Canadian cigarette market, executives within the Canadian cigarette industry could also point to the high brand loyalty displayed by Canadian smokers as evidence of the stability of the market. Of 29 new brands introduced from 1957–1960, only four survived. For example, in spite of the relatively low advertising and promotion budgets employed by the MacDonald Tobacco Company, its two "Export" brands maintained a sustained combined 23–28 percent market share.

Mr. George Weissman, President of Philip Morris International, and the President of Benson and Hedges (Canada) reflected as they considered the Canadian market that it was typical of markets around the world in that it exhibited in some areas rapid change and, in other areas, considerable stability. How would Canadian smokers react to the Parliament cigarettes? Clearly, it was different than the standard Canadian cigarette. Canadian cigarette tobacco was a straight Virginia-type flue-cured Burley tobacco without added flavorings to affect taste. The standard Canadian cigarette package was a slide-and-shell box. This package, which was popular in Canada, was a cardboard box shell which contained a sliding box that packed two rows of ten cigarettes one on top of the other with a foil paper between the two ten-cigarette layers. Parliament was an American-type cigarette with a recessed filter made from Virginia-type tobacco blended with darker colored Burley tobacco and packaged in a soft package or flip-top box. The distinguishing characteristic of the tobacco in the American-type cigarette, including Parliament, were the sugars, humectants (moistening agents), and flavorings (licorice, sugars, and alcohol) which were added to the tobacco, giving the cigarette a characteristic flavor and taste. Another distinguishing characteristic of Parliament and other American cigarettes was that they were less tightly packed than Canadian cigarettes. The American soft package was crushable, and the flip-top box a cardboard container with a top that flipped open exposing twenty cigarettes packed in two rows of seven and one row of six cigarettes.

On the other hand, Parliament was Philip Morris's number two brand in the United States and was doing quite well in the extremely competitive U.S. market (see Exhibit 7). Awareness studies had shown that Canadians were cognizant of the brand name, Parliament, as a result of the overlap of U.S. media into Canada. *Advertising Age* estimated that in 1960 Philip Morris was spending almost $40 million per annum on advertising, and it was estimated by one Philip Morris International executive that perhaps 5 percent of this expenditure was exposed to Canadians, not to mention any exposure resulting from Canadian travel in the U.S.

It was felt that the great similarities between the American and Canadian people in terms of culture, language, personality, etc., would assure acceptance of a brand which was a major factor in the United States if it were made available to Canadians. Moreover, U.S. brands had been introduced in Australia and had done very well, and it was felt by Philip Morris executives that there was considerable comparability between Australia and Canada.

EXHIBIT 7. Philip Morris U.S. Sales by Brand (billions of cigarettes)

		1961 est.	1960	1959	1958
Marlboro	(filter)	24.10	22.0	20.40	20.70
Parliament	(filter)	9.40	8.90	9.00	6.50
Alpine	(filter)	2.50	2.60	1.00	—
Philip Morris	(king)	3.80	3.80	3.80	4.40
″ ″	(regular)	4.60	5.50	6.60	7.80

Source: John C. Maxwell, Jr., undated mimeo, Montgomery, Scott Company, N.Y.C.

There was some reason for caution, however. A "Copy Claim Study" in Canada (see Exhibit 8) raised some questions about the appeal of U.S.-type cigarettes in Canada. In addition, similar research showed a preference for a hard, slide-and-shell package rather than the American soft cup variety. Further, it was known by Philip Morris executives that Canadians often exhibited a strong sense of nationalism in their consumer goods buying regardless of the product. Yet, as the President of Philip Morris International, Mr. Weissman, stated: "I can't believe that Parliament will sell well right up to the border and not within Canada. I've travelled in Canada since I was a boy, and those people are just like us."

EXHIBIT 8. Philip Morris International
Final Report—Canadian Copy Claim Report

A test of two copy claims was devised for Philip Morris International. The procedure was to have each smoker "test" a cigarette from a plain white package, and to react to the cigarette with various attitudinal words or phrases. Three groups of 800 people each were used in these tests. The first group, which we call the control or base group, smoked unmarked Parliament cigarettes from completely blank white packages and expressed their attitudes toward the cigarette. The second group smoked identical unmarked cigarettes from packages which had the phrase "American Type Cigarettes" printed on the package while the third group smoked cigarettes from packages labelled "Cigarettes Blended with the Darker Colored Burley Tobacco for Better Filter Smoking and Lower Tar Delivery." The phrases were written in English on one side of the package and in Canadian French on the other side.

RESULTS

1. The claim "Cigarettes blended with the darker colored burley tobacco for better filter smoking and lower tar delivery" was an *ineffective* claim.
2. The cultural difference between French and English speaking Canadians seems more significant than difference in sex, age, income, or type of cigarette usually smoked.

DISCUSSION

The purpose of these tests was to determine what change would occur in smokers' attitudes toward cigarettes which were designated as "American Type Cigarettes" as opposed to "Cigarettes blended with the darker colored burley for better filter smoking and lower tar delivery." After smoking one cigarette the people were asked to select one word or another from each pair of words to describe their attitude toward the cigarette. For example, "mild" or "strong," "cool" or "hot."

EXHIBIT 8. (Cont.)

Since one group of people smoked unmarked cigarettes in a blank package, we have a base point against which we can measure any increments or decrements of the number of people associating a particular attitude with cigarettes smoked from the "test" packages which bore the claims. We then concern ourselves with responses to the test cigarettes which received either a statistically significant higher or lower percentage of responses than were given to the blank package or control cigarettes. In other words, when an association is classified as significant, it means that in 95 out of 100 repetitions of the study the results would not be reversed.

While there were 14 such associations made toward each cigarette, the strongest pair of attitudes on the list is for a person to say "For me" as opposed to "Not for me." The following table shows two things. First, the French speaking people were not more favorably disposed toward the cigarettes used than were the English speaking smokers when there was no claim attached to the cigarettes. Second, the claim "American type cigarettes" significantly reduced the "For me" responses among the English speaking people and significantly increased the number of responses of "For me" among the French speaking sample. The "blended-burley-low tar" claim failed to increase the associations with "For me" among either the French or the English sample.

Percent Responding with "For Me"
As Opposed to "Not for Me"

Language Spoken	Blank	American Type Cigarettes	Cigarettes Blended with the Darker Colored Burley Tobacco
English	46	38	49
French	57	66	55

No other breakdown of the sample, such as men vs. women, young vs. old, etc., showed significant differences on the "For me" item.

A second method of looking at the association data is to analyze the total number of favorable associations as opposed to the total number of unfavorable associations expressed as a percentage. In other words, if every smoker selected each favorable association from each of the 14 pairs, we would have 100 percent favorable associations. In a sense, the total favorable percentage is a rough average of the percentage of people associating any one favorable word with the cigarette.

The following table shows that the overall reaction to the American type cigarette claim was more favorable among the French-Canadians than among the English speaking people and that the claim was also more effective than the "blended-burley-low tar" claim.

Percent of Total Favorable Responses

Language Spoken	Blank	American Type Cigarettes	Cigarettes Blended with the Darker Colored Burley Tobacco
English	67	63	69
French	64	76	68

We could caution the reader that the individual items taken singularly can often be misleading since there is a tendency for consumers to generalize their liking for a product over a series of items. As we have already stated, we feel that the critical item is whether people say "For me" or "Not for me" about the cigarette. Thus, the French-Canadians liked the "American type cigarettes" and attributed significantly higher associations on rich tobacco flavor, good, slow burning, effective filtration and non irritation, high quality tobacco, well made and desirable.

The "blended-burley-low tar" claim was ineffective among the French-Canadians.

EXHIBIT 8. (Cont.)

There were increases in associations with high quality tobacco, effective filtration and slow burning, but the taste and flavor connotations were not increased. One other item which did show a significant increase over the blank package cigarettes was costly as opposed to cheap.

In summary then, to the French speaking people the "American type cigarettes" had flavor, filtration and quality without being costly. The "blended-burley-low tar" cigarettes had filtration, quality and expense but lacked an increase in flavor associations.

To the English-speaking smokers, the "American type cigarettes" were associated with significant decreases in associations with clean, desirable and "For me". It appears that the English-speaking Canadians rejected the "American type cigarettes" purely on an emotional basis.

While the English sample rejected an "American type cigarette" even though it was given most of the same qualities as was the blank package, the "blended—burley—low tar" cigarettes were given some increases in qualities but no increase in preference over the blank pack cigarettes. Associations with good flavor, high quality tobacco, slow burning, desirable and well made were all increased for the "blended-burley-low tar" cigarettes; but even with these quality increases, the copy claim failed to draw an increase in the critical "For me" association.

To summarize the results of the English-speaking Canadian sample, they appear to have simply rejected the idea of an "American type cigarette," and although the "blended-burley-low tar" cigarettes showed increased associations in taste, quality and desirability, the concept was not sufficiently enticing to have an increase in acceptance of the cigarette.

Research Department
October 6, 1960

Source: Philip Morris Company Records.

QUESTIONS

1. What is the significance of the findings of the "Copy Claim" test results reported in Exhibit 8?
2. Should Philip Morris International introduce Parliament to the Canadian market? Why? Why not?
3. Recommend a marketing strategy for Canada for Philip Morris International.

APPENDIX / MARSTELLER INTERNATIONAL

In the latter part of 1961, Harold Burson, President of Marsteller International (MINT) recapped in a speech the economic and business considerations that were important to his agency's going abroad.

AMERICAN-STYLE ADVERTISING

How many times have we been told "that probably is a good ad in the United States but it certainly would never work in my country"? Here's what a recent issue of "Grey Matter," the perceptive publication of Grey Advertising, Inc., said on the subject:

The "you can'ts" and "you mustn'ts" tend to drown out the voices counseling courage and daring and point to the challenges of opportunity. The inclinations to look for the endemic differences in foreign countries have been stronger than the impulses to seek the universal characteristics of people. Far too many potentially powerful universal appeals have been needlessly discarded in favor of advertising approaches keyed narrowly to the assumed mores and attitudes of each individual country.

The article went on to admit that Pontiac's "wide track" campaign would have little appeal in countries where most roads are already too narrow for autos. And certainly no one would advocate advertising the warmth features of a garment in the tropics just because the campaign was successful back home. But for the products that would appear to have marketability in overseas countries, the evidence is mounting in the direction that good advertising, properly directed, is effective on a universal basis.

For Example: Travel almost anywhere in Europe and you'll never get away from that Esso tiger. I recall driving to Scarsdale with one of our European associates and pointing out the billboards which had just started admonishing motorists to "put a tiger in your tank." He told me flatly that advertising would never work in his country because the people are too literal in their thinking.

But someone at Esso must have thought differently, because tigers are now finding havens in European tanks and Esso sales have gone up as a result. In most cases the translation is literal, but it has been interesting to note that in some countries you'll have to look in the motor to find the tiger—not the tank.

Recently, the head of Norman Craig & Kummel spoke to this point. Here's what he said about several products that are well known to all of you.

In the case of Maidenform, "Dream" advertisements have been running in every corner of the globe for 15 years with absolutely no change, except translation. And yet, when we began this, you never heard such a barrage of protests. People said that nothing like that could possibly be run—certainly not in Spain, certainly not in Switzerland, certainly not in the Netherlands. "We don't show people like that," and "they don't understand dreams," and "Freud is unknown here," and you wouldn't believe what else we were told.

Similarly, in the case of Hertz, this methodology worked extremely well. Hertz, with its far-flung system, operates in over 70 countries. With the complications of the car rental business, with each country in a different "state of maturity," Hertz found the basic application of a common marketing methodology an enormous help in quickly and efficiently plotting its strategy for each country—looking forward to the day when the man flying into the driver's seat could be a worldwide symbol.

Still another case: for a long while, it was believed that tea drinking was so ingrained in Japanese life that it would be fruitless to advertise coffee. If all coffee manufacturers had believed this, they would have passed up what promises to be one of the vast untapped markets remaining in the world today. Advertisers have seized on the convenience of instant coffee and Japanese beverage consumption habits have changed to the point that coffee houses in Japan are now considered more "in" than tea houses.

INDUSTRIAL ADVERTISING OVERSEAS

What about the industrial field? The evidence is mounting in this area also, but, unfortunately, at a slower rate. Readership studies by McGraw-Hill in this area indicate that those ads which score high in the United States also score high when translated and published overseas. Our own inquiry analysis seems to indicate comparable results: that is, a good inquiry-producing ad in one country will produce well in other countries if the status of the market is comparable. As in the United States, businessmen and professional people are generally eager for information. When ads contain information of value, they are read—the world over.

The key to universality, in my opinion, is a knowledge of the market-place. This is equally true in the United States. A centrifuge manufacturer may be persuaded to advertise contamination-free features in food and pharmaceutical publications yet he would find another feature to advertise in synthetic fiber publications because the need for high purity is not nearly so critical. Transposed overseas, the lift truck manufacturer would very likely advertise labor-saving features in Germany or France where labor is both scarce and expensive, but he likely would find a different sales argument in Spain where labor is plentiful and cheap.

Nature of Overseas Markets

If there are similarities in domestic and overseas advertising—and there are—what are some of the differences?

But before treating differences, I think my remarks would be in better context if I took a few minutes to talk about the nature of overseas markets. One of the most important lessons we have learned from our experience abroad is that "there really is no such thing as international markets", consequently, there really is no such thing as international advertising.

Effective advertising involves a process of reaching a specific national market. There are no buyers who profess international citizenship; none save those under United Nations Trusteeship who live on international territory.

Customers live in nations that have fairly specific boundaries—even customers in those nations that have joined together in the European and other common markets. These countries all have their own distribution channels; many use different languages; almost all have different currencies, with differing credit arrangements.

When we speak of the international market, we actually are speaking of a collection of individual national markets, some more important than others. The more highly developed industrial markets—which usually are those of greatest importance to the typical American manufacturer operating overseas—have their own communications media on which people in the market place lay varying degrees of reliance.

The job of the international advertiser and his agency is to evaluate, market-by-market, country-by-country, where and to whom he wants his sales message disseminated. The result is a collection of countries and a collection of communications programs that can be lumped into the general category of international advertising.

So—all overseas marketing advertising and promotion must be treated country-by-country, market-by-market, product-by-product. This produces a tremendous administrative burden and a highly fractioned advertising budget.

CASE HISTORY OF AN AD

Let me illustrate by tracing for you the history of a single ad produced by our Geneva office. This is an actual case history involving a client in the plastics industry. The product—an industrial product—is marketed in England, France, Belgium, Holland, Germany, Italy, and Spain. Seven countries, seven languages (because in Belgium, in addition to French, we have to print in Flemish).

The first determination was where to run the ad. There is no Standard Rate & Data book for the world or even Europe. There are individual directories for the countries I've mentioned, but anyone who has used them will tell you the information on business and technical publications leaves much unanswered (like sometimes omitting the name of the top book in a given field). Eventually, however, 15 different publications were recommended for this particular ad.

Among media data obtained were page sizes of each publication and other mechanical specifications such as halftone screen. Page sizes among the 15 publications ranged from a page slightly smaller than *Reader's Digest* to something a little larger than *Life* or *Look*.

Our art and production staffs decided the ad should be prepared in three different sizes. Because of the great disparity in page size, it meant two different layouts and one modification.

Copy has to be written. We usually write in English—because most of the account executives in our overseas offices are Americans and because most of our clients—at least the men who approve the copy—are American or are U.S.-oriented.

Next we have to translate the ad into the six other languages. But we consider English—the form in which the text will run in the U.K.—as a separate language, too, so that makes seven.

And sometimes there is an intermediate step. If we are adapting text that has already been created for domestic use, we have to translate it *out* of "American" before we can translate it *into* another language. For example, we have to eliminate American idioms, convert abstractions into specifics, and make sure we are being very precise in what we intend to say.

Now we are ready to order the translations.

Learning About Translations

I wish I could report that we know the secret of getting good translations—good translations in any language, on any subject.

We don't—but I'm certain that no one else is further along this road than we are.

There are some things we've learned about translations. A translation can be technically correct and still not be an acceptable translation. As a literal word-for-word translation it might stand up in a classroom, but it wouldn't go as an ad because it would be considered childish or even absurd by the people to whom it is addressed. They would recognize it for what it was: a translation of something originally intended for somebody else.

Translation is a technical skill—an ability to convert words from one language to another. Translation does not imply any degree of literary skill—in other words, just because a man is an accurate translator, that's no assurance that he's also a good writer. Therefore we feel it's important to give the translated copy to a writer in the language of the translation and have him come up with the final polished text.

This is time consuming. It is costly—at least twice the cost of a straight translation in the conventional manner. But it's the only way we know to provide the literary standard that's often desired.

Duplication of Activity

Now what does this mean to the advertising agency? Since the ad was in seven languages, there were, in effect, seven different ads. Type had to be set in seven languages, and because translations were coming in at different times, we had to enter seven different type orders. Instead of a single set of engravings—we had to order engravings on seven separate occasions for the same ad.

This piecemeal activity produces, as you might expect, a torrent of paperwork. Instead of one engraving invoice, you're more likely to end up with seven; instead of one type bill, seven; instead of one charge from the art department, at least seven—and so on down the line. When you get bills from publishers, they are in as many languages as ads and they ask for payment in as many currencies.

I go into this detail because a lot of what I have been talking about is not visible to the client or to the publisher. They end up with one check, in the case of the publisher, or one consolidated bill, in the case of the advertiser.

When we start an ad in the United States we prepare a job folder. That folder follows the job throughout its course. Every charge against the job goes into the folder as it is received from the vendor or the publisher.

At the end of the job, there may be ten or so separate invoices that have to be verified, reconciled, tabulated and finally billed to the client. All of these charges are, of course, expressed in dollars. And one thing about most American vendors: they send bills fast.

The overseas story is a little different. Not ten or fifteen separate charges, but closer to a hundred. Seven currencies were involved, to be paid in local currencies, to be billed to our clients in dollars. And, most troublesome of all, a large number of bills were several months late in arriving. Two months after the job was finished, it was still not possible to submit a final bill and close out the job.

This would appear to be a complex way of doing business—and it is. But for those who do it day-after-day, it becomes a way of life—although none of my associates overseas has ever described the process as "a routine procedure."

TOTAL COMMUNICATIONS OVERSEAS

As a final word, I'd like to comment on the nature of the overseas advertising program—particularly as it applies to the industrial company.

You must realize that many U.S. industrial companies operating overseas are not big enough to have full-time advertising departments or even a manager.

Therefore, an agency such as our operating overseas reports to a sales manager or even a general manager; and both not only have a multitude of other duties, but are traveling so much of the time it is seldom we can get to see them.

The work we do is not advertising as we know it in the United States. Most often, it covers the broad spectrum of communications—ranging all the way from letterheads and calling cards to setting up sales meetings.

This, I believe, is good—and even, in some respects, in advance of the way we and other agencies work in the United States. The communications job is viewed in its totality. It is not segmented or compartmentalized. Therefore, there is greater opportunity to effect true coordination among advertising, sales promotion, publicity, sales training.

Typically, the primary requirement of a U.S. company in its early overseas stages is literature—basic technical and sales product information literature like spec sheets and catalogs. It is not untypical for the first year's promotion budget to be devoted almost entirely to printing literature in the languages of the market place. This is not an inexpensive project, when properly done—and frequently there is little remaining money for other promotional activities.

After literature requirements have been met, one begins to think of space advertising, publicity, trade shows—and, of course, sales aids and sales meetings. The pattern is seldom the same for two companies. One must ascertain the degree of development of each individual company and formulate a program to meet specific requirements. Such a program must relate to the marketing plan. And this is sometimes a good trick because companies operating overseas are even less likely than domestic companies to have written marketing plans.

I hope my remarks will not have the effect on the one hand of making you think overseas advertising is easy because of the similarities to advertising domestically. Or on the other hand, I hope the effect will not be to discourage you completely because of the complexities. The real truth is somewhere between—particularly for those who involve themselves deeply.

exporting
and
importing

No nation was ever ruined by trade.

Benjamin Franklin, 1706-90
(Thoughts on Commercial Subjects)

INTRODUCTION

Exporting supplies a customer in one country with products manufactured in another country. Until the post-World War II era, it was the major form of international market involvement. The changes that have swept the field of international marketing have affected this ancient multinational marketing activity. Today it is important to distinguish between *export selling* and *export marketing.* Export selling involves the sale of goods manufactured in one country to customers in other countries. The focus of export selling is on the product that is considered fixed and simply taken from the country's domestic product line and offered to customers in foreign markets. Typically, export selling involves independent distribution channels in the market country that are not managed by the manufacturer's marketing organization.

Export marketing, which is distinct from export selling, involves a shift in emphasis from the product to the customer. In export marketing no element of the marketing program, product, price, communications, or distribution is assumed. Each of these elements is revised on the basis of data obtained from the target market. The distinction between export marketing and export selling is determined by the degree of direct management involvement and control of the marketing program in the market countries rather than by the location of manufacturing facilities for the product.

The location of production facilities in an international company should be a function of factor costs, transportation charges, and tariff and duty charges that determine the costs of goods in a market. These production location considerations are substantially independent of the marketing decisions on a product's design and characteristics, its price, the channels employed, and the communications programs employed.

Between 1969 and 1976 world exports increased from \$246.4 billion to over \$906.5 billion, an annual compound growth for the period in excess of 20 percent. (See Table 15-1.) This increase was more than double the rate of growth of GNP throughout the world during this period. Exports now account for 15 percent of global GNP. The unmistakable fact is that exporting is becoming increasingly important in the world economy as national economies become more involved in supplying and servicing markets located outside their national boundaries. Virtually every large corporation, in particular every corporation referred to as multinational because of the scope and extent of its international involvement, is an active exporter. One percent of U.S. companies, the big multinationals, account for 85 percent of all U.S. exports.[1] The involvement of smaller U.S. enterprises in export activities is much less pronounced. Eugene Lang, president of Resources and Facilities Corporation of New York City, has estimated that there are 250,000 U.S. manufacturers in the small-business category that are not exporting and have no export objectives or programs for developing overseas markets. For many of these firms, exporting is a major untapped market opportunity. For the U.S. government or any other government concerned with its balance of payments, the export potential of uninvolved firms could be a major factor contributing to the elimination of a balance-of-payments deficit.

Thus *export marketing* refers to the integrated marketing of goods and services that are produced in a foreign country. Export marketing requires: an understanding of the global market environment and the application of all the skills of marketing; the use of marketing research and the identification of market potential; the product design decision, pricing decisions, distribution and channel decisions, and advertising and promotion decisions. It also requires organization, planning, and control. Each of these major topics is dealt with in a specialized chapter in this book. The purpose of this chapter is to focus specifically on some unique problems and aspects of export marketing.

NATIONAL POLICIES TOWARD EXPORTS

National policies toward exports could be summarized by a single term: schizophrenic. The nation-states of the world have for centuries combined two opposing policy attitudes toward the movement of goods across national boundaries. Nations take steps to encourage exports by outright subsidy and by indirect measures, such as tax rebates, and extensive government support programs in the area of promotion and producer education. The flow of goods in the other direction, imports, is generally restricted by national policy. Measures such as tariffs, import control, and a host of nontariff barriers are employed by nation-states to limit the inward flow of goods. Thus the international situation is a combination of measures de-

---

[1] "The Reluctant Exporter," *Business Week,* April 10, 1978, p. 56.

TABLE 15-1. World Trade: Value of Exports (In Billions of U.S. Dollars)

	1969	1970	1971	1972	1973	1974	1975	1976
World Total	246.4	283.5	317.0	376.1	523.7	772.0	795.8	906.5
Industrial Countries	179.7	208.1	233.3	276.3	376.5	503.6	537.3	597.5
Other Europe	10.0	11.8	13.2	16.5	22.8	30.3	32.0	36.5
Australia, S. Africa, New Zealand	8.8	9.3	10.0	12.5	18.3	22.2	23.1	26.5
Oil Exporting Countries	14.6	17.3	21.9	24.5	38.7	117.8	109.5	133.1
Other Less Developed Areas	33.3	37.1	38.6	46.3	67.4	98.1	94.0	115.5
Other Western Hemisphere	11.8	13.4	13.4	15.7	22.5	34.5	32.9	38.4
Other Middle East	2.4	2.5	2.7	3.3	4.4	7.5	7.2	7.9
Other Asia	12.4	13.9	15.5	19.1	29.3	40.2	39.3	52.6
Other Africa	6.7	7.3	6.9	8.2	11.2	15.9	14.5	16.3

Source: International Monetary Fund, *International Financial Statistics,* 1978, p. 45.

signed to encourage exports and restrict imports. The combination of policy measures is offsetting to some extent.

GOVERNMENT PROGRAMS SUPPORTING EXPORTS

There are three major governmental activities designed to support export activities of national firms. Tax incentives treat earnings from export activities preferentially either by applying a lower rate to earnings from these activities or by providing for a refund of taxes already paid where income is associated with exporting. Outright subsidies are used to reward export performance. And the third support area is governmental assistance to exporters, particularly in providing information concerning the location of markets and credit risks, and in promotion, including assistance in the establishment of trade fairs and other exhibits designed to promote sales to foreign customers.

The tax benefits of export-conscious governments include varying degrees of tax exemption or tax deferral on export income, accelerated depreciation of export-related assets, and generous tax treatment of overseas market development activities. Naturally, in many cases the actual treatment of export-related income is even more favorable than tax statutes would imply. Japanese and European trading nations have been particularly generous in providing these kinds of special aids to exporting companies.

The decision by the U.S. Congress in 1971 to help U.S. exporters through the creation of DISC (Domestic International Sales Corporation) is illustrative of the support arrangements offered by national governments. The DISC was created in response to similar government support, particularly in Europe and Japan. A DISC is entitled to defer federal income taxes on 50 percent of its export income as long as deferred income is in the corporation's export business, in export-related assets, or invested in Export-Import Bank paper. Within certain limits the profits of a DISC are taxable only at the time they are distributed to its stockholders.[2] In effect, DISC earnings are labeled as foreign source income and are not fully taxed until repatriated. The argument supporting DISC is that it provides a partially compensating offset to the tax advantages foreign exporters have in the value-added tax system. In brief, countries with a value-added tax system rely on this in lieu of a corporate income tax as a major source of revenue. Since the value-added tax is collected or added at the time of sale, foreign exporters do not pay the tax on sales to the United States. U.S. exporters, however, when selling to a value-added tax country, have the VAT tax added to their products. This in effect places U.S. exporters at a disadvantage because they are also taxed under the U.S. corporate income tax system. In effect, U.S. manufacturers selling to a VAT country pay a double tax. Foreign manufacturers selling to the United States receive tax relief.

By 1978, over ten thousand DISCs had been created. They sheltered $11

[2]U.S. Department of Commerce, "Obtain a Tax Deferral through a Domestic International Sales Corporation DISC," March 1977.

billion in profits. Although DISCs have been attacked by tax reformers, they appear to have a legitimate place in an imperfect world. Assuming that DISC tax preferences are divided between greater profits for manufacturers and lower prices for foreign customers, it can be argued that this is an unwarranted reallocation of wealth, and from a narrow national point of view particularly unwarranted to the extent that it is partially reallocated to foreign sources, the harsh reality of international competiton and the need to maintain equilibrium in the balance of payments forces nations to adopt DISC-type measures. A clearly preferable situation would be one in which tax systems around the world were harmonized, no special incentives were provided for export activities, and no barriers were raised to the international movement of goods.

GOVERNMENT EXPORT EXPANSION PROGRAMS—THE U.S. EXAMPLE

The United States is a classic example of a country with an export expansion problem. American businessmen lack export consciousness. Less than 10 percent of the approximately 350,000 U.S. manufacturers export at all, and most of these export only marginally. Major competing nations export up to 20 percent of their total production, whereas the United States exports only 4 percent. These percentages reflect the fact that the United States is a massive continental market accounting for one-quarter of global national income. The American businessman's foreign counterpart in the typical industrialized country abroad has exhausted his home market long before his U.S. counterpart. As a result, when the foreign company is forced by the smaller size of his home market to search internationally for expansion opportunities, his U.S. counterpart is still profitably expanding within the U.S. market. It is simply not true that all U.S. companies that are not exporting are missing an opportunity. Many of these companies are in fact devoting their efforts to the most profitable and feasible potential market for them—the U.S. market.

Nevertheless, the enormous size of the U.S. market has created a relative insularity and lack of export awareness that is increasingly a problem both from a private and from a public policy perspective. For companies, the export myopia creates dangerous competitive threats by giving up market position and volume to manufacturers in other parts of the world, who inevitably will decide to enter and compete in the U.S. market. From a public policy perspective, weak export performance creates balance-of-payments and currency pressures that are politically undesirable. The root cause of the poor U.S. export performance is a lack of will or determination to export. The Department of Commerce has estimated that there are twenty thousand U.S. companies who could successfully sell in foreign markets but are not doing so. The resulting asymmetry between the United States and the rest of the world is typified by the U.S. auto industry, which designs U.S.-manufactured cars for the U.S. market and exports almost none of its U.S. production. In contrast, Japanese and European auto companies sell over 2 million cars a year in the United States, roughly 20 percent of the total market.

Most of the international marketing information provided by the U.S. government is designed to expand U.S. exports. These sources are outlined in detail in Appendix I. The following list briefly describes those information services specifically tailored to assist U.S. exporters or prospective exporters.

Foreign Market Reports are prepared by U.S. foreign service officers and include information on commodities, industries, and economic conditions, as well as in-depth foreign market surveys. Automatic distribution of the reports by Standard Industrial Classification number or by country is available. There is a monthly index to the reports and surveys.

World Traders Data Report Service provides a detailed profile on individual foreign firms, including financial references, firm size, background, sales area, officers, reputation, and trading connections.

Foreign Traders Index is a computerized file on more than 150,000 foreign importing organizations in 135 countries.

Export Mailing List Service offers information in a print-out format or as address labels on lists of foreign organizations. These may be selected in one or more countries or geographical areas, or by product or product groups handled by those organizations.

Data Tape Service provides magnetic tape or direct input to the user's own computer, covering information on all firms in selected countries listed in the *Foreign Traders Index.*

Trade List Service is designed to help U.S. firms obtain names and addresses of foreign distributors, agents, purchasers, and other firms in the same product field. This service is indexed and is also offered as a subscription service.

Agent Distributor Service is a personalized service conducted by U.S. commercial officers overseas to provide firms with up to six foreign firms that have expressed an interest in a specific U.S. proposal. There is a small charge for the search, which usually takes a month or two.

Trade Opportunities Program provides current sales leads overseas through a computerized mail service, the TOP. Matching of U.S. and foreign firms is done by computer at a basic subscription cost.

Business Counseling Services range from information about setting up DISCs to lists of the latest trade fairs, U.S. trade missions, and how to obtain business facilities on a trip abroad. In addition, appointments may be scheduled with other government experts in specific areas of interest. This service may be obtained at the Department of Commerce in Washington or through any of the District Offices of the Commerce Department. For a complete list of these offices, see Appendix I.

Government Regulations of Exports—The U.S. Case

The U.S. government controls the exportation of U.S. goods to all countries except Canada. Control and licensing, which are exercised by the Department of Commerce, with few exceptions are based on the commodity to be exported and the country of destination. Two types of licenses are issued: general and validated. A *general license* is a privilege permitting exportation within limits without requiring that an application be filed or that a license document be issued. A *validated license,* a document authorizing exportation within the specific limitations it sets forth, is issued only upon formal application. Most goods can move from the United States to a free-world country under a general license. A validated license is required when shipments involve certain strategic goods regardless of destination and when shipping most goods to Soviet Bloc countries in Eastern Europe. Details of U.S. export control regulations can be obtained from the U.S. Department of Commerce.

TERMS OF ACCESS

The phrase *terms of access* refers to all the conditions that apply to the importation of goods manufactured in a foreign country. The major instruments covered by this phrase include import duties, import restrictions or quotas, foreign exchange regulations, and preference arrangements.

Tariff Systems

Tariff systems provide either a single rate of duty for each item applicable to all countries, or two or more rates, applicable to different countries or groups of countries. Tariffs are usually grouped into two classifications.

SINGLE-COLUMN TARIFF

The single-column tariff is the simplest type of tariff and consists of a schedule of duties in which the rate applies to imports from all countries on the same basis.

TWO-COLUMN TARIFF

Under the two-column tariff, the initial single column of duties is supplemented by a second column of "conventional" duties, which shows reduced rates agreed through tariff negotiations with other countries. The conventional rates, for example those agreed upon by "convention," are supplied to all countries enjoying MFN (most favored nation) treatment within the framework of GATT (General Agreement on Tariffs and Trade). Under GATT, nations agree to apply their most favorable tariff or lowest tariff rate to all nations who are signators to GATT, with some substantial exceptions.

Preferential Tariff

A preferential tariff is a reduced tariff rate applied to imports from certain countries. GATT prohibits the use of preferential tariffs with the major exceptions of historical preference schemes, such as· the British Commonwealth preferences and similar arrangements that existed before the GATT convention; preference schemes that are part of a formal economic integration treaty, such as free-trade areas or common markets; and the granting of preferential access to industrial country markets to companies based in less-developed countries.

Types of Duties

Customs duties are of two different types. They are calculated either as a specific amount per unit or specific duty, or as a percentage of the value of the goods or ad valorem, or as a combination of both of these methods.

Ad valorem duties. This duty is expressed as a percentage of the value of goods. The definition of *customs value* varies from country to country. Therefore an exporter is well advised to secure information about the valuation practices applied to his product in the country of destination. A uniform basis for the valuation of goods for customs purposes was elaborated by the Customs Cooperation Council in Brussels and was adopted in 1953. In countries adhering to the Brussels convention on customs valuation, the customs value is landed CIF cost at the port of entry. This cost should reflect the arm's-length price of the goods at the time the duty becomes payable. Major trading nations that are not members of the Brussels convention on customs valuation are the United States and Canda, which use FOB cost as the basis of valuation, and Japan, which uses CIF value.

Specific duties. These duties are expressed as a specific amount of currency per unit of weight, volume, length, or number of other units of measurement; for example, fifty U.S. cents per pound, one dollar per pair, twenty-five cents per square yard. Specific duties are usually expressed in the currency of the importing country, but there are exceptions, particularly in countries that have experienced sustained inflation. In the Chilean tariff, rates are given in gold pesos and, therefore, must be multiplied by an established conversion factor to obtain the corresponding amount of escudos.

Alternative duties. In this case both *ad valorem* and *specific* duties are set out in the custom tariff for a given product. Normally, the applicable rate is the one that yields the higher amount of duty, although there are cases where the lower is specified.

Compound or mixed duties. These duties provide for *specific* plus *ad valorem* rates to be levied on the same articles.

Antidumping duties. The term *dumping* refers to the sale of a product at a price lower than that normally charged in a domestic market or country of origin. To offset the impact of dumping, most countries have introduced legislation providing for the imposition of antidumping duties if injury is caused to domestic producers. Such duties take the form of special additional import charges designed to cover the difference between the export price and the "normal" price, which usually refers to the price paid by consumers in the exporting countries. Antidumping duties are almost invariably applied to articles that are produced in the importing country.

Other Import Charges

Variable import levies. Several countries, including Sweden and the European economic community, apply a system of variable import levies to their imports of various agricultural products. The objective of these levies is to raise the price of imported products to the domestic price level.

Temporary import surcharges. Temporary surcharges have been introduced from time to time by certain countries, such as the United Kingdom and the United States, to provide additional protection for local industry and, in particular, in response to balance-of-payments deficits.

Compensatory import taxes. In theory these taxes correspond with various internal taxes, such as value-added taxes and sales taxes. Such "border tax adjustments" must not, according to GATT, amount to additional protection for domestic producers or to a subsidy for exports. In practice, one of the major tax inequities today is the fact that manufacturers in value-added tax (VAT) countries do not pay a value-added tax on sales to non-VAT countries such as the United States while U.S. manufacturers who pay income taxes in the United States must also pay VAT taxes on sales in VAT countries.

Adaptation to meet local requirements. The impact of adaptation to conform to local safety and other requirements can be crippling. For example, the Ford Motor Company sells its Mustang in the Japanese market. Because of the markups and expensive adaptations that are required to adapt the U.S. product to conform to Japanese safety and other requirements the Mustang in Japan sells for approximately $15,000. Needless to say very few Mustangs are sold in Japan. An alternative approach to the Japanese market would be to begin with the Japanese customer to identify the customer's wants and needs and to design a product for that market or to adapt the Mustang design to a world design that would fit the needs and wants in both the U.S. and the Japanese market. The implementation of such a program would involve major marketing investments by the Ford Motor Company in establishing distribution, in advertising and promotion, in training and developing organizations to market the Mustang in Japan. It would also involve significant expenditures of especially energy in designing the Mustang to appeal to the needs of the Japanese customer.

The Kennedy Round

A major development of the 1960s was agreements negotiated in the 1963–67 period, popularly known as the "Kennedy Round." During these negotiations, tariff concessions on nonagricultural products by the four largest industrial participants—the United States, the United Kingdom, Japan, and the European Economic Community—averaged slightly more than 35 percent and covered about $20 billion of trade. On agricultural products, excluding grains, the average reduction by the major industrial countries amounted to about 20 percent and affected about one-half of the dutiable imports. Tariff reductions under the agreement took place in five equal installments. The first was concluded on January 1, 1968, and the last on January 1, 1972. Over sixty thousand items were involved, representing approximately $40 billion in world trade annually.

At the conclusion of the Kennedy Round negotiations, tariffs on dutiable nonagricultural products averaged 9.9 percent in the United States, 8.6 percent in the European Economic Community, 10.8 percent in the United Kingdom, and 10.7 percent in Japan.[3]

A second "Tokyo round" of trade negotiations was undertaken by the ninety-seven-nation General Agreement on Tariffs and Trade in the 1970s. The target in these negotiations, which were still underway in 1979, was to achieve another 35 percent tariff reduction.

The tariff barriers to trade in the post-Kennedy Round world have been substantially reduced for a broad range of goods. Consider, for example, a bottle of champagne selling for approximately $9.00 a bottle in the United States. The price of this champagne to the consumer in the U.S. market includes approximately $2.50 as landed CIF price, duty included. The remaining $6.50 is accounted for by advertising and distribution costs and profit in the U.S. market. The duty included in the $2.50 price to the American importer is approximately $0.25, or 10 percent of the landed price, duty included. A 10 percent increase of this duty sounds like a substantial price increase or price barrier. However, 10 percent of the duty is only 2.5 cents, which is not a barrier to the sale of a product that retails for $9.00.

Nontariff Barriers

With the success of the Kennedy Round tariff negotiations, attention has naturally turned to the remaining nontariff obstacles to trade. A *nontariff trade barrier* is defined by economists as any measure, public or private, that causes internationally traded goods and services to be allocated in such a way as to reduce potential real-world income. Potential real-world income is the attainable level when resources are allocated in the most economically efficient manner. To the businessman a nontariff barrier is any measure, other than tariffs, that provides a barrier or obstacle to the sale of his products in a foreign market. The major nontariff trade barriers are as follows:

1. *Quotas and Trade Control*—These are specific limits and controls. The trade distortion of a quota is even more severe than a tariff because once the quota has been filled, the price mechanism is not allowed to operate. The good is simply

---

[3] Robert E. Baldwin, *Non-Tariff Distortion of International Trade* (Washington, D.C.: Brookings Institution), p. 1.

unavailable at any price. *State trading* refers to the practice of monopolizing trade in certain commodities. In Communist countries all commodities are monopolized, but there are many examples of non-Communist government monopolies: the Swedish government controls the import of all alcoholic beverages and tobacco products, and the French government controls all imports of coal.

2. *Discriminatory Government and Private Procurement Policies*—These are the rules and regulations that discriminate against foreign suppliers and are commonly referred to as "Buy British" or "Buy American" policies.

3. *Restrictive Customs Procedures*—The rules and regulations for classifying and valuing commodities as a basis for levying import duties can be administered in a way that makes compliance difficult and expensive.

4. *Selective Monetary Controls and Discriminatory Exchange Rate Policies*— Discriminatory exchange rate policies distort trade in much the same way as selective import duties and export subsidies. Selective monetary policies are definite barriers to trade. For example, many countries from time to time require importers to place on deposit at no interest an amount equal to the value of imported goods. These regulations in effect raise the price of foreign goods by the cost of money for the term of the required deposit.

5. *Restrictive Administrative and Technical Regulations*—These include anti-dumping regulations, size regulations, and safety and health regulations. Some of these regulations are intended to keep out foreign goods while others are directed toward legitimate domestic objectives. For example, the safety and pollution regulations being developed in the United States for automobiles are motivated almost entirely by legitimate concerns about highway safety and pollution. However, an effect of these regulations, particularly on smaller foreign manufacturers, has been to make it so expensive to comply with U.S. safety requirements that they have withdrawn from the market.

In 1969 GATT published a 276-page report listing nontariff barriers to trade. This report, which listed such obscure items as an Italian sanitary tax on foreign snake poison, is already out of date. In 1971, for example, the California wine industry proposed that all wine sold in the U.S. market be bottled in the standard U.S.-size wine bottle, which was slightly different in size and shape than the standard European bottle. This typical nontariff barrier is particularly vicious because its full impact is hidden. It would have required any foreign producers to package or bottle wine for the U.S. market in a special "export" package. Thus, many wines that are sold in the United States in limited quantities would no longer be available because the producers would not have enough volume in U.S. sales to justify the expense of a special bottle. From the point of view of the California wine industry, however, this simple and apparently benign regulation would have had a much greater restrictive effect upon the competitiveness of foreign wine products than do the existing tariff levels on wines, which are quite modest. Fortunately, the proposal was defeated and the U.S. industry instead is switching to metric sizes.

Germany requires that imports of meal used to feed poultry and swine contain only 5 percent fat. Wellens & Company, Minneapolis, produces a meal that contains about 10 percent fat, and, according to the company president, "We simply don't sell any to the Germans. To change the meal's fat content would involve special machinery which would greatly increase production costs; it simply wouldn't be worth it." Wellens expects several other West European countries to adopt the 5 percent regulation, which the company claims does nothing for the animal's health.

Stanley Works of New Britain, Connecticut, was exporting thousands of electric drills to Mexico until 1967. Then the Mexican government banned the import of drills with handles that measured a half inch in diameter or less. The move effectively shut off drill imports because the only significant market in Mexico was for the smaller-size drills.

Packaging regulations often erect a hurdle for exports. Brazil, for example, requires that tires be removed from certain types of vehicles imported from the United States. This regulation adds approximately 5 percent to the cost of U.S.-made vehicles, principally because additional labor is needed to remove the tires before vehicles are shipped to Brazil.[4]

Producers of restrictive administrative regulations are incredibly creative in establishing barriers to trade. In 1969 the U.S. Department of Agriculture put a set of minimum size restrictions on all tomatoes sold in the U.S. market. The regulations provided that mature green tomatoes (those that ripen after they are picked) could not be sold unless they measured more than 2-9/32" in diameter. Vine-ripened tomatoes were required to measure at least 2-17/32" in diameter. Mexican tomato farmers were outraged because the regulations barred almost 50 percent of their crop from the U.S. market. Florida growers contended that the regulations were not discriminatory because they applied to both the Mexican and the U.S. crops. But the Mexicans pointed out that the regulations were more lenient on green than ripened tomatoes. Green tomatoes accounted for approximately 85 percent of the Florida tomato crop and only 10 percent of the Mexican crop. While U.S. housewives saw prices rise as much as 30 percent, Mexican tomato farmers were enraged while they watched tons of their tomatoes being fed to cattle or simply rotting in heaps along the highway. Rod Batiz, president of the twenty-thousand-member confederation of agriculture association, was quoted in the *Wall Street Journal* as saying, "The whole of Mexico feels stabbed in the back."[5]

The Florida growers who called for the size restriction said they could not understand the furor. Jack Peters, manager of the Florida Tomato Committee, a grower group that has authority under federal laws to draw up tomato-size maturity and grade requirements for the Agriculture Department, said, "What we're doing is good for the entire industry in Florida and Mexico.[6]

The example illustrates how difficult it is to deal with nontariff barriers to

[4] "Export Hurdles: U.S. Businessmen Say Non-Tariff Bars to Goods Pose Growing Problems," *Wall Street Journal*, November 26, 1968, p. 1.
[5] "Curbs on Tomatoes from Mexico Causes U.S. Prices to Rise," *Wall Street Journal*, March 4, 1969, p. 9.
[6] Ibid.

trade. The Mexicans can protest the decisions of the U.S. Department of Agriculture, but the Florida growers who were competing with the Mexican growers in effect wrote their own regulations. They maintained that the regulations worked for the benefit of everyone: growers on both sides of the border and the consumer. A strong case could be made for the harm done by these regulations to Mexican growers and U.S. consumers, but the mechanism for hearing this case does not really exist. The Mexican growers can influence this decision by pressuring the U.S. government through diplomatic channels, or try to appeal directly to consumers and thereby influence legislative and administrative action in government.

An important test of a ruling or regulation is whether it has a greater impact on foreign producers. If this is the case, and there is no apparent social benefit for consumers, the ruling is a nontariff barrier.

Tariff Classification

Before World War II specific duties were widely used and the tariffs of many countries, particularly those in Europe and Latin America, were extremely complex. Since the war the trend has been toward the conversion to ad valorem duties. Tariff administration has been simplified by the adoption by a large number of countries of the Brussels nomenclature (BTN). This nomenclature was worked out by an international committee of experts under the sponsorship of the Customs Cooperation Council, which in 1955 produced a convention that entered into force in 1959. The rules of this convention are now being applied by most GATT countries. Approximately two-thirds of all world trade is now conducted under tariffs based on the BTN system. It is significant, however, that among major trading nations neither the United States nor Canada uses the BTN.

The BTN groups articles mainly according to the material from which they are made. For less-developed countries, it is both easy to use and applicable to the goods they produce. An additional advantage of the BTN is its widespread use. A common basis for the classification of goods facilitates comparison of duties applied by different countries and simplifies international tariff negotiations.

In spite of the progress made in simplifying tariff procedures, the task of administrating a tariff presents an enormous problem. Even a tariff schedule of several thousand items cannot clearly describe every product that enters into international trade. The constant flow of new products and new materials used in manufacturing processes introduces new problems. Often, two or more alternative classifications must be considered in assessing the rate on a particular article depending upon how it is used or its component material. The classification of a product can make a substantial difference in the duty applied. There are two important implications of this fact for export marketers. The first is that exporters should seek the most favorable classification for their products in order to minimize the duty levied in the importing country. The second is that the difficulties of classification raise serious questions about the accuracy of data on international trade patterns. When using international trade data, it is important to bear in mind the enormous problems posed by classification and recognize that the numbers in trade reports may often reflect hasty and arbitrary classifications that distort the true picture of the trade flows. Evidence of the inaccuracy of trade classification practices is provided by frequent failure of import and export figures of the same commodity to reconcile between two countries.

THE DECISION TO INVESTIGATE EXPORT MARKETS

A company committed to growth has four basic expansion alternatives. *Vertical integration* involves moving from a finished product back to basic materials, or viceversa. For a steel manufacturer, this would involve moving forward from the manufacture of steel to the fabrication of metal products. For the metal fabricator, vertical integration would involve moving back to the manufacture of steel. A second expansion alternative is *horizontal expansion* of the product line. This involves moving to configurations and adaptations in the product that are variations on the company's basic line. For example, a sled manufacturer might introduce a low-price utility model and a high-price luxury model, thus expanding his sled line from one basic medium-price sled to three. A third and more venturesome expansion alternative is *product diversification.* This involves moving into an entirely new product technology area via acquisition. A fourth expansion alternative is geographical diversification, or the extension of existing products to new geographic markets. If the move into foreign markets involves the use of goods manufactured in the home or domestic market, the fourth expansion alternative is export marketing or export selling depending on the degree of involvement in foreign markets.

When should a company investigate export markets? This question must be answered by comparing the business opportunity in export markets with that in domestic markets. For each market, determine the export opportunity as shown below:

M = potential market size in market X_1

C = competitive offering

P_1 = product

P_2 = price (sum of manufacturing cost + transportation, insurance, taxes, duty, and trade margins)

P_3 = product distribution or availability

P_4 = advertising and promotion

TR = total revenue in market

Cost = manufacturing, marketing, tariff, and overhead costs

TR = $f(M, C, P_1, P_2, P_3, P_4)$

then,

Export opportunity = (TR) − Cost

Export opportunities should be compared with each other and with domestic opportunities to determine investigation priorities.

CHOOSING EXPORT MARKETS

Creating a Product/Market Profile

The first step in choosing export markets is to establish the key factors influencing sales and profitability of the product in question. If a company is getting started for the first time in exporting, its product market profile will have to be based upon its experience in its home market. The basic questions that must be answered can be summarized as the six *W*'s:

1. What need or function does our product serve?
2. Who buys our product?
3. Why is our product purchased?
4. When is our product purchased?
5. Where is our product purchased?
6. What are the critical factors determining sales and profitability of our product?

This profile, when applied to the Richardson Manufacturing Company, might yield the following answers:

1. Our product prepares a seed bed in a manner that preserves the moisture in the soil and conserves approximately 25 percent of the pulling power of a tractor.

2. Farmers who buy our product, particularly innovative farmers who are anxious to conserve their soil, increase their yields and reduce their cost.

3. They buy our product because they increase yields, reduce soil erosion, and reduce operating costs. They buy our product because they concluded that these three advantages outweigh the additional cost of our product.

4. The product is purchased at all times of the year, but most frequently before the cultivating season.

5. The product is purchased from a dealer who is close to the site of farming operations.

6. The critical factors influencing sales and profitability in our business are our product advantages, price distribution, and communication. In our business the principal communication tool is the personal selling effort of the dealer and sales representatives. We rely heavily on the influence of innovators and early adopters who provide a demonstration of the effectiveness of our new soil cultivation method and who are in effect our best salesmen.

This profile suggests that if Richardson is going to be effective in export markets, it must satisfy several criteria. First, it must have a price that is within a competitive range of alternative soil cultivation methods. Second, the company must obtain distribution of its product and must support this distribution with field-selling efforts that succeed in getting the product into the hands of innovative farmers who will provide a demonstration of its advantages through their own use.

Market Selection

Given the product/market profile for the company's product, the next step in choosing an export market is to appraise possible markets. To do this, six basic elements of information are required:

1. *Market potential.* What is the basic market potential for the product in foreign markets? The best place to start in getting an answer to this question is at your desk or library table. What are major factors determining demand for your company's product? Using some of the tools and techniques described in Chapter 9, it is possible with statistical analysis and published data to come up with a rough estimate of total potential demand for your company's product in particular markets. At this stage in the analysis, accuracy is unnecessary and irrelevant to the decision task. For a large number of products, gross national product will be a sufficient statistic for obtaining a sufficiently accurate estimate of total demand for the product. For many other products, additional statistical measures will considerably sharpen the estimate of total demand. For example, if you are interested in the demand for automobile tires, information on the total number of cars registered in any country in the world is easily obtained. This could be combined with information on gasoline consumption to come up with an estimate of the total mileage driven in the target market. When this figure is combined with tire life predictions, demand estimates are easily obtained.

Many products will defy such accurate estimation from published statistics. Frequently, the most useful statistical analysis for products for which specific data are unavailable is estimation by analogy. When the researcher has information on consumption or use of the product in a single market, if there is any basis for assuming that demand conditions for the product are similar in other markets, the method of estimation by analogy described in Chapter 9 can be applied.

2. *Terms of access.* This phrase covers the entire set of national controls that apply to important merchandise. It includes such items as import duties, import restrictions or quotas, foreign exchange regulations, and preference arrangements.

3. *Shipping cost.* Ask the shipping companies to give you some idea of shipping charges to various potential markets or consult a freight forwarding firm. Investigate the alternative ways of shipping, such as sea, air, or even parcel post if the product is very small.

4. *Appraising the level and quality of competition in the potential market.* Interviews with exporters, bankers, and other industry executives are extremely

useful at this stage. Using a country's commercial representatives abroad can also be valuable. When contacting country representatives abroad, it is important to provide as much specific information as possible. If a manufacturer simply writes and says, "I make lawnmowers. Is there a market for them in your territory?" the representative cannot provide much helpful information. On the other hand, if a manufacturer would write providing the following information: (a) sizes of lawnmowers manufactured, (b) descriptive brochures indicating features and advantages, and (c) estimated CIF and retail price in the target market, the commercial representative could provide a very useful report based upon a comparison of the company's product with market needs and offerings.

5. *Product fit.* With information on market potential, cost of access to the market, and local competition, the next step is to decide how well your company's product fits the market in question. In general, a product fits a market if it satisfies the following criteria: (1) the product is likely to appeal to customers in the potential market; (2) the product will not require more adaptation than is economically justifiable by the volume expected in the potential market; (3) import restrictions and/or high tariffs do not exclude or make the product so expensive in the target market as to effectively eliminate demand; (4) shipping costs to the target market are in line with the requirements for competitive price; and (5) the cost of assembling sales literature, catalogs, and technical bulletins is not out of line with the market potential. (This factor is particularly important in selling highly technical products.)

6. *Service.* If service is required for the product, can it be delivered at a cost that is consistent with the size of the market?

Table 15-2 presents a market selection framework that incorporates the information elements discussed above. Three countries, A, B, and C, are arranged in order of declining size of market. The competitive advantage of a hypothetical firm is zero in market A, 10 percent in market B, and 20 percent in market C. The product of the market size and competitive advantage index yields a market potential of 5 in market B and 4 in C.

The next stage in our analysis requires an assessment of the "terms of access" to the market. This phrase covers all the conditions affecting the entry of a foreign manufactured good through a market: import duties, import restrictions and quotas, foreign exchange regulations, nontariff barriers, and transportation costs. In Table 15-2 all of these conditions or terms are reduced to an index number, which is 60

TABLE 15-2. Market Selection Framework

Market	Market Size	Competitive Advantage		Market Potential	Terms of Access	Export Market Potential
A	100	0	=	0	100	0
B	50	.10	=	5	.60	3.0
C	20	.20	=	4	.90	3.6

percent for market B and 90 percent for market C. In other words, the "terms of access" are greater to market C than to B. As a result of the multiplication of the market's potential and the "terms of access" index, we now find that market C has become a market of greater potential than B. In this example, a company with limited resources would want to begin its export-marketing program in market C because this country (all things considered) offers the largest export market potential of the countries examined.

Visiting the Potential Market

After a desk research has zeroed in on potential markets, there is no substitute for a field visit to conclude research and begin the development of an actual export-marketing program. There are four major functions of a market visit. The first is to confirm assumptions that were made during the desk appraisal. All the information concerning terms of access, competition, and even the size of the market is based on secondary sources and may require adjustment or revision on the basis of firsthand data obtained in the market. A second major purpose is to gather additional data necessary to reach the final decision about whether to go ahead with an export-marketing program. There are certain kinds of information that simply cannot be obtained from secondary sources. For example, a manufacturer may have a list of potential distributors provided by the U.S. Department of Commerce. He may correspond with distributors on the list and have achieved some tentative idea of their availability. It is difficult, however, to complete an effective arrangement with foreign distributors without actually meeting face to face to allow both sides of the contract to appraise the capabilities and character of the other party.

A third reason for a visit to the export market is to develop, in cooperation with the local agent or distributor, a marketing plan. Agreement should be reached on necessary product modifications, pricing, advertising and promotion expenditures, and a distribution plan. If the plan calls for investment, agreement on the allocation of costs must also be reached.

A fourth important justification for a visit to a market is that it provides an opportunity to engage in direct selling. One excellent way to test a market is to exhibit in trade fairs. At a trade fair an exhibitor can study the reactions to his product compared with his competitors'. The exhibitor can also make contact with possible agents or customers.

A foreign manufacturer of athletic footwear makes most of his contacts and does nearly all of his selling in the United States, his main market, by partaking each winter in the national sporting goods show in Chicago. At the show he meets buyers from U.S. department stores and finds that he needs no other outlets. Specialized or "vertical" trade fairs are particularly useful in selling technical products because they offer an exhibitor an excellent demonstration ground and a group of potential buyers who talk his language. In addition, vertical fairs are attended by people in the trade who are potential agents or distributors, whereas the horizontal fair, which attracts all types of products and the general public, is usually not visited by special buying agents.

Developing an Export Program

After an export market has been selected, the export program must be developed. The following section outlines the major stages in the development of such a program.

PRODUCT SELECTION

The selection of the export market was based upon analysis of potential demand and competition in specific product areas. Further analysis is required to determine which products will be offered in the target market and what, if any, adaptations will be required or are indicated for these products. Some adaptations are mandatory: electrical products must be consistent with the voltage and cycle of electrical power in the target market. Other adaptations are optional: the instruction plates on a mechanical product may or may not be fitted or engraved in the language of the target market. Any company that is serious about export potential will make such optional adaptations because these adaptations are important for the competitive attractiveness of its product.

PRICING

There are two ways to price a product for an export market. One is to take the existing factory price and add on all of the costs required to place the product in the target market. (See Chapter 12.) A second method is to determine the price that would fit an effective total marketing program in the target market. Working from this guide, calculations can be taken back to the factory that will determine the factory price at which the market price could be achieved given all of the transportation, duty, packaging, and other costs associated with the export source. These two prices are the limits for a pricing study. It is possible that the first price will be too high to achieve a desired sales level in the target market. It is also possible that the second price will yield a factory price below cost. Clearly, the final price selected must yield a satisfactory contribution to overhead and profits and at the same time must be competitive in the target market.

An important consideration in this pricing exercise is the effect of increased sales on cost. Many firms are in a position of experiencing scale economies in their costs as sales increase. If scale economies are realized, the export-pricing decision should fully recognize the impact of increased sales on costs. Thus the price should be at least partially based on marginal rather than full cost, or more precisely on expected cost levels after sales increases are realized rather than costs at existing production levels.

The Japanese have used dramatically lower prices as a means of quickly obtaining a market position. When lower prices are offered on products with equivalent or better quality and style, and distribution, advertising, and promotion are adequate, this typically results in a tremendous increase in sales and share of market. The increased volume in turn results in lower unit costs.

TRADE TERMS

A number of terms covering the conditions of the delivery are commonly used in international trade. Many of these terms have through long use acquired precise meanings. Every commercial transaction is based upon a contract of sale, and the trade terms used in that contract have the important function of naming the exact point at which the ownership of merchandise is transferred from the seller to the buyer. The International Chamber of Commerce in Paris has published a pamphlet entitled *Incoterms 1953*. The latest edition of this pamphlet, published in 1955, is tabled showing how ten of the common clauses now in use in international trade are interpreted by eighteen different countries. In preparing this pamphlet, the ICC adopted the principle that a contract price settled on the basis of *Incoterms 1953* would provide for minimum liabilities on the part of the seller. Thus, parties to a transaction wishing to provide for greater liabilities than those in this set of rules must specify the additional liabilities. For example, if a buyer insists upon protection against wharf risk, the contract should then specify "*Incoterms 1953,* plus wharf risk insurance."

The simplest type of sale "as is, where is." Under this type of contract in export, the seller must guarantee the buyer that he will receive an export permit but his responsibility ends there. At the other extreme, the easiest terms of sale for the buyer are "Franco Delivered" including duty and local transportation to his warehouse. Under this contract, the buyer's only responsibility is to obtain an import permit if one is needed and to pass the customs entry at the seller's expense. Between these two terms there are many expenses that accrue to the goods as they move from the place of manufacture to the buyer's warehouse. Following are some of the steps involved in moving goods from a factory to a buyer's warehouse:

1. Obtaining an export permit if required (in the United States, nonstrategic goods are exported under a general license that requires no specific permit).
2. Obtaining a currency permit if required.
3. Packing the goods for export.
4. Transporting the goods to the place of departure (this would normally involve transport by truck or rail to a sea or airport).
5. Preparing a bill of lading.
6. Completing necessary customs export papers.
7. Preparing customs or consular invoices as required in the country of destination.
8. Arranging for ocean freight and preparation.
9. Obtaining marine insurance and certificate of the policy.

Who carries out these steps? This depends on the terms of the sale. In the following paragraphs some of the major terms are defined.

EX-FACTORY (OR EX-WORKS, EX-MILL, EX-PLANTATION, EX-WAREHOUSE)

In this contract the seller places goods at the disposal of the buyer at the time specified in the contract. The buyer takes delivery at the premises of the seller and bears all risks and expenses from that point on.

FAS (FREE ALONGSIDE SHIP) NAMED PORT OF SHIPMENT

Under this contract the seller must place goods alongside the vessel or other mode of transportation and pay all charges up to that point. The seller's legal responsibility ends once he has obtained a clean wharfage receipt.

FOB (FREE ON BOARD)

In an FOB contract the responsibility and liability of the seller does not end until the goods have actually been placed aboard a ship. Terms should preferably be "FOB ship (name port)." In an FOB contract the seller must:

1. Deliver the goods on board the vessel named by the buyer at the port of shipment on the date specified in the contract.
2. Bear all cost payable on or for the goods until they have effectively been placed aboard the ship or other mode of transportation
3. Suitably pack the goods for the mode of transportation specified
4. Provide documentation indicating proof of delivery of goods aboard the mode of transportation

In turn, with an FOB contract the buyer must:

1. Arrange for transportation specifying the mode of transportation to the port of departure
2. Bear all cost and risk from the time the goods have been placed on board the mode of transportation

CIF (COST, INSURANCE, FREIGHT) NAMED PORT OF DESTINATION

Under this contract, as in the FOB contract, the risk of loss or damage to goods is transferred to the buyer once they have been loaded on board ship, freight car, or airplane. But the seller has to pay the expense of transportation for the goods up to the port of destination, including the expense of insurance.

DELIVERED DUTY PAID

Under this contract the seller undertakes to deliver the goods to the buyer at the place he names in the country of import with all costs, including duties, paid. The seller is responsible under this contract for getting the import license if one is required.

EXPORT ORGANIZATION—MANUFACTURER'S COUNTRY

A manufacturer interested in export marketing has two broad alternatives organizationally. He can negotiate a representation agreement with one of the many external independent organizations that typically concentrate in a product area and sometimes in a geographic area. Alternatively, he can create his own in-house export department that will deal directly with foreign markets.

External Independent Export Organizations

The terms used to describe various types of export firms, "export merchant," "export broker," "combination export manager," "manufacturer's export representative or commission agent," and "export distributor," have never been used precisely to describe the services performed by an export organization. The definitions in Table 15-3 are suggested as reasonable approximations of current usage in the industry. Because of the variations in usage of these terms, the reader is

TABLE 15-3. Export Agents and Organizations—Definition

A. *No Assignment of Responsibility from a U.S. Client*

Purchasing Agent

Foreign purchasing agents are variously referred to as "buyer for export," "export commission house" or "export confirming house." They operate on behalf of, and are remunerated by, an overseas customer. They generally seek out the U.S. manufacturer whose price and quality match the demands of their overseas principals.

Foreign purchasing agents often represent large users of materials abroad—governments, utilities, and railroads, for example. They do not offer the U.S. manufacturer stable volume except when long-term supply contracts are agreed upon. Purchases may be completed as domestic transactions with the purchasing agent handling all export packing and shipping details, or the agent may rely on the manufacturer to handle the shipping arrangements.

Export Broker

The export broker receives a fee for bringing together the U.S. seller and the overseas buyer. The fee is usually paid by the seller, but sometimes the buyer pays it. The broker takes no title to the goods, and assumes no financial responsibility. A broker usually specializes in a specific commodity, such as grain or cotton, and is less frequently involved in the export of manufactured goods.

Export Merchant

Export merchants are sometimes referred to as "jobbers." They seek out needs in foreign markets and make purchases in the United States to fill these needs. Conversely, they often complement this activity by importing to fill needs in the United States. Export merchants often handle staple, openly traded products, for which brand names or manufacturers' identifications are not important.

TABLE 15–3 (cont.)

Export Merchant

Compensation is in the form of a markup the merchant bases on market conditions. Manufacturers sell to the export merchant in an ordinary domestic transaction. The merchant generally purchases from the lowbidding manufacturer or middleman. Many merchant houses, to stabilize their businesses, also operate as export distributors of export commission representatives.

B. Assignment of Responsibility from a U.S. Client

Combination Export Manager

Combination export manager (CEM) is the term used to designate an independent export firm that acts as the export sales department for more than one manufacturer. The combination export manager usually operates in its own name, but sometimes it operates in the name of a manufacturer-client for export markets. It may act as an independent distributor, purchasing and reselling goods at an established price or profit margin, or as a commission representative taking no title and bearing no financial risks in the sale.

Manufacturer's Export Representative

Combination export management firms often refer to themselves as manufacturer's export representatives whether they act as export distributors or export commission representatives.

Export Distributor

The export distributor assumes financial risk. The firm usually has exclusive right to sell a manufacturer's products in all or some markets outside the United States. The distributor pays for goods in the United States in a domestic transaction and handles all financial risks in the foreign sale. The firm ordinarily sells at manufacturer's list price abroad, receiving an agreed percentage of list price as remuneration. The distributor may operate in its own name or in the manufacturer's. It handles all shipping details. The export distributor usually represents several manufacturers and hence is a combination export manager.

Export Commission Representative

The export commission representative assumes no financial risk and is sometimes termed an "agent," although this term is generally avoided because of the legal connotations of the term. The commission representative is assigned all or some foreign markets by the manufacturer. The manufacturer carries all accounts, although the representative often provides credit checks and arranges financing. The representative may operate in its own name or in the manufacturer's. Generally, export commission representatives handle several accounts and hence are combination export managers.

Cooperative Exporter

The cooperative exporter, sometimes called a "mother hen," a "piggyback" exporter, or an "export vendor," is an export organization of a U.S. manufacturing company retained by other independent manufacturers to sell their products in some or all foreign markets. Cooperative exporters usually operate as export distributors for other manufacturers, but may operate in special cases as commission representatives. They are regarded as a form of a combination export manager.

TABLE 15-3 (cont.)

Webb-Pomerene Association

Webb-Pomerene associations are organizations jointly owned, maintained, or supported by competing U.S. manufacturers especially and exclusively for export trade. Special legislation gives them qualified exemption from antitrust laws. They may provide informational services to their members, as well as buy and sell abraod, and may engage in other activities such as setting prices and allocating orders.

Foreign Freight Forwarder

Foreign freight forwarders are licensed by the Federal Maritime Commission and are considered an integral part of the American merchant marine. They are highly specialized in traffic operations, overseas import regulations, customs clearances, and shipping rates and schedules. They assist manufacturers or combination export managers in determining and paying freight, fees, and insurance charges. Forwarders may also do export packing. For a fee paid by the overseas customer, they usually handle goods from port of exit to overseas port of entry. They may also move inland freight from factory to port and, through affiliates abroad, handle freight from foreign port to customer.

A licensed forwarder may receive brokerage or rebates from shipping companies for booked space. Some companies and manufacturers engage in freight forwarding or some phase of it on their own, but they may not, under law, receive brokerage from shipping lines.

Source: NICB, *Organizing for Exporting, Studies in Business Policy No. 126* (New York, N.Y. 1968).

warned to check and confirm the services performed by an independent export organization.

WEBB-POMERENE ASSOCIATIONS

The Webb-Pomerene Act of 1918 authorized the creation of associations of U.S. exporters to engage in export trade. The purpose of the act was to increase the competitive effectiveness of U.S. exporters, particularly those in competition with large European cartels. The act permits the exporters who combine to share costs of export operations to reap common rewards. The legislation further exempts companies in a Webb-Pomerene association from the normal strictures of antitrust legislation and enforcement.

Well over two hundred Webb-Pomerene associations have been formed since the legislation was passed in 1918, but many have been disbanded for various reasons, including changing market conditions and a decision by members to handle their own exports independently. Currently there are between thirty and forty active associations. Carbon Black Export Incorporated is one of the more successful Webb-Pomerene associations.

A Successful Webb-Pomerene Association

Carbon Black Export Inc.

One of the most successful "full" Webb-Pomerene associations is Carbon Black Export Inc. (CBE). This association, with 20 employees, has five of the seven major carbon black producers in its membership, and accounts for nearly $23 million in carbon black exports a year, about 75 percent of the total exports of this commodity. Current expenses are covered by an annual "deficit pro rata assessment" of its membership based on each member's use of CBE's facilities; this system initiated some years ago replaced equity participation used for the initial financing. The annual "deficit" arises from the decision of CBE not to act as a profit-making organization in its own right. Originally organized as an informational of trade association type of Webb-Pomerene grouping, CBE was reorganized in 1933 to provide more direct services to its members in their export trade. Under the reorganization, it acts as an "export coordinator."

CBE establishes the sales terms for its members on each sale, and in addition handles the mechanics of the sale. They include editing the order and letter of credit, checking product availability, allocating the order, expediting factory release and inland transport, consolidating shipments, arranging for foreign freight forwarding, preparing commercial invoices and drafts, and presenting and collecting the draft. Shipments are made in CBE's name and are insured under a marine insurance policy held by CBE. Because orders for carbon black stipulate a brand name, CBE some time ago abandoned its quota allocation policy. Individual members maintain their own sales representatives in foreign markets.

Source: NICB, *Organizing for Exporting. Studies in Business Policy No. 126.*

In-House Export Organization

Most larger companies handle export operations in their own organization. There is a rule of thumb that when a company's export sales exceed $200,000 to $500,000 a year, volume is sufficient to justify the establishment of an internal organization. The possible arrangements for handling exports are manifold:

1. As a part-time activity by domestic employees
2. Through an export partner who is part of the domestic marketing structure
3. Through an export department that is independent of the domestic marketing structure
4. Through an export department within an international division
5. For multidivisional companies, each of the above possibilities exists within each division

For the company that considers its export business sufficiently interesting to establish an in-house organization, the question of how to effectively organize depends on the company's appraisal of the opportunities in export marketing, and on its strategy for allocating its resources to markets on a global basis. It is entirely possible that a company would arrive at an optimal position by allocating export responsibility on a part-time basis to domestic employees. The advantages of this arrangement are twofold. First, it is a very low-cost arrangement requiring no additional specialized personnel; and second, the domestic employees assigned to the task can be thoroughly competent in terms of their product and customer knowledge, which although developed in the domestic market may be applicable to the target foreign markets. A key variable in the equation leading to the internal structure is the extent to which the target export market is different from the domestic market. If customer circumstances and characteristics are similar, the requirements for specialized regional knowledge are of course lessened.

EXPORT ORGANIZATION—MARKET COUNTRY

The export organization, regardless of whether it is located within the manufacturing company or in an external independent export organization, must make arrangements to distribute the product in the market country. The basic decision that every exporting organization faces is the extent to which it will rely upon direct market representation as opposed to representation by independent intermediaries.

Direct Market Representation

There are two major advantages to direct representation in a market. The first is *control* and the second is *communications.* Control is an important feature of direct representation. When a marketer wishes to develop a particular program, commit resources to some activity such as advertising, change price, or make any of a host of moves, direct representation allows these moves to be made without the need to negotiate and achieve consent of an independent party. When a product is not yet established in a market, special efforts are necessary to achieve sales. The advantage of direct representation is that these special efforts can be obtained as part of the marketer's investment. With indirect or independent representation, such an investment is often not forthcoming. This is in no way a criticism of independent representation. Because they acquire no contractual claim on the value of the market position developed, independent representatives in many cases would be foolish to invest significant time and money in a product. The other great advantage to direct representation is that the possibilities for feedback and information from the market are much greater. This information can vastly improve export-marketing decisions concerning product, price, communications, and distribution.

Direct representation does not mean that the exporter is selling directly to the consumer or customer. In most cases direct representation involves selling to wholesalers or retailers. For example, the major automobile exporters in Germany and Japan rely upon direct representation in the U.S. market in the form of their distributing agencies, which are owned and controlled by the manufacturing organization. The distributing agencies sell products to franchised dealers.

Independent Representation

In smaller markets it is usually not feasible to establish direct representation because the volume of sales does not justify the cost that would be involved. A small manufacturer usually lacks adequate sales volume to justify the cost of direct representation even in the larger markets. Whenever sales volume is small, use of an independent distributor is an effective method of sales distribution. Finding "good" distributors can be the key to export success. Several methods are described in Appendix II at the end of this chapter.

An inexpensive source of potential distributors and agents is the U.S. Department of Commerce trade lists arranged by 5-digit standard industrial classification numbers giving the names and addresses of foreign firms. These lists include the name, mailing address, chief executive, and the type of organization, plus other selected information. They are available for each principal SIC product category from the U.S. Department of Commerce, Washington, D.C.

TRADE CONTACT SURVEYS

Trade Contact Surveys conducted by the U.S. Foreign Service in a specified country are especially designed to locate agents, distributors, or licensees abroad. These surveys attempt to find firms that express an interest in the requesting company's business proposal and meet the requirements specified by the requesting company. The survey report includes pertinent marketing data in addition to names, addresses, and brief descriptions of the companies recommended. Applications for a survey should be submitted to the Department of Commerce and should be accompanied by sales literature.

Potential distributors can be solicited by mail, or even more effectively can be initially contacted by mail, screened, and then directly contacted on a market visit.

Piggyback Marketing

"Piggyback marketing" or the use of a "mother hen" sales force is an innovation in international distribution that has received much attention in recent years. This is an arrangement whereby one manufacturer obtains distribution of his products through another's distribution channels. The motivation for this arrangement exists on both sides of the contract. The active distribution partner obtains a fuller utilization of its distribution system and thereby increases the revenues generated by the system. The manufacturer using the piggyback arrangement does so at a cost that is much lower than that required for any direct arrangement. Successful piggyback marketing requires that the combined product lines be complementary. They must appeal to the same customer, and they must not be competitive with each other. If these requirements are met, the piggyback arrangement can be a very effective way of fully utilizing an international channel system to the advantage of both parties.

EXPORT PROMOTION

During 1976 over eight hundred fairs were held in major foreign markets. U.S. trade centers alone, for example, hold sixty product shows annually in major cities abroad. At these fairs, which are usually organized around a product, a group of products, or activity, manufacturers can exhibit their products and meet potentially interested customers. Appendix I at the end of this chapter contains a number of suggestions on how to obtain information on trade fairs.

EXPORT FINANCING[7]

Sales of merchandise by exporters to buyers abroad are generally made on the basis of one of the following forms of finance.

Export Letters of Credit

Except for cash in advance, export letters of credit as a means of obtaining payment afford the highest degree of protection to the exporter. Particularly in the case of the irrevocable letter of credit, the credit risk of the buyer is eliminated and replaced by that of the bank opening the letter of credit. If the credit is confirmed by a bank in the exporting country, the exportee is protected from foreign exchange restrictions in the country of destination. If a letter of credit is obtained, the exporter ordinarily receives dollars at the time of presentation of shipping documents to the bank holding the credit. In the case of irrevocable credits, the possibility of cancellation of the order prior to payment is eliminated.

Dollar (or Foreign Currency) Drafts Covering Exports

The draft may be on a sight basis for immediate payment or it may be drawn to be accepted for payment 30, 60, or 90 days after sight or date and at times for longer periods. Drafts directed to a bank for collection usually are accompanied by shipping documents consisting of a full set of bills of lading in negotiable form, airways bills of lading, or parcel post receipt, together with insurance certificates, commercial invoices, consular invoices, and any other documents that may be required in the country of destination.

Sales against Cash Deposit in Advance

When credit risks abroad are doubtful, when exchange restrictions within the country of destination are such that the return of funds from abroad may be delayed for an unreasonable period, or when the exporter for any other reason may be unwilling to sell on credit terms, he may request payment in whole or in part in cash in advance of shipment. Because of competition and restrictions against cash payment in many countries, the volume of business handled on a cash-in-advance basis is small.

[7]From *Export and Import Procedures,* Morgan Guaranty Trust Company of New York, 1968.

Sales on Open Account

Open account terms generally prevail in areas where exchange controls are minimal and exporters have had long-standing relations with good buyers in nearby or long-established markets. Open account terms also prevail when sales are made to branches or subsidiaries of the exporter. The main objection to open account sales is the absence of a tangible obligation. Normally, if a time draft is drawn and dishonored after acceptance, it can be used as a basis of legal action, whereas in the case of a dishonored open account transaction the legal procedure may be more complicated.

Sales on a Consignment Basis

As in the case of sales on open account, no tangible obligation is created by consignment sales. In countries with free ports or free trade zones, it can be arranged to have consigned merchandise placed under bonded warehouse control in the name of a foreign bank. Sales can then be arranged by the selling agent and arrangements made to release partial lots out of the consigned stock against regular payment terms. The merchandise is not cleared through customs until after the sale has been completed.

Although there is much concern regarding credit on the part of those companies who have never exported, the experience of Felix Norman, president of Hart-Carter International, is not unusual. During a four-year period, Hart-Carter exported $9 million worth of agricultural machinery to over 105 countries and never had a single default:

> With new export customers we utilize a letter of credit form of payment, whereby we merely present proof of shipment to a U.S. bank in which our foreign customer has established a credit. That way we get paid the day we ship.
>
> Later, as we gain experience with these customers, we reduce our credit requirements—even placing many on an open account basis.
>
> Almost without exception, we find these open accounts pay within thirty days of delivery and many pay sooner.[8]

EXPORT DOCUMENTATION AND CONTROL

Every country requires substantial documentation of export activity. Some countries, the United States included, also engage in substantial efforts to control the type of exporting that is carried out by domestic firms. Appendix I at the end of this chapter contains a summary of U.S. export documentation and control regulations and requirements.

---

[8]"Export Awareness, an Advertising Test," U.S. Department of Commerce, Bureau of International Commerce, July 1970.

The major difference between trade in one's own country and trade in a foreign country is documentation requirements. Documents must accompany every export shipment. If they are not correct, expensive delays and in some cases fines can result.

Some businessmen avoid exports because they feel they could not handle the documentation. Although documentation is difficult, it is something that can be learned and there are many experts to help. The Ministry or Department of Commerce in almost every country has staff specialists to help in this area, as do many chamber of commerce and trade associations. There are excellent reference books kept up to date by regular supplements.

Finally, a good freight forwarder includes obtaining and filling out documents in the many services that he offers to exporters.

NATIONAL EXPORT PERFORMANCE

Clearly, the most outstanding performance during recent years has been achieved by Japan. As Table 15-4 shows, there were eleven Japanese corporations whose exports were in excess of $1 billion per annum in 1976, as compared with only six U.S. companies in 1977 (see Table 15-5). The top-ranking Japanese exporting corporation, Nissan Motor, did almost $3 billion of export business in 1976. The Japanese performance during the 1960s demonstrates how an attractive product at an attractive price combined with an effective communications program can dramatically achieve results. The Japanese have succeeded in export marketing by adapting their offering and by always positioning themselves in the market with a competitive advantage.

If a company wishes to achieve any real success in export markets, it is absolutely vital to have some kind of competitive advantage. Unless a company's product is unique, customers in export markets have established sources of supply of comparable products. If a company is going to succeed in persuading potential customers to shift their source of supply or their purchasing pattern, there must be some demonstrable advantage or reason for making the shift. Change involves uncertainty and inevitably perceived risk, and in order to absorb this uncertainty and incur the risk, there must be a perceived potential advantage.

The Japanese have succeeded because they have responded to this fundamental marketing axiom. Price has been their most spectacular weapon for achieving market entry. The Latin American telecommunications market provides an interesting example of how effectively price can be used as a marketing and competitive tool. At the beginning of the 1960s Latin American telecommunications were supplied entirely by companies based in Europe and the United States. The Japanese entered the market with products that were comparable or inferior, depending upon the source of information. However, regardless of any appraisal of product quality, it was clear that the Japanese were aggressive in pricing their telecommunications products. As a result of the lead taken by the Japanese, prices of telecommunications equipment in Latin America dropped over 50 percent during

TABLE 15-4. The 11 Exporting Corporations of Japan

Rank '76	'75	Company	Export Value (US $1,000)	Export Ratio (%)	Export Value Growth ('75 = 100)	Technology Exports (US $1,000)	Investments Abroad (US $1,000)	Corporations Incorporated Abroad No.	Sales (US $1,000)	Corporations with Mfg. Operations Abroad No.	Sales (US $1,000)	No. of Employees Abroad
1	2	Nissan Motor	2,960,359	44.1	141	...	90,207	11	1,812,200	5	329,934	8,068
2	1	Nippon Steel	2,792,348	36.0	105	21,917	59,469	11	52,717	7	49,093	1,000
3	5	Toyota Motor	2,744,897	37.7	146	...	39,531	10	...	6	...	...
4	3	Sumitomo Metal Industries	1,678,852	48.1	82	1,497	3,259	7	107,283	3	31,534	330
5	4	Nippon Kokan	1,516,659	37.8	79	10,707	2,297	4	10,248	3	9,952	230
6	9	Matsushita Electric Industrial	1,450,593	24.6	165	...	...	54	...	29	...	20,000
7	8	Honda Motor	1,308,672	61.8	113	...	113,103	20	1,540,576	11	76,038	3,431
8	7	Kawasaki Steel	1,203,431	39.4	102	...	120,007	11	29,752	5	15,621	1,167
9	6	Mitsubishi Heavy Industries	1,188,221	31.2	83	30,876	79,334	9	75,624	7	75,624	4,486
10	10	Ishikawajima-Harima Heavy Industries	1,065,217	49.2	139	26,493	63,869	17	143,431	7	139,497	7,555
11	16	Sanyo Electric	1,032,424	45.9	160	...	30,417	28	747,472	21	502,303	17,915

Source: The President Directory, 1978, "The 200 Leading Exporting Corporations," pp. 84–87.

TABLE 15-5. The 20 Biggest U.S. Industrial Exporters

Company	Main Export Products	1977 Exports (millions of dollars)
General Electric	Gas turbines, aircraft engines, power generating equipment, appliances, motors	$2,100
Caterpillar Tractor	Earth-moving & materials-handling equipment	1,900
Boeing	Commercial aircraft	1,470
McDonnell Douglas	Commercial & military aircraft	1,130
Lockheed	Commercial & military aircraft, aerospace items	1,030
Du Pont	Synthetic fibers, plastics, agricultural chemicals, health care products	1,000
Dow Chemical	Plastic intermediates, caustic soda, magnesium	900
United Technologies	Jet engines, aircraft equipment, telephone & powercables, helicopters, elevators	890
Eastman Kodak	Photographic film, papers, chemicals & equipment	850
Sperry Rand	Computers, farm machinery, hydraulic equipment	850
Westinghouse Electric	Nuclear power plants, electrical generators & equipment, defense equipment	800
Weyerhauser	Logs, pulp, liner board, lumber	710
International Harvester	Trucks, farm & construction equipment, gas turbines	660
Union Carbide	Chemicals, agricultural products, plastics, metals, batteries	640
Textron	Helicopters, staplers & staples, pens, machine tools	540
Chrysler	Cars & trucks	530*
Monsanto	Chemicals, plastics, fibers	530
Northrup	Military aircraft	500
Rockwell International	Automotive, aerospace, electronic products	470
Grumman	Military & executive aircraft	430

*Excluding shipments under the U.S.-Canada automotive free trade pact.
Source: Business Week, April 10, 1978, p. 65.

TABLE 15-6. GNP and Exports, 43 Less-Developed Countries, 1960-69
(Annual Growth Rates in Percent)

GNP Growth Rate	Number of Countries	Mean GNP Growth Rate	Mean Export Growth Rate
0—4.0	10	3.2	3.5
4.1—6.0	19	5.1	6.9
more than 6.0	14	9.6	17.8

Source: Trade and Development: Trade Performance and Prospects of Developing Countries (Washington, D.C.: Agency for International Development, 1971).

the 1960s. The aggressive pricing policies of the Japanese companies enabled them to obtain over 25 percent of the Latin American telecommunications market in a span of less then ten years.

In the U.S. automobile market a combination of attractive pricing and product features, which were specifically made with the U.S. market in mind, have enabled the Japanese automobile manufacturers to obtain a significant share of one of the most competitive automobile markets in the world. This pricing and product package has been combined with a heavy and effective advertising program and also with a strong dealer network. It is clear that in the case of the U.S. automobile market, Japanese manufacturers have put together the four basic elements of the marketing mix: product, price, distribution, and communications. This is the essence of effective export marketing. When these basic elements are each considered and adjusted to ensure that the overall marketing mix is competitive, success is assured.

The impact of foreign trade on economic growth is multiple and complex, but recent experience clearly demonstrates that strong export performance is associated with rapid internal growth and a relatively efficient price system. The correlation coefficient between exports and GNP growth rates for the 1960–69 period was 0.94. This correlation can be seen in Table 15-6.

The link between exports and GNP growth rates reflects the fact that ability to compete in export markets requires attention to relative costs of production and avoidance of investment in noncompetitive industries. Trade creates incentives for better utilization of available resources and therefore affects productivity and overall growth. In addition, export success generates foreign exchange, which is available to finance imports of needed components and finished goods that are in demand. Adequate foreign exchange eliminates the possibility of a foreign exchange bottleneck that could limit growth.

BIBLIOGRAPHY

BOOKS

Getting Started in Export Trade. Geneva: International Trade Centre, UNCTAD/ GATT, 1970.

Horn, Paul V., and Henry Gomez, *International Trade.* Englewood Cliffs, N.J.: Prentice-Hall, 1959.

International Marketing Institute, *Export Marketing for Smaller Firms* (2nd ed.). Washington, D.C.: Small Business Administration, 1966.

Morgan Guaranty Trust Company, *Export and Import Procedures.* New York, September 1965.

Root, Franklin R., *Strategic Planning for Export Marketing.* Scranton, Pa.: International Textbook Company, 1966.

Schultz, George J., ed., *Foreign Trade Marketplace.* Detroit: Gale Research Co., 1977.

Stanley, Alexander O., *Handbook of International Marketing.* New York: McGraw-Hill, 1963.

Stuart, Robert D., *Penetrating the International Market,* Management Report Number 84. New York: American Management Association, 1965.

Technology and International Trade. Washington, D.C.: National Academy of Engineering, 1971.

Trade and Development: Trade Performance and Prospects of Developing Countries. Washington, D.C.: Agency for International Development, n.d.

Washington Researchers, *A Researcher's Guide to Washington.* Washington, D.C., 1978.

ARTICLES

"A Summary of Export Control Regulations," revised February 18, 1971. Washington, D.C.: Department of Commerce, Bureau of International Commerce, 1971.

Borch, F. J., "International Trade: What Is the Problem?" Speech given to the Economic Club of Detroit, October 12, 1971. Schenectady, N.Y.: Executive Speech Reprints, General Electric Company, 1971.

de la Torre, Jose, Jeffrey S. Arpan, Michael Jay Jedel, Erenest W. Ogram, Jr., and Brian Toyne, "Corporate Adjustments and Import Competition in the U.S. Apparel Industry," *Journal of International Business Studies,* Spring/Summer 1977, pp. 5–22.

Feinschreiber, Robert, "The U.S. Law Provides Two Export Incentives," *Columbia Journal of World Business,* 10, No. 2 (Summer 1975), 46–49.

Kearns, Henry, "Credit: A Key to Export Sales," *Columbia Journal of World Business,* March-April 1971, pp. 31–38.

——, "A Golden Age for U.S. Exporters," *Columbia Journal of World Business,* 8, No. 3 (Fall 1973), 113–15.

King, Audrey Marsh, "How to Find a Distributor," International Trade Forum, August 1968, pp. 28–30.

"Nontariff Distortions of Trade." New York: Committee for Economic Development, 1969.

Simpson, Claude L., Jr., and Duane Kujawa," The Export Decision Process: An Empirical Inquiry," *Journal of International Business Studies,* Fall 1974, pp. 107–18.

BROWN CRANES LIMITED
INTERNATIONAL MARKETING PROGRAM REVIEW

Brown Cranes Ltd. was established in 1938 to design, manufacture and market mobile cranes. Prior to 1955 the company's business was primarily concentrated on the production of one model—a 4 wheel, diesel powered, 10 ton crane. This model was an exceptionally sturdy and reliable machine (a survey in 1958 showed that every single 10 ton crane sold was still in service—in many cases still operating 24 hours a day). Its use was largely confined to the loading and unloading of railway trucks and similar work. The company marketed the product in 4 overseas markets: Australia, New Zealand, South Africa, and India.

In 1955 the company was acquired by the George Green Group—traditionally the UK's largest scrap metal merchant but which was by then a widely diversified engineering concern. The new management team appointed at that time identified two major factors which appeared to be limiting the growth potential of the crane business: first, a narrow product line, and second, virtually stagnant potential demand caused in part by the exceptionally long life associated with the Brown cranes.

The reorganization of Brown Cranes which followed the 1955 acquisition resulted in a company which in 1970 employed some 2000 people manufacturing mobile cranes with a life capacity from 15 cwt to 35 tons, and a price range of $2500-$60,000. Exhibit 1, unit crane sales for the 1960-69 period, shows clearly the success of the company's export sales program.

Following the Sterling devaluation of 1967 (from £ 1 = $2.80 to £ 1 = $2.40 or 14.3 percent) the company increased its prices by only 10 percent and found itself in a very strong competitive position. By 1970 orders currently available were approximately 300 percent greater than factory production capacity. This situation

EXHIBIT 1. Brown Cranes Limited, Unit Crane Sales, 1960-69.

Year End	Home	Export	Total	Export %
1960	840	466	1307	35
1961	1130	699	1834	38
1962	1149	855	2004	42
1963	866	1060	1926	55
1964	1109	1087	2196	49
1965	1187	1351	2539	53
1966	1257	1395	2652	54
1967	909	1489	2398	61
1968	980	1591	2571	62
1969	950	1650	2650	63

Note: 2600 cranes per annum is approximately maximum output of the plant.
Source: Company records.

was to be partially relieved in 1971 when a new factory was to be opened in the North of England where skilled labour was more readily available than in the midlands where the company's factory was located.

The company was optimistic about future potential demand. Its cranes were sold in 70 countries, including all of the former British colonies in Africa, Asia, and Latin America, although no attempt had been made to enter the North American or Japanese market. This was mainly due to the capacity shortage but was also a recognition of the considerably more sophisticated marketing and servicing operation that would be required to penetrate either of these markets. Until 1967, the Eastern European market had not been penetrated. However, in 1967 after prolonged negotiations an agreement was signed with the Polish government for the delivery of a minimum of $10,000,000 of partially assembled cranes over the 1967–73 period. In return, the company was to purchase an equivalent amount of material and components from Poland. This agreement was so successful that further negotiations were in progress for an expanded agreement. As of 1970, the contract had been very profitable. The company hoped to export cranes to other Comecon countries through the Polish trading company Polinex. Another possibility was sales to non-Comecon countries who had insufficient Sterling for direct purchase, but who had "soft-currency" agreements with Poland which might be tapped via the company's Polish agreement.

DISTRIBUTION STRUCTURE

The major burden of overseas distribution fell upon local agents. They were appointed only after a thorough analysis of their suitability had been conducted by Head Office staff. This was not so much due to the web of legal restrictions surrounding agency agreements in many countries[1] but mainly due to the central role played by the company's agents—they were primarily responsible for procuring orders for cranes and were also responsible for providing after-sales service.

Following a decision to enter a particular market approaches were made to suitable businesses in the area. Principal requirements included adequate capital resources (so that an adequate inventory of new cranes and spare parts could be held) and a record of dynamic and resourceful business performance. In addition, the selected agent normally was expected to be currently operating in a related field—e.g., excavators, dock-yard cranes, factory overhead cranes, or conceivably, agricultural dealers. This restrictive policy was justified by the low turnover in mobile cranes achieved by most dealers. A person operating one of the above businesses usually had salesmen visiting potential customers anyway, so that the marginal costs of carrying a line of mobile cranes was limited to the capital costs of inventories.

---

[1] Though problems had arisen in the past over the dismissal of agents, the company had never found legal restrictions insurmountable.

When the company was satisfied that a potential agent satisfied the above requirements, a thorough investigation of past performance and credit rating was undertaken, usually by staff of the holding company. Finally, no agent was appointed until a senior director personally interviewed the local management. Once this screening procedure was completed the agent was appointed and received the promotional aides and technical assistance outlined below under "Promotional Strategy."

The guide-lines for the selection of agents were by no means rigidly adhered to—each country was considered on its own merits. Indeed the selection procedure was substantially modified for smaller markets where agent qualification requirements were substantially related (though a personal interview was never dispensed with). Two examples illustrate the differences. The Swedish sales and service personnel had been trained to a very high standard. In Somalia, where the company had controlled 100 percent of the market for 10 years the agent was an individual who provided no-after-sales service and whose selling methods according to the marketing director "do not bear unduly close examination." In 20 percent of the company's country markets only very basic spare parts were kept by the agent. This arrangement was largely confined to countries where sales were limited to government orders—and where the government obtained its spare parts direct from England.

There was, however, a fairly sharp distinction drawn between these agents and full service agents. If an agent had a full distributorship his contract prescribed minimum inventory levels for almost all major spares, and further, it was required that at least one mechanic be sent to England to obtain the company Proficiency Certificate in the factory training program. Where the potential market was large enough at least three mechanics were required to take the course (at Brown Crane's expense) and substantial pressure was exerted to ensure the creation of a separate department dealing with the sales, and after-sales servicing, of Brown cranes.

On the average, one agent per year had his contract withdrawn (usually the smaller agencies) but the company was in general very satisfied with the sales effort of its agents. The close working relationship which existed in almost all cases was attributed to the frequent visits not only of company sales and service personnel but, and perhaps more importantly, to the visits of the three most senior executives of the company.

PRODUCT STRATEGY

The design department regularly produced an evaluation of the existing product line. Reference to foreign customers, agents, and company technical and sales personnel, produced the general sepcifications for a new crane shown in Exhibit 2. These specifications were enthusiastically received when presented to agents in early 1970.

EXHIBIT 2. Proposed New Crane Model Specifications.

---

1. *Flexible operational capability*—refined operations in restricted space, as well as high output capability (very different characteristics).
2. *30/35/Ton Lift Capacity*
3. *Truck Mounted/Self Propelled/Crawler Tracked*—Depending on trade, but basic design should be capable of ready adaption.
4. *Simplified Operation Controls*—This was particularly stressed by agents in underdeveloped countries where operators were particularly hard to find.
5. *Minimum Maintenance*—Automatic lubrication and good accessibility. These cranes frequently are required to work 24 hours a day.
6. *Up-to-Date Styling*—Not really stressed by either agents or customers. It is, however, company policy to overcome the present image of a "strong, reliable and old-fashioned" manufacturer caused by the existence of a large number of 15–20 year old Brown Cranes.
7. *Basic Design Flexible*
   a) To provide for special job characteristics—e.g. high level cabs in ports.
   b) To cater for widely varying climates—e.g. dust and sand protection devices. Special lagging on hydraulic piping for cold climates.
   c) To cater for innumerable national and local government regulations. These can even be contradictory—e.g. in most countries a special lock is required to prevent free-fall lowering, so avoiding accidents to pedestrians. In Sweden and France, however, free-fall lowering must be possible. (If crane is tipping over the only sure preventive device is to drop the load on the jib.)
8. *Government Design Standards on Safety Devices and Strength*—usually cheapest to standardize on the most stringent requirements. This is not always possible as such standards can impose an unacceptable loss of performance specification.
9. *All Jibs are Fabricated in 20-ft. Lengths*—and are especially designed to ensure safe and convenient local assembly.

Source: Brown Cranes Limited Design Department Memo dated 1/70.

PROMOTION STRATEGY

Sales Force

Lying at the center of the company's promotional philosophy was an uncompromising belief in the importance of fluency in foreign languages. The director of Technical Development (overseas manufacture and design) spoke Spanish and Polish fluently. The Chairman and the Managing Director both spoke three languages and the Marketing Director five. Eighty-five percent of export staff were at the least bilingual (languages spoken depended to an extent upon area of operation—see below). The Head Office regularly handled correspondence in French, German, Spanish, Italian, Portuguese, and Czech.

The world was divided into 6 territories, each controlled by a senior sales officer (see Exhibit 3) who had overall responsibility for:

1. Relationship with agents.
2. Organization of visits by service personnel and coordination of technical representation (see Exhibit 2).
3. Coordination of all promotional techniques used by agents and issuance of all promotional leaflets made by Head Office (see below).

EXHIBIT 3. The Organization

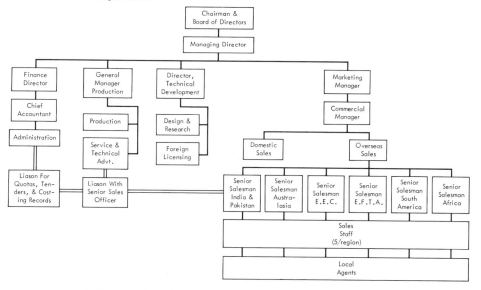

4. Preparation of quotes and tenders (bids) where necessary.
5. "Keeping in touch" with major customers and agents by travelling regularly in his area.

The extent to which Head Office Staff were in contact with agents in the field can be seen from Exhibit 4. Company executives attributed their success in overseas markets to this constant exchange of information and views between agents, customers and the senior representatives of the company. In the words of the marketing director, "If the chairman of your company is not prepared to fly to Ethiopia to secure a contract—you need a new chairman."

All sales staff were based in the UK, where they regularly attended training courses which exposed them to new promotional ideas, design changes, and new uses for Brown Cranes. A by-product of these courses was that junior salesmen

EXHIBIT 4. Table showing Extent of Foreign Travel Undertaken by Senior Executives and Members of Foreign Sales Staff (2 years)

Chairman	— Twice Round the World and other trips. Visited 34 countries
Managing Director	— Visited 28 countries.
General Manager (Plant)	— Visited 7 countries.
Director of Technical Development	— Visited 32 countries.
Marketing Director	— Since 1958 "double mile-million-aire". Has repeatedly visited over 75 countries.
Members of Export Sales Staff	— About 426 trips over the two year period. These staff stay on location often for extended periods.

were kept in relatively close contact, which ensured that a problem occurring in one area could be anticipated in others.

The Marketing Director defended this absence of local sales officers:

First, if one uses Englishmen, as is currently the case, it is cheaper for them to be based in England due to the high "foreign service allowances" required and the considerable expenses involved in moving a man and his whole family around the world. In addition, the system provides valuable flexibility. The alternative of using area Sales Headquarters and local sales staff is rejected on the grounds that a factory representative from England is more "acceptable" in, say, Peru than a Brazilian.

In general, therefore, the 35 sales personnel acted in a "staff" capacity, providing liaison between Head Office and agents around the world. The company considered that given such a large number of agents in so many countries, no other method of organization could achieve the required degree of flexibility, central control, and company-agent liaison for a given cost.

Other Promotional Devices

It is perhaps convenient to analyze the appropriation of promotional effort by examining each method separately—Costs of promotional efforts were borne by the head office. Distributor participation in promotional efforts was normally confined to the biggest dealers, for example the Swedish dealer. The different items developed are described below:

1. *"Range Leaflet."* A general leaflet showing colour photographs of entire range and brief details. Available in 14 languages.

2. *Detailed Leaflet on Each Individual Crane.* Again in colour, and available in 14 languages.

3. *A fully illustrated and technically detailed publication for each crane.* These were of exceptionally high quality and were very readable. Originally printed in 4 languages, they were made available in an unlimited range due to an ingenious technique of inserting transparent pages—so that diagrams etc. could be seen while English was replaced by the local language.

4. *Trade Brochures.* Introduced to meet the need for a descriptive brochure dealing with mobile crane application in a specific industry—Steelwork, timber, cargo handling (inc. ports), fuel, house construction, sugar industry.

This pamphlet was mailed to firms in appropriate industries to encourage the use of mobile cranes as a labour saving device. It was available in 5 languages.

The information for this brochure was obtained on notification by a salesman of a new use for a mobile crane. The company also had a policy of flying a technician to discuss any problem encountered by a customer. One example is the adaptation of a 30 ton mobile crane to handle containers which would normally have required a 50 ton dock-yard crane. The solution saved the customer about $70,000 and aroused considerable interest from other stevedores when included in the Cargo Trade Brochure the following month.

5. *Advertising.* Advertising was largely confined to Trade Journals and was not believed to be a particularly effective medium for an industrial product. Total advertising expenditure was around $50,000 and was usually confined to announcing company participation in a local Trade Fair (see below under direct mail).

6. *Film Shows and Refreshments.* Used quite frequently, and invariably at Trade Fairs.

Educational and publicity films made with magnetic sound track so that foreign language can be super-imposed.

7. *Demonstration Tours.* Bus equipped with literature and crane models is in constant use. Enthusiastic reception from agents so that consideration is now being given to the acquisition of a second one.

8. *Exhibition Programs and Participation in Trade Fairs.* The company regards these fairs as a major promotional device, due to the high proportion of visitors who are potential customers.

The stand is always well attended since mobile cranes fitted with maximum length jibs are always impressive and can be seen from every corner of the fair ground.

Represented at 15 fairs in 1969 (usually about 10).

9. *Company News Letter.* Circulated by direct mail bi-monthly to 8000 users and potential users. Since existing customers represent 60 percent of orders this is an effective medium. Brown Cranes also appear in every issue of the House magazine of the Holding Company whose circulation was 40,000.

10. *Crane Drivers Club—"The Jib."* Very successful club started about 1950. Contains stories and pictures of unusual loads and incidents in the operation of Brown cranes. Mailed to all users (one for each crane) monthly, and has had remarkably good response from drivers in many countries. The aim was to make Brown cranes popular with operators.

AFTER-SALES SERVICE

Since 60 percent of current orders were received from existing customers, the company felt that it was of the utmost importance that after-sales service be exceptionally good, particularly so because the company relied to a considerable extent on "word of mouth" promotion. Exhibit 5 shows the company's record.

All customers were encouraged to sign a contract servicing agreement with their local agent. This preventive maintenance is not only very profitable but also ensured satisfied customers.

The company employed a team of 10 highly skilled engineers who constantly traveled the world inspecting cranes, supervising overhauls, and giving technical advice. In addition, shortened courses were regularly held abroad for agents' mechanics, and customers' crane operators. These were free of charge.

EXHIBIT 5. Delivery Record of Spare Parts to Overseas Agents, 1969

Normal Requests

70% dispatched within 48 hours
15% dispatched within 2 weeks
15% over 2 weeks.
The delays on 30% of requests relate to orders for obsolete equipment,
which require special manufacture.
A special 24 hour delivery service direct to London Airport is available. All such
requests receive top priority over all other factory work.

Urgent Requests

80% left country on the same day
15% left country within 2 days
5% took longer than 2 days

PRICING POLICY

The agent was entirely free to set whatever selling price he thought was best. Factory prices varied from country to country based on the distance from England.

"Factory cost" was based upon ex-works price (cost + profit percentage) and the cost of shipment to the agent. It was company pricing policy to make this the minimum charge to the agent. In practice, the minimum price was offered to large agents who were stable, competitive, and who provided service. Smaller agents who did little or no servicing normally paid more than the minimum charge.

SOURCING AND MANUFACTURING POLICY

It was the policy of the Holding Company (The George Green Group) to avoid capital expenditures on foreign plant. However, licensing agreements had been signed with a Spanish and an Indian Company (due to prohibitive tariff barriers in these countries), an Australian Company (due to the distance from the U.K. to Australia) and a Polish Company (due to exchange unavailability as described earlier). A permanent factory representative was retained at each of the licensee manufacturing plants.

QUESTIONS

1. What are the major strengths and weaknesses of BCL's marketing program?
2. What changes, if any, would you recommend to BCL?

APPENDIX I
U.S. EXPORT CONTROL REGULATIONS

Export Control regulations specify which U.S. origin goods can move to which destination. In addition they attempt to insure that commodities, once exported, remain in the country of destination, unless otherwise authorized by the U.S. government.

Export controls were instituted under authority provided by the Export Control Act of 1948. The implementation of this legislation is the responsibility of the Bureau of International Commerce, U.S. Department of Commerce.

The controls were created for three reasons:

1. *National security* where the control of exports is deemed necessary for the security of the United States (i.e., denial of strategic goods to the USSR, Eastern Europe, or Mainland China).
2. *U.S. foreign policy* where controls augment the foreign policy of the United States (i.e., the embargo on goods to Southern Rhodesia).
3. *Short supply* where controls limit the loss of scarce materials from the domestic economy (i.e., nickel).

METHOD OF CONTROL

The U.S. government uses *licensing* to control the movement of commodities and technical data. The license is a statement of permission to export a specific commodity to a particular destination under limitations set forth in the license.

Commodities or technical data can be exported from the United States with the authorization of either a *general* or *validated* license. A *validated* license can only be obtained in response to a formal application whereas the *general* license does not require an application.

The exporter determines whether a particular commodity destined for a specific country requires a general or validated license. If the authorization requires a validated license the exporter must submit a formal application with certain supporting documents attached to the Department of Commerce. The application is reviewed on an individual basis which can take from three to six weeks or longer. If the application is approved, the exporter receives an *Export License* to export the commodity or technical data within the conditions specified by the license. If, however, the commodity qualifies under a general license authorization this means no application is required, that is, the goods are classified acceptable for export without individual consideration. In this case, the authorization is general so the Department of Commerce does not issue an individual license for the transaction.

Whether or not you need a validated license depends on the type of commodity being exported and the country of destination. In general, the more sophisticated the technology an item possesses, especially technology with military significance, the more likely it is to require a validated license. In order to classify countries the Department of Commerce divides them into eight groups, excluding the United States and Canada. The classification is made on the basis of the extent the U.S. government restricts the movement of commodities or technical data to a country. The more restrictive the movement the greater the number of commodities that will require a validated license and the more often denials of application will be issued.

In order to determine whether a commodity requires a validated license the exporter must consult the Commodity Control List (CCL) contained in the *U.S. Department of Commerce Export Control Regulations.* Country groups that require a validated license are listed by commodity.

PROCEDURE (VALIDATED LICENSE)

A U.S. exporter can apply for a Validated Export License by completing Department of Commerce form FC-419, *Application for Export License.* The form requests the names of the parties involved, a description of the commodity, the amount and value of the commodity to be exported, and of primary importance, the end use of the commodity in the country of destination. An application must be accompanied by additional documentation completed by the importer. The supporting documents are either an Import Certificate or a Single Transaction Statement (FC-842 or FC-843). To describe what form is appropriate necessitates some explanation.

IC/DV: The United States, along with Austria, Belgium, Denmark, France, Greece, Hong Kong, Italy, Japan, Luxembourg, Netherlands, Norway, Portugal, Turkey, United Kingdom, and West Germany, have agreed to participate in a mutual effort to prevent the unauthorized diversion of "strategic" commodities. The group of countries has accomplished this by an arrangement known as the IC/DV Procedure. The countries involved agreed on a common list of strategic commodities that all have agreed to control for each other. For example, if the United States exports to Turkey, the government of Turkey agrees to insure that the commodity does not leave Turkey unless authorized by the United States and vice versa. In the U.S. Commodity Control List each commodity is assigned an Export Commodity Control Number (ECC) and those commodities included in the IC/DV list are designated by an "A" after the ECC number. If the final destination for a good is an IC/DV country, the importer has to acquire an *Import Certificate* (IC) from his government. He supplies the foreign government with about the same information contained in the U.S. exporter's Application for Export License.

The foreign government issues the importer the Import Certificate which signifies he has registered the ensuing transaction with the foreign government. The effect is to obligate the importer to the conditions specified by the U.S. Export License or face the legal sanctions of the foreign government in addition to those applied by the U.S. government. After he receives the Import Certificate he sends the document to the U.S. exporter who attaches the Certificate to the Application for Export License and submits the application to the Department of Commerce. If the transaction is approved, the commodity is shipped, and then the foreign government follows up by verifying the delivery of the commodity to the approved destination with the stated end use. The foreign government then provides the U.S. Department of Commerce with a Delivery Verification (DV) statement.

Transaction Statement: In countries where the IC/DC Procedure is not used the importer has to fill out a *Transaction Statement.* Essentially it is a description of the transaction and a pledge by the importer to abide by the U.S.

Export Control regulations. Again this is returned to the U.S. exporter who attaches the Transaction Statement to the Application for Export License. If the importer violates the conditions of the license he is not subject to any legal sanctions in his home country as in the IC/DV countries. However, he is subject to sanctions applied by the U.S. government. If an importer violates the conditions of the license the U.S. government can deny the firm or individual the right to import from the United States, refuse visas for business travel in the United States, or deny AID assistance. These can be for a specified period or most common, for the duration of the U.S. Export Control Act. An important point to stress is if the firm is "blacklisted" (see list in Export Control Regulations) not only is the firm blacklisted but so are the principals. Once the goods are shipped, in some instances, personnel from the U.S. consulate will verify the delivery and end use of the commodity.

License: After the Application for Export License and supporting documentation have been received by the U.S. Department of Commerce, the application is reviewed and if approved a license is issued to the U.S. exporter. The goods are moved to a U.S. Customs location. To certify that the goods are approved for export the U.S. Customs official must receive the Export License, and a *Shippers Export Declaration.* These two documents do not leave the United States but are returned by the customs official to the Department of Commerce. The Shippers Export Declaration contains essentially the same information as supplied in the Application or the Export License. The purpose of the Declaration is to provide the Bureau of the Census with accurate statistical data on exports for balance of payments compilation and other purposes.

Destination Control Statement: Since the license and "Export Dec" do not move with the goods a *Destination Control Statement* is required to be entered on the bill of lading or airway bill and the commercial invoice. These statements notify the foreign customs officials the approved destination and that they are moving under license. For a validated license Statements 1 or 2 may be used. For a general license shipment any of the three may be used.

Statement 1.
"These (commodities) (technical data) licensed by the United States for ultimate destination (name of country). Diversion contrary to U.S. law prohibited."

Statement 2.
"These (commodities) (technical data) licensed by the United States for ultimate destination (name of country) and for distribution or resale in (name of country). Diversion contrary to U.S. law prohibited."

Statement 3.
"United States' law prohibits disposition of these commodities to the Soviet Bloc, Communist China, North Korea, Macao, Hong Kong, Communist controlled areas of Vietnam, Cuba, Southern Rhodesia, unless otherwise authorized by the United States."

RE-EXPORT

What if the importer desires to re-export? This can be handled in two ways. First, if the importer knows he wants to re-export at the time of application he can have it specified in the application. The license will be approved or

EXHIBIT 1. Country Groups

Group S	Southern Rhodesia	Most restrictive
Group Z	Communist China, North Korea, Communist-controlled areas of Vietnam and Cuba	
Group Y	Albania, Bulgaria, Czechoslovakia, East Germany (Soviet Zone of Germany and East Berlin), Estonia, Hungary, Latvia, Lithuania, Outer Mongolia, and the USSR	
Group W	Poland	
Group Q	Rumania	
Group X	Hong Kong and Macao	
Group V	All other countries, except Canada	
Group T	All countries of the Western Hemisphere, except Cuba	
		Least Restrictive

Note: Canada is not included in any country group since exports to that country are normally not controlled.

denied with the provision for re-export considered. The second situation is where, after export to a foreign destination, it is desired to re-export, the importer can apply for permission to re-export. The procedure is to complete a Request To Dispose of Commodities or Technical Data Previously Exported (1a-1145) which he can submit directly to the Department of Commerce or, most common, send it to the original U.S. exporter who submits it for approval. Upon approval by the Department of Commerce, the importer receives a license to re-export.

CONCLUSION

The Export Control Program has as its purpose the control of the use of U.S. commodities or technical data. To facilitate the movement of U.S. commodities the program provides 19 different types of General Licenses, means to amend licenses, procedures for emergency clearance, and other services. The best reference to ascertain the most appropriate method to export within the Export Control Regulations is to review *U.S. Department of Commerce, Export Control Regulations,* Supt. of Documents, Government Printing Office, Washington D.C., 20402, $20. The Regulations are also available for reference at any Department of Field Office, or at Columbia in the Watson Library, Columbia Graduate School of Business.

APPENDIX II

EIGHTEEN POINTERS TO MAKE YOUR
TRADE FAIR EXHIBIT MORE PRODUCTIVE

Exhibiting and selling abroad take the same advance planning, market research, attention to detail and hard work that result in successful show-and-sell events at home.

Before you decide to exhibit overseas, consider these valuable tips from experienced trade promotion specialists and seasoned exhibitors:

Decide Your Business Objectives before You Enter the Show

Why do you want to exhibit? Are you looking for on-the-spot sales or new customers? Do you want to introduce a new product or service? Do you want to find agents or distributors? Are you interested in joining venture or licensing arrangements? Perhaps you want to exhibit in order to gain exposure or study the market.

Select a Market with Care

Study the market before you enter an overseas trade show.

Exhibit Your Newest Product

Foreign customers want to see and buy your latest and best products. Don't show outdated merchandise.

Prepare Ahead

Give yourself plenty of time—up to 12 months—to prepare for an overseas trade fair. Remember, an outstanding exhibit cannot be put together overnight. You'll want ample time to contact prospective sales representatives and customers—through direct mail, advertising and personal calls—to invite them to visit your booth.

Learn All You Can about the Specific Fair

When you enter a foreign trade show, make certain you know all its rules, exhibiting hours, utility requirements and services and facilities available for your use.

Send a Decision-Maker to the Fair

Your man at the fair should be a decision-maker who knows your marketing goals. If you are exhibiting technical equipment, send along an engineer to explain the nuts-and-bolts.

Arrive Early, Stay Late

Plan to arrive at the fair site a few days before the show opens to be sure your booth is in order and exhibits are operating. If you can spare the time, stay over for a week or two after the fair ends in order to follow through with new leads.

Business and Pleasure Don't Mix

Exhibiting at trade fairs is serious business. Man your booth at all times—empty booths don't sell. Give your full attention to the visitor—he may be your next customer.

Don't Forget Advertising

While many exhibitors buy advertising space in the catalogs published by the sponsors of international trade fairs, it is good business to place an attractive ad in leading overseas trade journals and business periodicals before the fair opens. Invite the reader to view your product at the fair; tell him the location of your booth. You could also consider direct mail invitations to selected key prospects. Mailing lists can be obtained from trade organizations, agencies, publications, chambers of commerce, and government sources.

Learn Foreign Business Practices

Familiarize yourself with foreign business practices before you take a trip abroad. Check such things as local holidays, vacation, and seasonal market periods.

Select a Good Overseas Distributor

If possible, it's a good idea to line up a distributor before the fair. He can familiarize himself with your products and your organization during the exhibition and, of course, he will have an opportunity to meet and establish contacts with prospective customers who visit your booth.

Give Distributors Samples of Your Products

Confucius said that a picture is worth a thousand words; but once you have named your distributor, a sample of your product for him to show prospective customers will generate far more sales than a picture in a sales catalog.

Quote Full Prices

Be prepared to quote CIF (cost, insurance, freight) prices to your foreign buyers. An FOB price has little, if any, significance in international trading. Also be prepared to set delivery dates.

Service Your Foreign Customer

The quickest way to lose business is to fail to provide service. Once you make a sale, be prepared to provide complete service and fast delivery of spare parts.

Give Specifications in the Metric System

The English-speaking nations are out of step with the world when it comes to measurements. Most of the world uses the metric system. Be prepared to provide metric conversion tables applicable to your equipment.

Leap the Language Barrier

Have your sales literature, catalogs, specifications, and advertising prepared in the language of the country. Hire professional translators and interpreters. Learn a language yourself.

What about Credit and Payment?

Second payment policies for export accounts are little different from domestic policies. You should, of course, be concerned about credit standings of your foreign representatives. Consult the international department of your bank and other private credit agencies. You'll also want to look into government-sponsored credit risk insurance which offers low-cost protection against credit losses—commercial and political—as further incentive to spur world trade.

Protect Your Patents and Trademark Rights

If you own valuable patents and trademarks, you should get advance counsel from your patent attorney on extending this protection to overseas markets. Most nations offer some protection on patents and trademarks.

Source: International Trade Fairs, 1970, Pan American World Airways, Inc. Adapted by author. Used by permission.

part five

PLANNING, ORGANIZING, AND CONTROLLING THE MULTINATIONAL PROGRAM

multinational marketing planning

> One does not plan and then try to make circumstances
> fit these plans. One tries to make plans fit
> the circumstances.
>
> *General George Patton*

INTRODUCTION

This chapter focuses on the integration of each element of the marketing mix into a total plan that responds to expected opportunities and threats in the global marketing environment. In the international firm, marketing planning must be conducted not only at the national level but also at one or more headquarters levels. The challenge is the integration of national, regional, and international plans into an overall plan that best utilizes organizational resources to exploit global opportunities.

WHAT KIND OF INTERNATIONAL PLAN?

Standardized

A standardized multinational marketing plan offers a number of advantages. First of all, there are significant cost savings if standardization is practiced. A company that limits the number of models and variants of its product can achieve longer production runs and much greater economies of scale. This is elementary and has been demonstrated in actual practice thousands of times over. Henry Ford was probably the first industrialist to demonstrate the potential of mass production for achieving scale economies and creating a national market. Similarly, the Italian appliance industry during the 1960s achieved remarkable cost reduction through standardization and long production runs and in the process took a leadership position in Europe. Of course, cost savings can be achieved not only in production but also in packaging, in distribution, and in the creation of advertising materials.

There are other benefits of standardization. In an increasingly mobile world a standardized product is the same in every national market and is therefore uniform for increasing numbers of customers who travel across national boundaries. There are pressures today to standardize products so that the customer can develop standardized programs in its operations. Another benefit of standardization is that it extends successful products and good ideas into all markets.

There are, however, a number of obstacles to standardization. Market characteristics may be so different in so many major ways that it is impossible to offer a standardized product. There is simply no significant market in Europe for the 3,500–4,000 pound, 120" wheel base U.S. automobile. It is too big to fit in the streets, it consumes too much gasoline, it costs too much to license, and it does not appeal to the European sense of style. American automobile manufacturers who wish to compete in more than a very minor segment of the European market must adapt their product or develop entirely new products to suit the market preferences that exist within the European market. In cases where the same product can be sold, other elements of the marketing mix can be obstacles to standardization because of environmental differences or differences in company position. For example, consider the company whose market share position is quite different from market to market. Although other characteristics in markets may be relatively similar, different market share positions make standardization of promotional and pricing decisions extremely difficult. Where the local position is commanding, an advertising message that expands the total market for the product category will benefit the dominant company. But the same company may have a minor position in an adjoining market where its advertising strategy should be to obtain a share of the market for its particular product.

Decentralized

Many companies have followed a decentralized planning approach either as a result of poor results using the standardized approach or after noting the many differences from country to country in market environments. This approach has received perhaps more support in marketing than any other functional area. An executive of a major international company expressed what is probably a representative view: "Marketing is conspicuous by its absence from the functions which can be planned at the corporate headquarters level. It is in this phase of overseas business activity that the variations in social patterns and the subtlety of local conditions have the most pronounced effect on basic business strategy and tactics. For this reason, the responsibility for marketing planning must be carried out by those overseas executives who are most familiar with the local environment."[1]

A common feature of both the standardized and the decentralized approaches

---

[1] Millard H. Pryor, "Planning in a Worldwide Business," *Harvard Business Review*, January-February 1965.

is the absence of responsibility for analysis and planning at the headquarters level for multicountry marketing programs. In the standardized case such activities are assumed to be unnecessary. Once the marketing problem is solved for the United States, or the home country, it is solved for the world. In the decentralized company the need for analysis and planning to respond to local conditions is recognized, but it is assumed that knowledgeable efforts can only be attempted at the country level and that there is no opportunity for effective supranational participation in these activities.

International

A third approach to formulating an international marketing plan is the interactive, or international, approach. This is superior to either the standardized or the local plan because it draws on the strengths of each of these approaches in planning to formulate a synthesis. Under the interactive marketing planning approach, subsidiaries are responsible for identifying the major unique characteristics of their market and ensuring that the marketing plan fully responds to local characteristics.

Headquarters, both international and regional, is responsible for establishing a broad strategic framework for planning in such matters as deciding on major goals and objectives and on where to allocate resources. In addition, headquarters must coordinate and rationalize the product design, advertising, pricing, and distribution activities of each subsidiary operation. Headquarters must constantly be alert to the trade-offs of concentrating staff activities at headquarters locations in an attempt to achieve a high level of performance versus the advantages of decentralizing staff activities and assigning people directly to subsidiaries. Each decision must stand on its own merit, but international marketers are concluding that there are significant opportunities for the improvement of performance and cost saving by concentrating certain activities at headquarters locations. For example, as discussed in Chapter 14, some companies have already successfully centralized the preparation of advertising appeals and creative material at regional headquarters. Indeed the international approach to planning is practiced most frequently at the regional level because as compared to the world there is greater within-group similarity in a region.

Current Planning Practices

In a study of eighty-six separate marketing programs in nine U.S.-based multinational companies, R. J. Aylmer found that local management plays a vital role in the development of marketing programs.[2] In his sample, subsidiaries were responsible for 86 percent of advertising decisions, 74 percent of pricing decisions, and 61 percent of channel decisions. (See Table 16-1.) However, decisions concerning product design were imposed or jointly made with headquarters

[2]R. J. Aylmer, "Who Makes Decisions in the Multinational Firm?" *Journal of Marketing,* October 1970.

TABLE 16-1. Degree of Local Management Autonomy Classified According to Type of Local Marketing Decision[a]

Degree of Local Management Autonomy	Local Marketing Decision			
	Product Design	Adver-tising Approach	Retail Price	Distribution Outlets/'000 Population
Primary authority rested with local management	30%	86%	74%	61%
Local management shared authority with other levels in organization	15%	8%	20%	38%
Decision primarily imposed upon local management	55%	6%	6%	1%
	100%	100%	100%	100%
N (Marketing programs observed)	N = 86	N = 84[b]	N = 84[b]	N = 86

[a]For Western European affiliates of 9 U.S. based manufacturers.
[b]Classification information not available in two cases.

Source: Aylmer, *"Who Makes Decisions in the Multinational Firm?" p. 26.*

in 70 percent of the programs studied. Thus the key and strategic decisions regarding product design and performance characteristics were largely controlled or even dominated by headquarters, whereas the final task of developing a viable local strategy was left to local management.

In addition to environmental forces, Aylmer found that organizational factors affect location of authority for marketing decisions. The most important of these factors are the relative importance of the firm's international operations and the relative importance of the local affiliate's position within the firm. As a firm's international sales as a percentage of total sales increase, top management becomes increasingly involved as a participant in local decision making. In addition, as the size of local affiliates grows, the frequency of imposed decisions as opposed to shared decisions with headquarters declines. These patterns of development are consistent with the normative planning model suggested in this chapter. As companies grow and become increasingly sophisticated, they develop planning methods that draw on both local and international perspectives. This is international as opposed to standardized or decentralized planning.

Sorenson and Weichmann, in a survey of one hundred senior executives in twenty-seven leading multinationals in consumer package goods industries, found that on their index 63 percent of the total marketing programs were judged to be highly standardized.[3] The idea of standardization for the other elements of the marketing mix in the Sorenson and Weichmann study are shown in Figure 16-1.

[3]Ralph Z. Sorenson and Ulrich Weichmann, "How Multinationals View Marketing Standardization," *Harvard Business Review,* May-June 1975, pp. 38ff.

Elements of marketing program | Percent of total number of paired countries showing comparisons (rounded off)

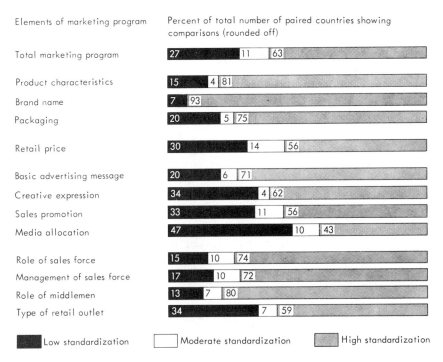

FIGURE 16-1. Index of Standardization of Marketing Decisions among European Subsidiaries of Selected Multinational Enterprises

Source: Sorenson and Weichmann, "How Multinationals View Marketing Standardization," p. 39.

The highest degree of standardization observed was in product physical characteristics, brand names, and packaging. In addition to advantages of longer production runs, executives mentioned the advantages of better international legal and trademark protection and the intangible advantages of having a worldwide as opposed to a merely national brand franchise. This is increasingly valuable as consumers become more mobile.

In contrast to product decisions, pricing decisions are much less standardized. Manufacturing costs, competitors' prices, taxes, company market position, tariffs and duties, and so on, vary from country to country making it extremely difficult to standardize prices.

In advertising and promotion, Sorenson and Weichmann found that almost three-quarters of the advertising messages had been highly standardized but that the frequency of standardization for media allocation was much lower. The explanation for this difference is the fact that advertising media availability varies considerably among countries.

The major finding, however, of the Sorenson-Weichmann study is that the real competitive advantage of the multinational company comes not from the extent to which it is able to standardize marketing programs but rather the extent to which it is able to standardize the marketing process. To the successful multinational, it is not really important whether marketing programs are internationally standardized or differentiated; what is important is that the process by which these programs are developed is standardized. A standardized process provides a disciplined framework for analyzing marketing problems and opportunities. It also provides a framework for the cross pollination of experience, ideas, and judgments from one market to another. Sorenson and Weichmann quote a headquarters executive:

> A total standardization of all the elements of the marketing mix is hardly thinkable. On the other hand, the intellectual method used for approaching a marketing problem, for analyzing that problem, and for synthesizing information in order to arrive at a decision, can absolutely be standardized on an international basis.
>
> It is desirable that marketing decisions be as decentralized as possible toward the field of economic battle. Nevertheless, if decision-making is done in each country according to the same intellectual process, it can be more easily understood by headquarters management: a standard process eliminating guesses in the subjective side of marketing permits one to arrive more easily at the standardization of certain elements of the marketing mix.[4]

PLANNING FOR MULTINATIONAL BRANDS[5]

One of the greatest potential strengths of a multinational brand is that better marketing decisions can be made by drawing upon a broad base of experience accumulated under different national conditions. Most valuable brand information is lost in a sea of records, but imaginative analysis of such information, and the development of new information systems, can make a wealth of information available for marketing planning.

One planning technique is the development of multinational cost and profit breakdowns. This technique requires the application of consistent cost and allocation criteria. One system in general use is "relevant costing" where all revenues and costs attributable to a brand, that is, revenues and costs that would not exist were the brand to disappear, are included in estimates. While it is an important first step to decide upon a standard system, it is important to ensure that it is being used in a uniform way. For example, free credit to the trade or free samples are sometimes not costed as relevant costs. Once this has been accomplished, the brand position can be displayed as in Figures 16-2 and 16-3.

These types of displays allow the international planner to consider for both short- and long-term periods something beyond trying to increase sales and market share in every country where the multinational brand is established. Analysis of potential payoff may point to concentration of funds in a limited number of more responsive national markets.

[4] Ibid., p. 54.
[5] Adapted from C.G.F. Nuttall, "Profit Planning for Multinational Brands," *International Advertiser*, 13, No. 1 (Winter 1972), 7-11.

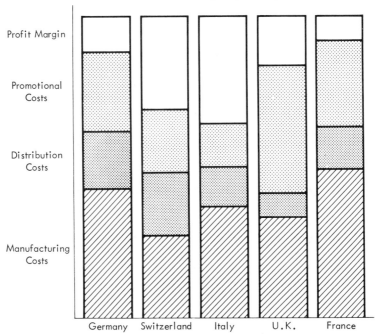

BRAND X

Breakdown of Marketing Costs and Profit Margins by Country.

Profit Margin

Promotional Costs

Distribution Costs

Manufacturing Costs

Germany Switzerland Italy U.K. France

FIGURE 16-2.

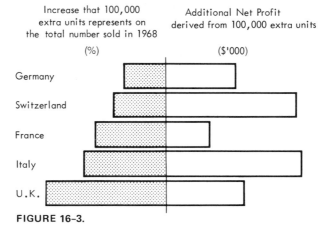

BRAND X

Increase that 100,000 extra units represents on the total number sold in 1968

Additional Net Profit derived from 100,000 extra units

(%)   ($'000)

Germany

Switzerland

France

Italy

U.K.

FIGURE 16-3.

REQUIREMENTS FOR A SUCCESSFUL INTERNATIONAL MARKETING PLAN

The successful international marketing plan is an integrated set of effective national marketing plans. Each national marketing plan must be based upon three types of information:

1. Knowledge of the market—of customers, competitors, the government, and so on
2. Knowledge of the product—its technology, its applications in various customer settings, and so on
3. Knowledge of the marketing function

Information or knowledge about the market in itself must come from people who are assigned to that market. Normally, this is the staff of the local operating subsidiary. Product knowledge is closely associated with engineers and production managers. For most industrial products, knowledge becomes very important part of the advertising and selling program for the product. For many customer products, technical information is not important to the buyer and therefore need not necessarily be combined or associated with advertising and selling activities. The third major input of a successful marketing plan is knowledge of the marketing function, including the analytic and conceptual tools of marketing.

A multinational company must decide how it will obtain these three key types of knowledge on a global basis. It must also decide how it will assign responsibility for formulating a marketing plan. If plan formulation is assigned to national subsidiaries, the international headquarters must ensure that the subsidiary planners are fully informed on the technical and engineering characteristics of the product as well as being up to date in their functional skills. One of the ways of doing this is to involve headquarters marketing staff specialists in the planning process so that they can ensure that the highest standard of product and functional knowledge is associated with the local marketing staff's market knowledge.

Thus the international plan is neither the product of the subsidiary nor the product of headquarters. It is neither "top down" nor "bottom up" but rather an interactive product that combines inputs from both the global and the local perspective. This balance is essential if the plan is to approximate the objective of global optimization as opposed to national suboptimization.

The international plan should be initiated by a global overview that attempts to assess the broad nature of opportunity and threat on a global basis and attempts to break down this assessment on a country-by-country basis with an indication of sales and earnings expectations for each country. These expectations are proposed by headquarters as guidance to each country subsidiary for the formulation of country plans. Guidance, when properly utilized, should be nothing more than guidance. If a subsidiary concludes that headquarters guidance is unrealistic, it should openly challenge headquarters and the challenge should produce a dialogue that searches for the realistic target.

After receiving guidance from headquarters, subsidiaries need to search for programs that in the context of the company's areas of operation will achieve the targets specified by the guidance. After preparing their plans, headquarters and subsidiaries come together to negotiate an agreement. Headquarters is seeking top performance from each subsidiary *and* the integration of its global plan. If a subsidiary is a supplier for home and third-country markets, production schedules and transfer prices must be agreed upon. If a subsidiary is to market a product produced elsewhere in the company, the sales and delivery plans must be coordinated. The subsidiary is seeking approval of a plan that it feels it can attain.

Key Questions for Global Marketing Planning

Figure 16-4 relates strategic and operational planning to analysis and control of a global marketing program and suggests ten key questions that should be addressed in the preparation of an international plan. The most important questions on the list are the first two: Who should make the decisions concerning each element of the plan? and What our key assumptions about target markets? Head-

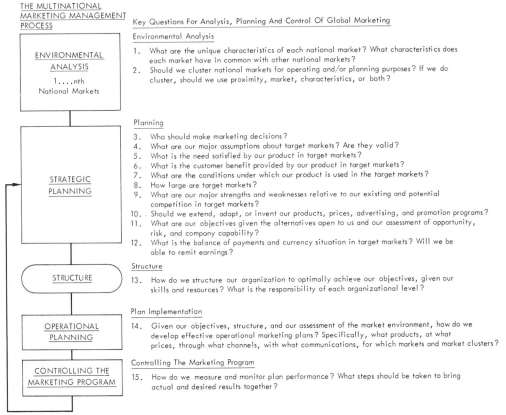

THE MULTINATIONAL
MARKETING MANAGEMENT
PROCESS

Key Questions For Analysis, Planning And Control Of Global Marketing

Environmental Analysis

ENVIRONMENTAL
ANALYSIS

1....nth
National Markets

1. What are the unique characteristics of each national market? What characteristics does each market have in common with other national markets?
2. Should we cluster national markets for operating and/or planning purposes? If we do cluster, should we use proximity, market, characteristics, or both?

Planning

STRATEGIC
PLANNING

3. Who should make marketing decisions?
4. What are our major assumptions about target markets? Are they valid?
5. What is the need satisfied by our product in target markets?
6. What is the customer benefit provided by our product in target markets?
7. What are the conditions under which our product is used in the target markets?
8. How large are target markets?
9. What are our major strengths and weaknesses relative to our existing and potential competition in target markets?
10. Should we extend, adapt, or invent our products, prices, advertising, and promotion programs?
11. What are our objectives given the alternatives open to us and our assessment of opportunity, risk, and company capability?
12. What is the balance of payments and currency situation in target markets? Will we be able to remit earnings?

Structure

STRUCTURE

13. How do we structure our organization to optimally achieve our objectives, given our skills and resources? What is the responsibility of each organizational level?

Plan Implementation

OPERATIONAL
PLANNING

14. Given our objectives, structure, and our assessment of the market environment, how do we develop effective operational marketing plans? Specifically, what products, at what prices, through what channels, with what communications, for which markets and market clusters?

Controlling The Marketing Program

CONTROLLING THE
MARKETING PROGRAM

15. How do we measure and monitor plan performance? What steps should be taken to bring actual and desired results together?

FIGURE 16-4. A Conceptual Framework for Multinational Marketing

quarters and subsidiaries must work together to answer these questions for each national market and for the international market.

GROUPING WORLD MARKETS FOR PRODUCT PLANNING

The large number of countries in the world (at present count, more than 140) demands some simplified grouping of markets for planning purposes.[6] A number of efforts to group world markets have been undertaken, most recently using factor and cluster analysis.[7] These efforts have been useful, but they are limited by their reliance on historical data that do not reflect the concerns of the practicing product planner about the future. To fill this gap, the author has developed a typology based on five criteria: market size, market accessibility, stage of market development, present and future prospects for growth, and political risk. The use of these criteria has resulted in the eighteen-cell matrix shown in Table 16–2.

The use of this matrix requires analysis of countries to categorize them according to their market accessibility and expected rate of future growth. Market accessibility will vary from company to company because of product differences, and expected future growth must necessarily reflect judgmental evaluation of country prospects. It is beyond the scope of this book to engage in this kind of detailed analysis. However, to give the reader an idea of the order of magnitude of the various categories in the typology, we have, by using the 1975 *World Bank Atlas,* assigned the 125 countries of the world with populations of more than one million to matrix categories using the following criteria:

1. Industrial countries: All countries except OPEC members with a GNP per capita of more than $1,000. Eastern Bloc planned economies in this range are shown separately.
2. Industrializing countries: All countries with a GNP per capita between $500 and $1,000, plus OPEC members with higher and lower GNPs per capita.
3. Promising less-developed countries: All countries with GNP per capita between $130 and $500, excluding OPEC members.
4. Unpromising less-developed countries: All countries with a GNP per capita less than $130.

The results of this exercise are shown in Table 16–2.

The Existing Markets: Industrial Countries

As Table 16–2 clearly reveals, the greatest opportunity in the world today lies in the industrial countries, particularly in the Western market economies. These

[6] This section is adapted from Warren J. Keegan, "New Myths and Old Realities," in *Multinational Product Management,* ed. Warren J. Keegan and Charles S. Mayer (New York: American Marketing Association, 1977).

[7] See, for example, Eugene D. Jaffe, *Grouping: A Strategy for International Marketing* (New York: American Management, 1974); and S. Prakash Sethi, "Comparative Cluster Analysis for World Markets," *Journal of Marketing Research,* 8 (August 1971), 348–54.

TABLE 16-2. World Markets for Product Planning—1973 Countries with Populations of One Million or More 1973 GNP (U.S. $ Thousands)

Typology Category	Large-Scale Economies GNP: > $100 Billion		Medium-Scale Economies GNP: $25–100 Billion		Small-Scale Economies GNP: < $25 Billion		Total		
	GNP	No.	GNP	No.	GNP	No.	GNP	No.	%
1. *Industrial countries*									
a. Western market economies	$2,690,220	7	$424,250	10	$ 109,450	11	$3,223,920	28	57
b. Eastern Bloc planned economies	506,490	1	162,530	3	54,190	3	723,210	7	13
2. *Industrializing countries*									
a. OPEC countries	—	0	27,830	1	47,310	4	75,140	5	1
b. Other industrializing countries	—	0	126,780	2	83,430	15	210,210	17	4
3. *Promising less-developed countries*	216,750	1	—	0	149,320	42	366,070	43	7
4. *Unpromising less-developed countries*	—	0	71,590	1	948,500	24	1,020,090	25	18
Total	$3,413,460	9	$812,980	17	$1,392,200	99	$5,618,640	125	100

Data source: World Bank Atlas (Washington, D.C., 1975). Table prepared by author.

countries not only represent the biggest markets but are also the most stable politically. Their political stability is assured by two forces. The first is the tendency of prosperous countries to prefer centrist government and rule of law as a strategy for keeping and building on what they have. Even in countries like France, which has a propensity to indulge in left-of-center political rhetoric, there is a realization that centrist policies have resulted in economic success and prosperity. This same rule explains at least part of the underlying support of successful non-democratic governments in countries like the USSR. A second force that limits the tendency of these countries to apply discriminatory policies to "foreign" enterprise is the fact that most of these countries are the home base for companies who have invested abroad and who in effect have created national hostages in the form of their own foreign investment position. Where this is not the case, as in Canada, there is an absence of countervailing pressure to limit nationalist policies and restrictions and a tendency for nationalist and discriminatory government actions directed toward "foreign" enterprise.

As the process of economic convergence between the East and West continues, we expect an accompanying expansion of trade and investment or investment-equivalent opportunities in the East. As Eastern economies continue to decentralize, it is likely that they will become increasingly successful in competing in Western markets; this will enable them to expand their Western purchases. At some point, Eastern companies will no doubt wish to strengthen their position in Western markets through investments in marketing and, eventually, even in manufacturing. When this interest develops, and is expressed, presently unimagined solutions to the obstacles to equity investment in Eastern countries will no doubt emerge. To be sure, this equity investment will probably not be called by that name, but the control and claim on income associated with equity investment could be obtained without the legal form of equity, thereby overcoming ideological objections to private ownership.

Important Potential: The Industrializing Countries

The rapidly industrializing countries, those whose real growth exceeds 5 percent per annum, present interesting risk-reward trade-offs. The present market size of countries with major potential, such as Brazil, is actually no larger than the increase in GNP in a single good year in the United States. The economic importance of countries like Brazil lies more in their potential than in their present size. If they successfully transform their economies and in effect thrust themselves into the industrial country class, they will then acquire both the market size and the political stability associated with industrial countries. If they do not succeed, they will probably become politically risky and economically stagnant.

Some Prospects: The Promising Less-Developed Countries

The promising less-developed countries are countries with prospects for future growth who have not yet demonstrated their ability to achieve sustained real growth in excess of 5 percent per annum. They have attracted fewer foreign investors and spawned fewer local entrepreneurs than faster-growing countries; therefore, their markets are typically less competitive than those of the rapidly industrializing countries. The payoff in these countries will materialize if they successfully achieve the status of a rapidly industrializing country and then eventually enter the industrial category. The risk is that they will fail or falter in their industrialization process and will react to their problems in ways that damage the quality of their business environment.

Few Prospects: The Unpromising Less-Developed Countries

The unpromising less-developed countries are those countries whose problems, either natural or man-made, seem to preclude any medium-term prospect for successful industrialization. These countries, by definition, are uninteresting investment opportunities. They need help, but the kind of help they need cannot realistically be provided by private investors responsible to shareholders for return on investment. They have small local markets with no prospect for significant growth, and their political stability is constantly being threatened by their lack of economic success.

The importance of developing countries to multinational manufacturing companies is largely a myth. As has been the case throughout human history, the poor of the world outnumber the rich.

PLANNING CONCEPTS

Competence Centers

A competence center is an organizational unit in a company that is designated the most sophisticated and experienced location in the company for the marketing or manufacture of a product. As the most sophisticated location of marketing or manufacturing know-how in the organization, the competence center is responsible for transferring this know-how to designated new markets. The competence center may be an operating unit anywhere in the world. The idea of the competence center is to get away from the traditional pattern of headquarters subsidiary relationships and allow direct subsidiary-to-subsidiary transfer of skill and know-how. Competence centers can be utilized to draw upon the experience of subsidiaries that have taken the responsibility for developing, producing, and marketing new products. Once the subsidiaries have successfully demonstrated their ability to manage a new product, rather than channel their experience through headquarters, the subsidiary can be designated as a competence center and given direct responsibility for transferring their know-how. Obviously, if such a practice is followed, it is necessary to provide adequate incentives and rewards to subsidiaries for carrying out the transfer effectively.

The basic idea behind the competence center is that competence in a multinational company can be globally dispersed. It can be a part of the international plan to develop product X in country Y and then to transfer country Y's experience directly to other markets without channeling it through a headquarters intermediary.

Orientation and Multinational Marketing Planning

The basic orientation of management toward international business is an important influence on planning.[8] A management group that assumes that all markets are alike and that its major source of competence and ability is in the home market is going to pursue a basically ethnocentric approach to multinational marketing because its assumptions will lead it to this approach. Conversely, a management that assumes that each national market is so different that they are effectively unique and therefore unrelated to any other national market is going to pursue a polycentric approach to international marketing planning because its assumptions demand such an approach. We have argued that neither the ethnocentric nor the polycentric assumptions are applicable to today's global market environment and that the effective manager will pursue a synthesis of the approaches, which can be termed geocentric. The geocentric assumption is that there are major differences from country to country and that these differences are important in the formulation of a national marketing plan, but at the same time there are important similarities among markets and these similarities must be recognized in order to develop an effective integrated and coordinated international marketing plan that maximizes the profitability of a worldwide marketing effort.

BIBLIOGRAPHY

BOOKS

Skinner, Wickham, *The Management of International Manufacturing.* New York: John Wiley, 1968.

Steiner, George A., and Warren M. Cannon, *Multinational Corporate Planning.* New York: Macmillan, 1966.

ARTICLES

Aylmer, R. J., "Who Makes Marketing Decisions in the Multinational Firm?" *Journal of Marketing,* October 1970.

Berg, Norman, "Strategic Planning in Conglomerate Companies," *Harvard Business Review,* May-June 1965.

[8] Howard V. Perlmutter, "The Tortuous Evolution of the Multinational Corporation," *Columbia Journal of World Business,* January-February 1969, pp. 9-18.

Brandt, W. K., and J. M. Hulbert, "Patterns of Communications in Multinational Corporations: An Empirical Study," *Journal of International Business Studies,* Spring 1976, pp. 57–64.

Buzzell, Robert D., "Can You Standardize Multinational Marketing?" *Harvard Business Review,* November-December 1968.

Cain, W. W., "International Planning: Mission Impossible?" *Columbia Journal of World Business,* July-August 1970.

Franko, Lawrence G., "Who Manages Multinational Enterprise?" *Columbia Journal of World Business,* 8 (Spring 1973), 30–42.

Goldman, Irwin, "The Special Problems of International Long Range Planning," *Management Review,* April 1965.

Keegan, Warren J., "Multinational Marketing: The Headquarters Role," *Columbia Journal of World Business,* January-February 1971.

Kuin, Pieter, "The Magic of Multinational Management," *Harvard Business Review,* November-December 1972, pp. 89–97.

Lorange, Peter, "Formal Planning in Multinational Corporations," *Columbia Journal of World Business,* 8 (Summer 1973), 83–87.

Perlmutter, Howard V., "The Tortuous Evolution of the Multinational Corporation," *Columbia Journal of World Business,* January-February 1969.

Pryor, Millard H., "Planning in a Worldwide Business," *Harvard Business Review,* January-February 1965.

Schollhammer, Hans, "Long Range Planning in Multinational Firms," *Columbia Journal of World Business,* September-October 1971.

Schwendiman, John S., "International Strategic Planning: Still in Its Infancy?" *Worldwide P & I Planning,* September-October 1971, pp. 52–61.

Sorenson, Ralph Z., and Ulrich E. Weichmann, "How Multinationals View Marketing Standardization," *Harvard Business Review,* May-June 1975, pp. 38–56.

POLAROID FRANCE (S.A.)
MARKETING PLANNING IN A MULTINATIONAL COMPANY

In July 1967, M. Jacques Dumon, General Manager of Polaroid France (S.A.), was preparing a preliminary marketing plan for 1968. M. Dumon was scheduled to present his proposals to the marketing executives at the headquarters office of the American parent firm, Polaroid Corporation, in September. Following this review, a final version of the plan would be adopted as a basis for Polaroid's operations in France during the forthcoming year.

In preparing his recommendations for 1968, M. Dumon was especially concerned with problems of pricing and promotion for the Model 20 "Swinger" camera. The Swinger had been introduced in France during the fall of 1966, and was the first Polaroid Land Camera available to French consumers at a retail price under NF 300.[1] Sales of the Swinger during 1966 and early 1967 had not reached expected levels, and M. Dumon was aware that the basic attitude of headquarters management toward overseas operations in 1968 was cautious, because Polaroid's unconsolidated foreign subsidiaries had incurred a combined loss of $907,000 in 1966. He recognized, therefore, that all proposals for 1968 would be subject to extremely careful scrutiny.

COMPANY BACKGROUND

Polaroid Corporation, with headquarters in Cambridge, Massachusetts, produced a wide line of photographic and related products for household and business uses, including cameras, film, photographic equipment, polarizing products, and X-ray products. Total 1966 sales in the United States amounted to $316.5 million, more than three times the amount of business done in 1962. Worldwide sales in 1966, including Polaroid's 13 subsidiaries, totaled $363 million. A summary of sales and profits for the period 1950–1966 is given in Exhibit 1.

The company was founded in 1937 by Dr. Edwin H. Land to produce polarizing products, including sunglasses, photographic filters, and glare-free lamps. By 1941, sales had reached $1 million. Following World War II, Dr. Land developed a new method for developing and printing photographs. The Polaroid Land Camera was announced in 1947, and the first models were sold in November 1948. The Polaroid Land Camera utilized a "one-step" process, in contrast with the "three-step" process required for conventional photography. In conventional still photography, the sequence involved in producing a black-and-white picture is as follows:

1. A photosensitive material ("film") is exposed to light. The light converts grains of silver bromide into specks of silver, the amount of silver deposited in a given area depending on the amount of light reaching that area.
2. The film is developed by immersing it in a chemical solution which converts the exposed grains into black silver. The unexposed grains are then dissolved with a second solution and washed away. This yields a finished "negative" in which all of the natural tones are reversed—i.e., black appears as white, and vice versa.
3. The negative is placed in contact with a sheet of light-sensitive paper and exposed to light. The developing process is then repeated to produce a finished "positive" print.

The second and third steps of conventional photography require that exposed film be processed in a commercial laboratory or in a home "darkroom." For the vast majority of amateur photographers, this means a delay of several days between taking a picture and receiving a finished print of it.

The technique developed by Dr. Land yielded finished prints from the

[1] New Franc = $.20 (approx.) in 1967.

EXHIBIT 1. Sales and Net Earnings of Polaroid Corporation in the United States and Canada 1950–1966 (Thousands of Dollars)

Year	Sales		Net Earnings	
	U.S.A. Only	U.S.A. & Canada	U.S.A. Only	U.S.A. & Canada
1950	N.A.	$ 6,390	N.A.	$ 726
1951	N.A.	9,259	N.A.	512
1952	N.A.	13,393	N.A.	597
1953	N.A.	26,034	N.A.	1,415
1954	N.A.	23,500	N.A.	1,153
1955	N.A.	26,421	N.A.	2,402
1956	N.A.	34,464	N.A.	3,667
1957	N.A.	48,043	N.A.	5,355
1958	N.A.	65,271	N.A.	7,211
1959	$ 89,487	89,919	$10,750	10,743
1960	98,734	99,446	8,838	8,813
1961	100,562	101,478	8,008	8,111
1962	102,589	103,738	9,872	9,965
1963	122,333	123,459	11,078	11,218
1964	138,077	139,351	18,105	18,323
1965	202,228	204,003	28,872	29,114
1966	316,551	322,399	47,594	47,963

Source: Company annual reports.

camera itself, with no delay for processing. Basic discoveries in photographic chemistry, and new materials based on these discoveries, permitted the entire process to be completed in 60 seconds (later, in 10 seconds) with no equipment other than the camera and film.

The Polaroid Land Camera was commercially successful almost from the beginning. In 1949, sales of cameras and film amounted to over $5 million.

PRODUCT LINE

Between 1949 and 1964, research and development activities at Polaroid provided the basis for a continuous improvement and diversification of Polaroid's camera product line.

The earliest versions of the Polaroid Land Camera produced sepia-colored prints of a quality inferior to that of conventional films. Subsequent improvements in the film permitted clear, black-and-white photographs and, beginning in 1963, color pictures as well. Another major innovation in 1963 was the introduction of the Automatic 100 Land Camera. The Model 100 utilized a film "pack" rather than the film roll which had been used in all earlier Polaroid cameras. With a film pack, the camera could be loaded more easily and quickly, since it was not necessary to wind the film around a series of rollers. Instead, the user simply opened the camera, inserted the pack, and closed the camera. In addition to the pack-loading feature, the Model 100 incorporated several other improvements over the earlier models. It weighed less than earlier models and had a better exposure control.

Following the introduction of the Model 100, Polaroid introduced three lower-priced pack cameras: the Model 101 in 1964, and Models 103 and 104 in 1965. In early 1967, a redesigned line of five pack cameras was introduced. Thus, in mid-1967, the models offered and their suggested retail prices in the U.S.A. were as follows:

Model 250	$159.95
Model 240	124.95
Model 230	94.95
Model 220	69.95
Model 210	49.95

All of these cameras produced both black-and-white and color photographs in a 3 1/4 in. × 4 1/4 in. format, and all had electric eye mechanisms for automatic exposure control. The main differences among the various models were in lens qualities and in materials. For example, the Model 250 features a Zeiss rangefinder-viewfinder, a three-piece precision lens, an all-metal body, and a leather carrying strap. The Model 210 had a plastic body, a nylon strap, a less expensive focusing system, a two-piece lens, and was not designed to accommodate the accessories (such as a portrait lens) which could be employed with the higher-priced models.

In late 1965, Polaroid introduced the Model 20 "Swinger" Land Camera in the United States.[2] The Swinger was a roll-film camera, capable of taking black-and-white photos only, in a 2 1/4 in. × 3 1/4 in. format and with a 15-second development time. It was made of white plastic; the suggested retail price, which was emphasized in national advertising, was $19.95. The introduction of the Swinger enabled Polaroid to compete for the first time in the large-volume market for inexpensive cameras; around three-fourths of all still cameras purchased each year sold for less than $50 at retail. Thus, the launching of the Swinger was a major contributing factor in the dramatic growth of the company's sales during 1965 and 1966 (see Exhibit 1). According to company reports, by "sometime in 1967" over 5 million Swinger cameras had been sold by Polaroid.

All of Polaroid's cameras were produced for the company by outside contractors. The company itself manufactured black-and-white and color film rolls (for pre-1963 cameras); film packs for pack cameras; and film rolls for the Swinger.

In addition to amateur cameras and film, Polaroid produced one camera (the Model 180) for professional photographers and highly skilled amateurs, as well as several different types of industrial photographic equipment and supplies. Special-purpose industrial products included a system for producing identification cards and badges; X-ray equipment and film; and the MP-3 Industrial View Land Camera, designed for such applications as photomicrography.

---

[2] The name "Swinger" was chosen so as to emphasize the appeal of the new camera to teenagers and young adults. The word "Swinger," in American slang, designated a youthful and exciting person. Presumably this usage was related to the much older word "swing," a popular type of jazz music in the 1930s and 1940s. Because of the worldwide popularity of this kind of music, the word "swing" had essentially the same meaning (and pronunciation) through Western Europe as in the U.S.A. The term "Swinger" was, however, strictly American.

Polaroid Corporation did not publish sales figures for individual products. According to the company's annual reports, photographic products accounted for between 93 percent and 97 percent of sales during the 1950s and 1960s. The remaining 3 percent to 7 percent of total volume was derived from sunglasses, polarizers, and other nonphotographic products. Trade sources estimated that cameras represented about 55 percent–60 percent of Polaroid's sales volume in the mid-1950s and around 40 percent in the mid-1960s.

THE U.S. CAMERA MARKET

The market for still cameras in the United States expanded dramatically during the early 1960s. According to trade estimates, some 14 million still cameras were sold in 1966, three times as many as in 1960. Estimates of total industry sales and of Polaroid's market share (in units) were as follows:[3]

Year	Industry Sales	Polaroid Market Share
	(million units)	(percent)
1954	4.5	4–5%
1959	4.9	—
1960	4.6	8
1962	5.3	—
1964	8.4	11
1965	11.0	—
1966	14.0	30–35

According to trade estimates, Polaroid camera sales in 1966 represented approximately 50 percent of the total *dollar value* of U.S. retail camera sales.

The rapid growth of the camera market was due, in the opinion of industry observers, to rising levels of consumer income and to the introduction of new products by Polaroid and by the Eastman Kodak Company. As described in the preceding section, Polaroid had introduced a series of new models in 1963, 1964, and 1965 at progressively lower prices and with various improvements in operating features.

In 1963, Kodak had introduced its new line of "Instamatic" cameras. Instamatic cameras, like Polaroid's pack film used rolls in earlier models. Instamatic cameras were designed to use 35-millimeter film which was enclosed in a special cartridge produced only by Kodak. Thus, although Kodak licensed other companies to manufacture cameras using Instamatic film, it was the only source of film for all such cameras.

Kodak's own line of Instamatic cameras included simple, fixed-focus models

[3]Industry sales estimates published in annual statistical reports, prepared by Augustus Wolfman of *Modern Photography* and *Photo Dealer* magazines; Polaroid market share estimates from various trade sources; for 1964, from Duncan M. Payne, *The European Operations of the Eastman Kodak Company,* Institut d'Etudes Européenes de Geneve, 1967, p. 28.

selling at retail for around $12 and more sophisticated models priced as high as $100. Thus, Instamatics competed in virtually all price segments of the camera market, except the under $10 category. According to trade estimates, Instamatics accounted for around a third of all still cameras sold in the United States in 1964 and 1965.

Still cameras were purchased primarily by "amateur" users for personal recreational use. In 1966, 70 percent to 75 percent of all U.S. households owned one or more still cameras. Some cameras, and a significant proportion of all film, were bought by business, institutional, and governmental users for use in research, sales promotion, record-keeping, etc. The principal objective of Polaroids's marketing programs was, however, the sale of Polaroid Land Cameras to household consumers.

Household consumers used several different types of cameras, ranging from very simple, inexpensive "box" cameras up to very complex 35-mm. instruments. According to Polaroid estimates, 35-mm. cameras (exclusive of Instamatics) represented only about 5 percent to 7 percent of total camera purchases in 1965. In terms of retail price categories, around 15 percent of all cameras were sold at retail prices under $10; between 60 percent and 65 percent were priced between $10 and $49; and 20 percent to 25 percent cost $50 or more. Nearly half of all cameras were for the purchasers' own use; over 40 percent were purchased as gifts; and almost 10 percent were obtained as prizes, premiums, or in return for trading stamps.

Because of the importance of gift-giving, camera sales were highly seasonal. November and December accounted for over 50 percent of total annual retail sales. The second most important selling season, May-June-July, accounted for nearly one-fourth of annual sales.

Up to 1963, the dominant type of customer for still cameras costing over $10 was the relatively affluent family with small children. The introduction of the Instamatics, the Swinger, and the relatively inexpensive Models 104 and 210 pack cameras resulted in a substantial broadening of the household market. The estimated distribution of purchasers by income groups and age groups in 1965–1966 was as follows:

	Purchasers of			
Income Group	All Still Cameras	Polaroid Pack Cameras	Polaroid Swingers	All U.S. Households
Under $3,000	4%	1%	3%	17%
$ 3,000–$4,999	11	9	20	18
5,000– 6,999	21	16		20
7,000– 9,999	31	31	38	26
10,000 or more	34	43	39	19

				All U.S.
Age of Principal User				Individuals
19 or younger	30%	23%	26%	22%
20–49 years	53	63	65	50
50 years or more	16	14	9	28

POLAROID MARKETING IN THE U.S.A.

Polaroid had no direct competition in the instant photography field. Although the patents on the original version of the Polaroid Land Camera had expired in 1965, Polaroid still held some 750 unexpired patents on various improvements in film chemistry and camera design that had been developed during the 1950s and 1960s. The company's products were, however, in active competition with many conventional types of cameras and films.

POLAROID ADVERTISING

At the time of its introduction in 1948, the first Polaroid Land Camera was a radical product innovation in photography. According to *Fortune* magazine,[4]

> Land's revolution was at first derided by all the experts . . . (including) virtually every camera dealer in the country, every "advanced" amateur photographer, and nearly everyone on Wall Street.

To overcome the skepticism of consumers and dealers, Polaroid placed considerable emphasis on national advertising. According to trade estimates, the company's advertising expenditures increased during the 1950s and 1960s as follows:[5]

Year	Estimated Advertising Expenditures	
1954	$ 1,700,000	
1957	3,000,000	
1958	4,000,000	
1960	7,500,000	
1963	8,000,000	(Color film and pack
1964	8,500,000	cameras introduced)
1965	12,000,000	(Swinger introduced)
1966	18,000,000	

Especially during the introductory phases of Polaroid marketing, the Land Camera lent itself ideally to the medium of television, where the method of operation and its results could be demonstrated. The company was among the first major sponsors of "big-time" network television programs in the 1950s, such as the Garry Moore and Perry Como music-variety shows. Advertising trade publications estimated that around 45 percent of Polaroid's total advertising budget was devoted to network television in the mid-1960s, about 30 percent to magazines, and less than 5 percent to newspapers.

Early Polaroid advertising in the United States was designed to acquaint consumers with the basic idea of instant photography. An illustrative advertisement from the mid-1950s is shown in Exhibit 2. Later, after the great majority of pro-

---

[4] Francis Bello, "The Magic That Made Polaroid," *Fortune,* April 1959.
[5] Estimates by *Advertising Age* and other trade sources.

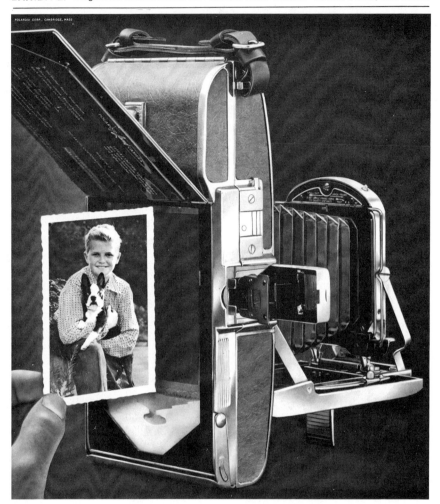

How to take a picture 1 minute and see it the next! Today's Polaroid Land Camera is a magnificent photographic instrument that not only takes beautiful pictures—but develops and prints them as well. With this camera in your hands, you are a magician, who can produce a finished print in 60 seconds. You are a professional photographer, fully equipped to produce expert pictures—clear, sharp, lasting black and white prints—on the spot. Whether you own several cameras or have never even owned one, you will have to own a Polaroid Land Camera. Ask your dealer to show you this remarkable instrument. There are three to choose from, including a new smaller, lower-priced model. *the amazing* **POLAROID** *Land* **CAMERA**

spective buyers were familiar with the concept of "a picture in a minute," the company's advertising efforts were devoted to announcements of successive changes in product features, such as color film and pack-loading cameras, and to publicizing the availability of lower-priced cameras. An example of a 1966 Swinger advertisement is given in Exhibit 3.

DISTRIBUTION AND PRICING

In the United States, Polaroid sold its cameras and film directly to around 15,000 retailers. Pack cameras were sold primarily by specialty photographic stores, department stores, and general merchandise "discount" stores. Swinger cameras and Polaroid films were carried by a greater number and variety of outlets, including

EXHIBIT 3. Magazine Advertisement for Swinger Camera—United States, 1966

many drugstores. Sales were made to many of the smaller outlets via wholesalers, but the bulk of Polaroid sales was made directly to stores and to buying offices of chain and mail-order firms.

Polaroid Corporation established "suggested" retail prices for cameras and film, but there were no legal or other restrictions on the freedom of dealers to set their own resale prices. The suggested retail prices provided gross margins for the retailers of around 33 1/3 percent on the Model 250, 28 percent on the Model 210, and 33 1/3 percent on the Swinger, and 33 1/3 percent on pack films. Because Polaroid Land Cameras were regarded by the larger retailers as attractive products to feature in "discount" promotions, the prevailing retail prices were often well below suggested levels. In mid-1967, consumers in large metropolitan areas could buy the Model 250 at a discount of around $129.95, the Model 210 for around $39.95, and the Swinger for as little as $14. The smaller "conventional" photographic stores sold Polaroid cameras and films at lesser discounts and, often, at full list price. Polaroid films were also often sold at prices significantly below the suggested or list figures:

| | Retail Price | |
Film Type	Suggested	Discount Price
Type 107—Black-and-White Pack	$2.85	$1.99 – 2.49
Type 108—Color Pack	5.39	3.99 – 4.99
Type 20—Black-and-White Swinger	2.10	1.49 – 1.79

Discounting by retailers was also common in the sale of competing cameras. Some of the larger and more aggressive discount stores sold cameras at prices very slightly above cost, and the smaller conventional stores found it very difficult to compete with such outlets. Partly for this reason, a substantial proportion of total retail camera sales were made by a relatively small number of dealers. For example, 40 percent of Polaroid's total sales were accounted for by 10 percent of its total number of sales accounts, and 60 percent of total sales by 20 percent of the accounts.

Sales were made to dealers by Polaroid's field sales force of some 55 salesmen. The salesmen were responsible for calling on dealers periodically, setting up displays in the stores, training retail salespersons, assisting dealers in planning retail advertising of Polaroid products, and introducing new products. From time to time, the salesmen conducted special promotional campaigns, such as used camera trade-in campaigns. For these programs, Polaroid would provide display and advertising materials to the dealers and the salesmen would assist them in promoting the sale of new Polaroid cameras via special trade-in allowances on used Polaroid cameras.

The frequency of salesmen's calls depended on a dealer's size and location. Small dealers located in remote areas were visited only once every four to six months. Large dealers located in major metropolitan areas were visited weekly.

Dealers' orders were almost always placed by telephone or mailed to one of Polaroid's six regional warehouses.

Polaroid salesmen were compensated on a salary basis. A typical salesman's territory included about 300 regular dealers, along with wholesalers and other types of accounts.

POLAROID OVERSEAS OPERATIONS

Up to 1964, Polaroid's sales outside the United States and Canada were relatively small. Cameras and film were exported from the United States and were subject to the high tariffs which most countries imposed on photographic products. As a result, prices of Polaroid products were so high as to make them virtually luxury items.

Beginning in 1965, Polaroid undertook a more aggressive program of developing international markets. Mr. Stanford Calderwood, Marketing Vice President of Polaroid, commented on this development at an international distributors' meeting in September 1966:

> In 1965, things began to change somewhat and the international curve began perking up as we introduced the Models 103 and 104. . . . In 1966, international sales began to climb very sharply because of the introduction of the Swinger. It is our goal—and we think it is an achievable goal—that in the next decade we can make the international business grow so it will be equal in size to the U.S.A. total.[6]

According to the company's *Annual Reports,* sales to dealers by Polaroid's overseas subsidiaries in 1966 amounted to $36 million, compared with $18.2 million in 1965. Beginning in 1965, the company had adopted a policy of pricing cameras and film "as if they were being made behind the Common Market and Commonwealth tariff barriers." Also in 1965, Polaroid established manufacturing facilities for Swinger film at Enschede, The Netherlands, and at the Vale of Leven, Scotland. Swinger camera production in the United Kingdom commenced in late 1965 at a plant set up by one of Polaroid's American camera suppliers.

Along with the establishment of manufacturing facilities, Polaroid

> . . . embarked on a program designed to stimulate increased demand for its products overseas. Margins were adjusted downward to bring prices to the foreign consumer more in line with those to U.S. consumers. . . . Greatly expanded magazine and newspaper advertising, as well as commercial television where available, carried the Polaroid instant-picture message in many languages.[7]

The costs of the expanded marketing program, coupled with delays in provid-

[6] *Intercom,* Polaroid International Communique, October 1966.
[7] Polaroid *Annual Report* for 1966, p. 13.

ing Swinger cameras from the new overseas factory, contributed to an operating loss of $907,000 by Polaroid's unconsolidated subsidiaries (excluding Canada) in 1966.

A portion of Polaroid's organization for international marketing, showing the activities affecting operations in Europe, is depicted in Exhibit 4. As shown there, the general managers of the European subsidiary companies reported to a European coordinator, located at the Polaroid International headquarters in Amsterdam, who in turn reported to Polaroid's-Vice President-Sales, Mr. Thomas Wyman. Mr. Wyman and his assistant manager for international sales also had frequent contact with the subsidiary managers by mail and through periodic visits.

Advertising policies were established by the company's Vice President-Advertising, Mr. Peter Wensberg, in consultation with representatives of Doyle Dane Bernbach, the company's advertising agency. The agency was also charged with directing the work of its subsidiary and affiliate agencies in other countries. Thus, advertising campaigns for European markets were developed by the overseas agencies within broad guidelines established by Mr. Wyman and by DDB–New York. Mr. Wensberg stated that ". . . we are great believers in the power of advertising," and that "much of the success of our advertising efforts over the years has been due to the fact that we have what we feel is the world's best advertising agency—Doyle Dane Bernbach, in New York."

EXHIBIT 4. Partial Organization Chart—European Marketing Activities, 1967

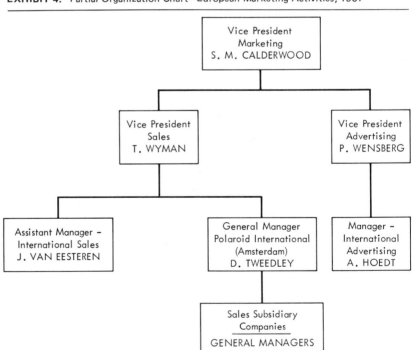

INTERNATIONAL PLANNING AND CONTROL

During 1965, Polaroid's marketing executives had developed a new planning and control system for overseas marketing operations. This system included a standardized format for financial accounting, standardized monthly performance reports, and annual operating plans for each subsidiary company. The system required that an annual operating plan be developed and submitted to Cambridge each fall, covering proposed operations during the next calendar year. The format of the plan called for:

1. A review of market conditions, including trends in total industry sales, competitive developments, distribution, and changes in consumer buying habits.
2. A statement of objectives for the year, expressed in concrete terms (e.g., "increase distribution by adding at least 20 more department stores and 100 more photographic stores").
3. A summary of planned marketing activities, including
   —sales force
   —advertising budget and media
   —publicity
   —market research
   —customer service
4. Estimated operating results for the year, including monthly sales forecasts for each major product, operating expenses, estimated profits, and cash flow.

Monthly reports to Cambridge indicated actual results in comparison with the plan, and significant discrepancies were explained via accompanying correspondence.

POLAROID FRANCE (S.A.)

Polaroid France (S.A.) was established in November 1961 as a wholly owned subsidiary of Polaroid Corporation. Up to 1964, sales in France were relatively small. With the introduction of the Models 103 and 104 cameras in 1964 and 1965, followed by the Swinger in late 1966, sales of Polaroid France increased rapidly.

M. Dumon became General Manager of Polaroid France early in 1966. During 1966, he was responsible for making preparations for the introduction of the Swinger, which took place in September. The addition of the Swinger involved a significant expansion of sales volume, advertising and promotional efforts, and retail distribution for Polaroid France. Consequently, M. Dumon had devoted most of his efforts during 1966 to discussions with the major advertising media, hiring additional personnel, and working with retailers to obtain distribution and promotional support for the new camera.

In mid-1967, Polaroid France employed 86 persons. The company's headquarters office and warehouse were located at Colombes, a suburb of Paris.

EXHIBIT 5. Organization Chart, 1967

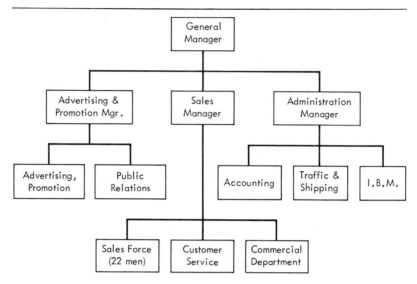

Reporting to M. Dumon were the sales manager, the advertising manager, and the manager-administration. An organization chart is given in Exhibit 5.

THE FRENCH CAMERA MARKET

The market for still cameras in France was about one-tenth as large as that in the United States. According to estimates by Polaroid's marketing research department, total camera sales to household and business users in France had increased slowly since 1963:

	Still Camera Sales (000 units)		
Year	Total	Over $50	Under $10
1963	1,200	210	390
1964	1,350	220	390
1965	1,300	220	400
1966	1,350	230	420

In comparison with the U.S. market, cameras selling for less than NF 50 ($10) comprised a larger proportion of total camera sales—around one-third. These inexpensive cameras were primarily simple, fixed-focus "box" cameras, many of which were imported. In France and elsewhere in Europe, Kodak offered less expensive models in the Instamatic line than those available in the U.S. According to one source, Kodak sales represented about half of the French camera market in 1965-1966.

Altogether, there were some 11,000 retail outlets for cameras in France.[8] Specialty photographic stores sold around three-fourths of all still cameras bought by French household consumers. Other important types of outlets included department stores (5 percent to 10 percent of total sales), supermarkets (5 percent), and opticians (2 percent). There were fewer general merchandise discount retailers in France than in the United States, and this type of outlet sold only 1 percent to 2 percent of all still cameras.[9] Some of the larger photo retailers were aggressive discounters, however, especially in the Paris metropolitan area. The large department stores, such as Galeries Lafayette and Au Printemps, also sold cameras at substantial discounts from suggested retail prices. Outside Paris, smaller conventional photo stores dominated the retailing scene. These smaller stores typically had markups on photographic products of 25 percent to 30 percent, while the larger stores operated on margins of around 20 percent. As in the United States, the dealers earned their highest margins on film processing (35 percent to 40 percent).

Market studies by Polaroid indicated that about one-third of total camera sales were made in Paris, although only 17 percent of the population lived in the region. An additional 15 percent of camera sales were accounted for by other major cities (population over 100,000).

In France, about a third of all still cameras were purchased to be given as gifts. This compared with a gift proportion of nearly half in the United States. Because gift-giving played a lesser role in the market, Christmas season sales naturally represented a smaller percentage of annual industry volume than in the United States. The peak selling season in France was during the spring and summer: May, June, and July accounted for more than half of annual camera sales, and November-December represented less than 15 percent.

According to Polaroid estimates, sales of Kodak Instamatic cameras amounted to over a fourth of the French market; 35-mm. cameras, including the Agfa "Rapid" line manufactured in Germany and designed to compete with Instamatics, had a market share of over 20 percent.

Camera purchases were relatively concentrated in the higher income groups:

Income Group	All Still Camera Buyers	All French Individuals Over 15 Years	Polaroid Buyers	
			Pack	Swinger
Under NF 6,000	3%	17%	1%	1%
NF 6,001— 8,400	15	17		
8,401—12,000	31	26	1	1
12,001—24,000	38	30	4	9
Over 24,000	19	11	94	89

[8] Payne, *European Operations of the Eastman Kodak Company*, p. 98.
[9] Some French "supermarkets" carried diversified lines of general merchandise in addition to food, however, and were essentially combinations of U.S. food supermarket and discount-department store types of outlets.

About two-thirds of all French camera users were men. Among both men and women, persons under 24 years of age accounted for 34 percent of all camera users.

Among Polaroid Swinger buyers, nearly 20 percent were under 21 years of age, and another 20 percent between 21 and 30. The corresponding figures for all cameras selling for less than NF 100 were 30 percent and 35 percent.

POLAROID MARKETING IN FRANCE

Prior to the introduction of the Models 103 and 104 pack cameras, Polaroid products were distributed in France on a limited scale. In 1963, only around 400 outlets carried Polaroid cameras. During 1965 and 1966, the marketing program had undergone a complete transformation. A broadened product line, lower prices, increased distribution, and more aggressive promotion all contributed to the company's growth.

DISTRIBUTION AND SALES FORCE

The number of outlets handling Polaroid products increased steadily from 1,300 in 1964 to 1,600 in 1965, and 3,400 in 1967. By mid-1967, M. Dumon estimated that Polaroid accounts represented around two-thirds of total retail camera sales among all photographic specialty stores, and 60 percent in the department store category. The largest 15 percent of Polaroid's accounts represented about 80 percent of the company's total sales.

Polaroid's sales force, which consisted of 10 men in mid-1966, had grown to 22 by July 1967. On average, each salesman made 8 calls per day. The salesmen were compensated on a straight salary basis. They called on the dealers, took orders, arranged for in-store promotions of Polaroid cameras and handled dealer problems relating to camera repairs, deliveries, etc.

PRICING

While Polaroid Corporation did not release cost figures for individual products, Polaroid France's gross margin on total sales (cameras and film) was approximately 30 percent (see Exhibit 8).

According to industry sources, Polaroid France's gross margin on the Swinger was probably slightly less than that earned on other cameras. These sources also indicated that gross margins on cameras were typically about twice what they were on film. If Polaroid was typical of the French camera industry, these sources added, it probably sold about 8 rolls of film for each camera during the first year in the user's hands.

Experience with other cameras suggested that the Swinger would probably have a useful life of five to six years.

Because cameras were easily shipped from one country to another, Polaroid

EXHIBIT 6. Retail Prices of Polaroid Cameras and Film of Major Competing Products U.S.A. and France, 1967

	U.S.A.	France*	
Camera Model or Film Type	Typical Prices	Typical Prices	Lowest Discount Prices
CAMERAS:			
Polaroid Swinger	$17.00	—	$19.08
Polaroid Model 104	40.00	$70.04	67.40
Kodak Instamatic 104	13.50	15.00	—
FILMS:			
Polaroid Type 20	1.77	2.01	—
Pack Film—Color	4.49	5.03	—
Pack Film—B. & W.	2.09	2.48	—
Kodak Instamatic Color Film:			
per pack (12 prints)	1.24	.97	—
per finished print	.44	.45	—

*French prices include taxes on "value added" of approximately 20% of retail price.

felt that it was essential to coordinate prices on an international level. Consequently, all selling prices for Polaroid France were prescribed within narrow limits by management in Cambridge. Following the changes in Polaroid's marketing policies in 1965, prices to dealers were reduced substantially. The price paid by a dealer depended on quantities ordered. On the average, dealer costs for Polaroid pack cameras and film provided gross profits for the retailer of about 33 percent if he resold at full list price. Typical retail selling prices for Polaroid cameras and film and for major competing products in the United States and France are shown in Exhibit 6. These prices were from 15 percent to 20 percent below suggested retail prices.

When the Swinger was introduced, it was believed that small dealers would be reluctant to handle it, unless there were some kind of guarantee of obtaining adequate margins. Resale price maintenance was permitted in France only when specifically authorized. Polaroid applied for, and received, permission to establish a retail price of NF 99 ($19.90) for the Swinger; under French law, dealers were permitted to deviate from this price by up to 5 percent, and the prevailing price in larger retail outlets was quickly established at NF 94. The price paid by the dealer to Polaroid was NF 84.

Retail prices of Polaroid cameras and film are shown in Exhibit 6.

ADVERTISING AND PROMOTION

During 1966, Polaroid France spent some $600,000 on advertising, of which slightly over half was devoted to the introduction of the Swinger. The budget for

Maintenant
vous pouvez avoir une photo en 15 secondes avec un appareil Polaroid qui ne coûte que
99 F

Le nouveau "Swinger" Polaroid, c'est vraiment autre chose.

Pour 99 F seulement, voilà un appareil qui vous donne des photos noir et blanc parfaites, bien contrastées, des gros plans et des scènes rapides sensationnels.

Et vous avez en main l'épreuve terminée en 15 secondes.

C'est à peine croyable. Si vous n'avez pas vécu ces 15 secondes, ces 15 "interminables" secondes, vous ignorez encore tout du vrai plaisir de la photo !

Et c'est si facile. Visez, tournez le bouton de temps de pose : quand le mot YES apparaît dans le viseur, déclenchez.

Tirez le film hors de l'appareil et comptez jusqu'à 15 · Détachez l'épreuve du négatif. Et voici, terminée, votre épreuve sur papier.

Le "Swinger", c'est un appareil comme vous n'avez jamais rêvé d'en posséder pour seulement 99 F.

Ne vous privez pas de ce plaisir. Offrez-vous le nouveau "Swinger" Polaroid. Il est sensationnel.

SWINGER POLAROID

15 secondes après, la voici.

1967 was somewhat lower at around $550,00. About 40 percent of the total was devoted to magazines, 50 percent to newspapers, and 10 percent to cinema advertising.[10]

Because Polaroid cameras were much less well known in France than in the United States, a major objective of Polaroid advertising was to increase consumers' awareness and understanding of the "instant picture" idea. According to studies by the company's marketing research department, in early 1966 fewer than 5 percent of French consumers demonstrated "proved awareness" of Polaroid Land Cameras, and the level of awareness had increased only slightly by early 1967. A consumer was classified as having "proved awareness" if he or she (1) indicated knowledge of the Polaroid brand name *and* (2) knew of the instant picture feature. The French level of awareness compared with an estimated 85 percent in the United States, 70 percent in Canada, 15 percent in Germany, and 26 percent in the United Kingdom. An illustrative Swinger advertisement from the 1966 introductory campaign is shown in Exhibit 7.

A major obstacle to increasing awareness of Polaroid was the fact that commercial television was not available in France. Polaroid marketing executives believed that television had been a major factor in the growth of Polaroid sales in the United States, and in other countries where commercial television was available— such as Germany and the United Kingdom—it was used extensively.

To demonstrate the concept of instant photography to French consumers, Polaroid placed considerable reliance on in-store sales demonstrations. The company encouraged dealers to perform demonstrations by offering a free roll or pack of film (8 exposures) for each 14 demonstration photos taken by the dealer. To qualify for this partial reimbursement, the retailer had to send the negative portions of 14 film exposures to the company.

In-store sales demonstrations were also conducted by Polaroid demonstrators. These demonstrators, who were paid NF 35 per day, visited retail stores on pre-arranged schedules to conduct demonstrations of Polaroid cameras before groups of potential customers. Polaroid France provided the films for the demonstrations, provided that the dealer ordered cameras in advance. For example, if the dealer ordered 15 pack cameras, the company provided 6 packs of black-and-white film and 3 packs of color film for use in the demonstrations.

Total expenditures for promotion in 1966 amounted to $200,000, and approximately the same amount was budgeted for 1967. Polaroid marketing executives were not satisfied with the dealers' participation in the promotion program. Mr. Wyman, Vice President–Sales of Polaroid Corporation, wrote to M. Dumon in May 1967, stating that

> . . . it appears that the dealer is not demonstrating cameras as frequently and as skillfully as we should like.

---

[10]Total advertising expenditures by all photographic manufacturers in France were estimated at $1.8 million in 1965.

	1966 Actual	1967 Original Plan	1967 Revised Estimate
Net sales	$ 5,640	$ 8,800	$ 7,300
Cost of goods sold	3,950	6,170	5,150
Gross margin	$ 1,690	$ 2,630	$ 2,150
Advertising & promotion costs	800	750	630
Selling costs	150	370	370
General & administrative costs	1,000	850	750
Operating profit	($ 260)	$ 660	$ 400

Unit Sales:

Pack cameras	25,000	30,000	25,000
Swinger cameras	85,000	115,000	95,000

1966–1967 RESULTS AND 1968 PROSPECTS

Sales and profits of Polaroid France during 1966 and the first half of 1967 had not lived up to expectations. As shown in Exhibit 8, a net loss was incurred in 1966. Moreover, by July it was apparent to M. Dumon and to the Polaroid headquarters marketing staff that the goals set for 1967 would not be attained. Hence, a revised plan was prepared calling for lower sales volume and lower levels of expenditure.

Polaroid's other European subsidiaries were also below the levels planned for 1967, but not to the same degree as in France. In several countries, including Italy, Switzerland, and Belgium, Polaroid's estimated share of the camera market was significantly higher than in France. Polaroid's market penetration was about the same in France, Germany, and the U.K., however, despite much higher levels of consumer awareness in the latter countries. In some other countries, the company's advertising expenditures were proportionately higher than in France; with the French 1966 expenditure per camera sold set as 100, indexes of cost per unit for Germany, the U.K., and Italy were 112, 133, and 120 respectively.

For 1968, it was anticipated that the French camera market would grow very slightly, if at all. No major competitive new product introductions were in the United States around mid-year, but production would probably not be adequate to meet worldwide demand until the end of the year. Consequently, M. Dumon's plans for 1968 were to be based on the same basic product line as in 1967.

In considering his marketing program for 1968, M. Dumon was especially concerned with the problems of pricing and promoting the Swinger. With regard to pricing, he wondered whether he should recommend that the company apply for a one-year continuance of government approval for resale price maintenance. The current approval was due to expire on August 1, 1967, and M. Dumon felt that there might be some advantages in allowing completely free pricing after that date. On the other hand, he did not want to lose any of the distribution which had been so carefully built up during the preceding year, on account of "cutthroat" price competition by the discount stores.

The problem of promotion was a chronic one for Polaroid. Awareness of the Polaroid name and instant picture feature had increased only slightly between early 1966 and early 1967, and even Polaroid camera owners displayed a lack of full understanding of some important features. For example, among a group of 100 Swinger owners interviewed in June 1967, nearly half did not realize that it was possible to obtain duplicates of Polaroid pictures from the company's print copy service.

Although the need for further consumer education about Polaroid photography seemed great, it was also clear that advertising had played a very important role in building demand during 1966 and 1967. Among a sample of Swinger owners interviewed in November 1966, 53 percent mentioned advertising as their original source of information about the camera, 5 percent mentioned conversations with photo dealers, and 5 percent in-store demonstrations.

M. Dumon wanted to recommend a program which would contribute to the company's longer term marketing goals in France. At the same time, he was aware of the need to improve current operating results. He had recently received a letter from Mr. Wyman, indicating that

> . . we must be in a position, with a prepared advance plan, to reduce expenditures and limit our activities to insure that we are producing a profit for the year.

QUESTIONS

1. Describe and evaluate Polaroid's U.S. marketing strategy. What factors account for Polaroid's success in the United States?
2. How does the French market differ from the U.S. market? Describe and evaluate Polaroid's strategy and marketing program in France.
3. What should Polaroid have done in France re marketing strategy? Re 1968 marketing plan and budget?

organization
for
international marketing

A prince should therefore have no other aim or thought, nor take
up any other thing for his study, but war and its organization
and discipline, for that is the only art that is necessary to one who
commands.

Niccolò Machiavelli, 1469–1527
(The Prince)

INTRODUCTION

Organization is a subject of major importance to any company that has decided to
market internationally. When a domestic company decides to expand internationally, the issue of how to organize arises immediately. Who should be responsible for
this expansion? Should product divisions operate directly or should an international
division be established? Should individual country subsidiaries report directly to the
company president, or should a special corporate officer be appointed to take full-
time responsibility for international activities? Once the first decision of how to
organize initial international operations has been reached, a growing company is
faced with a number of reappraisal points during the development of its international business activities. Should a company abandon its international division and,
if so, what alternative structure should be adopted? Should an area or regional
headquarters be formed? What should be the relationship of staff executives at corporate, regional, and subsidiary offices? Specifically, how should the marketing
function be organized? To what extent should regional and corporate marketing
executives become involved in subsidiary marketing management?

The goal in organizing for international marketing is to find a structure that
enables the company to respond to relevant differences in international market
environments and at the same time enables the company to extend valuable corporate knowledge, experience, and know-how from national markets to the entire
corporate system. It is this pull between the value of centralized knowledge and

coordination and the need for individualized response to the local situation that creates a constant tension in the international marketing organization.

At the outset it is important to recognize that there is no single correct organizational structure for international marketing. Geographical diversity is a consequence of a strategy of international expansion. The effect of operations in different countries and areas is to present a major new dimension of required response to the organization. A geographically dispersed company in addition to its knowledge of product, function, and the home territory, must acquire knowledge of the complex set of social, political, economic, and institutional arrangements that exist within each international market. Most companies, after initial ad hoc arrangements (all foreign subs reporting to a designated vice-president or to the president, for example), establish an international division to manage their geographically dispersed new business. It is clear, however, that the international division in the multiproduct company is an unstable organizational arrangement and that as a company grows, this initial organizational structure gives way to various alternative structures.[1]

PATTERNS OF INTERNATIONAL ORGANIZATIONAL DEVELOPMENT

The conflicting pressures of the need for (1) product and technical knowledge, (2) functional expertise in marketing, finance, planning, and so on, and (3) area and country knowledge make it difficult to achieve performance and balance in organizations that typically have country operations that range over a long spectrum of size, potential, and local management competence. Because the matrix of pressures that shape organizations are never exactly the same, no two organizations pass through organizational stages in exactly the same way, nor do they arrive at precisely the same organizational pattern. Nevertheless, some general patterns have developed.

Most companies undertake initial foreign expansion with an organization similar to that in Figures 17-1 and 17-2. When a company is organized on this basis, foreign subsidiaries report directly to the company president or other designated company officer, who carries out his responsibilities without assistance from a headquarters staff group. This is a typical initial arrangement for companies getting started in international marketing operations.

International Division Structure

As a company's international business grows, the complexity of coordinating and directing this activity extends beyond the scope of a single person. Pressure is created to assemble a staff group that will take responsibility for coordination and

---

[1] John M. Stopford, "Growth and Organizational Change in the Multinational Firm" (Unpublished doctoral dissertation, Harvard Business School, 1968). The interested reader will find in this dissertation a complete exposition of research examining the organizational structure used by 170 U.S. manufacturing firms for their international operations. Stopford's research demonstrated that the international division is merely the first of a series of organizational structures utilized by companies to accomplish their international objectives.

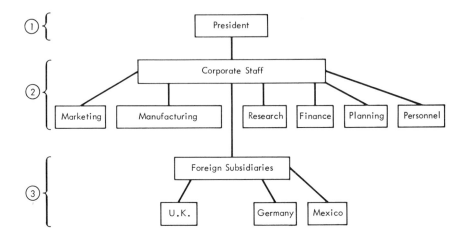

Legend:

① Executives with worldwide (domestic and foreign) responsibilities.

② Executives with domestic responsibilities only.

③ Executives with international multi-country responsibilities
    (excluding domestic or home country responsibilities.)

FIGURE 17-1. Functional Corporate Structure, Domestic Corporate Staff Orientation, Pre-International Division

direction of the growing international activities of the organization. Eventually, this pressure leads to the creation of the international division, as illustrated in Figures 17-3 and 17-4. The corporate staff may or may not be involved in the management of international marketing activities at this point. If the international division is fully developed in terms of staff appointments, there is a tendency for it to operate autonomously and independently of corporate staff. On the other hand, if the international division staff is small and limited, there is a tendency for a service such as marketing research to be supplied by the corporate staff organization.

The international division structure occurs in both the functional and the divisional organization. It allows an organization to concentrate in one headquarters location all of its expertise in dealing with foreign markets. In companies that have the bulk of their sales in a domestic market, this arrangement assures that an organizational location in the corporation gives its full attention to international markets.

A good example of an international division justified on these grounds is General Foods Corporation, which relies on General Foods International for the management of its international operations. One of GF's most important products is coffee. The Maxwell House Division of General Foods, which is responsible for coffee in the U.S. market only, accounts for over 90 percent of GF worldwide coffee sales. If this division were responsible for coffee on a worldwide basis, it would find itself with small businesses scattered around the world, and it would be

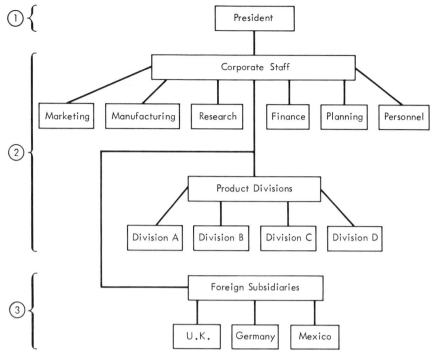

FIGURE 17-2. Divisional Corporate Structure, Domestically Oriented Product Division Staff, Pre-International Division

faced with the necessity of incurring large administrative and management overheads to maintain these small businesses. Moreover, the division does not have any staff experienced in international operations. It is felt at General Foods that the Maxwell House division would simply not give significant attention to international coffee sales, and therefore the management of the company feels that this business is best left in the hands of international specialists who can develop the business in conjunction with their activities in other product areas.

Regional Management Centers

The next stage of organizational evolution is the emergence of an area or regional headquarters as a level of management between the country organization and the international division headquarters. This division is illustrated in Figures 17-5 and 17-6. When business is conducted in a single region that is characterized by certain similarities in economic, social, geographical, and political conditions, after it reaches a certain size there is both justification and need for a management center. The center would coordinate interdependent decisions on such matters as pricing and sourcing and would participate in the planning and control of each country's operations with an eye toward applying company knowledge on a

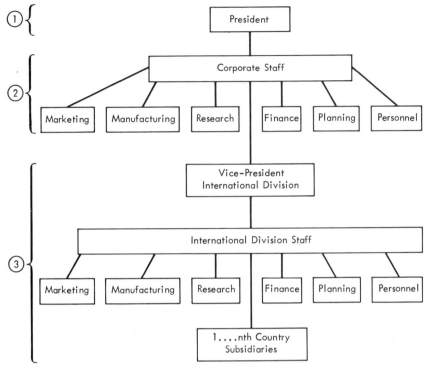

FIGURE 17-3. Functional Corporate Structure, Domestic Corporate Staff Orientation, International Division

regional basis and also toward regional optimization of the application of corporate resources.

The arguments in favor of regional management have been stated as follows:

> . . . the majority of regional managers agree that there is no better solution at the present time than an on-the-scene regional management unit, at least where there is a real need for coordinated, Europewide decision-making. Coordinated European planning and control is becoming necessary as the national subsidiary continues to lose its relevance as an independent operating unit. Regional management can probably achieve the best balance of geographical, product, and functional considerations required to implement corporate objectives effectively and to maximize profitability of the European area.[2]

The pressure for the creation of a regional headquarters comes from two sources. One is the scale and complexity of a company's operations within a region. Size generates revenues that can cover the cost of a regional headquarters, and complexity creates a pressure to respond at the regional level. A second important source of pressure is the nature of regions. A geographical region is by definition a group of countries related to each other by geographic proximity. When a region

---

[2]Charles R. Williams, "Regional Management Overseas," *Harvard Business Review*, January-February 1967, p. 91.

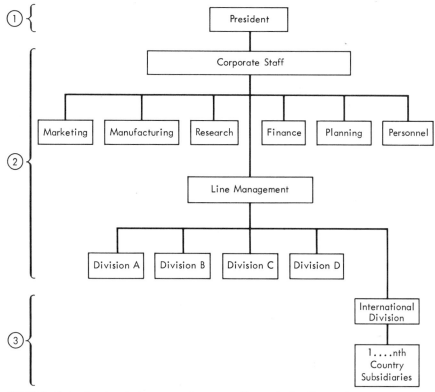

FIGURE 17-4. Divisional Corporate Structure, Domestically Oriented Corporate Staff, Domestically Oriented Product Divisions, International Division

is additionally unified by tariff reduction applying within the regional boundaries, by interregional communication media, by the development of interregional transportation systems, by various regional moves toward economic, social, and political cooperation, and by basic economic and cultural similarities, then the development of the region itself generates a pressure for the creation of a regional headquarters that will guide corporate activities in a way that will take advantage of the economic, social, and political integration that exists within the region.

One of the best examples of the combination of economic, social, and political integration with geographic proximity and relatively large scale operations has occurred in the European Common Market. In the EEC the progress toward economic, social, and political integration during the past two decades has created preconditions for the integration of business activities in EEC countries. However, these pressures in themselves are not sufficient to make it desirable for every company to create a regional headquarters. The company situation itself must be considered. Companies in a region can be placed in four categories:[3]

[3]The following material is drawn from Williams, "Regional Management Overseas." *Harvard Business Review,* January-February, 1967.

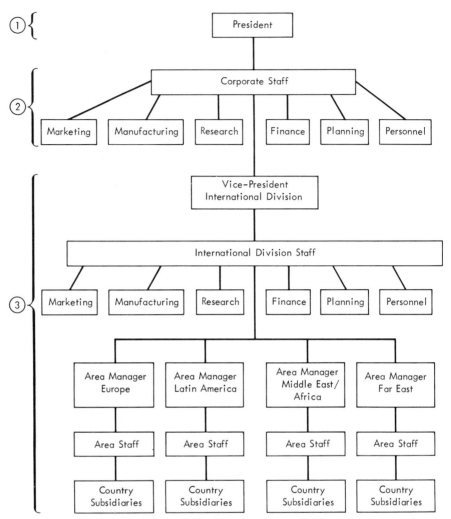

FIGURE 17-5. Functional Corporate Structure, Domestic Corporate Staff Orientation, International Division, Area Divisions

Category 1: initial operations, small annual sales in a handful of countries.

Category 2: regional operations dominated by one or two sizable national subsidiaries, each of which has its own substantial management staff.

Category 3: regional operations comprised of several large, strong, historically independent national operating subsidiaries.

Category 4: regional operations of companies of national subsidiaries that have been closely integrated according to a worldwide plan.

Categories 1 and 2 are the type of operations that have little need for a regional headquarters. The principal subsidiaries are so large that they can effectively function as operating units and in many cases are multicountry companies in their

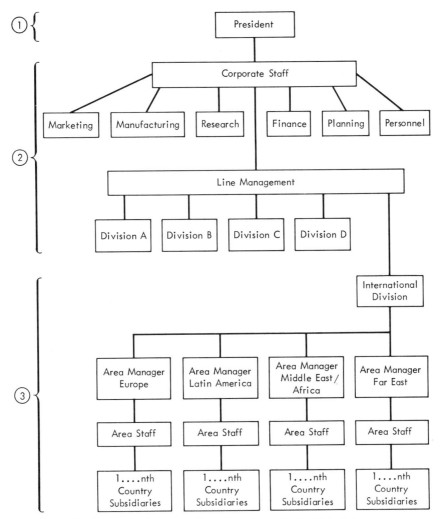

FIGURE 17-6. Divisional Corporate Structure, Domestically Oriented Corporate Staff, International Division, Area Subdivisions

own right. In any event, there is really little coordination between companies of vastly different size to be pursued.

Whenever a company's operations become sizable and are scattered over a number of subsidiaries, then the pressure for regional integration grows. This pressure is perhaps the greatest in the category 3 situation, where large unintegrated subsidiary companies are operating relatively autonomously and have therefore avoided the cost savings and rationalization moves that an overall direction would provide. Most companies today feel that the category 4 situation merits a regional headquarters in an area such as Europe where the opportunities for rationalization and area-wide coordination are significant.

The major disadvantage of a regional center is its cost. Whenever operations are under profit pressure, these costs become quite apparent and have in many companies been responsible for the abandonment of a regional headquarters. A $40,000 moving fee for getting a family overseas is not unusual. Extra compensation for living abroad and the cost of replacing incompetent employees can run up an enormous bill simply for transportation. Overhead cost for office space is expensive. Thus, creating an organizational unit adds manpower, transportation, and communication costs that must be justified by the unit's contribution to organizational effectiveness. In 1978 a three-man office in Germany was costing one U.S. company $500,000 per year. The scale of regional management must be in line with scale of operations in a region. A regional headquarters is premature whenever the size of the operations it manages is inadequate to cover the costs of the additional layer of management.

Thus the basic issue with regard to the regional headquarters is, Does it contribute enough to organizational effectiveness to justify its cost? Most companies would answer this question by saying yes, but only if the scale of operations is large enough to cover costs. Because the cost of a headquarters is highly variable depending upon its size and the extent to which local or regional nationals are employed, it is impossible to specify the amount of business or operating margin necessary to justify a regional headquarters. Each company must reach its own decision on this issue in the framework of its own cost estimates.

Another disadvantage of the regional headquarters is the communications barrier that distance from headquarters imposes. Some chief executives wish to have the heads of major regional operations nearby so that they will be readily available for consultation and discussion. Still another problem with the regional headquarters is the difficulty of obtaining effective execution of a regional management program. Many headquarters have been abandoned not because they were structurally unsound or because of a lack of opportunity to usefully apply a regional level of management, but because the companies' effective programs were never developed within the regional headquarters. Finally, some executives think that the regional headquarters imposes an additional layer of management in the planning and control process. Executives feel that the elimination of this management layer would improve organizational effectiveness by bringing headquarters and company management closer together.

Beyond the International Division

As companies develop their capability to operate in foreign markets with an international division, they usually find that the growing size and complexity of their international operation demands organizational modifications that fully apply organizational capabilities to market opportunities. In the functional single-product company, or product group, one modification involves the creation of geographical structure. In the multidivisional company, this involves the creation of the worldwide product division.

Geographical Structure

The geographical structure involves the assignment of operational responsibility for geographic areas of the world to line managers. The corporate headquarters retains responsibility for worldwide planning and control, and each area of the world—including the "home" or base market—is organizationally equal. For the company with U.S. origins, the United States is simply another geographic market under this organizational arrangement. The most common appearance of this structure is in companies with closely related product lines that are sold in similar end-use markets around the world. For example, the major international oil companies utilize the geographical structure, which is illustrated in Figure 17–7.

Worldwide Product Division Structure

When an organization assigns worldwide product responsibility to its product divisions, the product divisions must decide whether to rely upon an international division, thereby dividing their world into domestic and foreign, or to rely upon an area structure with each region of the world organizationally treated on an equal basis. In most cases when a divisional company shifts from a corporate international division to worldwide product divisions, there are two stages in the internationalization of the product divisions. The first stage occurs when international responsi-

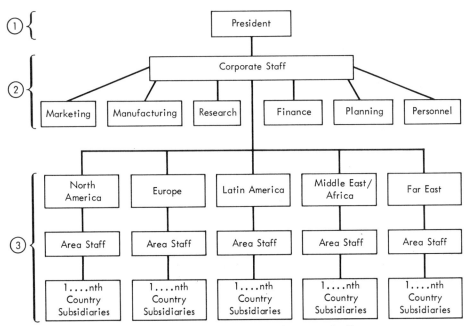

FIGURE 17–7. Geographic Corporate Structure, World Corporate Staff Orientation, Area Divisions Worldwide

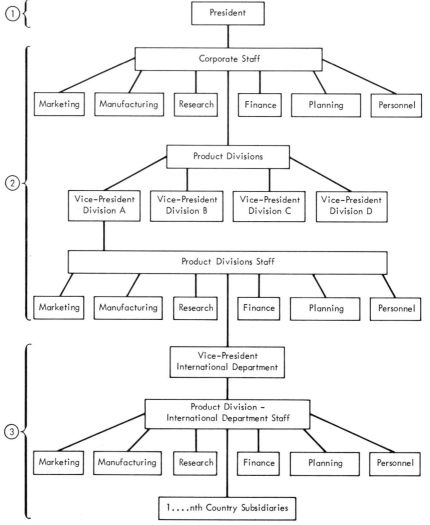

FIGURE 17-8. Divisional Corporate Structure, International Product Division with an International Department in the International Product Division

bility is shifted from a corporate international division to the product division international departments. The second occurs when the product divisions themselves shift international responsibility from international departments within the divisions to the total divisional organization. In effect, this shift is the utilization of a geographical structure within each product division. The worldwide product division with an international department is illustrated in Figure 17-8.

THE MATRIX STRUCTURE

The most sophisticated organizational arrangement brings to bear four basic competences on a worldwide basis. These competences are as follows:

1. Geographic knowledge. An understanding of the basic economic, social, cultural, political, governmental market and competitive dimensions of a country is essential. The country subsidiary is the major structural device employed today to enable the corporation to acquire geographic knowledge.
2. Product knowledge and know-how. Product managers with a worldwide responsibility can achieve this level of competence on a global basis. Another way of achieving global product competence is simply to duplicate product management organizations in domestic and international divisions, achieving high competence in both organizational units.
3. Functional competence in such fields as finance, production, and especially marketing. Corporate functional staff with worldwide responsibility contributes toward the development of functional competence on a global basis. In a handful of companies the appointment of country subsidiary functional managers is reviewed by the corporate functional manager who is responsible for the development of his functional activity in the organization on a global basis. What has emerged in a growing number of multinational companies is a dotted-line relationship between corporate, regional, and country staff. These relationships are illustrated in Figure 17-9. Dotted-line relationship ranges from nothing more than advice offered by corporate or regional staff to regional country staff to a much "heavier" line relationship where staff activities of a lower organizational level are directed and approved by higher-level staff. The relationship of staff organizations can become a source of tension and conflict in an organization if top management does not create a climate that encourages organizational integration. Headquarters staff wants to extend its control or influence over the activities of lower-level staff. For example, in marketing research, unless there is coordination of research design and activity, the international headquarters is unable to compare one market with another. If line management instead of recognizing the potential contribution of an integrated worldwide staff wishes to operate as autonomously as possible, the influence of corporate staff is perceived as undesirable. In such a situation the "stronger" party wins. This can be avoided if the level of management to which both line and staff report creates a climate and structure that expects and requires the cooperation of line and staff, and recognizes that each has responsibility for important aspects of the management of international markets.
4. A knowledge of the customer or industry and its needs. In certain large and very sophisticated international companies, staff with a responsibility for serving industries on a global basis exists to assist the line managers in the country organizations in their efforts to penetrate specific customer markets.

In the fully developed large-scale international company, product, function,

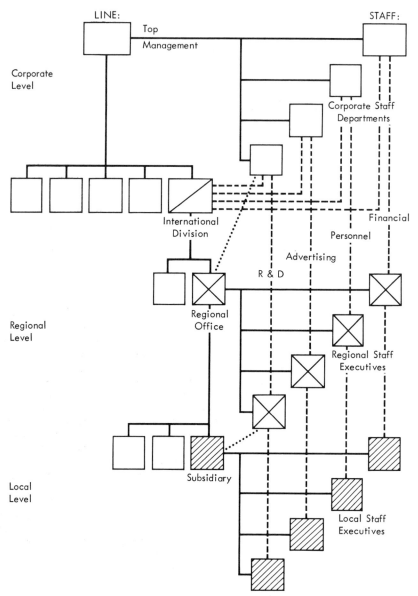

FIGURE 17-9. Organization Chart Showing Relationships Between Staff Executives in Corporate Departments, Regional Office, and Subsidiary

area, and customer know-how are simultaneously focused on the organization's worldwide marketing objectives. This type of total competence is a matrix organization. In the matrix organization the task of management is to achieve an organizational balance that brings together different perspectives and skills to accomplish the organization's objectives. Under this arrangement, instead of designating national organizations or product divisions as profit centers, both are responsible for profitability: the national organization for country profits, and the product divisions for national and worldwide product profitability. Figure 17–10 illustrates the matrix organization. This organization is the first one in the charts that starts with a bottom section that represents a single-country responsibility level, moves to representing the area or international level, and finally moves to representing global responsibility from the product divisions to the corporate staff, to the chief executive.

The key to successful matrix management is the extent to which managers in the organization are able to resolve conflicts and achieve integration of organization programs and plans. Thus the mere adoption of a matrix design or structure does not create a matrix organization. The matrix organization requires a fundamental

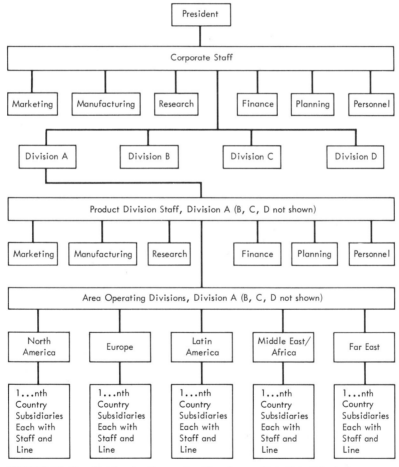

FIGURE 17–10. Divisional Corporate Structure, Globally Oriented Corporate Staff, Global Product Division (Globally Oriented Product Division Staff with Area Subdivisions)

change in management behavior, organizational culture, and technical systems. In a matrix, influence is based on technical competence and interpersonal sensitivity and not on formal authority. In a matrix culture, managers recognize the absolute need to resolve issues and choices at the lowest possible level and do not rely upon higher authority. A sure sign that managers do not understand matrix organizations is when issues and problems are regularly pushed to the CEO for resolution. Matrix organizations develop because companies refuse to accept the trade-offs of alternative traditional structures. For example, in traditional hierarchcial structures, there is a choice between country or national organization and worldwide product divisions as the profit center or accountability location for strategic business management. Which is more important—in-depth knowledge of language, customs, laws, and customers, or in-depth knowledge of technology, products, and markets? In the traditional design, organizations must choose. In the matrix, *both* locations are responsible for profits. Traditional structures minimize conflict, whereas matrix structures are acknowledged generators of conflict. The potential conflict in a matrix is accepted as inherent in the structure rather than as the consequence of poor management. Finally, a matrix requires a substantial investment in control systems—dual accounting, transfer pricing, corporate budgets, and so on.

Matrix Variations

The divisional company that disbands its international division in favor of assigning direct responsibility for international operations to its product divisions is seeking an organizational structure that is much more capable of directing the organization's product/market competence toward opportunities in international markets. Unfortunately, a company utilizing this structural arrangement will have multiple division organizational units operating simultaneously and independently in many countries where the market is not large enough to fully employ the resources committed. The major areas of duplication are in administrative and financial services. Another shortcoming of this arrangement is a lack of coordination of product division activities that could be centralized. For example, divisions may work entirely independent of each other in advertising to establish a corporate image. Another shortcoming is that the separation blocks the exchange of valuable information.

A matrix solution to this problem might involve the creation of so-called umbrella companies in each country, which are responsible for specified pooled activities such as administering reporting requirements to national authorities, coordinating corporate image-building activities, cash management and pooled services such as office management and transportation. Product divisions would have responsibility for country strategies and programs and would directly employ their own staff. They would have profit-and-loss accountabiltiy, and the umbrella organization would be a cost center whose costs would be allocated to each of the product divisions on the basis of a formula. This would be a matrix with heavy emphasis on product division responsibility and is illustrated in Figure 17-11. Another matrix could shift major emphasis for profit and loss to the country or

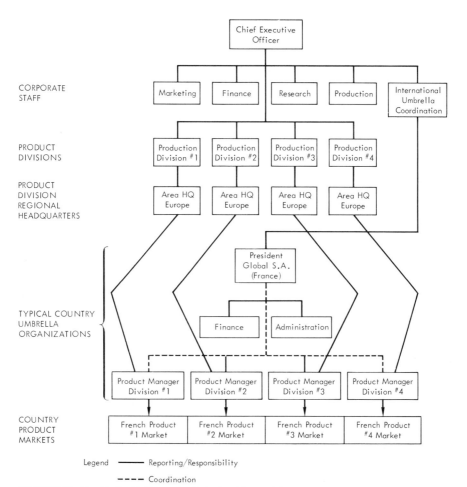

CORPORATE STAFF

PRODUCT DIVISIONS

PRODUCT DIVISION REGIONAL HEADQUARTERS

TYPICAL COUNTRY UMBRELLA ORGANIZATIONS

COUNTRY PRODUCT MARKETS

Legend ——— Reporting/Responsibility

- - - - Coordination

FIGURE 17-11. Umbrella Reporting Relationships and Structure

national organization. Still another matrix variation would be the attempt to divide responsibility equally between product and national organization.

RELATIONSHIP BETWEEN STRUCTURE, FOREIGN PRODUCT DIVERSIFICATION, AND SIZE

One writer has hypothesized the relationship between structure, foreign product diversification (defined as sales of a firm outside its major product line expressed as a percentage of the total sales), and size. This formulation posits that when size abroad grows, the emergence of an area division develops so that whenever size abroad is 50 percent of total size or more, several area divisions will probably be adopted. On the other hand, as a foreign product diversification increases, the likelihood that product divisions will operate on a worldwide basis increases. In a com-

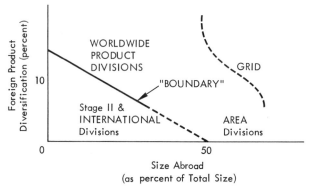

FIGURE 17-12. The Relationships between Structure, Foreign Product Diversification, and Size Abroad (as % of Total Size)

pany where there is both worldwide product diversity and large-scale business abroad as a percentage of total business, foreign operation will tend to move toward the matrix structure. Companies with limited foreign product diversification (under 10 percent) and limited size as a percentage of total size will utilize the international structure. This formulation is summarized schematically in Figure 17-12.

Organization Structure and National Origin

Before 1960 the American multidivisional structure was rarely found outside the United States. This structure was introduced in the United States as early as 1921 by Alfred P. Sloan at General Motors. The multidivisional structure in the United States had three distinctive characteristics. First, profit responsibility for operating decisions was assigned to general managers of self-contained business units. Second, there was a corporate headquarters which was concerned with strategic planning, appraisal, and the allocation of resources among the business divisions. Third, executives at the corporate headquarters were separated from operations and were psychologically committed to the whole organization rather than the individual businesses.[4]

During the 1960s European enterprises underwent a period of unprecedented reorganization. Essentially they adopted the American divisional structure. Today at the overall level there is little difference between European and American organizations. However, at the divisional level a comparison of European and U.S. multinational firms reveals that, in general, European firms typically give more responsibility to national organizations and typically give less attention to the home market and more attention to international markets than does the average American firm. These differences are really differences of focus and emphasis rather

---

[4]Lawrence G. Franko, "The Move toward a Multi-Division Structure in European Organizations," *Administrative Science Quarterly*, 19, No. 4 (December 1974), 493–506.

than differences in structure and can be traced to the size of the domestic market and the history of international growth. The initial geographic spread of U.S. firms was from regional to national operations. When the U.S. firm expanded internationally, the move was usually from its large U.S.-based position. For reasons discussed earlier in this chapter, these circumstances favor the international division as a structural device for concentrating limited knowledge, skills, and market positions in the largest possible mass.

A TYPICAL COMPANY EXPERIENCE

The experience of Raychem Incorporated in Europe illustrates the enormous complexity of effectively structuring international marketing operations. Raychem has four product categories, each of which is part of a related line. These categories are: wire and cable, heat-shrinkable materials, corrosion products utilizing heat-shrinkable materials, and machines and instruments to apply the company's heat-shrinkable products. These related products are sold to six major customer categories: aircraft, electronics, utilities, appliances, computers, and telecommunications. Raychem's European operations cover the entire continent of Europe, the United Kingdom, Israel, and South Africa. The European staff consists of a general manager, research and development, manufacturing, finance, MIS, and marketing.

Figure 17-13 illustrates the complexity of functional, geographic, and consumer characteristics when they are viewed on a three-industry, four-country, five-function basis. In this matrix there are sixty combinations of industry, country, and function that the organization must deal with. For example, in the marketing of the company's products to the aircraft industry in Germany, the need is to bring the company's competence in serving this industry to bear on customers located in Germany. The challenge of assisting the country's sales and marketing team in this effort is considerable. If headquarters is to be of assistance to the German manage-

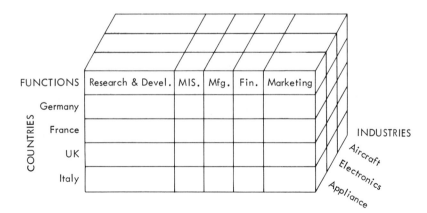

FIGURE 17-13. A One-Product Country, Industry, Function Matrix

ment, it must have a knowledge of marketing, the aircraft industry, and an interest in the unique characteristics of German customers.

When Raychem first organized a regional marketing function, it followed the policy of appointing bright and talented young men to the regional headquarters position. This proved to be disastrous because these men were inexperienced in the actual selling task for the company's products in specific industries. Because of their inadequate knowledge, they were in constant conflict with the country salesmen and were unable to contribute to effective marketing. Following this experience, the president of Raychem Europe decided to appoint marketing staff managers entirely from the ranks of successful country marketing and sales management. The specialist at European headquarters for the aircraft industry is now an experienced and extremely successful former German sales manager for the company's activities directed toward this industry.

According to the president of Raychem Europe, the area staff must be so good at their job that the local managers, motivated from the point of view of their own self-interest, seek out their help. The intelligent local manager realizes that when there is a competent staff person at the regional headquarters he can use this person as a sounding board and as a testing place for his own ideas, and in the process more effectively perform his function.

In order to make this arrangement work, the European area president must communicate to his general managers and their staffs in the different countries his commitment to the development of an effective headquarters staff. He must also communicate the rewards, which will accrue to managers and staffs who work effectively with the regional headquarters. On the other hand, he must communicate to the regional headquarters staff that their major function is to contribute toward the effectiveness of the individual country operations. They are aware that they, in general, are not in a position to direct action by country managers.

A second function of the headquarters staff is its role in advising the European manager on an overall European strategy for Raychem and also in assisting on a day-to-day basis the local managers in formulating their own strategic and operating plans.

The Raychem case illustrates the complexity of bringing a single related product group to market in a number of countries. When a company is involved in the marketing of unrelated products, a conceptual representation of their task requires the preparation of an industry, country, and function matrix for each related product group. Clearly, in these organizations there is pressure to rely on product divisions for the management of marketing efforts for the products concerned. The limiting factor is the size of each product division's business in each country.

BIBLIOGRAPHY

Business International, "Organizing for Worldwide Operations, Structuring and Implementing the Plan," February 1965.

Clee, Gilbert H., and Wilber M. Sachtjen, "Organizing a Worldwide Business," *Harvard Business Review,* November-December 1969, pp. 55-67.

Dance, W. D., "An Evolving Structure for Multinational Operations," *Columbia Journal of World Business,* November-December 1969, pp. 25-30.

Davis, Stanley, M., "Trends in the Organization of Multinational Corporations," *Columbia Journal of World Business,* Vol. 11, No. 2 (Summer 1976).

——, "Two Models of Organization: Unity of Command versus Balance of Power," *Sloan Management Review,* Fall 1974, pp. 29-40.

Fouraker, Lawrence E., and John M. Stopford, "Organizational Structure and the Multinational Strategy," *Administrative Science Quarterly,* June 1968, pp. 47-64.

Franko, Lawrence G., "The Move toward a Multidivional Structure in European Organizations," *ASQ,* Vol. 19, No. 4 (December 1974).

——, "Strategy Choice in Multinational Corporate Tolerance for Joint Ventures with Foreign Partners." Unpublished doctoral dissertation, Harvard Business School, August 1969.

Goggin, William C., "How the Multidimensional Structure Works at Dow Corning," *Harvard Business Review,* January-February 1974, pp. 54-65.

Kirchner, Donald P., "Now the Transnational Enterprise," *Harvard Business Review,* March-April 1964.

Mazzolini, Renato, "Behavioral and Strategic Obstacles to European Transnational Concentration," *Columbia Journal of World Business,* 8, No. 2 (Summer 1973), 68-78.

——, "The Obstacle Course for European Transnational Consolidations," *Columbia Journal of World Business,* 8, No. 1 (Spring 1973), 53-60.

"Organization and Control of International Operations," Conference Board Report No. 597, 1973.

Parks, F. Newton, "Survival of the European Headquarters," *Harvard Business Review,* March-April 1969, pp. 79-84.

Perlmutter, Howard V., "The Tortuous Evolution of the Multinational Corporation," *Columbia Journal of World Business,* January-February 1969, pp. 9-18.

Rutenburg, David P., "Organizational Archetypes of a Multinational Company," *Management Science,* February 1970, pp. B337-B349.

Schollhammer, Hans, "Organizational Structures of Multinational Corporations," *Academy of Management Journal,* September 1971.

Stopford, John M., "Growth and Organization Change in the Multinational Firm." Unpublished doctoral dissertation, Harvard Business School, June 1968.

Widing, J. William, Jr., "Reorganizing Your Worldwide Business," *Harvard Business Review,* May-June 1973, pp. 153-60.

Williams, Charles R., "Regional Management Overseas," *Harvard Business Review,* January-February 1967, pp. 87-91.

BANCIL CORPORATION

Struggling to clear his mind, Remy Gentile, marketing manager in France for the toiletry division of Bancil, stumbled to answer the ringing telephone.

"Allo?"

"Remy, Tom Wilson here. Sorry to bother you at this hour. Can you hear me?"

"Sacre Bleu! Do you know what time it is?"

"About 5:20 in Sunnyvale. I've been looking over the past quarter's results for our Peau Doux . . ."

"Tom, it's after 2 A.M. in Paris; hold the phone for a moment."

Remy was vexed with Tom Wilson, marketing vice president for the toiletry division and acting division marketing director for Europe, since they had discussed the Peau Doux situation via telex no more than a month ago. When he returned to the phone, Remy spoke in a more controlled manner.

"You mentioned the Peau Doux line, Tom."

"Yes, Remy, the last quarter's results were very disappointing. Though we've increased advertising by 30%, sales were less than 1% higher. What is even more distressing Remy, is that our competitors' sales have been growing at nearly 20% per year. Furthermore, our percent cost of goods sold has not decreased. Has Pierre Chevalier bought the new equipment to streamline the factory's operation?"

"No, Pierre has not yet authorized the purchase of the machine, and there is little that can be done to rationalize operations in the antiquated Peau Doux plant. Also, we have not yet succeeded in securing another distributor for the line."

"What! But that was part of the strategy with our increased advertising. I thought we agreed to . . ."

Tom Wilson hesitated for a moment. His mind was racing as he attempted to recall the specifics of the proposed toiletry division strategy for France. That strategy had guided his earlier recommendation to Gentile and Pierre Chevalier, the Bancil general manager in France, to increase advertising and to obtain a new distributor. Tom wanted to be forceful but tactful to insure Gentile's commitment to the strategy.

"Remy, let's think about what we discussed on my last trip to Paris. Do you recall we agreed to propose to Chevalier a plan to revitalize Peau Doux's growth? If my memory serves me well, it was to increase advertising by 25%, groom a new national distributor, reduce manufacturing costs with new equipment, increase prices, and purchase the 'L'aube' product line to spread our marketing overhead."

"Oui, oui. We explored some ideas and I thought they needed more study."

"Remy, as you recall Peau Doux has a low margin. Cutting costs is imperative. We expected to decrease costs by 5% by investing $45,000 in new equipment. Our test for the new strategy next year was to increase advertising this quarter and next quarter while contracting for a new distributor. The advertising was for naught. What happened?"

"I really don't know. I guess Pierre has some second thoughts."

Tom spoke faster as he grew more impatient. Gentile's asking Tom to repeat what he had said made him angrier. Tom realized that he must visit Paris to salvage what he could from the current test program on Peau Doux. He knew that the recent results would not support the proposed toiletry division strategy.

"Remy, I need to see what's going on and then decide how I can best assist you and Chevalier. I should visit Paris soon. How about early next week, say Monday and Tuesday?

"Oui, that is fine."

"I'll fly in on Sunday morning. Do you think you can join me for dinner that evening at the Vietnamese restaurant we dined at last time?"

"Oui."

"Please make reservations only for two. I'm coming alone. Good night, Remy."

"Oui. Bon soir."

COMPANY BACKGROUND

Bancil Corporation of Sunnyvale, California, was founded in 1903 by pharmacist Dominic Bancil. During its first half century, its products consisted primarily of analgesics (branded pain relievers like aspirin), an antiseptic mouthwash, and a first-aid cream. By 1974, some of the top-management positions were still held by members of the Bancil family, who typically had backgrounds as pharmacists or physicians. This tradition notwithstanding. John Stoopes, the present chief executive officer, was committed to developing a broad-based professional management team.

Bancil sales, amounting to $61 million in 1955, had grown to $380 million in 1970 and to $600 million in 1974. This sales growth had been aided by diversification and acquisition of allied businesses as well as by international expansion. Bancil's product line by 1970 included four major groups:

	Sales (in millions of dollars)	
	1970	1974
Agricultural and animal health products (weedkillers, fertilizers, feed additives)	$ 52	$141
Consumer products (Bancil original line plus hand creams, shampoos, and baby accessories)	205	276
Pharmaceutical products (tranquilizers, oral contraceptives, hormonal drugs)	62	107
Professional products (diagnostic reagents, automated chemical analyzers, and surgical gloves and instruments)	60	76

In 1974, Bancil's corporate organization was structured around these four product groups which, in turn, were divided into two or three divisions. Thus, in 1973 the consumer products group had been divided into the Dominic division, which handled Bancil's original product line, and the toiletry division, which was in charge of the newer product acquisitions. The objective of this separation was to direct greater attention to the toiletry products.

INTERNATIONAL OPERATIONS

International expansion had begun in the mid-1950s when Bancil exported through agents and distributors. Subsequently, marketing subsidiaries, called National Units (NUs), were created in Europe, Africa, Latin America, and Japan. All manufacturing took place in the United States. Virtually the entire export activity consisted of Bancil's analgesic Domicil. An innovative packaging concept, large amounts of creative advertising, and considerable sales push made Domicil a common word in most of the free world, reaching even the most remote areas of Africa, Asia, and South America. A vice president of international operations exercised control at this time through letters and occasional overseas trips. By the mid-1960s, overseas marketing of pharmaceutical and professional products began, frequently through a joint venture with a local company. Increasing sales led to the construction of production facilities for many of Bancil's products in England, Kenya, Mexico, Brazil, and Japan.

Bancil's international expansion received a strong commitment from top management. John Stoopes was not only a successful business executive but also a widely read intellectual with an avid interest in South American and African cultures. This interest generated an extraordinary sense of responsibility to the developing nations and a conviction that the mature industrial societies had an obligation to help in their development. He did not want Bancil to be viewed as a firm that drained resources and money from the developing world; rather, he desired to apply Bancil's resources to worldwide health and malnutrition problems. His personal commitment as an ardent humanist was a guideline for Bancil's international operations.

While Bancil had been successful during the 1960s in terms of both domestic diversification and international expansion, its efforts to achieve worldwide diversification had given rise to frustration. Even though the international division's specific purpose was to promote all Bancil products most advantageously throughout the world, the NUs had concentrated mainly on analgesics. As a result, the growth of the remaining products had been generally confined to the United States and thus these products were not realizing their fullest worldwide potential.

According to Bancil executives, these problems had their roots in the fact that the various product lines, though generically related, required different management strategies. For consumer products, advertising consumed 28% to 35% of sales; since production facilities did not require a large capital investment, considerable spare capacity was available to absorb impulses in demand created by advertising campaigns. For agricultural and animal health products, promotion was less than 1% of sales, but the capital-intensive production (a facility of minimum economic scale cost $18 million) required a marketing effort to stimulate demand consistently near full production capacity. Furthermore, the nature of the marketing activity for the professional and pharmaceutical products placed the burden on personal selling rather than on a mass-promotion effort.

In response to this situation, a reorganization in 1969 gave each product division worldwide responsibility for marketing its products. Regional marketing managers, reporting to the division's vice president of marketing, were given direct authority for most marketing decisions (e.g., advertising pricing, distribution channels) of their division's products in their area. The manufacturing division, with headquarters in Sunnyvale, had worldwide responsibility for production and quality control. (See Exhibit 1 for the 1969 organization chart.)

Corporate management also identified a need in key countries for a single local executive to represent Bancil Corporation's interests in local banking and

EXHIBIT 1. 1969 Organization Chart

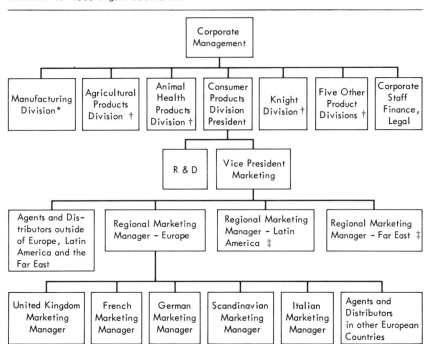

*The manufacturing division manufactured products for all the product divisions. Overseas manufacturing (not shown) reported to the manufacturing division in Sunnyvale.
† Organization similar to that of the consumer products division.
‡ Organization similar to that for Europe.

Source: Company records.

political circles. There was no single criterion for selecting, from the divisions' representatives in each country, the Bancil delegate, the title given to this position. A corporate officer remarked: "We chose who we thought was the best business executive in each country. There was no emphasis on functional specialty or on selecting an individual from the division with the greatest volume. In one country, the major candidates were opinionated and strong-willed, and we therefore chose the individual who was the least controversial. The Bancil delegate generally had a marketing background if marketing was the primary Bancil activity in the country or a production background if Bancil had several manufacturing facilities in the country."

While international sales had grown from $99 million in 1970 to $147 million in 1972, profit performance from 1971 to 1972 had been disappointing. A consultant's report stated:

> There are excessive communications between the NUs and Sunnyvale. The marketing managers and all the agents are calling for product-line information from the divisional headquarters. Five individuals are calling three times per week on an average, and many more are calling only slightly less often.

It appeared that a great deal of management time was spent on telex, long-distance communications, and travel. In response to these concerns, the divisions' staff increased in each country. Overhead nearly tripled, affecting the growth rate of profits from international operations.

With the exception of financial decisions which were dictated by corporate headquarters, most decisions on inventories, pricing, new product offerings, and facility development were made by corporate headquarters in conjunction with the local people. Local people, however, felt that the key decisions were being postponed. Conflicting demands also were a problem as every division drew on the local resources for manpower, inventories, receivables, and capital investment. These demands had been manageable, however, because even though profits were below target no cash shortages had developed.

Current Organization of International Operations

To improve the performance of its international operations, Bancil instituted a reorganization in mid-1973. The new organization was a matrix of NU general managers and area vice presidents, who were responsible for total resource allocation in their geographic area, and division presidents, who were responsible for their product lines worldwide. (See Exhibit 2 for a description of the matrix in 1975.)

The general manager was the chief executive in his country in charge of all Bancil products. He also was Bancil's representative on the board and executive committee of local joint ventures. The Bancil delegate usually had been chosen as the general manager. He was responsible for making the best use of financial, material, and personnel resources; pursuing approved strategies; searching for and identifying new business opportunities for Bancil in his NU; and developing Bancil's

EXHIBIT 2. Shared Responsibility Matrix.

		Europe — Andre Dufour			Latin America — Juan Vilas			Far East
		France P. Chevalier	Germany D. Rogge	Four Other National Units	Argentina and Uruguay S. Portillo	Brazil E. Covelli	Two Other National Units	Four Other National Units
Product Group Vice Presidents	Division Presidents							
Agricultural and Animal Health (3 divisions)	Rodgers Division							
	Division B							
	Division C							
Consumer Products (2 Divisions)	Dominic Division							
	Toiletry Division (Robert Vincent)							
Pharmaceuticals (2 divisions)	Division A							
	Division B							
Professional (3 divisions)	Knight Division							
	Division B							
	Division C							

Column header note: Above Europe and Latin America is "Vice President / International Operations / Clark B. Tucker", with "Area Vice Presidents" labeling the Europe/Latin America/Far East row and "General Managers" labeling the individual manager names.

Source: Company records.

reputation as a responsible corporate citizen. The general manager was assisted by a financial manager, one or more plant managers, product-line marketing managers, and other functional managers as required.

The divisions were responsible for operations in the United States and Canada and for worldwide expertise on their product lines. Divisions discharged the latter responsibility through local product-line marketing managers who reported on a line basis to the NU general manager and on a functional basis to a division area marketing director. The latter, in turn, reported to the divisional marketing vice president. Where divisions were involved in other functional activities, the organizational structure was similar to that for marketing. The flow of product-line expertise from the divisions to the NUs consisted of (1) operational inputs such as hiring/termination policies and the structure of merit programs and (2) technical/ professional inputs to the NU marketing, production, and other staff functions on the conduct of the division's business within the NU.

Only the Dominic division was represented in every NU. Some divisions lacked representation in several NUs, and in some cases a division did not have a marketing director in an area. For example, the Rodgers division had area marketing directors in Europe, the Far East, and Latin America, all reporting to the divisional vice president of marketing to whom the division's U.S. marketing personnel also reported. However, the Knight division, which had a structure similar to that of the Rodgers division, could justify area marketing directors only in Europe and Latin America.

The new matrix organization established for each country a National Unit Review Committee (NURC) with its membership consisting of the general manager (chairman), a financial manager, and a representative from each division with activities in the NU. Corporate executives viewed the NURC as the major mechanism for exercising shared profit responsibility. NURC met quarterly, or more frequently at the general manager's direction, to (1) review and approve divisional profit commitments generated by the general manager's staff; (2) insure that these profit commitments, viewed as a whole, were compatible with and representative of the best use of the NU's resources; (3) monitor the NU's progress against the agreed plans; and (4) review and approve salary ranges for key NU personnel. When the division's representatives acted as members of the NURC, they were expected to view themselves as responsible executives of the NU.

Strategic Planning and Control

NURC was also the framework within which general managers and division representatives established the NU's annual strategic plan and profit commitment. Strategy meetings commenced in May, at which time the general manager presented a forecast of Bancil's business in his NU for the next five years and the strategies he would pursue to exploit environmental opportunities. The general manager and the divisional representatives worked together between May and September to develop a mutually acceptable strategy and profit commitment. If genuine disagreement on principle arose during these deliberations, the issue could be resolved at the next level of responsibility. The profit commitment was reviewed at higher levels both within the area and within the product divisions, with the final approval coming from the corporate executive committee (CEC) which required compatible figures from the vice president of international operations and the product group executives. CEC, the major policy-making forum at Bancil, consisting of the chief executive officer, the group vice presidents, the vice president of international operations, and the corporate secretary, met monthly to resolve policy issues and to review operating performance.

For each country, results were reported separately for the various divisions represented, which, in turn, were consolidated into a combined NU statement. The NU as well as the divisions were held accountable, though at different levels, according to their responsibilities. The division profit flow (DPF) and NU net income are shown in the following example for the Argentine National Unit in 1974:

	Rodgers Division	Dominic Division	Toiletry Division	National Unit
Division sales	$250,000	$800,000	$1,250,000	$2,300,000
Division expenses	160,000	650,000	970,000	1,780,000
Division profit flow (DPF)	$ 90,000	$150,000	$ 280,000	$ 520,000
NU other expenses (general administrative, interest on loans, etc.)				350,000
NU income before taxes				$ 170,000
Less: Taxes				80,000
NU net income				$ 90,000
Working capital	$100,000	$300,000	$ 700,000	

The product divisions were responsible for worldwide division profit flow (DPF) defined as net sales less all direct expenses related to divisional activity, including marketing managers' salaries, sales force, and sales office expenses. The NU was responsible for net income after charging all local divisional expenses and all NU operating expenses such as general administration, taxes, and interest on borrowed funds. Because both the general managers and the divisions shared responsibility for profit in the international operations, the new structure was called a shared responsibility matrix (SRM). The vice president of international operations and the division presidents continually monitored various performance ratios and figures (see Exhibit 3). In 1975 international operations emphasized return on resources, cash generation, and cash remittance, while the division presidents emphasized product-line return on resources, competitive market share, share of advertising, and dates of new product introductions.

The impact of the 1973 organizational shift to the SRM had been greatest for the general managers. Previously, as Bancil delegates, they had not been measured on the basis of the NU's total performance for which they were now held responsible. Also, they now determined salary adjustments, hiring, dismissals, and appointments after consultations with the divisions. In addition, general managers continued to keep abreast of important political developments in their areas, such as the appointment of a new finance minister, a general work strike, imposition of punitive taxes, and the outbreak of political strife, a not-infrequent occurrence in some countries.

Under the new organizational structure, the area marketing directors felt that their influence was waning. While they were responsible for DPF, they were not sure that they had "enough muscle" to effect appropriate allocation of resources for their products in each of the countries they served. This view was shared by Nicholas Rosati, Knight division marketing manager in Italy, who commented on his job:

EXHIBIT 3. Control Figures and Ratios

Vice President of International Operations for National Unit		Division President for Product Line
X*	Sales	X
X	Operating Income: % Sales	X
X	General Manager Expense: % Sales	
X	Selling Expense: % Sales	X
X	Non-Production Expense: % Operating Income	
X	Operating Income per Staff Employee	
X	% Staff Turnover	
X	Accounts Receivable (days)	X
X	Inventories (days)	X
X	Fixed Assets	X
X	Resources Employed	X
X	Return on Resources	X
X	Cash Generation	
X	Cash Remittances	
X	Share of Market & Share of Advertising	X
X	Rate of new product introduction	X

*X indicates figure or ratio on organization's (national unit or division) performance of interest to the vice president of international operations and the division presidents.

Source: Company records.

> The European marketing director for the Knight division keeps telling me to make more calls on hospitals and laboratories. But it is useless to make calls to solicit more orders. The general manager for Italy came from the consumer products division. He will neither allocate additional manpower to service new accounts for the Knight division nor will he purchase sufficient inventory of our products so I can promise reasonable delivery times for new accounts.

Divisions, nevertheless, were anxious to increase their market penetration outside the United States and Canada, seeing such a strategy as their best avenue of growth. The recent increase in international sales and profits, which had by far exceeded that of domestic operations (see Exhibit 4), seemed to confirm the soundness of this view. Not all NU general managers shared this approach, as exemplified by a statement from Edmundo Covelli, the general manager of Brazil:

> The divisions are continually seeking to boost their sales and increase their DPF. They are not concerned with the working capital requirements to support the sales. With the inflation rate in Brazil, my interest rate of 40% on short-term loans has a significant effect on my profits.

The Peau Doux Issue

The telephone conversation described at the beginning of the case involved a disagreement between Tom Wilson, who was both marketing vice president for the

EXHIBIT 4. Sales and Profits for Bancil Corporation
Domestic and International (In Millions of Dollars)

Year	Domestic		International		Total	
	Sales	Profit	Sales	Profit	Sales	Profit
1955	$ 61	$ 5.5	–	–	$ 61	$ 5.5
1960	83	8.3	$ 6	$ 0.2	89	8.5
1965	121	13.5	23	1.3	144	14.8
1969	269	26.7	76	9.2	345	35.9
1970	280	27.1	99	12.3	379	39.4
1971	288	28.7	110	14.2	398	42.9
1972	313	32.5	147	15.8	460	48.3
1973	333	35.3	188	21.4	521	56.7
1974	358	36.7	242	30.9	600	67.6

Source: Company records.

toiletry division and acting division marketing director for Europe, and Pierre Chevalier, Bancil's general manager for France. It also involved Remy Gentile, who reported on a line basis to Chevalier and on a functional basis to Wilson.

Pierre Chevalier had been a general manager of France for 18 months after having been hired from a competitor in the consumer products business. Upon assuming the position, he identified several organizational and operational problems in France:

> When I took this job, I had five marketing managers, a financial manager, a production manager, and a medical specialist reporting to me. After the consumer products division split, the new toiletry division wanted its own marketing manager. Nine people reporting to me was too many. I hired Remy for his administrative talents and had him assume responsibility for the toiletry division in addition to having the other marketing managers report to him. That gave me more time to work with our production people to get the cost of goods down.

In less than two years as general manager. Chevalier had reduced the cost of goods sold by more than 3% by investing in new equipment and had improved the net income for the French NU by discontinuing products which had little profit potential.

Remy Gentile had been the marketing manager for the toiletry division in France for the past year. In addition, five other marketing managers (one for each Bancil Corporation division operating in France) reported to him. During the previous six years Gentile had progressed from salesman to sales supervisor to marketing manager within the Knight division in France. Although he had received mixed reviews from the toiletry division, particularly on his lack of mass-marketing experience, Chevalier had hired him because of his track record, his ability to learn fast, and his outstanding judgment.

The disagreement involved the Peau Doux line of hand creams which Bancil Corporation had purchased five years earlier to spread the general manager's overhead, especially in terms of marketing, over a broader product offering. Wilson's frustration resulted from Chevalier's ambivalence toward the division's strategy of increasing the marketing effort and cutting manufacturing costs on the Peau Doux line.

The total market in France for the Peau Doux product line was growing at an annual rate of 15%–20%, according to both Wilson and Gentile. However, Peau Doux, an old, highly regarded hand cream, had been traditionally distributed through pharmacies, whereas recently introduced hand creams had been successfully sold through supermarkets. The original Peau Doux sales force was not equipped to distribute the product through other outlets. To support a second sales force for supermarket distribution, the toiletry division sought to acquire the L'aube shampoo and face cream line. When Gentile had informed Chevalier of this strategy, the latter had questioned the wisdom of the move. The current volume of the Peau Doux line was $800,000. Though less than 10% of Chevalier's total volume, it comprised the entire toiletry division volume in France.

Tom Wilson viewed the Peau Doux problems primarily in terms of an inadequate marketing effort. On three occasions within the past year, he or his media experts from Sunnyvale had gone to Paris to troubleshoot the Peau Doux problems. On the last trip, Robert Vincent, the toiletry division president, had joined them. On the return flight to Sunnyvale, Wilson remarked to Vincent:

> I have the suspicion that Chevalier, in disregarding our expertise, is challenging our authority. It is apparent from his indifference to our concerns and his neglect in allocating capital for new machinery that he doesn't care about the Peau Doux line. Maybe he should be told what to do directly.

Vincent responded:

> Those are very strong words, Tom. I suggest we hold tight and do a very thorough job of preparing for the budget session on our strategy in France. If Chevalier does not accept or fundamentally revises our budget, we may take appropriate measures to make corporate management aware of the existing insensitivity to the toiletry division in France. This seems to be a critical issue. If we lose now, we may never get back in the French market in the future.

After Wilson and Vincent had departed for Sunnyvale, Chevalier commented to DuFour, his area vice president:

> I have the feeling that nothing we say will alter the thinking of Wilson and Vincent. They seem to be impervious to our arguments that mass advertising and merchandising in France do not fit the Peau Doux product concept.

Andre Dufour had been a practicing pharmacist for six years prior to joining Bancil Corporation as a sales supervisor in Paris in 1962. He had progressed to sales manager and marketing manager of the consumer products division in France. After the untimely death of the existing Bancil delegate for France in 1970, he had been selected to fill that position. With the advent of SRM he had become the general manager and had been promoted to vice president for Europe a year later. Dufour had a talent for identifying market needs and for thoroughly planning and deliberately executing strategies. He was also admired for his perservance and dedication to established objectives. Clark B. Tucker, vice president of international operations and Dufour's immediate supervisor, commented:

> When he was a pharmacist he developed an avocational interest in chess and desired to become proficient at the game. Within five years he successfully competed in several international tournaments and achieved the rank of International Grand Master.

In the fall of 1974, Dufour had become the acting vice president of international operations while his superior, Clark Tucker, was attending the 13-week Advanced Management Program at the Harvard Business School. Though Dufour had considerable difficulty with the English language, he favorably impressed the corporate management at Sunnyvale with his ability of getting to the heart of business problems.

The toiletry division had only limited international activities. In addition to the Peau Doux line in France, it marketed Cascada shampoos and Tempestad fragrances in Argentina. The Cascada and Tempestad lines had been acquired in 1971.

Tom Wilson and Manual Ramirez, toiletry division marketing director for Latin America, were ecstatic over the consumer acceptance and division performance of Cascada and Tempestad in Argentina. Revenue and DPF had quintupled since the acquisition. In his dealings with Gentile, Wilson frequently referred to the toiletry division's success in Argentina. Given this sales performance and the division's clearly stated responsibility for worldwide marketing of toiletry products, Wilson felt that his position in proposing the new strategy for France was strong.

On the other hand, Sergio Portillo, general manager of Argentina and Uruguay, and Juan Vilas, vice president for Latin American operations, had become alarmed by the cash drain from marketing the toiletry division products in Argentina. The high interest charges on funds for inventories and receivables seemed to negate the margins touted by the division executives. In describing the Cascada and Tempestad operation to Vilas, Portillo commented:

> I have roughly calculated our inventory turnover for the toiletry division products marketed in Argentina. Though my calcualtions are crude, the ratio based on gross sales is about four, which is less than one-half the inventory turnover of the remainder of our products.

Neither Portillo nor Vilas shared the toiletry division's enthusiasm and they suspected that Cascada and Tempestad were only slightly above break-even profitability. Chevalier and Dufour were aware of this concern with the toiletry products in Argentina.

As Chevalier contemplated the toiletry division strategy, he became convinced that more substantive arguments rather than just economic ones would support his position. In discussing his concerns with Dufour, Chevalier asked:

> Are the toiletry division product lines really part of what John Stoopes and we want to be Bancil's business? Hand creams, shampoos, and fragrances belong to firms like Colgate-Palmolive, Procter & Gamble, and Revlon. What is Bancil contributing to the local people's welfare by producing and marketing toiletries? We have several potentially lucrative alternatives for our resources. The Rodgers division's revenues have been increasing at 18%. We recently completed construction of a processing plant for Rodgers and we must get sales up to our new capacity. The Knight division is introducing an electronic blood analyzer that represents a technological breakthrough. We must expand and educate our sales force to take advantage of this opportunity.

Chevalier sensed that Gentile was becoming increasingly uneasy on this issue, and the feeling was contagious. They had never faced such a situation before. Under the previous organization, NUs had been required to comply, although sometimes reluctantly, with the decisions from Sunnyvale. However, SRM was not supposed to work this way. Chevalier and Gentile stood firmly behind their position, though they recognized the pressure on Tom Wilson and to a lesser degree on Vincent. They wondered what should be the next step and who should take it. Due to the strained relationship with Wilson, they did not rule out the possibility of Wilson and Vincent's taking the Peau Doux issue to the consumer products group vice president and having it resolved within the corporate executive committee.

QUESTIONS

1. What are the strategic business thrusts at Bancil? Which ones are the most critical for the future in the judgment of the corporate management?
2. Clearly identify the basic functioning of the new multiaxis structures implemented by the company. Where are the pressure points? Why was the structure changed? Will the new structure accomplish the purpose underlying the change? Under what conditions?
3. What are the opportunities and problems facing Chevalier, Dufour, and Vincent? Should the issue be resolved between Dufour and Vincent or by the corporate executive committee?
4. What should the president of the consumer products group division do, if anything?
5. How would you define the dimensions of the job for Dufour and Vincent?

multinational marketing management control

We have decided to call the entire field of control and communication theory, whether in the machine or in the animal, by the name of cybernetics, which we form from the Greek for steersman.

Norbert Wiener, 1894–1964
(Cybernetics, 1948)

INTRODUCTION

Multinational marketing presents formidable problems to managers responsible for marketing control. Each national market is different from every other market. Distance and differences in language, custom, and practices create communications problems. In larger companies the size of operations and number of country subsidiaries often result in the creation of an intermediate headquarters, which adds an organizational level to the control system. This chapter reviews multinational marketing control practices, compares these practices with domestic marketing control, and identifies the major factors that influence the design of a multinational control system.

CONTROL AND PLANNING

Every plan is conceived in the midst of uncertain major internal and external forces that influence marketing success. Market growth, customer response to a new product, competitive moves, government regulations, and costs are just a few of the uncertain factors about which assumptions must be made in order to formulate a plan. Therefore, when a company plans, it must also make provisions to monitor the results of plan implementation programs and make adjustments to plans where necessary. Planning necessitates control.

In the managerial literature, *control* is defined as the process of assuring "that the results of operations conform to established goals," or as "the process by which managers assure that resources are obtained and used effectively and efficiently in the accomplishment of the organization's objectives."[1] Marketing literature parallels these definitions. One marketing textbook, for example, defines *control* as "the process of taking steps to bring the actual and desired results closer together."[2]

Each of these definitions describes a process of activities and steps that are directed toward ensuring that planned organizational programs do in fact achieve desired objectives. Control activities are directed toward programs initiated by the planning process. In the ongoing enterprise, however, the data measures and evaluations generated by the control process are also a major input to the planning process. Thus planning and control are intertwined and interdependent. The planning process can be divided into two related phases: (1) strategic planning is the selection of opportunities defined in terms of products and markets, and the commitment of resources, both manpower and financial, to achieve these objectives; and (2) operational planning is the process in which strategic product market objectives and resource commitments to these objectives are translated into specific projects and programs. The relationship between strategic planning, operational planning, and control is illustrated in Figure 18-1.

In domestic operations, marketing control has become increasingly important and challenging. Because enterprise is getting larger, the distance between top managers and marketing operations is growing. Top managers must take steps to ensure that they receive information that measures the operation's success. The growing size of enterprise makes the analysis of an operation an increasingly challenging task. The environment is also changing rapidly, making it essential that control systems generate data that will be timely enough to allow management to take steps to correct problems.

In multinational operations, marketing control presents additional challenges. The rate of environmental change in a multinational company is a dimension of each of the national markets in which the company operates; and the multiplicity of environments, each changing at a different rate and each exhibiting unique characteristics, adds to the complexity of this dimension. In addition, the multiplicity of multinational environments challenges the multinational marketing control system with much greater environmental heterogeneity and therefore greater complexity in its control. Finally, multinational marketing causes special communications problems associated with the great distance between markets and headquarters, and differences among managers in languages, customs, and practices.

[1] Robert N. Anthony, *Planning and Control Systems: A Framework for Analysis* (Boston: Division of Research, Graduate School of Business Administration, Harvard University, 1965).
[2] Philip Kotler, *Marketing Management: Analysis Planning and Control*, 2nd ed. (Englewood Cliffs, N.J.: Prentice-Hall, 1972).

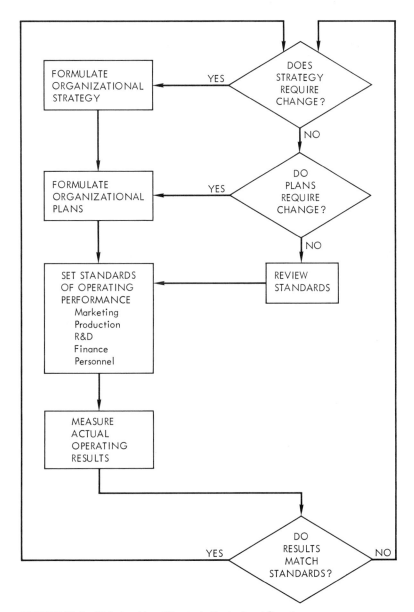

FIGURE 18-1. Relationship of Strategic Control and Planning

FORMAL CONTROL METHODS

Planning and Budgeting

The basic formal marketing control technique used by companies is planning and budgeting.[3] This practice is an extension of a basic technique used by companies in domestic marketing to international marketing. It involves expressing planned sales and profit objectives and expenditures on marketing programs in unit and money terms in a budget. The budget spells out the objectives and necessary expenditures to achieve these objectives. Control consists of measuring actual sales and expenditures. If there is no variance or favorable variance between actual and budget, no action is usually taken. If variance is unfavorable, this is a red flag that attracts the attention of line and staff executives at regional and international headquarters, and they will investigate and attempt to determine the cause of the unfavorable variance and what might be done to improve performance.

Evaluating Performance

In evaluating performance, actual performance is compared with budgeted performance as described in the previous section. Thus the key question is, How is the budget established? According to one researcher most companies in both domestic and international operations place heavy reliance upon two standards—last year's actual performance, and some kind of industry average or historical norm.[4] A more normative approach is to develop at headquarters an estimate concerning the kind of growth that would be desirable and attainable in each national market. This estimate can be based upon exhaustive studies of national and industry growth patterns.

In larger companies there is enough business volume in a number of products to justify staff product specialists at corporate headquarters who follow the performance of products worldwide. They have staff responsibility for their product from its introduction to its withdrawal from the company's product line. Normally a new product is first introduced in the largest and most-sophisticated markets. It is subsequently introduced in smaller and less-developed markets. As a result, the company's products are typically at different stages of the product life cycle in different markets. A major responsibility of staff specialists is to ensure that lessons learned in more-advanced markets are applied to the management of their products in smaller less-developed markets. Wherever possible they try to avoid making the same mistake twice, and they try to capitalize on what they have learned and apply it elsewhere. They also ensure that useful ideas from markets at similar stages of

---

[3] John J. Mauriel, "Evaluation and Control of Overseas Operations," *Management Accounting* (New York: National Association of Accountants, May 1969), pp. 35–39; James McIness, "Financial Control Systems for Multinational Operations: An Empirical Investigation," *Journal of International Business Studies* (Atlanta: School of Business Administration, Georgia State University and the Association for Education in International Business, Fall 1971), pp. 11–28.
[4] Mauriel, "Evaluation and Control of Overseas Operations," pp. 35–39.

development are fully applied. Smaller companies focus on key products in key markets. Key products are those that are important to the company's sales, profit objectives, and competitive position. They are frequently new products that require close attention in their introductory stage in a market. If any budget variances develop with a key product, headquarters intervenes directly to learn about the nature of the problem and to assist local management in dealing with the problem.

In theory, if conditions in the subsidiary's business environment change during a planning period, the budget would be changed to reflect changes in underlying assumptions. In practice, budgets of the companies studied are not changed during an operating period. Companies recognize that refusing to change a budget can result in unfavorable variances that are not controllable by the subsidiary management, but the view of most companies is that it is better to allow these unfavorable variances to occur than it is to allow budget revision during an implementation period. When a company does not permit budget revision, it is emphasizing the importance of careful planning and of achieving plan objectives. If uncontrollable and unforeseeable changes do occur, these can be noted as mitigating reasons or even as a full explanation for failure to achieve budget.

Influences on Marketing Budgets

In preparing a budget or plan, the following factors are important:

Market potential. How large is the potential market for the product being planned? In every domestic market, management must address this question in formulating a product plan. An international company that introduces a product in more than one national market must answer this question for each market. In most cases new products are introduced on a serial rather than simultaneous basis and can be defined as new international products as opposed to new products per se. A new international product is analogous to a product that has been introduced in a test market. The major opportunity of a test market is the chance to project the experience in the test market to a national market, whereas its major pitfall is that the characteristics of the test market will be unlike those of the national market, thus invalidating the projections made. The same opportunities and pitfalls apply in an amplified way to new international products.

Competition. A marketing plan or budget must be prepared in light of the competitive level in the market. The more entrenched the competition, the more difficult it is to achieve market share and the more likely a competitive reaction will occur to any move that promises significant success in the target market. Competitive moves are particularly important as a variable in international market planning because many companies are moving from strong competitive positions in their base markets to foreign markets where they have a minor position and must compete against entrenched companies. Domestic market standards and expectations of marketing performance are based on experience in markets where the company has a major position. These standards and expectations are simply not relevant to a market where the company is in a minor position trying to break into the market.

Impact of substitute products. One of the sources of competition for a product in a market is the frequent existence of substitute products. As a product is moved into markets at different stages of development, improbable substitute products often emerge. For example, in Colombia a major source of competition for manufactured boxes and other packaging products is woven bags and wood boxes made in the handicraft sector of the economy. Marketing officials of multinational companies in the packaging industry report that the garage operator producing a handmade product is very difficult competition because of costs of materials and labor in Colombia.

Process. The manner in which targets are communicated to subsidiary management is as important as the way in which they are derived. One of the most sophisticated methods used today is the so-called indicative planning method. Headquarters estimates of regional potential are disaggregated and communicated to subsidiary management as "guidance."[5] The subsidiaries are in no way bound by guidance. They are expected to produce their own plan, taking into account the headquarters guidance that is based on global data and their own data from the market, including a detailed review of customers, competitors, and other relevant market developments. This method produces excellent results because it combines a global perspective and estimate with specific country marketing plans that are developed from the objective to the program by the country management teams themselves. Headquarters, in providing "guidance," does not need to understand a market in depth. For example, it is not necessary that the headquarters of a manufacturer of electrical products know how to sell electric motors to a Frenchman. What headquarters can do is gather data on the expected expansion in generating capacity in France and use experience tables drawn from world studies that indicate what each megawatt of additional generating capacity will mean in terms of the growth in demand in France for electrical motors. The estimate of total market potential together with information on the competitiveness of the French subsidiary can be the basis for a "guidance" in terms of expected sales and earnings in France. The guidance may not be accepted by the French subsidiary. If the indicative planning method is used properly, the subsidiary educates the headquarters if its guidance is unrealistic. If headquarters does a good job, it will select an attainable but ambitious target. If the subsidiary does not see how it can achieve the headquarters goal, discussion and headquarters involvement in the planning process will either lead to a plan that will achieve the guidance objective or it will result in a revision of the guidance by headquarters.

Many companies communicate sales and earnings expectations rather than guidance to subsidiaries. In one typical case these expectations were high and were based upon successful experience in the U.S. market. Subsidiaries accepted

---

[5] This term was coined by French planners in the 1950s to describe the function of the French National Planning Ministry in setting industry targets.

the expectations and budgeted programs to achieve them even though they did not have plans developed to achieve the budgeted goals. The problem in this company was the fear subsidiaries had of challenging headquarters expectations. They felt it was better to fail to achieve headquarters expectations than to challenge them. The result in this case was an almost worldwide failure to achieve product plan objectives. If subsidiaries had taken headquarters initial goals for the product in question as guidance rather than as expectations, the result would have been a dialogue at the plan formulation stage between headquarters and subsidiaries that would have led to either the development of realistic plans to achieve headquarters guidance or the downward revision of the product's sales and earnings goals.

Other Measures of Performance

Another principal measure of marketing performance is share of market. In larger markets data are reported for subsidiaries and, where significant sales are involved, on a product-by-product basis. Share-of-market data in larger markets are often obtained from independent market audit groups. In smaller markets share-of-market data are often not available because the market is not large enough to justify the development of an independent commercial marketing audit service. Local managers or agents are asked to estimate their share-of-market position. In these smaller markets it is possible for a country manager or agent to hide a deteriorating market position or share of market behind absolute gains in sales and earnings. This is a valuable measure because it provides a comparison of company performance with that of other competitors in the market. Companies who do not obtain this measure, even if it is an estimate, are flying blind.

It is important that this share-of-market measure be of the whole market, not just the import component. Until recently, one major U.S. corporation reported its business in foreign markets as a percentage of U.S. exports to each market. By this measure, in a period of declining U.S. export competitiveness in a number of markets, the company appeared to be doing very well when in fact its market position was rapidly deteriorating.

INFORMAL CONTROL METHODS

In addition to budgeting, informal control methods play an important role, particularly in multinational companies. The main informal control method is the transfer of people from one market to another. When a person is transferred, he takes with him his experience in previous markets, which will normally include some standards for marketing performance. When investigating a new market that has lower standards than a previous market, the investigation will lead to revised standards or to discovery of why there is a difference. Another valuable informal control device is face-to-face contact between subsidiary staff and headquarters staff, as well as contact among subsidiary staff. These contacts provide an opportunity for an exchange of information and judgments that can be a valuable input to the planning and control process. Annual meetings that bring together staff from a region of the world often result in informal inputs to the process of setting standards.

VARIABLES INFLUENCING CONTROL

Domestic practices and the value of standardization. One of the major assets of any organization is its operational and successful managerial practices. If a company has successfully developed and used a control system in its home or domestic operation, then this system is clearly a candidate for export because (1) it works, (2) there are people who understand it, and (3) these people can in most instances be persuaded to transfer their know-how to a foreign subsidiary. Today companies are using a standard reporting format for both domestic and foreign operations. The amount of detail and frequency of reports should be a function of the size of the foreign subsidiary. One sophisticated international marketer has designated seven key markets and another fourteen major markets in its one-hundred-country multinational group. The amount and frequency of reporting is greatest for ordinary markets.

The advantage of a standard system (adapted for market size differences) is that it allows comparisons to be made on a global basis, and it facilitates the easy transfer of people and ideas because all managers in the organization are working with the same system.

Communications system. A major development affecting control in international marketing operations is the communications infrastructure. A century ago international marketers had at their disposal various means of surface travel—horse, carriage, and train—as well as various means of water travel, such as sailboats and steamships. Electronic communications were limited to the telegraph. The businessman who wanted to control international operations had two choices. He could either travel by land, sea, or a combination of both, or he could transmit written messages either by post or by telegraph. Given the speed, cost, and comfort of the communications methods available a century ago, it is understandable that businesses operated on a highly decentralized basis. Operating policies consisted of sending out handpicked men with instructions as to their general areas of operations. These men were versed in the ways of the company, and therefore it was assumed that company policies and procedures would be implemented by them. They had total responsibility for carrying out the company's operations in their area. At the end of the designated operating period, which was typically a year, the results of operations would be reported. In those days, subsidiaries were controlled according to Saint Augustine's rule for Christian conduct: "Love God and do what you like!" The implication of this is that if you love God, then you will only ever want to do things that are acceptable to Him.[6] Men who were sent out to manage company affairs were expected to approach things in the approved manner.

[6] Anthony Jay, *Management and Machiavelli* (New York: Holt, Rinehart & Winston, 1967).

Today the communications infrastructure is vastly enlarged. In addition to surface and sea travel, the airplane is now the major form of long-distance travel in the world. Face-to-face and written communications possibilities are vastly extended by highspeed jet aircraft. They allow managers to maintain regular direct contact with operating units all over the world. Given the importance of face-to-face communications in the information-acquisition process, it seems reasonable to conclude that the jet aircraft has been a major tool in making it possible to manage a global enterprise. The very limited success of small businesses in international operations can be attributed to the reluctance or inability of the small-business owner to invest money and time to travel to achieve instant familiarity with customers, agents, and distributors in foreign markets. The larger enterprise spends enormous sums to maintain contact with managers in foreign markets who are in direct contact with employees, customers, agents, and distributors in their market.

In addition to the face-to-face communications possibilities, electronic communication is also vastly expanded. The teletype and telephone enable rapid, direct, high-speed voice and data communication to take place on a global basis. Increasingly, the communications systems of large corporations (large companies account for an estimated 80 percent of U.S. foreign direct investment) are being developed so that communication of voice and data will be available on a worldwide basis. In many large companies internal communications systems allow direct dialing of any company telephone in the United States. A number of companies are planning to expand their internal communications so that a company telephone anywhere in the world can be dialed direct.

Distance. All other things being equal, the greater the distance between headquarters and an operating unit, the more autonomous the operating unit will be from headquarters. This relationship is due to physical and psychological differences. The physical distance imposes a time and cost barrier on communications because to travel to a distant point takes more time and therefore is more costly. To communicate by telephone, Telex, or other telecommunications methods is also more costly and time consuming as distances increase. Thus, with less communication, particularly face-to-face communication, there is a greater delegation of responsibility as distances increase in international operations. Nevertheless, one of the major changes in the environment of international business is the development of communications technology, which has reduced the time-and-cost barriers of distance by increasing the speed and raising the quality of Telex, voice, television, and air travel methods of communications.

The product. A major factor affecting the type of marketing control system developed for international operations is the product being controlled. A product that is technically sophisticated can be more extensively controlled because the product use is highly similar around the world. This similarity creates opportunities to apply standards of measurement and evaluation on an international basis. Computers, for example, are products that are applied today in the same manner in technologies wherever they are located in the world. The process-control computer for the petrochemical industry is the same type of application in Rotterdam as it is in Baton Rouge, Louisiana. The technology for the application of microcircuitry is a universal technology that is applied in the same way in Japan as it is in the United States.

Environmental sensitivity is the relevant product dimension influencing the extent to which "international" control can be exercised. If a product is similar or identical in the way it is applied and used around the world, that is, if it is culturally insensitive, then international standards and measures of performance can be developed. Computers and many industrial products fit this category. If a product is sensitive to environmental differences, then it is more difficult to apply international standards. Drugs and packaged food are two examples of environmentally sensitive products that normally require adaptation to meet the preferences of different cultures and systems of medical practice.

Environmental differences. The greater the environmental difference, the greater will be the delegation of responsibility and the more limited the control of the operating unit. For example, most U.S. companies with operations in Canada apply their most extensive control of international operations to Canadian operations. Indeed, many U.S. companies with extensive international operations, some of which are semiautonomous with regard to U.S. headquarters, operate in Canada as if Canada were a part of the U.S. market. A major reason for this is that the Canadian market is perceived as being highly similar to the U.S. market. Therefore, the standards of measurement and evaluation applicable to the U.S. market are seen as being applicable and relevant to Canadian operations.

The development that has most accelerated the extension of control of international operations in regions that are highly different from the home country area is the regional headquarters. Regional headquarters copes with environmental difference by focusing on a group of countries that is formed to maximize within-group similarities and between-group differences.

Environmental stability. The greater the degree of instability in a country, the less the relevance of external or planned standards and measures of performance. When a country moves into a period of sweeping political change, it is often impossible to predict environmental conditions. One company decided that whenever a subsidiary country went into a period of revolutionary change or turmoil it would scrap all plans and adopt a policy of simply delegating total on-the-spot discretion to local management to do whatever the managers thought best. Its experience had been that local management usually achieved much more than headquarters expected.

Subsidiary performance. A major variable influencing the kind of control exercised over international operations is the performance of subsidiary units. A subsidiary that is achieving budget is normally left alone. When a subsidiary fails to achieve budget, the variance between budgeted and actual performance is a sign that triggers intervention by headquarters. In addition, managers of successful profit centers have more leverage in holding off headquarters involvement in their operations. Subsidiaries reporting unfavorable variances find that headquarters is anxious to determine the cause of the problem, to correct the problem, and to maintain closer surveillance of operations to ensure that further difficulties do not emerge and develop undetected. Therefore a well-managed, successful subsidiary operation will be more loosely controlled than an operation in difficulty. At the same time, the sophisticated multinational company headquarters wants to know how everybody, including successful units, is doing. It needs data on performance to help establish standards and comparisons to use in evaluating the performance of subsidiaries.

Size of international operations. The larger the international operation in terms of sales and earnings, the greater is its ability to support its own headquarters staff specialists. The greater the specialization of a headquarters staff, the more extensive and penetrating is its control, or measurement and evaluation of performance. A large multinational company will have three or four levels of staff expertise focusing on operations in large country markets: country, region, and international and/or corporate. This fully developed staff organization is shown in Figure 18-2. A smaller company cannot afford to create a highly specialized multi-level staff and will therefore have less intensive control over its operations. A large multinational company assigns control responsibility to both line and staff executives. Normally, marketing control falls into the province of product group specialists and general managers. In smaller country markets, small staff organizations require a considerable simplification and abbreviation of the control process because the expertise and time required to generate and evaluate data are simply not available. One of the challenges to the large multinational company is the development of methods and procedures for the control of small subsidiaries that do not place an excessive data collection and reporting burden on the small subsidiary.

COMMUNICATIONS AND CONTROL IN THE MULTINATIONAL ENTERPRISE

In their study of American, European, and Japanese subsidiaries in Brazil, Brandt and Hulbert found that subsidiary managers were unanimously of the opinion that the flow of communications between home office and Brazil had doubled or quadrupled in recent years.[7] Despite the increasing flow of communications aided by computers, satellites, telecommunications, and jet airplanes, there are significant problems in collecting relevant quality information, getting it to the right people, and actually making it useful for decision making and resource allocation. Additionally, few managers, particularly at headquarters, seem to be aware of the costs in time, effort, and direct expense linked to communications.

[7]This section draws heavily upon William K. Brandt and James M. Hulbert, "Communications and Control in the Multinational Enterprise" (Unpublished manuscript, no date).

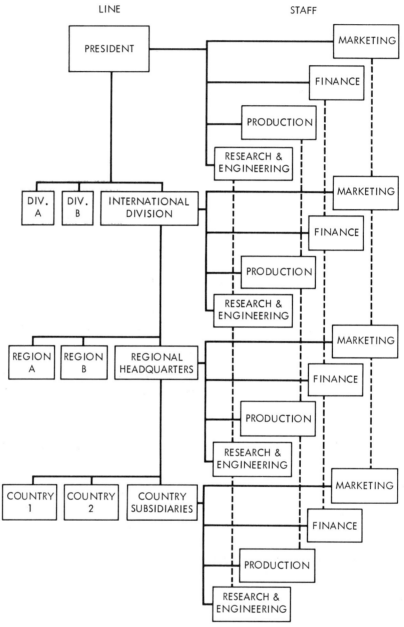

FIGURE 18-2. Organization Chart Showing the Relationship of Staff and Line Profit Centers in a Large Multinational Company

Types of Communications

Communications between home office and subsidiary in multinational companies can be divided into two broad categories: personal communication such as visits, meetings, telephone conversations; and impersonal communications such as regular or ad hoc reports, budget plans.

IMPERSONAL COMMUNICATIONS

Much information from subsidiaries to home office is reported on standardized forms which include statements of profit and loss, balance sheets, sales reports, sources and uses of funds, inventory positions, production schedules and output, production and marketing costs, budgets and budget deviations.

American subsidiaries in Brazil report to their home offices in far greater detail and with greater frequency than Japanese and European subsidiaries. Brandt and Hulbert found that managers in American firms complain bitterly about the burden of report requirements. Marketing managers in American companies estimated that they spent one day a week to "keep the home office happy." In contrast, their counterparts in European companies spent 10 percent of their time on such duties and in Japanese companies only 8 percent. American managers more frequently "touch base" to see whether the home office concurs with decisions or actions. In marked contrast, European managers tend to be proud of the fact that they seldom call headquarters.

Corporations with many overseas subsidiaries seem to do a better job of evaluating reports from subsidiaries than do those with few subsidiaries. This is not surprising, since with more foreign subsidiaries and greater sales and earnings, the home office must respond by adding staff and procedures to review and evaluate the reports required by the system.

PERSONAL COMMUNICATIONS

Managers of American companies in Brazil visited their home office an average of 2.4 times a year, as compared with 1.6 visits for European and 1.9 for the Japanese. Americans were visited far more often by executives responsible for Brazilian operations: home office honchos and the Brazilian chief executive met face to face 4.8 times a year on an average in American companies. In contrast, visits averaged 2.9 times a year for the European companies and 3.4 times a year for the Japanese companies.

Many European and American managers suffer from "overvisitation." It appears that at least for Brazil, there is a pattern of "vacation" visits which are perfunctory and are carried out simply because it is cold in New York.

Effects of Communications

Brandt and Hulbert concluded that the quantity of communications—number of reports, personal visits, or conferences—had no significant effect on perceived levels of understanding. The task of improving communications and control in multinational operations is to increase the quality and relevancy rather than quantity of information flows.

The need for improved communications in multinational operations is crucial. Many American companies are operating on the assumption that "more is better" and when in doubt send all information available. This burdens subsidiaries with the problem of sifting and sorting to find useful information and adds little to improving understanding in either home office or subsidiary. In contrast, some European companies use the opposite approach, which is to send nothing unless it is requested. This practice wastes time and also leads to decision making based on limited or inadequate information.

As companies develop standardized reporting formats, there is a pressing need for each subsidiary manager to sit down with headquarters and realistically assess the costs and benefits of providing the standardized information on the report form. Far too often a random request for specific data in one market gets locked into a worldwide reporting system, never again to be questioned as to why it is there or what purpose it serves.

For example, in one case a company president asked for market share data for a minor product in Finland. When he learned that no one at the home office knew the answer, he demanded that henceforth and forever more all overseas subsidiaries would report market share figures monthly, broken down by market segment for all products. While this is a valid and valuable exercise in the United States, it is a horrendous waste of time and money in many smaller overseas markets. Nonetheless, in this particular company the subsidiaries report market share data each month. Both the home office and the subsidiaries know the data are garbage, but they continue to play the game and really do not want to know how much it is costing them each year to play this game.

Control. Managers of European firms indicated much more freedom to make day-to-day decisions than did their American or Japanese counterparts. One concrete illustration of this was the much higher budgetary limit for chief executives of European firms than for those of Japanese or American firms. In European companies 23 percent had no effective limit, and 41 percent had a limit in the range of $50–$500,000 dollars. In American companies 67 percent had a limit of less than $5,000.

When the plan represents a commitment rather than a coordinating device, as it often does in American companies as compared with other multinationals, the so-called pressure-cooker syndrome may develop. Budgets and plans can, instead of providing standards and benchmarks, be perverted to pressure devices if managers feel that they are caught in a "pressure cooker." When this happens subsidiary managers respond predictably by doing everything possible to meet plan targets. In its most basic form this involves simple period-to-period manipulation of revenue and costs in order to make the bottom line, but more complex schemes might involve keeping a separate set of books or making major and undiscussed trade-offs in the short run in order to make the bottom line at the sacrifice of the longer-run profitability and health of the business.

Communications Guidelines

Effective communications requires both cooperation and adaptability on the part of home office and subsidiary executives. Each of these executives walks a thin line between chaos and rigidity. Systems are absolutely necessary in order to provide the possibility of integration and comparison across the international network. On the other hand, a rigid adherence to standardized systems results in garbage reports that provide the appearance of standardized and comparable information but actually are nothing of the sort.

All data reported by subsidiaries should meet the following test: Is this information necessary to help manage the subsidiary or the broader worldwide operation? Is the information worth the cost of collection? What is the cost of collection? These are routine questions in a well-managed market research operation, particularly when the information is being purchased in an outside buy. Inevitably there is a tendency within a company to assume that management time is a free good. This of course is not true.

SUMMARY

Lack of knowledge of basic market conditions is one of the major obstacles to the development of an effective control relationship between headquarters and subsidiary in international marketing. When headquarters commits itself to measure and evaluate subsidiary performance, the decision commits headquarters to participation in subsidiary planning. Measurement and evaluation of current performance are instrinsically involved in the cycle of planning for operations and programs in future time periods. In order to become effectively involved in this planning control cycle, headquarters must understand the basic characteristics and conditions of the subsidiary market. If there is inadequate understanding, headquarters may adversely or inadequately influence the design of the country marketing plan for future periods and may misunderstand the significance of operating results in current periods. The result of headquarters misunderstanding can involve major failures when headquarters succeeds in imposing an inappropriate plan on subsidiaries or in influencing subsidiaries to accept inappropriate objectives. Perhaps even more dangerously, headquarters misunderstanding can result in a failure of subsidiaries to achieve their full potential in a market. If headquarters does not understand the basic characteristics of a market, it will not be able to pinpoint subsidiary underperformance. The problem in international operations is a counterpart of the problem of managing product divisions in different technologies in a divisionalized company. In order to manage a product division, corporate management must understand the basic technology of the products being managed. If it does not understand the technology, divisional management virtually has free rein to develop its plan and explain its performance. For example, the disastrous unchecked expenditure of over $250 million by the Convair Division of General Dynamics was attributed to the lack of knowledge of the airframe industry by corporate management.

Companies expand headquarters understanding of foreign markets in one important way: by being actively involved in the subsidiary planning process. This involvement ensures that headquarters executives learn about each subsidiary and region's market conditions. A few sophisticated companies are assigning approximately equal numbers of domestic and foreign executives to their international headquarters in an effort to obtain an effective mix of U.S. product and system know-how and international environmental knowledge in the headquarters group.

The basic tool for controlling multinational marketing operations is the budget. The use of budgeting is an extension of a domestic practice suggesting once again that marketing tools and concepts are universal. Because the budget is derived from the marketing plan, it is clear that effective multinational marketing control begins with effective involvement in the national marketing planning process in each country market. To be effectively involved in the national marketing planning process, the multinational marketer must understand the relevant dimensions of each national market environment. This understanding at headquarters is expanded by the assignment of managers with international experience to headquarters jobs in marketing, and by working with subsidiaries in the development of local marketing plans. As understanding expands, the multinational marketer is better able to play a role in establishing realistic and challenging goals and helping subsidiaries overcome obstacles to their objectives. The major advantage of the multinational marketer in the task is his ability to draw upon worldwide operating experience.

BIBLIOGRAPHY

BOOKS

Ackoff, Russell L., *A Concept of Corporate Planning.* New York: Wiley Interscience, 1970.

Ahroni, Yair, *The Foreign Investment Decision Process.* Boston: Division of Research, Graduate School of Business Administration, Harvard University, 1966.

Alsegg, Robert J., *Control Relationships between American Corporations and Their European Subsidiaries,* AMA Research Study 107. New York: American Management Association, 1971.

Anthony, Robert N., *Planning and Control Systems: A Framework for Analysis.* Boston: Division of Research, Graduate School of Business Administration, Harvard University, 1965.

Behrman, Jack N., *Some Patterns in the Rise of the Multinational Enterprise,* Research Paper 18. Chapel Hill, N.C.: Graduate School of Business Administration, University of North Carolina, March 1969.

Bower, Joseph L., *Managing the Resource Allocation Process: A Study of Corporate Planning and Investment.* Boston: Division of Research, Graduate School of Business Administration, Harvard University, 1970.

Brooke, Michael Z., and H. Lee Remmers, *The Strategy of the Multinational Enterprise.* New York: American Elsevier Publishing, 1970.

The Conference Board, *Measuring the Profitability of Foreign Operations.* New York: Managing International Business, No. 7, 1970.

Jay, Anthony, *Management and Machiavelli.* New York: Holt, Rinehart & Winston, 1967.

Miller, Ernest C., *Objectives and Standards of Performance in Marketing Management,* AMA Research Study 85. New York: American Management Association, 1967.

Skinner, Wickham, *American Industry in Developing Economies.* New York: John Wiley, 1968.

Van der Hass, H., *The Enterprise in Transition: An Analysis of European and American Practice.* London: Tavistock Publications, 1967.

Vernon, Raymond, *Sovereignty at Bay, the Multinational Spread of U.S. Enterprises.* New York: Basic Books, 1971.

ARTICLES

Aggarwal, Raj, and James C. Baker, "Using Foreign Subsidiary Accounting Data: A Dilemma for the Multinational Corporation," *Columbia Journal of World Business,* 10, No. 3 (Fall 1975), 83–92.

Aylmer, R. J., "Who Makes Marketing Decisions in the Multinational Firm?" *Journal of Marketing,* 34 (October 1970), 25–30.

Bonini, Charles P., "Simulation of Organizational Behavior" in *Management Controls,* ed. Charles P. Bonini, Robert K. Jaedicke, and Harvey M. Wagner. New York: McGraw-Hill, 1964.

Brandt, William K., and James M. Hulbert, "Communications and Control in the Multinational Enterprise." Unpublished manuscript, no date.

Butler, W. Jack, and John Dearden, "Managing a Worldwide Business," *Harvard Business Review,* May-June 1965, pp. 93–102.

Cain, William W., "International Planning: Mission Impossible?" *Columbia Journal of World Business,* July-August 1970.

Hawkins, David F., "Controlling Foreign Operations," *Financial Executive,* February 1965, pp. 25–32, 56.

Keegan, Warren J., "Multinational Marketing Management." Cambridge: Marketing Science Institute *Working Paper,* January 1970.

——, "Multinational Marketing Planning: Headquarters Role," *Columbia Journal of World Business,* January-February 1971.

McIness, James, "Financial Control Systems for Multinational Operations: An Empirical Investigation," *Journal of International Business Studies,* Fall 1971, pp. 11–28.

Mauriel, John J., "Evaluation and Control of Overseas Operations," *Management Accounting,* pp. 35–39. New York: National Association of Accountants, May 1969.

Perlmutter, Howard V., "The Tortuous Evolution of the Multinational Corporation," *Columbia Journal of World Business,* January-February 1969.

Rocour, Jean-Luc, "Management of European Subsidiaries in the U.S.," *Management International.* Wiesbaden, Federal Republic of Germany: Betriebswirtschaftlicher, Verlag, No. 1, 1966.

Ruttenberg, David, "Tailoring Controls to Types of Multinational Companies." Unpublished paper, Carnegie-Mellon University, December 1968.

Sorenson, Ralph Z., and Ulrich E. Weichmann, "How Multinationals View Marketing Standardization," *Harvard Business Review,* May-June 1975, pp. 38ff.

Yoshino, M. Y., "Towards a Concept of Managerial Control for a World Enterprise," *Michigan Business Review,* March 1966, pp. 24–31.

Keegan, Warren J., "Scanning the International Business Environment: A Study of the Information Acquisition Process." Unpublished doctoral dissertation, Harvard Business School, June 1967.

GLOBAL FASTENERS, INC.

Joseph Standish, president of Global Fasteners, Inc. (GFI) leaned back in his chair and rubbed his eyes wearily as the arguments raged around him. While going "multinational" was undoubtedly the best route for GFI, it was no bed of roses, he mused. Apparently a firm had to do more than just declare that it was a multinational operation. With a shrug, he jerked his thoughts back to the meeting.

The June 1972 meeting to which Standish so reluctantly turned his thoughts concerned a major potential order for GFI in Great Britain. While all at the meeting were in agreement that GFI should get the order, there was considerable disagreement regarding *which* subsidiary should be permitted to bid on the job and supply the customer, Ellsworth Ltd. If GFI were successful in this particular bid, it would undoubtedly be in a favored position with Ellsworth in coming years and could expect a high volume of repeat sales over the next three to five years. The bid on the first phase of the contract would approximate $2.5 million, with sales volume expected to reach nearly $4.0 million annually over the next five years.

Attending the meeting were the managers of two foreign subsidiaries who wished to bid, one from the French subsidiary which was 85 percent owned by GFI and one from the Canadian subsidiary which was 100 percent owned. Also present were the marketing manager-International for industrial fasteners and GFI's legal counsel.

COMPANY AND INDUSTRY BACKGROUND

GFI was a moderately large U.S.-based corporation with total sales of $565 million in 1970, of which $85 million originated in the company's non-U.S. subsidiaries. GFI was generally considered to be a leader in the U.S. market as a supplier of fasteners to OEMs (original equipment manufacturer) in both consumer products and industrial products.

Outside the United States, the company's reputation and market position varied by region and industry. For example, the company was fairly strong in Latin

America, where the dominant position of U.S. manufacturers, as well as the strong trade position of the United States tended to put a U.S. orientation on the thinking of even Latin-owned operations. In Europe, the company's position tended to be weak with consumer products companies, and stronger in the industrial components market, principally because a number of the company's U.S. industrial customers had located in Europe. GFI did virtually no business in Africa, and only a limited volume in the Asian countries.

As could be expected, standard fasteners were basically a commodity item and were sold largely on the basis of price. However, for many applications there existed the possibility of orienting the company's product, through either design or materials technology, to meet specific customer needs. In these cases the salesman, the product design people, and the supplying subsidiary had to work closely together to meet special customer requirements. Also, GFI's customers, especially in consumer products, periodically redesigned their lines, often requiring a flurry of activity to meet new requirements. In addition to cost and product specifications, customers were generally concerned about the consistency and speed of delivery that their supplying companies could provide. For the most part there were few problems with respect to nationalistic bias; most companies were quite willing to source from nondomestic suppliers, once they were convinced that cost, product specifications, and delivery could be managed.

In the United States, GFI had two main production locations, one in the Chicago area and a newer plant in the Atlanta area. The Chicago plant was generally considered to be high cost because of labor rates, inefficient plant layout, and old equipment. Company engineers estimated that its "average" unit cost of manufacturing was some 10 to 15 percent higher than that of the Atlanta plant.

Until 1965, GFI's Canadian plant had been its major foreign operation, with sales of approximately $50 million in 1970. "Average" unit costs were slightly higher than those of GFI's Atlanta plant.

During the 1960s, GFI had joined in the general rush of U.S. corporations to invest in overseas facilities. In 1965, the company had acquired 60 percent ownership of a small operation in Brazil. By 1970, GFI do Brasil was the largest Brazilian manufacturer of fasteners, with sales of $4 million.

The company had started a wholly owned facility in Mexico in 1967, principally to service the U.S. car manufacturers in Mexico. In the last two years the Mexican operation had expanded into serving the appliance and machine tool industries. GFI's industrial engineers considered the Mexican plant to be potentially one of its low-cost locations. The average Mexican worker had proved to be adaptable and motivated. Only the limited domestic market in Mexico held the subsidiary back from achieving its full potential. At a sales volume of $20-$25 million, the Mexican plant's "average" unit cost could be as low as 65 percent of Atlanta costs. Sales were expected to hit $5 million in 1971.

The French subsidiary, Longchamps–GFI, had been acquired in 1965, with GFI purchasing 85 percent of the outstanding stock. With sales of approximately $26 million in 1970, Longchamps–GFI was only a moderately important factor in the European market. Prior to its acquisition, sales had largely been concentrated in

France. In recent years, through GFI branches and agents in other European countries, the French operation had begun to expand its export sales and take an active interest in non-French markets. "Average" unit costs were estimated at 85 percent of the Atlanta operation.

Organizationally, GFI assigned subsidiary market responsibility on the basis of home country markets—i.e., the French subsidiary had responsibility for the first claim to the French market, GFI Canada had responsibility for the first claim to the Canadian market, etc. Sales in markets outside the home market (third-country markets) were the responsibility of the International Division, which had been responsible for export marketing for the U.S. and Canadian plants. The only exception had been that GFI–Canada had maintained a separate sales branch in Great Britain, given the close cultural, political, and economic ties of the two countries. Since 1965 the International Division had attempted to act as a sales force for all divisions and subsidiaries in third country markets. Exhibits 1–5 are drawn from company files and summarize basic international economic facts.

EXHIBIT 1. Average Hourly Earnings in Manufacturing, 1967

United States	$2.83
Canada	2.22
France	0.67
Mexico	0.25
Brazil	n.a.

EXHIBIT 2. Consumer Price Movements (1963 = 100)

	1964	1965	1966	1967	1968	1969	1970
United States	101	103	106	109	114	120	127
Canada	102	104	108	112	117	122	126
France	103	106	109	112	117	124	131
Mexico	102	106	111	114	116	120	126
Brazil	187	303	444	575	714	880	1048

EXHIBIT 3. Trend in Industrial Wages (1963 = 100)

	1964	1965	1966	1967	1968	1969	1970
United States	103	106	111	115	122	130	137
Canada	104	109	115	123	132	143	154
France	107	114	120	128	193	154	173
Mexico	109	117	122	130	136	143	151
Brazil	n.a.						

EXHIBIT 4. Exchange Rate Movements (Local Currency Units per U.S. $)

	1964	1965	1966	1967	1968	1969	1970
Canada (dollar)	1.074	1.075	1.084	1.081	1.073	1.073	1.010
France (franc)	4.90	4.90	4.95	4.91	4.95	5.56	5.52
Mexico (peso)	12.49						
Brazil (cruzeiro)	1.85	2.22	2.22	2.75	3.83	4.35	4.95

EXHIBIT 5. Gross National Product (U.S. $—Billions)

	1964	1965	1966	1967	1968	1969	1970
United States	632	685	748	794	865	929	974
Canada	46	51	57	61	66	73	85
France	93	100	108	117	127	135	n.a.
Mexico	18	19	22	24	27	n.a.	n.a.
Brazil	12	16	24	26	26	30	n.a.

Gallic Logic

"Gentlemen, I can tell you that this is potentially a very important order for us. To be more precise, from the point of view of subsidiary profits, we are at present operating at 65 percent capacity. The British order would bring us up to 75 percent capacity in the first year alone, with important incremental profits. Also, Great Britain will shortly be in the EEC, and this order would give us a vital opening into their business community. As you know, given past tariff and various other customs barriers, we have been kept out of the market. Also, there has been, regrettably, some tendency on the part of the British to mistrust us. We would like to start dissolving that attitude.

"There are some other issues which have caused me some difficulties. Speaking frankly, it has not been easy to be a part of an American multinational firm. You are all familiar with J. S. Servan-Schreiber's book *The American Challenge*. We are constantly under pressure from our government to pursue an independent policy. It will be difficult to explain to any interested officials who may inquire why we were not permitted to bid on this very important piece of business, especially since it is within the EEC.

"In addition, I have the problem of minority stockholders. While they comprise only 15 percent of stockholdings, they are vocal and impeccable in their logic. We must keep them in mind when we make our decisions, or they will be keeping *me* and *us* in mind. And let's not forget our labor unions. I wouldn't like them to get on to this issue of 'outsiders' deciding on which jobs we can bid. Another thing you must remember is that we cannot easily adjust our work force as you can in the U.S. Our labor becomes almost a fixed cost, which further emphasizes the importance of these longer-term contracts to us.

"Well, to sum up, there are a number of economic and 'political' reasons why we should be permitted to bid on this job. I can assure you that we will come up with a very attractive price and still have acceptable incremental profit."

Canadian Tradition

"I must say, gentlemen, that we in Canada are upset about the possibility of other subsidiaries moving into our traditional markets. We have had a long and profitable relationship servicing the U.K. market. Our historical and political ties, as well as Commonwealth preferences, have given us a 'special relationship' with the British. Should we just throw all this out the window? While I admit that GFI–Canada has not done much business with Ellsworth Ltd. in the past, we have worked hard to develop this account and are now beginning to see some real results.

"I suppose each of us has his own special sales and profitability problems. And, we all can make a strong case. We were particularly hard hit in Canada as a re-sult of President Nixon's exchange rate actions. The U.S. is our largest trading part-ner and we now find ourselves with a revalued Canadian dollar, and perhaps even future 10 percent import surcharges. As a result, the future business situation in Canada looks somewhat bleak. While we are operating at close to 90 percent capac- *?* ity, this will drop substantially in the near future. In short, we also need the Ells- *CAN they handle* worth business.

"I might also say that we have been considering the addition of a new automated line which will substantially lower our costs and increase our quality for industrial-type fasteners. With the Ellsworth business as a base, we can easily justify this improvement in our ability to be competitive worldwide. Without it, the new line is still attractive but would not be fully utilized.

"I am really quite disturbed to think that we would not be given clear-cut preference on this job in a traditional market. Also, let's not be too hasty about putting Britain in the EEC. There are still hurdles to be jumped. And, even if they do go in, there will be at least a five-year period of transition. It would still be feasible to supply from Canada over the life of the Ellsworth contract."

International Division Interests

"My concern is that we not get into this kind of problem every time we get a request for an important quotation. Frankly, I don't know *where* this order should be filled, only that GFI should get it. I don't know the various costs and capacity conditions of each of our plants and subsidiaries at any one time and I doubt that we will in the foreseeable future. Perhaps we should have the Atlanta management at this meeting, for example. However, I think my sales people do know something about the price and service aspects which will determine who gets the order.

"My suggestion is that any subsidiary or plant which wishes to do so should be permitted to bid on any third-country job. Each manager knows best his current profit, cost, and capacity position. Let each come forth with his best proposal through a coordinating office at the International Division and we will pass them on to our salesmen or agents for presentation to the customer. Let the best, and hungriest, man win. However, we should protect the home market of each subsidiary.

"In practice, what we would do is have our salesmen and agents pass quotation requests to the International Division and we would send them on to the plants and subsidiaries that are capable of making the requested product. Where a long-term relationship has been built up between one of our producing locations and a customer, we would automatically send the request on to this plant or perhaps instruct field personnel to do this automatically and notify us. And, of course, if a customer requests a particular subsidiary we would automatically notify that subsidiary only. My best guess is that most of the bid requests we receive could be handled quickly and automatically. For the exceptional cases, as I said previously, we would notify each plant or subsidiary, receive their quotes, and pass them on to the customer through our field people.

"The system is easy to operate, clear, and fairly inexpensive. We don't have to get into emotional issues related to who has the best case for a job. We simply let each operating plant or subsidiary decide for itself whether business is profitable and at what price. I suggest we do this with the Ellsworth job."

Legal Qualms

"Before precedent-setting decisions are made, it would be well for us to review any possible antitrust implications. First, let us remember that U.S. antitrust law extends beyond our borders. We must be careful to not even appear to restrain trade or reduce competition.

"The key issue here as I see it is that of relationships between parent and subsidiary. As long as we operate through divisions or branch offices there can be no question of making agreements in contravention of the law. The corporation and its divisions are one juridical person. However, in the case of subsidiaries there are separate legal personages, and agreements in restraint of trade are a legal possibility.

"To avoid antitrust exposure, the parent company through appropriately appointed people must direct its subsidiaries with regard to who bids on what jobs or in which markets. In other words, there must be corporate control and direction. Also, the company must not be put in the position of holding itself and its subsidiaries out to customers as separate entities. The customer must be told that multiple GFI bids are *alternative,* not competing, bids. Our sales agents and personnel must always present multiple quotes as alternative bids and make it clear that they are all from members of the GFI group.

"A final point to remember is that anything less than majority ownership of a subsidiary means that there can be no question of control. Where we have less than majority ownership, control of who bids on what jobs would be seen as an illegal agreement, not as legitimate management direction. Therefore, treat minority-owned operations at arm's length and not as part of the GFI group."

QUESTIONS

1. What is the problem? ✓
2. Which plants should be permitted to bid on this job? Why?
3. What long-range policy, if any, should Mr. Standish set to cover this type of situation?

part six

THE FUTURE
OF MULTINATIONAL
MARKETING

the future
of multinational
marketing

We should all be concerned about the future because
we will have to spend the rest of our lives there.

Charles Franklin Kettering, 1876-1958
(Seed for Thought, 1949)

INTRODUCTION

Anyone who maintains that he can predict the future is either a charlatan or a
fool. Nevertheless , one of the more fascinating and valuable enterprises in human
endeavor is the effort to forecast future developments on the basis of patterns,
trends, and underlying factors that can be observed in the present situation. These
forecasts are vitally important as an input to the strategic planning process for
both domestic and international enterprises.

MULTINATIONAL CORPORATIONS IN THE EVOLVING
INTERNATIONAL ECONOMIC ORDER

Four major trends will undoubtedly affect the role and future of multinational
corporations in the evolving international economic order. First, there is a trend
toward symmetry in the relative importance of multinational corporations based
outside the United States as opposed to U.S.-based multinational corporations.
Recent data indicate that Japanese and European-based multinational companies
are expanding their foreign direct investment and operations in the United States
more rapidly than the expansion of U.S. companies' direct investment and operations outside the United States. This trend will result in increasing balance between
the size of the U.S. direct investment position in the world and the size of the
world's direct investment position in the United States. Another factor of major
significance is the emergence of multinational companies based in less-developed

countries. This trend is so new that it is little recognized, but, in fact, *Fortune* magazine's "overseas 500" companies now include twenty-three developing countries. Perhaps even more significantly, this represents a 200 percent increase over the past five years. This trend will result in an increasing balance in the investment positions of countries now labeled as less-developed and the developed countries. An increasing balance between U.S. and non-U.S. foreign direct investment and industrialized and less-developed investment will create a common interest in the international economic order in preserving a framework for international investment and operations. In effect, each investor country will be a hostage to its own investment position in the rest of the world. A condition of mutual interdependence will create a fundamentally stable environment for continued growth and expansion of international business.

A second trend that is clearly observable is the emergence of an increasingly large number of world-scale industries. Today we are witnessing a shakeout of firms in industries ranging from electronics to automobiles that is analogous to the shakeout that occurred in the national economy of the United States between 1850 and 1950. The farm equipment industry provides an interesting illustrative example of this process. In 1850 there were hundreds of farm equipment manufacturers. Between 1850 and 1950, firms in this industry expanded their operations from local to regional to national scale. In the process of this expansion, many weaker firms were weeded out because of their higher operating costs and lower available operating margins. Since 1950 the shakeout has continued, but the arena has shifted from the national to the world frame. The emergence of world-scale industries is also apparent in more recently established technologies, such as integrated circuits and television receivers.

The implications of this trend are of enormous significance from both a private and a public policy perspective. From the point of view of the corporation, it is necessary to identify and recognize the world-scale trend if it applies to the company's product scope. Zenith, for example, made the mistake of assuming that it was number one in the color television market because of its leading position in the U.S. market. This proved to be a disastrous illusion, as Zenith found it increasingly difficult to compete with Japanese companies that were operating not only in the U.S. market but throughout the world. A more accurate description of Zenith's position is that of perhaps a fourth- or fifth-ranked world competitor as opposed to the illusionary perception of Zenith as number one in the United States.

The public policy implications of this trend are especially important in the United States, which is operating under antitrust laws that are based on the implicit assumption that the frame for determining the competitiveness of an industry is the national market. In the late nineteenth century, when these laws were formulated, this assumption was valid. In the 1980s it is sadly out of date. U.S. policymakers must recognize that U.S. companies will increasingly need to amalgamate so that they can form viable world-scale competitive enterprises if they are to operate without protection in the international economic order. The United States faces a choice: a continued commitment to open competitive economy which will require a revision of the frame for evaluating industry competitiveness and which must necessarily allow the merger of independent organizations to form competitive world-scale units, or, alternatively, an abandonment of the long-standing U.S. commitment to an open economy and the international economic order and the erection of barriers to protect U.S. companies that are unable to compete in the evolving world-scale industry.

A third trend that is observable in multinational corporate orientation is an increasing move toward a geocentric or world orientation as opposed to an ethnocentric or home country orientation, or, alternatively, a polycentric or host country orientation. A *geocentric* company is one that consciously recognizes that it is operating in the international economic order and that its stakeholders are customers, employees, and shareholders in every area of operation. In addition, a geocentric company is one that recognizes the possibility of creating a global strategic plan for each of its businesses in order to allocate and apply resources most effectively. An *ethnocentric* company is one that recognizes home country stakeholders as being preeminent in their rights to and claims on corporate resources and rewards. The operating style of the ethnocentric company is highly centralized. It seeks to impose a top-down approach to planning and operating programs and operates on the implicit assumption that the home country way is the best way. Many U.S.-based multinationals have been highly ethnocentric in their orientation. A *polycentric* company is based on the assumption that the differences between countries are so great that the only effective way of managing an international company is to decentralize and locate a decision responsibility for resource allocation in national organizations. Some of the largest European multinational companies have been basically polycentric in their orientation. This is particularly true of companies based in countries like Switzerland and the Netherlands where there has never been a large home country organization that could impose an ethnocentric orientation on smaller national subsidiaries abroad. Indeed, for the smaller European countries, the situation is precisely the opposite: the largest organizations are national companies outside the home countries.

The geocentric company is based on the assumption that world markets consist of both similarities and differences and that the most effective strategies are those that reflect a full recognition of both similarities and differences. In marketing, this means that products will be adapted where necessary to conform to local market and competitive conditions, but there will also be an attempt to, wherever possible, standardize the product line and marketing procedures in order to minimize costs of research and development and manufacturing and to maximize the gains from scale and concentration of resources. This geocentric shift is evident in the creation of worldwide product divisions and the decision to locate strategic planning product market responsibility within these divisions. Another key measure of the extent to which a company is actually geocentric in its day-to-day operations is the extent to which men and women of many nationalities are promoted to positions of major product division and corporate responsibility. Whenever the corporate headquarters and product divisions are staffed with home country nationals, you can be sure that a basically ethnocentric orientation is present within the headquarters. This is often juxtaposed with a polycentric orientation in national organizations within the same enterprise. The mixing of nationalities in headquarters, product division, and national organizations is the surest way of breaking down the ethnocentric and polycentric attitudes that must give way before a company can operate geocentrically.

A fourth important trend in multinational corporations is an expanding appreciation of the need for active participation of the corporate and product division headquarters in business strategy formulation and implementation. The headquarters role, when expressed, is only effective when it fully incorporates responses to national conditions. Thus, strong, sensitive, and effective national organizations must be maintained as companies simultaneously develop the capability of active and constructive participation in the strategy formulation and implementation process.

MARKETING IN SOCIALIST COUNTRIES

Another significant development in marketing in the next decade will be the increasing interest and application of marketing concepts and tools in Socialist countries. An early sign of this development is the frequent participation of state officials and managers in marketing seminars held in the West. This is an exceedingly healthy and desirable trend because it is absolutely clear that East-West trade and economic cooperation will be limited in forthcoming decades by the ability of Socialist enterprise to compete effectively in Western markets. Over the medium term the West cannot hope to sell more to the East than it buys, for the obvious reason that the East must pay for its purchases in the West. A very important question is the extent to which Western companies will be permitted to engage in direct marketing operations in Socialist countries.

One possible set of developments that could result in opportunities for direct marketing by Western enterprise within Socialist countries will be the emergence of direct enterprise participation in Western markets by Socialist countries. If such participation develops (there are already some small efforts successfully under way on the part of Socialist industries, especially those in the so-called satellite countries of Eastern Europe), the participation of Western companies in the Socialist markets will be more than likely permitted under the rubric of reciprocity. This development is surely several years in the future, as it is only dimly perceived in Socialist countries today. A couple of years ago I had a conversation with the manager of a major Polish factory and I proposed that Poland begin to develop its own multinational corporations. His reaction—"Polish multinational enterprise? Are you kidding?"— was not entirely encouraging, but failure to perceive this possibility does not in my judgment make it any less likely that it will eventually come to pass. The continuing trend toward decentralization and the location of resource allocation responsibility at the enterprise level in Socialist countries will inevitably lead to increasing interest on the part of these enterprises in extending their sales and marketing operation on an international scale. This will be supported by the apparent continuing commitment of the political leadership in these countries to a rising standard of living. Every country, whether Socialist or capitalist, faces the same choice: participation in the international economic order with the associated advantages of economies of world scale, or operations conducted under autarchy with the associated disadvantages and limitations of national-scale operations.

DECLINE OF THE UNITED STATES

A final trend of special importance for U.S. marketers is the declining role of the United States in the international economic order. According to my estimates, in 1946 the United States accounted for 40-50 percent of gross world product. This percentage has been steadily declining since the end of World War II and today is approximately 23 percent. The declining aggregate size of the United States vis-à-vis the rest of the world means that in an increasing number of industries, the United States is no longer the home of the largest and most powerful enterprises. Today U.S. steel production is only slightly higher than that in Japan, and the U.S. automobile industry—once established as an industry without peer in the world—is only one and one-half times the size of the Japanese automobile industry. Increasingly, the U.S. company is facing strong competitors with resources that are equal to or greater than its own.

Another aspect of the relative decline of the United States as a preeminent world market is the leveling of per capita incomes in the industrialized countries. Today the United States is no longer the richest market in the world as measured by national income on a per capita basis.[1] This has important implications for product life cycle patterns. In the past, new products or major innovations were almost always introduced in the United States and only later sold in foreign markets. This was because the United States, with the highest income per capita, presented the first opportunity for expensive and often untested or unproven product innovations. Today, with several countries having higher national incomes per capita, it is now possible to present new products first elsewhere in the world.

In short, the United States is still the world's largest national market, but its relative size and relative income advantage have declined substantially and will probably continue to decline. This means that U.S. companies must increasingly face strong and established foreign competitors who will have opportunities to try out and establish product innovations outside of the United States before introducing them in the U.S. market. A major implication of these developments is that U.S. companies must increasingly monitor developments taking place in other parts of the world in order to stay abreast of the most advanced practices and the most important new-product development and introduction activities.

---

[1] The U.S. still leads the industrial countries of the world on a purchasing power parity comparison basis. In 1976, with the U.S. on a scale of 100, the following comparisons resulted: Canada, 91; Sweden, 77; West Germany, 76; Denmark, 72; Norway, 71; Japan, 70; United Kingdom, 59; and Italy, 46. See Jai-Hoon Yang, *Review,* Federal Reserve Bank of St. Louis, May 1978.

In the past, if one was informed about what was going on in the United States, one was informed about the frontiers of marketing practice. Today this is no longer the case. Marketing professionals who are committed to keeping up with the latest developments in the field must scan the world and not just the United States. In effect, there is no longer a separation between domestic and international marketing: they have become a part of a unified field.

MARKETING: A GLOBAL PROFESSION

Type of Person Needed for Multinational Marketing[2]

There are certain *general* specifications that a person should have if he is to do an outstanding job in multinational marketing. Before discussing the specific background a review of these *general* specifications is in order.

(A) A WORLD-BEATER IN THE DOMESTIC ARENA

If a candidate currently is working in Global Enterprise, he should be recognized as a "comer," as a well-rounded businessman who has built a monument on each of his jobs; may have worked in more than one function and has shown expertise in each; is *bright, inquiring,* and *interested;* knows the Global Enterprise Company and how to use its strengths both domestically and offshore; is an authority on his product lines; is the kind of person who might conceivably develop into general managership, since he will be pioneering and establishing a new business in oftentimes an unfamiliar market area. This person must be a broad-gauge stemwinder, not the average performer who is ready to be "put out to pasture." (The promotability of this person is vital, so the knowledge he will gain in multinational marketing work may be further multiplied as Global Enterprise becomes a worldwide company.) this is such an outstanding person that his career movement eventually took him to an offshore position) domestic departments would be interested in bringing him back to their headquarters organization some day.

Since offshore marketing sometimes requires an adaptation of standard products or normal domestic marketing practices, he must have, or be capable of establishing, excellent working relationships with his associates, particularly in engineering, manufacturing, and finance, so he can gain their cooperation in design, production schedules, pricing, and shifting, speeded-up delivery dates. He must get help and cooperation from many, many sources, so he must be able to integrate well.

If the candidate being considered is not currently with Global Enterprise, he will need to bring to the job expertise about either a particular foreign country, or market, or market approach; also must have shown adaptable characteristics that will enable him to learn in rapid fashion what he will need to know about

---

[2]This job description was developed by an international marketing executive at Global Enterprise, a large U.S.-based multinational company which prefers to remain anonymous. The words "he" and "his" are used generically.

Global Enterprise, its organization, nomenclature, policies, and strengths which he can use in the new assignment.

(B) CAREER SHOWS SOME MULTINATIONAL ORIENTATION

The candidate should have a genuine interest and desire to perform with distinction in multinational marketing work as one part of his career plan. He would be willing to parlay this particular experience to a challenging offshore job, should one develop. He is *not* the international "thrill seeker"; he is *not* the kind of person who is fascinated primarily with international travel; he is not interested in this kind of work solely because it may be today's "popular trend" or because company top management currently is interested in international business. He looks at an international assignment with the same interest as he would another challenging domestic assignment.

Needs to be broad-minded and have an international attitude with a minimum of racial, religious, and political prejudices; must have a normal interest in the history, culture, and mores of the countries with which he does business, without "going native"; must appreciate that the values placed on many things in personal and business life offshore are different from U.S.A.; should have talents for understanding and be willing to invest the personal time and effort to understand, the people and to learn their language. Must be sensitive immediately to the political scene offshore, have the interest and stick-to-itiveness to wade through the morass of foreign government regulations and restrictions which may be vital to his being able to do business in the country; should be a combination diplomat-judge-ward-alderman in each country where he operates, recognizing that the political arena in one country may differ remarkably from that in the next.

May have worked in IGE Export Division or may have been in export-import work at some time in his career. Or, has been offshore enough to find out from first-hand experience that he is gaited to this tough, demanding international business.

(C) COMPETENT PLANNER

Should be a strong business planner, must have a knowledge of where to get knowledge; will evaluate a confusing array of data—much of which is incomplete; separate the important from the unimportant; and develop a plan that fits the needs of the business and is responsive to the customer.

(D) CUSTOMER-ORIENTED

All good marketing people are *expected* to be customer-oriented. But the international marketing person based in the U.S.A. must have an extra charge of this orientation. Different voltages, left-hand threads, strange mounting specifications, and other requirements (which to the modern, standards-conscious, American businessman may be quaint and curious) are customer needs offshore and must be satisfied.

1. *Self-Sufficient*

Must be secure in himself and able to work on his own schedule for an extented period of time; needs to be competent professionally in his field; self-confidence is a "must", for when traveling offshore he will not have immediate counsel of his domestic counterparts; needs courage and willingness to make decisions, oftentimes with inadequate information and within a short period of time.

2. *Aggressive*

The doors to the customer do not open quite as easily internationally as they do domestically. So the marketing man who tries to sell offshore needs a high degree of aggressiveness (note: in some foreign countries—e.g., Japan—*overt* aggressiveness may be fatal in marketing a product); must have persistence, perseverance, dedication, and drive and be willing to work.

3. *Adaptable*

Must be flexible and adapt quickly to new people, different surroundings, and be prepared for the unexpected and the unusual experiences which cannot always be anticipated; hopefully will have demonstrated in previous work this flexibility (e.g., having supervised a widely dispersed sales force or sales territory in domestic work could be a plus toward a similar responsibility that involves regional differences, offshore). Also should be service-oriented, sensitive, and observant.

4. *Creative*

Must have imagination to see new approaches or adopt new approaches to accomplishing mission; have an alert, open mind.

5. *Communicative*

Should have above-average ability to cummunicate and patience in achieving understanding through communication where English may not be the principal language and where only one-third of a conversation may be understood; listening skills must be tuned to nuances, double-talk, or different word or phrase connotations; should have sufficient language aptitude to carry on a conversation in a foreign language after one hundred hours of training. (Note: Global Enterprise's International Division's Employee Relations Operation has a Modern Language Aptitude Test, developed by the Psychological Corporation, which can help determine a person's aptitude for learning a foreign language.)

6. *Patient*

Must have patience to put up with customer's delays (sometimes planned) in coming up with agreements; must expect to invest what will seem to be non-productive hours in trying to see people on a scheduled basis.

7. *Travel-oriented*

Must be able to withstand: rigors of foreign travel; being away from home for weeks at a time; day and night work schedules and rapid changes of time zones; loss of sleep; irregular eating of widely varying food; different standards of cleanliness and sanitation; and many strange climates and customs.

If married, should have a spouse who understands the travel requirements of the job.

8. *Management Potential*

Even though his first work may be entirely a one-person operation, should have a potential to manage people and a larger operation, if it materializes; may have demonstrated these skills in a previous job.

Impact of Marketing Approach on Job Specifications

To supplement the *general* specifications just discussed, there are other, more specific, guidelines that are important in the person's background, depending on the *market approach* that will be followed. It should be recognized that this information may have to be acquired with tailor-made training. For example:

IF THE MARKET APPROACH IS TO: A. DIRECT EXPORT

The individual must have thorough grounding in marketing aspects of the product. In addition, should have a sound knowledge of offshore trade channels which can be used to get his product to key customers. Knowledge would cover such distribution channels as sales representatives, distributors, wholesalers, and retailers. Should be familiar with pricing and credit procedures in each market area; also details of trademark registration; willing to work hard to learn what he does not know.

The importance of matching the specific demands of the offshore marketing approach to the work experience in which a person already has excelled domestically cannot be overemphasized. For example, if the best approach to getting the product to market offshore is through distributors, then the person to hire is the one who, in addition to having shown he has the general qualities for international marketing work, already has demonstrated his outstanding ability to take a product line to the domestic customers using distributors.

(*Note:* Working knowledge in the following four market approaches may be either by Departments or Divisions picking up the ball or by a special training program which Global's International Division could help to arrange.)

IF THE MARKET APPROACH IS TO: B. LICENSE

In addition to marketing knowledge, the individual needs to be familiar with: legal aspects of contracts; terms of agreement; importance of contract semantics; foreign tax obligations; other government regulations; opportunities for sublicensing, license amendments, royalties, and stock participation in licensee's company.

IF THE MARKET APPROACH IS TO: C. MANUFACTURE OFFSHORE

This market approach suggests the person in charge have depth of experience in production, in industrial relations, in foreign social legislation plus marketing know-how. Some observers point out that movement of U.S. industry to foreign countries is accompanied by movement of organized U.S. labor practices offshore, although in some foreign countries the labor unions are much stronger than in the United States.

IF THE MARKET APPROACH IS TO: D. EXPORT COMPONENTS AND ASSEMBLIES OFFSHORE

Certain countries demand that products sold within their borders be made there. The person in charge of this approach must have the same background and experience as the "manufacture offshore" person. In addition, he should know tax and tariff regulations on components, which countries curtail imports (e.g., Mexico), and the financial impact of foreign government regulations. In this market approach the experience a person may have gained in the domestic markets getting a knowledge in depth of the OEM business would provide immediate know-how which he could use in his international marketing work.

IF THE MARKET APPROACH IS TO: E. ACQUIRE A FOREIGN FIRM OR MERGE WITH IT

In this market approach, the person in charge needs to have strong financial background; knowledge of foreign government's political stability; its attitude toward majority or minority ownership by outside firms; also, must know how strengths and weaknesses of acquisitions can be melded with those of domestic company to form a stronger union which will result in increased sales and profits.

Few people would meet all of these requirements. Nevertheless, the man or woman who accepts the challenge of multinational marketing develops most of the qualities identified in Global's memorandum. Perhaps this explains why multinational marketers are being tapped to fill the chief executive officer's position in their companies.

BIBLIOGRAPHY

Cooper, Richard N., "A New International Economic Order for Mutual Gain," *Foreign Policy,* No. 26 (Spring 1977), pp. 65–139.

Gabriel, Peter P., "MNCs in the Third World: Is Conflict Unavoidable?" *Harvard Business Review,* July-August 1972, pp. 93–102.

Galbraith, John Kenneth, "The Defense of the Multinational Company," *Harvard Business Review,* March-April 1978, pp. 83–94.

Heenan, David A., "Global Cities of Tomorrow," *Harvard Business Review,* May-June 1977, pp. 79–92.

Maisonrouge, Jacques G., "The Mythology of Multinationalism," *Columbia Journal of World Business,* 9, No. 1 (Spring 1974), 7–12.

Nye, Joseph S., Jr., "Independence and Interdependence," *Foreign Policy,* No. 22 (Spring 1976), pp. 129–61.

Spencer, William I., "Who Controls MNCs?" *Harvard Business Review,* November-December 1975, pp. 97–108.

Stobaugh, Robert B., "Multinational Competition Encountered by U.S. Companies That Manufacture Abroad," *Journal of International Business Studies,* Spring/Summer 1977, pp. 33–44.

appendixes

APPENDIX I / DOCUMENTARY SOURCES OF INFORMATION

INFORMATION ON FOREIGN COUNTRIES—STATISTICAL

International Financial Statistics—Published monthly by the International Monetary Fund. This is one of the finest international sources of data available. The particular value of *International Financial Statistics* is that data provided by national sources are screened and reviewed before being included in the statistics. If the compilers of *International Financial Statistics* have any reason to believe that the data provided by a national government are "doctored," they simply exclude them from their publication. Another advantage of *International Financial Statistics* is that the data are comparable and provided on a monthly basis. Each monthly issue contains world tables on international liquidity, interest rates, exchange rates, prices of world trade commodities, export and import price indexes, consumer price indexes, and international trade tables for each of the 104 countries included. The statistics provide information on national accounts, government finance, interest rates, prices, and production, banking, international liquidity, and exchange rates.

Statistical Yearbook of the United Nations—The *Statistical Yearbook,* published annually, is a major source of world economic data. It includes information on population, manpower, agriculture, mining, manufacturing, construction, trade, transport, communications, consumption, balance of payments, wages and prices, national accounts, finance, international capital flows, health, housing, education, and mass communications. This valuable volume should be in the library of every active international market researcher.

National Governments—The single most valuable publication in most countries for information on the domestic market is the *National Statistical Abstract,* which pulls together the major economic and social indicators for the country and is published for virtually every country in the world on an annual basis. International marketers needing information that is not included in the statistical abstract should refer to published lists of available information provided by each government indicating more specialized publications and reports. The only current sources of trade and production data on a country are the national trade and production statistics.

In general, the quantity and quality of data provided by national governments are directly related to the size and wealth of the economy that the government represents. Thus the U.S. government, representing the largest and the richest nation in the world, is at the same time one of the best governmental sources of market data available. The *Statistical Abstract of the United States,* which runs over a thousand pages, is a gold mine of valuable market data. In this single source, the market researcher can obtain information on population, health, nutrition, education, law enforcement, climate, recreation and travel, employment and earnings, social insurance and welfare services, income and expenditures, prices, government finance, banking finance and insurance, detailed information in industrial sectors and so on.

U. S. Trade and Production Statistics are the most detailed in the world. The United States uses a seven-digit classification system to record trade and production data. Other governments use a four-digit system.

In addition to this voluminous data on the U.S. domestic economy and trade, the U.S. government also provides extensive data and information on international markets. These international data are provided as a service to U.S. manufacturers and as an expression of national policy encouraging the international extension of business activity, particularly the export activity. In this regard, the U.S. government is typical of those of industrialized countries. Space does not allow a summary of all national activities in this area, so the following review of U.S. government publications is provided not only as an indication of those information services available from the U.S. government but as a guide to the general kinds of data available from governments of all industrialized nations.

U.S. STATISTICAL PUBLICATIONS ON U.S. TRADE AND PRODUCTION SCHEDULES AND CLASSIFICATIONS

1. Statistical Series Guide

Guide to Foreign Trade Statistics—U.S. Department of Commerce, latest edition 1975, $4.05. The *Guide* lists all the statistical series compiled by the Department of Commerce and gives samples of the formats used and the information provided. This publication is a must for anyone who wishes to use U.S. trade statistics effectively. Some of the major statistical reports are:

(a) FT-410—Monthly cumulative data on exports, commodity by country listing.

(b) FT-135—Monthly cumulative data on imports, commodity by country listing.

2. Schedule A

Statistical Classification of Commodities Imported into the United States. Bureau of the Census, May 1976.

3. Schedule B

Statistical Classification of Domestic and Foreign Commodities Exported from the United States. Bureau of the Census, 1978. $16.25.

4. TSUSA

Tariff Schedule of the United States, Annotated. U.S. International Trade Commission Publication #843. Government Printing Office, 1978.

5. SIC

Standard Industrial Classification Manual, 1972. Office of the President, Office of Management and Budget, Washington, D.C. The SIC manual provides a listing of all categories used to classify U.S. domestic production. Superintendent of Documents, Washington, D.C. 20402. $6.75.

U.S. DEPARTMENT OF COMMERCE INFORMATION

The U.S. Department of Commerce provides extensive help to both exporters and importers through its District Offices, its Bureaus, and its many publications. The major surveys, reports, indexes, and periodicals, current as of Summer 1978, are listed below. Copies of thse periodicals can, for the most part, be ordered from (1) the Superintendent of Documents, Government Printing Office, Washington, D.C. 20402; (2) the National Technical Information Service, 5285 Port Royal Rd., Springfield, Va. 22151; or (3) the Department of Commerce, Washington, D.C. 20230.

Because the Department of Commerce, its Bureaus, and their publications undergo periodic changes in organization and title, no listing can ever be completely correct. The basic formats of the services provided tend, however, to remain constant.

International Marketing Information Series

As part of a marketing information program, the Department of Commerce makes available to the U.S. business community, on a continuing basis, six types of publications and reports:

1. *Global Market Surveys*—In-depth reports covering twenty to thirty of the best foreign markets for a single U.S. industry or a group of related industries.
2. *Country Market Sectorial Surveys*—Office of International Marketing, Industry and Trade Administration. In-depth reports covering the most promising U.S. export opportunities in a single foreign country. About fifteen leading industrial sectors are usually included.
3. *Overseas Business Reports*—Reports that include current and detailed marketing information on all of our leading trading partners. Most are revised annually. Each report contains basic information for exporters, importers, manufacturers, and researchers organized by country or region. Annual subscription for 50–60 reports per year, $46.
4. *Foreign Economic Trend Reports*—Prepared by the U.S. Foreign Service and the U.S. Department of Commerce. Annual or semiannual reports prepared on almost every country in the world. These are up-to-date economic summaries including such topics as balance of payments, credit availability, inflation, and investment climate. $37.50.
5. *Market Research Summaries*—Brief market summaries in support of overseas trade promotion events organized by the Department of Commerce.
6. *Overseas Export Promotion Calendar*—This provides an eighteen-month schedule of events sponsored by the Department of Commerce consisting of exhibitions in U.S. Trade Centers and in international trade fairs and trade missions.

All of the above may be obtained from the U.S. Department of Commerce, FCAT Br. Room 6880, Washington, D.C. 20230.

Trade Opportunities Program Bulletin—Indexes trade opportunities according to product codes and shows country of origin, type of opportunity, and notice number, followed by a full list of notices. U.S. Department of Commerce Industry & Trade Administration, TOP, Rm. 2323, Washington, D.C. 20230. Weekly service $100/hour.

World Traders Data Report Service (WTDR)—This service provides detailed commercial information prepared by U.S. Foreign Service on an individual foreign firm, upon request. Forms for this service can be obtained from local U.S. Department District Offices or by writing to the U.S. Department of Commerce, Washington, D.C. 20230. These are not credit reports, but they do contain names and addresses of sources of credit, financial, and commercial data. The typical report includes information on type of organization, method of operation, lines handled, size of firm, sales territory, names of owners and officers, capital, sales volume, general reputation in trade and financial circles, and names of the firm's trading connections. Each report is $15.

Foreign Trade Reports—Bureau of the Census. Monthly, with yearly totals in December. $122.20 per year; $10.20 per copy. Includes a wide variety of statistics on U.S. imports and exports, arranged according to various classification schedules. Indexed in the *Bureau of the Census Catalog* below.

Bureau of the Census Catalog—Bureau of the Census. A quarterly catalog which lists reports and monthly supplements. Four quarterly issues $14.

Foreign Market Reports Service—Indexes reports for subscription customers either by automatically sending reports on preselected subjects to firms or by supplying a printed Index from which items may be chosen. Subscriptions from NTIS OR the U.S. Department of Commerce. Price varies according to services selected.

Index to Foreign Market Reports—U.S. Department of Commerce, International Trade Administration, Bureau of Export Development. This monthly publication lists documents by Standard Industrial Class, by country, and by document number. It supplants the BDSA publications list and is available for $10.00 annual subscription or $3.25 for a single copy from the National Technical Information Service.

Market Share Reports—U.S. Department of Commerce. The reports provide basic data for a five-year period needed by exporters and prospective exporters to evaluate overall trends in the size of world markets for manufacturers; they measure changes in import data for specific products, compare the competitive positions of the U.S. and foreign exporters, select distribution centers for U.S. products abroad, and identify existing and potential markets for U.S. components, parts, and accessories. A catalog to these reports is free from the National Technical Information Service and Department of Commerce Field Offices.

Agent/Distributor Service—Designed for the marketer who needs assistance in identifying potential foreign agents or distributors, this service provides up to six names of prospects. The service is given by the Foreign Service through any Department of Commerce District Office and requires sixty days to complete.

Export Mailing List Service—An offshoot of the *Foreign Traders Index,* this service provides U.S. business firms lists of foreign organizations for export contact purposes in the form of printouts or mailing labels. It can cover one or more countries and includes firms selected by industry or by products handled.

Foreign Buyer Program—This program helps marketer make contact with foreign buyers who are visiting the United States. Business appointments are made, visits scheduled, and travel plans arranged to bring buyers and supplier together. Service is obtained through District Offices of the Department of Commerce.

Exhibitions—Four types of services are provided by the Department of Commerce:

1. *U.S. Trade Center Exhibitions*—Business executives are invited to exhibit at the department's permanent network of Trade Centers located throughout the world.
2. *Joint Export Establishment Promotions* (JEEP)—Between-show promotions are arranged in specially tailored promotion programs undertaken on a shared-cost basis.
3. *Commercial Exhibitions*—The department frequently sponsors participation in U.S. pavilions at major international exhibitions, such as the Paris Air Show.
4. *Catalog Exhibitions*—These are special displays featuring American product catalogs, sales brochures, and other pictorial materials at U.S. Foreign Service posts or in conjunction with trade shows, most often held in developing markets, where there are fewer product exhibitions.

Trade Missions—The Department of Commerce sponsors two types of trade missions. One is the specialized trade mission, which is planned and led by the department after extensive research shows a strong potential market opportunity. The second type is Industry Organized Government Approved (IOGA), which may be organized and led by state, trade, or similar business organizations. The department offers substantial support, including arrangements for business appointments for those meeting established criteria.

Business Counseling—The Business Counseling Section of the department's Bureau of International Commerce in Washington offers guidance and schedules appointments with appropriate officials in a variety of agencies. The District Offices, listed below, also offer counseling, identify markets for products and services, suggest possible agents and distributors, give sources of credit information, financing, insurance, and other special export help.

Product Marketing Service—For the business executive traveling abroad, the department offers help in locating secretaries, interpreters, offices, orientation to the city, lists of prime business contacts, and other services. A small daily fee is charged.

District Offices—The forty-three District Offices of the Department of Commerce are organized to help provide all of the above services and publications to any business person. More information may also be obtained from the Director, Bureau of International Commerce, U.S. Department of Commerce, Washington, D.C. 20230.

Albuquerque, N.M., 87102 505 Marquette N.W. Suite 1015 (505) 766-2386

Anchorage, 99501, 632 Sixth Ave., Hill Bldg., Suite 412 (907) 265-5307.

Atlanta, 30309, Suite 600, 1365 Peachtree St., NE (404) 881-7000.

Baltimore, 21202, 415 U.S. Customhouse, Gay and Lombard Sts. (301) 962-3560.

Birmingham, Ala., 35205, Suite 200-201, 908 S. 20th St. (205) 254-1331.

Boston, 02116, 10th Floor, 441 Stuart St. (617) 223-2312.

Buffalo, N.Y., 14202, Room 1312, Federal Bldg., 111 W. Huron St. (716) 842-3208.

Charleston, W.Va., 25301, 3000 New Federal Office Bldg., 500 Quarrier St. (304) 343-6181, Ext. 375.

Cheyenne, Wyo., 82001, 6022 O'Mahoney Federal Center, 2120 Capitol Ave. (307) 778-2151.

Chicago, 60603, Room 1406, Mid-Continental Plaza Bldg., 55 E. Monroe St. (312) 353-4450.

Cincinnati, 45202, 10504 Federal Building, 550 Main St. (513) 684-2944.

Cleveland, 44114, Room 600, 666 Euclid Ave. (216) 522-4750.

Columbia, S.C., 29204, Forest Center, 2611 Forest Dr. (803) 765-5345.

Dallas, 75202, Room 7A5, 1100 Commerce St. (214) 749-1515.

Denver, 80202, Room 161, New Custom House, 19th and Stout Sts. (303) 837-3246.

Des Moines, Iowa, 50309, 609 Federal Bldg., 210 Walnut St. (515) 284-4222.

Detroit, 48226, 445 Federal Bldg., 231 W. Lafayette (313) 226-3650.

Greensboro, N.C., 37402, 203 Federal Bldg., W. Market St., P.O. Box 1950 (919) 378-5345.

Hartford, Conn., 06103, Room 610-B, Federal Office Bldg., 450 Main St. (203) 244-3530.

Honolulu, 96813, 286 Alexander Young Bldg., 1015 Bishop St. (808) 546-8694.

Houston, 77002, 201 Fannin, 2625 Federal Bldg. Courthouse, 515 Rusk St. (713) 226-4231.

Indianapolis, 46204, 357 Federal Office Bldg., 46 E. Ohio St. (317) 269-6214.

Los Angeles, 90049, Room 800, 11777 San Vicente Blvd. (213) 824-7591.

Memphis, 38103, Room 710, 147 Jefferson Ave. (901) 521-3213.

Miami, 33130, Rm. 821, City National Bank Bldg., 25 W. Flagler St. (305) 350-5267.

Milwaukee, 53202, 605 Federal Office Bldg., 517 E. Wisconsin Ave., Room 605. (414) 224-3473.

Minneapolis, 55401, 218 Federal Bldg., 110 S. Fourth St. (612) 725-2133.

New Orleans, 70130, Room 432, International Trade Mart, 2 Canal St. (504) 589-6546.

New York, 10007, 37th Floor, Federal Office Bldg., 26 Federal Plaza, Foley Sq. (212) 264-0634.

Newark, N.J., 07102, Gateway Bldg. (4th floor) (201) 645-6214.

Omaha, Neb., 68102, Capitol Plaza, Suite 703A, 1815 Capitol Ave. (402) 221-3665.

Philadelphia, 19106, 9448 Federal Bldg., 600 Arch St. (215) 597-2850.

Phoenix, Ariz., 85004, 508 Greater Arizona Savings Bldg., 112 N. Central Ave. (602) 261-3285.

Pittsburgh, 15222, 2002 Federal Bldg., 1000 Liberty Ave. (412) 644-2850.

Portland, Ore., 97204, Room 618, 1220 S.W. 3rd Ave. (503) 221-3001.

Reno, Nev., 89502, 2028 Federal Bldg., 300 Booth St. (702) 784-5203.

Richmond, Va., 23240, 8010 Federal Bldg., 400 N. 8th St. (804) 782-2246.

St. Louis, 63105, Chromalloy Bldg., 120 S. Central Ave. (314) 425-3302.

Salt Lake City, 84138, 1203 Federal Bldg., 125 S. State St. (801) 524-5116.

San Francisco, 94102, Federal Bldg., Box 36013, 450 Golden Gate Ave. (415) 556-5860.

San Juan, P.R., 00918, 659 Federal Building. (809) 763-6363.

Savannah, 31402, 235 U.S. Courthouse and Post Office Bldg., 125-29 Bull St. (912) 232-4321.

Seattle, 98109, 706 Lake Union Bldg., 1700 Westlake Ave. North. (206) 442-5615.

Books, Pamphlets, Directories

The Agent/Distributor Service—A description of this service, the markets covered, and how to apply. Free from any District Office of the Department of Commerce.

The Carrier's Role in Export Control—Summarizes the main provisions of U.S. export control regulation which affect operations of U.S. and foreign flag carriers. 16 pp. Free.

Electric Current Abroad—Gives characteristics of electric current available in principal foreign cities. 1967.

Exporting. A Basic Guide to Exporting—This invaluable booklet contains advice on such topics as assessing export potential, selecting sales and distribution channels, locating foreign representatives, drawing up agreements, financing exports, and receiving payment. 1976. 63 pp. Superintendent of Documents, U.S. GPO, Washington, D.C. 20402. $1.25.

Export Contact List Services—A useful guide to Trade List and Data tape services and the Export Mailing List service. 1978. 16 pp. U.S. Department of Commerce, Industry and Trade Administration. Free.

Export Information Services—A guide to aids to U.S. business firms that are provided by the Bureau of International Commerce, 12 pp. Free.

Foreign Business Practices—Includes basic information on some of the laws and practices that affect export, licensing, and investment abroad. 1970. 64 pp. 75¢.

Foreign Investment Checklist—Cites factors U.S. business executives should consider when exploring investment opportunities abroad. Order only from District Offices. Free.

Foreign Investment Offices in the United States—Lists foreign chambers of commerce, development boards, and other offices that are sources of investment information. Order only from District Offices. Free.

How to Get the Most from Overseas Exhibitions—Advice for the U.S. firm that wishes to exhibit abroad. 1976. 20 pp. Free.

Industry-organized Trade Missions Overseas—Tells how U.S. business executives obtain help from the Department of Commerce in developing new markets overseas through industry-organized trade missions, and includes the stands required for government sponsorship. 1965. 12 pp. 25¢.

Marketing Aids for Higher Export Profits—Describes Department of Commerce services for the exporter. Order only from District Offices. Free.

New Look at Export Credit Guarantees, Insurance—A review of credit insurance and guarantee programs. Includes table showing type of coverage, purpose, types of goods covered, costs, etc. Reprint from *International Commerce* magazine, November 24, 1969. Free.

Ocean Freight Rate Guidelines for Shippers—Acquaints exporters with the manner in which ocean freight rates are established by shipping lines and conferences of such lines. Describes principal factors in ocean carrier rate-making; outlines ocean freight rate adjustment procedures; lists names, addresses, and trade areas of the steamship conferences and rate agreement groups serving the foreign commerce of the U.S. 50¢.

Sources of Credit Information on Foreign Firms—Ready reference to principal sources of foreign credit information in the U.S. and abroad. 1967. 108 pp. 50¢.

Sources of Information on U.S. firms—A guide for International traders including local sources, business directories, trade journals, etc. 1977. 28 pp.

Summary of U.S. Export Control Regulations—Includes helpful hints on applying for a license and specimens of forms used. 18 pp. 50¢.

U.S. Trade Center Facilities Abroad—A detailed description of display space, electrical and water provisions, and other facilities in trade centers as well as brief summaries of developed and developing markets. 1977. 44 pp.

Periodicals

Business

Commerce America (formerly *International Commerce*)—Contains international commerce and domestic business reports, economic highlights, and worldwide business outlook. Superintendent of Documents, Washington, D.C. 20402. $22 annually, $6 additional for foreign mailing, 90¢ for an individual copy.

Export Administration Regulations and *Export Administration Bulletins*—Compilation of official regulations and policies governing the export licensing of commodities and technical data. The *Regulations* is issued annually on June 1; the supplementary *Bulletins* appear throughout the year. Superintendent of Documents, Washington, D.C. 20402. Subscription to the *Regulations* and all *Bulletins* is $45.00 ($56.25 to foreign address). District Offices of the Department of Commerce will sell individual copies.

OTHER GOVERNMENT SOURCES

No Appendix can hope to cover the multitude of publications and agencies that can provide information to the multinational marketer. A sampling is offered below as an indication of the rich resources available. More comprehensive listings can be found in two excellent publications:

A Researcher's Guide to Washington, 1978 edition. Washington Researchers, Suite 325, 910 Seventeenth St., N.W., Washington, D.C. 20006. This comprehensive volume provides names, addresses, and telephone numbers to some 20,000 information sources in the federal government. $95.

Foreign Trade Marketplace, 1st edition, George J. Schultz. editor. Gale Research Co., Detroit, 1977. This work lists all people and organizations in foreign trade, including governments and private organizations, with addresses and telephone numbers. Government agencies, diplomatic officers, etc., are also listed. $48.

Books, Pamphlets, Directories

Aids to Business. (Overseas Investment)–Spells out what the Agency for International Development can do to assist U.S. firms interested in developing nations. Order from Superintendent of Documents, Washington, D.C. 20402. 30¢.

Background Notes–Short, factual pamphlets about individual countries and territories, covering information on land, people, history, government, political conditions, economy, and foreign relations. 150 Notes. Complete set of current stock, $6.00; one-year subscription for updates, $3.50.

Export Marketing for Smaller Firms–Small Business Administration publication describes how smaller business firms can either expand their export trade or enter the export market. Order from Superintendent of Documents, Washington, D.C. 20402.

Foreign Consular Offices in the United States–State Department listing of foreign consular offices and representatives in the United States, in U.S. territories and possessions, and Canal Zone. Annual. Order from Superintendent of Documents, Washington, D.C. 20402. 50¢.

Postal Manual–Explains the domestic and international mail services, rates, fees, and conditions of use. Order from Superintendent of Documents, Washington, D.C. 20402. Looseleaf edition, with supplements. Chapters 1–6, $33.

Periodicals, Services

Diplomatic List–State Department listing of officers (including commercial attachés) of foreign embassies and legations in Washington, D.C. Quarterly. Order from the Superintendent of Documents, Washington, D.C. 20402. 45¢ per copy, $1.50 annually.

U.S. DEPARTMENT OF LABOR

Monthly Labor Review–This is a comprehensive listing of all Department of Labor publications which include occasional studies on labor law and labor developments abroad. Annual. Order from Superintendent of Documents, GPO, Washington, D.C. 20402. $16.

U.S. DEPARTMENT OF AGRICULTURE

Foreign Gold and Exchange Reserves—Issued semiannually, appraises the external financial position of foreign countries, particularly as it relates to opportunities for selling U.S. farm products abroad. Important events in international finance and trade are reviewed. The report points out foreign countries that are financially able to buy farm products commercially; it also appraises the financial position of developing countries where U.S. farm products are sold concessionally.

Foreign Agriculture Trade of the United States—A monthly review, presents the current status and outlook for U.S. agricultural policy, production, and trade.

Agricultural Economy and Trade—Each country report in the Economic Research Service-Foreign Series surveys agricultural policy, production, and trade.

The World Agricultural Situation—Published annually in February (with more detailed statements by regions of the world published in April).

Copies of all these publications are available from the Economic, Statistical, and Cooperative Service, U.S. Department of Agriculture, Washington, D.C. 20250.

U.S. DEPARTMENT OF HEALTH, EDUCATION, AND WELFARE

Publications on Comparative Education—A number of country reports concerning education in various countries have been issued by the Office of Education of HEW. Sample titles: "Education in Japan: A Century of Modern Development" (1977); "Educational System of Israel" (1976); "Educational System of the German Democratic Republic" (1976); "Educational System of Yugoslavia" (1976). Single free copies are available from Publications Distribution Unit, Office of Education, U.S. Department of Health, Education, and Welfare, Washington, D.C. 20202. A list of available and forthcoming reports is given in "Publications of the Office of Education on Comparative Education" upon request from the HEW Office of Education.

ORGANIZATION FOR ECONOMIC COOPERATION AND DEVELOPMENT

OECD Economic Surveys—Each title in this series of economic studies is a booklet published annually by the Organization for Economic Cooperation and Development concerning one of the 21 OECD member countries. Each booklet contains information on recent trends of demand and output, prices and wages, foreign trade and payments, economic policy, and prospects and conclusions. OECD Publications Office, Suite 1305, 1750 Pennsylvania Avenue, N.W., Washington, D.C. Single copies, $2.50; subscription to full series, $45.00.

OECD Economic Outlook—A semiannual survey of economic trends and prospects in OECD countries. Prefaced by a general survey of the economic situation, it examines the current situation and prospects regarding demand and output, employment, costs and prices, and foreign trade for OECD as a whole and in some of the major countries. Attention is paid to the trend of current balances, monetary developments, and capital movements as factors affecting international monetary developments. Sincle copies, $7.00; annual subscription, $13.75.

OECD Financial Statistics—A bilingual publication supplying complete, up-to-date, authoritative information on financial markets in 16 European countries, the United States, Canada, and Japan. It focuses on capital operations and financial transactions with foreign countries; new security issues on national and Euro-markets; security portfolios of the different categories of investors; interest rates for 10 to 15 different financial instruments in each country; and other current financial information. Annual subscription, $75.00.

OECD Observer—Published in alternate months by the Organization for Economic Cooperation and Development Publication Office, Suite 1305, 1750 Pennsylvania Avenue, N.W., Washington, D.C. 20006. Single copy, $1.25; annual subscription, $6.25.

INTERNATIONAL MONETARY FUND

International Monetary Fund Survey—A biweekly survey of international economic trends. $10 mailing fee per year.

Surveys of Foreign Economies—Each volume surveys the monetary, fiscal, exchange control, and trading systems that are common to the groups of selected countries and presents detailed information for each country on natural resources, production development planning and progress, budgets and taxation, money and banking, and foreign trade, aid, and payments. The first seven volumes deal with Africa; volumes 1–3 are out of print. Vol. 4 (1971): Democratic Republic of the Congo, Malagasy, Zambia, Malawi, Mauritius. Vol. 5 (1973): Botswana, Lesotho, Swaziland, Burundi, Ecuatorial Guinea, Rwanda. Vol. 6 (1975): Gambia, Ghana, Liberia, Nigeria, Sierra Leone. Vol. 7 (1978): Algeria, Morocco, Tunesia. $5.00 each.

The IMF also publishes a *Direction of Trade* handbook, a *Balance of Payments Yearbook, International Financial Statistics,* and various *Staff Papers.*

UNITED NATIONS

The UN publishes a large volume of books, pamphlets, periodicals, and official records, including several annual surveys and bulletins concerning economic developments in various regions.

Economic Survey of Europe—Review of current developments in the European economy. Annual. About $3. *Economic Bulletin for Europe*—supplements the *Survey,* issued twice annually.

Economic Survey of Asia and the Far East—Review of current situation covering agriculture, industry, transport, trade, payments, etc. Annual. About $4.

Economic Bulletin for Asia and the Far East—supplements the *Survey*, issued three times annually.

Economic Survey of Latin America—Review of regional and internal economic developments. Annual. About $5. *Economic Bulletin for Latin America*—supplements the *Survey*, issued twice annually.

Economic Developments in the Middle East—Review of developments relating to agriculture industry, petroleum, foreign trade, and the balance of payments. Annual.

(See also *Statistical Yearbook of the United Nations* listed under "Information on Foreign Countries, Statistical")

Information on Foreign Countries—periodicals of governments and international agencies.

International Financial News Survey—published weekly. Apply to The Secretary, International Monetary Fund, 19th & H Streets, N.W., Washington, D.C. Free.

World Economic Survey—World economic report. A comprehensive review of world economic issues and trends. Orders from the UN Department of Economic and Social Affairs, New York, N.Y.

World Trade Annual—Data from the 24 principal trading countries of the world, providing statistics of trade by commodity by country. Order from the UN Statistical Office. New York, N.Y.

INTERNATIONAL TRADE CENTER

International Trade Forum—published quarterly by the International Trade Center UNCTAD/GATT, Palais des Nations, 1211 Geneva 10, Switzerland.

GATT PUBLICATIONS
(AVAILABLE FROM UN PUBLICATION SALES OFFICE)

Analytical Bibliography—Market Surveys by Products and Countries
Guide to Sources of Information on Foreign Trade Regulations
Role of the Freight Forwarder in Developing Countries
Foreign Trade Enterprises in Eastern Europe
Foreign Trade Enterprises in Yugoslavia
Compilation of Basic Information on Export Markets
Organization of Trade Missions—A Guide for Developing Countries
Compendium of Sources: Basic Commodity Statistics
Compendium of Sources: International Trade Statistics
Manual on Export Marketing Research for Developing Countries
World Directory of Industry & Trade Associations
Directory of Product and Industry Journals

FOREIGN MISSIONS

Missions of foreign governments are good sources of information about developments in their home countries. Some foreign governments, as well as foreign chambers of commerce, issue economic newsletters and other reports. For the addresses of Foreign Embassies in Washington, and the names of their commercial counselors or attachés, consult *The Diplomatic List*. A current copy of this quarterly State Department publication is available from the Superintendent of Documents, Washington, D.C. 20402. 45¢.

INDEPENDENT RESEARCH FIRMS

Some firms specialize in the preparation of information relevant to topics under consideration by decision makers. Washington Researchers, one such firm in the Washington, D.C., area, is in the business of providing custom service suited to individual needs. The firm is designed to help determine information requirements, locate sources of relevant information, and present only that information that affects the client's decision. The research is based on interviews with experts as well as existing data sources.

PROCESSED STATISTICAL INFORMATION

At least one organization, Predicasts, Inc., of Cleveland, Ohio, processes business information on industries, countries, companies, and subjects and publishes a variety of services. Two of these are of particular interest to multinational marketers. Entitled "Regional and Product Worldcasts," these publications systematically arrange published foreign forecasts from all government planning agencies, foreign and domestic journals, bankletters, international agencies, and special studies. Each abstract contains a one-line subject description, base period data, short- and long-range forecasts, a key to indicate extent of article, and source. Information is included on capacities, production, shipments, and sales distribution. Coverage includes all countries and ranges from detailed products to industries to the overall economy.

PRIVATE SOURCES

International agencies and national government statistics are valuable sources of statistical data on economic variables. Their major shortcoming, however, is that these data deal in aggregates and do not specifically focus on the particular products or markets of concern to a company. Aggregate statistics on economic and social variables are extremely valuable in describing the general characteristics and size of an economy and, therefore, of the particular market, but they are no substitute for specific data on the size of product and service markets, and data on the activities of specific companies. For this type of information, private sources are necessary. The following listing indicates the major private sources of published documentary information.

Information Services

Business International—This organization publishes a weekly newsletter and various reports on special topics. It is widely read by international business marketers and is a particularly good source of information on what companies are currently doing.

Economic Intelligence Unit—The Economist Intelligence Unit, or EIU, is a source of information on specific industry situations. Frequent reports are issued covering such topics as refrigerator sales in France and color-television sales in Germany.

Magazines and Newspapers

Asian W.S.J.

Major business and financial newspapers, such as the *Wall Street Journal*, *Nihon Keizai Shimbun,* and the *Financial Times,* are excellent sources of information not only on domestic economy but on international markets as well. The same is true of major newspapers such as the *New York Times* and *Frankfurter Algemeine.*

General Business Magazines—Most countries have business magazines targeted on a general management audience. In the U.S., *Business Week, Fortune,* and *Forbes* are excellent sources of information on international management and markets.

Trade Magazines—Another major source of specialized information on particular products and industries is trade publications. In the U.S. alone there are over 53,000 trade publications. Typically, these publications devote portions of each issue and, in some cases, entire issues to international markets. *Advertising Age,* for example, publishes an annual roundup of advertising expenditures by country. A typical issue of *Advertising Age* will contain an article on some aspect of advertising in foreign countries. Virtually every industry has at least one trade magazine, and these magazines are increasing their coverage of international aspects of industry operations.

Service Organizations

Service organizations such as banks and consultants are an important source of foreign market information. The banks, in particular, are a valuable source. Most large international banks have a combination of periodicals and special reports on international market developments. For example, in addition to its monthly "Morgan Guaranty Survey," which often carries an article on some aspect of the international economy, Morgan Guaranty also publishes special booklets entitled "Export and Import Procedures, which are relevant to multinational marketing sales.

Corporate Publications

Perhaps the single most valuable source of information on company and industry activity in international business is the reports of companies themselves.

The basic reporting documents of companies are, of course, their annual reports. U.S.-based companies as a group lead others in the disclosure of information concerning their operations. This is a result of both custom and legislation in the United States. The typical U.S. company annual report is a gold mine of information concerning the operations of the company. U.S. companies, however, are not the only companies that disclose useful information in their annual reports. An increasing number of non-U.S.-based multinational coporations are adopting a policy of substantial disclosure of their worldwide activities. The Nestlé Company of Vevey, Switzerland, is a good example of current practice in this area. Nestlé's annual report is translated into four languages: French, German, Italian, and English. The report gives a full description of Nestlé's sales by product and by geographic region together with an extensive description of the company's operations, problems, and intentions in each region of the world and in each of the product areas.

In addition to annual reports, most larger companies publish, from time to time, selected documents which describe aspects of their operations, including their international development. Often these publications are extremely valuable summary documents describing the company's international activity.

A third source of company information is the house organ. Although house organs are normally circulated only internally, an interested party can usually obtain copies and programs.

Thus a company's own publications are one of the finest sources of information about the company's operations. An analyst interested in gathering information on an industry can do this by assembling the reports, annual and otherwise, of companies in the industry and aggregating the information contained in these reports.

TRADE PUBLICATIONS

Trade and industry associations gather a considerable amount of information on opportunities in foreign markets for distribution to their membership. Anyone investigating a specific product should check with the appropriate trade association to see whether it has gathered material on the product of interest.

Very often, trade associations gather comprehensive statistical and narrative material for distribution to their membership in the form of an annual yearbook. These yearbooks, which are usually available to the public, constitute one of the most detailed and comprehensive information sources available on particular products and industries.

BIBLIOGRAPHIES

Three standard bibliographical services published in the United States are the *Business Periodicals Index, The Public Affairs Information Service,* and Funk and Scott's *Company Index. Business Periodicals Index* and Funk and Scott's *Index* organize information around subject and company. A valuable international bibliographic source is the *Foreign Commerce Handbooks* published by the Chamber of Commerce of the United States in Washington, D.C. Another international source is the *International Executive,* a quarterly bibliography focusing exclusively on the international business and related subjects and providing an abstract of books and articles. Two additional international bibliographic sources are the *International Business and Foreign Trade Information Sources* and *The Developing Nations Information Sources,* both published by the Gail Research Company, Detroit, Michigan.

DIRECTORIES

Directories are useful when information on a subject or the name of an association is needed. The following are recommended:

1. *The Standard Periodical Directory – 1975*
   3rd Edition, Edited by Leon Garry
   Oxbridge Publishing Co., 420 Lexington Ave.
   New York, N.Y. 10017
   $60
   Provides 53,000 publications under 2,225 classifications according to subject from Accounting through Zoology.
2. *Ulrich's International Periodicals Directory*
   13th Edition/1969–1970 (2 volumes)
   R. R. Bowker Co. (Xerox)
   1180 Avenue of the Americas
   New York, N.Y. 10036
   The publications are classified according to general subject and language and are extensively cross-indexed.
3. *Encyclopedia of Associations*
   7th Edition (3 volumes)
   Gale Research Company
   Book Tower, Detroit, Mich. 48226
   Volume I, National Organizations of the United States, $45.00
   Volume II, Geographic-Executive Index, $28.50
   Volume III, New Associations & Projects, $48.00

The main function of the third directory is to list associations; however, it also lists whatever publications the associations distribute. The first volume classifies the associations according to type, such as "I. Trade, Business, Commercial."

ABC Europe Production—Lists 500,000 names and addresses of exporting manufacturers in 29 European countries. Indexed in English, French, German, Italian, Portuguese, and Spanish. Annual. ABC Verlagshaus, Berliner Allee 8, 61 Darmstadt, West Germany. 4,200 pp. $50.

American Register of Exporters and Importers—Lists over 25,000 active American export and import firms, products handled, and allied data. Annual. American Register of Exporters and Importers Corp., 90 West Broadway, New York, N.Y. 10007. $40.

Bottin International—International register lists names and addresses of over

300,000 firms in 110 countries under 1,000 product classifications. Two major sections: the world by trades and the world by countries. In four languages: English, French, German, and Spanish. Published annually by Didot-Bottin, S.A., Paris 7, France. Order from Bottin International, U.S.A., 5714 W. Pico Blvd. Los Angeles, Calif. 90019. 2,500 pp. $55.

Custom House Guide—Lists companies, banks, and brokers servicing international trade by business categories and U.S. and Canadian port cities, 28,000 separate commodity listings; U.S. tariff schedules; customs regulations and general information. Annual Budd Publications, Inc., 134 13th Street, Philadelphia, Pa. 19107. 2,000 pp. $49. (Includes subscription to *American Import & Export Bulletin.*)

Exporter's Encyclopedia—Import regulations and procedures required for shipping to every country in the world, plus information on preparing export shipments. Lists world ports, steamship lines, airlines, government agencies, trade organizations. Special sections on packing, marine insurance, export terms, and many other aspects of foreign trade. Annual. Price includes twice-monthly supplementary bulletins and newsletters. Dun & Bradstreet International, P.O. Box 3224, Church Street Station, New York, N.Y. 10008. $120.

Guide to Foreign Business Directories—Provides lists of general, special, and local directories, arranged by country, with a separate list of international directories published in the U.S. Government Printing Office, Washington, D.C.

Guide to Foreign Information Sources—Lists foreign embassies and legations in the United States; other organizations and services relating to major areas of the world. Chamber of Commerce of the United States, 1615 H. St., N.W., Washington, D.C. 20006. $1.

Kelly's Manufacturers and Merchants Directory—Lists firms in the United States and other principal trading countries of the world. Annual. Kelly's Directories Ltd., 220 E. 42nd St., New York, N.Y. 10017.

Reference Book for World Traders—Loose-leaf handbook covering information required for planning exports to and imports from all foreign countries, as well as market research throughout the world. Kept up to date by monthly supplements. Croner Publications, Inc., 211–03 Jamaica Ave., Queens Village, N.Y. 11428. 2 vols. $35.

Trade Directories of the World—Loose-leaf reference work, kept up to date by monthly amendments. Contains data on some 2,000 business and trade directories covering the U.S. and 150 foreign countries, as well as 393 trade categories. Includes frequency of publication, price, number of pages, publisher, publisher's address, as well as short synopses of the directories. Croner Publications, Inc., 211–03 Jamaica Ave., Queens Village, New York, N.Y. 11428. $25.

World Directory of Freight Conferences—Loose-leaf reference work, kept up to date by monthly amendments. Lists more than 350 freight conferences operating outward from the United States, Great Britain, and all other countries of the world. Includes titles of the freight conferences, areas covered, terms, rebate periods, secretaries, names and addresses, and list of members. Croner Publications Ltd., 46-50 Coomb Road, New Malden, Surrey, UK, KT3-4QL. About $20.

American Import and Export Bulletin—Laws, rulings, articles, news, and trade opportunities. Monthly. Budd Publications, Inc., 134 13th Street, Philadelphia, Pa. 19107. (Included in subscription to *Custom House Guide.*)

Brandon's Shipper and Forwarder—Complete advance ship-sailing schedules, news articles, directory, and other information on foreign trade and shipping. Weekly. New York Foreign Freight Forwarders and Brokers Association, Inc., 1 World Trade Center, Suite 3169, New York, N.Y. 10648. $15 per year.

Commodity Trade Statistics—Quarterly data covering about 80 percent of world commodity trade, showing quantity, value, origin, and destination. About 30 issues annually. Sales Section, United Nations, Room LX-2300, New York, N.Y. 10017. $64 per year.

Shipping Digest—Lists sailing dates from all U.S. and Canadian ports; includes news articles and directory material. Covers all phases of foreign trade shipping. Shipping Digest, Inc., 25 Broadway, New York, N.Y. 10004. $15 per year. ($20 to foreign address.)

World Marketing—Concentrated coverage of overseas trade, including market developments and international trade possibilities. Twice monthly. Dun & Bradstreet Publications, P.O. Box 3224, Church Street Station, New York, N.Y. 10008. $30 per year. Included in subscription to *Exporter's Encyclopedia*.

APPENDIX II / HOW TO LOOK UP
TRADE, TARIFF, AND PRODUCTION DATA

In order to locate trade and tariff data you must learn how to use commodity classification systems.

WHAT ARE THE MAJOR CLASSIFICATION SYSTEMS?

For international trade there are two main systems in use, the BTN and the SITC (Standard Industrial Trade Classification). The BTN (Brussels Tariff Nomenclature) was first adopted in 1955 by European countries; the system has since been adopted by many less-developed countries. Commodities are classified primarily by the principal material they contain or from which they are made. BTN has fewer categories than the SITC, which means there are a large number of items in each category. Since the less-developed countries have few products to classify, this is a more convenient system. If a country wants sensitivity within a category, it can extend the usual two- or three-digit number system to over ten digits for a particular group of commodities.

In order to achieve comparability of economic statistics among countries involved in international trade, the United Nations has encouraged use of the SITC system. At present over 80 percent of the countries use the SITC system or some slight variation for measuring international flows. The SITC system is based on type of commodity; for example, food chemicals, or transport equipment. SITC has about 1,300 categories using a five-digit system to indicate a specific category. The different systems are compared in Figure 1.

United States. The United States uses an expanded version of the SITC system to measure exports and imports and to levy duties on imports.

	U.S. Systems
Imports	Schedule A(SITC)
Exports	Schedule B(SITC)
Tariffs	Tariff Schedule-USA(TSUSA)
Domestic production	Standard Industrial Classification (SIC)

The U.S. Schedule A and Schedule B SITC systems differ from the United Nations SITC in that they are more detailed and contain about 3,500 categories each. The TSUSA system is the most detailed, containing over 10,000 categories. These three systems are completey correlated, so that any item in one can be translated into a category in any of the others. The U.S. Department of Commerce publishes three catalogs or schedules that list the categories of each system, their assigned number, and a description of the items included in the category.

Since Schedule A (Imports) and Schedule B (Exports) differ only slightly, only one catalog is published to cover both systems. It lists only *Schedule B* numbers.

The second Commerce catalog is the *Tariff Schedule, USA,* which lists the number, commodity description, and tariff for all items imported into the United States.

The third publication is the *Cross-Classifications* and provides a catalog of the correlations between the SIC, Schedule A, Schedule B, and Tariff Schedule, USA. This means that a category number in Schedule B can be referenced in the *Cross-Classifications* and the corresponding category number in the Tariff Schedule can be found.

U.S. trade statistics. The U.S. Department of Commerce publishes a variety of statistical series covering imports and exports. The various series are compiled with varying detail. For example, information on imports provided from TSUSA sources is more detailed than series compiled using the Schedule A system because TSUSA has more categories. The Department of Commerce publishes a book-

FIGURE 1. Classification Systems Compared by Major Characteristics

Classification System	Use	Number of Classifications*	Number	Description**	
					Least Detail → Most Detail
Brussels Tariff Nomenclature (BTN)	Imports, Exports	800	22.07	Wine of Fresh Grapes	
Standard Industrial Classification (SIC)	U.S. Domestic Production	2,000	208.40	Wine, All Types	
United Nations Standard Industrial Classification (SITC)	Imports, Exports Other than U.S.	1,312	—	—	
Schedule A SITC	U.S. Imports	3,500	112.10	Wine of Fresh Grapes	
Schedule B SITC	U.S. Exports	3,500	112.10	Wine of Fresh Grapes	
Tariff Schedule, USA (TSUSA)	Duties on U.S. Imports	10,000	167.10 20	Champagne and other Sparkling Wines, Value not over $6./Gallon	

*These are approximate estimates which can vary depending on their use.
**Listings are for wine.

let describing the various statistical series available in addition to giving examples of their format and the information they provide. This is called the *Guide to Foreign Trade Statistics: 1971*. Price $1.50. The *Guide* has an information locator on page V that lists the statistical series vailable from the department. The "Foreign Trade (FT)" series are recommended as good statistical series for summarizing flows in and out of the United States.

HOW TO LOOK UP IMPORTS, EXPORTS, AND DUTIES

To find U.S. imports of champagne, first locate the key word "champagne" in Part 2 of either the Schedule B classification catalog or the *Cross-Classifications* catalog. If you were not sure of the exact term for a bubbly wine, you could look up the key word "beverage." The key word is keyed to a number that is the item category listed in the front of the catalog. This category provides a complete catalog of items coded and allows you to pick the classification number that most closely identifies the item or products of interst. The classification method is illustrated in the following example.

Sample Listing of Commodity Key Words (Schedule B)

Key Word	Schedule B Number
Beverages	1100000
Alcoholic Beverages	1120000
Fermented Alcoholic Beverages	1121000
Wine of Fresh Grapes	1121200
Champagne	1121210

All catalogs have broad categories that divide into progressively more detailed subcategories in a logical sequence. By using the key words properly it is easy to find the information you need.

HOW TO LOOK UP AN IMPORT DUTY FOR THE U.S.A.

To find the U.S. import duty on champagne, first locate the TSUSA number for champagne in the rear of the *Tariff Schedule, USA–1978* using the alphabetic index. Then find the category in the front part of the schedule that will list the category number, description of the commodity, and the tariff. An alternative is to find the category number in, for instance, the *Schedule B* catalog, translate the number into a TSUSA number using the *Cross-Classifications* catalog, then find the duty in the *Tariff Schedule, USA–1978*. This is illustrated in Figure 2. Sample pages from the various schedules are shown in Appendix I-1 in Figure 2.

U.S. DEPARTMENT OF COMMERCE STATISTICS

The catalogs and statistical series published by the Department of Commerce can be referenced in any Field Office of the department. See list of District Field offices under "Department of Commerce" in Appendix I.

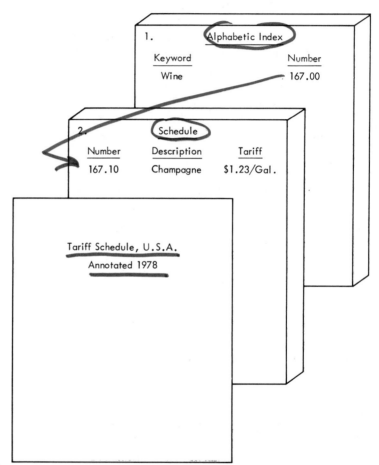

FIGURE 2. How to Find a U.S. Tariff Rate

For classification of parts for machinery or other equipment, or for items of mixed materials, including alloys, see page XXVI of the Introduction.

FIGURE 2. (Cont.)

SECTION 1. BEVERAGES AND TOBACCO

Schedule B number	Commodity description, and items included (List of items not necessarily complete)	Unit of quantity
	BEVERAGES	
	Non-alcoholic beverages, except fruit and vegetable juices:	
111.0010	Bottled and canned soft drinks, and mineral waters	Gal.
	CLUB SODA OXYGENATE↑ COLA POLAND WA↑ GINGER ALE POTASH WA↑ HUNYADI JANOS WATER.↑) QUININE TO↑ LEMON SODA ROOT BEER LEMONADE SARSAPARIL	
111.0020	Nonalcoholic beverages, except soft drinks and m	3al.
	For classification of juices, see 0535005-05.	
	CHOC LAC SKIM MILK, LIQUID, CHOCOLATE- WHOLE LIQUID MILK, CHOCOLATE MALT- COCKTAIL MIXES FLAVORED FLAVORED EGG NOG UNFERMENTED BREWERS WORT WHOLE MILK, FRESH, CHOCOLATE- MALT BEVERAGE (NON-ALCOHOLIC FLAVORED BEVERAGE MADE OF MALT AND HOPS)	
	Alcoholic beverages:	
112.1000	Wines of fresh grapes, and grape must..	Wine Gal.
	For classification of unfermented grape must, see 0535030.	
	ALTAR CINZANO RHINE BORDEAUX CLARET SHERRY BURGUNDY CRUSE SPARKLING CALIFORNIA MADEIRA STILL, UNFLAVORED CANARY MALAGA VERMOUTH CHABLIS MUSCATEL VOURAY CHAMPAGNE RED AND WHITE PORT ZINFANDEL	
112.2000	Cider and fermented beverages, except wines of fresh grapes and grape must	Gal.
	GINGER BEER RICE WINE SAKE HARD CIDER	
112.3000	Beer, ale, stout, and porter	Gal.
	BREWERS WORT	
112.4010	Brandy	Pf. Gal.
112.4013	Bourbon whiskey in containers each holding one gallon or less (formerly part of 1124020)...........	Pf. Gal.
112.4018	Bourbon whiskey in containers each holding more than one gallon (formerly part of 1124020)...........	Pf. Gal.
112.4023	Whiskey (except bourbon), in containers each holding one gallon or less (formerly part of 1124020)..........	Pf. Gal.
	BLENDED RYE SCOTCH	
112.4028	Whiskey (except bourbon), in containers each holding more than one gallon (formerly part of 1124020)	Pf. Gal.
	BLENDED RYE SCOTCH	
112.4032	Rum, in containers each holding one gallon or less (formerly part of 1124033)...........	Pf. Gal.
112.4034	Rum, in containers each holding more than one gallon (formerly part of 1124033)	Pf. Gal.
112.4036	Distilled alcoholic beverages (liquors, liqueurs, and compounds containing spirits), in containers each holding one gallon or less, except brandy, rum, and whiskey (formerly part of 1124038)...........	Pf. Gal.
	AGUARDIENTE (SPIRITS) CURACO NEUTRAL GRAIN SPIRITS AMER PICON↑ GENEVA GIN POMERANZA (SPIRITS) BENEDICTINE↑ GIN RATAFIA BITTERS KIRSCHWASSER SLOE GIN CALONE-PUNCH MESCAL (SPIRITS) TAFFIA CHERRY HEERING.↑ MIXED ALCOHOLIC COCKTAILS TEQUILA CORDIALS NEUTRAL CANE SPIRITS VODKA CREME DE MENTHE	
112.4039	Distilled alcoholic beverages (liquors, liqueurs, and compounds containing spirits), in containers each holding more than one gallon, except brandy, rum, and whiskey (formerly part of 1124038)...........	Pf. Gal.
	AGUARDIENTE (SPIRITS) CURACO NEUTRAL GRAIN SPIRITS AMER PICON↑ GENEVA GIN POMERANZA (SPIRITS) BENEDICTINE↑ GIN RATAFIA BITTERS KIRSCHWASSER SLOE GIN CALONE-PUNCH MESCAL (SPIRITS) TAFFIA CHERRY HEERING↑ MIXED ALCOHOLIC COCKTAILS TEQUILA CORDIALS NEUTRAL CANE SPIRITS VODKA CREME DE MENTHE	

Schedule B
Commodity Listing
Appendix I-2

FIGURE 2. (Cont.)

Section 6. Correlation Between Schedule A Import Classifications and TSUSA, SITC, and FT 990 Codes—Continued

Schedule A number	Commodity description and TSUSA numbers	Unit of quantity	SITC code	FT 990 code[1]
091.0	LARD, OLEO, OTHER BUTTER SUBSTITUTES			
091.0000	LARD, OLEOMARGARINE, AND OTHER BUTTER SUBSTI 116.30 00 177.50 00	LB	09100	006
099	FOOD PREPARATIONS, NES			
099.0	FOOD PREPARATIONS, NES			
099.0100	CHICORY ROOTS, GROUND OR OTHERWISE PREPARED 160.35 00	LB	09901	006
099.0300	MUSTARD, GROUND OR PREPARED 161.59 00	LB	09903	006
C99.0420	SOY SAUCE, THIN 132.45 00	LB	09904	006
099.044	SAUCES, EXCEPT THIN SOY 182.46 00	LB	09904	006
099.0460	PREPARATIONS CONTAINING OVER 50% BY WEIGHT OF MONOSODIUM GLUTAMATE. 493.42 00	-	09904	006
099.0500	SOUPS AND BROTHS. 182.50 00 182.52 00	LB	09905	006
099.0630	PAPAIN, DRIED BREWERS YEAST AND FICIN, CRUDE. 437.48 00	LB	09906	006
099.0640	YEAST, NATURAL, ACTIVE AND INACTIVE NES 182.40 00 437.47 00	LB	09906	006
099.0700	VINEGAR AND SUBSTITUTES FOR VINEGAR 182.55 00 182.58 00	PFG	09907	006
099.0900	FOOD PREPARATIONS, MISCELLANEOUS, NES 118.25 00 1-5.48 40 182.11 00 182.90 00 182.92 00 182.95 40	-	09909	006
	SECTION 1--BEVERAGES AND TOBACCO			
11	BEVERAGES			
111	BEVERAGES--NONALCOHOLIC, NES			
111.0	BEVERAGES, NES--NONALCOHOLIC			
111.0100	MINERAL WATERS AND ICE. 166.10 00 522.51 00	-	11101	024
111.0200	CHOCOLATE MILK DRINK, GINGER ALE, GINGER BEER, LEMONADE, SODA WATER AND BEVERAGES, NSPF . . 118.15 00 166.20 00 166.40 00	GAL	11102	024
112	BEVERAGES--ALCOHOLIC			
112.1	WINE, EXCEPT PRUNE WINE AND RICE WINE			
112.1210	CHAMPAGNE AND OTHER SPARKLING WINES 167.10 20 167.10 40	GAL	11212	025
112.1220	WINE, STILL, PRODUCED FROM GRAPE, LESS THAN 14% ALCOHOL 167.30 20 167.30 40 167.32 00	GAL	11212	025
112.1230	WINE, GRAPE, MARSALA. 167.34 00	GAL	11212	025
112.1240	WINE, SHERRY. 167.35 20 167.35 40	GAL	11212	025
112.1250	WINE, GRAPE, OVER 14% ALCOHOL, NES. 167.37 20 167.37 40	GAL	11212	025
112.1300	VERMOUTH. 167.40 00 167.42 00	GAL	11213	025
112.2	CIDER AND FERMENTED BEVERAGES, NES			
112.2000	FRUIT JUICE, CIDER, PRUNE WINE, RICE WINE, AND OTHER FERMENTED ALCOHOLIC BEVERAGES, NES . . 165.70 00 167.15 00 167.20 00 167.25 00 167.50 00	GAL	11220	025
112.3	ALE, BEER, PORTER, STOUT			
112.3000	ALE, PORTER, STOUT, AND BEER. 167.05 20 167.05 40	GAL	11230	025
112.4	BEVERAGES--DISTILLED, ALCOHOLIC			
112.4010	BRANDY. 168.19 00 168.20 00 168.21 00 168.22 00	PFG	11240	026
112.4020	CORDIALS, LIQUEURS, KIRSCHWASSER, AND RATAFIA 168.25 00 168.25 00	PFG	11240	026
112.4030	GIN 168.35 20 168.35 40	PFG	11240	026
112.4040	RUM 168.40 20 168.40 40	PFG	11240	026
112.4050	WHISKEY, SCOTCH AND IRISH 168.45 20 168.45 40	PFG	11240	026
112.4060	WHISKEY, EXCEPT SCOTCH AND IRISH. 168.46 20 168.46 40	PFG	11240	026

[1]Principal Commodity Codes--for Bureau of the Census use only.

Cross-Classification between Schedule A and TSUSA Appendix I-3

FIGURE 2. (Cont.)

TARIFF SCHEDULES OF THE UNITED STATES ANNOTATED (1971)

SCHEDULE 1. - ANIMAL AND VEGETABLE PRODUCTS
Part 12. - Beverages

Page 63

1 - 12 - B,C
166.10 - 167.35

Item	Stat. Suf- fix	Articles	Units of Quantity	Rates of Duty	
				1	2
		Subpart B. - Non-Alcoholic Beverages		↗	↖
		Subpart B headnote:		Most Favored Nation Countries	Non-Most Favored Nation Countries
		Tariff Schedule-USA Commodity and Tariff Listing (using TSUSA numbers) Appendix I-5			
166.10	00	All mineral waters, natural, imitation, or arti- ficial..	Gal.....	1.5¢ per gal.	10¢ per gal.
166.20	00	Ginger ale, ginger beer, lemonade, and soda water........	Gal.....	1¢ per gal.	15¢ per gal.
166.30	00	Vegetable juices, including mixed vegetable juices......	Gal.....	1¢ per gal.	15¢ per gal.
166.40	00	Beverages, not specially provided for..................	Gal.....	1¢ per gal.	15¢ per gal.
		Subpart C. - Fermented Alcoholic Beverages			
		Subpart C headnote:			
		1. Beverages in this subpart, containing over 24 percent of ethyl alcohol by volume when imported, are classed as spirits under item 168.50.			
167.05	20 40	Ale, porter, stout, and beer............................ In containers each holding not over 1 gallon....... In containers each holding over 1 gallon...........	.... Gal. Gal.	7¢ per gal.	50¢ per gal.
167.10	20 40	Champagne and other sparkling wines..................... Valued not over $6 per gallon..................... Valued over $6 per gallon.........................	.... Gal. Gal.	$1.23 per gal.	$6 per gal.
167.15	00	Cider, fermented, whether still or sparkling...........	Gal.....	3¢ per gal.	5¢ per gal.
167.20	00	Prune wine..	Gal.....	27¢ per gal. + $1.98 per proof gallon on ethyl alcohol content	70¢ per gal. + $5 per proof gallon on ethyl alcohol content
167.25	00	Rice wine or sake.......................................	Gal.....	30¢ per gal.	$1.25 per gal.
		Still wines produced from grapes: Containing not over 14 percent of alcohol by volume:			
167.30	20 40	In containers each holding not over 1 gallon.................................... Valued not over $4 per gallon............ Valued over $4 per gallon................	.... Gal. Gal.	37.5¢ per gal.	$1.25 per gal.
167.32	00	In containers each holding over 1 gallon...... Containing over 14 percent of alcohol by volume:	Gal.....	62.5¢ per gal.	$1.25 per gal.
167.34	00	In containers each holding not over 1 gallon, if entitled under regulations of the United States Internal Revenue Service to a type designation which includes the name "Marsala" and if so designated on the approved label............	Gal.....	33¢ per gal.	$1.25 per gal.
167.35	20 40	Sherry.................................... In containers each holding not over 1 gallon............................... In containers each holding over 1 gallon...............................	.... Gal. Gal.	$1 per gal.	$1.25 per gal.

FIGURE 2. (Cont.)

Tariff Schedule-USA
Alphabetic Index
Appendix I-4

FIGURE 2. (Cont.)

APPENDIX III / HOW TO USE THE INTERNATIONAL MARKETING INFORMATION RESOURCES OF THE U.S. DEPARTMENT OF COMMERCE FIELD OFFICES

PURPOSE

The U.S. Department of Commerce publishes extensive information—in the form of reports, statistical series, and lists—on foreign markets. The purpose of this information is to encourage the export of U.S. goods to foreign destinations. The individual seeking information faces the problem that the sources are so numerous it is frequently difficult to find useful information. The purpose of this Appendix is to assist you in using this source of information.

WHAT INFORMATION CAN COMMERCE SUPPLY?

Suppose we are interested in exporting table wine to Argentina. Commerce publications will cover everything from the general economic conditions in Argentina to a description of the particular market conditions affecting the import of wine. Statistical series will show how much (dollar value and gallons) wine the United States has exported to Argentina and how much wine Argentina has imported from the United States.

Commerce also keeps information on the duties and import restrictions Argentina imposes on wine. It will also provide the regulations pertaining to the export of wine under the U.S. Export Control Act. The act regulates or restricts the movement of certain commodities to certain countries (i.e., export of computers to the Communist countries).

HOW IS THE INFORMATION CLASSIFIED?

All sources are classified by *country* or by *commodity*. Commodities are classified by number using the various classification systems. Most reports are classified according to the SIC (Standard Industrial Classification) number, but some use Schedule B or TSUSA.

HOW IS INFORMATION PROVIDED?

Statistical information is available for reference at all field offices (see list in Appendix I). These statistical series can be in bound form, on microfilm, or on computer printouts.

Reports are usually in small booklet form. Some can be referenced in the

Field Office Library, but most have to be ordered from Washington, D.C., and take approximately four weeks to arrive.

Duties and regulations for both the U.S. Export Control program and all foreign countries are available at the Field Office upon request. (Export Controls Room and Laws & Regulations Room.)

Trade lists are lists of names of potential agents or representatives for a specific commodity. Trade lists are free to students.

REPORTS

The reports are of two types, recurring and special. *Recurring* reports are published regularly by the department. *Special* reports are published for commodities that have high export potential. The special reports cover these listed commodities:

1. Data Processing Equipment
2. Food Processing Equipment
3. Valves, Pumps, and Compressors
4. Medical and Scientific Equipment

Special reports are very detailed, covering economic, market, competitive, governmental, and social conditions within a country.

Commerce publishes two indexes that list all their reports both by country and by commodity. All commodities are listed according to their SIC (Standard Industrial Classification) number. *The Checklist of International Business Publications* contains all recurring reports published by the department. For some recurring and all special reports, use the *Index to Foreign Production and Commercial Reports.* The *Index* is available in a quarterly edition and an annual edition. The annual is the most useful.

Both the *Checklist* and the *Index* can be referenced in *Foreign Trade Statistics* or a Field Office Library, with a limited supply available free on request.

OTHER SERVICES

There are a number of Foreign Trade Specialists in Field Offices who are knowledgeable about certain world regions or commodities. If you want to see a specialist, first make an appointment with the receptionist in the Field Office entrance area. Specialists usually give seminars or visit firms interested in export and are out of the office three days per week.

DESK OFFICERS

In Washington the Office of International Commercial Relations has people who gather information on particular countries. These are the "Country Desk Officers," who are expert in one or several countries. Information is sent to the Desk Officer from the U.S. Consulates in the countries assigned to him. These people are a valuable source of information. To call a Desk Officer, check with the personnel in the Foreign Trade Statistics Room, who will let you use the Washington tie-line.

LIBRARY

Field Office Libraries maintain information for both the Bureau of International Commerce and the Bureau of Domestic Commerce. Due to space limitations, Field Office Libraries do not have a complete collection of all reports published by the department. Available reports are filed by country of commodity name. Libraries also have some information on foreign duties and regulations in addition to a good selection of foreign business directories.

APPENDIX IV / POPULATION, GNP AT MARKET PRICES, AND GNP PER CAPITA FOR 1974, 1975, AND 1976

Member countries of the World Bank and countries with mid-1975 populations of one million or more.

Region Country	1974 Population (000)	1974 GNP at market prices Amount (US$ millions)	1974 GNP at market prices Per capita (US$)	1975 Population (000)	1975 GNP at market prices Amount (US$ millions)	1975 GNP at market prices Per capita (US$)	1976 (preliminary) Population (000)	1976 (preliminary) GNP at market prices Amount (US$ millions)	1976 (preliminary) GNP at market prices Per capita (US$)
AFRICA									
Nigeria	73,044	22,200	300	75,023	25,600	340	77,056	29,320	380
Egypt, Arab Republic of	36,417	8,390	230	37,230	9,540	260	38,086	10,530	280
Ethiopia	27,240	2,480	90	27,950	2,730	100	28,678	2,960	100
South Africa	24,940	28,950	1,160	25,470	32,270	1,270	26,030	34,850	1,340
Zaire	24,071	3,180	130	24,721	3,450	140	25,389	3,510	140
Morocco	16,291	7,080	430	16,680	7,860	470	17,197	9,220	540
Algeria	15,215	11,780	770	15,747	13,680	870	16,235	16,060	990
Sudan[1]	15,227	3,720	240	15,550	4,140	270	15,880	4,610	290
Tanzania[2]	14,351	2,140	150	14,738	2,440	170	15,136	2,700	180
Kenya	12,910	2,690	210	13,350	2,970	220	13,800	3,280	240
Uganda	11,186	2,580	230	11,556	2,680	230	11,937	2,820	240
Ghana	9,610	5,330	560	9,870	5,860	590	10,136	5,920	580
Mozambique[1]	9,030	1,730	190	9,240	1,640	180	9,455	1,600	170
Madagascar	8,562	1,560	180	8,833	1,720	200	9,112	1,870	200
Cameroon	7,300	1,900	260	7,435	2,050	280	7,606	2,240	290
Ivory Coast	6,387	2,990	470	6,700	3,630	540	7,028	4,280	610
Rhodesia	6,100	3,220	530	6,310	3,460	550	6,527	3,560	550
Upper Volta	5,900	550	90	6,032	640	110	6,170	710	110
Mali	5,560	440	80	5,697	530	90	5,840	590	100
Tunisia	5,459	3,430	630	5,594	4,090	730	5,732	4,790	840
Guinea	5,390	640	120	5,540	750	130	5,695	880	150
Angola[1]	6,050	2,340	390	5,470	2,030	370	5,470	1,830	330
Malawi	4,917	580	120	5,044	660	130	5,176	700	140
Senegal	4,869	1,540	320	5,000	1,800	360	5,135	1,980	390
Zambia	4,781	1,900	400	4,920	2,090	420	5,063	2,200	440
Niger	4,480	530	120	4,592	590	130	4,730	740	160
Rwanda	4,058	360	90	4,137	430	100	4,217	480	110
Chad	3,952	390	100	4,035	460	120	4,120	510	120
Burundi	3,655	370	100	3,732	410	110	3,811	460	120
Somalia[1]	3,100	310	100	3,180	340	110	3,252	370	110
Benin	3,027	330	110	3,110	390	130	3,200	430	130
Sierra Leone	2,911	550	190	2,982	610	200	3,053	610	200
Libya	2,352	10,260	4,360	2,442	13,510	5,530	2,535	16,000	6,310
Togo	2,176	540	250	2,220	560	250	2,280	600	260
Central African Empire	1,748	380	220	1,787	390	220	1,827	420	230
Liberia	1,500	610	410	1,549	640	410	1,600	720	450
Congo, People's Republic of the	1,300	620	480	1,329	670	510	1,360	700	520
Mauritania	1,290	380	300	1,322	420	320	1,355	460	340
Lesotho[1]	1,191	160	130	1,217	190	160	1,244	210	170
Mauritius	871	500	580	883	540	610	894	600	680
Botswana[1]	654	250	380	666	230	350	679	280	410
Gabon	528	1,160	2,200	536	1,360	2,540	544	1,410	2,590
Guinea-Bissau[1]	520	60	110	530	70	120	530	70	140
Gambia, The	506	80	160	519	90	180	540	100	180
Swaziland[1]	478	170	360	494	220	440	510	240	470
Comoros	322	70	220	333	70	200	344	60	180
Equatorial Guinea[1]	318	90	300	320	100	320	320	110	330
São Tomé and Príncipe[1]	79	30	400	80	40	460	80	40	490

NOTE: Data for GNP at market prices and GNP per capita are rounded to US$ tens of millions and US$10, respectively, and are expressed in current US$.

Footnotes are listed at end of table.

Member countries of the World Bank and countries with mid-1975 populations of one million or more.

Region Country	1974 GNP at market prices			1975 GNP at market prices			1976 (preliminary) GNP at market prices		
	Population (000)	Amount (US$ millions)	Per capita (US$)	Population (000)	Amount (US$ millions)	Per capita (US$)	Population (000)	Amount (US$ millions)	Per capita (US$)
ASIA									
China, People's Republic of [1,3]	809,251	269,160	330	822,800	315,250	380	835,800	343,090	410
India	595,579	72,150	120	608,072	85,960	140	620,440	95,880	150
Japan	110,160	444,770	4,040	111,570	496,260	4,450	112,770	553,140	4,910
Bangladesh	76,200	6,490	90	78,600	7,280	90	80,400	8,470	110
Pakistan	67,213	9,640	140	69,229	11,270	160	71,306	12,190	170
Viet Nam	n.a.	n.a.	n.a.	n.a.	n.a.	n.a.	47,600	n.a.	n.a.
Philippines	41,072	13,760	340	42,231	15,930	380	43,293	17,810	410
Thailand	40,780	12,710	310	41,870	14,600	350	42,960	16,230	380
Korea, Republic of	34,690	16,760	480	35,280	19,850	560	35,969	24,050	670
Iran	32,500	45,430	1,400	33,390	55,510	1,660	34,300	66,250	1,930
Burma	29,521	2,910	100	30,170	3,320	110	30,827	3,730	120
China, Republic of	15,710	13,300	850	16,000	14,890	930	16,300	17,500	1,070
Korea, Democratic People's Republic of [1,3]	15,443	6,300	410	15,848	7,100	450	16,254	7,610	470
Afghanistan	13,410	1,800	130	13,700	2,060	150	14,000	2,300	160
Sri Lanka	13,393	2,250	170	13,603	2,540	190	13,819	2,750	200
Nepal	12,320	1,200	100	12,587	1,340	110	12,857	1,490	120
Malaysia	11,976	8,560	720	12,308	9,340	760	12,653	10,900	860
Iraq	10,770	10,210	950	11,120	13,880	1,250	11,481	15,940	1,390
Saudi Arabia	8,008	24,760	3,090	8,296	33,240	4,010	8,594	38,510	4,480
Syrian Arab Republic	7,168	4,220	590	7,410	5,330	720	7,655	5,970	780
Yemen Arab Republic [1]	5,837	920	160	5,936	1,210	200	6,037	1,540	250
Hong Kong	4,249	6,830	1,610	4,367	7,700	1,760	4,460	9,410	2,110
Israel [4]	3,359	12,090	3,600	3,469	13,160	3,790	3,563	13,980	3,920
Lao People's Democratic Republic [1]	3,260	250	80	3,200	300	90	3,250	310	90
Lebanon [1]	3,065	3,290	1,070	3,164	n.a.	n.a.	n.a.	n.a.	n.a.
Jordan	2,620	1,200	460	2,700	1,240	460	2,792	1,710	610
Singapore	2,219	4,820	2,170	2,250	5,500	2,450	2,278	6,150	2,700
Yemen, People's Democratic Republic of [1]	1,633	350	220	1,677	410	250	1,723	480	280
Mongolia [1,3]	1,403	1,080	770	1,446	1,250	860	1,491	1,280	860
Bhutan [1]	1,150	70	60	1,176	80	70	1,203	90	70
Kuwait	947	10,670	11,270	1,005	15,270	15,190	1,064	16,480	15,480
Oman	750	1,140	1,520	773	1,790	2,320	796	2,130	2,680
United Arab Emirates	548	7,680	14,020	653	8,880	13,600	694	9,710	13,990
Bahrain	245	560	2,310	260	570	2,210	276	660	2,410
Qatar	190	1,950	10,270	200	2,200	10,970	210	2,390	11,400
Cambodia	n.a.	n.a.	n.a.	n.a.	n.a.	n.a.	n.a.	n.a.	n.a.

Footnotes are listed at end of table.

Region Country	1974 GNP at market prices			1975 GNP at market prices			1976 (preliminary) GNP at market prices		
	Population (000)	Amount (US$ millions)	Per capita (US$)	Population (000)	Amount (US$ millions)	Per capita (US$)	Population (000)	Amount (US$ millions)	Per capita (US$)
EUROPE									
USSR[1,3]	252,065	580,400	2,300	254,393	649,470	2,550	256,670	708,170	2,760
Germany, Federal Republic of	62,040	389,760	6,280	61,830	412,480	6,670	62,000	457,540	7,380
United Kingdom	55,970	197,630	3,530	55,960	211,700	3,780	56,070	225,150	4,020
Italy	55,410	149,250	2,690	55,810	156,590	2,810	56,190	171,250	3,050
France	52,560	290,280	5,520	52,790	314,080	5,950	52,920	346,730	6,550
Turkey	39,301	30,530	780	40,198	36,030	900	41,243	40,960	990
Spain	35,099	88,180	2,510	35,348	97,140	2,750	35,701	104,090	2,920
Poland[1,3]	33,691	76,560	2,270	34,022	88,320	2,600	34,343	98,130	2,860
Yugoslavia	21,155	29,040	1,370	21,350	33,080	1,550	21,520	36,170	1,680
Romania[5]	21,029	21,910	1,040	21,245	26,450	1,240	21,446	31,070	1,450
German Democratic Republic[1,3]	16,925	58,350	3,450	16,850	65,830	3,910	16,794	70,880	4,220
Czechoslovakia[1,3]	14,686	47,640	3,240	14,802	53,450	3,610	14,917	57,250	3,840
Netherlands	13,540	73,330	5,420	13,650	78,550	5,750	13,770	85,320	6,200
Hungary[1,3]	10,479	20,270	1,930	10,541	22,690	2,150	10,599	24,140	2,280
Belgium	9,770	57,020	5,840	9,799	61,470	6,270	9,830	66,660	6,780
Portugal	9,247	14,580	1,580	9,577	15,060	1,570	9,732	16,480	1,690
Greece	9,020	18,450	2,050	9,101	21,320	2,340	9,128	23,600	2,590
Bulgaria[1,3]	8,679	15,690	1,810	8,722	18,420	2,110	8,761	20,270	2,310
Sweden	8,160	60,680	7,440	8,200	66,830	8,150	8,220	71,290	8,670
Austria	7,550	34,220	4,530	7,520	36,650	4,870	7,520	40,080	5,330
Switzerland	6,440	53,310	8,280	6,400	53,840	8,410	6,410	56,900	8,880
Denmark	5,050	31,770	6,290	5,060	34,450	6,810	5,070	37,770	7,450
Finland	4,690	23,300	4,970	4,710	25,520	5,420	4,730	26,570	5,620
Norway	3,990	24,090	6,040	4,010	27,110	6,760	4,030	29,920	7,420
Ireland	3,090	6,890	2,230	3,130	7,470	2,390	3,164	8,090	2,560
Albania[1,3]	2,349	1,020	430	2,404	1,220	510	2,460	1,330	540
Cyprus	645	840	1,310	630	780	1,240	630	930	1,480
Luxembourg	355	2,120	5,970	358	2,150	6,020	361	2,330	6,460
Iceland	220	1,220	5,540	223	1,320	5,930	226	1,380	6,100

Footnotes are listed at end of table.

Member countries of the World Bank and countries with mid-1975 populations of one million or more.

Region / Country	1974			1975			1976 (preliminary)		
		GNP at market prices			GNP at market prices			GNP at market prices	
	Population (000)	Amount (US$ millions)	Per capita (US$)	Population (000)	Amount (US$ millions)	Per capita (US$)	Population (000)	Amount (US$ millions)	Per capita (US$)
NORTH and CENTRAL AMERICA									
United States	211,980	1,415,980	6,680	213,540	1,519,890	7,120	215,120	1,698,060	7,890
Mexico	57,899	55,510	960	59,928	63,200	1,050	62,025	67,640	1,090
Canada	22,480	143,740	6,390	22,830	158,100	6,930	23,180	174,120	7,510
Cuba¹,³	9,190	6,300	690	9,332	7,460	800	9,464	8,120	860
Guatemala	6,078	3,220	530	6,275	3,590	570	6,478	4,070	630
Dominican Republic	4,562	2,940	640	4,695	3,390	720	4,835	3,750	780
Haiti	4,514	780	170	4,584	850	190	4,674	930	200
El Salvador	3,887	1,610	410	4,006	1,830	460	4,129	2,030	490
Puerto Rico	3,030	6,550	2,160	3,090	7,120	2,300	3,160	7,670	2,430
Honduras	2,806	960	340	2,890	1,050	360	2,977	1,160	390
Nicaragua	2,188	1,410	640	2,261	1,580	700	2,335	1,760	750
Jamaica	2,008	2,070	1,030	2,042	2,270	1,110	2,078	2,230	1,070
Costa Rica	1,918	1,670	870	1,965	1,890	960	2,013	2,090	1,040
Panama	1,618	1,920	1,180	1,668	2,150	1,290	1,718	2,260	1,310
Trinidad and Tobago	1,072	1,920	1,790	1,082	2,170	2,000	1,093	2,450	2,240
Barbados¹	244	310	1,260	246	350	1,410	247	380	1,550
Bahamas¹	197	660	3,370	204	630	3,110	211	700	3,310
Grenada	108	40	350	110	40	390	112	50	420
SOUTH AMERICA									
Brazil	103,981	97,250	940	106,996	110,130	1,030	109,960	125,570	1,140
Argentina	25,050	36,540	1,460	25,383	39,330	1,550	25,719	39,920	1,550
Colombia	22,944	11,920	520	23,576	13,630	580	24,226	15,400	630
Peru	14,953	10,460	700	15,387	11,670	760	15,833	12,610	800
Venezuela	11,632	23,980	2,060	11,993	27,320	2,280	12,360	31,750	2,570
Chile	10,068	10,790	1,070	10,253	10,130	990	10,453	10,980	1,050
Ecuador	6,830	3,540	520	7,069	4,180	590	7,316	4,690	640
Bolivia	5,470	1,760	320	5,634	2,040	360	5,794	2,280	390
Uruguay	2,754	3,200	1,160	2,764	3,600	1,300	2,800	3,900	1,390
Paraguay	2,484	1,320	530	2,553	1,470	580	2,625	1,680	640
Guyana	758	340	450	770	400	510	783	430	540
OCEANIA and INDONESIA									
Indonesia	129,083	25,680	200	132,112	29,120	220	135,191	32,440	240
Australia	13,340	71,470	5,360	13,500	77,010	5,700	13,660	83,380	6,100
New Zealand	3,010	12,270	4,080	3,070	13,130	4,280	3,090	13,120	4,250
Papua New Guinea	2,683	1,250	470	2,756	1,290	470	2,829	1,400	490
Fiji	564	570	1,010	569	620	1,090	580	670	1,150
Western Samoa	151	40	290	152	50	320	153	50	350

NOTE: Data for GNP at market prices and GNP per capita are rounded to US$ tens of millions and US$10, respectively, and are expressed in current US$.

1 Estimates of GNP per capita are tentative.
2 Mainland Tanzania.
3 For estimation of GNP per capita, see Technical Note
4 GNP per capita estimates do not reflect the significant devaluation of the pound in November 1977.
5 These estimates are not comparable to those for the other centrally planned economies. They have been arrived at, following the Bank Atlas methodology, by adjusting official Romanian national accounts data and converting them into US dollars at the effective exchange rate for foreign trade transactions, which approximates Lei 20 per US dollar.
n.a.—Not available.

Source: World Bank Atlas 1977, World Bank, Washington, D.C.

name index

subject index